SCHAUM'S OUTLINE OF

THEORY AND PROBLEMS

OF

LINEAR
ALGEBRA
SI (METRIC) EDITION

BY

SEYMOUR LIPSCHUTZ, Ph.D.

Associated Professor of Mathematics
Temple University

SCHAUM'S OUTLINE SERIES
McGraw-Hill Book Company

New York · St Louis · San Francisco · Auckland · Bogotá
Guatemala · Hamburg · Lisbon · London
Madrid · Mexico · Montreal · New Delhi · Panama · Paris
San Juan · São Paulo · Singapore · Sydney · Tokyo · Toronto

Theory and Problems of
LINEAR ALGEBRA SI (Metric) Edition

When ordering this title use ISBN 0-07-099012-3

Printed in Singapore

Preface

Linear algebra has in recent years become an essential part of the mathematical background required of mathematicians, engineers, physicists and other scientists. This requirement reflects the importance and wide applications of the subject matter.

This book is designed for use as a textbook for a formal course in linear algebra or as a supplement to all current standard texts. It aims to present an introduction to linear algebra which will be found helpful to all readers regardless of their fields of specialization. More material has been included than can be covered in most first courses. This has been done to make the book more flexible, to provide a useful book of reference, and to stimulate further interest in the subject.

Each chapter begins with clear statements of pertinent definitions, principles and theorems together with illustrative and other descriptive material. This is followed by graded sets of solved and supplementary problems. The solved problems serve to illustrate and amplify the theory, bring into sharp focus those fine points without which the student continually feels himself on unsafe ground, and provide the repetition of basic principles so vital to effective learning. Numerous proofs of theorems are included among the solved problems. The supplementary problems serve as a complete review of the material of each chapter.

The first three chapters treat of vectors in Euclidean space, linear equations and matrices. These provide the motivation and basic computational tools for the abstract treatment of vector spaces and linear mappings which follow. A chapter on eigenvalues and eigenvectors, preceded by determinants, gives conditions for representing a linear operator by a diagonal matrix. This naturally leads to the study of various canonical forms, specifically the triangular, Jordan and rational canonical forms. In the last chapter, on inner product spaces, the spectral theorem for symmetric operators is obtained and is applied to the diagonalization of real quadratic forms. For completeness, the appendices include sections on sets and relations, algebraic structures and polynomials over a field.

I wish to thank many friends and colleagues, especially Dr. Martin Silverstein and Dr. Hwa Tsang, for invaluable suggestions and critical review of the manuscript. I also want to express my gratitude to Daniel Schaum and Nicola Monti for their very helpful cooperation.

SEYMOUR LIPSCHUTZ

Temple University
January, 1968

CONTENTS

Page

Chapter **1** VECTORS IN R^n AND C^n 1

Introduction. Vectors in R^n. Vector addition and scalar multiplication. Dot product. Norm and distance in R^n. Complex numbers. Vectors in C^n.

Chapter **2** LINEAR EQUATIONS 18

Introduction. Linear equation. System of linear equations. Solution of a system of linear equations. Solution of a homogeneous system of linear equations.

Chapter **3** MATRICES 35

Introduction. Matrices. Matrix addition and scalar multiplication. Matrix multiplication. Transpose. Matrices and systems of linear equations. Echelon matrices. Row equivalence and elementary row operations. Square matrices. Algebra of square matrices. Invertible matrices. Block matrices.

Chapter **4** VECTOR SPACES AND SUBSPACES 63

Introduction. Examples of vector spaces. Subspaces. Linear combinations, linear spans. Row space of a matrix. Sums and direct sums.

Chapter **5** BASIS AND DIMENSION 86

Introduction. Linear dependence. Basis and dimension. Dimension and subspaces. Rank of a matrix. Applications to linear equations. Coordinates.

Chapter **6** LINEAR MAPPINGS 121

Mappings. Linear mappings. Kernel and image of a linear mapping. Singular and nonsingular mappings. Linear mappings and systems of linear equations. Operations with linear mappings. Algebra of linear operators. Invertible operators.

Chapter **7** MATRICES AND LINEAR OPERATORS 150

Introduction. Matrix representation of a linear operator. Change of basis. Similarity. Matrices and linear mappings.

Chapter **8** DETERMINANTS 171

Introduction. Permutations. Determinant. Properties of determinants. Minors and cofactors. Classical adjoint. Applications to linear equations. Determinant of a linear operator. Multilinearity and determinants.

Chapter **9** EIGENVALUES AND EIGENVECTORS 197

Introduction. Polynomials of matrices and linear operators. Eigenvalues and eigenvectors. Diagonalization and eigenvectors. Characteristic polynomial, Cayley-Hamilton theorem. Minimum polynomial. Characteristic and minimum polynomials of linear operators.

CONTENTS

                                                                          Page

Chapter *10* CANONICAL FORMS 222
              Introduction. Triangular form. Invariance. Invariant direct-sum decom-
              positions. Primary decomposition. Nilpotent operators, Jordan canonical
              form. Cyclic subspaces. Rational canonical form. Quotient spaces.

Chapter *11* LINEAR FUNCTIONALS AND THE DUAL SPACE 249
              Introduction. Linear functionals and the dual space. Dual basis. Second dual
              space. Annihilators. Transpose of a linear mapping.

Chapter *12* BILINEAR, QUADRATIC AND HERMITIAN FORMS 261
              Bilinear forms. Bilinear forms and matrices. Alternating bilinear forms.
              Symmetric bilinear forms, quadratic forms. Real symmetric bilinear forms.
              Law of inertia. Hermitian forms.

Chapter *13* INNER PRODUCT SPACES 279
              Introduction. Inner product spaces. Cauchy-Schwarz inequality. Orthogo-
              nality. Orthonormal sets. Gram-Schmidt orthogonalization process. Linear
              functionals and adjoint operators. Analogy between $A(V)$ and $\mathbf{C}$, special
              operators. Orthogonal and unitary operators. Orthogonal and unitary mat-
              rices. Change of orthonormal basis. Positive operators. Diagonalization and
              canonical forms in Euclidean spaces. Diagonalization and canonical forms in
              unitary spaces. Spectral theorem.

Appendix A SETS AND RELATIONS 315
              Sets, elements. Set operations. Product sets. Relations. Equivalence
              relations.

Appendix B ALGEBRAIC STRUCTURES 320
              Introduction. Groups. Rings, integral domains and fields. Modules.

Appendix C POLYNOMIALS OVER A FIELD 327
              Introduction. Ring of polynomials. Notation. Divisibility. Factorization.

INDEX 331

Chapter 1

Vectors in R^n and C^n

INTRODUCTION

In various physical applications there appear certain quantities, such as temperature and speed, which possess only "magnitude". These can be represented by real numbers and are called *scalars*. On the other hand, there are also quantities, such as force and velocity, which possess both "magnitude" and "direction". These quantities can be represented by arrows (having appropriate lengths and directions and emanating from some given reference point O) and are called *vectors*. In this chapter we study the properties of such vectors in some detail.

We begin by considering the following operations on vectors.

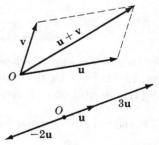

(i) *Addition*: The resultant $\mathbf{u} + \mathbf{v}$ of two vectors $\mathbf{u}$ and $\mathbf{v}$ is obtained by the so-called parallelogram law, i.e. $\mathbf{u} + \mathbf{v}$ is the diagonal of the parallelogram formed by $\mathbf{u}$ and $\mathbf{v}$ as shown on the right.

(ii) *Scalar multiplication*: The product $k\mathbf{u}$ of a real number k by a vector $\mathbf{u}$ is obtained by multiplying the magnitude of $\mathbf{u}$ by k and retaining the same direction if $k \geqq 0$ or the opposite direction if $k < 0$, as shown on the right.

Now we assume the reader is familiar with the representation of the points in the plane by ordered pairs of real numbers. If the origin of the axes is chosen at the reference point O above, then every vector is uniquely determined by the coordinates of its endpoint. The relationship between the above operations and endpoints follows.

(i) *Addition*: If (a, b) and (c, d) are the endpoints of the vectors $\mathbf{u}$ and $\mathbf{v}$, then $(a + c, b + d)$ will be the endpoint of $\mathbf{u} + \mathbf{v}$, as shown in Fig. (a) below.

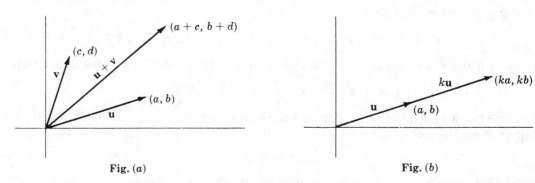

Fig. (a) Fig. (b)

(ii) *Scalar multiplication*: If (a, b) is the endpoint of the vector $\mathbf{u}$, then (ka, kb) will be the endpoint of the vector $k\mathbf{u}$, as shown in Fig. (b) above.

Mathematically, we identify a vector with its endpoint; that is, we call the ordered pair (a, b) of real numbers a vector. In fact, we shall generalize this notion and call an n-tuple $(a_1, a_2, \ldots, a_n)$ of real numbers a vector. We shall again generalize and permit the coordinates of the n-tuple to be complex numbers and not just real numbers. Furthermore, in Chapter 4, we shall abstract properties of these n-cuples and formally define the mathematical system called a *vector space*.

We assume the reader is familiar with the elementary properties of the real number field which we denote by $\mathbf{R}$.

VECTORS IN $\mathbf{R}^n$

The set of all n-tuples of real numbers, denoted by $\mathbf{R}^n$, is called *n-space*. A particular n-tuple in $\mathbf{R}^n$, say

$$u = (u_1, u_2, \ldots, u_n)$$

is called a *point* or *vector*; the real numbers u_i are called the *components* (or: *coordinates*) of the vector u. Moreover, when discussing the space $\mathbf{R}^n$ we use the term *scalar* for the elements of $\mathbf{R}$, i.e. for the real numbers.

> **Example 1.1:**   Consider the following vectors:
>
> $$(0, 1), \quad (1, -3), \quad (1, 2, \sqrt{3}, 4), \quad (-5, \tfrac{1}{2}, 0, \pi)$$
>
> The first two vectors have two components and so are points in $\mathbf{R}^2$; the last two vectors have four components and so are points in $\mathbf{R}^4$.

Two vectors u and v are *equal*, written $u = v$, if they have the same number of components, i.e. belong to the same space, and if corresponding components are equal. The vectors $(1, 2, 3)$ and $(2, 3, 1)$ are not equal, since corresponding elements are not equal.

> **Example 1.2:**   Suppose $(x - y, x + y, z - 1) = (4, 2, 3)$. Then, by definition of equality of vectors,
>
> $$x - y = 4$$
> $$x + y = 2$$
> $$z - 1 = 3$$
>
> Solving the above system of equations gives $x = 3$, $y = -1$, and $z = 4$.

VECTOR ADDITION AND SCALAR MULTIPLICATION

Let u and v be vectors in $\mathbf{R}^n$:

$$u = (u_1, u_2, \ldots, u_n) \quad \text{and} \quad v = (v_1, v_2, \ldots, v_n)$$

The *sum* of u and v, written $u + v$, is the vector obtained by adding corresponding components:

$$u + v = (u_1 + v_1, u_2 + v_2, \ldots, u_n + v_n)$$

The *product* of a real number k by the vector u, written ku, is the vector obtained by multiplying each component of u by k:

$$ku = (ku_1, ku_2, \ldots, ku_n)$$

Observe that $u + v$ and ku are also vectors in $\mathbf{R}^n$. We also define

$$-u = -1u \quad \text{and} \quad u - v = u + (-v)$$

The sum of vectors with different numbers of components is not defined.

Example 1.3:   Let $u = (1, -3, 2, 4)$ and $v = (3, 5, -1, -2)$.   Then

$$u + v \;=\; (1+3, -3+5, 2-1, 4-2) \;=\; (4, 2, 1, 2)$$
$$5u \;=\; (5 \cdot 1, 5 \cdot (-3), 5 \cdot 2, 5 \cdot 4) \;=\; (5, -15, 10, 20)$$
$$2u - 3v \;=\; (2, -6, 4, 8) + (-9, -15, 3, 6) \;=\; (-7, -21, 7, 14)$$

Example 1.4:   The vector $(0, 0, \ldots, 0)$ in $\mathbf{R}^n$, denoted by 0, is called the *zero vector*. It is similar to the scalar 0 in that, for any vector $u = (u_1, u_2, \ldots, u_n)$,

$$u + 0 \;=\; (u_1 + 0, u_2 + 0, \ldots, u_n + 0) \;=\; (u_1, u_2, \ldots, u_n) \;=\; u$$

Basic properties of the vectors in $\mathbf{R}^n$ under the operations of vector addition and scalar multiplication are described in the following theorem.

Theorem 1.1:   For any vectors $u, v, w \in \mathbf{R}^n$ and any scalars $k, k' \in \mathbf{R}$:

(i) $(u + v) + w = u + (v + w)$	(v) $k(u + v) = ku + kv$
(ii) $u + 0 = u$	(vi) $(k + k')u = ku + k'u$
(iii) $u + (-u) = 0$	(vii) $(kk')u = k(k'u)$
(iv) $u + v = v + u$	(viii) $1u = u$

Remark: Suppose u and v are vectors in $\mathbf{R}^n$ for which $u = kv$ for some nonzero scalar $k \in \mathbf{R}$. Then u is said to be in the *same direction* as v if $k > 0$, and in the *opposite direction* if $k < 0$.

DOT PRODUCT

Let u and v be vectors in $\mathbf{R}^n$:

$$u = (u_1, u_2, \ldots, u_n) \quad \text{and} \quad v = (v_1, v_2, \ldots, v_n)$$

The *dot* or *inner* product of u and v, denoted by $u \cdot v$, is the scalar obtained by multiplying corresponding components and adding the resulting products:

$$u \cdot v \;=\; u_1 v_1 + u_2 v_2 + \cdots + u_n v_n$$

The vectors u and v are said to be *orthogonal* (or: *perpendicular*) if their dot product is zero: $u \cdot v = 0$.

Example 1.5:   Let $u = (1, -2, 3, -4)$, $v = (6, 7, 1, -2)$ and $w = (5, -4, 5, 7)$.   Then

$$u \cdot v \;=\; 1 \cdot 6 + (-2) \cdot 7 + 3 \cdot 1 + (-4) \cdot (-2) \;=\; 6 - 14 + 3 + 8 \;=\; 3$$
$$u \cdot w \;=\; 1 \cdot 5 + (-2) \cdot (-4) + 3 \cdot 5 + (-4) \cdot 7 \;=\; 5 + 8 + 15 - 28 \;=\; 0$$

Thus u and w are orthogonal.

Basic properties of the dot product in $\mathbf{R}^n$ follow.

Theorem 1.2:   For any vectors $u, v, w \in \mathbf{R}^n$ and any scalar $k \in \mathbf{R}$:

(i) $(u + v) \cdot w = u \cdot w + v \cdot w$	(iii) $u \cdot v = v \cdot u$
(ii) $(ku) \cdot v = k(u \cdot v)$	(iv) $u \cdot u \geqq 0$, and $u \cdot u = 0$ iff $u = 0$

Remark: The space $\mathbf{R}^n$ with the above operations of vector addition, scalar multiplication and dot product is usually called *Euclidean n-space*.

NORM AND DISTANCE IN $\mathbf{R}^n$

Let u and v be vectors in $\mathbf{R}^n$: $u = (u_1, u_2, \ldots, u_n)$ and $v = (v_1, v_2, \ldots, v_n)$.   The *distance* between the points u and v, written $d(u, v)$, is defined by

$$d(u, v) \;=\; \sqrt{(u_1 - v_1)^2 + (u_2 - v_2)^2 + \cdots + (u_n - v_n)^2}$$

The *norm* (or: *length*) of the vector u, written $\|u\|$, is defined to be the nonnegative square root of $u \cdot u$:

$$\|u\| = \sqrt{u \cdot u} = \sqrt{u_1^2 + u_2^2 + \cdots + u_n^2}$$

By Theorem 1.2, $u \cdot u \geq 0$ and so the square root exists. Observe that

$$d(u, v) = \|u - v\|$$

   Example 1.6: Let $u = (1, -2, 4, 1)$ and $v = (3, 1, -5, 0)$. Then

$$d(u, v) = \sqrt{(1-3)^2 + (-2-1)^2 + (4+5)^2 + (1-0)^2} = \sqrt{95}$$

$$\|v\| = \sqrt{3^2 + 1^2 + (-5)^2 + 0^2} = \sqrt{35}$$

Now if we consider two points, say $p = (a, b)$ and $q = (c, d)$ in the plane $\mathbf{R}^2$, then

$$\|p\| = \sqrt{a^2 + b^2} \qquad \text{and} \qquad d(p, q) = \sqrt{(a-c)^2 + (b-d)^2}$$

That is, $\|p\|$ corresponds to the usual Euclidean length of the arrow from the origin to the point p, and $d(p, q)$ corresponds to the usual Euclidean distance between the points p and q, as shown below:

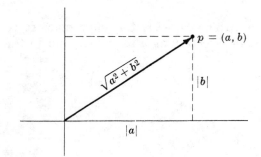 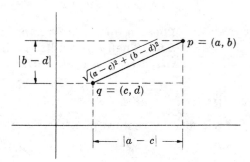

A similar result holds for points on the line $\mathbf{R}$ and in space $\mathbf{R}^3$.

Remark: A vector e is called a *unit vector* if its norm is 1: $\|e\| = 1$. Observe that, for any nonzero vector $u \in \mathbf{R}^n$, the vector $e_u = u/\|u\|$ is a unit vector in the same direction as u.

We now state a fundamental relationship known as the Cauchy-Schwarz inequality.

Theorem 1.3 (Cauchy-Schwarz):   For any vectors $u, v \in \mathbf{R}^n$, $|u \cdot v| \leq \|u\| \, \|v\|$.

Using the above inequality, we can now define the angle θ between any two nonzero vectors $u, v \in \mathbf{R}^n$ by

$$\cos \theta = \frac{u \cdot v}{\|u\| \, \|v\|}$$

Note that if $u \cdot v = 0$, then $\theta = 90°$ (or: $\theta = \pi/2$). This then agrees with our previous definition of orthogonality.

COMPLEX NUMBERS

The set of complex numbers is denoted by $\mathbf{C}$. Formally, a complex number is an ordered pair (a, b) of real numbers; equality, addition and multiplication of complex numbers are defined as follows:

$$(a, b) = (c, d) \quad \text{iff} \quad a = c \text{ and } b = d$$

$$(a, b) + (c, d) = (a+c, b+d)$$

$$(a, b)(c, d) = (ac - bd, ad + bc)$$

We identify the real number a with the complex number $(a, 0)$:
$$a \leftrightarrow (a, 0)$$
This is possible since the operations of addition and multiplication of **real numbers** are preserved under the correspondence:
$$(a, 0) + (b, 0) = (a + b, 0) \quad \text{and} \quad (a, 0)(b, 0) = (ab, 0)$$
Thus we view $\mathbf{R}$ as a subset of $\mathbf{C}$ and replace $(a, 0)$ by a whenever convenient and possible.

The complex number $(0, 1)$, denoted by i, has the important property that
$$i^2 = ii = (0, 1)(0, 1) = (-1, 0) = -1 \quad \text{or} \quad i = \sqrt{-1}$$
Furthermore, using the facts
$$(a, b) = (a, 0) + (0, b) \quad \text{and} \quad (0, b) = (b, 0)(0, 1)$$
we have
$$(a, b) = (a, 0) + (b, 0)(0, 1) = a + bi$$
The notation $a + bi$ is more convenient than (a, b). For example, the sum and product of complex numbers can be obtained by simply using the commutative and distributive laws and $i^2 = -1$:
$$(a + bi) + (c + di) = a + c + bi + di = (a + c) + (b + d)i$$
$$(a + bi)(c + di) = ac + bci + adi + bdi^2 = (ac - bd) + (bc + ad)i$$
The *conjugate* of the complex number $z = (a, b) = a + bi$ is denoted and defined by
$$\bar{z} = a - bi$$
(Notice that $z\bar{z} = a^2 + b^2$.) If, in addition, $z \neq 0$, then the inverse z^{-1} of z and division by z are given by
$$z^{-1} = \frac{\bar{z}}{z\bar{z}} = \frac{a}{a^2 + b^2} + \frac{-b}{a^2 + b^2}i \quad \text{and} \quad \frac{w}{z} = wz^{-1}$$
where $w \in \mathbf{C}$. We also define
$$-z = -1z \quad \text{and} \quad w - z = w + (-z)$$

Example 1.7:   Suppose $z = 2 + 3i$ and $w = 5 - 2i$.   Then
$$z + w = (2 + 3i) + (5 - 2i) = 2 + 5 + 3i - 2i = 7 + i$$
$$zw = (2 + 3i)(5 - 2i) = 10 + 15i - 4i - 6i^2 = 16 + 11i$$
$$\bar{z} = \overline{2 + 3i} = 2 - 3i \quad \text{and} \quad \bar{w} = \overline{5 - 2i} = 5 + 2i$$
$$\frac{w}{z} = \frac{5 - 2i}{2 + 3i} = \frac{(5 - 2i)(2 - 3i)}{(2 + 3i)(2 - 3i)} = \frac{4 - 19i}{13} = \frac{4}{13} - \frac{19}{13}i$$

Just as the real numbers can be represented by the points on a line, the complex numbers can be represented by the points in the plane. Specifically, we let the point (a, b) in the plane represent the complex number $z = a + bi$, i.e. whose *real part* is a and whose *imaginary part* is b. The *absolute value* of z, written $|z|$, is defined as the distance from z to the origin:

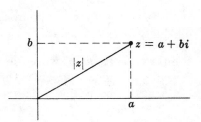

$$|z| = \sqrt{a^2 + b^2}$$
Note that $|z|$ is equal to the norm of the vector (a, b). Also, $|z| = \sqrt{z\bar{z}}$.

Example 1.8:   Suppose $z = 2 + 3i$ and $w = 12 - 5i$.   Then
$$|z| = \sqrt{4 + 9} = \sqrt{13} \quad \text{and} \quad |w| = \sqrt{144 + 25} = 13$$

Remark: In Appendix B we define the algebraic structure called a *field*. We emphasize that the set $\mathbf{C}$ of complex numbers with the above operations of addition and multiplication is a field.

VECTORS IN $\mathbf{C}^n$

The set of all n-tuples of complex numbers, denoted by $\mathbf{C}^n$, is called *complex n-space*. Just as in the real case, the elements of $\mathbf{C}^n$ are called *points* or *vectors*, the elements of $\mathbf{C}$ are called *scalars*, and *vector addition* in $\mathbf{C}^n$ and *scalar multiplication* on $\mathbf{C}^n$ are given by

$$(z_1, z_2, \ldots, z_n) + (w_1, w_2, \ldots, w_n) = (z_1 + w_1, z_2 + w_2, \ldots, z_n + w_n)$$

$$z(z_1, z_2, \ldots, z_n) = (zz_1, zz_2, \ldots, zz_n)$$

where $z_i, w_i, z \in \mathbf{C}$.

Example 1.9: $(2 + 3i, 4 - i, 3) + (3 - 2i, 5i, 4 - 6i) = (5 + i, 4 + 4i, 7 - 6i)$

$2i(2 + 3i, 4 - i, 3) = (-6 + 4i, 2 + 8i, 6i)$

Now let u and v be arbitrary vectors in $\mathbf{C}^n$:

$$u = (z_1, z_2, \ldots, z_n), \qquad v = (w_1, w_2, \ldots, w_n), \qquad z_i, w_i \in \mathbf{C}$$

The *dot*, or *inner*, product of u and v is defined as follows:

$$u \cdot v = z_1 \overline{w}_1 + z_2 \overline{w}_2 + \cdots + z_n \overline{w}_n$$

Note that this definition reduces to the previous one in the real case, since $w_i = \overline{w}_i$ when w_i is real. The norm of u is defined by

$$\|u\| = \sqrt{u \cdot u} = \sqrt{z_1 \bar{z}_1 + z_2 \bar{z}_2 + \cdots + z_n \bar{z}_n} = \sqrt{|z_1|^2 + |z_2|^2 + \cdots + |z_n|^2}$$

Observe that $u \cdot u$ and so $\|u\|$ are real and positive when $u \neq 0$, and 0 when $u = 0$.

Example 1.10:   Let $u = (2 + 3i, 4 - i, 2i)$ and $v = (3 - 2i, 5, 4 - 6i)$. Then

$$u \cdot v = (2 + 3i)(\overline{3 - 2i}) + (4 - i)(\overline{5}) + (2i)(\overline{4 - 6i})$$
$$= (2 + 3i)(3 + 2i) + (4 - i)(5) + (2i)(4 + 6i)$$
$$= 13i + 20 - 5i - 12 + 8i = 8 + 16i$$

$$u \cdot u = (2 + 3i)(\overline{2 + 3i}) + (4 - i)(\overline{4 - i}) + (2i)(\overline{2i})$$
$$= (2 + 3i)(2 - 3i) + (4 - i)(4 + i) + (2i)(-2i)$$
$$= 13 + 17 + 4 = 34$$

$$\|u\| = \sqrt{u \cdot u} = \sqrt{34}$$

The space $\mathbf{C}^n$ with the above operations of vector addition, scalar multiplication and dot product, is called *complex Euclidean n-space*.

Remark: If $u \cdot v$ were defined by $u \cdot v = z_1 w_1 + \cdots + z_n w_n$, then it is possible for $u \cdot u = 0$ even though $u \neq 0$, e.g. if $u = (1, i, 0)$. In fact, $u \cdot u$ may not even be real.

Solved Problems

VECTORS IN $\mathbf{R}^n$

1.1. Compute: (i) $(3, -4, 5) + (1, 1, -2)$; (ii) $(1, 2, -3) + (4, -5)$; (iii) $-3(4, -5, -6)$; (iv) $-(-6, 7, -8)$.

    (i)   Add corresponding components: $(3, -4, 5) + (1, 1, -2) = (3 + 1, -4 + 1, 5 - 2) = (4, -3, 3)$.

    (ii) The sum is not defined since the vectors have different numbers of components.

    (iii) Multiply each component by the scalar: $-3(4, -5, -6) = (-12, 15, 18)$.

    (iv) Multiply each component by -1: $-(-6, 7, -8) = (6, -7, 8)$.

1.2. Let $u = (2, -7, 1)$, $v = (-3, 0, 4)$, $w = (0, 5, -8)$. Find (i) $3u - 4v$, (ii) $2u + 3v - 5w$.

    First perform the scalar multiplication and then the vector addition.

    (i) $3u - 4v = 3(2, -7, 1) - 4(-3, 0, 4) = (6, -21, 3) + (12, 0, -16) = (18, -21, -13)$

    (ii) $2u + 3v - 5w = 2(2, -7, 1) + 3(-3, 0, 4) - 5(0, 5, -8)$

$$= (4, -14, 2) + (-9, 0, 12) + (0, -25, 40)$$

$$= (4 - 9 + 0, -14 + 0 - 25, 2 + 12 + 40) = (-5, -39, 54)$$

1.3. Find x and y if $(x, 3) = (2, x + y)$.

    Since the two vectors are equal, the corresponding components are equal to each other:

$$x = 2, \qquad 3 = x + y$$

Substitute $x = 2$ into the second equation to obtain $y = 1$. Thus $x = 2$ and $y = 1$.

1.4. Find x and y if $(4, y) = x(2, 3)$.

    Multiply by the scalar x to obtain $(4, y) = x(2, 3) = (2x, 3x)$.

    Set the corresponding components equal to each other: $4 = 2x$, $y = 3x$.

    Solve the linear equations for x and y: $x = 2$ and $y = 6$.

1.5. Find x, y and z if $(2, -3, 4) = x(1, 1, 1) + y(1, 1, 0) + z(1, 0, 0)$.

    First multiply by the scalars x, y and z and then add:

$$(2, -3, 4) = x(1, 1, 1) + y(1, 1, 0) + z(1, 0, 0)$$

$$= (x, x, x) + (y, y, 0) + (z, 0, 0)$$

$$= (x + y + z, x + y, x)$$

Now set the corresponding components equal to each other:

$$x + y + z = 2, \qquad x + y = -3, \qquad x = 4$$

To solve the system of equations, substitute $x = 4$ into the second equation to obtain $4 + y = -3$ or $y = -7$. Then substitute into the first equation to find $z = 5$. Thus $x = 4$, $y = -7$, $z = 5$.

1.6. Prove Theorem 1.1: For any vectors $u, v, w \in \mathbf{R}^n$ and any scalars $k, k' \in \mathbf{R}$,

    (i) $(u + v) + w = u + (v + w)$ (v) $k(u + v) = ku + kv$

    (ii) $u + 0 = u$ (vi) $(k + k')u = ku + k'u$

    (iii) $u + (-u) = 0$ (vii) $(kk')u = k(k'u)$

    (iv) $u + v = v + u$ (viii) $1u = u$

Let u_i, v_i and w_i be the ith components of u, v and w, respectively.

(i)   By definition, $u_i + v_i$ is the ith component of $u + v$ and so $(u_i + v_i) + w_i$ is the ith component of $(u + v) + w$. On the other hand, $v_i + w_i$ is the ith component of $v + w$ and so $u_i + (v_i + w_i)$ is the ith component of $u + (v + w)$. But u_i, v_i and w_i are real numbers for which the associative law holds, that is,

$$(u_i + v_i) + w_i \; = \; u_i + (v_i + w_i) \qquad \text{for} \quad i = 1, \ldots, n$$

Accordingly, $(u + v) + w = u + (v + w)$ since their corresponding components are equal.

(ii)   Here, $0 = (0, 0, \ldots, 0)$; hence

$$u + 0 \; = \; (u_1, u_2, \ldots, u_n) + (0, 0, \ldots, 0)$$
$$= \; (u_1 + 0, u_2 + 0, \ldots, u_n + 0) \; = \; (u_1, u_2, \ldots, u_n) \; = \; u$$

(iii)   Since $-u = -1(u_1, u_2, \ldots, u_n) = (-u_1, -u_2, \ldots, -u_n)$,

$$u + (-u) \; = \; (u_1, u_2, \ldots, u_n) + (-u_1, -u_2, \ldots, -u_n)$$
$$= \; (u_1 - u_1, u_2 - u_2, \ldots, u_n - u_n) \; = \; (0, 0, \ldots, 0) \; = \; 0$$

(iv)   By definition, $u_i + v_i$ is the ith component of $u + v$, and $v_i + u_i$ is the ith component of $v + u$. But u_i and v_i are real numbers for which the commutative law holds, that is,

$$u_i + v_i \; = \; v_i + u_i, \qquad i = 1, \ldots, n$$

Hence $u + v = v + u$ since their corresponding components are equal.

(v)   Since $u_i + v_i$ is the ith component of $u + v$, $k(u_i + v_i)$ is the ith component of $k(u + v)$. Since ku_i and kv_i are the ith components of ku and kv respectively, $ku_i + kv_i$ is the ith component of $ku + kv$. But k, u_i and v_i are real numbers; hence

$$k(u_i + v_i) \; = \; ku_i + kv_i, \qquad i = 1, \ldots, n$$

Thus $k(u + v) = ku + kv$, as corresponding components are equal.

(vi)   Observe that the first plus sign refers to the addition of the two scalars k and k' whereas the second plus sign refers to the vector addition of the two vectors ku and $k'u$.

By definition, $(k + k')u_i$ is the ith component of the vector $(k + k')u$. Since ku_i and $k'u_i$ are the ith components of ku and $k'u$ respectively, $ku_i + k'u_i$ is the ith component of $ku + k'u$. But k, k' and u_i are real numbers; hence

$$(k + k')u_i \; = \; ku_i + k'u_i, \qquad i = 1, \ldots, n$$

Thus $(k + k')u = ku + k'u$, as corresponding components are equal.

(vii)   Since $k'u_i$ is the ith component of $k'u$, $k(k'u_i)$ is the ith component of $k(k'u)$. But $(kk')u_i$ is the ith component of $(kk')u$ and, since k, k' and u_i are real numbers,

$$(kk')u_i \; = \; k(k'u_i), \qquad i = 1, \ldots, n$$

Hence $(kk')u = k(k'u)$, as corresponding components are equal.

(viii) $1 \cdot u = 1(u_1, u_2, \ldots, u_n) = (1u_1, 1u_2, \ldots, 1u_n) = (u_1, u_2, \ldots, u_n) = u.$

1.7.   Show that $0u = 0$ for any vector u, where clearly the first 0 is a scalar and the second 0 a vector.

     Method 1: $0u = 0(u_1, u_2, \ldots, u_n) = (0u_1, 0u_2, \ldots, 0u_n) = (0, 0, \ldots, 0) = 0$

     Method 2:   By Theorem 1.1, $0u = (0 + 0)u = 0u + 0u$

         Adding $-0u$ to both sides gives us the required result.

DOT PRODUCT

1.8.   Compute $u \cdot v$ where: (i) $u = (2, -3, 6)$, $v = (8, 2, -3)$; (ii) $u = (1, -8, 0, 5)$, $v = (3, 6, 4)$; (iii) $u = (3, -5, 2, 1)$, $v = (4, 1, -2, 5)$.

(i)   Multiply corresponding components and add: $u \cdot v = 2 \cdot 8 + (-3) \cdot 2 + 6 \cdot (-3) = -8.$

(ii)   The dot product is not defined between vectors with different numbers of components.

(iii)   Multiply corresponding components and add: $u \cdot v = 3 \cdot 4 + (-5) \cdot 1 + 2 \cdot (-2) + 1 \cdot 5 = 8.$

1.9. Determine k so that the vectors u and v are orthogonal where
  (i) $u = (1, k, -3)$ and $v = (2, -5, 4)$
  (ii) $u = (2, 3k, -4, 1, 5)$ and $v = (6, -1, 3, 7, 2k)$

  In each case, compute $u \cdot v$, set it equal to 0, and solve for k.

  (i) $u \cdot v = 1 \cdot 2 + k \cdot (-5) + (-3) \cdot 4 = 2 - 5k - 12 = 0, \quad -5k - 10 = 0, \quad k = -2$

  (ii) $u \cdot v = 2 \cdot 6 + 3k \cdot (-1) + (-4) \cdot 3 + 1 \cdot 7 + 5 \cdot 2k$
  $\qquad\quad\ = 12 - 3k - 12 + 7 + 10k = 0, \quad k = -1$

1.10. Prove Theorem 1.2:   For any vectors $u, v, w \in \mathbf{R}^n$ and any scalar $k \in \mathbf{R}$,
  (i) $(u + v) \cdot w = u \cdot w + v \cdot w$ (iii) $u \cdot v = v \cdot u$
  (ii) $(ku) \cdot v = k(u \cdot v)$ (iv) $u \cdot u \geqq 0$, and $u \cdot u = 0$ iff $u = 0$

  Let $u = (u_1, u_2, \ldots, u_n)$, $v = (v_1, v_2, \ldots, v_n)$, $w = (w_1, w_2, \ldots, w_n)$.

  (i)   Since $u + v = (u_1 + v_1, u_2 + v_2, \ldots, u_n + v_n)$,
  $$(u + v) \cdot w = (u_1 + v_1)w_1 + (u_2 + v_2)w_2 + \cdots + (u_n + v_n)w_n$$
  $$= u_1 w_1 + v_1 w_1 + u_2 w_2 + v_2 w_2 + \cdots + u_n w_n + v_n w_n$$
  $$= (u_1 w_1 + u_2 w_2 + \cdots + u_n w_n) + (v_1 w_1 + v_2 w_2 + \cdots + v_n w_n)$$
  $$= u \cdot w + v \cdot w$$

  (ii) Since $ku = (ku_1, ku_2, \ldots, ku_n)$,
  $$(ku) \cdot v = ku_1 v_1 + ku_2 v_2 + \cdots + ku_n v_n = k(u_1 v_1 + u_2 v_2 + \cdots + u_n v_n) = k(u \cdot v)$$

  (iii) $u \cdot v = u_1 v_1 + u_2 v_2 + \cdots + u_n v_n = v_1 u_1 + v_2 u_2 + \cdots + v_n u_n = v \cdot u$

  (iv) Since u_i^2 is nonnegative for each i, and since the sum of nonnegative real numbers is nonnegative,
  $$u \cdot u = u_1^2 + u_2^2 + \cdots + u_n^2 \geqq 0$$
  Furthermore, $u \cdot u = 0$ iff $u_i = 0$ for each i, that is, iff $u = 0$.

DISTANCE AND NORM IN $\mathbf{R}^n$

1.11. Find the distance $d(u, v)$ between the vectors u and v where: (i) $u = (1, 7)$, $v = (6, -5)$;
  (ii) $u = (3, -5, 4)$, $v = (6, 2, -1)$; (iii) $u = (5, 3, -2, -4, -1)$, $v = (2, -1, 0, -7, 2)$.

  In each case use the formula $d(u, v) = \sqrt{(u_1 - v_1)^2 + \cdots + (u_n - v_n)^2}$.

  (i) $d(u, v) = \sqrt{(1 - 6)^2 + (7 + 5)^2} = \sqrt{25 + 144} = \sqrt{169} = 13$

  (ii) $d(u, v) = \sqrt{(3 - 6)^2 + (-5 - 2)^2 + (4 + 1)^2} = \sqrt{9 + 49 + 25} = \sqrt{83}$

  (iii) $d(u, v) = \sqrt{(5 - 2)^2 + (3 + 1)^2 + (-2 + 0)^2 + (-4 + 7)^2 + (-1 - 2)^2} = \sqrt{47}$

1.12. Find k such that $d(u, v) = 6$ where $u = (2, k, 1, -4)$ and $v = (3, -1, 6, -3)$.
  $$(d(u, v))^2 = (2 - 3)^2 + (k + 1)^2 + (1 - 6)^2 + (-4 + 3)^2 = k^2 + 2k + 28$$
  Now solve $k^2 + 2k + 28 = 6^2$ to obtain $k = 2, -4$.

1.13. Find the norm $\|u\|$ of the vector u if (i) $u = (2, -7)$, (ii) $u = (3, -12, -4)$.

  In each case use the formula $\|u\| = \sqrt{u_1^2 + u_2^2 + \cdots + u_n^2}$.

  (i) $\|u\| = \sqrt{2^2 + (-7)^2} = \sqrt{4 + 49} = \sqrt{53}$

  (ii) $\|u\| = \sqrt{3^2 + (-12)^2 + (-4)^2} = \sqrt{9 + 144 + 16} = \sqrt{169} = 13$

1.14. Determine k such that $\|u\| = \sqrt{39}$ where $u = (1, k, -2, 5)$.

$$\|u\|^2 = 1^2 + k^2 + (-2)^2 + 5^2 = k^2 + 30$$

Now solve $k^2 + 30 = 39$ and obtain $k = 3, -3$.

1.15. Show that $\|u\| \geqq 0$, and $\|u\| = 0$ iff $u = 0$.

By Theorem 1.2, $u \cdot u \geqq 0$, and $u \cdot u = 0$ iff $u = 0$. Since $\|u\| = \sqrt{u \cdot u}$, the result follows.

1.16. Prove Theorem 1.3 (Cauchy-Schwarz):

For any vectors $u = (u_1, \ldots, u_n)$ and $v = (v_1, \ldots, v_n)$ in $\mathbf{R}^n$, $|u \cdot v| \leqq \|u\| \, \|v\|$.

We shall prove the following stronger statement: $|u \cdot v| \leqq \displaystyle\sum_{i=1}^{n} |u_i v_i| \leqq \|u\| \, \|v\|$.

If $u = 0$ or $v = 0$, then the inequality reduces to $0 \leqq 0 \leqq 0$ and is therefore true. Hence we need only consider the case in which $u \neq 0$ and $v \neq 0$, i.e. where $\|u\| \neq 0$ and $\|v\| \neq 0$. Furthermore,

$$|u \cdot v| = |u_1 v_1 + \cdots + u_n v_n| \leqq |u_1 v_1| + \cdots + |u_n v_n| = \sum |u_i v_i|$$

Thus we need only prove the second inequality.

Now for any real numbers $x, y \in \mathbf{R}$, $0 \leqq (x - y)^2 = x^2 - 2xy + y^2$ or, equivalently,

$$2xy \leqq x^2 + y^2 \tag{1}$$

Set $x = |u_i|/\|u\|$ and $y = |v_i|/\|v\|$ in (1) to obtain, for any i,

$$2 \, \frac{|u_i|}{\|u\|} \, \frac{|v_i|}{\|v\|} \leqq \frac{|u_i|^2}{\|u\|^2} + \frac{|v_i|^2}{\|v\|^2} \tag{2}$$

But, by definition of the norm of a vector, $\|u\| = \sum u_i^2 = \sum |u_i|^2$ and $\|v\| = \sum v_i^2 = \sum |v_i|^2$. Thus summing (2) with respect to i and using $|u_i v_i| = |u_i| \, |v_i|$, we have

$$2 \, \frac{\sum |u_i v_i|}{\|u\| \, \|v\|} \leqq \frac{\sum |u_i|^2}{\|u\|^2} + \frac{\sum |v_i|^2}{\|v\|^2} = \frac{\|u\|^2}{\|u\|^2} + \frac{\|v\|^2}{\|v\|^2} = 2$$

that is,

$$\frac{\sum |u_i v_i|}{\|u\| \, \|v\|} \leqq 1$$

Multiplying both sides by $\|u\| \, \|v\|$, we obtain the required inequality.

1.17. Prove Minkowski's inequality:

For any vectors $u = (u_1, \ldots, u_n)$ and $v = (v_1, \ldots, v_n)$ in $\mathbf{R}^n$, $\|u + v\| \leqq \|u\| + \|v\|$.

If $\|u + v\| = 0$, the inequality clearly holds. Thus we need only consider the case $\|u + v\| \neq 0$.

Now $|u_i + v_i| \leqq |u_i| + |v_i|$ for any real numbers $u_i, v_i \in \mathbf{R}$. Hence

$$\begin{aligned}
\|u + v\|^2 &= \sum (u_i + v_i)^2 = \sum |u_i + v_i|^2 \\
&= \sum |u_i + v_i| \, |u_i + v_i| \leqq \sum |u_i + v_i| \, (|u_i| + |v_i|) \\
&= \sum |u_i + v_i| \, |u_i| + \sum |u_i + v_i| \, |v_i|
\end{aligned}$$

But by the Cauchy-Schwarz inequality (see preceding problem),

$$\sum |u_i + v_i| \, |u_i| \leqq \|u + v\| \, \|u\| \quad \text{and} \quad \sum |u_i + v_i| \, |v_i| \leqq \|u + v\| \, \|v\|$$

Thus $\quad \|u + v\|^2 \leqq \|u + v\| \, \|u\| + \|u + v\| \, \|v\| = \|u + v\| \, (\|u\| + \|v\|)$

Dividing by $\|u + v\|$, we obtain the required inequality.

√ **1.18.** Prove that the norm in $\mathbf{R}^n$ satisfies the following laws:

[N_1]: For any vector u, $\|u\| \geqq 0$; and $\|u\| = 0$ iff $u = 0$.

[N_2]: For any vector u and any scalar k, $\|ku\| = |k| \, \|u\|$.

[N_3]: For any vectors u and v, $\|u + v\| \leqq \|u\| + \|v\|$.

[N_1] was proved in Problem 1.15, and [N_3] in Problem 1.17. Hence we need only prove that [N_2] holds.

Suppose $u = (u_1, u_2, \ldots, u_n)$ and so $ku = (ku_1, ku_2, \ldots, ku_n)$. Then

$$\|ku\|^2 = (ku_1)^2 + (ku_2)^2 + \cdots + (ku_n)^2 = k^2 u_1^2 + k^2 u_2^2 + \cdots + k^2 u_n^2$$
$$= k^2(u_1^2 + u_2^2 + \cdots + u_n^2) = k^2 \|u\|^2$$

The square root of both sides of the equality gives us the required result.

COMPLEX NUMBERS

1.19. Simplify: (i) $(5 + 3i)(2 - 7i)$; (ii) $(4 - 3i)^2$; (iii) $\dfrac{1}{3 - 4i}$; (iv) $\dfrac{2 - 7i}{5 + 3i}$; (v) i^3, i^4, i^{31}; (vi) $(1 + 2i)^3$; (vii) $\left(\dfrac{1}{2 - 3i}\right)^2$.

(i) $(5 + 3i)(2 - 7i) = 10 + 6i - 35i - 21i^2 = 31 - 29i$

(ii) $(4 - 3i)^2 = 16 - 24i + 9i^2 = 7 - 24i$

(iii) $\dfrac{1}{3 - 4i} = \dfrac{(3 + 4i)}{(3 - 4i)(3 + 4i)} = \dfrac{3 + 4i}{25} = \dfrac{3}{25} + \dfrac{4}{25}i$

(iv) $\dfrac{2 - 7i}{5 + 3i} = \dfrac{(2 - 7i)(5 - 3i)}{(5 + 3i)(5 - 3i)} = \dfrac{-11 - 41i}{34} = -\dfrac{11}{34} - \dfrac{41}{34}i$

(v) $i^3 = i^2 \cdot i = (-1)i = -i$; $i^4 = i^2 \cdot i^2 = 1$; $i^{31} = (i^4)^7 \cdot i^3 = 1^7 \cdot (-i) = -i$

(vi) $(1 + 2i)^3 = 1 + 6i + 12i^2 + 8i^3 = 1 + 6i - 12 - 8i = -11 - 2i$

(vii) $\left(\dfrac{1}{2 - 3i}\right)^2 = \dfrac{1}{-5 - 12i} = \dfrac{(-5 + 12i)}{(-5 - 12i)(-5 + 12i)} = \dfrac{-5 + 12i}{169} = -\dfrac{5}{169} + \dfrac{12}{169}i$

1.20. Let $z = 2 - 3i$ and $w = 4 + 5i$. Find:

(i) $z + w$ and zw; (ii) z/w; (iii) $\bar{z}$ and $\overline{w}$; (iv) $|z|$ and $|w|$.

(i) $z + w = 2 - 3i + 4 + 5i = 6 + 2i$

$zw = (2 - 3i)(4 + 5i) = 8 - 12i + 10i - 15i^2 = 23 - 2i$

(ii) $\dfrac{z}{w} = \dfrac{2 - 3i}{4 + 5i} = \dfrac{(2 - 3i)(4 - 5i)}{(4 + 5i)(4 - 5i)} = \dfrac{-7 - 22i}{41} = -\dfrac{7}{41} - \dfrac{22}{41}i$

(iii) Use $\overline{a + bi} = a - bi$: $\bar{z} = \overline{2 - 3i} = 2 + 3i$; $\overline{w} = \overline{4 + 5i} = 4 - 5i$.

(iv) Use $|a + bi| = \sqrt{a^2 + b^2}$: $|z| = |2 - 3i| = \sqrt{4 + 9} = \sqrt{13}$; $|w| = |4 + 5i| = \sqrt{16 + 25} = \sqrt{41}$.

√ **1.21.** Prove: For any complex numbers $z, w \in \mathbf{C}$,

(i) $\overline{z + w} = \bar{z} + \overline{w}$,   (ii) $\overline{zw} = \bar{z} \, \overline{w}$,   (iii) $\bar{\bar{z}} = z$.

Suppose $z = a + bi$ and $w = c + di$ where $a, b, c, d \in \mathbf{R}$.

(i) $\overline{z + w} = \overline{(a + bi) + (c + di)} = \overline{(a + c) + (b + d)i}$
$= (a + c) - (b + d)i = a + c - bi - di$
$= (a - bi) + (c - di) = \bar{z} + \overline{w}$

(ii) $\overline{zw} = \overline{(a + bi)(c + di)} = \overline{(ac - bd) + (ad + bc)i}$
$= (ac - bd) - (ad + bc)i = (a - bi)(c - di) = \bar{z} \, \overline{w}$

(iii) $\bar{\bar{z}} = \overline{\overline{a + bi}} = \overline{a - bi} = a - (-b)i = a + bi = z$

1.22. Prove: For any complex numbers $z, w \in \mathbf{C}$, $|zw| = |z|\,|w|$.

Suppose $z = a + bi$ and $w = c + di$ where $a, b, c, d \in \mathbf{R}$. Then

$$|z|^2 = a^2 + b^2, \quad |w|^2 = c^2 + d^2, \quad \text{and} \quad zw = (ac - bd) + (ad + bc)i$$

Thus
$$\begin{aligned}|zw|^2 &= (ac - bd)^2 + (ad + bc)^2 \\ &= a^2c^2 - 2abcd + b^2d^2 + a^2d^2 + 2abcd + b^2c^2 \\ &= a^2(c^2 + d^2) + b^2(c^2 + d^2) = (a^2 + b^2)(c^2 + d^2) = |z|^2\,|w|^2\end{aligned}$$

The square root of both sides gives us the desired result.

1.23. Prove: For any complex numbers $z, w \in \mathbf{C}$, $|z + w| \leq |z| + |w|$.

Suppose $z = a + bi$ and $w = c + di$ where $a, b, c, d \in \mathbf{R}$. Consider the vectors $u = (a, b)$ and $v = (c, d)$ in $\mathbf{R}^2$. Note that

$$|z| = \sqrt{a^2 + b^2} = \|u\|, \quad |w| = \sqrt{c^2 + d^2} = \|v\|$$

and
$$|z + w| = |(a + c) + (b + d)i| = \sqrt{(a + c)^2 + (b + d)^2} = \|(a + c, b + d)\| = \|u + v\|$$

By Minkowski's inequality (Problem 1.17), $\|u + v\| \leq \|u\| + \|v\|$ and so

$$|z + w| = \|u + v\| \leq \|u\| + \|v\| = |z| + |w|$$

VECTORS IN $\mathbf{C}^n$

1.24. Let $u = (3 - 2i, 4i, 1 + 6i)$ and $v = (5 + i, 2 - 3i, 5)$. Find:

(i) $u + v$, (ii) $4iu$, (iii) $(1 + i)v$, (iv) $(1 - 2i)u + (3 + i)v$.

(i) Add corresponding components: $u + v = (8 - i, 2 + i, 6 + 6i)$.

(ii) Multiply each component of u by the scalar $4i$: $4iu = (8 + 12i, -16, -24 + 4i)$.

(iii) Multiply each component of v by the scalar $1 + i$:
$$(1 + i)v = (5 + 6i + i^2, 2 - i - 3i^2, 5 + 5i) = (4 + 6i, 5 - i, 5 + 5i)$$

(iv) First perform the scalar multiplication and then the vector addition:
$$\begin{aligned}(1 - 2i)u + (3 + i)v &= (-1 - 8i, 8 + 4i, 13 + 4i) + (14 + 8i, 9 - 7i, 15 + 5i) \\ &= (13, 17 - 3i, 28 + 9i)\end{aligned}$$

1.25. Find $u \cdot v$ and $v \cdot u$ where: (i) $u = (1 - 2i, 3 + i)$, $v = (4 + 2i, 5 - 6i)$; (ii) $u = (3 - 2i, 4i, 1 + 6i)$, $v = (5 + i, 2 - 3i, 7 + 2i)$.

Recall that the conjugates of the second vector appear in the dot product:
$$(z_1, \ldots, z_n) \cdot (w_1, \ldots, w_n) = z_1\overline{w}_1 + \cdots + z_n\overline{w}_n$$

(i)
$$\begin{aligned}u \cdot v &= (1 - 2i)\overline{(4 + 2i)} + (3 + i)\overline{(5 - 6i)} \\ &= (1 - 2i)(4 - 2i) + (3 + i)(5 + 6i) = -10i + 9 + 23i = 9 + 13i\end{aligned}$$

$$\begin{aligned}v \cdot u &= (4 + 2i)\overline{(1 - 2i)} + (5 - 6i)\overline{(3 + i)} \\ &= (4 + 2i)(1 + 2i) + (5 - 6i)(3 - i) = 10i + 9 - 23i = 9 - 13i\end{aligned}$$

(ii)
$$\begin{aligned}u \cdot v &= (3 - 2i)\overline{(5 + i)} + (4i)\overline{(2 - 3i)} + (1 + 6i)\overline{(7 + 2i)} \\ &= (3 - 2i)(5 - i) + (4i)(2 + 3i) + (1 + 6i)(7 - 2i) = 20 + 35i\end{aligned}$$

$$\begin{aligned}v \cdot u &= (5 + i)\overline{(3 - 2i)} + (2 - 3i)\overline{(4i)} + (7 + 2i)\overline{(1 + 6i)} \\ &= (5 + i)(3 + 2i) + (2 - 3i)(-4i) + (7 + 2i)(1 - 6i) = 20 - 35i\end{aligned}$$

In both examples, $v \cdot u = \overline{u \cdot v}$. This holds true in general, as seen in Problem 1.27.

1.26. Find $\|u\|$ where: (i) $u = (3 + 4i, 5 - 2i, 1 - 3i)$;   (ii) $u = (4 - i, 2i, 3 + 2i, 1 - 5i)$.

Recall that $z\bar{z} = a^2 + b^2$ when $z = a + bi$. Use

$$\|u\|^2 = u \cdot u = z_1\bar{z}_1 + z_2\bar{z}_2 + \cdots + z_n\bar{z}_n \quad \text{where} \quad z = (z_1, z_2, \ldots, z_n)$$

(i) $\|u\|^2 = (3)^2 + (4)^2 + (5)^2 + (-2)^2 + (1)^2 + (-3)^2 = 64$,   or $\|u\| = 8$

(ii) $\|u\|^2 = 4^2 + (-1)^2 + 2^2 + 3^2 + 2^2 + 1^2 + (-5)^2 = 60$,   or $\|u\| = \sqrt{60} = 2\sqrt{15}$

1.27. Prove: For any vectors $u, v \in \mathbf{C}^n$ and any scalar $z \in \mathbf{C}$, (i) $u \cdot v = \overline{v \cdot u}$, (ii) $(zu) \cdot v = z(u \cdot v)$, (iii) $u \cdot (zv) = \bar{z}(u \cdot v)$.   (Compare with Theorem 1.2.)

Suppose $u = (z_1, z_2, \ldots, z_n)$ and $v = (w_1, w_2, \ldots, w_n)$.

(i)   Using the properties of the conjugate established in Problem 1.21,

$$\overline{v \cdot u} = \overline{w_1\bar{z}_1 + w_2\bar{z}_2 + \cdots + w_n\bar{z}_n} = \overline{w_1\bar{z}_1} + \overline{w_2\bar{z}_2} + \cdots + \overline{w_n\bar{z}_n}$$
$$= \overline{w}_1 z_1 + \overline{w}_2 z_2 + \cdots + \overline{w}_n z_n = z_1\overline{w}_1 + z_2\overline{w}_2 + \cdots + z_n\overline{w}_n = u \cdot v$$

(ii)   Since $zu = (zz_1, zz_2, \ldots, zz_n)$,

$$(zu) \cdot v = zz_1\overline{w}_1 + zz_2\overline{w}_2 + \cdots + zz_n\overline{w}_n = z(z_1\overline{w}_1 + z_2\overline{w}_2 + \cdots + z_n\overline{w}_n) = z(u \cdot v)$$

(iii)   **Method 1.**   Since $zv = (zw_1, zw_2, \ldots, zw_n)$,

$$u \cdot (zv) = z_1\overline{zw_1} + z_2\overline{zw_2} + \cdots + z_n\overline{zw_n} = z_1\bar{z}\overline{w}_1 + z_2\bar{z}\overline{w}_2 + \cdots + z_n\bar{z}\overline{w}_n$$
$$= \bar{z}(z_1\overline{w}_1 + z_2\overline{w}_2 + \cdots + z_n\overline{w}_n) = \bar{z}(u \cdot v)$$

Method 2.   Using (i) and (ii),

$$u \cdot (zv) = \overline{(zv) \cdot u} = \overline{z(v \cdot u)} = \bar{z}\,(\overline{v \cdot u}) = \bar{z}\,(u \cdot v)$$

MISCELLANEOUS PROBLEMS

1.28. Let $u = (3, -2, 1, 4)$ and $v = (7, 1, -3, 6)$.   Find:

(i) $u + v$; (ii) $4u$; (iii) $2u - 3v$; (iv) $u \cdot v$; (v) $\|u\|$ and $\|v\|$; (vi) $d(u, v)$.

(i) $u + v = (3 + 7, -2 + 1, 1 - 3, 4 + 6) = (10, -1, -2, 10)$

(ii) $4u = (4 \cdot 3, 4 \cdot (-2), 4 \cdot 1, 4 \cdot 4) = (12, -8, 4, 16)$

(iii) $2u - 3v = (6, -4, 2, 8) + (-21, -3, 9, -18) = (-15, -7, 11, -10)$

(iv) $u \cdot v = 21 - 2 - 3 + 24 = 40$

(v) $\|u\| = \sqrt{9 + 4 + 1 + 16} = \sqrt{30}$, $\|v\| = \sqrt{49 + 1 + 9 + 36} = \sqrt{95}$

(vi) $d(u, v) = \sqrt{(3 - 7)^2 + (-2 - 1)^2 + (1 + 3)^2 + (4 - 6)^2} = \sqrt{45} = 3\sqrt{5}$

1.29. Let $u = (7 - 2i, 2 + 5i)$ and $v = (1 + i, -3 - 6i)$.   Find:

(i) $u + v$; (ii) $2iu$; (iii) $(3 - i)v$; (iv) $u \cdot v$; (v) $\|u\|$ and $\|v\|$.

(i) $u + v = (7 - 2i + 1 + i, 2 + 5i - 3 - 6i) = (8 - i, -1 - i)$

(ii) $2iu = (14i - 4i^2, 4i + 10i^2) = (4 + 14i, -10 + 4i)$

(iii) $(3 - i)v = (3 + 3i - i - i^2, -9 - 18i + 3i + 6i^2) = (4 + 2i, -15 - 15i)$

(iv) $u \cdot v = (7 - 2i)(\overline{1 + i}) + (2 + 5i)(\overline{-3 - 6i})$
$$= (7 - 2i)(1 - i) + (2 + 5i)(-3 + 6i) = 5 - 9i - 36 - 3i = -31 - 12i$$

(v) $\|u\| = \sqrt{7^2 + (-2)^2 + 2^2 + 5^2} = \sqrt{82}$, $\|v\| = \sqrt{1^2 + 1^2 + (-3)^2 + (-6)^2} = \sqrt{47}$

1.30. Any pair of points $P = (a_i)$ and $Q = (b_i)$ in $\mathbf{R}^n$ defines the *directed line segment from P to Q*, written $\overrightarrow{PQ}$. We identify $\overrightarrow{PQ}$ with the vector $v = Q - P$:

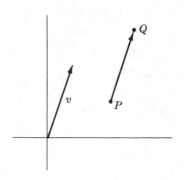

$$\overrightarrow{PQ} \;=\; v \;=\; (b_1 - a_1, \, b_2 - a_2, \, \ldots, \, b_n - a_n)$$

Find the vector v identified with $\overrightarrow{PQ}$ where:

(i) $P = (2, 5), \;\; Q = (-3, 4)$

(ii) $P = (1, -2, 4), \;\; Q = (6, 0, -3)$

(i) $v \;=\; Q - P \;=\; (-3 - 2, \, 4 - 5) \;=\; (-5, -1)$

(ii) $v \;=\; Q - P \;=\; (6 - 1, \, 0 + 2, \, -3 - 4) \;=\; (5, 2, -7)$

1.31. The set H of elements in $\mathbf{R}^n$ which are solutions of a linear equation in n unknowns $x_1, \ldots, x_n$ of the form

$$c_1 x_1 + c_2 x_2 + \cdots + c_n x_n \;=\; b \tag{$*$}$$

with $u = (c_1, \ldots, c_n) \neq 0$ in $\mathbf{R}^n$, is called a *hyperplane* of $\mathbf{R}^n$, and $(*)$ is called an *equation* of H. (We frequently identify H with $(*)$.) Show that the directed line segment $\overrightarrow{PQ}$ of any pair of points $P, Q \in H$ is orthogonal to the coefficient vector u; the vector u is said to be *normal* to the hyperplane H.

Suppose $P = (a_1, \ldots, a_n)$ and $Q = (b_1, \ldots, b_n)$. Then the a_i and the b_i are solutions of the given equation:

$$c_1 a_1 + c_2 a_2 + \cdots + c_n a_n \;=\; b, \qquad c_1 b_1 + c_2 b_2 + \cdots + c_n b_n \;=\; b$$

Let

$$v \;=\; \overrightarrow{PQ} \;=\; Q - P \;=\; (b_1 - a_1, \, b_2 - a_2, \, \ldots, \, b_n - a_n)$$

Then

$$\begin{aligned} u \cdot v \;&=\; c_1(b_1 - a_1) + c_2(b_2 - a_2) + \cdots + c_n(b_n - a_n) \\ &=\; c_1 b_1 - c_1 a_1 + c_2 b_2 - c_2 a_2 + \cdots + c_n b_n - c_n a_n \\ &=\; (c_1 b_1 + c_2 b_2 + \cdots + c_n b_n) - (c_1 a_1 + c_2 a_2 + \cdots + c_n a_n) \;=\; b - b \;=\; 0 \end{aligned}$$

Hence v, that is, $\overrightarrow{PQ}$, is orthogonal to u.

1.32. Find an equation of the hyperplane H in $\mathbf{R}^4$ if: (i) H passes through $P = (3, -2, 1, -4)$ and is normal to $u = (2, 5, -6, -2)$; (ii) H passes through $P = (1, -2, 3, 5)$ and is parallel to the hyperplane H' determined by $4x - 5y + 2z + w = 11$.

(i)   An equation of H is of the form $2x + 5y - 6z - 2w = k$ since it is normal to u. Substitute P into this equation to obtain $k = -2$. Thus an equation of H is $2x + 5y - 6z - 2w = -2$.

(ii) H and H' are parallel iff corresponding normal vectors are in the same or opposite direction. Hence an equation of H is of the form $4x - 5y + 2z + w = k$. Substituting P into this equation, we find $k = 25$. Thus an equation of H is $4x - 5y + 2z + w = 25$.

1.33. The line l in $\mathbf{R}^n$ passing through the point $P = (a_i)$ and in the direction of $u = (u_i) \neq 0$ consists of the points $X = P + tu, \; t \in \mathbf{R}$, that is, consists of the points $X = (x_i)$ obtained from

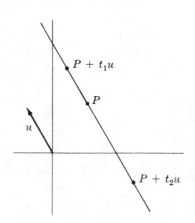

$$(*) \begin{cases} x_1 \;=\; a_1 + u_1 t \\ x_2 \;=\; a_2 + u_2 t \\ \cdots\cdots\cdots\cdots \\ x_n \;=\; a_n + u_n t \end{cases}$$

where t takes on all real values. The variable t is called a *parameter*, and $(*)$ is called a *parametric representation* of l.

(i) Find a parametric representation of the line passing through P and in the direction of u where: (a) $P = (2,5)$ and $u = (-3,4)$; (b) $P = (4,-2,3,1)$ and $u = (2,5,-7,11)$.

(ii) Find a parametric representation of the line passing through the points P and Q where: (a) $P = (7,-2)$ and $Q = (9,3)$; (b) $P = (5,4,-3)$ and $Q = (1,-3,2)$.

(i) In each case use the formula (*).

$$(a)\quad \begin{cases} x = 2 - 3t \\ y = 5 + 4t \end{cases} \qquad (b)\quad \begin{cases} x = 4 + 2t \\ y = -2 + 5t \\ z = 3 - 7t \\ w = 1 + 11t \end{cases}$$

(In $\mathbf{R}^2$ we usually eliminate t from the two equations and represent the line by a single equation: $4x + 3y = 23$.)

(ii) First compute $u = \overrightarrow{PQ} = Q - P$. Then use the formula (*).

$$(a)\quad u = Q - P = (2,5) \qquad\qquad (b)\quad u = Q - P = (-4,-7,5)$$

$$\begin{cases} x = 7 + 2t \\ y = -2 + 5t \end{cases} \qquad\qquad \begin{cases} x = 5 - 4t \\ y = 4 - 7t \\ z = -3 + 5t \end{cases}$$

(Note that in each case we could also write $u = \overrightarrow{QP} = P - Q$.)

Supplementary Problems

VECTORS IN $\mathbf{R}^n$

1.34. Let $u = (1,-2,5)$, $v = (3,1,-2)$. Find: (i) $u + v$; (ii) $-6u$; (iii) $2u - 5v$; (iv) $u \cdot v$; (v) $||u||$ and $||v||$; (vi) $d(u,v)$.

1.35. Let $u = (2,-1,0,-3)$, $v = (1,-1,-1,3)$, $w = (1,3,-2,2)$. Find: (i) $2u - 3v$; (ii) $5u - 3v - 4w$; (iii) $-u + 2v - 2w$; (iv) $u \cdot v$, $u \cdot w$ and $v \cdot w$; (v) $d(u,v)$ and $d(v,w)$.

1.36. Let $u = (2,1,-3,0,4)$, $v = (5,-3,-1,2,7)$. Find: (i) $u + v$; (ii) $3u - 2v$; (iii) $u \cdot v$; (iv) $||u||$ and $||v||$; (v) $d(u,v)$.

1.37. Determine k so that the vectors u and v are orthogonal. (i) $u = (3,k,-2)$, $v = (6,-4,-3)$. (ii) $u = (5,k,-4,2)$, $v = (1,-3,2,2k)$. (iii) $u = (1,7,k+2,-2)$, $v = (3,k,-3,k)$.

1.38. Determine x and y if: (i) $(x,x+y) = (y-2,6)$; (ii) $x(1,2) = -4(y,3)$.

1.39. Determine x and y if: (i) $x(3,2) = 2(y,-1)$; (ii) $x(2,y) = y(1,-2)$.

1.40. Determine x, y and z if:

(i) $(3,-1,2) = x(1,1,1) + y(1,-1,0) + z(1,0,0)$

(ii) $(-1,3,3) = x(1,1,0) + y(0,0,-1) + z(0,1,1)$

1.41. Let $e_1 = (1,0,0)$, $e_2 = (0,1,0)$, $e_3 = (0,0,1)$. Show that for any vector $u = (a,b,c)$ in $\mathbf{R}^3$: (i) $u = ae_1 + be_2 + ce_3$; (ii) $u \cdot e_1 = a$, $u \cdot e_2 = b$, $u \cdot e_3 = c$.

1.42. Generalize the result in the preceding problem as follows. Let $e_i \in \mathbf{R}^n$ be the vector with 1 in the ith coordinate and 0 elsewhere:

$$e_1 = (1, 0, 0, \ldots, 0, 0), \quad e_2 = (0, 1, 0, \ldots, 0, 0), \quad \ldots, \quad e_n = (0, 0, 0, \ldots, 0, 1)$$

Show that for any vector $u = (a_1, a_2, \ldots, a_n)$,

$$\text{(i)} \quad u = a_1 e_1 + a_2 e_2 + \cdots + a_n e_n, \qquad \text{(ii)} \quad u \cdot e_i = a_i \text{ for } i = 1, \ldots, n$$

1.43. Suppose $u \in \mathbf{R}^n$ has the property that $u \cdot v = 0$ for every $v \in \mathbf{R}^n$. Show that $u = 0$.

1.44. Using $d(u, v) = \|u - v\|$ and the norm properties $[N_1]$, $[N_2]$ and $[N_3]$ in Problem 1.18, show that the distance function satisfies the following properties for any vectors $u, v, w \in \mathbf{R}^n$:

(i) $d(u, v) \geqq 0$, and $d(u, v) = 0$ iff $u = v$;   (ii) $d(u, v) = d(v, u)$;   (iii) $d(u, w) \leqq d(u, v) + d(v, w)$.

COMPLEX NUMBERS

1.45. Simplify: (i) $(4 - 7i)(9 + 2i)$; (ii) $(3 - 5i)^2$; (iii) $\dfrac{1}{4 - 7i}$; (iv) $\dfrac{9 + 2i}{3 - 5i}$; (v) $(1 - i)^3$.

1.46. Simplify: (i) $\dfrac{1}{2i}$; (ii) $\dfrac{2 + 3i}{7 - 3i}$; (iii) i^{15}, i^{25}, i^{34}; (iv) $\left(\dfrac{1}{3 - i}\right)^2$.

1.47. Let $z = 2 - 5i$ and $w = 7 + 3i$. Find: (i) $z + w$; (ii) zw; (iii) z/w; (iv) $\bar{z}, \bar{w}$; (v) $|z|, |w|$.

1.48. Let $z = 2 + i$ and $w = 6 - 5i$. Find: (i) z/w; (ii) $\bar{z}, \bar{w}$; (iii) $|z|, |w|$.

1.49. Show that: (i) $zz^{-1} = 1$; (ii) $|z| = |\bar{z}|$; (iii) real part of $z = \frac{1}{2}(z + \bar{z})$; (iv) imaginary part of $z = (z - \bar{z})/2i$.

1.50. Show that $zw = 0$ implies $z = 0$ or $w = 0$.

VECTORS IN $\mathbf{C}^n$

1.51. Let $u = (1 + 7i, 2 - 6i)$ and $v = (5 - 2i, 3 - 4i)$. Find: (i) $u + v$; (ii) $(3 + i)u$; (iii) $2iu + (4 - 7i)v$; (iv) $u \cdot v$ and $v \cdot u$; (v) $\|u\|$ and $\|v\|$.

1.52. Let $u = (3 - 7i, 2i, -1 + i)$ and $v = (4 - i, 11 + 2i, 8 - 3i)$. Find: (i) $u - v$; (ii) $(3 + i)v$; (iii) $u \cdot v$ and $v \cdot u$; (iv) $\|u\|$ and $\|v\|$.

1.53. Prove: For any vectors $u, v, w \in \mathbf{C}^n$:

(i) $(u + v) \cdot w = u \cdot w + v \cdot w$; (ii) $w \cdot (u + v) = w \cdot u + w \cdot v$. (Compare with Theorem 1.2.)

1.54. Prove that the norm in $\mathbf{C}^n$ satisfies the following laws:

$[N_1]$: For any vector u, $\|u\| \geqq 0$; and $\|u\| = 0$ iff $u = 0$.

$[N_2]$: For any vector u and any complex number z, $\|zu\| = |z|\,\|u\|$.

$[N_3]$: For any vectors u and v, $\|u + v\| \leqq \|u\| + \|v\|$.

(Compare with Problem 1.18.)

MISCELLANEOUS PROBLEMS

1.55. Find an equation of the hyperplane in $\mathbf{R}^3$ which:

(i)   passes through $(2, -7, 1)$ and is normal to $(3, 1, -11)$;

(ii) contains $(1, -2, 2)$, $(0, 1, 3)$ and $(0, 2, -1)$;

(iii) contains $(1, -5, 2)$ and is parallel to $3x - 7y + 4z = 5$.

1.56. Determine the value of k such that $2x - ky + 4z - 5w = 11$ is perpendicular to $7x + 2y - z + 2w = 8$. (Two hyperplanes are perpendicular iff corresponding normal vectors are orthogonal.)

1.57. Find a parametric representation of the line which:
    (i)   passes through $(7, -1, 8)$ in the direction of $(1, 3, -5)$
    (ii)   passes through $(1, 9, -4, 5)$ and $(2, -3, 0, 4)$
    (iii) passes through $(4, -1, 9)$ and is perpendicular to the plane $3x - 2y + z = 18$

1.58. Let P, Q and R be the points on the line determined by
$$x_1 = a_1 + u_1 t, \quad x_2 = a_2 + u_2 t, \quad \ldots, \quad x_n = a_n + u_n t$$
which correspond respectively to the values t_1, t_2 and t_3 for t. Show that if $t_1 < t_2 < t_3$, then $d(P, Q) + d(Q, R) = d(P, R)$.

Answers to Supplementary Problems

1.34. (i) $u + v = (4, -1, 3)$;   (ii) $-6u = (-6, 12, -30)$;   (iii) $2u - 5v = (-13, -9, 20)$;   (iv) $u \cdot v = -9$;
     (v) $\|u\| = \sqrt{30}$, $\|v\| = \sqrt{14}$; (vi) $d(u, v) = \sqrt{62}$

1.35. (i) $2u - 3v = (1, 1, 3, -15)$; (ii) $5u - 3v - 4w = (3, -14, 11, -32)$; (iii) $-u + 2v - 2w = (-2, -7, 2, 5)$;
     (iv) $u \cdot v = -6$, $u \cdot w = -7$, $v \cdot w = 6$; (v) $d(u, v) = \sqrt{38}$, $d(v, w) = 3\sqrt{2}$

1.36. (i) $u + v = (7, -2, -4, 2, 11)$; (ii) $3u - 2v = (-4, 9, -7, -4, -2)$; (iii) $u \cdot v = 38$; (iv) $\|u\| = \sqrt{30}$,
     $\|v\| = 2\sqrt{22}$; (v) $d(u, v) = \sqrt{42}$

1.37. (i) $k = 6$; (ii) $k = 3$; (iii) $k = 3/2$

1.38. (i) $x = 2$, $y = 4$; (ii) $x = -6$, $y = 3/2$

1.39. (i) $x = -1$, $y = -3/2$; (ii) $x = 0$, $y = 0$;   or $x = -2$, $y = -4$

1.40. (i) $x = 2$, $y = 3$, $z = -2$; (ii) $x = -1$, $y = 1$, $z = 4$

1.43. We have that $u \cdot u = 0$ which implies that $u = 0$.

1.45. (i) $50 - 55i$; (ii) $-16 - 30i$; (iii) $(4 + 7i)/65$; (iv) $(1 + 3i)/2$; (v) $-2 - 2i$.

1.46. (i) $-\frac{1}{2}i$; (ii) $(5 + 27i)/58$; (iii) $-i, i, -1$; (iv) $(4 + 3i)/50$.

1.47. (i) $z + w = 9 - 2i$; (ii) $zw = 29 - 29i$; (iii) $z/w = (-1 - 41i)/58$; (iv) $\bar{z} = 2 + 5i$, $\bar{w} = 7 - 3i$;
     (v) $|z| = \sqrt{29}$, $|w| = \sqrt{58}$.

1.48. (i) $z/w = (7 + 16i)/61$; (ii) $\bar{z} = 2 - i$, $\bar{w} = 6 + 5i$; (iii) $|z| = \sqrt{5}$, $|w| = \sqrt{61}$.

1.50. If $zw = 0$, then $|zw| = |z| \, |w| = |0| = 0$. Hence $|z| = 0$ or $|w| = 0$; and so $z = 0$ or $w = 0$.

1.51. (i) $u + v = (6 + 5i, \ 5 - 10i)$ (iv) $u \cdot v = 21 + 27i$, $v \cdot u = 21 - 27i$
     (ii) $(3 + i)u = (-4 + 22i, \ 12 - 16i)$ (v) $\|u\| = 3\sqrt{10}$, $\|v\| = 3\sqrt{6}$
     (iii) $2iu + (4 - 7i)v = (-8 - 41i, \ -4 - 33i)$

1.52. (i) $u - v = (-1 - 6i, -11, -9 + 4i)$ (iii) $u \cdot v = 12 + 2i$, $v \cdot u = 12 - 2i$
     (ii) $(3 + i)v = (13 + i, \ 31 + 17i, \ 27 - i)$ (iv) $\|u\| = 8$, $\|v\| = \sqrt{215}$

1.55. (i) $3x + y - 11z = -12$; (ii) $13x + 4y + z = 7$; (iii) $3x - 7y + 4z = 46$.

1.56. $k = 0$

1.57. (i) $\begin{cases} x = 7 + t \\ y = -1 + 3t \\ z = 8 - 5t \end{cases}$ (ii) $\begin{cases} x = 1 + t \\ y = 9 - 12t \\ z = -4 + 4t \\ w = 5 - t \end{cases}$ (iii) $\begin{cases} x = 4 + 3t \\ y = -1 - 2t \\ z = 9 + t \end{cases}$

Chapter 2

Linear Equations

INTRODUCTION

The theory of linear equations plays an important and motivating role in the subject of linear algebra. In fact, many problems in linear algebra are equivalent to studying a system of linear equations, e.g. finding the kernel of a linear mapping and characterizing the subspace spanned by a set of vectors. Thus the techniques introduced in this chapter will be applicable to the more abstract treatment given later. On the other hand, some of the results of the abstract treatment will give us new insights into the structure of "concrete" systems of linear equations.

For simplicity, we assume that all equations in this chapter are over the real field **R**. We emphasize that the results and techniques also hold for equations over the complex field **C** or over any arbitrary field K.

LINEAR EQUATION

By a linear equation over the real field **R**, we mean an expression of the form

$$a_1 x_1 + a_2 x_2 + \cdots + a_n x_n = b \tag{1}$$

where the $a_i, b \in \mathbf{R}$ and the x_i are *indeterminants* (or: *unknowns* or *variables*). The scalars a_i are called the *coefficients* of the x_i respectively, and b is called the *constant term* or simply *constant* of the equation. A set of values for the unknowns, say

$$x_1 = k_1, \ x_2 = k_2, \ \ldots, \ x_n = k_n$$

is a *solution* of (1) if the statement obtained by substituting k_i for x_i,

$$a_1 k_1 + a_2 k_2 + \cdots + a_n k_n = b$$

is true. This set of values is then said to *satisfy* the equation. If there is no ambiguity about the position of the unknowns in the equation, then we denote this solution by simply the n-tuple

$$u = (k_1, k_2, \ldots, k_n)$$

> **Example 2.1:** Consider the equation $x + 2y - 4z + w = 3$.
>
> The 4-tuple $u = (3, 2, 1, 0)$ is a solution of the equation since
>
> $$3 + 2 \cdot 2 - 4 \cdot 1 + 0 = 3 \quad \text{or} \quad 3 = 3$$
>
> is a true statement. However, the 4-tuple $v = (1, 2, 4, 5)$ is not a solution of the equation since
>
> $$1 + 2 \cdot 2 - 4 \cdot 4 + 5 = 3 \quad \text{or} \quad -6 = 3$$
>
> is not a true statement.

Solutions of the equation (1) can be easily described and obtained. There are three cases:

Case (i): One of the coefficients in (1) is not zero, say $a_1 \neq 0$. Then we can rewrite the equation as follows

$$a_1 x_1 = b - a_2 x_2 - \cdots - a_n x_n \quad \text{or} \quad x_1 = a_1^{-1} b - a_1^{-1} a_2 x_2 - \cdots - a_1^{-1} a_n x_n$$

By arbitrarily assigning values to the unknowns $x_2, \ldots, x_n$, we obtain a value for x_1; these values form a solution of the equation. Furthermore, every solution of the equation can be obtained in this way. Note in particular that the linear equation in one unknown,

$$ax = b, \quad \text{with } a \neq 0$$

has the unique solution $x = a^{-1}b$.

> **Example 2.2:**   Consider the equation $2x - 4y + z = 8$.
>
>   We rewrite the equation as
>
> $$2x = 8 + 4y - z \quad \text{or} \quad x = 4 + 2y - \tfrac{1}{2}z$$
>
>   Any value for y and z will yield a value for x, and the three values will be a solution of the equation. For example, let $y = 3$ and $z = 2$; then $x = 4 + 2 \cdot 3 - \tfrac{1}{2} \cdot 2 = 9$. In other words, the 3-tuple $u = (9, 3, 2)$ is a solution of the equation.

Case (ii): All the coefficients in (1) are zero, but the constant is not zero. That is, the equation is of the form

$$0x_1 + 0x_2 + \cdots + 0x_n = b, \quad \text{with } b \neq 0$$

Then the equation has no solution.

Case (iii): All the coefficients in (1) are zero, and the constant is also zero. That is, the equation is of the form

$$0x_1 + 0x_2 + \cdots + 0x_n = 0$$

Then every n-tuple of scalars in **R** is a solution of the equation.

SYSTEM OF LINEAR EQUATIONS

We now consider a system of m linear equations in the n unknowns $x_1, \ldots, x_n$:

$$
\begin{aligned}
a_{11}x_1 + a_{12}x_2 + \cdots + a_{1n}x_n &= b_1 \\
a_{21}x_1 + a_{22}x_2 + \cdots + a_{2n}x_n &= b_2 \\
&\cdots\cdots\cdots\cdots\cdots\cdots\cdots \\
a_{m1}x_1 + a_{m2}x_2 + \cdots + a_{mn}x_n &= b_m
\end{aligned}
\tag{*}
$$

where the a_{ij}, b_i belong to the real field **R**. The system is said to be *homogeneous* if the constants $b_1, \ldots, b_m$ are all 0. An n-tuple $u = (k_1, \ldots, k_n)$ of real numbers is a *solution* (or: a *particular solution*) if it satisfies each of the equations; the set of all such solutions is termed the *solution set* or the *general solution*.

The system of linear equations

$$
\begin{aligned}
a_{11}x_1 + a_{12}x_2 + \cdots + a_{1n}x_n &= 0 \\
a_{21}x_1 + a_{22}x_2 + \cdots + a_{2n}x_n &= 0 \\
&\cdots\cdots\cdots\cdots\cdots\cdots\cdots \\
a_{m1}x_1 + a_{m2}x_2 + \cdots + a_{mn}x_n &= 0
\end{aligned}
\tag{**}
$$

is called the homogeneous system associated with (*). The above system always has a solution, namely the zero n-tuple $0 = (0, 0, \ldots, 0)$ called the *zero* or *trivial* solution. Any other solution, if it exists, is called a *nonzero* or *nontrivial* solution.

The fundamental relationship between the systems (*) and (**) follows.

Theorem 2.1: Suppose u is a particular solution of the nonhomogeneous system (∗) and suppose W is the general solution of the associated homogeneous system (∗∗). Then

$$u + W = \{u + w : w \in W\}$$

is the general solution of the nonhomogeneous system (∗).

We emphasize that the above theorem is of theoretical interest and does not help us to obtain explicit solutions of the system (∗). This is done by the usual method of elimination described in the next section.

SOLUTION OF A SYSTEM OF LINEAR EQUATIONS

Consider the above system (∗) of linear equations. We reduce it to a simpler system as follows:

Step 1. Interchange equations so that the first unknown x_1 has a nonzero coefficient in the first equation, that is, so that $a_{11} \neq 0$.

Step 2. For each $i > 1$, apply the operation

$$L_i \;\rightarrow\; -a_{i1}L_1 + a_{11}L_i$$

That is, replace the ith linear equation L_i by the equation obtained by multiplying the first equation L_1 by $-a_{i1}$, multiplying the ith equation L_i by a_{11}, and then adding.

We then obtain the following system which (Problem 2.13) is *equivalent* to (∗), i.e. has the same solution set as (∗):

$$a_{11}x_1 + a'_{12}x_2 + a'_{13}x_3 + \cdots + a'_{1n}x_n = b'_1$$
$$a'_{2j_2}x_{j_2} + \cdots\cdots + a'_{2n}x_n = b'_2$$
$$\cdots\cdots\cdots\cdots\cdots\cdots\cdots\cdots\cdots\cdots$$
$$a'_{mj_2}x_{j_2} + \cdots\cdots + a'_{mn}x_n = b'_m$$

where $a_{11} \neq 0$. Here x_{j_2} denotes the first unknown with a nonzero coefficient in an equation other than the first; by Step 2, $x_{j_2} \neq x_1$. This process which eliminates an unknown from succeeding equations is known as (Gauss) elimination.

Example 2.3: Consider the following system of linear equations:

$$2x + 4y - z + 2v + 2w = 1$$
$$3x + 6y + z - v + 4w = -7$$
$$4x + 8y + z + 5v - w = 3$$

We eliminate the unknown x from the second and third equations by applying the following operations:

$$L_2 \rightarrow -3L_1 + 2L_2 \quad \text{and} \quad L_3 \rightarrow -2L_1 + L_3$$

We compute

$$\begin{array}{rl} -3L_1: & -6x - 12y + 3z - 6v - 6w = -3 \\ 2L_2: & 6x + 12y + 2z - 2v + 8w = -14 \\ \hline -3L_1 + 2L_2: & 5z - 8v + 2w = -17 \end{array}$$

and

$$\begin{array}{rl} -2L_1: & -4x - 8y + 2z - 4v - 4w = -2 \\ L_3: & 4x + 8y + z + 5v - w = 3 \\ \hline -2L_1 + L_3: & 3z + v - 5w = 1 \end{array}$$

Thus the original system has been reduced to the following equivalent system:

$$2x + 4y - z + 2v + 2w = 1$$

$$5z - 8v + 2w = -17$$

$$3z + v - 5w = 1$$

Observe that y has also been eliminated from the second and third equations. Here the unknown z plays the role of the unknown x_{j_2} above.

We note that the above equations, excluding the first, form a subsystem which has fewer equations and fewer unknowns than the original system (*). We also note that:

   (i)   if an equation $0x_1 + \cdots + 0x_n = b, \; b \neq 0$ occurs, then the system is *inconsistent* and has no solution;

   (ii) if an equation $0x_1 + \cdots + 0x_n = 0$ occurs, then the equation can be deleted without affecting the solution.

Continuing the above process with each new "smaller" subsystem, we obtain by induction that the system (*) is either inconsistent or is reducible to an equivalent system in the following form

$$a_{11}x_1 + a_{12}x_2 + a_{13}x_3 + \cdots\cdots\cdots\cdots\cdots + a_{1n}x_n = b_1$$

$$a_{2j_2}x_{j_2} + a_{2,j_2+1}x_{j_2+1} + \cdots\cdots + a_{2n}x_n = b_2$$

$$\cdots\cdots\cdots\cdots\cdots\cdots\cdots\cdots\cdots\cdots\cdots\cdots$$

$$a_{rj_r}x_{j_r} + a_{r,j_r+1}x_{j_r+1} + \cdots + a_{rn}x_n = b_r$$

(***)

where $1 < j_2 < \cdots < j_r$ and where the leading coefficients are not zero:

$$a_{11} \neq 0, \; a_{2j_2} \neq 0, \; \ldots, \; a_{rj_r} \neq 0$$

(For notational convenience we use the same symbols a_{ij}, b_k in the system (***) as we used in the system (*), but clearly they may denote different scalars.)

Definition: The above system (***) is said to be in *echelon form*; the unknowns x_i which do not appear at the beginning of any equation $(i \neq 1, j_2, \ldots, j_r)$ are termed *free variables*.

The following theorem applies.

Theorem 2.2:   The solution of the system (***) in echelon form is as follows.   There are two cases:

   (i) $r = n$. That is, there are as many equations as unknowns.   Then the system has a unique solution.

   (ii) $r < n$. That is, there are fewer equations than unknowns.   Then we can arbitrarily assign values to the $n - r$ free variables and obtain a solution of the system.

Note in particular that the above theorem implies that the system (***) and any equivalent systems are consistent. Thus if the system (*) is consistent and reduces to case (ii) above, then we can assign many different values to the free variables and so obtain many solutions of the system. The following diagram illustrates this situation.

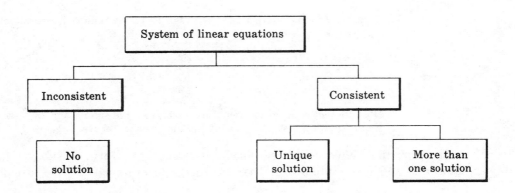

In view of Theorem 2.1, the unique solution above can only occur when the associated homogeneous system has only the zero solution.

Example 2.4:   We reduce the following system by applying the operations $L_2 \to -3L_1 + 2L_2$ and $L_3 \to -3L_1 + 2L_3$, and then the operation $L_3 \to -3L_2 + L_3$:

$$
\begin{aligned}
2x + y - 2z + 3w &= 1 \\
3x + 2y - z + 2w &= 4 \\
3x + 3y + 3z - 3w &= 5
\end{aligned}
\qquad
\begin{aligned}
2x + y - 2z + 3w &= 1 \\
y + 4z - 5w &= 5 \\
3y + 12z - 15w &= 7
\end{aligned}
\qquad
\begin{aligned}
2x + y - 2z + 3w &= 1 \\
y + 4z - 5w &= 5 \\
0 &= -8
\end{aligned}
$$

The equation $0 = -8$, that is, $0x + 0y + 0z + 0w = -8$, shows that the original system is inconsistent, and so has no solution.

Example 2.5:   We reduce the following system by applying the operations $L_2 \to -L_1 + L_2$, $L_3 \to -2L_1 + L_3$ and $L_4 \to -2L_1 + L_4$, and then the operations $L_3 \to L_2 - L_3$ and $L_4 \to -2L_2 + L_4$:

$$
\begin{aligned}
x + 2y - 3z &= 4 \\
x + 3y + z &= 11 \\
2x + 5y - 4z &= 13 \\
2x + 6y + 2z &= 22
\end{aligned}
\qquad
\begin{aligned}
x + 2y - 3z &= 4 \\
y + 4z &= 7 \\
y + 2z &= 5 \\
2y + 8z &= 14
\end{aligned}
\qquad
\begin{aligned}
x + 2y - 3z &= 4 \\
y + 4z &= 7 \\
2z &= 2 \\
0 &= 0
\end{aligned}
$$

$$
\begin{aligned}
x + 2y - 3z &= 4 \\
y + 4z &= 7 \\
2z &= 2
\end{aligned}
$$

Observe first that the system is consistent since there is no equation of the form $0 = b$, with $b \neq 0$. Furthermore, since in echelon form there are three equations in the three unknowns, the system has a unique solution. By the third equation, $z = 1$. Substituting $z = 1$ into the second equation, we obtain $y = 3$. Substituting $z = 1$ and $y = 3$ into the first equation, we find $x = 1$. Thus $x = 1$, $y = 3$ and $z = 1$ or, in other words, the 3-tuple $(1, 3, 1)$, is the unique solution of the system.

Example 2.6:   We reduce the following system by applying the operations $L_2 \to -2L_1 + L_2$ and $L_3 \to -5L_1 + L_3$, and then the operation $L_3 \to -2L_2 + L_3$:

$$
\begin{aligned}
x + 2y - 2z + 3w &= 2 \\
2x + 4y - 3z + 4w &= 5 \\
5x + 10y - 8z + 11w &= 12
\end{aligned}
\qquad
\begin{aligned}
x + 2y - 2z + 3w &= 2 \\
z - 2w &= 1 \\
2z - 4w &= 2
\end{aligned}
\qquad
\begin{aligned}
x + 2y - 2z + 3w &= 2 \\
z - 2w &= 1 \\
0 &= 0
\end{aligned}
$$

$$
\begin{aligned}
x + 2y - 2z + 3w &= 2 \\
z - 2w &= 1
\end{aligned}
$$

The system is consistent, and since there are more unknowns than equations in echelon form, the system has an infinite number of solutions. In fact, there are two free variables, y and w, and so a particular solution can be obtained by giving y and w any values. For example, let $w = 1$ and $y = -2$. Substituting $w = 1$ into the second equation, we obtain $z = 3$. Putting $w = 1$, $z = 3$ and $y = -2$ into the first equation, we find $x = 9$. Thus $x = 9$, $y = -2$, $z = 3$ and $w = 1$ or, in other words, the 4-tuple $(9, -2, 3, 1)$ is a particular solution of the system.

Remark: We find the general solution of the system in the above example as follows. Let the free variables be assigned arbitrary values; say, $y = a$ and $w = b$. Substituting $w = b$ into the second equation, we obtain $z = 1 + 2b$. Putting $y = a$, $z = 1 + 2b$ and $w = b$ into the first equation, we find $x = 4 - 2a + b$. Thus the general solution of the system is

$$x = 4 - 2a + b, \quad y = a, \quad z = 1 + 2b, \quad w = b$$

or, in other words, $(4 - 2a + b, a, 1 + 2b, b)$, where a and b are arbitrary numbers. Frequently, the general solution is left in terms of the free variables y and w (instead of a and b) as follows:

$$x = 4 - 2y + w, \quad z = 1 + 2w \quad \text{or} \quad (4 - 2y + w, y, 1 + 2w, w)$$

We will investigate further the representation of the general solution of a system of linear equations in a later chapter.

Example 2.7: Consider two equations in two unknowns:

$$a_1 x + b_1 y = c_1$$
$$a_2 x + b_2 y = c_2$$

According to our theory, exactly one of the following three cases must occur:

(i)   The system is inconsistent.
(ii) The system is equivalent to two equations in echelon form.
(iii) The system is equivalent to one equation in echelon form.

When linear equations in two unknowns with real coefficients can be represented as lines in the plane $\mathbf{R}^2$, the above cases can be interpreted geometrically as follows:

(i)   The two lines are parallel.
(ii) The two lines intersect in a unique point.
(iii) The two lines are coincident.

SOLUTION OF A HOMOGENEOUS SYSTEM OF LINEAR EQUATIONS

If we begin with a homogeneous system of linear equations, then the system is clearly consistent since, for example, it has the zero solution $0 = (0, 0, \ldots, 0)$. Thus it can always be reduced to an equivalent homogeneous system in echelon form:

$$a_{11}x_1 + a_{12}x_2 + a_{13}x_3 + \cdots\cdots\cdots\cdots + a_{1n}x_n = 0$$
$$a_{2j_2}x_{j_2} + a_{2,j_2+1}x_{j_2+1} + \cdots\cdots + a_{2n}x_n = 0$$
$$\cdots\cdots\cdots\cdots\cdots\cdots\cdots\cdots\cdots$$
$$a_{rj_r}x_{j_r} + a_{r,j_r+1}x_{j_r+1} + \cdots + a_{rn}x_n = 0$$

Hence we have the two possibilities:

(i) $r = n$. Then the system has only the zero solution.
(ii) $r < n$. Then the system has a nonzero solution.

If we begin with fewer equations than unknowns then, in echelon form, $r < n$ and hence the system has a nonzero solution. That is,

Theorem 2.3: A homogeneous system of linear equations with more unknowns than equations has a nonzero solution.

Example 2.8: The homogeneous system

$$x + 2y - 3z + w = 0$$
$$x - 3y + z - 2w = 0$$
$$2x + y - 3z + 5w = 0$$

has a nonzero solution since there are four unknowns but only three equations.

Example 2.9: We reduce the following system to echelon form:

$$x + y - z = 0 \qquad x + y - z = 0 \qquad x + y - z = 0$$
$$2x - 3y + z = 0 \qquad -5y + 3z = 0 \qquad -5y + 3z = 0$$
$$x - 4y + 2z = 0 \qquad -5y + 3z = 0$$

The system has a nonzero solution, since we obtained only two equations in the three unknowns in echelon form. For example, let $z = 5$; then $y = 3$ and $x = 2$. In other words, the 3-tuple $(2, 3, 5)$ is a particular nonzero solution.

Example 2.10: We reduce the following system to echelon form:

$$x + y - z = 0 \qquad x + y - z = 0 \qquad x + y - z = 0$$
$$2x + 4y - z = 0 \qquad 2y + z = 0 \qquad 2y + z = 0$$
$$3x + 2y + 2z = 0 \qquad -y + 5z = 0 \qquad 11z = 0$$

Since in echelon form there are three equations in three unknowns, the system has only the zero solution $(0, 0, 0)$.

Solved Problems

SOLUTION OF LINEAR EQUATIONS

$$2x - 3y + 6z + 2v - 5w = 3$$

2.1. Solve the system:
$$y - 4z + v \qquad\qquad = 1$$
$$v - 3w = 2$$

The system is in echelon form. Since the equations begin with the unknowns x, y and v respectively, the other unknowns, z and w, are the free variables.

To find the general solution, let, say, $z = a$ and $w = b$. Substituting into the third equation,

$$v - 3b = 2 \quad \text{or} \quad v = 2 + 3b$$

Substituting into the second equation,

$$y - 4a + 2 + 3b = 1 \quad \text{or} \quad y = 4a - 3b - 1$$

Substituting into the first equation,

$$2x - 3(4a - 3b - 1) + 6a + 2(2 + 3b) - 5b = 3 \quad \text{or} \quad x = 3a - 5b - 2$$

Thus the general solution of the system is

$$x = 3a - 5b - 2, \quad y = 4a - 3b - 1, \quad z = a, \quad v = 2 + 3b, \quad w = b$$

or $(3a - 5b - 2, 4a - 3b - 1, a, 2 + 3b, b)$, where a and b are arbitrary real numbers. Some texts leave the general solution in terms of the free variables z and w instead of a and b as follows:

$$x = 3z - 5w - 2$$
$$y = 4z - 3w - 1 \quad \text{or} \quad (3z - 5w - 2,\; 4z - 3w - 1,\; z,\; 2 + 3w,\; w)$$
$$v = 2 + 3w$$

After finding the general solution, we can find a particular solution by substituting into the general solution. For example, let $a = 2$ and $b = 1$; then

$$x = -1, \; y = 4, \; z = 2, \; v = 5, \; w = 1 \quad \text{or} \quad (-1, 4, 2, 5, 1)$$

is a particular solution of the given system.

2.2. Solve the system:
$$\begin{aligned} x + 2y - 3z &= -1 \\ 3x - y + 2z &= 7 \\ 5x + 3y - 4z &= 2 \end{aligned}$$

Reduce to echelon form. Eliminate x from the second and third equations by the operations $L_2 \to -3L_1 + L_2$ and $L_3 \to -5L_1 + L_3$:

$$\begin{array}{ll}
-3L_1: & -3x - 6y + 9z = 3 \\
L_2: & 3x - y + 2z = 7 \\
\hline
-3L_1 + L_2: & -7y + 11z = 10
\end{array}
\qquad
\begin{array}{ll}
-5L_1: & -5x - 10y + 15z = 5 \\
L_3: & 5x + 3y - 4z = 2 \\
\hline
-5L_1 + L_3: & -7y + 11z = 7
\end{array}$$

Thus we obtain the equivalent system

$$\begin{aligned} x + 2y - 3z &= -1 \\ -7y + 11z &= 10 \\ -7y + 11z &= 7 \end{aligned}$$

The second and third equations show that the system is inconsistent, for if we subtract we obtain $0x + 0y + 0z = 3$ or $0 = 3$.

2.3. Solve the system:
$$\begin{aligned} 2x + y - 2z &= 10 \\ 3x + 2y + 2z &= 1 \\ 5x + 4y + 3z &= 4 \end{aligned}$$

Reduce to echelon form. Eliminate x from the second and third equations by the operations $L_2 \to -3L_1 + 2L_2$ and $L_3 \to -5L_1 + 2L_3$:

$$\begin{array}{ll}
-3L_1: & -6x - 3y + 6z = -30 \\
2L_2: & 6x + 4y + 4z = 2 \\
\hline
-3L_1 + 2L_2: & y + 10z = -28
\end{array}
\qquad
\begin{array}{ll}
-5L_1: & -10x - 5y + 10z = -50 \\
2L_3: & 10x + 8y + 6z = 8 \\
\hline
-5L_1 + 2L_3: & 3y + 16z = -42
\end{array}$$

Thus we obtain the following system from which we eliminate y from the third equation by the operation $L_3 \to -3L_2 + L_3$:

$$\begin{aligned} 2x + y - 2z &= 10 \\ y + 10z &= -28 \\ 3y + 16z &= -42 \end{aligned} \qquad \text{to} \qquad \begin{aligned} 2x + y - 2z &= 10 \\ y + 10z &= -28 \\ -14z &= 42 \end{aligned}$$

In echelon form there are three equations in the three unknowns; hence the system has a unique solution. By the third equation, $z = -3$. Substituting into the second equation, we find $y = 2$. Substituting into the first equation, we obtain $x = 1$. Thus $x = 1$, $y = 2$ and $z = -3$, i.e. the 3-tuple $(1, 2, -3)$, is the unique solution of the system.

$$x + 2y - 3z = 6$$

2.4. Solve the system: $\quad 2x - y + 4z = 2$

$$4x + 3y - 2z = 14$$

Reduce the system to echelon form. Eliminate x from the second and third equations by the operations $L_2 \to -2L_1 + L_2$ and $L_3 \to -4L_1 + L_3$:

$$-2L_1:\quad -2x - 4y + 6z = -12 \qquad\qquad -4L_1:\quad -4x - 8y + 12z = -24$$

$$L_2:\quad 2x - y + 4z = 2 \qquad\qquad\qquad L_3:\quad 4x + 3y - 2z = 14$$

$$-5y + 10z = -10 \qquad\qquad\qquad\qquad -5y + 10z = -10$$

$$\text{or}\quad y - 2z = 2 \qquad\qquad\qquad\qquad \text{or}\quad y - 2z = 2$$

Thus the system is equivalent to

$$x + 2y - 3z = 6$$
$$y - 2z = 2 \qquad \text{or simply} \qquad \begin{array}{l} x + 2y - 3z = 6 \\ y - 2z = 2 \end{array}$$
$$y - 2z = 2$$

(Since the second and third equations are identical, we can disregard one of them.)

In echelon form there are only two equations in the three unknowns; hence the system has an infinite number of solutions and, in particular, $3 - 2 = 1$ free variable which is z.

To obtain the general solution let, say, $z = a$. Substitute into the second equation to obtain $y = 2 + 2a$. Substitute into the first equation to obtain $x + 2(2 + 2a) - 3a = 6$ or $x = 2 - a$. Thus the general solution is

$$x = 2 - a, \quad y = 2 + 2a, \quad z = a \qquad \text{or} \qquad (2 - a, 2 + 2a, a)$$

where a is any real number.

The value, say, $a = 1$ yields the particular solution $x = 1$, $y = 4$, $z = 1$ or $(1, 4, 1)$.

$$x - 3y + 4z - 2w = 5$$

2.5. Solve the system: $\quad 2y + 5z + w = 2$

$$y - 3z = 4$$

The system is not in echelon form since, for example, y appears as the first unknown in both the second and third equations. However, if we rewrite the system so that w is the second unknown, then we obtain the following system which is in echelon form:

$$x - 2w - 3y + 4z = 5$$
$$w + 2y + 5z = 2$$
$$y - 3z = 4$$

Now if a 4-tuple (a, b, c, d) is given as a solution, it is not clear if b should be substituted for w or for y; hence for theoretical reasons we consider the two systems to be distinct. Of course this does not prohibit us from using the new system to obtain the solution of the original system.

Let $z = a$. Substituting into the third equation, we find $y = 4 + 3a$. Substituting into the second equation, we obtain $w + 2(4 + 3a) + 5a = 2$ or $w = -6 - 11a$. Substituting into the first equation,

$$x - 2(-6 - 11a) - 3(4 + 3a) + 4a = 5 \qquad \text{or} \qquad x = 5 - 17a$$

Thus the general solution of the original system is

$$x = 5 - 17a, \quad y = 4 + 3a, \quad z = a, \quad w = -6 - 11a$$

where a is any real number.

2.6.   Determine the values of a so that the following system in unknowns x, y and z has:
(i) no solution, (ii) more than one solution, (iii) a unique solution:

$$x + y - z = 1$$
$$2x + 3y + az = 3$$
$$x + ay + 3z = 2$$

Reduce the system to echelon form. Eliminate x from the second and third equations by the operations $L_2 \rightarrow -2L_1 + L_2$ and $L_3 \rightarrow -L_1 + L_3$:

$-2L_1$:	$-2x - 2y + 2z = -2$	$-L_1$:	$-x - y + z = -1$
L_2:	$2x + 3y + az = 3$	L_3:	$x + ay + 3z = 2$

$$y + (a+2)z = 1 (a-1)y + 4z = 1$$

Thus the equivalent system is

$$x + y - z = 1$$
$$y + (a+2)z = 1$$
$$(a-1)y + 4z = 1$$

Now eliminate y from the third equation by the operation $L_3 \rightarrow -(a-1)L_2 + L_3$,

$-(a-1)L_2$:	$-(a-1)y + (2-a-a^2)z = 1-a$
L_3:	$(a-1)y + 4z = 1$

$$(6 - a - a^2)z = 2 - a$$
$$\text{or} \quad (3+a)(2-a)z = 2 - a$$

to obtain the equivalent system

$$x + y - z = 1$$
$$y + (a+2)z = 1$$
$$(3+a)(2-a)z = 2 - a$$

which has a unique solution if the coefficient of z in the third equation is not zero, that is, if $a \neq 2$ and $a \neq -3$. In case $a = 2$, the third equation is $0 = 0$ and the system has more than one solution. In case $a = -3$, the third equation is $0 = 5$ and the system has no solution.

Summarizing, we have: (i) $a = -3$, (ii) $a = 2$, (iii) $a \neq 2$ and $a \neq -3$.

2.7.   Which condition must be placed on a, b and c so that the following system in unknowns x, y and z has a solution?

$$x + 2y - 3z = a$$
$$2x + 6y - 11z = b$$
$$x - 2y + 7z = c$$

Reduce to echelon form. Eliminating x from the second and third equation by the operations $L_2 \rightarrow -2L_1 + L_2$ and $L_3 \rightarrow -L_1 + L_3$, we obtain the equivalent system

$$x + 2y - 3z = a$$
$$2y - 5z = b - 2a$$
$$-4y + 10z = c - a$$

Eliminating y from the third equation by the operation $L_3 \rightarrow 2L_2 + L_3$, we finally obtain the equivalent system

$$x + 2y - 3z = a$$
$$2y - 5z = b - 2a$$
$$0 = c + 2b - 5a$$

The system will have no solution if the third equation is of the form $0 = k$, with $k \neq 0$; that is, if $c + 2b - 5a \neq 0$. Thus the system will have at least one solution if

$$c + 2b - 5a = 0 \qquad \text{or} \qquad 5a = 2b + c$$

Note, in this case, that the system will have more than one solution. In other words, the system cannot have a unique solution.

HOMOGENEOUS SYSTEMS OF LINEAR EQUATIONS

2.8. Determine whether each system has a nonzero solution:

$$
\begin{aligned}
x - 2y + 3z - 2w &= 0 \\
3x - 7y - 2z + 4w &= 0 \\
4x + 3y + 5z + 2w &= 0 \\
\text{(i)}
\end{aligned}
\qquad
\begin{aligned}
x + 2y - 3z &= 0 \\
2x + 5y + 2z &= 0 \\
3x - y - 4z &= 0 \\
\text{(ii)}
\end{aligned}
\qquad
\begin{aligned}
x + 2y - z &= 0 \\
2x + 5y + 2z &= 0 \\
x + 4y + 7z &= 0 \\
x + 3y + 3z &= 0 \\
\text{(iii)}
\end{aligned}
$$

(i)   The system must have a nonzero solution since there are more unknowns than equations.

(ii) Reduce to echelon form:

$$
\begin{aligned}
x + 2y - 3z &= 0 \\
2x + 5y + 2z &= 0 \\
3x - y - 4z &= 0
\end{aligned}
\quad \text{to} \quad
\begin{aligned}
x + 2y - 3z &= 0 \\
y + 8z &= 0 \\
-7y + 5z &= 0
\end{aligned}
\quad \text{to} \quad
\begin{aligned}
x + 2y - 3z &= 0 \\
y + 8z &= 0 \\
61z &= 0
\end{aligned}
$$

In echelon form there are exactly three equations in the three unknowns; hence the system has a unique solution, the zero solution.

(iii) Reduce to echelon form:

$$
\begin{aligned}
x + 2y - z &= 0 \\
2x + 5y + 2z &= 0 \\
x + 4y + 7z &= 0 \\
x + 3y + 3z &= 0
\end{aligned}
\qquad
\begin{aligned}
x + 2y - z &= 0 \\
y + 4z &= 0 \\
2y + 8z &= 0 \\
y + 4z &= 0
\end{aligned}
\qquad
\begin{aligned}
x + 2y - z &= 0 \\
y + 4z &= 0
\end{aligned}
$$

In echelon form there are only two equations in the three unknowns; hence the system has a nonzero solution.

2.9. The vectors $u_1, \ldots, u_m$ in, say, $\mathbf{R}^n$ are said to be *linearly dependent*, or simply *dependent*, if there exist scalars $k_1, \ldots, k_m$, not all of them zero, such that $k_1 u_1 + \cdots + k_m u_m = 0$. Otherwise they are said to be *independent*. Determine whether the vectors u, v and w are dependent or independent where:

(i) $u = (1, 1, -1)$, $v = (2, -3, 1)$, $w = (8, -7, 1)$

(ii) $u = (1, -2, -3)$, $v = (2, 3, -1)$, $w = (3, 2, 1)$

(iii) $u = (a_1, a_2)$, $v = (b_1, b_2)$, $w = (c_1, c_2)$

In each case:

(a) let $xu + yv + zw = 0$ where x, y and z are unknown scalars;

(b) find the equivalent homogeneous system of equations;

(c) determine whether the system has a nonzero solution. If the system does, then the vectors are dependent; if the system does not, then they are independent.

(i)   Let $xu + yv + zw = 0$:

$$x(1, 1, -1) + y(2, -3, 1) + z(8, -7, 1) = (0, 0, 0)$$

or

$$(x, x, -x) + (2y, -3y, y) + (8z, -7z, z) = (0, 0, 0)$$

or

$$(x + 2y + 8z, \ x - 3y - 7z, \ -x + y + z) = (0, 0, 0)$$

Set corresponding components equal to each other and reduce the system to echelon form:

$$
\begin{array}{llll}
x + 2y + 8z = 0 & x + 2y + 8z = 0 & x + 2y + 8z = 0 & x + 2y + 8z = 0 \\
x - 3y - 7z = 0 & -5y - 15z = 0 & y + 3z = 0 & y + 3z = 0 \\
-x + y + z = 0 & 3y + 9z = 0 & y + 3z = 0 &
\end{array}
$$

In echelon form there are only two equations in the three unknowns; hence the system has a nonzero solution. Accordingly, the vectors are dependent.

Remark: We need not solve the system to determine dependence or independence; we only need to know if a nonzero solution exists.

(ii)
$$
\begin{aligned}
x(1, -2, -3) + y(2, 3, -1) + z(3, 2, 1) &= (0, 0, 0) \\
(x, -2x, -3x) + (2y, 3y, -y) + (3z, 2z, z) &= (0, 0, 0) \\
(x + 2y + 3z, -2x + 3y + 2z, -3x - y + z) &= (0, 0, 0)
\end{aligned}
$$

$$
\begin{array}{lll}
x + 2y + 3z = 0 & x + 2y + 3z = 0 & x + 2y + 3z = 0 \\
-2x + 3y + 2z = 0 & 7y + 8z = 0 & 7y + 8z = 0 \\
-3x - y + z = 0 & 5y + 10z = 0 & 30z = 0
\end{array}
$$

In echelon form there are exactly three equations in the three unknowns; hence the system has only the zero solution. Accordingly, the vectors are independent.

(iii)
$$
\begin{aligned}
x(a_1, a_2) + y(b_1, b_2) + z(c_1, c_2) &= (0, 0) \\
(a_1 x, a_2 x) + (b_1 y, b_2 y) + (c_1 z, c_2 z) &= (0, 0) \qquad \text{and so} \qquad \begin{array}{l} a_1 x + b_1 y + c_1 z = 0 \\ a_2 x + b_2 y + c_2 z = 0 \end{array} \\
(a_1 x + b_1 y + c_1 z, a_2 x + b_2 y + c_2 z) &= (0, 0)
\end{aligned}
$$

The system has a nonzero solution by Theorem 2.3, i.e. because there are more unknowns than equations; hence the vectors are dependent. In other words, we have proven that *any* three vectors in $\mathbf{R}^2$ are dependent.

2.10.   Suppose in a homogeneous system of linear equations the coefficients of one of the unknowns are all zero.   Show that the system has a nonzero solution.

Suppose $x_1, \ldots, x_n$ are the unknowns of the system, and x_j is the unknown whose coefficients are all zero.   Then each equation of the system is of the form

$$
a_1 x_1 + \cdots + a_{j-1} x_{j-1} + 0 x_j + a_{j+1} x_{j+1} + \cdots + a_n x_n = 0
$$

Then for example $(0, \ldots, 0, 1, 0, \ldots, 0)$, where 1 is the jth component, is a nonzero solution of each equation and hence of the system.

MISCELLANEOUS PROBLEMS

2.11.   Prove Theorem 2.1:   Suppose u is a particular solution of the homogeneous system (*) and suppose W is the general solution of the associated homogeneous system (**). Then
$$
u + W = \{u + w : w \in W\}
$$
is the general solution of the nonhomogeneous system (*).

Let U denote the general solution of the nonhomogeneous system (*).   Suppose $u \in U$ and that $u = (u_1, \ldots, u_n)$.   Since u is a solution of (*), we have for $i = 1, \ldots, m$,

$$
a_{i1} u_1 + a_{i2} u_2 + \cdots + a_{in} u_n = b_i
$$

Now suppose $w \in W$ and that $w = (w_1, \ldots, w_n)$.   Since w is a solution of the homogeneous system (**), we have for $i = 1, \ldots, m$,

$$
a_{i1} w_1 + a_{i2} w_2 + \cdots + a_{in} w_n = 0
$$

Therefore, for $i = 1, \ldots, m$,

$$a_{i1}(u_1 + w_1) + a_{i2}(u_2 + w_2) + \cdots + a_{in}(u_n + w_n)$$

$$= a_{i1}u_1 + a_{i1}w_1 + a_{i2}u_2 + a_{i2}w_2 + \cdots + a_{in}u_n + a_{in}w_n$$

$$= (a_{i1}u_1 + a_{i2}u_2 + \cdots + a_{in}u_n) + (a_{i1}w_1 + a_{i2}w_2 + \cdots + a_{in}w_n)$$

$$= b_i + 0 = b_i$$

That is, $u + w$ is a solution of (*). Thus $u + w \in U$, and hence

$$u + W \subset U$$

Now suppose $v = (v_1, \ldots, v_n)$ is any arbitrary element of U, i.e. solution of (*). Then, for $i = 1, \ldots, m$,

$$a_{i1}v_1 + a_{i2}v_2 + \cdots + a_{in}v_n = b_i$$

Observe that $v = u + (v - u)$. We claim that $v - u \in W$. For $i = 1, \ldots, m$,

$$a_{i1}(v_1 - u_1) + a_{i2}(v_2 - u_2) + \cdots + a_{in}(v_n - u_n)$$

$$= (a_{i1}v_1 + a_{i2}v_2 + \cdots + a_{in}v_n) - (a_{i1}u_1 + a_{i2}u_2 + \cdots + a_{in}u_n)$$

$$= b_i - b_i = 0$$

Thus $v - u$ is a solution of the homogeneous system (*), i.e. $v - u \in W$. Then $v \in u + W$, and hence

$$U \subset u + W$$

Both inclusion relations give us $U = u + W$; that is, $u + W$ is the general solution of the nonhomogeneous system (**).

2.12. Consider the system (*) of linear equations (page 18). Multiplying the ith equation by c_i, and adding, we obtain the equation

$$(c_1 a_{11} + \cdots + c_m a_{m1})x_1 + \cdots + (c_1 a_{1n} + \cdots + c_m a_{mn})x_n = c_1 b_1 + \cdots + c_m b_m \quad (1)$$

Such an equation is termed a *linear combination* of the equations in (*). Show that any solution of (*) is also a solution of the linear combination (1).

Suppose $u = (k_1, \ldots, k_n)$ is a solution of (*). Then

$$a_{i1}k_1 + a_{i2}k_2 + \cdots + a_{in}k_n = b_i, \qquad i = 1, \ldots, m \qquad\qquad (2)$$

To show that u is a solution of (1), we must verify the equation

$$(c_1 a_{11} + \cdots + c_m a_{m1})k_1 + \cdots + (c_1 a_{1n} + \cdots + c_m a_{mn})k_n = c_1 b_1 + \cdots + c_m b_m$$

But this can be rearranged into

$$c_1(a_{11}k_1 + \cdots + a_{1n}k_n) + \cdots + c_m(a_{m1} + \cdots + a_{mn}k_n) = c_1 b_1 + \cdots + c_m b_m$$

or, by (2), $$c_1 b_1 + \cdots + c_m b_m = c_1 b_1 + \cdots + c_m b_m$$

which is clearly a true statement.

2.13. In the system (*) of linear equations, suppose $a_{11} \neq 0$. Let (#) be the system obtained from (*) by the operation $L_i \rightarrow -a_{i1}L_1 + a_{11}L_i$, $i \neq 1$. Show that (*) and (#) are equivalent systems, i.e. have the same solution set.

In view of the above operation on (*), each equation in (#) is a linear combination of equations in (*); hence by the preceding problem any solution of (*) is also a solution of (#).

On the other hand, applying the operation $L_i \rightarrow \dfrac{1}{a_{11}}(-a_{i1}L_1 + L_i)$ to (#), we obtain the original system (*). That is, each equation in (*) is a linear combination of equations in (#); hence each solution of (#) is also a solution of (*).

Both conditions show that (*) and (#) have the same solution set.

2.14. Prove Theorem 2.2: Consider a system in echelon form:

$$a_{11}x_1 + a_{12}x_2 + a_{13}x_3 + \cdots\cdots\cdots\cdots\cdots + a_{1n}x_n = b_1$$
$$a_{2j_2}x_{j_2} + a_{2,j_2+1}x_{j_2+1} + \cdots\cdots + a_{2n}x_n = b_2$$
$$\cdots\cdots\cdots\cdots\cdots\cdots\cdots\cdots\cdots\cdots\cdots\cdots\cdots$$
$$a_{rj_r}x_{j_r} + a_{r,j_r+1}x_{j_r+1} + \cdots + a_{rn}x_n = b_r$$

where $1 < j_2 < \cdots < j_r$ and where $a_{11} \neq 0$, $a_{2j_2} \neq 0$, ..., $a_{rj_r} \neq 0$. The solution is as follows. There are two cases:

(i) $r = n$. Then the system has a unique solution.

(ii) $r < n$. Then we can arbitrarily assign values to the $n - r$ free variables and obtain a solution of the system.

The proof is by induction on the number r of equations in the system. If $r = 1$, then we have the single linear equation

$$a_1x_1 + a_2x_2 + a_3x_3 + \cdots + a_nx_n = b, \qquad \text{where } a_1 \neq 0$$

The free variables are $x_2, \ldots, x_n$. Let us arbitrarily assign values to the free variables; say, $x_2 = k_2$, $x_3 = k_3$, ..., $x_n = k_n$. Substituting into the equation and solving for x_1,

$$x_1 = \frac{1}{a_1}(b - a_2k_2 - a_3k_3 - \cdots - a_nk_n)$$

These values constitute a solution of the equation; for, on substituting, we obtain

$$a_1\left[\frac{1}{a_1}(b - a_2k_2 - \cdots - a_nk_n)\right] + a_2k_2 + \cdots + a_nk_n = b \qquad \text{or} \qquad b = b$$

which is a true statement.

Furthermore if $r = n = 1$, then we have $ax = b$, where $a \neq 0$. Note that $x = b/a$ is a solution since $a(b/a) = b$ is true. Moreover if $x = k$ is a solution, i.e. $ak = b$, then $k = b/a$. Thus the equation has a unique solution as claimed.

Now assume $r > 1$ and that the theorem is true for a system of $r - 1$ equations. We view the $r - 1$ equations

$$a_{2j_2}x_{j_2} + a_{2,j_2+1}x_{j_2+1} + \cdots\cdots\cdots\cdots\cdots + a_{2n}x_n = b_2$$
$$\cdots\cdots\cdots\cdots\cdots\cdots\cdots\cdots\cdots\cdots\cdots\cdots\cdots$$
$$a_{rj_r}x_{j_r} + a_{r,j_r+1}x_{j_r+1} + \cdots + a_{rn}x_n = b_r$$

as a system in the unknowns $x_{j_2}, \ldots, x_n$. Note that the system is in echelon form. By induction we can arbitrarily assign values to the $(n - j_2 + 1) - (r - 1)$ free variables in the reduced system to obtain a solution (say, $x_{j_2} = k_{j_2}$, ..., $x_n = k_n$). As in case $r = 1$, these values and arbitrary values for the additional $j_2 - 2$ free variables (say, $x_2 = k_2$, ..., $x_{j_2-1} = k_{j_2-1}$), yield a solution of the first equation with

$$x_1 = \frac{1}{a_{11}}(b_1 - a_{12}k_2 - \cdots - a_{1n}k_n)$$

(Note that there are $(n - j_2 + 1) - (r - 1) + (j_2 - 2) = n - r$ free variables.) Furthermore, these values for $x_1, \ldots, x_n$ also satisfy the other equations since, in these equations, the coefficients of $x_1, \ldots, x_{j_2-1}$ are zero.

Now if $r = n$, then $j_2 = 2$. Thus by induction we obtain a unique solution of the subsystem and then a unique solution of the entire system. Accordingly, the theorem is proven.

2.15. A system (*) of linear equations is defined to be *consistent* if no linear combination of its equations is the equation

$$0x_1 + 0x_2 + \cdots + 0x_n = b, \qquad \text{where } b \neq 0 \tag{1}$$

Show that the system (*) is consistent if and only if it is reducible to echelon form.

Suppose (*) is reducible to echelon form. Then it has a solution which, by Problem 2.12, is a solution of every linear combination of its equations. Since (1) has no solution, it cannot be a linear combination of the equations in (*). That is, (*) is consistent.

On the other hand, suppose (*) is not reducible to echelon form. Then, in the reduction process, it must yield an equation of the form (1). That is, (1) is a linear combination of the equations in (*). Accordingly (*) is not consistent, i.e. (*) is inconsistent.

Supplementary Problems

SOLUTION OF LINEAR EQUATIONS

2.16. Solve:
(i) $\begin{aligned} 2x + 3y &= 1 \\ 5x + 7y &= 3 \end{aligned}$
(ii) $\begin{aligned} 2x + 4y &= 10 \\ 3x + 6y &= 15 \end{aligned}$
(iii) $\begin{aligned} 4x - 2y &= 5 \\ -6x + 3y &= 1 \end{aligned}$

2.17. Solve:
(i) $\begin{aligned} 2x + y - 3z &= 5 \\ 3x - 2y + 2z &= 5 \\ 5x - 3y - z &= 16 \end{aligned}$
(ii) $\begin{aligned} 2x + 3y - 2z &= 5 \\ x - 2y + 3z &= 2 \\ 4x - y + 4z &= 1 \end{aligned}$
(iii) $\begin{aligned} x + 2y + 3z &= 3 \\ 2x + 3y + 8z &= 4 \\ 3x + 2y + 17z &= 1 \end{aligned}$

2.18. Solve:
(i) $\begin{aligned} 2x + 3y &= 3 \\ x - 2y &= 5 \\ 3x + 2y &= 7 \end{aligned}$
(ii) $\begin{aligned} x + 2y - 3z + 2w &= 2 \\ 2x + 5y - 8z + 6w &= 5 \\ 3x + 4y - 5z + 2w &= 4 \end{aligned}$
(iii) $\begin{aligned} x + 2y - z + 3w &= 3 \\ 2x + 4y + 4z + 3w &= 9 \\ 3x + 6y - z + 8w &= 10 \end{aligned}$

2.19. Solve:
(i) $\begin{aligned} x + 2y + 2z &= 2 \\ 3x - 2y - z &= 5 \\ 2x - 5y + 3z &= -4 \\ x + 4y + 6z &= 0 \end{aligned}$
(ii) $\begin{aligned} x + 5y + 4z - 13w &= 3 \\ 3x - y + 2z + 5w &= 2 \\ 2x + 2y + 3z - 4w &= 1 \end{aligned}$

2.20. Determine the values of k such that the system in unknowns x, y and z has: (i) a unique solution, (ii) no solution, (iii) more than one solution:

(a) $\begin{aligned} kx + y + z &= 1 \\ x + ky + z &= 1 \\ x + y + kz &= 1 \end{aligned}$
(b) $\begin{aligned} x + 2y + kz &= 1 \\ 2x + ky + 8z &= 3 \end{aligned}$

2.21. Determine the values of k such that the system in unknowns x, y and z has: (i) a unique solution, (ii) no solution, (iii) more than one solution:

(a) $\begin{aligned} x + y + kz &= 2 \\ 3x + 4y + 2z &= k \\ 2x + 3y - z &= 1 \end{aligned}$
(b) $\begin{aligned} x \quad\quad - 3z &= -3 \\ 2x + ky - z &= -2 \\ x + 2y + kz &= 1 \end{aligned}$

2.22. Determine the condition on a, b and c so that the system in unknowns x, y and z has a solution:

(i) $\begin{aligned} x + 2y - 3z &= a \\ 3x - y + 2z &= b \\ x - 5y + 8z &= c \end{aligned}$
(ii) $\begin{aligned} x - 2y + 4z &= a \\ 2x + 3y - z &= b \\ 3x + y + 2z &= c \end{aligned}$

HOMOGENEOUS SYSTEMS

2.23. Determine whether each system has a nonzero solution:

(i) $\begin{aligned} x + 3y - 2z &= 0 \\ x - 8y + 8z &= 0 \\ 3x - 2y + 4z &= 0 \end{aligned}$
(ii) $\begin{aligned} x + 3y - 2z &= 0 \\ 2x - 3y + z &= 0 \\ 3x - 2y + 2z &= 0 \end{aligned}$
(iii) $\begin{aligned} x + 2y - 5z + 4w &= 0 \\ 2x - 3y + 2z + 3w &= 0 \\ 4x - 7y + z - 6w &= 0 \end{aligned}$

2.24. Determine whether each system has a nonzero solution:

$$
\begin{array}{ll}
\text{(i)} &
\begin{aligned}
x - 2y + 2z &= 0 \\
2x + y - 2z &= 0 \\
3x + 4y - 6z &= 0 \\
3x - 11y + 12z &= 0
\end{aligned}
& \quad \text{(ii)} &
\begin{aligned}
2x - 4y + 7z + 4v - 5w &= 0 \\
9x + 3y + 2z - 7v + w &= 0 \\
5x + 2y - 3z + v + 3w &= 0 \\
6x - 5y + 4z - 3v - 2w &= 0
\end{aligned}
\end{array}
$$

2.25. Determine whether the vectors u, v and w are dependent or independent (see Problem 2.9) where:

(i) $u = (1, 3, -1)$, $v = (2, 0, 1)$, $w = (1, -1, 1)$

(ii) $u = (1, 1, -1)$, $v = (2, 1, 0)$, $w = (-1, 1, 2)$

(iii) $u = (1, -2, 3, 1)$, $v = (3, 2, 1, -2)$, $w = (1, 6, -5, -4)$

MISCELLANEOUS PROBLEMS

2.26. Consider two general linear equations in two unknowns x and y over the real field **R**:

$$
\begin{aligned}
ax + by &= e \\
cx + dy &= f
\end{aligned}
$$

Show that:

(i)   if $\dfrac{a}{c} \neq \dfrac{b}{d}$, i.e. if $ad - bc \neq 0$, then the system has the unique solution $x = \dfrac{de - bf}{ad - bc}$, $y = \dfrac{af - ce}{ad - bc}$;

(ii) if $\dfrac{a}{c} = \dfrac{b}{d} \neq \dfrac{e}{f}$, then the system has no solution;

(iii) if $\dfrac{a}{c} = \dfrac{b}{d} = \dfrac{e}{f}$, then the system has more than one solution.

2.27. Consider the system
$$
\begin{aligned}
ax + by &= 1 \\
cx + dy &= 0
\end{aligned}
$$

Show that if $ad - bc \neq 0$, then the system has the unique solution $x = d/(ad - bc)$, $y = -c/(ad - bc)$. Also show that if $ad - bc = 0$, and either $c \neq 0$ or $d \neq 0$, then the system has no solution.

2.28. Show that an equation of the form $0x_1 + 0x_2 + \cdots + 0x_n = 0$ may be added or deleted from a system without affecting the solution set.

2.29. Consider a system of linear equations with the same number of equations as unknowns:

$$
\begin{aligned}
a_{11}x_1 + a_{12}x_2 + \cdots + a_{1n}x_n &= b_1 \\
a_{21}x_1 + a_{22}x_2 + \cdots + a_{2n}x_n &= b_2 \\
& \cdots\cdots\cdots\cdots\cdots\cdots\cdots \\
a_{n1}x_1 + a_{n2}x_2 + \cdots + a_{nn}x_n &= b_n
\end{aligned}
\tag{1}
$$

(i)   Suppose the associated homogeneous system has only the zero solution. Show that (1) has a unique solution for every choice of constants b_i.

(ii) Suppose the associated homogeneous system has a nonzero solution. Show that there are constants b_i for which (1) does not have a solution. Also show that if (1) has a solution, then it has more than one.

Answers to Supplementary Problems

2.16.   (i) $x = 2,\ y = -1$;   (ii) $x = 5 - 2a,\ y = a$;   (iii) no solution

2.17.   (i) $(1, -3, -2)$;   (ii) no solution;   (iii) $(-1 - 7a,\ 2 + 2a,\ a)$ or $\begin{cases} x = -1 - 7z \\ y = 2 + 2z \end{cases}$

2.18.   (i) $x = 3,\ y = -1$

(ii) $(-a + 2b,\ 1 + 2a - 2b,\ a,\ b)$ or $\begin{cases} x = -z + 2w \\ y = 1 + 2z - 2w \end{cases}$

(iii) $(7/2 - 5b/2 - 2a,\ a,\ 1/2 + b/2,\ b)$ or $\begin{cases} x = 7/2 - 5w/2 - 2y \\ z = 1/2 + w/2 \end{cases}$

2.19.   (i) $(2, 1, -1)$;   (ii) no solution

2.20.   (a) (i) $k \neq 1$ and $k \neq -2$;   (ii) $k = -2$;   (iii) $k = 1$

(b) (i) never has a unique solution;   (ii) $k = 4$;   (iii) $k \neq 4$

2.21.   (a) (i) $k \neq 3$;   (ii) always has a solution;   (iii) $k = 3$

(b) (i) $k \neq 2$ and $k \neq -5$;   (ii) $k = -5$;   (iii) $k = 2$

2.22.   (i) $2a - b + c = 0$.   (ii) Any values for a, b and c yields a solution.

2.23.   (i) yes;   (ii) no;   (iii) yes, by Theorem 2.3.

2.24.   (i) yes;   (ii) yes, by Theorem 2.3.

2.25.   (i) dependent;   (ii) independent;   (iii) dependent

Chapter 3

Matrices

INTRODUCTION

In working with a system of linear equations, only the coefficients and their respective positions are important. Also, in reducing the system to echelon form, it is essential to keep the equations carefully aligned. Thus these coefficients can be efficiently arranged in a rectangular array called a "matrix". Moreover, certain abstract objects introduced in later chapters, such as "change of basis", "linear operator" and "bilinear form", can also be represented by these rectangular arrays, i.e. matrices.

In this chapter, we will study these matrices and certain algebraic operations defined on them. The material introduced here is mainly computational. However, as with linear equations, the abstract treatment presented later on will give us new insight into the structure of these matrices.

Unless otherwise stated, all the "entries" in our matrices shall come from some arbitrary, but fixed, field K. (See Appendix B.) The elements of K are called *scalars*. Nothing essential is lost if the reader assumes that K is the real field $\mathbf{R}$ or the complex field $\mathbf{C}$.

Lastly, we remark that the elements of $\mathbf{R}^n$ or $\mathbf{C}^n$ are conveniently represented by "row vectors" or "column vectors", which are special cases of matrices.

MATRICES

Let K be an arbitrary field. A rectangular array of the form

$$\begin{pmatrix} a_{11} & a_{12} & \ldots & a_{1n} \\ a_{21} & a_{22} & \ldots & a_{2n} \\ \cdots\cdots\cdots\cdots\cdots\cdots \\ a_{m1} & a_{m2} & \ldots & a_{mn} \end{pmatrix}$$

where the a_{ij} are scalars in K, is called a *matrix over K*, or simply a *matrix* if K is implicit. The above matrix is also denoted by (a_{ij}), $i = 1, \ldots, m$, $j = 1, \ldots, n$, or simply by (a_{ij}). The m horizontal n-tuples

$$(a_{11}, a_{12}, \ldots, a_{1n}), \ (a_{21}, a_{22}, \ldots, a_{2n}), \ \ldots, \ (a_{m1}, a_{m2}, \ldots, a_{mn})$$

are the *rows* of the matrix, and the n vertical m-tuples

$$\begin{pmatrix} a_{11} \\ a_{21} \\ .. \\ a_{m1} \end{pmatrix}, \quad \begin{pmatrix} a_{12} \\ a_{22} \\ .. \\ a_{m2} \end{pmatrix}, \quad \ldots, \quad \begin{pmatrix} a_{1n} \\ a_{2n} \\ .. \\ a_{mn} \end{pmatrix}$$

are its *columns*. Note that the element a_{ij}, called the *ij-entry* or *ij-component*, appears in the ith row and the jth column. A matrix with m rows and n columns is called an m by n matrix, or $m \times n$ matrix; the pair of numbers (m, n) is called its *size* or *shape*.

Example 3.1:   The following is a 2×3 matrix: $\begin{pmatrix} 1 & -3 & 4 \\ 0 & 5 & -2 \end{pmatrix}$.

Its rows are $(1, -3, 4)$ and $(0, 5, -2)$; its columns are $\begin{pmatrix} 1 \\ 0 \end{pmatrix}$, $\begin{pmatrix} -3 \\ 5 \end{pmatrix}$ and $\begin{pmatrix} 4 \\ -2 \end{pmatrix}$.

Matrices will usually be denoted by capital letters $A, B, \ldots$, and the elements of the field K by lower case letters $a, b, \ldots$. Two matrices A and B are *equal*, written $A = B$, if they have the same shape and if corresponding elements are equal. Thus the equality of two $m \times n$ matrices is equivalent to a system of mn equalities, one for each pair of elements.

Example 3.2:   The statement $\begin{pmatrix} x+y & 2z+w \\ x-y & z-w \end{pmatrix} = \begin{pmatrix} 3 & 5 \\ 1 & 4 \end{pmatrix}$ is equivalent to the following system of equations:

$$\begin{cases} x + y = 3 \\ x - y = 1 \\ 2z + w = 5 \\ z - w = 4 \end{cases}$$

The solution of the system is $x = 2$, $y = 1$, $z = 3$, $w = -1$.

Remark: A matrix with one row is also referred to as a *row vector*, and with one column as a *column vector*. In particular, an element in the field K can be viewed as a 1×1 matrix.

MATRIX ADDITION AND SCALAR MULTIPLICATION

Let A and B be two matrices with the same size, i.e. the same number of rows and of columns, say, $m \times n$ matrices:

$$A = \begin{pmatrix} a_{11} & a_{12} & \ldots & a_{1n} \\ a_{21} & a_{22} & \ldots & a_{2n} \\ \ldots\ldots\ldots\ldots\ldots\ldots \\ a_{m1} & a_{m2} & \ldots & a_{mn} \end{pmatrix} \quad \text{and} \quad B = \begin{pmatrix} b_{11} & b_{12} & \ldots & b_{1n} \\ b_{21} & b_{22} & \ldots & b_{2n} \\ \ldots\ldots\ldots\ldots\ldots\ldots \\ b_{m1} & b_{m2} & \ldots & b_{mn} \end{pmatrix}$$

The *sum* of A and B, written $A + B$, is the matrix obtained by adding corresponding entries:

$$A + B = \begin{pmatrix} a_{11}+b_{11} & a_{12}+b_{12} & \ldots & a_{1n}+b_{1n} \\ a_{21}+b_{21} & a_{22}+b_{22} & \ldots & a_{2n}+b_{2n} \\ \ldots\ldots\ldots\ldots\ldots\ldots\ldots\ldots\ldots \\ a_{m1}+b_{m1} & a_{m2}+b_{m2} & \ldots & a_{mn}+b_{mn} \end{pmatrix}$$

The *product* of a scalar k by the matrix A, written $k \cdot A$ or simply kA, is the matrix obtained by multiplying each entry of A by k:

$$kA = \begin{pmatrix} ka_{11} & ka_{12} & \ldots & ka_{1n} \\ ka_{21} & ka_{22} & \ldots & ka_{2n} \\ \ldots\ldots\ldots\ldots\ldots\ldots \\ ka_{m1} & ka_{m2} & \ldots & ka_{mn} \end{pmatrix}$$

Observe that $A + B$ and kA are also $m \times n$ matrices. We also define

$$-A = -1 \cdot A \quad \text{and} \quad A - B = A + (-B)$$

The sum of matrices with different sizes is not defined.

Example 3.3: Let $A = \begin{pmatrix} 1 & -2 & 3 \\ 4 & 5 & -6 \end{pmatrix}$ and $B = \begin{pmatrix} 3 & 0 & 2 \\ -7 & 1 & 8 \end{pmatrix}$. Then

$$A + B = \begin{pmatrix} 1+3 & -2+0 & 3+2 \\ 4-7 & 5+1 & -6+8 \end{pmatrix} = \begin{pmatrix} 4 & -2 & 5 \\ -3 & 6 & 2 \end{pmatrix}$$

$$3A = \begin{pmatrix} 3 \cdot 1 & 3 \cdot (-2) & 3 \cdot 3 \\ 3 \cdot 4 & 3 \cdot 5 & 3 \cdot (-6) \end{pmatrix} = \begin{pmatrix} 3 & -6 & 9 \\ 12 & 15 & -18 \end{pmatrix}$$

$$2A - 3B = \begin{pmatrix} 2 & -4 & 6 \\ 8 & 10 & -12 \end{pmatrix} + \begin{pmatrix} -9 & 0 & -6 \\ 21 & -3 & -24 \end{pmatrix} = \begin{pmatrix} -7 & -4 & 0 \\ 29 & 7 & -36 \end{pmatrix}$$

Example 3.4: The $m \times n$ matrix whose entries are all zero,

$$\begin{pmatrix} 0 & 0 & \dots & 0 \\ 0 & 0 & \dots & 0 \\ \dots\dots\dots\dots\dots \\ 0 & 0 & \dots & 0 \end{pmatrix}$$

is called the *zero matrix* and will be denoted by 0. It is similar to the scalar 0 in that, for any $m \times n$ matrix $A = (a_{ij})$, $A + 0 = (a_{ij} + 0) = (a_{ij}) = A$.

Basic properties of matrices under the operations of matrix addition and scalar multiplication follow.

Theorem 3.1:   Let V be the set of all $m \times n$ matrices over a field K. Then for any matrices $A, B, C \in V$ and any scalars $k_1, k_2 \in K$,

    (i) $(A + B) + C = A + (B + C)$ (v) $k_1(A + B) = k_1 A + k_1 B$

    (ii) $A + 0 = A$ (vi) $(k_1 + k_2)A = k_1 A + k_2 A$

    (iii) $A + (-A) = 0$ (vii) $(k_1 k_2)A = k_1(k_2 A)$

    (iv) $A + B = B + A$ (viii) $1 \cdot A = A$ and $0A = 0$

Using (vi) and (viii) above, we also have that $A + A = 2A$, $A + A + A = 3A$, ...

Remark: Suppose vectors in $\mathbf{R}^n$ are represented by row vectors (or by column vectors); say,

$$u = (a_1, a_2, \dots, a_n) \quad \text{and} \quad v = (b_1, b_2, \dots, b_n)$$

Then viewed as matrices, the sum $u + v$ and the scalar product ku are as follows:

$$u + v = (a_1 + b_1, a_2 + b_2, \dots, a_n + b_n) \quad \text{and} \quad ku = (ka_1, ka_2, \dots, ka_n)$$

But this corresponds precisely to the sum and scalar product as defined in Chapter 1. In other words, the above operations on matrices may be viewed as a generalization of the corresponding operations defined in Chapter 1.

MATRIX MULTIPLICATION

The product of matrices A and B, written AB, is somewhat complicated. For this reason, we include the following introductory remarks.

(i) Let $A = (a_i)$ and $B = (b_i)$ belong to $\mathbf{R}^n$, and A represented by a row vector and B by a column vector. Then their dot product $A \cdot B$ may be found by combining the matrices as follows:

$$A \cdot B = (a_1, a_2, \dots, a_n) \begin{pmatrix} b_1 \\ b_2 \\ \cdot\cdot \\ b_n \end{pmatrix} = a_1 b_1 + a_2 b_2 + \cdots + a_n b_n$$

Accordingly, we define the matrix product of a row vector A by a column vector B as above.

(ii) **Consider the equations**
$$o_{11}x_1 + b_{12}x_2 + b_{13}x_3 = y_1$$
$$b_{21}x_1 + b_{22}x_2 + b_{23}x_3 = y_2$$
$\qquad\qquad\qquad\qquad\qquad\qquad\qquad\qquad\qquad\qquad\qquad\qquad\qquad\qquad\qquad$ (1)

This system is equivalent to the matrix equation

$$\begin{pmatrix} b_{11} & b_{12} & b_{13} \\ b_{21} & b_{22} & b_{23} \end{pmatrix} \begin{pmatrix} x_1 \\ x_2 \\ x_3 \end{pmatrix} = \begin{pmatrix} y_1 \\ y_2 \end{pmatrix} \qquad \text{or simply} \quad BX = Y$$

where $B = (b_{ij})$, $X = (x_i)$ and $Y = (y_i)$, if we combine the matrix B and the column vector X as follows:

$$BX = \begin{pmatrix} b_{11} & b_{12} & b_{13} \\ b_{21} & b_{22} & b_{23} \end{pmatrix} \begin{pmatrix} x_1 \\ x_2 \\ x_3 \end{pmatrix} = \begin{pmatrix} b_{11}x_1 + b_{12}x_2 + b_{13}x_3 \\ b_{21}x_1 + b_{22}x_2 + b_{23}x_3 \end{pmatrix} = \begin{pmatrix} B_1 \cdot X \\ B_2 \cdot X \end{pmatrix}$$

where B_1 and B_2 are the rows of B. Note that the product of a matrix and a column vector yields another column vector.

(iii) Now consider the equations
$$a_{11}y_1 + a_{12}y_2 = z_1$$
$$a_{21}y_1 + a_{22}y_2 = z_2$$
$\qquad\qquad\qquad\qquad\qquad\qquad\qquad\qquad\qquad\qquad\qquad\qquad\qquad\qquad\qquad$ (2)

which we can represent, as above, by the matrix equation

$$\begin{pmatrix} a_{11} & a_{12} \\ a_{21} & a_{22} \end{pmatrix} \begin{pmatrix} y_1 \\ y_2 \end{pmatrix} = \begin{pmatrix} z_1 \\ z_2 \end{pmatrix} \qquad \text{or simply} \quad AY = Z$$

where $A = (a_{ij})$, $Y = (y_i)$ as above, and $Z = (z_i)$. Substituting the values of y_1 and y_2 of (1) into the equations of (2), we obtain

$$a_{11}(b_{11}x_1 + b_{12}x_2 + b_{13}x_3) + a_{12}(b_{21}x_1 + b_{22}x_2 + b_{23}x_3) = z_1$$
$$a_{21}(b_{11}x_1 + b_{12}x_2 + b_{13}x_3) + a_{22}(b_{21}x_1 + b_{22}x_2 + b_{23}x_3) = z_2$$

or, on rearranging terms,

$$(a_{11}b_{11} + a_{12}b_{21})x_1 + (a_{11}b_{12} + a_{12}b_{22})x_2 + (a_{11}b_{13} + a_{12}b_{23})x_3 = z_1$$
$$(a_{21}b_{11} + a_{22}b_{21})x_1 + (a_{21}b_{12} + a_{22}b_{22})x_2 + (a_{21}b_{13} + a_{22}b_{23})x_3 = z_2$$
$\qquad\qquad\qquad\qquad\qquad\qquad\qquad\qquad\qquad\qquad\qquad\qquad\qquad\qquad\qquad$ (3)

On the other hand, using the matrix equation $BX = Y$ and substituting for Y into $AY = Z$, we obtain the expression

$$ABX = Z$$

This will represent the system (3) if we define the product of A and B as follows:

$$AB = \begin{pmatrix} a_{11} & a_{12} \\ a_{21} & a_{22} \end{pmatrix} \begin{pmatrix} b_{11} & b_{12} & b_{13} \\ b_{21} & b_{22} & b_{23} \end{pmatrix} = \begin{pmatrix} a_{11}b_{11} + a_{12}b_{21} & a_{11}b_{12} + a_{12}b_{22} & a_{11}b_{13} + a_{12}b_{23} \\ a_{21}b_{11} + a_{22}b_{21} & a_{21}b_{12} + a_{22}b_{22} & a_{21}b_{13} + a_{22}b_{23} \end{pmatrix}$$

$$= \begin{pmatrix} A_1 \cdot B^1 & A_1 \cdot B^2 & A_1 \cdot B^3 \\ A_2 \cdot B^1 & A_2 \cdot B^2 & A_2 \cdot B^3 \end{pmatrix}$$

where A_1 and A_2 are the rows of A and B^1, B^2 and B^3 are the columns of B. We emphasize that if these computations are done in general, then the main requirement is that the number of y_i in (1) and (2) must be the same. This will then correspond to the fact that the number of columns of the matrix A must equal the number of rows of the matrix B.

With the above introduction, we now formally define matrix multiplication.

Definition: Suppose $A = (a_{ij})$ and $B = (b_{ij})$ are matrices such that the number of columns of A is equal to the number of rows of B; say, A is an $m \times p$ matrix and B is a $p \times n$ matrix. Then the *product* AB is the $m \times n$ matrix whose ij-entry is obtained by multiplying the ith row A_i of A by the jth column B^j of B:

$$AB = \begin{pmatrix} A_1 \cdot B^1 & A_1 \cdot B^2 & \ldots & A_1 \cdot B^n \\ A_2 \cdot B^1 & A_2 \cdot B^2 & \ldots & A_2 \cdot B^n \\ \ldots\ldots\ldots\ldots\ldots\ldots\ldots\ldots\ldots \\ A_m \cdot B^1 & A_m \cdot B^2 & \ldots & A_m \cdot B^n \end{pmatrix}$$

That is,

$$\begin{pmatrix} a_{11} & \ldots & a_{1p} \\ \cdot & & \cdot \\ a_{i1} & \ldots & a_{ip} \\ \cdot & & \cdot \\ a_{m1} & \ldots & a_{mp} \end{pmatrix} \begin{pmatrix} b_{11} & \ldots & b_{1j} & \ldots & b_{1n} \\ \cdot & \ldots & \cdot & \ldots & \cdot \\ \cdot & \ldots & \cdot & \ldots & \cdot \\ \cdot & \ldots & \cdot & \ldots & \cdot \\ b_{p1} & \ldots & b_{pj} & \ldots & b_{pn} \end{pmatrix} = \begin{pmatrix} c_{11} & \ldots & c_{1n} \\ \cdot & & \cdot \\ \cdot & c_{ij} & \cdot \\ \cdot & & \cdot \\ c_{m1} & \ldots & c_{mn} \end{pmatrix}$$

where $\quad c_{ij} = a_{i1}b_{1j} + a_{i2}b_{2j} + \cdots + a_{ip}b_{pj} = \sum\limits_{k=1}^{p} a_{ik}b_{kj}.$

We emphasize that the product AB is not defined if A is an $m \times p$ matrix and B is a $q \times n$ matrix, where $p \neq q$.

Example 3.5:
$$\begin{pmatrix} r & s \\ t & u \end{pmatrix} \begin{pmatrix} a_1 & a_2 & a_3 \\ b_1 & b_2 & b_3 \end{pmatrix} = \begin{pmatrix} ra_1 + sb_1 & ra_2 + sb_2 & ra_3 + sb_3 \\ ta_1 + ub_1 & ta_2 + ub_2 & ta_3 + ub_3 \end{pmatrix}$$

Example 3.6:
$$\begin{pmatrix} 1 & 2 \\ 3 & 4 \end{pmatrix} \begin{pmatrix} 1 & 1 \\ 0 & 2 \end{pmatrix} = \begin{pmatrix} 1 \cdot 1 + 2 \cdot 0 & 1 \cdot 1 + 2 \cdot 2 \\ 3 \cdot 1 + 4 \cdot 0 & 3 \cdot 1 + 4 \cdot 2 \end{pmatrix} = \begin{pmatrix} 1 & 5 \\ 3 & 11 \end{pmatrix}$$

$$\begin{pmatrix} 1 & 1 \\ 0 & 2 \end{pmatrix} \begin{pmatrix} 1 & 2 \\ 3 & 4 \end{pmatrix} = \begin{pmatrix} 1 \cdot 1 + 1 \cdot 3 & 1 \cdot 2 + 1 \cdot 4 \\ 0 \cdot 1 + 2 \cdot 3 & 0 \cdot 2 + 2 \cdot 4 \end{pmatrix} = \begin{pmatrix} 4 & 6 \\ 6 & 8 \end{pmatrix}$$

The above example shows that matrix multiplication is not commutative, i.e. the products AB and BA of matrices need not be equal.

Matrix multiplication does, however, satisfy the following properties:

Theorem 3.2: (i) $(AB)C = A(BC)$, (associative law)

(ii) $A(B + C) = AB + AC$, (left distributive law)

(iii) $(B + C)A = BA + CA$, (right distributive law)

(iv) $k(AB) = (kA)B = A(kB)$, where k is a scalar

We assume that the sums and products in the above theorem are defined.

We remark that $0A = 0$ and $B0 = 0$ where 0 is the zero matrix.

TRANSPOSE

The *transpose* of a matrix A, written A^t, is the matrix obtained by writing the rows of A, in order, as columns:

$$\begin{pmatrix} a_{11} & a_{12} & \ldots & a_{1n} \\ a_{21} & a_{22} & \ldots & a_{2n} \\ \ldots\ldots\ldots\ldots\ldots\ldots \\ a_{m1} & a_{m2} & \ldots & a_{mn} \end{pmatrix}^t = \begin{pmatrix} a_{11} & a_{21} & \ldots & a_{m1} \\ a_{12} & a_{22} & \ldots & a_{m2} \\ \ldots\ldots\ldots\ldots\ldots\ldots \\ a_{1n} & a_{2n} & \ldots & a_{mn} \end{pmatrix}$$

Observe that if A is an $m \times n$ matrix, then A^t is an $n \times m$ matrix.

Example 3.7:
$$\begin{pmatrix} 1 & 2 & 3 \\ 4 & -5 & -6 \end{pmatrix}^t = \begin{pmatrix} 1 & 4 \\ 2 & -5 \\ 3 & -6 \end{pmatrix}$$

The transpose operation on matrices satisfies the following properties:

Theorem 3.3:   (i) $(A + B)^t = A^t + B^t$

(ii) $(A^t)^t = A$

(iii) $(kA)^t = kA^t$, for k a scalar

(iv) $(AB)^t = B^t A^t$

MATRICES AND SYSTEMS OF LINEAR EQUATIONS

The following system of linear equations

$$\begin{aligned}
a_{11}x_1 + a_{12}x_2 + \cdots + a_{1n}x_n &= b_1 \\
a_{21}x_1 + a_{22}x_2 + \cdots + a_{2n}x_n &= b_2 \\
&\cdots\cdots\cdots\cdots\cdots\cdots\cdots\cdots\cdots\cdots \\
a_{m1}x_1 + a_{m2}x_2 + \cdots + a_{mn}x_n &= b_m
\end{aligned} \qquad (1)$$

is equivalent to the matrix equation

$$\begin{pmatrix} a_{11} & a_{12} & \ldots & a_{1n} \\ a_{21} & a_{22} & \ldots & a_{2n} \\ \cdots\cdots\cdots\cdots\cdots\cdots \\ a_{m1} & a_{m2} & \ldots & a_{mn} \end{pmatrix} \begin{pmatrix} x_1 \\ x_2 \\ \cdot\cdot \\ x_n \end{pmatrix} = \begin{pmatrix} b_1 \\ b_2 \\ \cdot\cdot \\ b_m \end{pmatrix} \quad \text{or simply} \quad AX = B \qquad (2)$$

where $A = (a_{ij})$, $X = (x_i)$ and $B = (b_i)$.   That is, every solution of the system (1) is a solution of the matrix equation (2), and vice versa.   Observe that the associated homogeneous system of (1) is then equivalent to the matrix equation $AX = 0$.

The above matrix A is called the *coefficient matrix* of the system (1), and the matrix

$$\begin{pmatrix} a_{11} & a_{12} & \ldots & a_{1n} & b_1 \\ a_{21} & a_{22} & \ldots & a_{2n} & b_2 \\ \cdots\cdots\cdots\cdots\cdots\cdots\cdots\cdots \\ a_{m1} & a_{m2} & \ldots & a_{mn} & b_m \end{pmatrix}$$

is called the *augmented matrix* of (1).   Observe that the system (1) is completely determined by its augmented matrix.

Example 3.8:   The coefficient matrix and the augmented matrix of the system

$$2x + 3y - 4z = 7$$
$$x - 2y - 5z = 3$$

are respectively the following matrices:

$$\begin{pmatrix} 2 & 3 & -4 \\ 1 & -2 & -5 \end{pmatrix} \quad \text{and} \quad \begin{pmatrix} 2 & 3 & -4 & 7 \\ 1 & -2 & -5 & 3 \end{pmatrix}$$

Observe that the system is equivalent to the matrix equation

$$\begin{pmatrix} 2 & 3 & -4 \\ 1 & -2 & -5 \end{pmatrix} \begin{pmatrix} x \\ y \\ z \end{pmatrix} = \begin{pmatrix} 7 \\ 3 \end{pmatrix}$$

In studying linear equations it is usually simpler to use the language and theory of matrices, as indicated by the following theorems.

Theorem 3.4: Suppose $u_1, u_2, \ldots, u_n$ are solutions of a homogeneous system of linear equations $AX = 0$. Then every linear combination of the u_i of the form $k_1u_1 + k_2u_2 + \cdots + k_nu_n$ where the k_i are scalars, is also a solution of $AX = 0$. Thus, in particular, every multiple ku of any solution u of $AX = 0$ is also a solution of $AX = 0$.

Proof. We are given that $Au_1 = 0$, $Au_2 = 0$, $\ldots$, $Au_n = 0$. Hence

$$
\begin{aligned}
A(ku_1 + ku_2 + \cdots + ku_n) &= k_1Au_1 + k_2Au_2 + \cdots + k_nAu_n \\
&= k_10 + k_20 + \cdots + k_n0 = 0
\end{aligned}
$$

Accordingly, $k_1u_1 + \cdots + k_nu_n$ is a solution of the homogeneous system $AX = 0$.

Theorem 3.5: Suppose the field K is infinite (e.g. if K is the real field **R** or the complex field **C**). Then the system $AX = B$ has no solution, a unique solution or an infinite number of solutions.

Proof. It suffices to show that if $AX = B$ has more than one solution, then it has infinitely many. Suppose u and v are distinct solutions of $AX = B$; that is, $Au = B$ and $Av = B$. Then, for any $k \in K$,

$$
A(u + k(u - v)) = Au + k(Au - Av) = B + k(B - B) = B
$$

In other words, for each $k \in K$, $u + k(u - v)$ is a solution of $AX = B$. Since all such solutions are distinct (Problem 3.31), $AX = B$ has an infinite number of solutions as claimed.

ECHELON MATRICES

A matrix $A = (a_{ij})$ is an *echelon matrix*, or is said to be in *echelon form*, if the number of zeros preceding the first nonzero entry of a row increases row by row until only zero rows remain; that is, if there exist nonzero entries

$$
a_{1j_1}, a_{2j_2}, \ldots, a_{rj_r}, \qquad \text{where} \quad j_1 < j_2 < \cdots < j_r
$$

with the property that

$$
a_{ij} = 0 \quad \text{for } i \le r, \; j < j_i, \; \text{and for } i > r
$$

We call $a_{1j_1}, \ldots, a_{rj_r}$ the *distinguished elements* of the echelon matrix A.

Example 3.9: The following are echelon matrices where the distinguished elements have been circled:

$$
\begin{pmatrix}
②&3&2&0&4&5&-6\\
0&0&⑦&1&-3&2&0\\
0&0&0&0&0&⑥&2\\
0&0&0&0&0&0&0
\end{pmatrix}
\quad
\begin{pmatrix}
①&2&3\\
0&0&④\\
0&0&0\\
0&0&0
\end{pmatrix}
\quad
\begin{pmatrix}
0&①&3&0&0&4&0\\
0&0&0&①&0&-3&0\\
0&0&0&0&①&2&0\\
0&0&0&0&0&0&①
\end{pmatrix}
$$

In particular, an echelon matrix is called a *row reduced echelon matrix* if the distinguished elements are:

(i)   the only nonzero entries in their respective columns;

(ii) each equal to 1.

The third matrix above is an example of a row reduced echelon matrix, the other two are not. Note that the zero matrix 0, for any number of rows or of columns, is also a row reduced echelon matrix.

ROW EQUIVALENCE AND ELEMENTARY ROW OPERATIONS

A matrix A is said to be *row equivalent* to a matrix B if B can be obtained from A by a finite sequence of the following operations called *elementary row operations*:

$[E_1]$: Interchange the ith row and the jth row: $R_i \leftrightarrow R_j$.

$[E_2]$: Multiply the ith row by a nonzero scalar k: $R_i \rightarrow kR_i$, $k \neq 0$.

$[E_3]$: Replace the ith row by k times the jth row plus the ith row: $R_i \rightarrow kR_j + R_i$.

In actual practice we apply $[E_2]$ and then $[E_3]$ in one step, i.e. the operation

$[E]$: Replace the ith row by k' times the jth row plus k (nonzero) times the ith row: $R_i \rightarrow k'R_j + kR_i$, $k \neq 0$.

The reader no doubt recognizes the similarity of the above operations and those used in solving systems of linear equations. In fact, two systems with row equivalent augmented matrices have the same solution set (Problem 3.71). The following algorithm is also similar to the one used with linear equations (page 20).

*Algorithm which **row reduces** a matrix to echelon form:*

Step 1. Suppose the j_1 column is the first column with a nonzero entry. Interchange the rows so that this nonzero entry appears in the first row, that is, so that $a_{1j_1} \neq 0$.

Step 2. For each $i > 1$, apply the operation

$$R_i \rightarrow -a_{ij_1}R_1 + a_{1j_1}R_i$$

Repeat Steps 1 and 2 with the submatrix formed by all the rows excluding the first. Continue the process until the matrix is in echelon form.

Remark: The term *row reduce* shall mean to transform by elementary row operations.

Example 3.10: The following matrix A is row reduced to echelon form by applying the operations $R_2 \rightarrow -2R_1 + R_2$ and $R_3 \rightarrow -3R_1 + R_3$, and then the operation $R_3 \rightarrow -5R_2 + 4R_3$:

$$A = \begin{pmatrix} 1 & 2 & -3 & 0 \\ 2 & 4 & -2 & 2 \\ 3 & 6 & -4 & 3 \end{pmatrix} \text{ to } \begin{pmatrix} 1 & 2 & -3 & 0 \\ 0 & 0 & 4 & 2 \\ 0 & 0 & 5 & 3 \end{pmatrix} \text{ to } \begin{pmatrix} 1 & 2 & -3 & 0 \\ 0 & 0 & 4 & 2 \\ 0 & 0 & 0 & 2 \end{pmatrix}$$

Now suppose $A = (a_{ij})$ is a matrix in echelon form with distinguished elements $a_{1j_1}, \ldots, a_{rj_r}$. Apply the operations

$$R_k \rightarrow -a_{kj_i}R_i + a_{ij_i}R_k, \qquad k = 1, \ldots, i-1$$

for $i = 2$, then $i = 3, \ldots, i = r$. Thus A is replaced by an echelon matrix whose distinguished elements are the only nonzero entries in their respective columns. Next, multiply R_i by $a_{ij_i}^{-1}$, $i \leqq r$. Thus, in addition, the distinguished elements are each 1. In other words, the above process row reduces an echelon matrix to one in row reduced echelon form.

Example 3.11: On the following echelon matrix A, apply the operation $R_1 \rightarrow -4R_2 + 3R_1$ and then the operations $R_1 \rightarrow R_3 + R_1$ and $R_2 \rightarrow -5R_3 + 2R_2$:

$$A = \begin{pmatrix} 2 & 3 & 4 & 5 & 6 \\ 0 & 0 & 3 & 2 & 5 \\ 0 & 0 & 0 & 0 & 2 \end{pmatrix} \text{ to } \begin{pmatrix} 6 & 9 & 0 & 7 & -2 \\ 0 & 0 & 3 & 2 & 5 \\ 0 & 0 & 0 & 0 & 2 \end{pmatrix} \text{ to } \begin{pmatrix} 6 & 9 & 0 & 7 & 0 \\ 0 & 0 & 6 & 4 & 0 \\ 0 & 0 & 0 & 0 & 2 \end{pmatrix}$$

Next multiply R_1 by 1/6, R_2 by 1/6 and R_3 by 1/2 to obtain the row reduced echelon matrix

$$\begin{pmatrix} 1 & 3/2 & 0 & 7/6 & 0 \\ 0 & 0 & 1 & 2/3 & 0 \\ 0 & 0 & 0 & 0 & 1 \end{pmatrix}$$

The above remarks show that any arbitrary matrix A is row equivalent to at least one row reduced echelon matrix. In the next chapter we prove, Theorem 4.8, that A is row equivalent to only one such matrix; we call it the *row canonical form* of A.

CHAP. 3]   MATRICES   **43**

SQUARE MATRICES

A matrix with the same number of rows as columns is called a *square matrix*. A square matrix with n rows and n columns is said to be of *order n*, and is called an n-square matrix. The *diagonal* (or: *main diagonal*) of the n-square matrix $A = (a_{ij})$ consists of the elements $a_{11}, a_{22}, \ldots, a_{nn}$.

Example 3.12: The following is a 3-square matrix: $\begin{pmatrix} 1 & 2 & 3 \\ 4 & 5 & 6 \\ 7 & 8 & 9 \end{pmatrix}$.

Its diagonal elements are 1, 5 and 9.

An *upper triangular matrix* or simply a *triangular matrix* is a square matrix whose entries below the main diagonal are all zero:

$$\begin{pmatrix} a_{11} & a_{12} & \ldots & a_{1n} \\ 0 & a_{22} & \ldots & a_{2n} \\ \cdots\cdots\cdots\cdots\cdots \\ 0 & 0 & \ldots & a_{nn} \end{pmatrix} \quad \text{or} \quad \begin{pmatrix} a_{11} & a_{12} & \ldots & a_{1n} \\ & a_{22} & \ldots & a_{2n} \\ & & \cdots\cdots \\ & & & a_{nn} \end{pmatrix}$$

Similarly, a *lower triangular matrix* is a square matrix whose entries above the main diagonal are all zero.

A *diagonal matrix* is a square matrix whose non-diagonal entries are all zero:

$$\begin{pmatrix} a_1 & 0 & \ldots & 0 \\ 0 & a_2 & \ldots & 0 \\ \cdots\cdots\cdots\cdots\cdots \\ 0 & 0 & \ldots & a_n \end{pmatrix} \quad \text{or} \quad \begin{pmatrix} a_1 & & & \\ & a_2 & & \\ & & \ddots & \\ & & & a_n \end{pmatrix}$$

In particular, the n-square matrix with 1's on the diagonal and 0's elsewhere, denoted by I_n or simply I, is called the *unit* or *identity* matrix; e.g.,

$$I_3 \;=\; \begin{pmatrix} 1 & 0 & 0 \\ 0 & 1 & 0 \\ 0 & 0 & 1 \end{pmatrix}$$

This matrix I is similar to the scalar 1 in that, for any n-square matrix A,

$$AI \;=\; IA \;=\; A$$

The matrix kI, for a scalar $k \in K$, is called a *scalar matrix*; it is a diagonal matrix whose diagonal entries are each k.

ALGEBRA OF SQUARE MATRICES

Recall that not every two matrices can be added or multiplied. However, if we only consider square matrices of some given order n, then this inconvenience disappears. Specifically, the operations of addition, multiplication, scalar multiplication, and transpose can be performed on any $n \times n$ matrices and the result is again an $n \times n$ matrix.

In particular, if A is any n-square matrix, we can form powers of A:

$$A^2 = AA, \; A^3 = A^2A, \; \ldots \quad \text{and} \quad A^0 = I$$

We can also form polynomials in the matrix A: for any polynomial

$$f(x) \;=\; a_0 + a_1x + a_2x^2 + \cdots + a_nx^n$$

where the a_i are scalars, we define $f(A)$ to be the matrix

$$f(A) = a_0 I + a_1 A + a_2 A^2 + \cdots + a_n A^n$$

In the case that $f(A)$ is the zero matrix, then A is called a *zero* or *root* of the polynomial $f(x)$.

Example 3.13: Let $A = \begin{pmatrix} 1 & 2 \\ 3 & -4 \end{pmatrix}$; then $A^2 = \begin{pmatrix} 1 & 2 \\ 3 & -4 \end{pmatrix}\begin{pmatrix} 1 & 2 \\ 3 & -4 \end{pmatrix} = \begin{pmatrix} 7 & -6 \\ -9 & 22 \end{pmatrix}$.

If $f(x) = 2x^2 - 3x + 5$, then

$$f(A) = 2\begin{pmatrix} 7 & -6 \\ -9 & 22 \end{pmatrix} - 3\begin{pmatrix} 1 & 2 \\ 3 & -4 \end{pmatrix} + 5\begin{pmatrix} 1 & 0 \\ 0 & 1 \end{pmatrix} = \begin{pmatrix} 16 & -18 \\ -27 & 61 \end{pmatrix}$$

If $g(x) = x^2 + 3x - 10$, then

$$g(A) = \begin{pmatrix} 7 & -6 \\ -9 & 22 \end{pmatrix} + 3\begin{pmatrix} 1 & 2 \\ 3 & -4 \end{pmatrix} - 10\begin{pmatrix} 1 & 0 \\ 0 & 1 \end{pmatrix} = \begin{pmatrix} 0 & 0 \\ 0 & 0 \end{pmatrix}$$

Thus A is a zero of the polynomial $g(x)$.

INVERTIBLE MATRICES

A square matrix A is said to be *invertible* if there exists a matrix B with the property that

$$AB = BA = I$$

where I is the identity matrix. Such a matrix B is unique; for

$$AB_1 = B_1 A = I \quad \text{and} \quad AB_2 = B_2 A = I \quad \text{implies} \quad B_1 = B_1 I = B_1(AB_2) = (B_1 A)B_2 = IB_2 = B_2$$

We call such a matrix B the *inverse* of A and denote it by A^{-1}. Observe that the above relation is symmetric; that is, if B is the inverse of A, then A is the inverse of B.

Example 3.14: $\begin{pmatrix} 2 & 5 \\ 1 & 3 \end{pmatrix}\begin{pmatrix} 3 & -5 \\ -1 & 2 \end{pmatrix} = \begin{pmatrix} 6-5 & -10+10 \\ 3-3 & -5+6 \end{pmatrix} = \begin{pmatrix} 1 & 0 \\ 0 & 1 \end{pmatrix}$

$\begin{pmatrix} 3 & -5 \\ -1 & 2 \end{pmatrix}\begin{pmatrix} 2 & 5 \\ 1 & 3 \end{pmatrix} = \begin{pmatrix} 6-5 & 15-15 \\ -2+2 & -5+6 \end{pmatrix} = \begin{pmatrix} 1 & 0 \\ 0 & 1 \end{pmatrix}$

Thus $\begin{pmatrix} 2 & 5 \\ 1 & 3 \end{pmatrix}$ and $\begin{pmatrix} 3 & -5 \\ -1 & 2 \end{pmatrix}$ are invertible and are inverses of each other.

We show (Problem 3.37) that for square matrices, $AB = I$ if and only if $BA = I$; hence it is necessary to test only one product to determine whether two given matrices are inverses, as in the next example.

Example 3.15: $\begin{pmatrix} 1 & 0 & 2 \\ 2 & -1 & 3 \\ 4 & 1 & 8 \end{pmatrix}\begin{pmatrix} -11 & 2 & 2 \\ -4 & 0 & 1 \\ 6 & -1 & -1 \end{pmatrix} = \begin{pmatrix} -11+0+12 & 2+0-2 & 2+0-2 \\ -22+4+18 & 4+0-3 & 4-1-3 \\ -44-4+48 & 8+0-8 & 8+1-8 \end{pmatrix} = \begin{pmatrix} 1 & 0 & 0 \\ 0 & 1 & 0 \\ 0 & 0 & 1 \end{pmatrix}$

Thus the two matrices are invertible and are inverses of each other.

We now calculate the inverse of a general 2×2 matrix $A = \begin{pmatrix} a & b \\ c & d \end{pmatrix}$. We seek scalars x, y, z, w such that

$$\begin{pmatrix} a & b \\ c & d \end{pmatrix}\begin{pmatrix} x & y \\ z & w \end{pmatrix} = \begin{pmatrix} 1 & 0 \\ 0 & 1 \end{pmatrix} \quad \text{or} \quad \begin{pmatrix} ax+bz & ay+bw \\ cx+dz & cy+dw \end{pmatrix} = \begin{pmatrix} 1 & 0 \\ 0 & 1 \end{pmatrix}$$

which reduces to solving the following two systems of linear equations in two unknowns:

$$\begin{cases} ax + bz = 1 \\ cx + dz = 0 \end{cases} \qquad \begin{cases} ay + bw = 0 \\ cy + dw = 1 \end{cases}$$

If we let $|A| = ad - bc$, then by Problem 2.27, page 33, the above systems have solutions if and only if $|A| \neq 0$; such solutions are unique and are as follows:

$$x = \frac{d}{ad-bc} = \frac{d}{|A|}, \quad y = \frac{-b}{ad-bc} = \frac{-b}{|A|}, \quad z = \frac{-c}{ad-bc} = \frac{-c}{|A|}, \quad w = \frac{a}{ad-bc} = \frac{a}{|A|}$$

Accordingly,
$$A^{-1} = \begin{pmatrix} d/|A| & -b/|A| \\ -c/|A| & a/|A| \end{pmatrix} = \frac{1}{|A|} \begin{pmatrix} d & -b \\ -c & a \end{pmatrix}$$

Remark: The reader no doubt recognizes $|A| = ad - bc$ as the determinant of the matrix A; thus we see that a 2×2 matrix has an inverse if and only if its determinant is not zero. This relationship, which holds true in general, will be further investigated in Chapter 9 on determinants.

BLOCK MATRICES

Using a system of horizontal and vertical lines, we can partition a matrix A into smaller matrices called *blocks* (or: *cells*) of A. The matrix A is then called a *block matrix*. Clearly, a given matrix may be divided into blocks in different ways; for example,

$$\begin{pmatrix} 1 & -2 & 0 & 1 & 3 \\ 2 & 3 & 5 & 7 & -2 \\ 3 & 1 & 4 & 5 & 9 \end{pmatrix} = \left(\begin{array}{cc|cc|c} 1 & -2 & 0 & 1 & 3 \\ 2 & 3 & 5 & 7 & -2 \\ \hline 3 & 1 & 4 & 5 & 9 \end{array}\right) = \left(\begin{array}{ccc|cc} 1 & -2 & 0 & 1 & 3 \\ \hline 2 & 3 & 5 & 7 & -2 \\ \hline 3 & 1 & 4 & 5 & 9 \end{array}\right)$$

The convenience of the partition into blocks is that the result of operations on block matrices can be obtained by carrying out the computation with the blocks, just as if they were the actual elements of the matrices. This is illustrated below.

Suppose A is partitioned into blocks; say

$$A = \begin{pmatrix} A_{11} & A_{12} & \dots & A_{1n} \\ A_{21} & A_{22} & \dots & A_{2n} \\ \dots\dots\dots\dots\dots\dots\dots \\ A_{m1} & A_{m2} & \dots & A_{mn} \end{pmatrix}$$

Multiplying each block by a scalar k, multiplies each element of A by k; thus

$$kA = \begin{pmatrix} kA_{11} & kA_{12} & \dots & kA_{1n} \\ kA_{21} & kA_{22} & \dots & kA_{2n} \\ \dots\dots\dots\dots\dots\dots\dots \\ kA_{m1} & kA_{m2} & \dots & kA_{mn} \end{pmatrix}$$

Now suppose a matrix B is partitioned into the same number of blocks as A; say

$$B = \begin{pmatrix} B_{11} & B_{12} & \dots & B_{1n} \\ B_{21} & B_{22} & \dots & B_{2n} \\ \dots\dots\dots\dots\dots\dots\dots \\ B_{m1} & B_{m2} & \dots & B_{mn} \end{pmatrix}$$

Furthermore, suppose the corresponding blocks of A and B have the same size. Adding these corresponding blocks, adds the corresponding elements of A and B. Accordingly,

$$A + B = \begin{pmatrix} A_{11}+B_{11} & A_{12}+B_{12} & \ldots & A_{1n}+B_{1n} \\ A_{21}+B_{21} & A_{22}+B_{22} & \ldots & A_{2n}+B_{2n} \\ \hdotsfor{4} \\ A_{m1}+B_{m1} & A_{m2}+B_{m2} & \ldots & A_{mn}+B_{mn} \end{pmatrix}$$

The case of matrix multiplication is less obvious but still true. That is, suppose matrices U and V are partitioned into blocks as follows

$$U = \begin{pmatrix} U_{11} & U_{12} & \ldots & U_{1p} \\ U_{21} & U_{22} & \ldots & U_{2p} \\ \hdotsfor{4} \\ U_{m1} & U_{m2} & \ldots & U_{mp} \end{pmatrix} \quad \text{and} \quad V = \begin{pmatrix} V_{11} & V_{12} & \ldots & V_{1n} \\ V_{21} & V_{22} & \ldots & V_{2n} \\ \hdotsfor{4} \\ V_{p1} & V_{22} & \ldots & V_{pn} \end{pmatrix}$$

such that the number of columns of each block U_{ik} is equal to the number of rows of each block V_{kj}. Then

$$UV = \begin{pmatrix} W_{11} & W_{12} & \ldots & W_{1n} \\ W_{21} & W_{22} & \ldots & W_{2n} \\ \hdotsfor{4} \\ W_{m1} & W_{m2} & \ldots & W_{mn} \end{pmatrix}$$

where
$$W_{ij} = U_{i1}V_{1j} + U_{i2}V_{2j} + \cdots + U_{ip}V_{pj}$$

The proof of the above formula for UV is straightforward, but detailed and lengthy. It is left as a supplementary problem (Problem 3.68).

Solved Problems

MATRIX ADDITION AND SCALAR MULTIPLICATION

3.1. Compute:

(i) $\begin{pmatrix} 1 & 2 & -3 & 4 \\ 0 & -5 & 1 & -1 \end{pmatrix} + \begin{pmatrix} 3 & -5 & 6 & -1 \\ 2 & 0 & -2 & -3 \end{pmatrix}$

(ii) $\begin{pmatrix} 1 & 2 & -3 \\ 0 & -4 & 1 \end{pmatrix} + \begin{pmatrix} 3 & 5 \\ 1 & -2 \end{pmatrix}$ (iii) $-3\begin{pmatrix} 1 & 2 & -3 \\ 4 & -5 & 6 \end{pmatrix}$

(i) Add corresponding entries:

$$\begin{pmatrix} 1 & 2 & -3 & 4 \\ 0 & -5 & 1 & -1 \end{pmatrix} + \begin{pmatrix} 3 & -5 & 6 & -1 \\ 2 & 0 & -2 & -3 \end{pmatrix}$$
$$= \begin{pmatrix} 1+3 & 2-5 & -3+6 & 4-1 \\ 0+2 & -5+0 & 1-2 & -1-3 \end{pmatrix} = \begin{pmatrix} 4 & -3 & 3 & 3 \\ 2 & -5 & -1 & -4 \end{pmatrix}$$

(ii) The sum is not defined since the matrices have different shapes.

(iii) Multiply each entry in the matrix by the scalar -3:

$$-3\begin{pmatrix} 1 & 2 & -3 \\ 4 & -5 & 6 \end{pmatrix} = \begin{pmatrix} -3 & -6 & 9 \\ -12 & 15 & -18 \end{pmatrix}$$

3.2. Let $A = \begin{pmatrix} 2 & -5 & 1 \\ 3 & 0 & -4 \end{pmatrix}$, $B = \begin{pmatrix} 1 & -2 & -3 \\ 0 & -1 & 5 \end{pmatrix}$, $C = \begin{pmatrix} 0 & 1 & -2 \\ 1 & -1 & -1 \end{pmatrix}$. Find $3A + 4B - 2C$.

First perform the scalar multiplication, and then the matrix addition:

$$3A + 4B - 2C = \begin{pmatrix} 6 & -15 & 3 \\ 9 & 0 & -12 \end{pmatrix} + \begin{pmatrix} 4 & -8 & -12 \\ 0 & -4 & 20 \end{pmatrix} + \begin{pmatrix} 0 & -2 & 4 \\ -2 & 2 & 2 \end{pmatrix} = \begin{pmatrix} 10 & -25 & -5 \\ 7 & -2 & 10 \end{pmatrix}$$

3.3. Find x, y, z and w if $3\begin{pmatrix} x & y \\ z & w \end{pmatrix} = \begin{pmatrix} x & 6 \\ -1 & 2w \end{pmatrix} + \begin{pmatrix} 4 & x+y \\ z+w & 3 \end{pmatrix}$.

First write each side as a single matrix:

$$\begin{pmatrix} 3x & 3y \\ 3z & 3w \end{pmatrix} = \begin{pmatrix} x+4 & x+y+6 \\ z+w-1 & 2w+3 \end{pmatrix}$$

Set corresponding entries equal to each other to obtain the system of four equations,

$$\begin{aligned}
3x &= x+4 & & & 2x &= 4 \\
3y &= x+y+6 & & & 2y &= 6+x \\
3z &= z+w-1 & \text{or} & & 2z &= w-1 \\
3w &= 2w+3 & & & w &= 3
\end{aligned}$$

The solution is: $x = 2$, $y = 4$, $z = 1$, $w = 3$.

3.4. Prove Theorem 3.1(v): Let A and B be $m \times n$ matrices and k a scalar. Then $k(A+B) = kA + kB$.

Suppose $A = (a_{ij})$ and $B = (b_{ij})$. Then $a_{ij} + b_{ij}$ is the ij-entry of $A + B$, and so $k(a_{ij} + b_{ij})$ is the ij-entry of $k(A + B)$. On the other hand, ka_{ij} and kb_{ij} are the ij-entries of kA and kB respectively and so $ka_{ij} + kb_{ij}$ is the ij-entry of $kA + kB$. But k, a_{ij} and b_{ij} are scalars in a field; hence

$$k(a_{ij} + b_{ij}) = ka_{ij} + kb_{ij}, \qquad \text{for every } i, j$$

Thus $k(A + B) = kA + kB$, as corresponding entries are equal.

Remark: Observe the similarity of this proof and the proof of Theorem 1.1(v) in Problem 1.6, page 7. In fact, all other sections in the above theorem are proven in the same way as the corresponding sections of Theorem 1.1.

MATRIX MULTIPLICATION

3.5. Let $(r \times s)$ denote a matrix with shape $r \times s$. Find the shape of the following products if the product is defined:

(i) $(2 \times 3)(3 \times 4)$ (iii) $(1 \times 2)(3 \times 1)$ (v) $(3 \times 4)(3 \times 4)$

(ii) $(4 \times 1)(1 \times 2)$ (iv) $(5 \times 2)(2 \times 3)$ (vi) $(2 \times 2)(2 \times 4)$

Recall that an $m \times p$ matrix and a $q \times n$ matrix are multiplicable only when $p = q$, and then the product is an $m \times n$ matrix. Thus each of the above products is defined if the "inner" numbers are equal, and then the product will have the shape of the "outer" numbers in the given order.

(i)   The product is a 2×4 matrix.

(ii) The product is a 4×2 matrix.

(iii) The product is not defined since the inner numbers 2 and 3 are not equal.

(iv) The product is a 5×3 matrix.

(v)   The product is not defined even though the matrices have the same shape.

(vi) The product is a 2×4 matrix.

3.6. Let $A = \begin{pmatrix} 1 & 3 \\ 2 & -1 \end{pmatrix}$ and $B = \begin{pmatrix} 2 & 0 & -4 \\ 3 & -2 & 6 \end{pmatrix}$. Find (i) AB, (ii) BA.

(i) Since A is 2×2 and B is 2×3, the product AB is defined and is a 2×3 matrix. To obtain the entries in the first row of AB, multiply the first row $(1, 3)$ of A by the columns $\begin{pmatrix} 2 \\ 3 \end{pmatrix}$, $\begin{pmatrix} 0 \\ -2 \end{pmatrix}$ and $\begin{pmatrix} -4 \\ 6 \end{pmatrix}$ of B, respectively:

$$\begin{pmatrix} 1 & 3 \\ 2 & -1 \end{pmatrix}\begin{pmatrix} 2 & 0 & -4 \\ 3 & -2 & 6 \end{pmatrix} = \begin{pmatrix} 1 \cdot 2 + 3 \cdot 3 & 1 \cdot 0 + 3 \cdot (-2) & 1 \cdot (-4) + 3 \cdot 6 \\ & & \end{pmatrix}$$

$$= \begin{pmatrix} 2 + 9 & 0 - 6 & -4 + 18 \\ & & \end{pmatrix} = \begin{pmatrix} 11 & -6 & 14 \\ & & \end{pmatrix}$$

To obtain the entries in the second row of AB, multiply the second row $(2, -1)$ of A by the columns of B, respectively:

$$\begin{pmatrix} 1 & 3 \\ 2 & -1 \end{pmatrix}\begin{pmatrix} 2 & 0 & -4 \\ 3 & -2 & 6 \end{pmatrix} = \begin{pmatrix} 11 & -6 & 14 \\ 2 \cdot 2 + (-1) \cdot 3 & 2 \cdot 0 + (-1) \cdot (-2) & 2 \cdot (-4) + (-1) \cdot 6 \end{pmatrix}$$

Thus $\qquad\qquad\qquad AB = \begin{pmatrix} 11 & -6 & 14 \\ 1 & 2 & -14 \end{pmatrix}$

(ii) Note that B is 2×3 and A is 2×2. Since the inner numbers 3 and 2 are not equal, the product BA is not defined.

3.7. Given $A = (2, 1)$ and $B = \begin{pmatrix} 1 & -2 & 0 \\ 4 & 5 & -3 \end{pmatrix}$, find (i) AB, (ii) BA.

(i) Since A is 1×2 and B is 2×3, the product AB is defined and is a 1×3 matrix, i.e. a row vector with 3 components. To obtain the components of AB, multiply the row of A by each column of B:

$$AB = (2, 1)\begin{pmatrix} 1 & -2 & 0 \\ 4 & 5 & -3 \end{pmatrix} = (2 \cdot 1 + 1 \cdot 4,\ 2 \cdot (-2) + 1 \cdot 5,\ 2 \cdot 0 + 1 \cdot (-3)) = (6, 1, -3)$$

(ii) Note that B is 2×3 and A is 1×2. Since the inner numbers 3 and 1 are not equal, the product BA is not defined.

3.8. Given $A = \begin{pmatrix} 2 & -1 \\ 1 & 0 \\ -3 & 4 \end{pmatrix}$ and $B = \begin{pmatrix} 1 & -2 & -5 \\ 3 & 4 & 0 \end{pmatrix}$, find (i) AB, (ii) BA.

(i) Since A is 3×2 and B is 2×3, the product AB is defined and is a 3×3 matrix. To obtain the first row of AB, multiply the first row of A by each column of B, respectively:

$$\begin{pmatrix} 2 & -1 \\ 1 & 0 \\ -3 & 4 \end{pmatrix}\begin{pmatrix} 1 & -2 & -5 \\ 3 & 4 & 0 \end{pmatrix} = \begin{pmatrix} 2 - 3 & -4 - 4 & -10 + 0 \\ & & \\ & & \end{pmatrix} = \begin{pmatrix} -1 & -8 & -10 \\ & & \\ & & \end{pmatrix}$$

To obtain the second row of AB, multiply the second row of A by each column of B, respectively:

$$\begin{pmatrix} 2 & -1 \\ 1 & 0 \\ -3 & 4 \end{pmatrix}\begin{pmatrix} 1 & -2 & -5 \\ 3 & 4 & 0 \end{pmatrix} = \begin{pmatrix} -1 & -8 & -10 \\ 1 + 0 & -2 + 0 & -5 + 0 \\ & & \end{pmatrix} = \begin{pmatrix} -1 & -8 & -10 \\ 1 & -2 & -5 \\ & & \end{pmatrix}$$

To obtain the third row of AB, multiply the third row of A by each column of B, respectively:

$$\begin{pmatrix} 2 & -1 \\ 1 & 0 \\ -3 & 4 \end{pmatrix}\begin{pmatrix} 1 & -2 & -5 \\ 3 & 4 & 0 \end{pmatrix} = \begin{pmatrix} -1 & -8 & -10 \\ 1 & -2 & -5 \\ -3+12 & 6+16 & 15+0 \end{pmatrix} = \begin{pmatrix} -1 & -8 & -10 \\ 1 & -2 & -5 \\ 9 & 22 & 15 \end{pmatrix}$$

Thus $\qquad\qquad AB = \begin{pmatrix} -1 & -8 & -10 \\ 1 & -2 & -5 \\ 9 & 22 & 15 \end{pmatrix}$

(ii) Since B is 2×3 and A is 3×2, the product BA is defined and is a 2×2 matrix. To obtain the first row of BA, multiply the first row of B by each column of A, respectively:

$$\begin{pmatrix} 1 & -2 & -5 \\ 3 & 4 & 0 \end{pmatrix}\begin{pmatrix} 2 & -1 \\ 1 & 0 \\ -3 & 4 \end{pmatrix} = \begin{pmatrix} 2-2+15 & -1+0-20 \end{pmatrix} = \begin{pmatrix} 15 & -21 \end{pmatrix}$$

To obtain the second row of BA, multiply the second row of B by each column of A, respectively:

$$\begin{pmatrix} 1 & -2 & -5 \\ 3 & 4 & 0 \end{pmatrix}\begin{pmatrix} 2 & -1 \\ 1 & 0 \\ -3 & 4 \end{pmatrix} = \begin{pmatrix} 15 & -21 \\ 6+4+0 & -3+0+0 \end{pmatrix} = \begin{pmatrix} 15 & -21 \\ 10 & -3 \end{pmatrix}$$

Thus $\qquad\qquad BA = \begin{pmatrix} 15 & -21 \\ 10 & -3 \end{pmatrix}$

Remark: Observe that in this case both AB and BA are defined, but they are not equal; in fact they do not even have the same shape.

3.9. Let $A = \begin{pmatrix} 2 & -1 & 0 \\ 1 & 0 & -3 \end{pmatrix}$ and $B = \begin{pmatrix} 1 & -4 & 0 & 1 \\ 2 & -1 & 3 & -1 \\ 4 & 0 & -2 & 0 \end{pmatrix}$.

(i) Determine the shape of AB. (ii) Let c_{ij} denote the element in the ith row and jth column of the product matrix AB, that is, $AB = (c_{ij})$. Find: c_{23}, c_{14} and c_{21}.

(i) Since A is 2×3 and B is 3×4, the product AB is a 2×4 matrix.

(ii) Now c_{ij} is defined as the product of the ith row of A by the jth column of B. Hence:

$$c_{23} = (1, 0, -3)\begin{pmatrix} 0 \\ 3 \\ -2 \end{pmatrix} = 1 \cdot 0 + 0 \cdot 3 + (-3) \cdot (-2) = 0 + 0 + 6 = 6$$

$$c_{14} = (2, -1, 0)\begin{pmatrix} 1 \\ -1 \\ 0 \end{pmatrix} = 2 \cdot 1 + (-1) \cdot (-1) + 0 \cdot 0 = 2 + 1 + 0 = 3$$

$$c_{21} = (1, 0, -3)\begin{pmatrix} 1 \\ 2 \\ 4 \end{pmatrix} = 1 \cdot 1 + 0 \cdot 2 + (-3) \cdot 4 = 1 + 0 - 12 = -11$$

3.10. Compute: (i) $\begin{pmatrix} 1 & 6 \\ -3 & 5 \end{pmatrix}\begin{pmatrix} 4 & 0 \\ 2 & -1 \end{pmatrix}$ (iii) $\begin{pmatrix} 1 \\ -6 \end{pmatrix}\begin{pmatrix} 1 & 6 \\ -3 & 5 \end{pmatrix}$ (v) $(2, -1)\begin{pmatrix} 1 \\ -6 \end{pmatrix}$

(ii) $\begin{pmatrix} 1 & 6 \\ -3 & 5 \end{pmatrix}\begin{pmatrix} 2 \\ -7 \end{pmatrix}$ (iv) $\begin{pmatrix} 1 \\ 6 \end{pmatrix}(3, 2)$

(i) The first factor is 2×2 and the second is 2×2, so the product is defined and is a 2×2 matrix:

$$\begin{pmatrix} 1 & 6 \\ -3 & 5 \end{pmatrix}\begin{pmatrix} 4 & 0 \\ 2 & -1 \end{pmatrix} \;=\; \begin{pmatrix} 1\cdot 4 + 6\cdot 2 & 1\cdot 0 + 6\cdot(-1) \\ (-3)\cdot 4 + 5\cdot 2 & (-3)\cdot 0 + 5\cdot(-1) \end{pmatrix} \;=\; \begin{pmatrix} 16 & -6 \\ -2 & -5 \end{pmatrix}$$

(ii) The first factor is 2×2 and the second is 2×1, so the product is defined and is a 2×1 matrix:

$$\begin{pmatrix} 1 & 6 \\ -3 & 5 \end{pmatrix}\begin{pmatrix} 2 \\ -7 \end{pmatrix} \;=\; \begin{pmatrix} 1\cdot 2 + 6\cdot(-7) \\ (-3)\cdot 2 + 5\cdot(-7) \end{pmatrix} \;=\; \begin{pmatrix} -40 \\ -41 \end{pmatrix}$$

(iii) Now the first factor is 2×1 and the second is 2×2. Since the inner numbers 1 and 2 are distinct, the product is not defined.

(iv) Here the first factor is 2×1 and the second is 1×2, so the product is defined and is a 2×2 matrix:

$$\begin{pmatrix} 1 \\ 6 \end{pmatrix}(3,\,2) \;=\; \begin{pmatrix} 1\cdot 3 & 1\cdot 2 \\ 6\cdot 3 & 6\cdot 2 \end{pmatrix} \;=\; \begin{pmatrix} 3 & 2 \\ 18 & 12 \end{pmatrix}$$

(v) The first factor is 1×2 and the second is 2×1, so the product is defined and is a 1×1 matrix which we frequently write as a scalar.

$$(2,\,-1)\begin{pmatrix} 1 \\ -6 \end{pmatrix} \;=\; (2\cdot 1 + (-1)\cdot(-6)) \;=\; (8) \;=\; 8$$

3.11. Prove Theorem 3.2(i): $(AB)C = A(BC)$.

Let $A = (a_{ij})$, $B = (b_{jk})$ and $C = (c_{kl})$. Furthermore, let $AB = S = (s_{ik})$ and $BC = T = (t_{jl})$. Then

$$s_{ik} \;=\; a_{i1}b_{1k} + a_{i2}b_{2k} + \cdots + a_{im}b_{mk} \;=\; \sum_{j=1}^{m} a_{ij}b_{jk}$$

$$t_{jl} \;=\; b_{j1}c_{1l} + b_{j2}c_{2l} + \cdots + b_{jn}c_{nl} \;=\; \sum_{k=1}^{n} b_{jk}c_{kl}$$

Now multiplying S by C, i.e. (AB) by C, the element in the ith row and lth column of the matrix $(AB)C$ is

$$s_{i1}c_{1l} + s_{i2}c_{2l} + \cdots + s_{in}c_{nl} \;=\; \sum_{k=1}^{n} s_{ik}c_{kl} \;=\; \sum_{k=1}^{n}\sum_{j=1}^{m} (a_{ij}b_{jk})c_{kl}$$

On the other hand, multiplying A by T, i.e. A by BC, the element in the ith row and lth column of the matrix $A(BC)$ is

$$a_{i1}t_{1l} + a_{i2}t_{2l} + \cdots + a_{im}t_{ml} \;=\; \sum_{j=1}^{m} a_{ij}t_{jl} \;=\; \sum_{j=1}^{m}\sum_{k=1}^{n} a_{ij}(b_{jk}c_{kl})$$

Since the above sums are equal, the theorem is proven.

3.12. Prove Theorem 3.2(ii): $A(B + C) = AB + AC$.

Let $A = (a_{ij})$, $B = (b_{jk})$ and $C = (c_{jk})$. Furthermore, let $D = B + C = (d_{jk})$, $E = AB = (e_{ik})$ and $F = AC = (f_{ik})$. Then

$$d_{jk} \;=\; b_{jk} + c_{jk}$$

$$e_{ik} \;=\; a_{i1}b_{1k} + a_{i2}b_{2k} + \cdots + a_{im}b_{mk} \;=\; \sum_{j=1}^{m} a_{ij}b_{jk}$$

$$f_{ik} \;=\; a_{i1}c_{1k} + a_{i2}c_{2k} + \cdots + a_{im}c_{mk} \;=\; \sum_{j=1}^{m} a_{ij}c_{jk}$$

Hence the element in the ith row and kth column of the matrix $AB + AC$ is

$$e_{ik} + f_{ik} \;=\; \sum_{j=1}^{m} a_{ij}b_{jk} + \sum_{j=1}^{m} a_{ij}c_{jk} \;=\; \sum_{j=1}^{m} a_{ij}(b_{jk} + c_{jk})$$

On the other hand, the element in the ith row and kth column of the matrix $AD = A(B + C)$ is

$$a_{i1}d_{1k} + a_{i2}d_{2k} + \cdots + a_{im}d_{mk} \;=\; \sum_{j=1}^{m} a_{ij}d_{jk} \;=\; \sum_{j=1}^{m} a_{ij}(b_{jk} + c_{jk})$$

Thus $A(B + C) = AB + AC$ since the corresponding elements are equal.

TRANSPOSE

3.13. Find the transpose A^t of the matrix $A = \begin{pmatrix} 1 & 0 & 1 & 0 \\ 2 & 3 & 4 & 5 \\ 4 & 4 & 4 & 4 \end{pmatrix}$.

Rewrite the rows of A as the columns of A^t: $A^t = \begin{pmatrix} 1 & 2 & 4 \\ 0 & 3 & 4 \\ 1 & 4 & 4 \\ 0 & 5 & 4 \end{pmatrix}$.

3.14. Let A be an arbitrary matrix. Under what conditions is the product AA^t defined?

Suppose A is an $m \times n$ matrix; then A^t is $n \times m$. Thus the product AA^t is always defined. Observe that A^tA is also defined. Here AA^t is an $m \times m$ matrix, whereas A^tA is an $n \times n$ matrix.

3.15. Let $A = \begin{pmatrix} 1 & 2 & 0 \\ 3 & -1 & 4 \end{pmatrix}$. Find (i) AA^t, (ii) A^tA.

To obtain A^t, rewrite the rows of A as columns: $A^t = \begin{pmatrix} 1 & 3 \\ 2 & -1 \\ 0 & 4 \end{pmatrix}$.   Then

$$AA^t = \begin{pmatrix} 1 & 2 & 0 \\ 3 & -1 & 4 \end{pmatrix}\begin{pmatrix} 1 & 3 \\ 2 & -1 \\ 0 & 4 \end{pmatrix}$$

$$= \begin{pmatrix} 1\cdot1 + 2\cdot2 + 0\cdot0 & 1\cdot3 + 2\cdot(-1) + 0\cdot4 \\ 3\cdot1 + (-1)\cdot2 + 4\cdot0 & 3\cdot3 + (-1)\cdot(-1) + 4\cdot4 \end{pmatrix} = \begin{pmatrix} 5 & 1 \\ 1 & 26 \end{pmatrix}$$

$$A^tA = \begin{pmatrix} 1 & 3 \\ 2 & -1 \\ 0 & 4 \end{pmatrix}\begin{pmatrix} 1 & 2 & 0 \\ 3 & -1 & 4 \end{pmatrix}$$

$$= \begin{pmatrix} 1\cdot1 + 3\cdot3 & 1\cdot2 + 3\cdot(-1) & 1\cdot0 + 3\cdot4 \\ 2\cdot1 + (-1)\cdot3 & 2\cdot2 + (-1)\cdot(-1) & 2\cdot0 + (-1)\cdot4 \\ 0\cdot1 + 4\cdot3 & 0\cdot2 + 4\cdot(-1) & 0\cdot0 + 4\cdot4 \end{pmatrix} = \begin{pmatrix} 10 & -1 & 12 \\ -1 & 5 & -4 \\ 12 & -4 & 16 \end{pmatrix}$$

3.16. Prove Theorem 3.3(iv): $(AB)^t = B^tA^t$.

Let $A = (a_{ij})$ and $B = (b_{jk})$. Then the element in the ith row and jth column of the matrix AB is

$$a_{i1}b_{1j} + a_{i2}b_{2j} + \cdots + a_{im}b_{mj} \tag{1}$$

Thus (1) is the element which appears in the jth row and ith column of the transpose matrix $(AB)^t$.

On the other hand, the jth row of B^t consists of the elements from the jth column of B:

$$(b_{1j} \quad b_{2j} \quad \ldots \quad b_{mj}) \tag{2}$$

Furthermore, the ith column of A^t consists of the elements from the ith row of A:

$$\begin{pmatrix} a_{i1} \\ a_{i2} \\ \cdot\cdot \\ \cdot\cdot \\ \cdot\cdot \\ a_{im} \end{pmatrix} \tag{3}$$

Consequently, the element appearing in the jth row and ith column of the matrix B^tA^t is the product of (2) by (3) which gives (1). Thus $(AB)^t = B^tA^t$.

ECHELON MATRICES AND ELEMENTARY ROW OPERATIONS

3.17. Circle the distinguished elements in each of the following echelon matrices. Which are row reduced echelon matrices?

$$\begin{pmatrix} 1 & 2 & -3 & 0 & 1 \\ 0 & 0 & 5 & 2 & -4 \\ 0 & 0 & 0 & 7 & 3 \end{pmatrix}, \quad \begin{pmatrix} 0 & 1 & 7 & -5 & 0 \\ 0 & 0 & 0 & 0 & 1 \\ 0 & 0 & 0 & 0 & 0 \end{pmatrix}, \quad \begin{pmatrix} 1 & 0 & 5 & 0 & 2 \\ 0 & 1 & 2 & 0 & 4 \\ 0 & 0 & 0 & 1 & 7 \end{pmatrix}$$

The distinguished elements are the first nonzero entries in the rows; hence

$$\begin{pmatrix} ① & 2 & -3 & 0 & 1 \\ 0 & 0 & ⑤ & 2 & -4 \\ 0 & 0 & 0 & ⑦ & 3 \end{pmatrix}, \quad \begin{pmatrix} 0 & ① & 7 & -5 & 0 \\ 0 & 0 & 0 & 0 & ① \\ 0 & 0 & 0 & 0 & 0 \end{pmatrix}, \quad \begin{pmatrix} ① & 0 & 5 & 0 & 2 \\ 0 & ① & 2 & 0 & 4 \\ 0 & 0 & 0 & ① & 7 \end{pmatrix}$$

An echelon matrix is row reduced if its distinguished elements are each 1 and are the only nonzero entries in their respective columns. Thus the second and third matrices are row reduced, but the first is not.

3.18. Given $A = \begin{pmatrix} 1 & -2 & 3 & -1 \\ 2 & -1 & 2 & 2 \\ 3 & 1 & 2 & 3 \end{pmatrix}$. (i) Reduce A to echelon form. (ii) Reduce A to row canonical form, i.e. to row reduced echelon form.

(i) Apply the operations $R_2 \to -2R_1 + R_2$ and $R_3 \to -3R_1 + R_3$, and then the operation $R_3 \to -7R_2 + 3R_3$ to reduce A to echelon form:

$$A \quad \text{to} \quad \begin{pmatrix} 1 & -2 & 3 & -1 \\ 0 & 3 & -4 & 4 \\ 0 & 7 & -7 & 6 \end{pmatrix} \quad \text{to} \quad \begin{pmatrix} 1 & -2 & 3 & -1 \\ 0 & 3 & -4 & 4 \\ 0 & 0 & 7 & -10 \end{pmatrix}$$

(ii) **Method 1.** Apply the operation $R_1 \to 2R_2 + 3R_1$, and then the operations $R_1 \to -R_3 + 7R_1$ and $R_2 \to 4R_3 + 7R_2$ to the last matrix in (i) to further reduce A:

$$\text{to} \quad \begin{pmatrix} 3 & 0 & 1 & 5 \\ 0 & 3 & -4 & 4 \\ 0 & 0 & 7 & -10 \end{pmatrix} \quad \text{to} \quad \begin{pmatrix} 21 & 0 & 0 & 45 \\ 0 & 21 & 0 & -12 \\ 0 & 0 & 7 & -10 \end{pmatrix}$$

Finally, multiply R_1 by 1/21, R_2 by 1/21 and R_3 by 1/7 to obtain the row canonical form of A:

$$\begin{pmatrix} 1 & 0 & 0 & 15/7 \\ 0 & 1 & 0 & -4/7 \\ 0 & 0 & 1 & -10/7 \end{pmatrix}$$

Method 2. In the last matrix in (i), multiply R_2 by 1/3 and R_3 by 1/7 to obtain an echelon matrix where the distinguished elements are each 1:

$$\begin{pmatrix} 1 & -2 & 3 & -1 \\ 0 & 1 & -4/3 & 4/3 \\ 0 & 0 & 1 & -10/7 \end{pmatrix}$$

Now apply the operation $R_1 \to 2R_2 + R_1$, and then the operations $R_2 \to (4/3)R_3 + R_2$ and $R_1 \to (-1/3)R_3 + R_1$ to obtain the above row canonical form of A.

Remark: Observe that one advantage of the first method is that fractions did not appear until the very last step.

3.19. Determine the row canonical form of $A = \begin{pmatrix} 0 & 1 & 3 & -2 \\ 2 & 1 & -4 & 3 \\ 2 & 3 & 2 & -1 \end{pmatrix}$.

$$A \text{ to } \begin{pmatrix} 2 & 1 & -4 & 3 \\ 0 & 1 & 3 & -2 \\ 2 & 3 & 2 & -1 \end{pmatrix} \text{ to } \begin{pmatrix} 2 & 1 & -4 & 3 \\ 0 & 1 & 3 & -2 \\ 0 & 2 & 6 & -4 \end{pmatrix} \text{ to } \begin{pmatrix} 2 & 1 & -4 & 3 \\ 0 & 1 & 3 & -2 \\ 0 & 0 & 0 & 0 \end{pmatrix}$$

$$\text{to } \begin{pmatrix} 2 & 0 & -7 & 5 \\ 0 & 1 & 3 & -2 \\ 0 & 0 & 0 & 0 \end{pmatrix} \text{ to } \begin{pmatrix} 1 & 0 & -7/2 & 5/2 \\ 0 & 1 & 3 & -2 \\ 0 & 0 & 0 & 0 \end{pmatrix}$$

Note that the third matrix is already in echelon form.

3.20. Reduce $A = \begin{pmatrix} 6 & 3 & -4 \\ -4 & 1 & -6 \\ 1 & 2 & -5 \end{pmatrix}$ to echelon form, and then to row reduced echelon form, i.e. to its **row canonical form**.

The computations are usually simpler if the "pivotal" element is 1. Hence first interchange the first and third rows:

$$A \text{ to } \begin{pmatrix} 1 & 2 & -5 \\ -4 & 1 & -6 \\ 6 & 3 & -4 \end{pmatrix} \text{ to } \begin{pmatrix} 1 & 2 & -5 \\ 0 & 9 & -26 \\ 0 & -9 & 26 \end{pmatrix} \text{ to } \begin{pmatrix} 1 & 2 & -5 \\ 0 & 9 & -26 \\ 0 & 0 & 0 \end{pmatrix}$$

$$\text{to } \begin{pmatrix} 1 & 2 & -5 \\ 0 & 1 & -26/9 \\ 0 & 0 & 0 \end{pmatrix} \text{ to } \begin{pmatrix} 1 & 0 & 7/9 \\ 0 & 1 & -26/9 \\ 0 & 0 & 0 \end{pmatrix}$$

Note that the third matrix is already in echelon form.

3.21. Show that each of the following elementary row operations has an inverse operation of the same type.

[E_1]: Interchange the ith row and the jth row: $R_i \leftrightarrow R_j$.

[E_2]: Multiply the ith row by a nonzero scalar k: $R_i \to kR_i$, $k \neq 0$.

[E_3]: Replace the ith row by k times the jth row plus the ith row: $R_i \to kR_j + R_i$.

(i) Interchanging the same two rows twice, we obtain the original matrix; that is, this operation is its own inverse.

(ii) Multiplying the ith row by k and then by k^{-1}, or by k^{-1} and then by k, we obtain the original matrix. In other words, the operations $R_i \to kR_i$ and $R_i \to k^{-1}R_i$ are inverses.

(iii) Applying the operation $R_i \to kR_j + R_i$ and then the operation $R_i \to -kR_j + R_i$, or applying the operation $R_i \to -kR_j + R_i$ and then the operation $R_i \to kR_j + R_i$, we obtain the original matrix. In other words, the operations $R_i \to kR_j + R_i$ and $R_i \to -kR_j + R_i$ are inverses.

SQUARE MATRICES

3.22. Let $A = \begin{pmatrix} 1 & 2 \\ 4 & -3 \end{pmatrix}$. Find (i) A^2, (ii) A^3, (iii) $f(A)$, where $f(x) = 2x^3 - 4x + 5$.

(i) $A^2 = AA = \begin{pmatrix} 1 & 2 \\ 4 & -3 \end{pmatrix}\begin{pmatrix} 1 & 2 \\ 4 & -3 \end{pmatrix}$

$= \begin{pmatrix} 1\cdot1+2\cdot4 & 1\cdot2+2\cdot(-3) \\ 4\cdot1+(-3)\cdot4 & 4\cdot2+(-3)\cdot(-3) \end{pmatrix} = \begin{pmatrix} 9 & -4 \\ -8 & 17 \end{pmatrix}$

(ii) $A^3 = AA^2 = \begin{pmatrix} 1 & 2 \\ 4 & -3 \end{pmatrix}\begin{pmatrix} 9 & -4 \\ -8 & 17 \end{pmatrix}$

$$= \begin{pmatrix} 1 \cdot 9 + 2 \cdot (-8) & 1 \cdot (-4) + 2 \cdot 17 \\ 4 \cdot 9 + (-3) \cdot (-8) & 4 \cdot (-4) + (-3) \cdot 17 \end{pmatrix} = \begin{pmatrix} -7 & 30 \\ 60 & -67 \end{pmatrix}$$

(iii) To find $f(A)$, first substitute A for x and $5I$ for the constant 5 in the given polynomial $f(x) = 2x^3 - 4x + 5$:

$$f(A) = 2A^3 - 4A + 5I = 2\begin{pmatrix} -7 & 30 \\ 60 & -67 \end{pmatrix} - 4\begin{pmatrix} 1 & 2 \\ 4 & -3 \end{pmatrix} + 5\begin{pmatrix} 1 & 0 \\ 0 & 1 \end{pmatrix}$$

Then multiply each matrix by its respective scalar:

$$= \begin{pmatrix} -14 & 60 \\ 120 & -134 \end{pmatrix} + \begin{pmatrix} -4 & -8 \\ -16 & 12 \end{pmatrix} + \begin{pmatrix} 5 & 0 \\ 0 & 5 \end{pmatrix}$$

Lastly, add the corresponding elements in the matrices:

$$= \begin{pmatrix} -14 - 4 + 5 & 60 - 8 + 0 \\ 120 - 16 + 0 & -134 + 12 + 5 \end{pmatrix} = \begin{pmatrix} -13 & 52 \\ 104 & -117 \end{pmatrix}$$

3.23. Referring to Problem 3.22, show that A is a zero of the polynomial $g(x) = x^2 + 2x - 11$.

A is a zero of $g(x)$ if the matrix $g(A)$ is the zero matrix. Compute $g(A)$ as was done for $f(A)$, i.e. first substitute A for x and $11I$ for the constant 11 in $g(x) = x^2 + 2x - 11$:

$$g(A) = A^2 + 2A - 11I = \begin{pmatrix} 9 & -4 \\ -8 & 17 \end{pmatrix} + 2\begin{pmatrix} 1 & 2 \\ 4 & -3 \end{pmatrix} - 11\begin{pmatrix} 1 & 0 \\ 0 & 1 \end{pmatrix}$$

Then multiply each matrix by the scalar preceding it:

$$g(A) = \begin{pmatrix} 9 & -4 \\ -8 & 17 \end{pmatrix} + \begin{pmatrix} 2 & 4 \\ 8 & -6 \end{pmatrix} + \begin{pmatrix} -11 & 0 \\ 0 & -11 \end{pmatrix}$$

Lastly, add the corresponding elements in the matrices:

$$g(A) = \begin{pmatrix} 9 + 2 - 11 & -4 + 4 + 0 \\ -8 + 8 + 0 & 17 - 6 - 11 \end{pmatrix} = \begin{pmatrix} 0 & 0 \\ 0 & 0 \end{pmatrix}$$

Since $g(A) = 0$, A is a zero of the polynomial $g(x)$.

3.24. Given $A = \begin{pmatrix} 1 & 3 \\ 4 & -3 \end{pmatrix}$. Find a nonzero column vector $u = \begin{pmatrix} x \\ y \end{pmatrix}$ such that $Au = 3u$.

First set up the matrix equation $Au = 3u$:

$$\begin{pmatrix} 1 & 3 \\ 4 & -3 \end{pmatrix}\begin{pmatrix} x \\ y \end{pmatrix} = 3\begin{pmatrix} x \\ y \end{pmatrix}$$

Write each side as a single matrix (column vector):

$$\begin{pmatrix} x + 3y \\ 4x - 3y \end{pmatrix} = \begin{pmatrix} 3x \\ 3y \end{pmatrix}$$

Set corresponding elements equal to each other to obtain the system of equations (and reduce to echelon form):

$$\begin{array}{ll} x + 3y = 3x \\ 4x - 3y = 3y \end{array} \text{ or } \begin{array}{ll} 2x - 3y = 0 \\ 4x - 6y = 0 \end{array} \text{ or } \begin{array}{ll} 2x - 3y = 0 \\ 0 = 0 \end{array} \text{ or } \quad 2x - 3y = 0$$

The system reduces to one homogeneous equation in two unknowns, and so has an infinite number of solutions. To obtain a nonzero solution let, say, $y = 2$; then $x = 3$. That is, $x = 3$, $y = 2$ is a solution of the system. Thus the vector $u = \begin{pmatrix} 3 \\ 2 \end{pmatrix}$ is nonzero and has the property that $Au = 3u$.

3.25. Find the inverse of $\begin{pmatrix} 3 & 5 \\ 2 & 3 \end{pmatrix}$.

Method 1. We seek scalars x, y, z and w for which

$$\begin{pmatrix} 3 & 5 \\ 2 & 3 \end{pmatrix}\begin{pmatrix} x & y \\ z & w \end{pmatrix} = \begin{pmatrix} 1 & 0 \\ 0 & 1 \end{pmatrix} \quad \text{or} \quad \begin{pmatrix} 3x + 5z & 3y + 5w \\ 2x + 3z & 2y + 3w \end{pmatrix} = \begin{pmatrix} 1 & 0 \\ 0 & 1 \end{pmatrix}$$

or which satisfy $\quad \begin{cases} 3x + 5z = 1 \\ 2x + 3z = 0 \end{cases} \quad$ and $\quad \begin{cases} 3y + 5w = 0 \\ 2y + 3w = 1 \end{cases}$

The solution of the first system is $x = -3$, $z = 2$, and of the second system is $y = 5$, $w = -3$. Thus the inverse of the given matrix is $\begin{pmatrix} -3 & 5 \\ 2 & -3 \end{pmatrix}$.

Method 2. We derived the general formula for the inverse A^{-1} of the 2×2 matrix $A = \begin{pmatrix} a & b \\ c & d \end{pmatrix}$:

$$A^{-1} = \frac{1}{|A|}\begin{pmatrix} d & -b \\ -c & a \end{pmatrix} \quad \text{where} \quad |A| = ad - bc$$

Thus if $A = \begin{pmatrix} 3 & 5 \\ 2 & 3 \end{pmatrix}$, then $|A| = 9 - 10 = -1$ and $A^{-1} = -1\begin{pmatrix} 3 & -5 \\ -2 & 3 \end{pmatrix} = \begin{pmatrix} -3 & 5 \\ 2 & -3 \end{pmatrix}$.

MISCELLANEOUS PROBLEMS

3.26. Compute AB using block multiplication, where

$$A = \begin{pmatrix} 1 & 2 & | & 1 \\ 3 & 4 & | & 0 \\ \hline 0 & 0 & | & 2 \end{pmatrix} \quad \text{and} \quad B = \begin{pmatrix} 1 & 2 & 3 & | & 1 \\ 4 & 5 & 6 & | & 1 \\ \hline 0 & 0 & 0 & | & 1 \end{pmatrix}$$

Here $A = \begin{pmatrix} E & F \\ 0 & G \end{pmatrix}$ and $B = \begin{pmatrix} R & S \\ 0 & T \end{pmatrix}$ where E, F, G, R, S and T are the given blocks. Hence

$$AB = \begin{pmatrix} ER & ES + FT \\ 0 & GT \end{pmatrix} = \begin{pmatrix} \begin{pmatrix} 9 & 12 & 15 \\ 19 & 26 & 33 \end{pmatrix} & \begin{pmatrix} 3 \\ 7 \end{pmatrix} + \begin{pmatrix} 1 \\ 0 \end{pmatrix} \\ (0 \quad 0 \quad 0) & (2) \end{pmatrix} = \begin{pmatrix} 9 & 12 & 15 & 4 \\ 19 & 26 & 33 & 7 \\ 0 & 0 & 0 & 2 \end{pmatrix}$$

3.27. Suppose $B = (R_1, R_2, \ldots, R_n)$, i.e. that R_i is the ith row of B. Suppose BA is defined. Show that $BA = (R_1 A, R_2 A, \ldots, R_n A)$, i.e. that $R_i A$ is the ith row of BA.

Let $A^1, A^2, \ldots, A^m$ denote the columns of A. By definition of matrix multiplication, the ith row of BA is $(R_i \cdot A^1, R_i \cdot A^2, \ldots, R_i \cdot A^m)$. But by matrix multiplication, $R_i A = (R_i \cdot A^1, R_i \cdot A^2, \ldots, R_i \cdot A^m)$. Thus the ith row of BA is $R_i A$.

3.28. Let $e_i = (0, \ldots, 1, \ldots, 0)$ be the row vector with 1 in the ith position and 0 elsewhere. Show that $e_i A = R_i$, the ith row of A.

Observe that e_i is the ith row of I, the identity matrix. By the preceding problem, the ith row of IA is $e_i A$. But $IA = A$. Accordingly, $e_i A = R_i$, the ith row of A.

3.29. Show: (i) If A has a zero row, then AB has a zero row.

(ii) If B has a zero column, then AB has a zero column.

(iii) Any matrix with a zero row or a zero column is not invertible.

(i) Let R_i be the zero row of A, and $B^1, \ldots, B^n$ the columns of B. Then the ith row of AB is

$$(R_i \cdot B^1, R_i \cdot B^2, \ldots, R_i \cdot B^n) = (0, 0, \ldots, 0)$$

(ii)   Let C_j be the zero column of B, and $A_1, \ldots, A_m$ the rows of A. Then the jth column of AB is

$$\begin{pmatrix} A_1 \cdot C_j \\ A_2 \cdot C_j \\ \cdot \cdot \\ A_m \cdot C_j \end{pmatrix} = \begin{pmatrix} 0 \\ 0 \\ \cdot \cdot \\ 0 \end{pmatrix}$$

(iii)   A matrix A is invertible means that there exists a matrix A^{-1} such that $AA^{-1} = A^{-1}A = I$. But the identity matrix I has no zero row or zero column; hence by (i) and (ii) A cannot have a zero row or a zero column. In other words, a matrix with a zero row or a zero column cannot be invertible.

3.30. Let A and B be invertible matrices (of the same order). Show that the product AB is also invertible and $(AB)^{-1} = B^{-1}A^{-1}$. Thus by induction, $(A_1A_2\cdots A_n)^{-1} = A_n^{-1}\cdots A_2^{-1}A_1^{-1}$ where the A_i are invertible.

$$(AB)(B^{-1}A^{-1}) = A(BB^{-1})A^{-1} = AIA^{-1} = AA^{-1} = I$$

and $\qquad (B^{-1}A^{-1})(AB) = B^{-1}(A^{-1}A)B = B^{-1}IB = B^{-1}B = I$

Thus $(AB)^{-1} = B^{-1}A^{-1}$.

3.31. Let u and v be distinct vectors. Show that, for each scalar $k \in K$, the vectors $u + k(u - v)$ are distinct.

It suffices to show that if
$$u + k_1(u - v) = u + k_2(u - v) \qquad (1)$$
then $k_1 = k_2$. Suppose (1) holds. Then
$$k_1(u - v) = k_2(u - v) \qquad \text{or} \qquad (k_1 - k_2)(u - v) = 0$$
Since u and v are distinct, $u - v \neq 0$. Hence $k_1 - k_2 = 0$ and $k_1 = k_2$.

ELEMENTARY MATRICES AND APPLICATIONS*

3.32. A matrix obtained from the identity matrix by a single elementary row operation is called an *elementary matrix*. Determine the 3-square elementary matrices corresponding to the operations $R_1 \leftrightarrow R_2$, $R_3 \to -7R_3$ and $R_2 \to -3R_1 + R_2$.

Apply the operations to the identity matrix $I_3 = \begin{pmatrix} 1 & 0 & 0 \\ 0 & 1 & 0 \\ 0 & 0 & 1 \end{pmatrix}$ to obtain

$$E_1 = \begin{pmatrix} 0 & 1 & 0 \\ 1 & 0 & 0 \\ 0 & 0 & 1 \end{pmatrix}, \quad E_2 = \begin{pmatrix} 1 & 0 & 0 \\ 0 & 1 & 0 \\ 0 & 0 & -7 \end{pmatrix}, \quad E_3 = \begin{pmatrix} 1 & 0 & 0 \\ -3 & 1 & 0 \\ 0 & 0 & 1 \end{pmatrix}$$

3.33. Prove: Let e be an elementary row operation and E the corresponding m-square elementary matrix, i.e. $E = e(I_m)$. Then for any $m \times n$ matrix A, $e(A) = EA$. That is, the result $e(A)$ of applying the operation e on the matrix A can be obtained by multiplying A by the corresponding elementary matrix E.

Let R_i be the ith row of A; we denote this by writing $A = (R_1, \ldots, R_m)$. By Problem 3.27, if B is a matrix for which AB is defined, then $AB = (R_1B, \ldots, R_mB)$. We also let
$$e_i = (0, \ldots, 0, \hat{1}, 0, \ldots, 0), \qquad \wedge = i$$

*This section is rather detailed and may be omitted in a first reading. It is not needed except for certain results in Chapter 9 on determinants.

Here $\wedge = i$ means that 1 is the ith component. By Problem 3.28, $e_i A = R_i$. We also remark that $I = (e_1, \ldots, e_m)$ is the identity matrix.

(i) Let e be the elementary row operation $R_i \leftrightarrow R_j$. Then, for $\wedge = i$ and $\mathbf{\wedge} = j$,

$$E \; = \; e(I) \; = \; (e_1, \ldots, \widehat{e_j}, \ldots, \widehat{\widehat{e_i}}, \ldots, e_m)$$

and

$$e(A) \; = \; (R_1, \ldots, \widehat{R_j}, \ldots, \widehat{\widehat{R_i}}, \ldots, R_m)$$

Thus

$$EA \; = \; (e_1 A, \ldots, \widehat{e_j A}, \ldots, \widehat{\widehat{e_i A}}, \ldots, e_m A) \; = \; (R_1, \ldots, \widehat{R_j}, \ldots, \widehat{\widehat{R_i}}, \ldots, R_m) \; = \; e(A)$$

(ii) Now let e be the elementary row operation $R_i \to k R_i$, $k \neq 0$. Then, for $\wedge = i$,

$$E \; = \; e(I) \; = \; (e_1, \ldots, \widehat{k e_i}, \ldots, e_m) \quad \text{and} \quad e(A) \; = \; (R_1, \ldots, \widehat{k R_i}, \ldots, R_m)$$

Thus
$$EA \; = \; (e_1 A, \ldots, \widehat{k e_i A}, \ldots, e_m A) \; = \; (R_1, \ldots, \widehat{k R_i}, \ldots, R_m) \; = \; e(A)$$

(iii) Lastly, let e be the elementary row operation $R_i \to k R_j + R_i$. Then, for $\wedge = i$,

$$E \; = \; e(I) \; = \; (e_1, \ldots, \widehat{k e_j + e_i}, \ldots, e_m) \quad \text{and} \quad e(A) \; = \; (R_1, \ldots, \widehat{k R_j + R_i}, \ldots, R_m)$$

Using $(k e_j + e_i) A = k(e_j A) + e_i A = k R_j + R_i$, we have

$$EA \; = \; (e_1 A, \ldots, \widehat{(k e_j + e_i) A}, \ldots, e_m A) \; = \; (R_1, \ldots, \widehat{k R_j + R_i}, \ldots, R_m) \; = \; e(A)$$

Thus we have proven the theorem.

3.34. Show that A is row equivalent to B if and only if there exist elementary matrices $E_1, \ldots, E_s$ such that $E_s \cdots E_2 E_1 A = B$.

By definition, A is row equivalent to B if there exist elementary row operations $e_1, \ldots, e_s$ for which $e_s(\cdots(e_2(e_1(A)))\cdots) = B$. But, by the preceding problem, the above holds if and only if $E_s \cdots E_2 E_1 A = B$ where E_i is the elementary matrix corresponding to e_i.

3.35. Show that the elementary matrices are invertible and that their inverses are also elementary matrices.

Let E be the elementary matrix corresponding to the elementary row operation e: $e(I) = E$. Let e' be the inverse operation of e (see Problem 3.21) and E' its corresponding elementary matrix. Then, by Problem 3.33,

$$I \; = \; e'(e(I)) \; = \; e'E \; = \; E'E \quad \text{and} \quad I \; = \; e(e'(I)) \; = \; eE' \; = \; EE'$$

Therefore E' is the inverse of E.

3.36. Prove that the following are equivalent:

(i) A is invertible.

(ii) A is row equivalent to the identity matrix I.

(iii) A is a product of elementary matrices.

Suppose A is invertible and suppose A is row equivalent to the row reduced echelon matrix B. Then there exist elementary matrices $E_1, E_2, \ldots, E_s$ such that $E_s \cdots E_2 E_1 A = B$. Since A is invertible and each elementary matrix E_i is invertible, the product is invertible. But if $B \neq I$, then B has a zero row (Problem 3.47); hence B is not invertible (Problem 3.29). Thus $B = I$. In other words, (i) implies (ii).

Now if (ii) holds, then there exist elementary matrices $E_1, E_2, \ldots, E_s$ such that

$$E_s \cdots E_2 E_1 A \; = \; I, \quad \text{and so} \quad A \; = \; (E_s \cdots E_2 E_1)^{-1} \; = \; E_1^{-1} E_2^{-1} \cdots E_s^{-1}$$

By the preceding problem, the E_i^{-1} are also elementary matrices. Thus (ii) implies (iii).

Now if (iii) holds $(A = E_1 E_2 \ldots E_s)$, then (i) must follow since the product of invertible matrices is invertible.

3.37. Let A and B be square matrices of the same order. Show that if $AB = I$, then $B = A^{-1}$. Thus $AB = I$ if and only if $BA = I$.

> Suppose A is not invertible. Then A is not row equivalent to the identity matrix I, and so A is row equivalent to a matrix with a zero row. In other words, there exist elementary matrices $E_1, \ldots, E_s$ such that $E_s \cdots E_2 E_1 A$ has a zero row. Hence $E_s \cdots E_2 E_1 AB$ has a zero row. Accordingly, AB is row equivalent to a matrix with a zero row and so is not row equivalent to I. But this contradicts the fact that $AB = I$. Thus A is invertible. Consequently,
>
> $$B = IB = (A^{-1}A)B = A^{-1}(AB) = A^{-1}I = A^{-1}$$

3.38. Suppose A is invertible and, say, it is row reducible to the identity matrix I by the sequence of elementary operations $e_1, \ldots, e_n$. (i) Show that this sequence of elementary row operations applied to I yields A^{-1}. (ii) Use this result to obtain the inverse of $A = \begin{pmatrix} 1 & 0 & 2 \\ 2 & -1 & 3 \\ 4 & 1 & 8 \end{pmatrix}$.

(i) Let E_i be the elementary matrix corresponding to the operation e_i. Then, by hypothesis and Problem 3.34, $E_n \cdots E_2 E_1 A = I$. Thus $(E_n \cdots E_2 E_1 I)A = I$ and hence $A^{-1} = E_n \cdots E_2 E_1 I$. In other words, A^{-1} can be obtained from I by applying the elementary row operations $e_1, \ldots, e_n$.

(ii) Form the block matrix (A, I) and row reduce it to row canonical form:

$$(A, I) = \begin{pmatrix} 1 & 0 & 2 & | & 1 & 0 & 0 \\ 2 & -1 & 3 & | & 0 & 1 & 0 \\ 4 & 1 & 8 & | & 0 & 0 & 1 \end{pmatrix} \text{ to } \begin{pmatrix} 1 & 0 & 2 & | & 1 & 0 & 0 \\ 0 & -1 & -1 & | & -2 & 1 & 0 \\ 0 & 1 & 0 & | & -4 & 0 & 1 \end{pmatrix}$$

$$\text{to } \begin{pmatrix} 1 & 0 & 2 & | & 1 & 0 & 0 \\ 0 & -1 & -1 & | & -2 & 1 & 0 \\ 0 & 0 & -1 & | & -6 & 1 & 1 \end{pmatrix} \text{ to } \begin{pmatrix} 1 & 0 & 0 & | & -11 & 2 & 2 \\ 0 & -1 & 0 & | & 4 & 0 & -1 \\ 0 & 0 & -1 & | & -6 & 1 & 1 \end{pmatrix}$$

$$\text{to } \begin{pmatrix} 1 & 0 & 0 & | & -11 & 2 & 2 \\ 0 & 1 & 0 & | & -4 & 0 & 1 \\ 0 & 0 & 1 & | & 6 & -1 & -1 \end{pmatrix}$$

Observe that the final block matrix is in the form (I, B). Hence A is invertible and B is its inverse:

$$A^{-1} = \begin{pmatrix} -11 & 2 & 2 \\ -4 & 0 & 1 \\ 6 & -1 & -1 \end{pmatrix}$$

Remark: In case the final block matrix is not of the form (I, B), then the given matrix is not row equivalent to I and so is not invertible.

Supplementary Problems

MATRIX OPERATIONS

In Problems 3.39-3.41, let

$$A = \begin{pmatrix} 1 & -1 & 2 \\ 0 & 3 & 4 \end{pmatrix}, \quad B = \begin{pmatrix} 4 & 0 & -3 \\ -1 & -2 & 3 \end{pmatrix}, \quad C = \begin{pmatrix} 2 & -3 & 0 & 1 \\ 5 & -1 & -4 & 2 \\ -1 & 0 & 0 & 3 \end{pmatrix}, \quad D = \begin{pmatrix} 2 \\ -1 \\ 3 \end{pmatrix}$$

3.39. Find: (i) $A + B$, (ii) $A + C$, (iii) $3A - 4B$.

3.40. Find: (i) AB, (ii) AC, (iii) AD, (iv) BC, (v) BD, (vi) CD.

3.41. Find: (i) A^t, (ii) A^tC, (iii) D^tA^t, (iv) B^tA, (v) D^tD, (vi) DD^t.

3.42. Let $e_1 = (1, 0, 0)$, $e_2 = (0, 1, 0)$ and $e_3 = (0, 0, 1)$.   Given $A = \begin{pmatrix} a_1 & a_2 & a_3 & a_4 \\ b_1 & b_2 & b_3 & b_4 \\ c_1 & c_2 & c_3 & c_4 \end{pmatrix}$, find (i) e_1A, (ii) e_2A, (iii) e_3A.

3.43. Let $e_i = (0, \ldots, 0, 1, 0, \ldots, 0)$ where 1 is the ith component. Show the following:

(i) $Be_j^t = C_j$, the jth column of B. (By Problem 3.28, $e_iA = R_i$.)

(ii) If $e_iA = e_iB$ for each i, then $A = B$.

(iii) If $Ae_i^t = Be_i^t$ for each i, then $A = B$.

ECHELON MATRICES AND ELEMENTARY ROW OPERATIONS

3.44. Reduce A to echelon form and then to its row canonical form, where

(i) $A = \begin{pmatrix} 1 & 2 & -1 & 2 & 1 \\ 2 & 4 & 1 & -2 & 3 \\ 3 & 6 & 2 & -6 & 5 \end{pmatrix}$,   (ii) $A = \begin{pmatrix} 2 & 3 & -2 & 5 & 1 \\ 3 & -1 & 2 & 0 & 4 \\ 4 & -5 & 6 & -5 & 7 \end{pmatrix}$.

3.45. Reduce A to echelon form and then to its row canonical form, where

(i) $A = \begin{pmatrix} 1 & 3 & -1 & 2 \\ 0 & 11 & -5 & 3 \\ 2 & -5 & 3 & 1 \\ 4 & 1 & 1 & 5 \end{pmatrix}$,   (ii) $A = \begin{pmatrix} 0 & 1 & 3 & -2 \\ 0 & 4 & -1 & 3 \\ 0 & 0 & 2 & 1 \\ 0 & 5 & -3 & 4 \end{pmatrix}$.

3.46. Describe all the possible 2×2 matrices which are in row reduced echelon form.

3.47. Suppose A is a square row reduced echelon matrix. Show that if $A \neq I$, the identity matrix, then A has a zero row.

3.48. Show that every square echelon matrix is upper triangular, but not vice versa.

3.49. Show that row equivalence is an equivalence relation:

(i) A is row equivalent to A;

(ii) A row equivalent to B implies B row equivalent to A;

(iii) A row equivalent to B and B row equivalent to C implies A row equivalent to C.

SQUARE MATRICES

3.50. Let $A = \begin{pmatrix} 2 & 2 \\ 3 & -1 \end{pmatrix}$. (i) Find A^2 and A^3. (ii) If $f(x) = x^3 - 3x^2 - 2x + 4$, find $f(A)$. (iii) If $g(x) = x^2 - x - 8$, find $g(A)$.

3.51. Let $B = \begin{pmatrix} 1 & 3 \\ 5 & 3 \end{pmatrix}$. (i) If $f(x) = 2x^2 - 4x + 3$, find $f(B)$. (ii) If $g(x) = x^2 - 4x - 12$, find $g(B)$. (iii) Find a nonzero column vector $u = \begin{pmatrix} x \\ y \end{pmatrix}$ such that $Bu = 6u$.

3.52. Matrices A and B are said to commute if $AB = BA$. Find all matrices $\begin{pmatrix} x & y \\ z & w \end{pmatrix}$ which commute with $\begin{pmatrix} 1 & 1 \\ 0 & 1 \end{pmatrix}$.

3.53. Let $A = \begin{pmatrix} 1 & 2 \\ 0 & 1 \end{pmatrix}$. Find A^n.

3.54. Let $A = \begin{pmatrix} 2 & 0 \\ 0 & 3 \end{pmatrix}$ and $B = \begin{pmatrix} 7 & 0 \\ 0 & 11 \end{pmatrix}$.

Find: (i) $A + B$, (ii) AB, (iii) A^2 and A^3, (iv) A^n, (v) $f(A)$ for a polynomial $f(x)$.

3.55. Let $D = \begin{pmatrix} 3 & 0 \\ 0 & 3 \end{pmatrix}$, $A = \begin{pmatrix} a_1 & a_2 & \cdots & a_n \\ b_1 & b_2 & \cdots & b_n \end{pmatrix}$, $B = \begin{pmatrix} c_1 & d_1 \\ c_2 & d_2 \\ \cdots\cdots \\ c_n & d_n \end{pmatrix}$. Find DA and BD.

3.56. Suppose the 2-square matrix B commutes with every 2-square matrix A, i.e. $AB = BA$. Show that $B = \begin{pmatrix} k & 0 \\ 0 & k \end{pmatrix}$ for some scalar k, i.e. B is a scalar matrix.

3.57. Let D_k be the m-square scalar matrix with diagonal elements k. Show that:
(i) for any $m \times n$ matrix A, $D_k A = kA$; (ii) for any $n \times m$ matrix B, $BD_k = kB$.

3.58. Show that the sum, product and scalar multiple of:
(i)   upper triangular matrices is upper triangular;
(ii) lower triangular matrices is lower triangular;
(iii) diagonal matrices is diagonal;
(iv) scalar matrices is scalar.

INVERTIBLE MATRICES

3.59. Find the inverse of each matrix: (i) $\begin{pmatrix} 3 & 2 \\ 7 & 5 \end{pmatrix}$, (ii) $\begin{pmatrix} 2 & -3 \\ 1 & 3 \end{pmatrix}$.

3.60. Find the inverse of each matrix: (i) $\begin{pmatrix} -1 & 2 & -3 \\ 2 & 1 & 0 \\ 4 & -2 & 5 \end{pmatrix}$, (ii) $\begin{pmatrix} 2 & 1 & -1 \\ 0 & 2 & 1 \\ 5 & 2 & -3 \end{pmatrix}$.

3.61. Find the inverse of $\begin{pmatrix} 1 & 3 & 4 \\ 3 & -1 & 6 \\ -1 & 5 & 1 \end{pmatrix}$.

3.62. Show that the operations of inverse and transpose commute; that is, $(A^t)^{-1} = (A^{-1})^t$. Thus, in particular, A is invertible if and only if A^t is invertible.

3.63. When is a diagonal matrix $A = \begin{pmatrix} a_1 & 0 & \cdots & 0 \\ 0 & a_2 & \cdots & 0 \\ \cdots\cdots\cdots\cdots\cdots \\ 0 & 0 & \cdots & a_n \end{pmatrix}$ invertible, and what is its inverse?

3.64. Show that A is row equivalent to B if and only if there exists an invertible matrix P such that $B = PA$.

3.65. Show that A is invertible if and only if the system $AX = 0$ has only the zero solution.

MISCELLANEOUS PROBLEMS

3.66. Prove Theorem 3.2: (iii) $(B + C)A = BA + CA$; (iv) $k(AB) = (kA)B = A(kB)$, where k is a scalar. (Parts (i) and (ii) were proven in Problem 3.11 and 3.12.)

3.67. Prove Theorem 3.3: (i) $(A + B)^t = A^t + B^t$; (ii) $(A^t)^t = A$; (iii) $(kA)^t = kA^t$, for k a scalar. (Part (iv) was proven in Problem 3.16.)

3.68. Suppose $A = (A_{ik})$ and $B = (B_{kj})$ are block matrices for which AB is defined and the number of columns of each block A_{ik} is equal to the number of rows of each block B_{kj}. Show that $AB = (C_{ij})$ where $C_{ij} = \sum_k A_{ik} B_{kj}$.

3.69. The following operations are called *elementary column operations*:

[E_1]:   Interchange the ith column and the jth column.

[E_2]:   Multiply the ith column by a nonzero scalar k.

[E_3]:   Replace the ith column by k times the jth column plus the ith column.

Show that each of the operations has an inverse operation of the same type.

3.70. A matrix A is said to be *equivalent* to a matrix B if B can be obtained from A by a finite sequence of operations, each being an elementary row or column operation. Show that matrix equivalence is an equivalence relation.

3.71. Show that two consistent systems of linear equations have the same solution set if and only if their augmented matrices are row equivalent. (We assume that zero rows are added so that both augmented matrices have the same number of rows.)

Answers to Supplementary Problems

3.39. (i) $\begin{pmatrix} 5 & -1 & -1 \\ -1 & 1 & 7 \end{pmatrix}$ (ii) Not defined.   (iii) $\begin{pmatrix} -13 & -3 & 18 \\ 4 & 17 & 0 \end{pmatrix}$

3.40. (i) Not defined.   (iii) $\begin{pmatrix} 9 \\ 9 \end{pmatrix}$ (v) $\begin{pmatrix} -1 \\ 9 \end{pmatrix}$

(ii) $\begin{pmatrix} -5 & -2 & 4 & 5 \\ 11 & -3 & -12 & 18 \end{pmatrix}$ (iv) $\begin{pmatrix} 11 & -12 & 0 & -5 \\ -15 & 5 & 8 & 4 \end{pmatrix}$ (vi) Not defined.

3.41. (i) $\begin{pmatrix} 1 & 0 \\ -1 & 3 \\ 2 & 4 \end{pmatrix}$ (ii) Not defined.   (iii) $(9, 9)$ (iv) $\begin{pmatrix} 4 & -7 & 4 \\ 0 & -6 & -8 \\ -3 & 12 & 6 \end{pmatrix}$ (v) 14   (vi) $\begin{pmatrix} 4 & -2 & 6 \\ -2 & 1 & -3 \\ 6 & -3 & 9 \end{pmatrix}$

3.42. (i) (a_1, a_2, a_3, a_4) (ii) (b_1, b_2, b_3, b_4) (iii) (c_1, c_2, c_3, c_4)

3.44. (i) $\begin{pmatrix} 1 & 2 & -1 & 2 & 1 \\ 0 & 0 & 3 & -6 & 1 \\ 0 & 0 & 0 & -6 & 1 \end{pmatrix}$ and $\begin{pmatrix} 1 & 2 & 0 & 0 & 4/3 \\ 0 & 0 & 1 & 0 & 0 \\ 0 & 0 & 0 & 1 & -1/6 \end{pmatrix}$

(ii) $\begin{pmatrix} 2 & 3 & -2 & 5 & 1 \\ 0 & -11 & 10 & -15 & 5 \\ 0 & 0 & 0 & 0 & 0 \end{pmatrix}$ and $\begin{pmatrix} 1 & 0 & 4/11 & 5/11 & 13/11 \\ 0 & 1 & -10/11 & 15/11 & -5/11 \\ 0 & 0 & 0 & 0 & 0 \end{pmatrix}$

3.45. (i) $\begin{pmatrix} 1 & 3 & -1 & 2 \\ 0 & 11 & -5 & 3 \\ 0 & 0 & 0 & 0 \\ 0 & 0 & 0 & 0 \end{pmatrix}$ and $\begin{pmatrix} 1 & 0 & 4/11 & 13/11 \\ 0 & 1 & -5/11 & 3/11 \\ 0 & 0 & 0 & 0 \\ 0 & 0 & 0 & 0 \end{pmatrix}$

(ii) $\begin{pmatrix} 0 & 1 & 3 & -2 \\ 0 & 0 & -13 & 11 \\ 0 & 0 & 0 & 35 \\ 0 & 0 & 0 & 0 \end{pmatrix}$ and $\begin{pmatrix} 0 & 1 & 0 & 0 \\ 0 & 0 & 1 & 0 \\ 0 & 0 & 0 & 1 \\ 0 & 0 & 0 & 0 \end{pmatrix}$

3.46. $\begin{pmatrix} 0 & 0 \\ 0 & 0 \end{pmatrix}$, $\begin{pmatrix} 0 & 1 \\ 0 & 0 \end{pmatrix}$, $\begin{pmatrix} 1 & 0 \\ 0 & 1 \end{pmatrix}$ or $\begin{pmatrix} 1 & k \\ 0 & 0 \end{pmatrix}$ where k is any scalar.

3.48. $\begin{pmatrix} 0 & 1 & 1 \\ 0 & 1 & 1 \\ 0 & 0 & 1 \end{pmatrix}$ is upper triangular but not an echelon matrix.

3.50. (i) $A^2 = \begin{pmatrix} 10 & 2 \\ 3 & 7 \end{pmatrix}$, $A^3 = \begin{pmatrix} 26 & 18 \\ 27 & -1 \end{pmatrix}$; (ii) $f(A) = \begin{pmatrix} -4 & 8 \\ 12 & -16 \end{pmatrix}$; (iii) $g(A) = \begin{pmatrix} 0 & 0 \\ 0 & 0 \end{pmatrix}$

3.51. (i) $f(B) = \begin{pmatrix} 31 & 12 \\ 20 & 39 \end{pmatrix}$; (ii) $g(B) = \begin{pmatrix} 0 & 0 \\ 0 & 0 \end{pmatrix}$; (iii) $u = \begin{pmatrix} 3 \\ 5 \end{pmatrix}$ or $\begin{pmatrix} 3k \\ 5k \end{pmatrix}$, $k \neq 0$.

3.52. Only matrices of the form $\begin{pmatrix} a & b \\ 0 & a \end{pmatrix}$ commute with $\begin{pmatrix} 1 & 1 \\ 0 & 1 \end{pmatrix}$.

3.53. $A^n = \begin{pmatrix} 1 & 2n \\ 0 & 1 \end{pmatrix}$

3.54. (i) $A + B = \begin{pmatrix} 9 & 0 \\ 0 & 14 \end{pmatrix}$ (iii) $A^2 = \begin{pmatrix} 4 & 0 \\ 0 & 9 \end{pmatrix}$, $A^3 = \begin{pmatrix} 8 & 0 \\ 0 & 27 \end{pmatrix}$ (v) $f(A) = \begin{pmatrix} f(2) & 0 \\ 0 & f(3) \end{pmatrix}$

(ii) $AB = \begin{pmatrix} 14 & 0 \\ 0 & 33 \end{pmatrix}$ (iv) $A^n = \begin{pmatrix} 2^n & 0 \\ 0 & 3^n \end{pmatrix}$

3.55. (i) $DA = \begin{pmatrix} 3a_1 & 3a_2 & \dots & 3a_n \\ 3b_1 & 3b_2 & \dots & 3b_n \end{pmatrix} = 3A$ (ii) $BD = \begin{pmatrix} 3c_1 & 3d_1 \\ 3c_2 & 3d_2 \\ \dots\dots\dots \\ 3c_n & 3d_n \end{pmatrix} = 3B$

3.59. (i) $\begin{pmatrix} 5 & -2 \\ -7 & 3 \end{pmatrix}$ (ii) $\begin{pmatrix} 1/3 & 1/3 \\ -1/9 & 2/9 \end{pmatrix}$

3.60. (i) $\begin{pmatrix} -5 & 4 & -3 \\ 10 & -7 & 6 \\ 8 & -6 & 5 \end{pmatrix}$ (ii) $\begin{pmatrix} 8 & -1 & -3 \\ -5 & 1 & 2 \\ 10 & -1 & -4 \end{pmatrix}$

3.61. $\begin{pmatrix} 31/2 & -17/2 & -11 \\ 9/2 & -5/2 & -3 \\ -7 & 4 & 5 \end{pmatrix}$

3.62. Given $AA^{-1} = I$. Then $I = I^t = (AA^{-1})^t = (A^{-1})^t A^t$. That is, $(A^{-1})^t = (A^t)^{-1}$.

3.63. A is invertible iff each $a_i \neq 0$. Then $A^{-1} = \begin{pmatrix} a_1^{-1} & 0 & \dots & 0 \\ 0 & a_2^{-1} & \dots & 0 \\ \dots\dots\dots\dots\dots \\ 0 & 0 & \dots & a_n^{-1} \end{pmatrix}$.

Chapter 4

Vector Spaces and Subspaces

INTRODUCTION

In Chapter 1 we studied the concrete structures $\mathbf{R}^n$ and $\mathbf{C}^n$ and derived various properties. Now certain of these properties will play the role of axioms as we define abstract "vector spaces" or, as they are sometimes called, "linear spaces". In particular, the conclusions (i) through (viii) of Theorem 1.1, page 3, become axioms $[A_1]$-$[A_4]$, $[M_1]$-$[M_4]$ below. We will see that, in a certain sense, we get nothing new. In fact, we prove in Chapter 5 that every vector space over $\mathbf{R}$ which has "finite dimension" (defined there) can be identified with $\mathbf{R}^n$ for some n.

The definition of a vector space involves an arbitrary field (see Appendix B) whose elements are called *scalars*. We adopt the following notation (unless otherwise stated or implied):

$$K \quad \text{the field of scalars,}$$
$$a, b, c \text{ or } k \quad \text{the elements of } K,$$
$$V \quad \text{the given vector space,}$$
$$u, v, w \quad \text{the elements of } V.$$

We remark that nothing essential is lost if the reader assumes that K is the real field $\mathbf{R}$ or the complex field $\mathbf{C}$.

Lastly, we mention that the "dot product", and related notions such as orthogonality, is not considered as part of the fundamental vector space structure, but as an additional structure which may or may not be introduced. Such spaces shall be investigated in the latter part of the text.

Definition: Let K be a given field and let V be a nonempty set with rules of addition and scalar multiplication which assigns to any $u, v \in V$ a *sum* $u + v \in V$ and to any $u \in V, k \in K$ a *product* $ku \in V$. Then V is called a *vector space over K* (and the elements of V are called *vectors*) if the following axioms hold:

$[A_1]$: For any vectors $u, v, w \in V$, $(u + v) + w = u + (v + w)$.

$[A_2]$: There is a vector in V, denoted by 0 and called the *zero vector*, for which $u + 0 = u$ for any vector $u \in V$.

$[A_3]$: For each vector $u \in V$ there is a vector in V, denoted by $-u$, for which $u + (-u) = 0$.

$[A_4]$: For any vectors $u, v \in V$, $u + v = v + u$.

$[M_1]$: For any scalar $k \in K$ and any vectors $u, v \in V$, $k(u + v) = ku + kv$.

$[M_2]$: For any scalars $a, b \in K$ and any vector $u \in V$, $(a + b)u = au + bu$.

$[M_3]$: For any scalars $a, b \in K$ and any vector $u \in V$, $(ab)u = a(bu)$.

$[M_4]$: For the unit scalar $1 \in K$, $1u = u$ for any vector $u \in V$.

The above axioms naturally split into two sets. The first four are only concerned with the additive structure of V and can be summarized by saying that V is a *commutative group* (see Appendix B) under addition. It follows that any sum of vectors of the form

$$v_1 + v_2 + \cdots + v_m$$

requires no parenthesis and does not depend upon the order of the summands, the zero vector 0 is unique, the *negative* $-u$ of u is unique, and the *cancellation law* holds:

$$u + w = v + w \quad \text{implies} \quad u = v$$

for any vectors $u, v, w \in V$. Also, *subtraction* is defined by

$$u - v = u + (-v)$$

On the other hand, the remaining four axioms are concerned with the "action" of the field K on V. Observe that the labelling of the axioms reflects this splitting. Using these additional axioms we prove (Problem 4.1) the following simple properties of a vector space.

Theorem 4.1:   Let V be a vector space over a field K.

   (i)   For any scalar $k \in K$ and $0 \in V$, $k0 = 0$.

   (ii) For $0 \in K$ and any vector $u \in V$, $0u = 0$.

   (iii) If $ku = 0$, where $k \in K$ and $u \in V$, then $k = 0$ or $u = 0$.

   (iv) For any scalar $k \in K$ and any vector $u \in V$, $(-k)u = k(-u) = -ku$.

EXAMPLES OF VECTOR SPACES

We now list a number of important examples of vector spaces. The first example is a generalization of the space $\mathbf{R}^n$.

Example 4.1:   Let K be an arbitrary field. The set of all n-tuples of elements of K with vector addition and scalar multiplication defined by

$$(a_1, a_2, \ldots, a_n) + (b_1, b_2, \ldots, b_n) = (a_1 + b_1, a_2 + b_2, \ldots, a_n + b_n)$$

and

$$k(a_1, a_2, \ldots, a_n) = (ka_1, ka_2, \ldots, ka_n)$$

where $a_i, b_i, k \in K$, is a vector space over K; we denote this space by K^n. The zero vector in K^n is the n-tuple of zeros, $0 = (0, 0, \ldots, 0)$. The proof that K^n is a vector space is identical to the proof of Theorem 1.1, which we may now regard as stating that $\mathbf{R}^n$ with the operations defined there is a vector space over $\mathbf{R}$.

Example 4.2:   Let V be the set of all $m \times n$ matrices with entries from an arbitrary field K. Then V is a vector space over K with respect to the operations of matrix addition and scalar multiplication, by Theorem 3.1.

Example 4.3:   Let V be the set of all polynomials $a_0 + a_1 t + a_2 t^2 + \cdots + a_n t^n$ with coefficients a_i from a field K. Then V is a vector space over K with respect to the usual operations of addition of polynomials and multiplication by a constant.

Example 4.4:   Let K be an arbitrary field and let X be any nonempty set. Consider the set V of all functions from X into K. The sum of any two functions $f, g \in V$ is the function $f + g \in V$ defined by

$$(f + g)(x) = f(x) + g(x)$$

and the product of a scalar $k \in K$ and a function $f \in V$ is the function $kf \in V$ defined by

$$(kf)(x) = k f(x)$$

Then V with the above operations is a vector space over K (Problem 4.5). The zero vector in V is the zero function $\mathbf{0}$ which maps each $x \in X$ into $0 \in K$: $\mathbf{0}(x) = 0$ for every $x \in X$. Furthermore, for any function $f \in V$, $-f$ is that function in V for which $(-f)(x) = -f(x)$, for every $x \in X$.

Example 4.5:   Suppose E is a field which contains a subfield K. Then E can be considered to be a vector space over K, taking the usual addition in E to be the vector addition and defining the scalar product kv of $k \in K$ and $v \in E$ to be the product of k and v as element of the field E. Thus the complex field $\mathbf{C}$ is a vector space over the real field $\mathbf{R}$, and the real field $\mathbf{R}$ is a vector space over the rational field $\mathbf{Q}$.

SUBSPACES

Let W be a subset of a vector space over a field K. W is called a *subspace* of V if W is itself a vector space over K with respect to the operations of vector addition and scalar multiplication on V. Simple criteria for identifying subspaces follow.

Theorem 4.2: W is a subspace of V if and only if

   (i) W is nonempty,

   (ii) W is closed under vector addition: $v, w \in W$ implies $v + w \in W$,

   (iii) W is closed under scalar multiplication: $v \in W$ implies $kv \in W$ for every $k \in K$.

Corollary 4.3: W is a subspace of V if and only if (i) $0 \in W$ (or $W \neq \emptyset$), and (ii) $v, w \in W$ implies $av + bw \in W$ for every $a, b \in K$.

Example 4.6:   Let V be any vector space. Then the set $\{0\}$ consisting of the zero vector alone, and also the entire space V are subspaces of V.

Example 4.7:   (i)   Let V be the vector space $\mathbf{R}^3$. Then the set W consisting of those vectors whose third component is zero, $W = \{(a, b, 0) : a, b \in \mathbf{R}\}$, is a subspace of V.

   (ii)   Let V be the space of all square $n \times n$ matrices (see Example 4.2). Then the set W consisting of those matrices $A = (a_{ij})$ for which $a_{ij} = a_{ji}$, called *symmetric matrices*, is a subspace of V.

   (iii)   Let V be the space of polynomials (see Example 4.3). Then the set W consisting of polynomials with degree $\leq n$, for a fixed n, is a subspace of V.

   (iv)   Let V be the space of all functions from a nonempty set X into the real field $\mathbf{R}$. Then the set W consisting of all bounded functions in V is a subspace of V. (A function $f \in V$ is *bounded* if there exists $M \in \mathbf{R}$ such that $|f(x)| \leq M$ for every $x \in X$.)

Example 4.8:   Consider any homogeneous system of linear equations in n unknowns with, say, real coefficients:

$$a_{11}x_1 + a_{12}x_2 + \cdots + a_{1n}x_n = 0$$
$$a_{21}x_1 + a_{22}x_2 + \cdots + a_{2n}x_n = 0$$
$$\cdots\cdots\cdots\cdots\cdots\cdots\cdots\cdots\cdots\cdots\cdots\cdots$$
$$a_{m1}x_1 + a_{m2}x_2 + \cdots + a_{mn}x_n = 0$$

Recall that any particular solution of the system may be viewed as a point in $\mathbf{R}^n$. The set W of all solutions of the homogeneous system is a subspace of $\mathbf{R}^n$ (Problem 4.16) called the *solution space*. We comment that the solution set of a nonhomogeneous system of linear equations in n unknowns is not a subspace of $\mathbf{R}^n$.

Example 4.9: Let U and W be subspaces of a vector space V. We show that the intersection $U \cap W$ is also a subspace of V. Clearly $0 \in U$ and $0 \in W$ since U and W are subspaces; whence $0 \in U \cap W$. Now suppose $u, v \in U \cap W$. Then $u, v \in U$ and $u, v \in W$ and, since U and W are subspaces,

$$au + bv \in U \qquad \text{and} \qquad au + bv \in W$$

for any scalars $a, b \in K$. Accordingly, $au + bv \in U \cap W$ and so $U \cap W$ is a subspace of V.

The result in the preceding example generalizes as follows.

Theorem 4.4: The intersection of any number of subspaces of a vector space V is a subspace of V.

LINEAR COMBINATIONS, LINEAR SPANS

Let V be a vector space over a field K and let $v_1, \ldots, v_m \in V$. Any vector in V of the form

$$a_1 v_1 + a_2 v_2 + \cdots + a_m v_m$$

where the $a_i \in K$, is called a *linear combination* of $v_1, \ldots, v_m$. The following theorem applies.

Theorem 4.5: Let S be a nonempty subset of V. The set of all linear combinations of vectors in S, denoted by $L(S)$, is a subspace of V containing S. Furthermore, if W is any other subspace of V containing S, then $L(S) \subset W$.

In other words, $L(S)$ is the smallest subspace of V containing S; hence it is called the subspace *spanned* or *generated* by S. For convenience, we define $L(\emptyset) = \{0\}$.

Example 4.10: Let V be the vector space $\mathbf{R}^3$. The linear span of any nonzero vector u consists of all scalar multiples of u; geometrically, it is the line through the origin and the point u. The linear space of any two vectors u and v which are not multiples of each other is the plane through the origin and the points u and v.

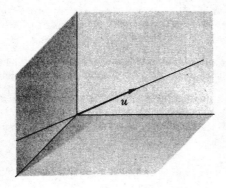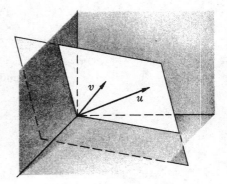

Example 4.11: The vectors $e_1 = (1, 0, 0)$, $e_2 = (0, 1, 0)$ and $e_3 = (0, 0, 1)$ generate the vector space $\mathbf{R}^3$. For any vector $(a, b, c) \in \mathbf{R}^3$ is a linear combination of the e_i; specifically,

$$\begin{aligned} (a, b, c) &= a(1, 0, 0) + b(0, 1, 0) + c(0, 0, 1) \\ &= a e_1 + b e_2 + c e_3 \end{aligned}$$

Example 4.12: The polynomials $1, t, t^2, t^3, \ldots$ generate the vector space V of all polynomials (in t): $V = L(1, t, t^2, \ldots)$. For any polynomial is a linear combination of 1 and powers of t.

Example 4.13: Determine whether or not the vector $v = (3, 9, -4, -2)$ is a linear combination of the vectors $u_1 = (1, -2, 0, 3)$, $u_2 = (2, 3, 0, -1)$ and $u_3 = (2, -1, 2, 1)$, i.e. belongs to the space spanned by the u_i.

Set v as a linear combination of the u_i using unknowns x, y and z; that is, set $v = xu_1 + yu_2 + zu_3$:

$$(3, 9, -4, -2) = x(1, -2, 0, 3) + y(2, 3, 0, -1) + z(2, -1, 2, 1)$$
$$= (x + 2y + 2z, -2x + 3y - z, 2z, 3x - y + z)$$

Form the equivalent system of equations by setting corresponding components equal to each other, and then reduce to echelon form:

$$
\begin{aligned}
x + 2y + 2z &= 3 \\
-2x + 3y - z &= 9 \\
2z &= -4 \\
3x - y + z &= -2
\end{aligned}
\quad \text{or} \quad
\begin{aligned}
x + 2y + 2z &= 3 \\
7y + 3z &= 15 \\
2z &= -4 \\
-7y - 5z &= -11
\end{aligned}
\quad \text{or} \quad
\begin{aligned}
x + 2y + 2z &= 3 \\
7y + 3z &= 15 \\
2z &= -4 \\
-2z &= 4
\end{aligned}
$$

$$
\text{or} \quad
\begin{aligned}
x + 2y + 2z &= 3 \\
7y + 3z &= 15 \\
2z &= -4
\end{aligned}
$$

Note that the above system is consistent and so has a solution; hence v is a linear combination of the u_i. Solving for the unknowns we obtain $x = 1$, $y = 3$, $z = -2$. Thus $v = u_1 + 3u_2 - 2u_3$.

Note that if the system of linear equations were not consistent, i.e. had no solution, then the vector v would not be a linear combination of the u_i.

ROW SPACE OF A MATRIX

Let A be an arbitrary $m \times n$ matrix over a field K:

$$
A = \begin{pmatrix}
a_{11} & a_{21} & \dots & a_{1n} \\
a_{21} & a_{22} & \dots & a_{2n} \\
\dots & \dots & \dots & \dots \\
a_{m1} & a_{m2} & \dots & a_{mn}
\end{pmatrix}
$$

The rows of A,

$$R_1 = (a_{11}, a_{21}, \dots, a_{1n}), \quad \dots, \quad R_m = (a_{m1}, a_{m2}, \dots, a_{mn})$$

viewed as vectors in K^n, span a subspace of K^n called the *row space* of A. That is,

$$\text{row space of } A = L(R_1, R_2, \dots, R_m)$$

Analogously, the columns of A, viewed as vectors in K^m, span a subspace of K^m called the *column space* of A.

Now suppose we apply an elementary row operation on A,

(i) $R_i \leftrightarrow R_j$, (ii) $R_i \to kR_i$, $k \neq 0$, or (iii) $R_i \to kR_j + R_i$

and obtain a matrix B. Then each row of B is clearly a row of A or a linear combination of rows of A. Hence the row space of B is contained in the row space of A. On the other hand, we can apply the inverse elementary row operation on B and obtain A; hence the row space of A is contained in the row space of B. Accordingly, A and B have the same row space. This leads us to the following theorem.

Theorem 4.6: Row equivalent matrices have the same row space.

We shall prove (Problem 4.31), in particular, the following fundamental result concerning row reduced echelon matrices.

Theorem 4.7:   Row reduced echelon matrices have the same row space if and only if they have the same nonzero rows.

Thus every matrix is row equivalent to a unique row reduced echelon matrix called its *row canonical form*.

We apply the above results in the next example.

> **Example 4.14:**   Show that the space U generated by the vectors
> $$u_1 = (1, 2, -1, 3), \quad u_2 = (2, 4, 1, -2), \quad \text{and} \quad u_3 = (3, 6, 3, -7)$$
> and the space V generated by the vectors
> $$v_1 = (1, 2, -4, 11) \quad \text{and} \quad v_2 = (2, 4, -5, 14)$$
> are equal; that is, $U = V$.
>
> **Method 1.**   Show that each u_i is a linear combination of v_1 and v_2, and show that each v_i is a linear combination of u_1, u_2 and u_3. Observe that we have to show that six systems of linear equations are consistent.
>
> **Method 2.**   Form the matrix A whose rows are the u_i, and row reduce A to row canonical form:
> $$A = \begin{pmatrix} 1 & 2 & -1 & 3 \\ 2 & 4 & 1 & -2 \\ 3 & 6 & 3 & -7 \end{pmatrix} \text{ to } \begin{pmatrix} 1 & 2 & -1 & 3 \\ 0 & 0 & 3 & -8 \\ 0 & 0 & 6 & -16 \end{pmatrix} \text{ to } \begin{pmatrix} 1 & 2 & -1 & 3 \\ 0 & 0 & 3 & -8 \\ 0 & 0 & 0 & 0 \end{pmatrix}$$
> $$\text{to } \begin{pmatrix} 1 & 2 & 0 & 1/3 \\ 0 & 0 & 1 & -8/3 \\ 0 & 0 & 0 & 0 \end{pmatrix}$$
>
> Now form the matrix B whose rows are v_1 and v_2, and row reduce B to row canonical form:
> $$B = \begin{pmatrix} 1 & 2 & -4 & 11 \\ 2 & 4 & -5 & 14 \end{pmatrix} \text{ to } \begin{pmatrix} 1 & 2 & -4 & 11 \\ 0 & 0 & 3 & -8 \end{pmatrix} \text{ to } \begin{pmatrix} 1 & 2 & 0 & 1/3 \\ 0 & 0 & 1 & -8/3 \end{pmatrix}$$
>
> Since the nonzero rows of the reduced matrices are identical, the row spaces of A and B are equal and so $U = V$.

SUMS AND DIRECT SUMS

Let U and W be subspaces of a vector space V. The sum of U and W, written $U + W$, consists of all sums $u + w$ where $u \in U$ and $w \in W$:
$$U + W = \{u + w : u \in U, w \in W\}$$

Note that $0 = 0 + 0 \in U + W$, since $0 \in U, 0 \in W$. Furthermore, suppose $u + w$ and $u' + w'$ belong to $U + W$, with $u, u' \in U$ and $w, w' \in W$. Then
$$(u + w) + (u' + w') = (u + u') + (w + w') \in U + W$$

and, for any scalar k, $\qquad k(u + w) = ku + kw \in U + W$

Thus we have proven the following theorem.

Theorem 4.8:   The sum $U + W$ of the subspaces U and W of V is also a subspace of V.

> **Example 4.15:**   Let V be the vector space of 2 by 2 matrices over **R**. Let U consist of those matrices in V whose second row is zero, and let W consist of those matrices in V whose second column is zero:
> $$U = \left\{ \begin{pmatrix} a & b \\ 0 & 0 \end{pmatrix} : a, b \in \mathbf{R} \right\}, \qquad W = \left\{ \begin{pmatrix} a & 0 \\ c & 0 \end{pmatrix} : a, c \in \mathbf{R} \right\}$$

Now U and W are subspaces of V. We have:

$$U + W = \left\{ \begin{pmatrix} a & b \\ c & 0 \end{pmatrix} : a, b, c \in \mathbf{R} \right\} \quad \text{and} \quad U \cap W = \left\{ \begin{pmatrix} a & 0 \\ 0 & 0 \end{pmatrix} : a \in \mathbf{R} \right\}$$

That is, $U + W$ consists of those matrices whose lower right entry is 0, and $U \cap W$ consists of those matrices whose second row and second column are zero.

Definition: The vector space V is said to be the *direct sum* of its subspaces U and W, denoted by

$$V = U \oplus W$$

if every vector $v \in V$ can be written in one and only one way as $v = u + w$ where $u \in U$ and $w \in W$.

The following theorem applies.

Theorem 4.9:   The vector space V is the direct sum of its subspaces U and W if and only if: (i) $V = U + W$, and (ii) $U \cap W = \{0\}$.

Example 4.16:   In the vector space $\mathbf{R}^3$, let U be the xy plane and let W be the yz plane:

$$U = \{(a, b, 0) : a, b \in \mathbf{R}\} \quad \text{and} \quad W = \{(0, b, c) : b, c \in \mathbf{R}\}$$

Then $\mathbf{R}^3 = U + W$ since every vector in $\mathbf{R}^3$ is the sum of a vector in U and a vector in W. However, $\mathbf{R}^3$ is not the direct sum of U and W since such sums are not unique; for example,

$$(3, 5, 7) = (3, 1, 0) + (0, 4, 7) \quad \text{and also} \quad (3, 5, 7) = (3, -4, 0) + (0, 9, 7)$$

Example 4.17:   In $\mathbf{R}^3$, let U be the xy plane and let W be the z axis:

$$U = \{(a, b, 0) : a, b \in \mathbf{R}\} \quad \text{and} \quad W = \{(0, 0, c) : c \in \mathbf{R}\}$$

Now any vector $(a, b, c) \in \mathbf{R}^3$ can be written as the sum of a vector in U and a vector in V in one and only one way:

$$(a, b, c) = (a, b, 0) + (0, 0, c)$$

Accordingly, $\mathbf{R}^3$ is the direct sum of U and W, that is, $\mathbf{R}^3 = U \oplus W$.

Solved Problems

VECTOR SPACES

4.1.   Prove Theorem 4.1: Let V be a vector space over a field K.

(i)   For any scalar $k \in K$ and $0 \in V$, $k0 = 0$.

(ii) For $0 \in K$ and any vector $u \in V$, $0u = 0$.

(iii) If $ku = 0$, where $k \in K$ and $u \in V$, then $k = 0$ or $u = 0$.

(iv) For any $k \in K$ and any $u \in V$, $(-k)u = k(-u) = -ku$.

(i)   By axiom $[A_2]$ with $u = 0$, we have $0 + 0 = 0$. Hence by axiom $[M_1]$, $k0 = k(0 + 0) = k0 + k0$. Adding $-k0$ to both sides gives the desired result.

(ii) By a property of K, $0 + 0 = 0$. Hence by axiom $[M_2]$, $0u = (0 + 0)u = 0u + 0u$. Adding $-0u$ to both sides yields the required result.

(iii) Suppose $ku = 0$ and $k \neq 0$. Then there exists a scalar k^{-1} such that $k^{-1}k = 1$; hence

$$u = 1u = (k^{-1}k)u = k^{-1}(ku) = k^{-1}0 = 0$$

(iv) Using $u + (-u) = 0$, we obtain $0 = k0 = k(u + (-u)) = ku + k(-u)$. Adding $-ku$ to both sides gives $-ku = k(-u)$.

Using $k + (-k) = 0$, we obtain $0 = 0u = (k + (-k))u = ku + (-k)u$. Adding $-ku$ to both sides yields $-ku = (-k)u$. Thus $(-k)u = k(-u) = -ku$.

4.2. Show that for any scalar k and any vectors u and v, $k(u-v) = ku - kv$.

Using the definition of subtraction $(u - v = u + (-v))$ and the result of Theorem 4.1(iv) $(k(-v) = -kv)$,

$$k(u-v) = k(u+(-v)) = ku + k(-v) = ku + (-kv) = ku - kv$$

4.3. In the statement of axiom $[M_2]$, $(a + b)u = au + bu$, which operation does each plus sign represent?

The $+$ in $(a+b)u$ denotes the addition of the two scalars a and b; hence it represents the addition operation in the field K. On the other hand, the $+$ in $au + bu$ denotes the addition of the two vectors au and bu; hence it represents the operation of vector addition. Thus each $+$ represents a different operation.

4.4. In the statement of axiom $[M_3]$, $(ab)u = a(bu)$, which operation does each product represent?

In $(ab)u$ the product ab of the scalars a and b denotes multiplication in the field K, whereas the product of the scalar ab and the vector u denotes scalar multiplication.

In $a(bu)$ the product bu of the scalar b and the vector u denotes scalar multiplication; also, the product of the scalar a and the vector bu denotes scalar multiplication.

4.5. Let V be the set of all functions from a nonempty set X into a field K. For any functions $f, g \in V$ and any scalar $k \in K$, let $f + g$ and kf be the functions in V defined as follows:

$$(f+g)(x) = f(x) + g(x) \quad \text{and} \quad (kf)(x) = kf(x), \quad \forall x \in X$$

(The symbol $\forall$ means "for every".) Prove that V is a vector space over K.

Since X is nonempty, V is also nonempty. We now need to show that all the axioms of a vector space hold.

$[A_1]$: Let $f, g, h \in V$. To show that $(f+g) + h = f + (g+h)$, it is necessary to show that the function $(f+g) + h$ and the function $f + (g+h)$ both assign the same value to each $x \in X$. Now,

$$((f+g)+h)(x) = (f+g)(x) + h(x) = (f(x) + g(x)) + h(x), \quad \forall x \in X$$
$$(f+(g+h))(x) = f(x) + (g+h)(x) = f(x) + (g(x) + h(x)), \quad \forall x \in X$$

But $f(x)$, $g(x)$ and $h(x)$ are scalars in the field K where addition of scalars is associative; hence

$$(f(x) + g(x)) + h(x) = f(x) + (g(x) + h(x))$$

Accordingly, $(f+g) + h = f + (g+h)$.

$[A_2]$: Let $\mathbf{0}$ denote the zero function: $\mathbf{0}(x) = 0$, $\forall x \in X$. Then for any function $f \in V$,

$$(f+\mathbf{0})(x) = f(x) + \mathbf{0}(x) = f(x) + 0 = f(x), \quad \forall x \in X$$

Thus $f + \mathbf{0} = f$, and $\mathbf{0}$ is the zero vector in V.

[A_3]: For any function $f \in V$, let $-f$ be the function defined by $(-f)(x) = -f(x)$. Then,

$$(f + (-f))(x) = f(x) + (-f)(x) = f(x) - f(x) = 0 = 0(x), \quad \forall x \in X$$

Hence $f + (-f) = 0$.

[A_4]: Let $f, g \in V$. Then

$$(f + g)(x) = f(x) + g(x) = g(x) + f(x) = (g + f)(x), \quad \forall x \in X$$

Hence $f + g = g + f$. (Note that $f(x) + g(x) = g(x) + f(x)$ follows from the fact that $f(x)$ and $g(x)$ are scalars in the field K where addition is commutative.)

[M_1]: Let $f, g \in V$ and $k \in K$. Then

$$(k(f + g))(x) = k((f + g)(x)) = k(f(x) + g(x)) = kf(x) + kg(x)$$
$$= (kf)(x) + (kg)(x) = (kf + kg)(x), \quad \forall x \in X$$

Hence $k(f + g) = kf + kg$. (Note that $k(f(x) + g(x)) = kf(x) + kg(x)$ follows from the fact that k, $f(x)$ and $g(x)$ are scalars in the field K where multiplication is distributive over addition.)

[M_2]: Let $f \in V$ and $a, b \in K$. Then

$$((a + b)f)(x) = (a + b)f(x) = af(x) + bf(x) = (af)(x) + bf(x)$$
$$= (af + bf)(x), \quad \forall x \in X$$

Hence $(a + b)f = af + bf$.

[M_3]: Let $f \in V$ and $a, b \in K$. Then,

$$((ab)f)(x) = (ab)f(x) = a(bf(x)) = a(bf)(x) = (a(bf))(x), \quad \forall x \in X$$

Hence $(ab)f = a(bf)$.

[M_4]: Let $f \in V$. Then, for the unit $1 \in K$, $(1f)(x) = 1f(x) = f(x)$, $\forall x \in X$. Hence $1f = f$.

Since all the axioms are satisfied, V is a vector space over K.

4.6. Let V be the set of ordered pairs of real numbers: $V = \{(a, b): a, b \in \mathbf{R}\}$. Show that V is not a vector space over R with respect to each of the following operations of addition in V and scalar multiplication on V:

(i) $(a, b) + (c, d) = (a + c, b + d)$ and $k(a, b) = (ka, b)$;

(ii) $(a, b) + (c, d) = (a, b)$ and $k(a, b) = (ka, kb)$;

(iii) $(a, b) + (c, d) = (a + c, b + d)$ and $k(a, b) = (k^2a, k^2b)$.

In each case show that one of the axioms of a vector space does not hold.

(i) Let $r = 1$, $s = 2$, $v = (3, 4)$. Then

$$(r + s)v = 3(3, 4) = (9, 4)$$
$$rv + sv = 1(3, 4) + 2(3, 4) = (3, 4) + (6, 4) = (9, 8)$$

Since $(r + s)v \neq rv + sv$, axiom [M_2] does not hold.

(ii) Let $v = (1, 2)$, $w = (3, 4)$. Then

$$v + w = (1, 2) + (3, 4) = (1, 2)$$
$$w + v = (3, 4) + (1, 2) = (3, 4)$$

Since $v + w \neq w + v$, axiom [A_4] does not hold.

(iii) Let $r = 1$, $s = 2$, $v = (3, 4)$. Then

$$(r + s)v = 3(3, 4) = (27, 36)$$
$$rv + sv = 1(3, 4) + 2(3, 4) = (3, 4) + (12, 16) = (15, 20)$$

Thus $(r + s)v \neq rv + sv$, and so axiom [M_2] does not hold.

SUBSPACES

4.7. Prove Theorem 4.2: W is a subspace of V if and only if (i) W is nonempty, (ii) $v, w \in W$ implies $v + w \in W$, and (iii) $v \in W$ implies $kv \in W$ for every scalar $k \in K$.

Suppose W satisfies (i), (ii) and (iii). By (i), W is nonempty; and by (ii) and (iii), the operations of vector addition and scalar multiplication are well defined for W. Moreover, the axioms $[A_1]$, $[A_4]$, $[M_1]$, $[M_2]$, $[M_3]$ and $[M_4]$ hold in W since the vectors in W belong to V. Hence we need only show that $[A_2]$ and $[A_3]$ also hold in W. By (i), W is nonempty, say $u \in W$. Then by (iii), $0u = 0 \in W$ and $v + 0 = v$ for every $v \in W$. Hence W satisfies $[A_2]$. Lastly, if $v \in W$ then $(-1)v = -v \in W$ and $v + (-v) = 0$; hence W satisfies $[A_3]$. Thus W is a subspace of V.

Conversely, if W is a subspace of V then clearly (i), (ii) and (iii) hold.

4.8. Prove Corollary 4.3: W is a subspace of V if and only if (i) $0 \in W$ and (ii) $v, w \in W$ implies $av + bw \in W$ for all scalars $a, b \in K$.

Suppose W satisfies (i) and (ii). Then, by (i), W is nonempty. Furthermore, if $v, w \in W$ then, by (ii), $v + w = 1v + 1w \in W$; and if $v \in W$ and $k \in K$ then, by (ii), $kv = kv + 0v \in W$. Thus by Theorem 4.2, W is a subspace of V.

Conversely, if W is a subspace of V then clearly (i) and (ii) hold in W.

4.9. Let $V = \mathbf{R}^3$. Show that W is a subspace of V where:

(i) $W = \{(a, b, 0) : a, b \in \mathbf{R}\}$, i.e. W is the xy plane consisting of those vectors whose third component is 0;

(ii) $W = \{(a, b, c) : a + b + c = 0\}$, i.e. W consists of those vectors each with the property that the sum of its components is zero.

(i) $0 = (0, 0, 0) \in W$ since the third component of 0 is 0. For any vectors $v = (a, b, 0)$, $w = (c, d, 0)$ in W, and any scalars (real numbers) k and k',

$$\begin{aligned} kv + k'w &= k(a, b, 0) + k'(c, d, 0) \\ &= (ka, kb, 0) + (k'c, k'd, 0) = (ka + k'c, kb + k'd, 0) \end{aligned}$$

Thus $kv + k'w \in W$, and so W is a subspace of V.

(ii) $0 = (0, 0, 0) \in W$ since $0 + 0 + 0 = 0$. Suppose $v = (a, b, c)$, $w = (a', b', c')$ belong to W, i.e. $a + b + c = 0$ and $a' + b' + c' = 0$. Then for any scalars k and k',

$$\begin{aligned} kv + k'w &= k(a, b, c) + k'(a', b', c') \\ &= (ka, kb, kc) + (k'a', k'b', k'c') \\ &= (ka + k'a', kb + k'b', kc + k'c') \end{aligned}$$

and furthermore,

$$\begin{aligned} (ka + k'a') + (kb + k'b') + (kc + k'c') &= k(a + b + c) + k'(a' + b' + c') \\ &= k0 + k'0 = 0 \end{aligned}$$

Thus $kv + k'w \in W$, and so W is a subspace of V.

4.10. Let $V = \mathbf{R}^3$. Show that W is not a subspace of V where:

(i) $W = \{(a, b, c) : a \geqq 0\}$, i.e. W consists of those vectors whose first component is nonnegative;

(ii) $W = \{(a, b, c) : a^2 + b^2 + c^2 \leqq 1\}$, i.e. W consists of those vectors whose length does not exceed 1;

(iii) $W = \{(a, b, c) : a, b, c \in \mathbf{Q}\}$, i.e. W consists of those vectors whose components are rational numbers.

In each case, show that one of the properties of, say, Theorem 4.2 does not hold.

(i) $v = (1, 2, 3) \in W$ and $k = -5 \in \mathbf{R}$. But $kv = -5(1, 2, 3) = (-5, -10, -15)$ does not belong to W since -5 is negative. Hence W is not a subspace of V.

(ii) $v = (1, 0, 0) \in W$ and $w = (0, 1, 0) \in W$. But $v + w = (1, 0, 0) + (0, 1, 0) = (1, 1, 0)$ does not belong to W since $1^2 + 1^2 + 0^2 = 2 > 1$. Hence W is not a subspace of V.

(iii) $v = (1, 2, 3) \in W$ and $k = \sqrt{2} \in \mathbf{R}$. But $kv = \sqrt{2}\,(1, 2, 3) = (\sqrt{2},\, 2\sqrt{2},\, 3\sqrt{2})$ does not belong to W since its components are not rational numbers. Hence W is not a subspace of V.

4.11. Let V be the vector space of all square $n \times n$ matrices over a field K. Show that W is a subspace of V where:

(i) W consists of the symmetric matrices, i.e. all matrices $A = (a_{ij})$ for which $a_{ji} = a_{ij}$;

(ii) W consists of all matrices which commute with a given matrix T; that is, $W = \{A \in V : AT = TA\}$.

(i) $0 \in W$ since all entries of 0 are 0 and hence equal. Now suppose $A = (a_{ij})$ and $B = (b_{ij})$ belong to W, i.e. $a_{ji} = a_{ij}$ and $b_{ji} = b_{ij}$. For any scalars $a, b \in K$, $aA + bB$ is the matrix whose ij-entry is $aa_{ij} + bb_{ij}$. But $aa_{ji} + bb_{ji} = aa_{ij} + bb_{ij}$. Thus $aA + bB$ is also symmetric, and so W is a subspace of V.

(ii) $0 \in W$ since $0T = 0 = T0$. Now suppose $A, B \in W$; that is, $AT = TA$ and $BT = TB$. For any scalars $a, b \in K$,

$$(aA + bB)T \;=\; (aA)T + (bB)T \;=\; a(AT) + b(BT) \;=\; a(TA) + b(TB)$$
$$=\; T(aA) + T(bB) \;=\; T(aA + bB)$$

Thus $aA + bB$ commutes with T, i.e. belongs to W; hence W is a subspace of V.

4.12. Let V be the vector space of all 2×2 matrices over the real field $\mathbf{R}$. Show that W is not a subspace of V where:

(i) W consists of all matrices with zero determinant;

(ii) W consists of all matrices A for which $A^2 = A$.

(i)   (Recall that $\det \begin{pmatrix} a & b \\ c & d \end{pmatrix} = ad - bc$.) The matrices $A = \begin{pmatrix} 1 & 0 \\ 0 & 0 \end{pmatrix}$ and $B = \begin{pmatrix} 0 & 0 \\ 0 & 1 \end{pmatrix}$ belong to W since $\det (A) = 0$ and $\det (B) = 0$. But $A + B = \begin{pmatrix} 1 & 0 \\ 0 & 1 \end{pmatrix}$ does not belong to W since $\det (A + B) = 1$. Hence W is not a subspace of V.

(ii) The unit matrix $I = \begin{pmatrix} 1 & 0 \\ 0 & 1 \end{pmatrix}$ belongs to W since

$$I^2 \;=\; \begin{pmatrix} 1 & 0 \\ 0 & 1 \end{pmatrix}\begin{pmatrix} 1 & 0 \\ 0 & 1 \end{pmatrix} \;=\; \begin{pmatrix} 1 & 0 \\ 0 & 1 \end{pmatrix} \;=\; I$$

But $2I = \begin{pmatrix} 2 & 0 \\ 0 & 2 \end{pmatrix}$ does not belong to W since

$$(2I)^2 \;=\; \begin{pmatrix} 2 & 0 \\ 0 & 2 \end{pmatrix}\begin{pmatrix} 2 & 0 \\ 0 & 2 \end{pmatrix} \;=\; \begin{pmatrix} 4 & 0 \\ 0 & 4 \end{pmatrix} \;\neq\; 2I$$

Hence W is not a subspace of V.

4.13. Let V be the vector space of all functions from the real field $\mathbf{R}$ into $\mathbf{R}$. Show that W is a subspace of V where:

(i) $W = \{f : f(3) = 0\}$, i.e. W consists of those functions which map 3 into 0;

(ii) $W = \{f : f(7) = f(1)\}$, i.e. W consists of those functions which assign the same value to 7 and 1;

(iii) W consists of the odd functions, i.e. those functions f for which $f(-x) = -f(x)$.

Here **0** denotes the zero function: $0(x) = 0$, for every $x \in R$.

(i) $0 \in W$ since $0(3) = 0$. Suppose $f, g \in W$, i.e. $f(3) = 0$ and $g(3) = 0$. Then for any real numbers a and b,
$$(af + bg)(3) = af(3) + bg(3) = a0 + b0 = 0$$
Hence $af + bg \in W$, and so W is a subspace of V.

(ii) $0 \in W$ since $0(7) = 0 = 0(1)$. Suppose $f, g \in W$, i.e. $f(7) = f(1)$ and $g(7) = g(1)$. Then, for any real numbers a and b,
$$(af + bg)(7) = af(7) + bg(7) = af(1) + bg(1) = (af + bg)(1)$$
Hence $af + bg \in W$, and so W is a subspace of V.

(iii) $0 \in W$ since $0(-x) = 0 = -0 = -0(x)$. Suppose $f, g \in W$, i.e. $f(-x) = -f(x)$ and $g(-x) = -g(x)$. Then for any real numbers a and b,
$$(af + bg)(-x) = af(-x) + bg(-x) = -af(x) - bg(x) = -(af(x) + bg(x)) = -(af + bg)(x)$$
Hence $af + bg \in W$, and so W is a subspace of V.

4.14. Let V be the vector space of all functions from the real field **R** into **R**. Show that W is not a subspace of V where:

(i) $W = \{f : f(7) = 2 + f(1)\}$;

(ii) W consists of all nonnegative functions, i.e. all functions f for which $f(x) \geqq 0$, $\forall x \in R$.

(i)   Suppose $f, g \in W$, i.e. $f(7) = 2 + f(1)$ and $g(7) = 2 + g(1)$. Then
$$\begin{aligned}(f + g)(7) &= f(7) + g(7) = 2 + f(1) + 2 + g(1) \\ &= 4 + f(1) + g(1) = 4 + (f+g)(1) \neq 2 + (f+g)(1)\end{aligned}$$
Hence $f + g \notin W$, and so W is not a subspace of V.

(ii) Let $k = -2$ and let $f \in V$ be defined by $f(x) = x^2$. Then $f \in W$ since $f(x) = x^2 \geqq 0$, $\forall x \in R$. But $(kf)(5) = kf(5) = (-2)(5^2) = -50 < 0$. Hence $kf \notin W$, and so W is not a subspace of V.

4.15. Let V be the vector space of polynomials $a_0 + a_1 t + a_2 t^2 + \cdots + a_n t^n$ with real coefficients, i.e. $a_i \in R$. Determine whether or not W is a subspace of V where:

(i) W consists of all polynomials with integral coefficients;

(ii) W consists of all polynomials with degree $\leqq 3$;

(iii) W consists of all polynomials $b_0 + b_1 t^2 + b_2 t^4 + \cdots + b_n t^{2n}$, i.e. polynomials with only even powers of t.

(i)   No, since scalar multiples of vectors in W do not always belong to W. For example, $v = 3 + 5t + 7t^2 \in W$ but $\frac{1}{2}v = \frac{3}{2} + \frac{5}{2}t + \frac{7}{2}t^2 \notin W$. (Observe that W is "closed" under vector addition, i.e. sums of elements in W belong to W.)

(ii) and (iii). Yes. For, in each case, W is nonempty, the sum of elements in W belong to W, and the scalar multiples of any element in W belong to W.

4.16. Consider a homogeneous system of linear equations in n unknowns $x_1, \ldots, x_n$ over a field K:
$$\begin{aligned}a_{11}x_1 + a_{12}x_2 + \cdots + a_{1n}x_n &= 0 \\ a_{21}x_1 + a_{22}x_2 + \cdots + a_{2n}x_n &= 0 \\ \cdots\cdots\cdots\cdots\cdots\cdots\cdots\cdots & \\ a_{m1}x_1 + a_{m2}x_2 + \cdots + a_{mn}x_n &= 0\end{aligned}$$

Show that the solution set W is a subspace of the vector space K^n.

$0 = (0, 0, \ldots, 0) \in W$ since, clearly,
$$a_{i1}0 + a_{i2}0 + \cdots + a_{in}0 = 0, \qquad \text{for } i = 1, \ldots, m$$

Suppose $u = (u_1, u_2, \ldots, u_n)$ and $v = (v_1, v_2, \ldots, v_n)$ belong to W, i.e. for $i = 1, \ldots, m$

$$a_{i1}u_1 + a_{i2}u_2 + \cdots + a_{in}u_n = 0$$
$$a_{i1}v_1 + a_{i2}v_2 + \cdots + a_{in}v_n = 0$$

Let a and b be scalars in K. Then

and, for $i = 1, \ldots, m$, $au + bv = (au_1 + bv_1, au_2 + bv_2, \ldots, au_n + bv_n)$

$$a_{i1}(au_1 + bv_1) + a_{i2}(au_2 + bv_2) + \cdots + a_{in}(au_n + bv_n)$$
$$= a(a_{i1}u_1 + a_{i2}u_2 + \cdots + a_{in}u_n) + b(a_{i1}v_1 + a_{i2}v_2 + \cdots + a_{in}v_n)$$
$$= a0 + b0 = 0$$

Hence $au + bv$ is a solution of the system, i.e. belongs to W. Accordingly, W is a subspace of K^n.

LINEAR COMBINATIONS

4.17. Write the vector $v = (1, -2, 5)$ as a linear combination of the vectors $e_1 = (1, 1, 1)$, $e_2 = (1, 2, 3)$ and $e_3 = (2, -1, 1)$.

We wish to express v as $v = xe_1 + ye_2 + ze_3$, with x, y and z as yet unknown scalars. Thus we require

$$(1, -2, 5) = x(1, 1, 1) + y(1, 2, 3) + z(2, -1, 1)$$
$$= (x, x, x) + (y, 2y, 3y) + (2z, -z, z)$$
$$= (x + y + 2z, x + 2y - z, x + 3y + z)$$

Form the equivalent system of equations by setting corresponding components equal to each other, and then reduce to echelon form:

$$\begin{array}{rcr} x + y + 2z &=& 1 \\ x + 2y - z &=& -2 \\ x + 3y + z &=& 5 \end{array} \quad \text{or} \quad \begin{array}{rcr} x + y + 2z &=& 1 \\ y - 3z &=& -3 \\ 2y - z &=& 4 \end{array} \quad \text{or} \quad \begin{array}{rcr} x + y + 2z &=& 1 \\ y - 3z &=& -3 \\ 5z &=& 10 \end{array}$$

Note that the above system is consistent and so has a solution. Solve for the unknowns to obtain $x = -6$, $y = 3$, $z = 2$. Hence $v = -6e_1 + 3e_2 + 2e_3$.

4.18. Write the vector $v = (2, -5, 3)$ in $\mathbf{R}^3$ as a linear combination of the vectors $e_1 = (1, -3, 2)$, $e_2 = (2, -4, -1)$ and $e_3 = (1, -5, 7)$.

Set v as a linear combination of the e_i using the unknowns x, y and z: $v = xe_1 + ye_2 + ze_3$.

$$(2, -5, 3) = x(1, -3, 2) + y(2, -4, -1) + z(1, -5, 7)$$
$$= (x + 2y + z, -3x - 4y - 5z, 2x - y + 7z)$$

Form the equivalent system of equations and reduce to echelon form:

$$\begin{array}{rcr} x + 2y + z &=& 2 \\ -3x - 4y - 5z &=& -5 \\ 2x - y + 7z &=& 3 \end{array} \quad \text{or} \quad \begin{array}{rcr} x + 2y + z &=& 2 \\ 2y - 2z &=& 1 \\ -5y + 5z &=& -1 \end{array} \quad \text{or} \quad \begin{array}{rcr} x + 2y + z &=& 2 \\ 2y - 2z &=& 1 \\ 0 &=& 3 \end{array}$$

The system is inconsistent and so has no solution. Accordingly, v cannot be written as a linear combination of the vectors e_1, e_2 and e_3.

4.19. For which value of k will the vector $u = (1, -2, k)$ in $\mathbf{R}^3$ be a linear combination of the vectors $v = (3, 0, -2)$ and $w = (2, -1, -5)$?

Set $u = xv + yw$:

$$(1, -2, k) = x(3, 0, -2) + y(2, -1, -5) = (3x + 2y, -y, -2x - 5y)$$

Form the equivalent system of equations:

$$3x + 2y = 1, \quad -y = -2, \quad -2x - 5y = k$$

By the first two equations, $x = -1$, $y = 2$. Substitute into the last equation to obtain $k = -8$.

4.20. Write the polynomial $v = t^2 + 4t - 3$ over $\mathbf{R}$ as a linear combination of the polynomials $e_1 = t^2 - 2t + 5$, $e_2 = 2t^2 - 3t$ and $e_3 = t + 3$.

Set v as a linear combination of the e_i using the unknowns x, y and z: $v = xe_1 + ye_2 + ze_3$.

$$t^2 + 4t - 3 = x(t^2 - 2t + 5) + y(2t^2 - 3t) + z(t + 3)$$
$$= xt^2 - 2xt + 5x + 2yt^2 - 3yt + zt + 3z$$
$$= (x + 2y)t^2 + (-2x - 3y + z)t + (5x + 3z)$$

Set coefficients of the same powers of t equal to each other, and reduce the system to echelon form:

$$\begin{array}{lll}
x + 2y \quad\quad = 1 & x + 2y \quad\quad = 1 & x + 2y \quad\quad = 1 \\
-2x - 3y + z = 4 \quad\text{or}\quad & y + z = 6 \quad\text{or}\quad & y + z = 6 \\
5x \quad\quad + 3z = -3 & -10y + 3z = -8 & 13z = 52
\end{array}$$

Note that the system is consistent and so has a solution. Solve for the unknowns to obtain $x = -3$, $y = 2$, $z = 4$. Thus $v = -3e_1 + 2e_2 + 4e_3$.

4.21. Write the matrix $E = \begin{pmatrix} 3 & 1 \\ 1 & -1 \end{pmatrix}$ as a linear combination of the matrices $A = \begin{pmatrix} 1 & 1 \\ 1 & 0 \end{pmatrix}$, $B = \begin{pmatrix} 0 & 0 \\ 1 & 1 \end{pmatrix}$ and $C = \begin{pmatrix} 0 & 2 \\ 0 & -1 \end{pmatrix}$.

Set E as a linear combination of A, B, C using the unknowns x, y, z: $E = xA + yB + zC$.

$$\begin{pmatrix} 3 & 1 \\ 1 & -1 \end{pmatrix} = x\begin{pmatrix} 1 & 1 \\ 1 & 0 \end{pmatrix} + y\begin{pmatrix} 0 & 0 \\ 1 & 1 \end{pmatrix} + z\begin{pmatrix} 0 & 2 \\ 0 & -1 \end{pmatrix}$$
$$= \begin{pmatrix} x & x \\ x & 0 \end{pmatrix} + \begin{pmatrix} 0 & 0 \\ y & y \end{pmatrix} + \begin{pmatrix} 0 & 2z \\ 0 & -z \end{pmatrix} = \begin{pmatrix} x & x + 2z \\ x + y & y - z \end{pmatrix}$$

Form the equivalent system of equations by setting corresponding entries equal to each other:

$$x = 3, \quad x + y = 1, \quad x + 2z = 1, \quad y - z = -1$$

Substitute $x = 3$ in the second and third equations to obtain $y = -2$ and $z = -1$. Since these values also satisfy the last equation, they form a solution of the system. Hence $E = 3A - 2B - C$.

4.22. Suppose u is a linear combination of the vectors $v_1, \ldots, v_m$ and suppose each v_i is a linear combination of the vectors $w_1, \ldots, w_n$:

$$u = a_1v_1 + a_2v_2 + \cdots + a_mv_m \quad\text{and}\quad v_i = b_{i1}w_1 + b_{i2}w_2 + \cdots + b_{in}w_n$$

Show that u is also a linear combination of the w_i. Thus if $S \subset L(T)$, then $L(S) \subset L(T)$.

$$u = a_1v_1 + a_2v_2 + \cdots + a_mv_m$$
$$= a_1(b_{11}w_1 + \cdots + b_{1n}w_n) + a_2(b_{21}w_1 + \cdots + b_{2n}w_n) + \cdots + a_m(b_{m1}w_1 + \cdots + b_{mn}w_n)$$
$$= (a_1b_{11} + a_2b_{21} + \cdots + a_mb_{m1})w_1 + \cdots + (a_1b_{1n} + a_2b_{2n} + \cdots + a_mb_{mn})w_n$$

or simply $\quad u = \displaystyle\sum_{i=1}^{m} a_iv_i = \sum_{i=1}^{m} a_i\left(\sum_{j=1}^{n} b_{ij}w_j\right) = \sum_{j=1}^{n}\left(\sum_{i=1}^{m} a_ib_{ij}\right)w_j$

LINEAR SPANS, GENERATORS

4.23. Show that the vectors $u = (1, 2, 3)$, $v = (0, 1, 2)$ and $w = (0, 0, 1)$ generate $\mathbf{R}^3$.

We need to show that an arbitrary vector $(a, b, c) \in \mathbf{R}^3$ is a linear combination of u, v and w.

Set $(a, b, c) = xu + yv + zw$:

$$(a, b, c) = x(1, 2, 3) + y(0, 1, 2) + z(0, 0, 1) = (x, 2x + y, 3x + 2y + z)$$

Then form the system of equations

$$\begin{array}{ll} x \qquad\qquad = a & z + 2y + 3x = c \\ 2x + \ y \qquad = b \qquad \text{or} & y + 2x = b \\ 3x + 2y + z = c & \qquad\quad x = a \end{array}$$

The above system is in echelon form and is consistent; in fact $x = a$, $y = b - 2a$, $z = c - 2b + a$ is a solution. Thus u, v and w generate $\mathbf{R}^3$.

4.24. Find conditions on a, b and c so that $(a, b, c) \in \mathbf{R}^3$ belongs to the space generated by $u = (2, 1, 0)$, $v = (1, -1, 2)$ and $w = (0, 3, -4)$.

Set (a, b, c) as a linear combination of u, v and w using unknowns x, y and z: $(a, b, c) = xu + yv + zw$.

$$(a, b, c) = x(2, 1, 0) + y(1, -1, 2) + z(0, 3, -4) = (2x + y, \ x - y + 3z, \ 2y - 4z)$$

Form the equivalent system of linear equations and reduce it to echelon form:

$$\begin{array}{lll} 2x + y \qquad = a & 2x + y \qquad = a & 2x + y \qquad = a \\ x - y + 3z = b \quad \text{or} & 3y - 6z = a - 2b \quad \text{or} & 3y - 6z = a - 2b \\ 2y - 4z = c & 2y - 4z = c & \qquad\quad 0 = 2a - 4b - 3c \end{array}$$

The vector (a, b, c) belongs to the space generated by u, v and w if and only if the above system is consistent, and it is consistent if and only if $2a - 4b - 3c = 0$. Note, in particular, that u, v and w do not generate the whole space $\mathbf{R}^3$.

4.25. Show that the xy plane $W = \{(a, b, 0)\}$ in $\mathbf{R}^3$ is generated by u and v where: (i) $u = (1, 2, 0)$ and $v = (0, 1, 0)$; (ii) $u = (2, -1, 0)$ and $v = (1, 3, 0)$.

In each case show that an arbitrary vector $(a, b, 0) \in W$ is a linear combination of u and v.

(i)   Set $(a, b, 0) = xu + yv$:

$$(a, b, 0) = x(1, 2, 0) + y(0, 1, 0) = (x, \ 2x + y, \ 0)$$

Then form the system of equations

$$\begin{array}{ll} x \quad = a & y + 2x = b \\ 2x + y = b \qquad \text{or} & \quad x = a \\ 0 = 0 & \end{array}$$

The system is consistent; in fact $x = a$, $y = b - 2a$ is a solution. Hence u and v generate W.

(ii)   Set $(a, b, 0) = xu + yv$:

$$(a, b, 0) = x(2, -1, 0) + y(1, 3, 0) = (2x + y, \ -x + 3y, \ 0)$$

Form the following system and reduce it to echelon form:

$$\begin{array}{ll} 2x + \ y = a & 2x + y = a \\ -x + 3y = b \qquad \text{or} & \quad 7y = a + 2b \\ 0 = 0 & \end{array}$$

The system is consistent and so has a solution. Hence W is generated by u and v. (Observe that we do not need to solve for x and y; it is only necessary to know that a solution exists.)

4.26. Show that the vector space V of polynomials over any field K cannot be generated by a finite number of vectors.

Any finite set S of polynomials contains one of maximum degree, say m. Then the linear span $L(S)$ of S cannot contain polynomials of degree greater than m. Accordingly, $V \neq L(S)$, for any finite set S.

4.27. Prove Theorem 4.5: Let S be a nonempty subset of V. Then $L(S)$, the set of all linear combinations of vectors in S, is a subspace of V containing S. Furthermore, if W is any other subspace of V containing S, then $L(S) \subset W$.

If $v \in S$, then $1v = v \in L(S)$; hence S is a subset of $L(S)$. Also, $L(S)$ is nonempty since S is nonempty. Now suppose $v, w \in L(S)$; say,

$$v = a_1 v_1 + \cdots + a_m v_m \qquad \text{and} \qquad w = b_1 w_1 + \cdots + b_n w_n$$

where $v_i, w_j \in S$ and a_i, b_j are scalars. Then

$$v + w = a_1 v_1 + \cdots + a_m v_m + b_1 w_1 + \cdots + b_n w_n$$

and, for any scalar k,

$$kv = k(a_1 v_1 + \cdots + a_m v_m) = ka_1 v_1 + \cdots + ka_m v_m$$

belong to $L(S)$ since each is a linear combination of vectors in S. Accordingly, $L(S)$ is a subspace of V.

Now suppose W is a subspace of V containing S and suppose $v_1, \ldots, v_m \in S \subset W$. Then all multiples $a_1 v_1, \ldots, a_m v_m \in W$, where $a_i \in K$, and hence the sum $a_1 v_1 + \cdots + a_m v_m \in W$. That is, W contains all linear combinations of elements of S. Consequently, $L(S) \subset W$ as claimed.

ROW SPACE OF A MATRIX

4.28. Determine whether the following matrices have the same row space:

$$A = \begin{pmatrix} 1 & 1 & 5 \\ 2 & 3 & 13 \end{pmatrix}, \qquad B = \begin{pmatrix} 1 & -1 & -2 \\ 3 & -2 & -3 \end{pmatrix}, \qquad C = \begin{pmatrix} 1 & -1 & -1 \\ 4 & -3 & -1 \\ 3 & -1 & 3 \end{pmatrix}$$

Row reduce each matrix to row canonical form:

$$A = \begin{pmatrix} 1 & 1 & 5 \\ 2 & 3 & 13 \end{pmatrix} \text{ to } \begin{pmatrix} 1 & 1 & 5 \\ 0 & 1 & 3 \end{pmatrix} \text{ to } \begin{pmatrix} 1 & 0 & 2 \\ 0 & 1 & 3 \end{pmatrix}$$

$$B = \begin{pmatrix} 1 & -1 & -2 \\ 3 & -2 & -3 \end{pmatrix} \text{ to } \begin{pmatrix} 1 & -1 & -2 \\ 0 & 1 & 3 \end{pmatrix} \text{ to } \begin{pmatrix} 1 & 0 & 1 \\ 0 & 1 & 3 \end{pmatrix}$$

$$C = \begin{pmatrix} 1 & -1 & -1 \\ 4 & -3 & -1 \\ 3 & -1 & 3 \end{pmatrix} \text{ to } \begin{pmatrix} 1 & -1 & -1 \\ 0 & 1 & 3 \\ 0 & 2 & 6 \end{pmatrix} \text{ to } \begin{pmatrix} 1 & -1 & -1 \\ 0 & 1 & 3 \\ 0 & 0 & 0 \end{pmatrix} \text{ to } \begin{pmatrix} 1 & 0 & 2 \\ 0 & 1 & 3 \\ 0 & 0 & 0 \end{pmatrix}$$

Since the nonzero rows of the reduced form of A and of the reduced form of C are the same, A and C have the same row space. On the other hand, the nonzero rows of the reduced form of B are not the same as the others, and so B has a different row space.

4.29. Consider an arbitrary matrix $A = (a_{ij})$. Suppose $u = (b_1, \ldots, b_n)$ is a linear combination of the rows $R_1, \ldots, R_m$ of A; say $u = k_1 R_1 + \cdots + k_m R_m$. Show that, for each i, $b_i = k_1 a_{1i} + k_2 a_{2i} + \cdots + k_m a_{mi}$ where $a_{1i}, \ldots, a_{mi}$ are the entries of the ith column of A.

We are given $u = k_1 R_1 + \cdots + k_m R_m$; hence

$$(b_1, \ldots, b_n) = k_1(a_{11}, \ldots, a_{1n}) + \cdots + k_m(a_{m1}, \ldots, a_{mn})$$

$$= (k_1 a_{11} + \cdots + k_m a_{m1}, \ldots, k_1 a_{m1} + \cdots + k_m a_{mn})$$

Setting corresponding components equal to each other, we obtain the desired result.

4.30. Prove: Let $A = (a_{ij})$ be an echelon matrix with distinguished entries $a_{1j_1}, a_{2j_2}, \ldots, a_{rj_r}$, and let $B = (b_{ij})$ be an echelon matrix with distinguished entries $b_{1k_1}, b_{2k_2}, \ldots, b_{sk_s}$:

Suppose A and B have the same row space. Then the distinguished entries of A and of B are in the same position: $j_1 = k_1$, $j_2 = k_2$, $\ldots$, $j_r = k_r$, and $r = s$.

Clearly $A = 0$ if and only if $B = 0$, and so we need only prove the theorem when $r \geqq 1$ and $s \geqq 1$. We first show that $j_1 = k_1$. Suppose $j_1 < k_1$. Then the j_1th column of B is zero. Since the first row of A is in the row space of B, we have by the preceding problem, $a_{1j_1} = c_1 0 + c_2 0 + \cdots + c_m 0 = 0$ for scalars c_i. But this contradicts the fact that the distinguished element $a_{1j_1} \neq 0$. Hence $j_1 \geqq k_1$, and similarly $k_1 \geqq j_1$. Thus $j_1 = k_1$.

Now let A' be the submatrix of A obtained by deleting the first row of A, and let B' be the submatrix of B obtained by deleting the first row of B. We prove that A' and B' have the same row space. The theorem will then follow by induction since A' and B' are also echelon matrices.

Let $R = (a_1, a_2, \ldots, a_n)$ be any row of A' and let $R_1, \ldots, R_m$ be the rows of B. Since R is in the row space of B, there exist scalars $d_1, \ldots, d_m$ such that $R = d_1 R_1 + d_2 R_2 + \cdots + d_m R_m$. Since A is in echelon form and R is not the first row of A, the j_1th entry of R is zero: $a_i = 0$ for $i = j_1 = k_1$. Furthermore, since B is in echelon form, all the entries in the k_1th column of B are 0 except the first: $b_{1k_1} \neq 0$, but $b_{2k_1} = 0, \ldots, b_{mk_1} = 0$. Thus

$$0 = a_{k_1} = d_1 b_{1k_1} + d_2 0 + \cdots + d_m 0 = d_1 b_{1k_1}$$

Now $b_{1k_1} \neq 0$ and so $d_1 = 0$. Thus R is a linear combination of $R_2, \ldots, R_m$ and so is in the row space of B'. Since R was any row of A', the row space of A' is contained in the row space of B'. Similarly, the row space of B' is contained in the row space of A'. Thus A' and B' have the same row space, and so the theorem is proved.

4.31. Prove Theorem 4.7: Let $A = (a_{ij})$ and $B = (b_{ij})$ be row reduced echelon matrices. Then A and B have the same row space if and only if they have the same nonzero rows.

Obviously, if A and B have the same nonzero rows then they have the same row space. Thus we only have to prove the converse.

Suppose A and B have the same row space, and suppose $R \neq 0$ is the ith row of A. Then there exist scalars $c_1, \ldots, c_s$ such that

$$R = c_1 R_1 + c_2 R_2 + \cdots + c_s R_s \qquad (1)$$

where the R_i are the nonzero rows of B. The theorem is proved if we show that $R = R_i$, or $c_i = 1$ but $c_k = 0$ for $k \neq i$.

Let a_{ij_i} be the distinguished entry in R, i.e. the first nonzero entry of R. By (1) and Problem 4.29,

$$a_{ij_i} = c_1 b_{1j_i} + c_2 b_{2j_i} + \cdots + c_s b_{sj_i} \qquad (2)$$

But by the preceding problem b_{ij_i} is a distinguished entry of B and, since B is row reduced, it is the only nonzero entry in the j_ith column of B. Thus from (2) we obtain $a_{ij_i} = c_i b_{ij_i}$. However, $a_{ij_i} = 1$ and $b_{ij_i} = 1$ since A and B are row reduced; hence $c_i = 1$.

Now suppose $k \neq i$, and b_{kj_k} is the distinguished entry in R_k. By (1) and Problem 4.29,

$$a_{ij_k} = c_1 b_{1j_k} + c_2 b_{2j_k} + \cdots + c_s b_{sj_k} \qquad (3)$$

Since B is row reduced, b_{kj_k} is the only nonzero entry in the j_kth column of B; hence by (3), $a_{ij_k} = c_k b_{kj_k}$. Furthermore, by the preceding problem a_{kj_k} is a distinguished entry of A and, since A is row reduced, $a_{ij_k} = 0$. Thus $c_k b_{kj_k} = 0$ and, since $b_{kj_k} = 1$, $c_k = 0$. Accordingly $R = R_i$ and the theorem is proved.

4.32. Determine whether the following matrices have the same column space:

$$A = \begin{pmatrix} 1 & 3 & 5 \\ 1 & 4 & 3 \\ 1 & 1 & 9 \end{pmatrix}, \qquad B = \begin{pmatrix} 1 & 2 & 3 \\ -2 & -3 & -4 \\ 7 & 12 & 17 \end{pmatrix}$$

Observe that A and B have the same column space if and only if the transposes A^t and B^t have the same row space. Thus reduce A^t and B^t to row reduced echelon form:

$$A^t = \begin{pmatrix} 1 & 1 & 1 \\ 3 & 4 & 1 \\ 5 & 3 & 9 \end{pmatrix} \text{ to } \begin{pmatrix} 1 & 1 & 1 \\ 0 & 1 & -2 \\ 0 & -2 & 4 \end{pmatrix} \text{ to } \begin{pmatrix} 1 & 1 & 1 \\ 0 & 1 & -2 \\ 0 & 0 & 0 \end{pmatrix} \text{ to } \begin{pmatrix} 1 & 0 & 3 \\ 0 & 1 & -2 \\ 0 & 0 & 0 \end{pmatrix}$$

$$B^t = \begin{pmatrix} 1 & -2 & 7 \\ 2 & -3 & 12 \\ 3 & -4 & 17 \end{pmatrix} \text{ to } \begin{pmatrix} 1 & -2 & 7 \\ 0 & 1 & -2 \\ 0 & 2 & -4 \end{pmatrix} \text{ to } \begin{pmatrix} 1 & -2 & 7 \\ 0 & 1 & -2 \\ 0 & 0 & 0 \end{pmatrix} \text{ to } \begin{pmatrix} 1 & 0 & 3 \\ 0 & 1 & -2 \\ 0 & 0 & 0 \end{pmatrix}$$

Since A^t and B^t have the same row space, A and B have the same column space.

4.33. Let R be a row vector and B a matrix for which RB is defined. Show that RB is a linear combination of the rows of B. Furthermore, if A is a matrix for which AB is defined, show that the row space of AB is contained in the row space of B.

Suppose $R = (a_1, a_2, \ldots, a_m)$ and $B = (b_{ij})$. Let $B_1, \ldots, B_m$ denote the rows of B and $B^1, \ldots, B^n$ its columns. Then

$$\begin{aligned}
RB &= (R \cdot B^1, R \cdot B^2, \ldots, R \cdot B^n) \\
&= (a_1 b_{11} + a_2 b_{21} + \cdots + a_m b_{m1}, \; a_1 b_{12} + a_2 b_{22} + \cdots + a_m b_{m2}, \; \ldots, \; a_1 b_{1n} + a_2 b_{2n} + \cdots + a_m b_{mn}) \\
&= a_1(b_{11}, b_{12}, \ldots, b_{1n}) + a_2(b_{21}, b_{22}, \ldots, b_{2n}) + \cdots + a_m(b_{m1}, b_{m2}, \ldots, b_{mn}) \\
&= a_1 B_1 + a_2 B_2 + \cdots + a_m B_m
\end{aligned}$$

Thus RB is a linear combination of the rows of B, as claimed.

By Problem 3.27, the rows of AB are $R_i B$ where R_i is the ith row of A. Hence by the above result each row of AB is in the row space of B. Thus the row space of AB is contained in the row space of B.

SUMS AND DIRECT SUMS

4.34. Let U and W be subspaces of a vector space V. Show that:

   (i) U and W are contained in $U + W$;

   (ii) $U + W$ is the smallest subspace of V containing U and W, that is, $U + W$ is the linear span of U and W: $U + W = L(U, W)$.

   (i)   Let $u \in U$. By hypothesis W is a subspace of V and so $0 \in W$. Hence $u = u + 0 \in U + W$. Accordingly, U is contained in $U + W$. Similarly, W is contained in $U + W$.

   (ii) Since $U + W$ is a subspace of V (Theorem 4.8) containing both U and W, it must also contain the linear span of U and W: $L(U, W) \subset U + W$.

        On the other hand, if $v \in U + W$ then $v = u + w = 1u + 1w$ where $u \in U$ and $w \in W$; hence v is a linear combination of elements in $U \cup W$ and so belongs to $L(U, W)$. Thus $U + W \subset L(U, W)$.

        The two inclusion relations give us the required result.

4.35. Suppose U and W are subspaces of a vector space V, and that $\{u_i\}$ generates U and $\{w_j\}$ generates W. Show that $\{u_i, w_j\}$, i.e. $\{u_i\} \cup \{w_j\}$, generates $U + W$.

Let $v \in U + W$. Then $v = u + w$ where $u \in U$ and $w \in W$. Since $\{u_i\}$ generates U, u is a linear combination of u_i's; and since $\{w_j\}$ generates W, w is a linear combination of w_j's:
$$u = a_1 u_{i_1} + a_2 u_{i_2} + \cdots + a_n u_{i_n}, \qquad a_j \in K$$
$$w = b_1 w_{j_1} + b_2 w_{j_2} + \cdots + b_m w_{j_m}, \qquad b_j \in K$$

Thus $\qquad v = u + w = a_1 u_{i_1} + a_2 u_{i_2} + \cdots + a_n u_{i_n} + b_1 w_{j_1} + b_2 w_{j_2} + \cdots + b_m w_{j_m}$

and so $\{u_i, w_j\}$ generates $U + W$.

4.36. Prove Theorem 4.9: The vector space V is the direct sum of its subspaces U and W if and only if (i) $V = U + W$ and (ii) $U \cap W = \{0\}$.

Suppose $V = U \oplus W$. Then any $v \in V$ can be uniquely written in the form $v = u + w$ where $u \in U$ and $w \in W$. Thus, in particular, $V = U + W$. Now suppose $v \in U \cap W$. Then:

(1) $v = v + 0$ where $v \in U$, $0 \in W$; and (2) $v = 0 + v$ where $0 \in U$, $v \in W$

Since such a sum for v must be unique, $v = 0$. Accordingly, $U \cap W = \{0\}$.

On the other hand, suppose $V = U + W$ and $U \cap W = \{0\}$. Let $v \in V$. Since $V = U + W$, there exist $u \in U$ and $w \in W$ such that $v = u + w$. We need to show that such a sum is unique. Suppose also that $v = u' + w'$ where $u' \in U$ and $w' \in W$. Then
$$u + w = u' + w' \quad \text{and so} \quad u - u' = w' - w$$

But $u - u' \in U$ and $w' - w \in W$; hence by $U \cap W = \{0\}$,
$$u - u' = 0, \quad w' - w = 0 \quad \text{and so} \quad u = u', \quad w = w'$$

Thus such a sum for $v \in V$ is unique and $V = U \oplus W$.

4.37. Let U and W be the subspaces of $\mathbf{R}^3$ defined by
$$U = \{(a, b, c): a = b = c\} \quad \text{and} \quad W = \{(0, b, c)\}$$
(Note that W is the yz plane.) Show that $\mathbf{R}^3 = U \oplus W$.

Note first that $U \cap W = \{0\}$, for $v = (a, b, c) \in U \cap W$ implies that
$$a = b = c \text{ and } a = 0 \quad \text{which implies} \quad a = 0, \ b = 0, \ c = 0$$
i.e. $v = (0, 0, 0)$.

We also claim that $\mathbf{R}^3 = U + W$. For if $v = (a, b, c) \in \mathbf{R}^3$, then $v = (a, a, a) + (0, b - a, c - a)$ where $(a, a, a) \in U$ and $(0, b - a, c - a) \in W$. Both conditions, $U \cap W = \{0\}$ and $\mathbf{R}^3 = U + W$, imply $\mathbf{R}^3 = U \oplus W$.

4.38. Let V be the vector space of n-square matrices over a field $\mathbf{R}$. Let U and W be the subspaces of symmetric and antisymmetric matrices, respectively. Show that $V = U \oplus W$. (The matrix M is symmetric iff $M = M^t$, and anti-symmetric iff $M^t = -M$.)

We first show that $V = U + W$. Let A be any arbitrary n-square matrix. Note that
$$A = \tfrac{1}{2}(A + A^t) + \tfrac{1}{2}(A - A^t)$$

We claim that $\tfrac{1}{2}(A + A^t) \in U$ and that $\tfrac{1}{2}(A - A^t) \in W$. For
$$(\tfrac{1}{2}(A + A^t))^t = \tfrac{1}{2}(A + A^t)^t = \tfrac{1}{2}(A^t + A^{tt}) = \tfrac{1}{2}(A + A^t)$$
that is, $\tfrac{1}{2}(A + A^t)$ is symmetric. Furthermore,
$$(\tfrac{1}{2}(A - A^t))^t = \tfrac{1}{2}(A - A^t)^t = \tfrac{1}{2}(A^t - A) = -\tfrac{1}{2}(A - A^t)$$
that is, $\tfrac{1}{2}(A - A^t)$ is antisymmetric.

We next show that $U \cap W = \{0\}$. Suppose $M \in U \cap W$. Then $M = M^t$ and $M^t = -M$ which implies $M = -M$ or $M = 0$. Hence $U \cap W = \{0\}$. Accordingly, $V = U \oplus W$.

Supplementary Problems

VECTOR SPACES

4.39. Let V be the set of infinite sequences $(a_1, a_2, \ldots)$ in a field K with addition in V and scalar multiplication on V defined by

$$(a_1, a_2, \ldots) + (b_1, b_2, \ldots) = (a_1 + b_1, a_2 + b_2, \ldots)$$

$$k(a_1, a_2, \ldots) = (ka_1, ka_2, \ldots)$$

where $a_i, b_j, k \in K$. Show that V is a vector space over K.

4.40. Let V be the set of ordered pairs (a, b) of real numbers with addition in V and scalar multiplication on V defined by
$$(a, b) + (c, d) = (a + c, b + d) \quad \text{and} \quad k(a, b) = (ka, 0)$$

Show that V satisfies all of the axioms of a vector space except $[M_4]$: $1u = u$. Hence $[M_4]$ is not a consequence of the other axioms.

4.41. Let V be the set of ordered pairs (a, b) of real numbers. Show that V is not a vector space over $\mathbf{R}$ with addition in V and scalar multiplication on V defined by:

(i) $(a, b) + (c, d) = (a + d, b + c)$ and $k(a, b) = (ka, kb)$;

(ii) $(a, b) + (c, d) = (a + c, b + d)$ and $k(a, b) = (a, b)$;

(iii) $(a, b) + (c, d) = (0, 0)$ and $k(a, b) = (ka, kb)$;

(iv) $(a, b) + (c, d) = (ac, bd)$ and $k(a, b) = (ka, kb)$.

4.42. Let V be the set of ordered pairs (z_1, z_2) of complex numbers. Show that V is a vector space over the real field $\mathbf{R}$ with addition in V and scalar multiplication on V defined by

$$(z_1, z_2) + (w_1, w_2) = (z_1 + w_1, z_2 + w_2) \quad \text{and} \quad k(z_1, z_2) = (kz_1, kz_2)$$

where $z_1, z_2, w_1, w_2 \in \mathbf{C}$ and $k \in \mathbf{R}$.

4.43. Let V be a vector space over K, and let F be a subfield of K. Show that V is also a vector space over F where vector addition with respect to F is the same as that with respect to K, and where scalar multiplication by an element $k \in F$ is the same as multiplication by k as an element of K.

4.44. Show that $[A_4]$, page 63, can be derived from the other axioms of a vector space.

4.45. Let U and W be vector spaces over a field K. Let V be the set of ordered pairs (u, w) where u belongs to U and w to W: $V = \{(u, w): u \in U, w \in W\}$. Show that V is a vector space over K with addition in V and scalar multiplication on V defined by

$$(u, w) + (u', w') = (u + u', w + w') \quad \text{and} \quad k(u, w) = (ku, kw)$$

where $u, u' \in U$, $w, w' \in W$ and $k \in K$. (This space V is called the *external direct sum* of U and W.)

SUBSPACES

4.46. Consider the vector space V in Problem 4.39, of infinite sequences $(a_1, a_2, \ldots)$ in a field K. Show that W is a subspace of V if:

(i) W consists of all sequences with 0 as the first component;

(ii) W consists of all sequences with only a finite number of nonzero components.

4.47. Determine whether or not W is a subspace of $\mathbf{R}^3$ if W consists of those vectors $(a, b, c) \in \mathbf{R}^3$ for which: (i) $a = 2b$; (ii) $a \le b \le c$; (iii) $ab = 0$; (iv) $a = b = c$; (v) $a = b^2$; (vi) $k_1 a + k_2 b + k_3 c = 0$, where $k_i \in \mathbf{R}$.

4.48. Let V be the vector space of n-square matrices over a field K. Show that W is a subspace of V if W consists of all matrices which are (i) antisymmetric ($A^t = -A$), (ii) (upper) triangular, (iii) diagonal, (iv) scalar.

4.49.   Let $AX = B$ be a nonhomogeneous system of linear equations in n unknowns over a field K. Show that the solution set of the system is not a subspace of K^n.

4.50.   Let V be the vector space of all functions from the real field $\mathbf{R}$ into $\mathbf{R}$. Show that W is a subspace of V in each of the following cases.

   (i) W consists of all bounded functions. (Here $f : \mathbf{R} \to \mathbf{R}$ is bounded if there exists $M \in \mathbf{R}$ such that $|f(x)| \leq M$, $\forall x \in \mathbf{R}$.)

   (ii) W consists of all even functions. (Here $f : \mathbf{R} \to \mathbf{R}$ is even if $f(-x) = f(x)$, $\forall x \in \mathbf{R}$.)

   (iii) W consists of all continuous functions.

   (iv) W consists of all differentiable functions.

   (v) W consists of all integrable functions in, say, the interval $0 \leq x \leq 1$.

   (The last three cases require some knowledge of analysis.)

4.51.   Discuss whether or not $\mathbf{R}^2$ is a subspace of $\mathbf{R}^3$.

4.52.   Prove Theorem 4.4: The intersection of any number of subspaces of a vector space V is a subspace of V.

4.53.   Suppose U and W are subspaces of V for which $U \cup W$ is also a subspace. Show that either $U \subset W$ or $W \subset U$.

LINEAR COMBINATIONS

4.54.   Consider the vectors $u = (1, -3, 2)$ and $v = (2, -1, 1)$ in $\mathbf{R}^3$.

   (i)   Write $(1, 7, -4)$ as a linear combination of u and v.

   (ii)   Write $(2, -5, 4)$ as a linear combination of u and v.

   (iii) For which value of k is $(1, k, 5)$ a linear combination of u and v?

   (iv)   Find a condition on a, b and c so that (a, b, c) is a linear combination of u and v.

4.55.   Write u as a linear combination of the polynomials $v = 2t^2 + 3t - 4$ and $w = t^2 - 2t - 3$ where (i) $u = 3t^2 + 8t - 5$, (ii) $u = 4t^2 - 6t - 1$.

4.56.   Write E as a linear combination of $A = \begin{pmatrix} 1 & 1 \\ 0 & -1 \end{pmatrix}$, $B = \begin{pmatrix} 1 & 1 \\ -1 & 0 \end{pmatrix}$ and $C = \begin{pmatrix} 1 & -1 \\ 0 & 0 \end{pmatrix}$

   where: (i) $E = \begin{pmatrix} 3 & -1 \\ 1 & -2 \end{pmatrix}$;   (ii) $E = \begin{pmatrix} 2 & 1 \\ -1 & -2 \end{pmatrix}$.

LINEAR SPANS, GENERATORS

4.57.   Show that $(1, 1, 1)$, $(0, 1, 1)$ and $(0, 1, -1)$ generate $\mathbf{R}^3$, i.e. that any vector (a, b, c) is a linear combination of the given vectors.

4.58.   Show that the yz plane $W = \{(0, b, c)\}$ in $\mathbf{R}^3$ is generated by: (i) $(0, 1, 1)$ and $(0, 2, -1)$; (ii) $(0, 1, 2)$, $(0, 2, 3)$ and $(0, 3, 1)$.

4.59.   Show that the complex numbers $w = 2 + 3i$ and $z = 1 - 2i$ generate the complex field $\mathbf{C}$ as a vector space over the real field $\mathbf{R}$.

4.60.   Show that the polynomials $(1 - t)^3$, $(1 - t)^2$, $1 - t$ and 1 generate the space of polynomials of degree ≤ 3.

4.61.   Find one vector in $\mathbf{R}^3$ which generates the intersection of U and W where U is the xy plane: $U = \{(a, b, 0)\}$, and W is the space generated by the vectors $(1, 2, 3)$ and $(1, -1, 1)$.

4.62.   Prove: $L(S)$ is the intersection of all the subspaces of V containing S.

4.63. Show that $L(S) = L(S \cup \{0\})$. That is, by joining or deleting the zero vector from a set, we do not change the space generated by the set.

4.64. Show that if $S \subset T$, then $L(S) \subset L(T)$.

4.65. Show that $L(L(S)) = L(S)$.

ROW SPACE OF A MATRIX

4.66. Determine which of the following matrices have the same row space:

$$A = \begin{pmatrix} 1 & -2 & -1 \\ 3 & -4 & 5 \end{pmatrix}, \quad B = \begin{pmatrix} 1 & -1 & 2 \\ 2 & 3 & -1 \end{pmatrix}, \quad C = \begin{pmatrix} 1 & -1 & 3 \\ 2 & -1 & 10 \\ 3 & -5 & 1 \end{pmatrix}$$

4.67. Let
$$u_1 = (1, 1, -1), \quad u_2 = (2, 3, -1), \quad u_3 = (3, 1, -5)$$
$$v_1 = (1, -1, -3), \quad v_2 = (3, -2, -8), \quad v_3 = (2, 1, -3)$$

Show that the subspace of $\mathbf{R}^3$ generated by the u_i is the same as the subspace generated by the v_i.

4.68. Show that if any row of an echelon (row reduced echelon) matrix is deleted, then the resulting matrix is still in echelon (row reduced echelon) form.

4.69. Prove the converse of Theorem 4.6: Matrices with the same row space (and the same size) are row equivalent.

4.70. Show that A and B have the same column space iff A^t and B^t have the same row space.

4.71. Let A and B be matrices for which AB is defined. Show that the column space of AB is contained in the column space of A.

SUMS AND DIRECT SUMS

4.72. We extend the notion of sum to arbitrary nonempty subsets (not necessarily subspaces) S and T of a vector space V by defining $S + T = \{s + t : s \in S, \ t \in T\}$. Show that this operation satisfies:

(i)   commutative law: $S + T = T + S$;

(ii) associative law: $(S_1 + S_2) + S_3 = S_1 + (S_2 + S_3)$;

(iii) $S + \{0\} = \{0\} + S = S$;

(iv) $S + V = V + S = V$.

4.73. Show that for any subspace W of a vector space V, $W + W = W$.

4.74. Give an example of a subset S of a vector space V which is not a subspace of V but for which (i) $S + S = S$, (ii) $S + S \subset S$ (properly contained).

4.75. We extend the notion of sum of subspaces to more than two summands as follows. If $W_1, W_2, \ldots, W_n$ are subspaces of V, then
$$W_1 + W_2 + \cdots + W_n = \{w_1 + w_2 + \cdots + w_n : w_i \in W_i\}$$
Show that:

(i) $L(W_1, W_2, \ldots, W_n) = W_1 + W_2 + \cdots + W_n$;

(ii) if S_i generates W_i, $i = 1, \ldots, n$, then $S_1 \cup S_2 \cup \cdots \cup S_n$ generates $W_1 + W_2 + \cdots + W_n$.

4.76. Suppose U, V and W are subspaces of a vector space. Prove that
$$(U \cap V) + (U \cap W) \ \subset \ U \cap (V + W)$$

Find subspaces of $\mathbf{R}^2$ for which equality does not hold.

4.77. Let U, V and W be the following subspaces of $\mathbf{R}^3$:
$$U = \{(a,b,c): a+b+c=0\}, \quad V = \{(a,b,c): a=c\}, \quad W = \{(0,0,c): c \in \mathbf{R}\}$$
Show that (i) $\mathbf{R}^3 = U + V$, (ii) $\mathbf{R}^3 = U + W$, (iii) $\mathbf{R}^3 = V + W$. When is the sum direct?

4.78. Let V be the vector space of all functions from the real field $\mathbf{R}$ into $\mathbf{R}$. Let U be the subspace of even functions and W the subspace of odd functions. Show that $V = U \oplus W$. (Recall that f is even iff $f(-x) = f(x)$, and f is odd iff $f(-x) = -f(x)$.)

4.79. Let $W_1, W_2, \ldots$ be subspaces of a vector space V for which $W_1 \subset W_2 \subset \cdots$. Let $W = W_1 \cup W_2 \cup \cdots$. Show that W is a subspace of V.

4.80. In the preceding problem, suppose S_i generates W_i, $i = 1, 2, \ldots$. Show that $S = S_1 \cup S_2 \cup \cdots$ generates W.

4.81. Let V be the vector space of n-square matrices over a field K. Let U be the subspace of upper triangular matrices and W the subspace of lower triangular matrices. Find (i) $U + W$, (ii) $U \cap W$.

4.82. Let V be the external direct sum of the vector spaces U and W over a field K. (See Problem 4.45.) Let
$$\hat{U} = \{(u,0): u \in U\}, \quad \hat{W} = \{(0,w): w \in W\}$$
Show that (i) $\hat{U}$ and $\hat{W}$ are subspaces of V, (ii) $V = \hat{U} \oplus \hat{W}$.

Answers to Supplementary Problems

4.47. (i) Yes.   (iv) Yes.

(ii) No; e.g. $(1,2,3) \in W$ but $-2(1,2,3) \notin W$.   (v) No; e.g. $(9,3,0) \in W$ but $2(9,3,0) \notin W$.

(iii) No; e.g. $(1,0,0)$, $(0,1,0) \in W$,   (vi) Yes.
but not their sum.

4.50. (i) Let $f, g \in W$ with M_f and M_g bounds for f and g respectively. Then for any scalars $a, b \in \mathbf{R}$,
$$|(af+bg)(x)| = |af(x)+bg(x)| \leq |af(x)| + |bg(x)| = |a|\,|f(x)| + |b|\,|g(x)| \leq |a|M_f + |b|M_g$$
That is, $|a|M_f + |b|M_g$ is a bound for the function $af + bg$.

(ii) $(af+bg)(-x) = af(-x) + bg(-x) = af(x) + bg(x) = (af+bg)(x)$

4.51. No. Although one may "identify" the vector $(a,b) \in \mathbf{R}^2$ with, say, $(a,b,0)$ in the xy plane in $\mathbf{R}^3$, they are distinct elements belonging to distinct, disjoint sets.

4.54. (i) $-3u + 2v$. (ii) Impossible. (iii) $k = -8$. (iv) $a - 3b - 5c = 0$.

4.55. (i) $u = 2v - w$. (ii) Impossible.

4.56. (i) $E = 2A - B + 2C$. (ii) Impossible.

4.61. $(2, -5, 0)$.

4.66. A and C.

4.67. Form the matrix A whose rows are the u_i and the matrix B whose rows are the v_i, and then show that A and B have the same row canonical forms.

4.74. (i) In $\mathbf{R}^2$, let $S = \{(0,0), (0,1), (0,2), (0,3), \ldots\}$.

(ii) In $\mathbf{R}^2$, let $S = \{(0,5), (0,6), (0,7), \ldots\}$.

4.77. The sum is direct in (ii) and (iii).

4.78. *Hint.* $f(x) = \frac{1}{2}(f(x) + f(-x)) + \frac{1}{2}(f(x) - f(-x))$, where $\frac{1}{2}(f(x) + f(-x))$ is even and $\frac{1}{2}(f(x) - f(-x))$ is odd.

4.81. (i) $V = U + W$. (ii) $U \cap W$ is the space of diagonal matrices.

Chapter 5

Basis and Dimension

INTRODUCTION

Some of the fundamental results proven in this chapter are:

(i) The "dimension" of a vector space is well defined (Theorem 5.3).

(ii) If V has dimension n over K, then V is "isomorphic" to K^n (Theorem 5.12).

(iii) A system of linear equations has a solution if and only if the coefficient and augmented matrices have the same "rank" (Theorem 5.10).

These concepts and results are nontrivial and answer certain questions raised and investigated by mathematicians of yesterday.

We will begin the chapter with the definition of linear dependence and independence. This concept plays an essential role in the theory of linear algebra and in mathematics in general.

LINEAR DEPENDENCE

Definition: Let V be a vector space over a field K. The vectors $v_1, \ldots, v_m \in V$ are said to be *linearly dependent over K*, or simply *dependent*, if there exist scalars $a_1, \ldots, a_m \in K$, not all of them 0, such that

$$a_1 v_1 + a_2 v_2 + \cdots + a_m v_m = 0 \qquad (*)$$

Otherwise, the vectors are said to be *linearly independent over K*, or simply *independent*.

Observe that the relation $(*)$ will always hold if the a's are all 0. If this relation holds only in this case, that is,

$$a_1 v_1 + a_2 v_2 + \cdots + a_m v_m = 0 \qquad \text{only if} \quad a_1 = 0, \ldots, a_m = 0$$

then the vectors are linearly independent. On the other hand, if the relation $(*)$ also holds when one of the a's is not 0, then the vectors are linearly dependent.

Observe that if 0 is one of the vectors $v_1, \ldots, v_m$, say $v_1 = 0$, then the vectors must be dependent; for

$$1 v_1 + 0 v_2 + \cdots + 0 v_m = 1 \cdot 0 + 0 + \cdots + 0 = 0$$

and the coefficient of v_1 is not 0. On the other hand, any nonzero vector v is, by itself, independent; for

$$kv = 0, \ v \neq 0 \quad \text{implies} \quad k = 0$$

Other examples of dependent and independent vectors follow.

Example 5.1: The vectors $u = (1, -1, 0)$, $v = (1, 3, -1)$ and $w = (5, 3, -2)$ are dependent since, for $3u + 2v - w = 0$,

$$3(1, -1, 0) + 2(1, 3, -1) - (5, 3, -2) = (0, 0, 0)$$

Example 5.2:   We show that the vectors $u = (6, 2, 3, 4)$, $v = (0, 5, -3, 1)$ and $w = (0, 0, 7, -2)$ are independent. For suppose $xu + yv + zw = 0$ where x, y and z are unknown scalars. Then

$$(0, 0, 0, 0) \; = \; x(6, 2, 3, 4) \, + \, y(0, 5, -3, 1) \, + \, z(0, 0, 7, -2)$$

$$= \; (6x, \, 2x + 5y, \, 3x - 3y + 7z, \, 4x + y - 2z)$$

and so, by the equality of the corresponding components,

$$6x \qquad\qquad\quad = \; 0$$
$$2x + 5y \qquad\quad = \; 0$$
$$3x - 3y + 7z \; = \; 0$$
$$4x + \;\; y - 2z \; = \; 0$$

The first equation yields $x = 0$; the second equation with $x = 0$ yields $y = 0$; and the third equation with $x = 0$, $y = 0$ yields $z = 0$. Thus

$$xu + yv + zw \; = \; 0 \qquad \text{implies} \qquad x = 0, \; y = 0, \; z = 0$$

Accordingly u, v and w are independent.

Observe that the vectors in the preceding example form a matrix in echelon form:

$$\begin{pmatrix} 6 & 2 & 3 & 4 \\ 0 & 5 & -3 & 1 \\ 0 & 0 & 7 & -2 \end{pmatrix}$$

Thus we have shown that the (nonzero) rows of the above echelon matrix are independent. This result holds true in general; we state it formally as a theorem since it will be frequently used.

Theorem 5.1:   The nonzero rows of a matrix in echelon form are linearly independent.

For more than one vector, the concept of dependence can be defined equivalently as follows:

The vectors $v_1, \ldots, v_m$ are linearly dependent if and only if one of them is a linear combination of the others.

For suppose, say, v_i is a linear combination of the others:

$$v_i \; = \; a_1 v_1 + \, \cdots \, + a_{i-1} v_{i-1} + a_{i+1} v_{i+1} + \, \cdots \, + a_m v_m$$

Then by adding $-v_i$ to both sides, we obtain

$$a_1 v_1 + \, \cdots \, + a_{i-1} v_{i-1} - v_i + a_{i+1} v_{i+1} + \, \cdots \, + a_m v_m \; = \; 0$$

where the coefficient of v_i is not 0; hence the vectors are linearly dependent. Conversely, suppose the vectors are linearly dependent, say,

$$b_1 v_1 + \, \cdots \, + b_j v_j + \, \cdots \, + b_m v_m \; = \; 0 \qquad \text{where } b_j \neq 0$$

Then $\qquad v_j \; = \; -b_j^{-1} b_1 v_1 - \, \cdots \, - b_j^{-1} b_{j-1} v_{j-1} - b_j^{-1} b_{j+1} v_{j+1} - \, \cdots \, - b_j^{-1} b_m v_m$

and so v_j is a linear combination of the other vectors.

We now make a slightly stronger statement than that above; this result has many important consequences.

Lemma 5.2:   The nonzero vectors $v_1, \ldots, v_m$ are linearly dependent if and only if one of them, say v_i, is a linear combination of the preceding vectors:

$$v_i \; = \; k_1 v_1 + k_2 v_2 + \, \cdots \, + k_{i-1} v_{i-1}$$

Remark 1.   The set $\{v_1, \ldots, v_m\}$ is called a *dependent* or *independent set* according as the vectors $v_1, \ldots, v_m$ are dependent or independent. We also define the empty set $\emptyset$ to be independent.

Remark 2.   If two of the vectors $v_1, \ldots, v_m$ are equal, say $v_1 = v_2$, then the vectors are dependent. For
$$v_1 - v_2 + 0v_3 + \cdots + 0v_m = 0$$
and the coefficient of v_1 is not 0.

Remark 3.   Two vectors v_1 and v_2 are dependent if and only if one of them is a multiple of the other.

Remark 4.   A set which contains a dependent subset is itself dependent. Hence any subset of an independent set is independent.

Remark 5.   If the set $\{v_1, \ldots, v_m\}$ is independent, then any rearrangement of the vectors $\{v_{i_1}, v_{i_2}, \ldots, v_{i_m}\}$ is also independent.

Remark 6.   In the real space $\mathbf{R}^3$, dependence of vectors can be described geometrically as follows: any two vectors u and v are dependent if and only if they lie on the same line through the origin; and any three vectors u, v and w are dependent if and only if they lie on the same plane through the origin:

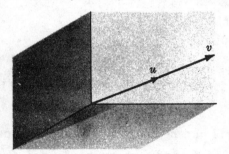   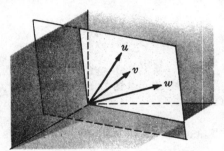

u and v are dependent.   u, v and w are dependent.

BASIS AND DIMENSION

We begin with a definition.

Definition: A vector space V is said to be of *finite dimension* n or to be *n-dimensional*, written $\dim V = n$, if there exists linearly independent vectors $e_1, e_2, \ldots, e_n$ which span V. The sequence $\{e_1, e_2, \ldots, e_n\}$ is then called a *basis* of V.

The above definition of dimension is well defined in view of the following theorem.

Theorem 5.3:   Let V be a finite dimensional vector space. Then every basis of V has the same number of elements.

The vector space $\{0\}$ is defined to have dimension 0. (In a certain sense this agrees with the above definition since, by definition, $\emptyset$ is independent and generates $\{0\}$.) When a vector space is not of finite dimension, it is said to be of *infinite dimension*.

> **Example 5.3:**   Let K be any field. Consider the vector space K^n which consists of n-tuples of elements of K. The vectors
> $$e_1 = (1, 0, 0, \ldots, 0, 0)$$
> $$e_2 = (0, 1, 0, \ldots, 0, 0)$$
> $$\cdots\cdots\cdots\cdots\cdots\cdots\cdots$$
> $$e_n = (0, 0, 0, \ldots, 0, 1)$$
> form a basis, called the *usual basis*, of K^n. Thus K^n has dimension n.

Example 5.4:   Let U be the vector space of all 2×3 matrices over a field K. Then the matrices

$$\begin{pmatrix} 1 & 0 & 0 \\ 0 & 0 & 0 \end{pmatrix}, \quad \begin{pmatrix} 0 & 1 & 0 \\ 0 & 0 & 0 \end{pmatrix}, \quad \begin{pmatrix} 0 & 0 & 1 \\ 0 & 0 & 0 \end{pmatrix},$$

$$\begin{pmatrix} 0 & 0 & 0 \\ 1 & 0 & 0 \end{pmatrix}, \quad \begin{pmatrix} 0 & 0 & 0 \\ 0 & 1 & 0 \end{pmatrix}, \quad \begin{pmatrix} 0 & 0 & 0 \\ 0 & 0 & 1 \end{pmatrix}$$

form a basis of U. Thus $\dim U = 6$. More generally, let V be the vector space of all $m \times n$ matrices over K and let $E_{ij} \in V$ be the matrix with ij-entry 1 and 0 elsewhere. Then the set $\{E_{ij}\}$ is a basis, called the *usual basis*, of V (Problem 5.32); consequently $\dim V = mn$.

Example 5.5:   Let W be the vector space of polynomials (in t) of degree $\le n$. The set $\{1, t, t^2, \ldots, t^n\}$ is linearly independent and generates W. Thus it is a basis of W and so $\dim W = n + 1$.

We comment that the vector space V of all polynomials is not finite dimensional since (Problem 4.26) no finite set of polynomials generates V.

The above fundamental theorem on dimension is a consequence of the following important "replacement lemma":

Lemma 5.4:   Suppose the set $\{v_1, v_2, \ldots, v_n\}$ generates a vector space V. If $\{w_1, \ldots, w_m\}$ is linearly independent, then $m \le n$ and V is generated by a set of the form

$$\{w_1, \ldots, w_m, v_{i_1}, \ldots, v_{i_{n-m}}\}$$

Thus, in particular, any $n + 1$ or more vectors in V are linearly dependent.

Observe in the above lemma that we have replaced m of the vectors in the generating set by the m independent vectors and still retained a generating set.

Now suppose S is a subset of a vector space V. We call $\{v_1, \ldots, v_m\}$ a *maximal independent subset* of S if:

(i) it is an independent subset of S; and

(ii) $\{v_1, \ldots, v_m, w\}$ is dependent for any $w \in S$.

The following theorem applies.

Theorem 5.5:   Suppose S generates V and $\{v_1, \ldots, v_m\}$ is a maximal independent subset of S. Then $\{v_1, \ldots, v_m\}$ is a basis of V.

The main relationship between the dimension of a vector space and its independent subsets is contained in the next theorem.

Theorem 5.6:   Let V be of finite dimension n. Then:

(i) Any set of $n + 1$ or more vectors is linearly dependent.

(ii) Any linearly independent set is part of a basis, i.e. can be extended to a basis.

(iii) A linearly independent set with n elements is a basis.

Example 5.6:   The four vectors in K^4

$$(1, 1, 1, 1), \quad (0, 1, 1, 1), \quad (0, 0, 1, 1), \quad (0, 0, 0, 1)$$

are linearly independent since they form a matrix in echelon form. Furthermore, since $\dim K^4 = 4$, they form a basis of K^4.

Example 5.7:   The four vectors in $\mathbf{R}^3$,

$$(257, -132, 58), \quad (43, 0, -17), \quad (521, -317, 94), \quad (328, -512, -731)$$

must be linearly dependent since they come from a vector space of dimension 3.

DIMENSION AND SUBSPACES

The following theorems give basic relationships between the dimension of a vector space and the dimension of a subspace.

Theorem 5.7:   Let W be a subspace of an n-dimensional vector space V. Then $\dim W \leqslant n$. In particular if $\dim W = n$, then $W = V$.

> **Example 5.8:**   Let W be a subspace of the real space $\mathbf{R}^3$. Now $\dim \mathbf{R}^3 = 3$; hence by the preceding theorem the dimension of W can only be 0, 1, 2 or 3. The following cases apply:
>
>   (i) $\dim W = 0$, then $W = \{0\}$, a point;
>   (ii) $\dim W = 1$, then W is a line through the origin;
>   (iii) $\dim W = 2$, then W is a plane through the origin;
>   (iv) $\dim W = 3$, then W is the entire space $\mathbf{R}^3$.

Theorem 5.8:   Let U and W be finite-dimensional subspaces of a vector space V. Then $U + W$ has finite dimension and

$$\dim (U + V) \;=\; \dim U \,+\, \dim W \,-\, \dim (U \cap W)$$

Note that if V is the direct sum of U and W, i.e. $V = U \oplus W$, then $\dim V = \dim U + \dim W$ (Problem 5.48).

> **Example 5.9:**   Suppose U and W are the xy plane and yz plane, respectively, in $\mathbf{R}^3$: $U = \{(a, b, 0)\}$, $W = \{(0, b, c)\}$. Since $\mathbf{R}^3 = U + W$, $\dim (U + W) = 3$. Also, $\dim U = 2$ and $\dim W = 2$. By the above theorem,
>
> $$3 = 2 + 2 - \dim (U \cap W) \qquad \text{or} \qquad \dim (U \cap W) = 1$$
>
> Observe that this agrees with the fact that $U \cap W$ is the y axis, i.e. $U \cap W = \{(0, b, 0)\}$, and so has dimension 1.

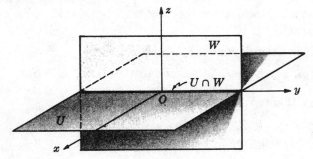

RANK OF A MATRIX

Let A be an arbitrary $m \times n$ matrix over a field K. Recall that the row space of A is the subspace of K^n generated by its rows, and the column space of A is the subspace of K^m generated by its columns. The dimensions of the row space and of the column space of A are called, respectively, the *row rank* and the *column rank* of A.

Theorem 5.9:   The row rank and the column rank of the matrix A are equal.

Definition: The *rank* of the matrix A, written rank (A), is the common value of its row rank and column rank.

Thus the rank of a matrix gives the maximum number of independent rows, and also the maximum number of independent columns. We can obtain the rank of a matrix as follows.

Suppose $A = \begin{pmatrix} 1 & 2 & 0 & -1 \\ 2 & 6 & -3 & -3 \\ 3 & 10 & -6 & -5 \end{pmatrix}$. We reduce A to echelon form using the elementary row operations:

$$A \text{ to } \begin{pmatrix} 1 & 2 & 0 & -1 \\ 0 & 2 & -3 & -1 \\ 0 & 4 & -6 & -2 \end{pmatrix} \text{ to } \begin{pmatrix} 1 & 2 & 0 & -1 \\ 0 & 2 & -3 & -1 \\ 0 & 0 & 0 & 0 \end{pmatrix}$$

Recall that row equivalent matrices have the same row space. Thus the nonzero rows of the echelon matrix, which are independent by Theorem 5.1, form a basis of the row space of A. Hence the rank of A is 2.

APPLICATIONS TO LINEAR EQUATIONS

Consider a system of m linear equations in n unknowns $x_1, \ldots, x_n$ over a field K:

$$a_{11}x_1 + a_{12}x_2 + \cdots + a_{1n}x_n = b_1$$
$$a_{21}x_1 + a_{22}x_2 + \cdots + a_{2n}x_n = b_2$$
$$\cdots\cdots\cdots\cdots\cdots\cdots\cdots\cdots\cdots$$
$$a_{m1}x_1 + a_{m2}x_2 + \cdots + a_{mn}x_n = b_m$$

or the equivalent matrix equation

$$AX = B$$

where $A = (a_{ij})$ is the coefficient matrix, and $X = (x_i)$ and $B = (b_i)$ are the column vectors consisting of the unknowns and of the constants, respectively. Recall that the *augmented matrix* of the system is defined to be the matrix

$$(A, B) = \begin{pmatrix} a_{11} & a_{12} & \ldots & a_{1n} & b_1 \\ a_{21} & a_{22} & \ldots & a_{2n} & b_2 \\ \cdots\cdots\cdots\cdots\cdots\cdots\cdots\cdots \\ a_{m1} & a_{m2} & \ldots & a_{mn} & b_m \end{pmatrix}$$

Remark 1. The above linear equations are said to be dependent or independent according as the corresponding vectors, i.e. the rows of the augmented matrix, are dependent or independent.

Remark 2. Two systems of linear equations are equivalent if and only if the corresponding augmented matrices are row equivalent, i.e. have the same row space.

Remark 3. We can always replace a system of equations by a system of independent equations, such as a system in echelon form. The number of independent equations will always be equal to the rank of the augmented matrix.

Observe that the above system is also equivalent to the vector equation

$$x_1 \begin{pmatrix} a_{11} \\ a_{21} \\ .. \\ a_{m1} \end{pmatrix} + x_2 \begin{pmatrix} a_{12} \\ a_{22} \\ .. \\ a_{m2} \end{pmatrix} + \cdots + x_n \begin{pmatrix} a_{1n} \\ a_{2n} \\ .. \\ a_{mn} \end{pmatrix} = \begin{pmatrix} b_1 \\ b_2 \\ .. \\ b_m \end{pmatrix}$$

Thus the system $AX = B$ has a solution if and only if the column vector B is a linear combination of the columns of the matrix A, i.e. belongs to the column space of A. This gives us the following basic existence theorem.

Theorem 5.10: The system of linear equations $AX = B$ has a solution if and only if the coefficient matrix A and the augmented matrix (A, B) have the same rank.

Recall (Theorem 2.1) that if the system $AX = B$ does have a solution, say v, then its general solution is of the form $v + W = \{v + w : w \in W\}$ where W is the general solution of the associated homogeneous system $AX = 0$. Now W is a subspace of K^n and so has a dimension. The next theorem, whose proof is postponed until the next chapter (page 127), applies.

Theorem 5.11:   The dimension of the solution space W of the homogeneous system of linear equations $AX = 0$ is $n - r$ where n is the number of unknowns and r is the rank of the coefficient matrix A.

In case the system $AX = 0$ is in echelon form, then it has precisely $n - r$ free variables (see page 21), say, $x_{i_1}, x_{i_2}, \ldots, x_{i_{n-r}}$. Let v_j be the solution obtained by setting $x_{i_j} = 1$, and all other free variables $= 0$. Then the solutions $v_1, \ldots, v_{n-r}$ are linearly independent (Problem 5.43) and so form a basis for the solution space.

Example 5.10:   Find the dimension and a basis of the solution space W of the system of linear equations

$$x + 2y - 4z + 3r - s = 0$$
$$x + 2y - 2z + 2r + s = 0$$
$$2x + 4y - 2z + 3r + 4s = 0$$

Reduce the system to echelon form:

$$x + 2y - 4z + 3r - s = 0$$
$$2z - r + 2s = 0 \qquad \text{and then}$$
$$6z - 3r + 6s = 0$$

$$x + 2y - 4z + 3r - s = 0$$
$$2z - r + 2s = 0$$

There are 5 unknowns and 2 (nonzero) equations in echelon form; hence $\dim W = 5 - 2 = 3$. Note that the free variables are y, r and s. Set:

(i) $y = 1$, $r = 0$, $s = 0$,   (ii) $y = 0$, $r = 1$, $s = 0$,   (iii) $y = 0$, $r = 0$, $s = 1$

to obtain the following respective solutions:

$$v_1 = (-2, 1, 0, 0, 0), \quad v_2 = (-1, 0, \tfrac{1}{2}, 1, 0), \quad v_3 = (-3, 0, -1, 0, 1)$$

The set $\{v_1, v_2, v_3\}$ is a basis of the solution space W.

COORDINATES

Let $\{e_1, \ldots, e_n\}$ be a basis of an n-dimensional vector space V over a field K, and let v be any vector in V. Since $\{e_i\}$ generates V, v is a linear combination of the e_i:

$$v = a_1 e_1 + a_2 e_2 + \cdots + a_n e_n, \quad a_i \in K$$

Since the e_i are independent, such a representation is unique (Problem 5.7), i.e. the n scalars $a_1, \ldots, a_n$ are completely determined by the vector v and the basis $\{e_i\}$. We call these scalars the *coordinates* of v in $\{e_i\}$, and we call the n-tuple $(a_1, \ldots, a_n)$ the *coordinate vector* of v relative to $\{e_i\}$ and denote it by $[v]_e$ or simply $[v]$:

$$[v]_e = (a_1, a_2, \ldots, a_n)$$

Example 5.11:   Let V be the vector space of polynomials with degree ≤ 2:

$$V = \{at^2 + bt + c : a, b, c \in \mathbf{R}\}$$

The polynomials

$$e_1 = 1, \quad e_2 = t - 1 \quad \text{and} \quad e_3 = (t-1)^2 = t^2 - 2t + 1$$

form a basis for V. Let $v = 2t^2 - 5t + 6$. Find $[v]_e$, the coordinate vector of v relative to the basis $\{e_1, e_2, e_3\}$.

Set v as a linear combination of the e_i using the unknowns x, y and z: $v = xe_1 + ye_2 + ze_3$.

$$2t^2 - 5t + 6 = x(1) + y(t-1) + z(t^2 - 2t + 1)$$
$$= x + yt - y + zt^2 - 2zt + z$$
$$= zt^2 + (y - 2z)t + (x - y + z)$$

Then set the coefficients of the same powers of t equal to each other:

$$x - y + z = 6$$
$$y - 2z = -5$$
$$z = 2$$

The solution of the above system is $x = 3$, $y = -1$, $z = 2$. Thus

$$v = 3e_1 - e_2 + 2e_3, \quad \text{and so} \quad [v]_e = (3, -1, 2)$$

Example 5.12: Consider the real space $\mathbf{R}^3$. Find the coordinate vector of $v = (3, 1, -4)$ relative to the basis $f_1 = (1, 1, 1)$, $f_2 = (0, 1, 1)$, $f_3 = (0, 0, 1)$.

Set v as a linear combination of the f_i using the unknowns x, y and z: $v = xf_1 + yf_2 + zf_3$.

$$(3, 1, -4) = x(1, 1, 1) + y(0, 1, 1) + z(0, 0, 1)$$
$$= (x, x, x) + (0, y, y) + (0, 0, z)$$
$$= (x, x+y, x+y+z)$$

Then set the corresponding components equal to each other to obtain the equivalent system of equations

$$x = 3$$
$$x + y = 1$$
$$x + y + z = -4$$

having solution $x = 3$, $y = -2$, $z = -5$. Thus $[v]_f = (3, -2, -5)$.

We remark that relative to the usual basis $e_1 = (1, 0, 0)$, $e_2 = (0, 1, 0)$, $e_3 = (0, 0, 1)$, the coordinate vector of v is identical to v itself: $[v]_e = (3, 1, -4) = v$.

We have shown above that to each vector $v \in V$ there corresponds, relative to a given basis $\{e_1, \ldots, e_n\}$, an n-tuple $[v]_e$ in K^n. On the other hand, if $(a_1, \ldots, a_n) \in K^n$, then there exists a vector in V of the form $a_1e_1 + \cdots + a_ne_n$. Thus the basis $\{e_i\}$ determines a one-to-one correspondence between the vectors in V and the n-tuples in K^n. Observe also that if

$$v = a_1e_1 + \cdots + a_ne_n \quad \text{corresponds to} \quad (a_1, \ldots, a_n)$$

and

$$w = b_1e_1 + \cdots + b_ne_n \quad \text{corresponds to} \quad (b_1, \ldots, b_n)$$

then

$$v + w = (a_1 + b_1)e_1 + \cdots + (a_n + b_n)e_n \quad \text{corresponds to} \quad (a_1, \ldots, a_n) + (b_1, \ldots, b_n)$$

and, for any scalar $k \in K$,

$$kv = (ka_1)e_1 + \cdots + (ka_n)e_n \quad \text{corresponds to} \quad k(a_1, \ldots, a_n)$$

That is, $\quad [v + w]_e = [v]_e + [w]_e \quad \text{and} \quad [kv]_e = k[v]_e$

Thus the above one-to-one correspondence between V and K^n preserves the vector space operations of vector addition and scalar multiplication; we then say that V and K^n are *isomorphic*, written $V \cong K^n$. We state this result formally.

Theorem 5.12: Let V be an n-dimensional vector space over a field K. Then V and K^n are isomorphic.

The next example gives a practical application of the above result.

Example 5.13:   Determine whether the following matrices are dependent or independent:

$$A = \begin{pmatrix} 1 & 2 & -3 \\ 4 & 0 & 1 \end{pmatrix}, \quad B = \begin{pmatrix} 1 & 3 & -4 \\ 6 & 5 & 4 \end{pmatrix}, \quad C = \begin{pmatrix} 3 & 8 & -11 \\ 16 & 10 & 9 \end{pmatrix}$$

The coordinate vectors of the above matrices relative to the basis in Example 5.4, page 89, are

$$[A] = (1, 2, -3, 4, 0, 1), \quad [B] = (1, 3, -4, 6, 5, 4), \quad [C] = (3, 8, -11, 16, 10, 9)$$

Form the matrix M whose rows are the above coordinate vectors:

$$M = \begin{pmatrix} 1 & 2 & -3 & 4 & 0 & 1 \\ 1 & 3 & -4 & 6 & 5 & 4 \\ 3 & 8 & -11 & 16 & 10 & 9 \end{pmatrix}$$

Row reduce M to echelon form:

$$M \text{ to } \begin{pmatrix} 1 & 2 & -3 & 4 & 0 & 1 \\ 0 & 1 & -1 & 2 & 5 & 3 \\ 0 & 2 & -2 & 4 & 10 & 6 \end{pmatrix} \text{ to } \begin{pmatrix} 1 & 2 & -3 & 4 & 0 & 1 \\ 0 & 1 & -1 & 2 & 5 & 3 \\ 0 & 0 & 0 & 0 & 0 & 0 \end{pmatrix}$$

Since the echelon matrix has only two nonzero rows, the coordinate vectors $[A]$, $[B]$ and $[C]$ generate a space of dimension 2 and so are dependent. Accordingly, the original matrices A, B and C are dependent.

Solved Problems

LINEAR DEPENDENCE

5.1.   Determine whether or not u and v are linearly dependent if:

     (i) $u = (3, 4), \ v = (1, -3)$ (iii) $u = (4, 3, -2), \ v = (2, -6, 7)$

     (ii) $u = (2, -3), \ v = (6, -9)$ (iv) $u = (-4, 6, -2), \ v = (2, -3, 1)$

     (v) $u = \begin{pmatrix} 1 & -2 & 4 \\ 3 & 0 & -1 \end{pmatrix}, \ v = \begin{pmatrix} 2 & -4 & 8 \\ 6 & 0 & -2 \end{pmatrix}$ (vi) $u = \begin{pmatrix} 1 & 2 & -3 \\ 6 & -5 & 4 \end{pmatrix}, \ v = \begin{pmatrix} 6 & -5 & 4 \\ 1 & 2 & -3 \end{pmatrix}$

     (vii) $u = 2 - 5t + 6t^2 - t^3, \ v = 3 + 2t - 4t^2 + 5t^3$

     (viii) $u = 1 - 3t + 2t^2 - 3t^3, \ v = -3 + 9t - 6t^2 + 9t^3$

     Two vectors u and v are dependent if and only if one is a multiple of the other.

     (i) No. (ii) Yes; for $v = 3u$. (iii) No. (iv) Yes; for $u = -2v$. (v) Yes; for $v = 2u$. (vi) No. (vii) No. (viii) Yes; for $v = -3u$.

5.2.   Determine whether or not the following vectors in $\mathbf{R}^3$ are linearly dependent:

     (i) $(1, -2, 1), (2, 1, -1), (7, -4, 1)$ (iii) $(1, 2, -3), (1, -3, 2), (2, -1, 5)$

     (ii) $(1, -3, 7), (2, 0, -6), (3, -1, -1), (2, 4, -5)$ (iv) $(2, -3, 7), (0, 0, 0), (3, -1, -4)$

     (i)   **Method 1.** Set a linear combination of the vectors equal to the zero vector using unknown scalars x, y and z:

$$x(1, -2, 1) + y(2, 1, -1) + z(7, -4, 1) = (0, 0, 0)$$

Then $\qquad\qquad (x, -2x, x) \; + \; (2y, y, -y) \; + \; (7z, -4z, z) \;\; = \;\; (0, 0, 0)$

or $\qquad\qquad\quad (x + 2y + 7z, \; -2x + y - 4z, \; x - y + z) \;\; = \;\; (0, 0, 0)$

Set corresponding components equal to each other to obtain the equivalent homogeneous system, and reduce to echelon form:

$$\begin{array}{lll}
x + 2y + 7z = 0 & & x + 2y + 7z = 0 \\
-2x + y - 4z = 0 \quad\text{or} & & \quad 5y + 10z = 0 \quad\text{or} \\
x - y + z = 0 & & \quad -3y - 6z = 0
\end{array}
\qquad
\begin{array}{l}
x + 2y + 7z = 0 \\[4pt]
\quad y + 2z = 0
\end{array}$$

The system, in echelon form, has only two nonzero equations in the three unknowns; hence the system has a nonzero solution. Thus the original vectors are linearly dependent.

Method 2. Form the matrix whose rows are the given vectors, and reduce to echelon form using the elementary row operations:

$$\begin{pmatrix} 1 & -2 & 1 \\ 2 & 1 & -1 \\ 7 & -4 & 1 \end{pmatrix} \quad\text{to}\quad \begin{pmatrix} 1 & -2 & 1 \\ 0 & 5 & -3 \\ 0 & 10 & -6 \end{pmatrix} \quad\text{to}\quad \begin{pmatrix} 1 & -2 & 1 \\ 0 & 5 & -3 \\ 0 & 0 & 0 \end{pmatrix}$$

Since the echelon matrix has a zero row, the vectors are dependent. (The three given vectors generate a space of dimension 2.)

(ii) Yes, since any four (or more) vectors in $\mathbf{R}^3$ are dependent.

(iii) Form the matrix whose rows are the given vectors, and row reduce the matrix to echelon form:

$$\begin{pmatrix} 1 & 2 & -3 \\ 1 & -3 & 2 \\ 2 & -1 & 5 \end{pmatrix} \quad\text{to}\quad \begin{pmatrix} 1 & 2 & -3 \\ 0 & -5 & 5 \\ 0 & -5 & 11 \end{pmatrix} \quad\text{to}\quad \begin{pmatrix} 1 & 2 & -3 \\ 0 & -5 & 5 \\ 0 & 0 & 6 \end{pmatrix}$$

Since the echelon matrix has no zero rows, the vectors are independent. (The three given vectors generate a space of dimension 3.)

(iv) Since $0 = (0, 0, 0)$ is one of the vectors, the vectors are dependent.

5.3. Let V be the vector space of 2×2 matrices over $\mathbf{R}$. Determine whether the matrices $A, B, C \in V$ are dependent where:

(i) $A = \begin{pmatrix} 1 & 1 \\ 1 & 1 \end{pmatrix}, \quad B = \begin{pmatrix} 1 & 0 \\ 0 & 1 \end{pmatrix}, \quad C = \begin{pmatrix} 1 & 1 \\ 0 & 0 \end{pmatrix}$

(ii) $A = \begin{pmatrix} 1 & 2 \\ 3 & 1 \end{pmatrix}, \quad B = \begin{pmatrix} 3 & -1 \\ 2 & 2 \end{pmatrix}, \quad C = \begin{pmatrix} 1 & -5 \\ -4 & 0 \end{pmatrix}$

(i) Set a linear combination of the matrices A, B and C equal to the zero matrix using unknown scalars x, y and z; that is, set $xA + yB + zC = 0$. Thus:

$$x\begin{pmatrix} 1 & 1 \\ 1 & 1 \end{pmatrix} + y\begin{pmatrix} 1 & 0 \\ 0 & 1 \end{pmatrix} + z\begin{pmatrix} 1 & 1 \\ 0 & 0 \end{pmatrix} = \begin{pmatrix} 0 & 0 \\ 0 & 0 \end{pmatrix}$$

or $\qquad\qquad \begin{pmatrix} x & x \\ x & x \end{pmatrix} + \begin{pmatrix} y & 0 \\ 0 & y \end{pmatrix} + \begin{pmatrix} z & z \\ 0 & 0 \end{pmatrix} = \begin{pmatrix} 0 & 0 \\ 0 & 0 \end{pmatrix}$

or $\qquad\qquad\qquad\quad \begin{pmatrix} x + y + z & x + z \\ x & x + y \end{pmatrix} = \begin{pmatrix} 0 & 0 \\ 0 & 0 \end{pmatrix}$

Set corresponding entries equal to each other to obtain the equivalent homogeneous system of equations:

$$x + y + z = 0$$
$$x + z = 0$$
$$x = 0$$
$$x + y = 0$$

Solving the above system we obtain only the zero solution, $x = 0$, $y = 0$, $z = 0$. We have shown that $xA + yB + zC$ implies $x = 0$, $y = 0$, $z = 0$; hence the matrices A, B and C are linearly independent.

(ii) Set a linear combination of the matrices A, B and C equal to the zero vector using unknown scalars x, y and z; that is, set $xA + yB + zC = 0$. Thus:

$$x \begin{pmatrix} 1 & 2 \\ 3 & 1 \end{pmatrix} + y \begin{pmatrix} 3 & -1 \\ 2 & 2 \end{pmatrix} + z \begin{pmatrix} 1 & -5 \\ -4 & 0 \end{pmatrix} = \begin{pmatrix} 0 & 0 \\ 0 & 0 \end{pmatrix}$$

or

$$\begin{pmatrix} x & 2x \\ 3x & x \end{pmatrix} + \begin{pmatrix} 3y & -y \\ 2y & 2y \end{pmatrix} + \begin{pmatrix} z & -5z \\ -4z & 0 \end{pmatrix} = \begin{pmatrix} 0 & 0 \\ 0 & 0 \end{pmatrix}$$

or

$$\begin{pmatrix} x + 3y + z & 2x - y - 5z \\ 3x + 2y - 4z & x + 2y \end{pmatrix} = \begin{pmatrix} 0 & 0 \\ 0 & 0 \end{pmatrix}$$

Set corresponding entries equal to each other to obtain the equivalent homogeneous system of linear equations and reduce to echelon form:

$$
\begin{aligned}
x + 3y + z &= 0 \\
2x - y - 5z &= 0 \\
3x + 2y - 4z &= 0 \\
x + 2y &= 0
\end{aligned}
\qquad \text{or} \qquad
\begin{aligned}
x + 3y + z &= 0 \\
-7y - 7z &= 0 \\
-7y - 7z &= 0 \\
-y - z &= 0
\end{aligned}
$$

or finally

$$x + 3y + z = 0$$
$$y + z = 0$$

The system in echelon form has a free variable and hence a nonzero solution, for example, $x = 2$, $y = -1$, $z = 1$. We have shown that $xA + yB + zC = 0$ does not imply that $x = 0$, $y = 0$, $z = 0$; hence the matrices are linearly dependent.

5.4. Let V be the vector space of polynomials of degree ≤ 3 over $\mathbf{R}$. Determine whether $u, v, w \in V$ are independent or dependent where:

(i) $u = t^3 - 3t^2 + 5t + 1$, $v = t^3 - t^2 + 8t + 2$, $w = 2t^3 - 4t^2 + 9t + 5$

(ii) $u = t^3 + 4t^2 - 2t + 3$, $v = t^3 + 6t^2 - t + 4$, $w = 3t^3 + 8t^2 - 8t + 7$

(i) Set a linear combination of the polynomials u, v and w equal to the zero polynomial using unknown scalars x, y and z; that is, set $xu + yv + zw = 0$. Thus:

$$x(t^3 - 3t^2 + 5t + 1) + y(t^3 - t^2 + 8t + 2) + z(2t^3 - 4t^2 + 9t + 5) = 0$$

or

$$xt^3 - 3xt^2 + 5xt + x + yt^3 - yt^2 + 8yt + 2y + 2zt^3 - 4zt^2 + 9zt + 5z = 0$$

or

$$(x + y + 2z)t^3 + (-3x - y - 4z)t^2 + (5x + 8y + 9z)t + (x + 2y + 5z) = 0$$

The coefficients of the powers of t must each be 0:

$$
\begin{aligned}
x + y + 2z &= 0 \\
-3x - y - 4z &= 0 \\
5x + 8y + 9z &= 0 \\
x + 2y + 5z &= 0
\end{aligned}
$$

Solving the above homogeneous system, we obtain only the zero solution: $x = 0$, $y = 0$, $z = 0$; hence u, v and w are independent.

(ii) Set a linear combination of the polynomials u, v and w equal to the zero polynomial using unknown scalars x, y and z; that is, set $xu + yv + zw = 0$. Thus:

$$x(t^3 + 4t^2 - 2t + 3) + y(t^3 + 6t^2 - t + 4) + z(3t^3 + 8t^2 - 8t + 7) = 0$$

or $\qquad xt^3 + 4xt^2 - 2xt + 3x + yt^3 + 6yt^2 - yt + 4y + 3zt^3 + 8zt^2 - 8zt + 7z = 0$

or $\qquad (x + y + 3z)t^3 + (4x + 6y + 8z)t^2 + (-2x - y - 8z)t + (3x + 4y + 7z) = 0$

Set the coefficients of the powers of t each equal to 0 and reduce the system to echelon form:

$$
\begin{array}{lll}
\begin{aligned}
x + \ y + 3z &= 0 \\
4x + 6y + 8z &= 0 \\
-2x - \ y - 8z &= 0 \\
3x + 4y + 7z &= 0
\end{aligned}
&\text{or}&
\begin{aligned}
x + y + 3z &= 0 \\
2y - 4z &= 0 \\
y - 2z &= 0 \\
y - 2z &= 0
\end{aligned}
\end{array}
$$

or finally
$$
\begin{aligned}
x + y + 3z &= 0 \\
y - 2z &= 0
\end{aligned}
$$

The system in echelon form has a free variable and hence a nonzero solution. We have shown that $xu + yv + zw = 0$ does not imply that $x = 0$, $y = 0$, $z = 0$; hence the polynomials are linearly dependent.

5.5. Let V be the vector space of functions from $\mathbf{R}$ into $\mathbf{R}$. Show that $f, g, h \in V$ are independent where: (i) $f(t) = e^{2t}$, $g(t) = t^2$, $h(t) = t$; (ii) $f(t) = \sin t$, $g(t) = \cos t$, $h(t) = t$.

In each case set a linear combination of the functions equal to the zero function $\mathbf{0}$ using unknown scalars x, y and z: $xf + yg + zh = 0$; and then show that $x = 0$, $y = 0$, $z = 0$. We emphasize that $xf + yg + zh = \mathbf{0}$ means that, for every value of t, $xf(t) + yg(t) + zh(t) = 0$.

(i) In the equation $xe^{2t} + yt^2 + zt = 0$, substitute

$$
\begin{aligned}
t = 0 \quad &\text{to obtain} \quad xe^0 + y0 + z0 = 0 \quad \text{or} \quad x = 0 \\
t = 1 \quad &\text{to obtain} \quad xe^2 + y + z = 0 \\
t = 2 \quad &\text{to obtain} \quad xe^4 + 4y + 2z = 0
\end{aligned}
$$

Solve the system $\begin{cases} x = 0 \\ xe^2 + y + z = 0 \\ xe^4 + 4y + 2z = 0 \end{cases}$ to obtain only the zero solution: $x = 0$, $y = 0$, $z = 0$.

Hence f, g and h are independent.

(ii) **Method 1.** In the equation $x \sin t + y \cos t + zt = 0$, substitute

$$
\begin{aligned}
t = 0 \quad &\text{to obtain} \quad x \cdot 0 + y \cdot 1 + z \cdot 0 = 0 \quad &&\text{or} \quad y = 0 \\
t = \pi/2 \quad &\text{to obtain} \quad x \cdot 1 + y \cdot 0 + z\pi/2 = 0 \quad &&\text{or} \quad x + \pi z/2 = 0 \\
t = \pi \quad &\text{to obtain} \quad x \cdot 0 + y(-1) + z \cdot \pi = 0 \quad &&\text{or} \quad -y + \pi z = 0
\end{aligned}
$$

Solve the system $\begin{cases} y = 0 \\ x + \pi z/2 = 0 \\ -y + \pi z = 0 \end{cases}$ to obtain only the zero solution: $x = 0$, $y = 0$, $z = 0$. Hence f, g and h are independent.

Method 2. Take the first, second and third derivatives of $x \sin t + y \cos t + zt = 0$ with respect to t to get

$$x \cos t - y \sin t + z = 0 \tag{1}$$

$$-x \sin t - y \cos t = 0 \tag{2}$$

$$-x \cos t + y \sin t = 0 \tag{3}$$

Add (*1*) and (*3*) to obtain $z = 0$. Multiply (*2*) by $\sin t$ and (*3*) by $\cos t$, and then add:

$$\sin t \times (2): \quad -x \sin^2 t - y \sin t \cos t = 0$$
$$\cos t \times (3): \quad -x \cos^2 t + y \sin t \cos t = 0$$

$$\rule{6cm}{0.4pt}$$

$$-x(\sin^2 t + \cos^2 t) \qquad = 0 \quad \text{or} \quad x = 0$$

Lastly, multiply (*2*) by $-\cos t$ and (*3*) by $\sin t$; and then add to obtain

$$y(\cos^2 t + \sin^2 t) = 0 \quad \text{or} \quad y = 0$$

Since $\qquad\qquad x \sin t + y \cos t + zt = 0 \qquad$ implies $\qquad x = 0, \ y = 0, \ z = 0$

f, g and h are independent.

5.6. Let u, v and w be independent vectors. Show that $u + v$, $u - v$ and $u - 2v + w$ are also independent.

Suppose $x(u+v) + y(u-v) + z(u-2v+w) = 0$ where x, y and z are scalars. Then $xu + xv + yu - yv + zu - 2zv + zw = 0$ or

$$(x + y + z)u + (x - y - 2z)v + zw = 0$$

But u, v and w are linearly independent; hence the coefficients in the above relation are each 0:

$$x + y + \ z = 0$$
$$x - y - 2z = 0$$
$$z = 0$$

The only solution to the above system is $x = 0$, $y = 0$, $z = 0$. Hence $u + v$, $u - v$ and $u - 2v + w$ are independent.

5.7. Let $v_1, v_2, \ldots, v_m$ be independent vectors, and suppose u is a linear combination of the v_i, say $u = a_1 v_1 + a_2 v_2 + \cdots + a_m v_m$ where the a_i are scalars. Show that the above representation of u is unique.

Suppose $u = b_1 v_1 + b_2 v_2 + \cdots + b_m v_m$ where the b_i are scalars. Subtracting,

$$0 = u - u = (a_1 - b_1)v_1 + (a_2 - b_2)v_2 + \cdots + (a_m - b_m)v_m$$

But the v_i are linearly independent; hence the coefficients in the above relation are each 0:

$$a_1 - b_1 = 0, \quad a_2 - b_2 = 0, \quad \ldots, \quad a_m - b_m = 0$$

Hence $a_1 = b_1$, $a_2 = b_2$, $\ldots$, $a_m = b_m$ and so the above representation of u as a linear combination of the v_i is unique.

5.8. Show that the vectors $v = (1 + i, 2i)$ and $w = (1, 1 + i)$ in $\mathbf{C}^2$ are linearly dependent over the complex field $\mathbf{C}$ but are linearly independent over the real field $\mathbf{R}$.

Recall that 2 vectors are dependent iff one is a multiple of the other. Since the first coordinate of w is 1, v can be a multiple of w iff $v = (1 + i)w$. But $1 + i \notin R$; hence v and w are independent over $\mathbf{R}$. Since

$$(1 + i)w = (1 + i)(1, 1 + i) = (1 + i, 2i) = v$$

and $1 + i \in \mathbf{C}$, they are dependent over $\mathbf{C}$.

5.9. Suppose $S = \{v_1, \ldots, v_m\}$ contains a dependent subset, say $\{v_1, \ldots, v_r\}$. Show that S is also dependent. Hence every subset of an independent set is independent.

Since $\{v_1, \ldots, v_r\}$ is dependent, there exist scalars $a_1, \ldots, a_r$, not all 0, such that

$$a_1 v_1 + a_2 v_2 + \cdots + a_r v_r = 0$$

Hence there exist scalars $a_1, \ldots, a_r, 0, \ldots, 0$, not all 0, such that

$$a_1 v_1 + \cdots + a_r v_r + 0 v_{r+1} + \cdots + 0 v_m = 0$$

Accordingly, S is dependent.

5.10. Suppose $\{v_1, \ldots, v_m\}$ is independent, but $\{v_1, \ldots, v_m, w\}$ is dependent. Show that w is a linear combination of the v_i.

Method 1. Since $\{v_1, \ldots, v_m, w\}$ is dependent, there exist scalars $a_1, \ldots, a_m, b$, not all 0, such that $a_1 v_1 + \cdots + a_m v_m + bw = 0$. If $b = 0$, then one of the a_i is not zero and $a_1 v_1 + \cdots + a_m v_m = 0$. But this contradicts the hypothesis that $\{v_1, \ldots, v_m\}$ is independent. Accordingly, $b \neq 0$ and so

$$w = b^{-1}(-a_1 v_1 - \cdots - a_m v_m) = -b^{-1} a_1 v_1 - \cdots - b^{-1} a_m v_m$$

That is, w is a linear combination of the v_i.

Method 2. If $w = 0$, then $w = 0 v_1 + \cdots + 0 v_m$. On the other hand, if $w \neq 0$ then, by Lemma 5.2, one of the vectors in $\{v_1, \ldots, v_m, w\}$ is a linear combination of the preceding vectors. This vector cannot be one of the v's since $\{v_1, \ldots, v_m\}$ is independent. Hence w is a linear combination of the v_i.

PROOFS OF THEOREMS

5.11. Prove Lemma 5.2: The nonzero vectors $v_1, \ldots, v_m$ are linearly dependent if and only if one of them, say v_i, is a linear combination of the preceding vectors: $v_i = a_1 v_1 + \cdots + a_{i-1} v_{i-1}$.

Suppose $v_i = a_1 v_1 + \cdots + a_{i-1} v_{i-1}$. Then

$$a_1 v_1 + \cdots + a_{i-1} v_{i-1} - v_i + 0 v_{i+1} + \cdots + 0 v_m = 0$$

and the coefficient of v_i is not 0. Hence the v_i are linearly dependent.

Conversely, suppose the v_i are linearly dependent. Then there exist scalars $a_1, \ldots, a_m$, not all 0, such that $a_1 v_1 + \cdots + a_m v_m = 0$. Let k be the largest integer such that $a_k \neq 0$. Then

$$a_1 v_1 + \cdots + a_k v_k + 0 v_{k+1} + \cdots + 0 v_m = 0 \quad \text{or} \quad a_1 v_1 + \cdots + a_k v_k = 0$$

Suppose $k = 1$; then $a_1 v_1 = 0$, $a_1 \neq 0$ and so $v_1 = 0$. But the v_i are nonzero vectors; hence $k > 1$ and

$$v_k = -a_k^{-1} a_1 v_1 - \cdots - a_k^{-1} a_{k-1} v_{k-1}$$

That is, v_k is a linear combination of the preceding vectors.

5.12. Prove Theorem 5.1: The nonzero rows $R_1, \ldots, R_n$ of a matrix in echelon form are linearly independent.

Suppose $\{R_n, R_{n-1}, \ldots, R_1\}$ is dependent. Then one of the rows, say R_m, is a linear combination of the preceding rows:

$$R_m = a_{m+1} R_{m+1} + a_{m+2} R_{m+2} + \cdots + a_n R_n \tag{*}$$

Now suppose the kth component of R_m is its first nonzero entry. Then, since the matrix is in echelon form, the kth components of $R_{m+1}, \ldots, R_n$ are all 0, and so the kth component of (*) is $a_{m+1} \cdot 0 + a_{m+2} \cdot 0 + \cdots + a_n \cdot 0 = 0$. But this contradicts the assumption that the kth component of R_m is not 0. Thus $R_1, \ldots, R_n$ are independent.

5.13. Suppose $\{v_1, \ldots, v_m\}$ generates a vector space V. Prove:

(i) If $w \in V$, then $\{w, v_1, \ldots, v_m\}$ is linearly dependent and generates V.

(ii) If v_i is a linear combination of the preceding vectors, then $\{v_1, \ldots, v_{i-1}, v_{i+1}, \ldots, v_m\}$ generates V.

(i) If $w \in V$, then w is a linear combination of the v_i since $\{v_i\}$ generates V. Accordingly, $\{w, v_1, \ldots, v_m\}$ is linearly dependent. Clearly, w with the v_i generate V since the v_i by themselves generate V. That is, $\{w, v_1, \ldots, v_m\}$ generates V.

(ii) Suppose $v_i = k_1 v_1 + \cdots + k_{i-1} v_{i-1}$. Let $u \in V$. Since $\{v_i\}$ generates V, u is a linear combination of the v_i, say, $u = a_1 v_1 + \cdots + a_m v_m$. Substituting for v_i, we obtain

$$u = a_1 v_1 + \cdots + a_{i-1} v_{i-1} + a_i(k_1 v_1 + \cdots + k_{i-1} v_{i-1}) + a_{i+1} v_{i+1} + \cdots + a_m v_m$$

$$= (a_1 + a_i k_1) v_1 + \cdots + (a_{i-1} + a_i k_{i-1}) v_{i-1} + a_{i+1} v_{i+1} + \cdots + a_m v_m$$

Thus $\{v_1, \ldots, v_{i-1}, v_{i+1}, \ldots, v_m\}$ generates V. In other words, we can delete v_i from the generating set and still retain a generating set.

5.14. Prove Lemma 5.4: Suppose $\{v_1, \ldots, v_n\}$ generates a vector space V. If $\{w_1, \ldots, w_m\}$ is linearly independent, then $m \leqq n$ and V is generated by a set of the form $\{w_1, \ldots, w_m, v_{i_1}, \ldots, v_{i_{n-m}}\}$. Thus, in particular, any $n+1$ or more vectors in V are linearly dependent.

It suffices to prove the theorem in the case that the v_i are all not 0. (Prove!) Since the $\{v_i\}$ generates V, we have by the preceding problem that

$$\{w_1, v_1, \ldots, v_n\} \tag{1}$$

is linearly dependent and also generates V. By Lemma 5.2, one of the vectors in (1) is a linear combination of the preceding vectors. This vector cannot be w_1, so it must be one of the v's, say v_j. Thus by the preceding problem we can delete v_j from the generating set (1) and obtain the generating set

$$\{w_1, v_1, \ldots, v_{j-1}, v_{j+1}, \ldots, v_n\} \tag{2}$$

Now we repeat the argument with the vector w_2. That is, since (2) generates V, the set

$$\{w_1, w_2, v_1, \ldots, v_{j-1}, v_{j+1}, \ldots, v_n\} \tag{3}$$

is linearly dependent and also generates V. Again by Lemma 5.2, one of the vectors in (3) is a linear combination of the preceding vectors. We emphasize that this vector cannot be w_1 or w_2 since $\{w_1, \ldots, w_m\}$ is independent; hence it must be one of the v's, say v_k. Thus by the preceding problem we can delete v_k from the generating set (3) and obtain the generating set

$$\{w_1, w_2, v_1, \ldots, v_{j-1}, v_{j+1}, \ldots, v_{k-1}, v_{k+1}, \ldots, v_n\}$$

We repeat the argument with w_3 and so forth. At each step we are able to add one of the w's and delete one of the v's in the generating set. If $m \leqq n$, then we finally obtain a generating set of the required form:

$$\{w_1, \ldots, w_m, v_{i_1}, \ldots, v_{i_{n-m}}\}$$

Lastly, we show that $m > n$ is not possible. Otherwise, after n of the above steps, we obtain the generating set $\{w_1, \ldots, w_n\}$. This implies that w_{n+1} is a linear combination of $w_1, \ldots, w_n$ which contradicts the hypothesis that $\{w_i\}$ is linearly independent.

5.15. Prove Theorem 5.3: Let V be a finite dimensional vector space. Then every basis of V has the same number of vectors.

Suppose $\{e_1, e_2, \ldots, e_n\}$ is a basis of V, and suppose $\{f_1, f_2, \ldots\}$ is another basis of V. Since $\{e_i\}$ generates V, the basis $\{f_1, f_2, \ldots\}$ must contain n or less vectors, or else it is dependent by the preceding problem. On the other hand, if the basis $\{f_1, f_2, \ldots\}$ contains less than n vectors, then $\{e_1, \ldots, e_n\}$ is dependent by the preceding problem. Thus the basis $\{f_1, f_2, \ldots\}$ contains exactly n vectors, and so the theorem is true.

5.16. Prove Theorem 5.5: Suppose $\{v_1, \ldots, v_m\}$ is a maximal independent subset of a set S which generates a vector space V. Then $\{v_1, \ldots, v_m\}$ is a basis of V.

Suppose $w \in S$. Then, since $\{v_i\}$ is a maximal independent subset of S, $\{v_1, \ldots, v_m, w\}$ is linearly dependent. By Problem 5.10, w is a linear combination of the v_i, that is, $w \in L(v_i)$. Hence $S \subset L(v_i)$. This leads to $V = L(S) \subset L(v_i) \subset V$. Accordingly, $\{v_i\}$ generates V and, since it is independent, it is a basis of V.

5.17. Suppose V is generated by a finite set S. Show that V is of finite dimension and, in particular, a subset of S is a basis of V.

Method 1. Of all the independent subsets of S, and there is a finite number of them since S is finite, one of them is maximal. By the preceding problem this subset of S is a basis of V.

Method 2. If S is independent, it is a basis of V. If S is dependent, one of the vectors is a linear combination of the preceding vectors. We may delete this vector and still retain a generating set. We continue this process until we obtain a subset which is independent and generates V, i.e. is a basis of V.

5.18. Prove Theorem 5.6: Let V be of finite dimension n. Then:
(i)   Any set of $n+1$ or more vectors is linearly dependent.
(ii) Any linearly independent set is part of a basis.
(iii) A linearly independent set with n elements is a basis.

Suppose $\{e_1, \ldots, e_n\}$ is a basis of V.

(i)   Since $\{e_1, \ldots, e_n\}$ generates V, any $n+1$ or more vectors is dependent by Lemma 5.4.

(ii) Suppose $\{v_1, \ldots, v_r\}$ is independent. By Lemma 5.4, V is generated by a set of the form

$$S = \{v_1, \ldots, v_r, e_{i_1}, \ldots, e_{i_{n-r}}\}$$

By the preceding problem, a subset of S is a basis. But S contains n elements and every basis of V contains n elements. Thus S is a basis of V and contains $\{v_1, \ldots, v_r\}$ as a subset.

(iii) By (ii), an independent set T with n elements is part of a basis. But every basis of V contains n elements. Thus, T is a basis.

5.19. Prove Theorem 5.7: Let W be a subspace of an n-dimensional vector space V. Then $\dim W \leqq n$. In particular, if $\dim W = n$, then $W = V$.

Since V is of dimension n, any $n+1$ or more vectors are linearly dependent. Furthermore, since a basis of W consists of linearly independent vectors, it cannot contain more than n elements. Accordingly, $\dim W \leqq n$.

In particular, if $\{w_1, \ldots, w_n\}$ is a basis of W, then since it is an independent set with n elements it is also a basis of V. Thus $W = V$ when $\dim W = n$.

5.20. Prove Theorem 5.8: $\dim(U+W) = \dim U + \dim W - \dim(U \cap W)$.

Observe that $U \cap W$ is a subspace of both U and W. Suppose $\dim U = m$, $\dim W = n$ and $\dim(U \cap W) = r$. Suppose $\{v_1, \ldots, v_r\}$ is a basis of $U \cap W$. By Theorem 5.6(ii), we can extend $\{v_i\}$ to a basis of U and to a basis of W; say,

$$\{v_1, \ldots, v_r, u_1, \ldots, u_{m-r}\} \quad \text{and} \quad \{v_1, \ldots, v_r, w_1, \ldots, w_{n-r}\}$$

are bases of U and W respectively. Let

$$B = \{v_1, \ldots, v_r, u_1, \ldots, u_{m-r}, w_1, \ldots, w_{n-r}\}$$

Note that B has exactly $m+n-r$ elements. Thus the theorem is proved if we can show that B is a basis of $U+W$. Since $\{v_i, u_j\}$ generates U and $\{v_i, w_k\}$ generates W, the union $B = \{v_i, u_j, w_k\}$ generates $U+W$. Thus it suffices to show that B is independent.

Suppose

$$a_1 v_1 + \cdots + a_r v_r + b_1 u_1 + \cdots + b_{m-r} u_{m-r} + c_1 w_1 + \cdots + c_{n-r} w_{n-r} = 0 \qquad (1)$$

where a_i, b_j, c_k are scalars. Let

$$v = a_1 v_1 + \cdots + a_r v_r + b_1 u_1 + \cdots + b_{m-r} u_{m-r} \qquad (2)$$

By (1), we also have that

$$v = -c_1 w_1 - \cdots - c_{n-r} w_{n-r} \qquad (3)$$

Since $\{v_i, u_j\} \subset U$, $v \in U$ by (2); and since $\{w_k\} \subset W$, $v \in W$ by (3). Accordingly, $v \in U \cap W$. Now $\{v_i\}$ is a basis of $U \cap W$ and so there exist scalars $d_1, \ldots, d_r$ for which $v = d_1 v_1 + \cdots + d_r v_r$. Thus by (3) we have

$$d_1 v_1 + \cdots + d_r v_r + c_1 w_1 + \cdots + c_{n-r} w_{n-r} = 0$$

But $\{v_i, w_k\}$ is a basis of W and so is independent. Hence the above equation forces $c_1 = 0, \ldots, c_{n-r} = 0$. Substituting this into (1), we obtain

$$a_1 v_1 + \cdots + a_r v_r + b_1 u_1 + \cdots + b_{m-r} u_{m-r} = 0$$

But $\{v_i, u_j\}$ is a basis of U and so is independent. Hence the above equation forces $a_1 = 0, \ldots, a_r = 0$, $b_1 = 0, \ldots, b_{m-r} = 0$.

Since the equation (1) implies that the a_i, b_j and c_k are all 0, $B = \{v_i, u_j, w_k\}$ is independent and the theorem is proved.

5.21. Prove Theorem 5.9: The row rank and the column rank of any matrix are equal.

Let A be an arbitrary $m \times n$ matrix:

$$A = \begin{pmatrix} a_{11} & a_{12} & \cdots & a_{1n} \\ a_{21} & a_{22} & \cdots & a_{2n} \\ \cdots\cdots\cdots\cdots\cdots\cdots \\ a_{m1} & a_{m2} & \cdots & a_{mn} \end{pmatrix}$$

Let $R_1, R_2, \ldots, R_m$ denote its rows:

$$R_1 = (a_{11}, a_{12}, \ldots, a_{1n}), \quad \ldots, \quad R_m = (a_{m1}, a_{m2}, \ldots, a_{mn})$$

Suppose the row rank is r and that the following r vectors form a basis for the row space:

$$S_1 = (b_{11}, b_{12}, \ldots, b_{1n}), \ S_2 = (b_{21}, b_{22}, \ldots, b_{2n}), \ \ldots, \ S_r = (b_{r1}, b_{r2}, \ldots, b_{rn})$$

Then each of the row vectors is a linear combination of the S_i:

$$R_1 = k_{11} S_1 + k_{12} S_2 + \cdots + k_{1r} S_r$$
$$R_2 = k_{21} S_1 + k_{22} S_2 + \cdots + k_{2r} S_r$$
$$\cdots\cdots\cdots\cdots\cdots\cdots\cdots\cdots\cdots$$
$$R_m = k_{m1} S_1 + k_{m2} S_2 + \cdots + k_{mr} S_r$$

where the k_{ij} are scalars. Setting the ith components of each of the above vector equations equal to each other, we obtain the following system of equations, each valid for $i = 1, \ldots, n$:

$$a_{1i} = k_{11} b_{1i} + k_{12} b_{2i} + \cdots + k_{1r} b_{ri}$$
$$a_{2i} = k_{21} b_{1i} + k_{22} b_{2i} + \cdots + k_{2r} b_{ri}$$
$$\cdots\cdots\cdots\cdots\cdots\cdots\cdots\cdots\cdots$$
$$a_{mi} = k_{m1} b_{1i} + k_{m2} b_{2i} + \cdots + k_{mr} b_{ri}$$

Thus for $i = 1, \ldots, n$:

$$\begin{pmatrix} a_{1i} \\ a_{2i} \\ \cdot\cdot \\ a_{mi} \end{pmatrix} = b_{1i} \begin{pmatrix} k_{11} \\ k_{21} \\ \cdot\cdot \\ k_{m1} \end{pmatrix} + b_{2i} \begin{pmatrix} k_{12} \\ k_{22} \\ \cdot\cdot \\ k_{m2} \end{pmatrix} + \cdots + b_{ri} \begin{pmatrix} k_{1r} \\ k_{2r} \\ \cdot\cdot \\ k_{mr} \end{pmatrix}$$

In other words, each of the columns of A is a linear combination of the r vectors

$$\begin{pmatrix} k_{11} \\ k_{21} \\ \cdot\cdot \\ k_{m1} \end{pmatrix}, \quad \begin{pmatrix} k_{12} \\ k_{22} \\ \cdot\cdot \\ k_{m2} \end{pmatrix}, \quad \ldots, \quad \begin{pmatrix} k_{1r} \\ k_{2r} \\ \cdot\cdot \\ k_{mr} \end{pmatrix}$$

Thus the column space of the matrix A has dimension at most r, i.e. column rank $\leqq r$. Hence, column rank $\leqq$ row rank.

Similarly (or considering the transpose matrix A^t) we obtain row rank $\leqq$ column rank. Thus the row rank and column rank are equal.

BASIS AND DIMENSION

5.22. Determine whether or not the following form a basis for the vector space $\mathbf{R}^3$:

(i) $(1, 1, 1)$ and $(1, -1, 5)$

(ii) $(1, 2, 3)$, $(1, 0, -1)$, $(3, -1, 0)$ and $(2, 1, -2)$

(iii) $(1, 1, 1)$, $(1, 2, 3)$ and $(2, -1, 1)$

(iv) $(1, 1, 2)$, $(1, 2, 5)$ and $(5, 3, 4)$

(i) and (ii). No; for a basis of $\mathbf{R}^3$ must contain exactly 3 elements, since $\mathbf{R}^3$ is of dimension 3.

(iii) The vectors form a basis if and only if they are independent. Thus form the matrix whose rows are the given vectors, and row reduce to echelon form:

$$\begin{pmatrix} 1 & 1 & 1 \\ 1 & 2 & 3 \\ 2 & -1 & 1 \end{pmatrix} \text{ to } \begin{pmatrix} 1 & 1 & 1 \\ 0 & 1 & 2 \\ 0 & -3 & -1 \end{pmatrix} \text{ to } \begin{pmatrix} 1 & 1 & 1 \\ 0 & 1 & 2 \\ 0 & 0 & 5 \end{pmatrix}$$

The echelon matrix has no zero rows; hence the three vectors are independent and so form a basis for $\mathbf{R}^3$.

(iv) Form the matrix whose rows are the given vectors, and row reduce to echelon form:

$$\begin{pmatrix} 1 & 1 & 2 \\ 1 & 2 & 5 \\ 5 & 3 & 4 \end{pmatrix} \text{ to } \begin{pmatrix} 1 & 1 & 2 \\ 0 & 1 & 3 \\ 0 & -2 & -6 \end{pmatrix} \text{ to } \begin{pmatrix} 1 & 1 & 2 \\ 0 & 1 & 3 \\ 0 & 0 & 0 \end{pmatrix}$$

The echelon matrix has a zero row, i.e. only two nonzero rows; hence the three vectors are dependent and so do not form a basis for $\mathbf{R}^3$.

5.23. Let W be the subspace of $\mathbf{R}^4$ generated by the vectors $(1, -2, 5, -3)$, $(2, 3, 1, -4)$ and $(3, 8, -3, -5)$. (i) Find a basis and the dimension of W. (ii) Extend the basis of W to a basis of the whole space $\mathbf{R}^4$.

(i) Form the matrix whose rows are the given vectors, and row reduce to echelon form:

$$\begin{pmatrix} 1 & -2 & 5 & -3 \\ 2 & 3 & 1 & -4 \\ 3 & 8 & -3 & -5 \end{pmatrix} \text{ to } \begin{pmatrix} 1 & -2 & 5 & 3 \\ 0 & 7 & -9 & 2 \\ 0 & 14 & -18 & 4 \end{pmatrix} \text{ to } \begin{pmatrix} 1 & -2 & 5 & -3 \\ 0 & 7 & -9 & 2 \\ 0 & 0 & 0 & 0 \end{pmatrix}$$

The nonzero rows $(1, -2, 5, -3)$ and $(0, 7, -9, 2)$ of the echelon matrix form a basis of the row space, that is, of W. Thus, in particular, dim $W = 2$.

(ii) We seek four independent vectors which include the above two vectors. The vectors $(1, -2, 5, -3)$, $(0, 7, -9, 2)$, $(0, 0, 1, 0)$ and $(0, 0, 0, 1)$ are independent (since they form an echelon matrix), and so they form a basis of $\mathbf{R}^4$ which is an extension of the basis of W.

5.24. Let W be the space generated by the polynomials

$$v_1 = t^3 - 2t^2 + 4t + 1 \qquad v_3 = t^3 + 6t - 5$$
$$v_2 = 2t^3 - 3t^2 + 9t - 1 \qquad v_4 = 2t^3 - 5t^2 + 7t + 5$$

Find a basis and the dimension of W.

The coordinate vectors of the given polynomials relative to the basis $\{t^3, t^2, t, 1\}$ are respectively

$$[v_1] = (1, -2, 4, 1) \qquad [v_3] = (1, 0, 6, -5)$$
$$[v_2] = (2, -3, 9, -1) \qquad [v_4] = (2, -5, 7, 5)$$

Form the matrix whose rows are the above coordinate vectors, and row reduce to echelon form:

$$\begin{pmatrix} 1 & -2 & 4 & 1 \\ 2 & -3 & 9 & -1 \\ 1 & 0 & 6 & -5 \\ 2 & -5 & 7 & 5 \end{pmatrix} \quad\text{to}\quad \begin{pmatrix} 1 & -2 & 4 & 1 \\ 0 & 1 & 1 & -3 \\ 0 & 2 & 2 & -6 \\ 0 & -1 & -1 & 3 \end{pmatrix} \quad\text{to}\quad \begin{pmatrix} 1 & -2 & 4 & 1 \\ 0 & 1 & 1 & -3 \\ 0 & 0 & 0 & 0 \\ 0 & 0 & 0 & 0 \end{pmatrix}$$

The nonzero rows $(1, -2, 4, 1)$ and $(0, 1, 1, -3)$ of the echelon matrix form a basis of the space generated by the coordinate vectors, and so the corresponding polynomials

$$t^3 - 2t^2 + 4t + 1 \quad\text{and}\quad t^2 + t - 3$$

form a basis of W. Thus $\dim W = 2$.

5.25. Find the dimension and a basis of the solution space W of the system

$$x + 2y + 2z - s + 3t = 0$$
$$x + 2y + 3z + s + t = 0$$
$$3x + 6y + 8z + s + 5t = 0$$

Reduce the system to echelon form:

$$\begin{aligned} x + 2y + 2z - s + 3t &= 0 \\ z + 2s - 2t &= 0 \\ 2z + 4s - 4t &= 0 \end{aligned} \qquad\text{or}\qquad \begin{aligned} x + 2y + 2z - s + 3t &= 0 \\ z + 2s - 2t &= 0 \end{aligned}$$

The system in echelon form has 2 (nonzero) equations in 5 unknowns; hence the dimension of the solution space W is $5 - 2 = 3$. The free variables are y, s and t. Set

(i) $y = 1$, $s = 0$, $t = 0$,   (ii) $y = 0$, $s = 1$, $t = 0$,   (iii) $y = 0$, $s = 0$, $t = 1$

to obtain the respective solutions

$$v_1 = (-2, 1, 0, 0, 0), \quad v_2 = (5, 0, -2, 1, 0), \quad v_3 = (-7, 0, 2, 0, 1)$$

The set $\{v_1, v_2, v_3\}$ is a basis of the solution space W.

5.26. Find a homogeneous system whose solution set W is generated by

$$\{(1, -2, 0, 3), (1, -1, -1, 4), (1, 0, -2, 5)\}$$

Method 1. Let $v = (x, y, z, w)$. Form the matrix M whose first rows are the given vectors and whose last row is v; and then row reduce to echelon form:

$$M = \begin{pmatrix} 1 & -2 & 0 & 3 \\ 1 & -1 & -1 & 4 \\ 1 & 0 & -2 & 5 \\ x & y & z & w \end{pmatrix} \text{ to } \begin{pmatrix} 1 & -2 & 0 & 3 \\ 0 & 1 & -1 & 1 \\ 0 & 2 & -2 & 2 \\ 0 & 2x+y & z & -3x+w \end{pmatrix} \text{ to } \begin{pmatrix} 1 & -2 & 0 & 3 \\ 0 & 1 & -1 & 1 \\ 0 & 0 & 2x+y+z & -5x-y+w \\ 0 & 0 & 0 & 0 \end{pmatrix}$$

The original first three rows show that W has dimension 2. Thus $v \in W$ if and only if the additional row does not increase the dimension of the row space. Hence we set the last two entries in the third row on the right equal to 0 to obtain the required homogeneous system

$$2x + y + z = 0$$
$$5x + y - w = 0$$

Method 2. We know that $v = (x, y, z, w) \in W$ if and only if v is a linear combination of the generators of W:

$$(x, y, z, w) = r(1, -2, 0, 3) + s(1, -1, -1, 4) + t(1, 0, -2, 5)$$

The above vector equation in unknowns r, s and t is equivalent to the following system:

$$\begin{array}{llll}
r + s + t = x & & r + s + t = x & \\
-2r - s \quad = y & & s + 2t = 2x + y & \\
\quad -s - 2t = z & \text{or} & -s - 2t = z & \text{or} \\
3r + 4s + 5t = w & & s + 2t = w - 3x &
\end{array}
\begin{array}{l}
r + s + t = x \\
s + 2t = 2x + y \\
0 = 2x + y + z \\
0 = 5x + y - w
\end{array}
\quad (1)$$

Thus $v \in W$ if and only if the above system has a solution, i.e. if

$$2x + y + z = 0$$
$$5x + y - w = 0$$

The above is the required homogeneous system.

Remark: Observe that the augmented matrix of the system (1) is the transpose of the matrix M used in the first method.

5.27. Let U and W be the following subspaces of $\mathbf{R}^4$:
$$U = \{(a,b,c,d): b+c+d = 0\}, \quad W = \{(a,b,c,d): a+b=0,\ c=2d\}$$
Find the dimension and a basis of (i) U, (ii) W, (iii) $U \cap W$.

(i) We seek a basis of the set of solutions (a,b,c,d) of the equation
$$b + c + d = 0 \quad \text{or} \quad 0 \cdot a + b + c + d = 0$$
The free variables are a, c and d. Set

    (1) $a=1,\ c=0,\ d=0$,   (2) $a=0,\ c=1,\ d=0$,   (3) $a=0,\ c=0,\ d=1$

to obtain the respective solutions
$$v_1 = (1,0,0,0), \quad v_2 = (0,-1,1,0), \quad v_3 = (0,-1,0,1)$$
The set $\{v_1, v_2, v_3\}$ is a basis of U, and $\dim U = 3$.

(ii) We seek a basis of the set of solutions (a,b,c,d) of the system
$$\begin{array}{ll} a + b = 0 & \quad a + b = 0 \\ c = 2d & \quad c - 2d = 0 \end{array} \text{ or }$$
The free variables are b and d. Set

    (1) $b=1,\ d=0$,   (2) $b=0,\ d=1$

to obtain the respective solutions
$$v_1 = (-1,1,0,0), \quad v_2 = (0,0,2,1)$$
The set $\{v_1, v_2\}$ is a basis of W, and $\dim W = 2$.

(iii) $U \cap W$ consists of those vectors (a,b,c,d) which satisfy the conditions defining U and the conditions defining W, i.e. the three equations
$$\begin{array}{ll}
b + c + d = 0 & \quad a + b \quad\quad = 0 \\
a + b \quad\quad = 0 & \text{or} \quad b + c + d = 0 \\
c \quad = 2d & \quad c - 2d = 0
\end{array}$$
The free variable is d. Set $d = 1$ to obtain the solution $v = (3,-3,2,1)$. Thus $\{v\}$ is a basis of $U \cap W$, and $\dim(U \cap W) = 1$.

5.28. Find the dimension of the vector space spanned by:

(i) $(1,-2,3,-1)$ and $(1,1,-2,3)$

(ii) $(3,-6,3,-9)$ and $(-2,4,-2,6)$

(iii) $t^3 + 2t^2 + 3t + 1$ and $2t^3 + 4t^2 + 6t + 2$

(iv) $t^3 - 2t^2 + 5$ and $t^2 + 3t - 4$

(v) $\begin{pmatrix} 1 & 2 \\ 1 & 2 \end{pmatrix}$ and $\begin{pmatrix} 1 & 1 \\ 2 & 2 \end{pmatrix}$

(vi) $\begin{pmatrix} 1 & 1 \\ -1 & -1 \end{pmatrix}$ and $\begin{pmatrix} -3 & -3 \\ 3 & 3 \end{pmatrix}$

(vii) 3 and -3

Two nonzero vectors span a space W of dimension 2 if they are independent, and of dimension 1 if they are dependent. Recall that two vectors are dependent if and only if one is a multiple of the other. Hence: (i) 2, (ii) 1, (iii) 1, (iv) 2, (v) 2, (vi) 1, (vii) 1.

5.29. Let V be the vector space of 2 by 2 symmetric matrices over K. Show that $\dim V = 3$. (Recall that $A = (a_{ij})$ is symmetric iff $A = A^t$ or, equivalently, $a_{ij} = a_{ji}$.)

An arbitrary 2 by 2 symmetric matrix is of the form $A = \begin{pmatrix} a & b \\ b & c \end{pmatrix}$ where $a, b, c \in K$. (Note that there are three "variables".) Setting

(i) $a = 1, b = 0, c = 0$,   (ii) $a = 0, b = 1, c = 0$,   (iii) $a = 0, b = 0, c = 1$

we obtain the respective matrices

$$E_1 = \begin{pmatrix} 1 & 0 \\ 0 & 0 \end{pmatrix}, \quad E_2 = \begin{pmatrix} 0 & 1 \\ 1 & 0 \end{pmatrix}, \quad E_3 = \begin{pmatrix} 0 & 0 \\ 0 & 1 \end{pmatrix}$$

We show that $\{E_1, E_2, E_3\}$ is a basis of V, that is, that it (1) generates V and (2) is independent.

(1) For the above arbitrary matrix A in V, we have

$$A = \begin{pmatrix} a & b \\ b & c \end{pmatrix} = aE_1 + bE_2 + cE_3$$

Thus $\{E_1, E_2, E_3\}$ generates V.

(2) Suppose $xE_1 + yE_2 + zE_3 = 0$, where x, y, z are unknown scalars. That is, suppose

$$x\begin{pmatrix} 1 & 0 \\ 0 & 0 \end{pmatrix} + y\begin{pmatrix} 0 & 1 \\ 1 & 0 \end{pmatrix} + z\begin{pmatrix} 0 & 0 \\ 0 & 1 \end{pmatrix} = \begin{pmatrix} 0 & 0 \\ 0 & 0 \end{pmatrix} \quad \text{or} \quad \begin{pmatrix} x & y \\ y & z \end{pmatrix} = \begin{pmatrix} 0 & 0 \\ 0 & 0 \end{pmatrix}$$

Setting corresponding entries equal to each other, we obtain $x = 0, y = 0, z = 0$. In other words,

$$xE_1 + yE_2 + zE_3 = 0 \quad \text{implies} \quad x = 0, \ y = 0, \ z = 0$$

Accordingly, $\{E_1, E_2, E_3\}$ is independent.

Thus $\{E_1, E_2, E_3\}$ is a basis of V and so the dimension of V is 3.

5.30. Let V be the space of polynomials in t of degree $\leq n$. Show that each of the following is a basis of V:

(i) $\{1, t, t^2, \ldots, t^{n-1}, t^n\}$,   (ii) $\{1, 1-t, (1-t)^2, \ldots, (1-t)^{n-1}, (1-t)^n\}$.

Thus $\dim V = n + 1$.

(i) Clearly each polynomial in V is a linear combination of $1, t, \ldots, t^{n-1}$ and t^n. Furthermore, $1, t, \ldots, t^{n-1}$ and t^n are independent since none is a linear combination of the preceding polynomials. Thus $\{1, t, \ldots, t^n\}$ is a basis of V.

(ii) (Note that by (i), $\dim V = n + 1$; and so any $n + 1$ independent polynomials form a basis of V.) Now each polynomial in the sequence $1, 1-t, \ldots, (1-t)^n$ is of degree higher than the preceding ones and so is not a linear combination of the preceding ones. Thus the $n + 1$ polynomials $1, 1-t, \ldots, (1-t)^n$ are independent and so form a basis of V.

5.31. Let V be the vector space of ordered pairs of complex numbers over the real field $\mathbf{R}$ (see Problem 4.42). Show that V is of dimension 4.

We claim that the following is a basis of V:

$$B = \{(1, 0), (i, 0), (0, 1), (0, i)\}$$

Suppose $v \in V$. Then $v = (z, w)$ where z, w are complex numbers, and so $v = (a + bi, c + di)$ where a, b, c, d are real numbers. Then

$$v = a(1, 0) + b(i, 0) + c(0, 1) + d(0, i)$$

Thus B generates V.

The proof is complete if we show that B is independent.   Suppose

$$x_1(1, 0) + x_2(i, 0) + x_3(0, 1) + x_4(0, i) = 0$$

where $x_1, x_2, x_3, x_4 \in R$.   Then

$$(x_1 + x_2 i, x_3 + x_4 i) = (0, 0) \quad \text{and so} \quad \begin{cases} x_1 + x_2 i = 0 \\ x_3 + x_4 i = 0 \end{cases}$$

Accordingly $x_1 = 0,\ x_2 = 0,\ x_3 = 0,\ x_4 = 0$ and so B is independent.

5.32. Let V be the vector space of $m \times n$ matrices over a field K. Let $E_{ij} \in V$ be the matrix with 1 as the ij-entry and 0 elsewhere. Show that $\{E_{ij}\}$ is a basis of V. Thus $\dim V = mn$.

We need to show that $\{E_{ij}\}$ generates V and is independent.

Let $A = (a_{ij})$ be any matrix in V. Then $A = \sum\limits_{i,j} a_{ij} E_{ij}$. Hence $\{E_{ij}\}$ generates V.

Now suppose that $\sum\limits_{i,j} x_{ij} E_{ij} = 0$ where the x_{ij} are scalars. The ij-entry of $\sum\limits_{i,j} x_{ij} E_{ij}$ is x_{ij}, and the ij-entry of 0 is 0. Thus $x_{ij} = 0,\ i = 1, \ldots, m,\ j = 1, \ldots, n$. Accordingly the matrices E_{ij} are independent.

Thus $\{E_{ij}\}$ is a basis of V.

Remark: Viewing a vector in K^n as a $1 \times n$ matrix, we have shown by the above result that the usual basis defined in Example 5.3, page 88, is a basis of K^n and that $\dim K^n = n$.

SUMS AND INTERSECTIONS

5.33. Suppose U and W are distinct 4-dimensional subspaces of a vector space V of dimension 6. Find the possible dimensions of $U \cap W$.

Since U and W are distinct, $U + W$ properly contains U and W; hence $\dim(U + W) > 4$. But $\dim(U + W)$ cannot be greater than 6, since $\dim V = 6$. Hence we have two possibilities: (i) $\dim(U + W) = 5$, or (ii) $\dim(U + W) = 6$. Using Theorem 5.8 that $\dim(U + W) = \dim U + \dim W - \dim(U \cap W)$, we obtain

$$\text{(i)} \quad 5 = 4 + 4 - \dim(U \cap W) \quad \text{or} \quad \dim(U \cap W) = 3$$

$$\text{(ii)} \quad 6 = 4 + 4 - \dim(U \cap W) \quad \text{or} \quad \dim(U \cap W) = 2$$

That is, the dimension of $U \cap W$ must be either 2 or 3.

5.34. Let U and W be the subspaces of $\mathbf{R}^4$ generated by

$$\{(1, 1, 0, -1), (1, 2, 3, 0), (2, 3, 3, -1)\} \quad \text{and} \quad \{(1, 2, 2, -2), (2, 3, 2, -3), (1, 3, 4, -3)\}$$

respectively.   Find   (i) $\dim(U + W)$, (ii) $\dim(U \cap W)$.

(i) $U + W$ is the space spanned by all six vectors. Hence form the matrix whose rows are the given six vectors, and then row reduce to echelon form:

$$\begin{pmatrix} 1 & 1 & 0 & -1 \\ 1 & 2 & 3 & 0 \\ 2 & 3 & 3 & -1 \\ 1 & 2 & 2 & -2 \\ 2 & 3 & 2 & -3 \\ 1 & 3 & 4 & -3 \end{pmatrix} \text{ to } \begin{pmatrix} 1 & 1 & 0 & -1 \\ 0 & 1 & 3 & 1 \\ 0 & 1 & 3 & 1 \\ 0 & 1 & 2 & -1 \\ 0 & 1 & 2 & -1 \\ 0 & 2 & 4 & -2 \end{pmatrix} \text{ to } \begin{pmatrix} 1 & 1 & 0 & -1 \\ 0 & 1 & 3 & 1 \\ 0 & 1 & 2 & -1 \\ 0 & 0 & 0 & 0 \\ 0 & 0 & 0 & 0 \\ 0 & 0 & 0 & 0 \end{pmatrix} \text{ to } \begin{pmatrix} 1 & 1 & 0 & -1 \\ 0 & 1 & 3 & 1 \\ 0 & 0 & -1 & -2 \\ 0 & 0 & 0 & 0 \\ 0 & 0 & 0 & 0 \\ 0 & 0 & 0 & 0 \end{pmatrix}$$

Since the echelon matrix has three nonzero rows, $\dim(U + W) = 3$.

(ii) First find dim U and dim W. Form the two matrices whose rows are the generators of U and W respectively and then row reduce each to echelon form:

$$\begin{pmatrix} 1 & 1 & 0 & -1 \\ 1 & 2 & 3 & 0 \\ 2 & 3 & 3 & -1 \end{pmatrix} \text{ to } \begin{pmatrix} 1 & 1 & 0 & -1 \\ 0 & 1 & 3 & 1 \\ 0 & 1 & 3 & 1 \end{pmatrix} \text{ to } \begin{pmatrix} 1 & 1 & 0 & -1 \\ 0 & 1 & 3 & 1 \\ 0 & 0 & 0 & 0 \end{pmatrix}$$

and

$$\begin{pmatrix} 1 & 2 & 2 & -2 \\ 2 & 3 & 2 & -3 \\ 1 & 3 & 4 & -3 \end{pmatrix} \text{ to } \begin{pmatrix} 1 & 2 & 2 & -2 \\ 0 & -1 & -2 & 1 \\ 0 & 1 & 2 & -1 \end{pmatrix} \text{ to } \begin{pmatrix} 1 & 2 & 2 & -2 \\ 0 & -1 & -2 & 1 \\ 0 & 0 & 0 & 0 \end{pmatrix}$$

Since each of the echelon matrices has two nonzero rows, dim $U = 2$ and dim $W = 2$. Using Theorem 5.8 that dim$(U + W) =$ dim $U +$ dim $W -$ dim$(U \cap W)$, we have

$$3 = 2 + 2 - \dim(U \cap W) \quad \text{or} \quad \dim(U \cap W) = 1$$

5.35. Let U be the subspace of $\mathbf{R}^5$ generated by

$$\{(1, 3, -2, 2, 3), (1, 4, -3, 4, 2), (2, 3, -1, -2, 9)\}$$

and let W be the subspace generated by

$$\{(1, 3, 0, 2, 1), (1, 5, -6, 6, 3), (2, 5, 3, 2, 1)\}$$

Find a basis and the dimension of (i) $U + W$, (ii) $U \cap W$.

(i) $U + W$ is the space generated by all six vectors. Hence form the matrix whose rows are the six vectors and then row reduce to echelon form:

$$\begin{pmatrix} 1 & 3 & -2 & 2 & 3 \\ 1 & 4 & -3 & 4 & 2 \\ 2 & 3 & -1 & -2 & 9 \\ 1 & 3 & 0 & 2 & 1 \\ 1 & 5 & -6 & 6 & 3 \\ 2 & 5 & 3 & 2 & 1 \end{pmatrix} \text{ to } \begin{pmatrix} 1 & 3 & -2 & 2 & 3 \\ 0 & 1 & -1 & 2 & -1 \\ 0 & -3 & 3 & -6 & 3 \\ 0 & 0 & 2 & 0 & -2 \\ 0 & 2 & -4 & 4 & 0 \\ 0 & -1 & 7 & -2 & -5 \end{pmatrix}$$

$$\text{to } \begin{pmatrix} 1 & 3 & -2 & 2 & 3 \\ 0 & 1 & -1 & 2 & -1 \\ 0 & 0 & 0 & 0 & 0 \\ 0 & 0 & 2 & 0 & -2 \\ 0 & 0 & -2 & 0 & 2 \\ 0 & 0 & 6 & 0 & -6 \end{pmatrix} \text{ to } \begin{pmatrix} 1 & 3 & -2 & 2 & 3 \\ 0 & 1 & -1 & 2 & -1 \\ 0 & 0 & 2 & 0 & -2 \\ 0 & 0 & 0 & 0 & 0 \\ 0 & 0 & 0 & 0 & 0 \\ 0 & 0 & 0 & 0 & 0 \end{pmatrix}$$

The set of nonzero rows of the echelon matrix,

$$\{(1, 3, -2, 2, 3), (0, 1, -1, 2, -1), (0, 0, 2, 0, -2)\}$$

is a basis of $U + W$; thus dim$(U + W) = 3$.

(ii) First find homogeneous systems whose solution sets are U and W respectively. Form the matrix whose first rows are the generators of U and whose last row is (x, y, z, s, t) and then row reduce to echelon form:

$$\begin{pmatrix} 1 & 3 & -2 & 2 & 3 \\ 1 & 4 & -3 & 4 & 2 \\ 2 & 3 & -1 & -2 & 9 \\ x & y & z & s & t \end{pmatrix} \text{ to } \begin{pmatrix} 1 & 3 & -2 & 2 & 3 \\ 0 & 1 & -1 & 2 & -1 \\ 0 & -3 & 3 & -6 & 3 \\ 0 & -3x+y & 2x+z & -2x+s & -3x+t \end{pmatrix}$$

$$\text{to } \begin{pmatrix} 1 & 3 & -2 & 2 & 3 \\ 0 & 1 & -1 & 2 & -1 \\ 0 & 0 & -x+y+z & 4x-2y+s & -6x+y+t \\ 0 & 0 & 0 & 0 & 0 \end{pmatrix}$$

Set the entries of the third row equal to 0 to obtain the homogeneous system whose solution set is U:

$$-x + y + z = 0, \quad 4x - 2y + s = 0, \quad -6x + y + t = 0$$

Now form the matrix whose first rows are the generators of W and whose last row is (x, y, z, s, t) and then row reduce to echelon form:

$$\begin{pmatrix} 1 & 3 & 0 & 2 & 1 \\ 1 & 5 & -6 & 6 & 3 \\ 2 & 5 & 3 & 2 & 1 \\ x & y & z & s & t \end{pmatrix} \text{ to } \begin{pmatrix} 1 & 3 & 0 & 2 & 1 \\ 0 & 2 & -6 & 4 & 2 \\ 0 & -1 & 3 & -2 & -1 \\ 0 & -3x+y & z & -2x+s & -x+t \end{pmatrix}$$

$$\begin{pmatrix} 1 & 3 & 0 & 2 & 1 \\ 0 & 1 & -3 & 2 & 1 \\ 0 & 0 & -9x+3y+z & 4x-2y+s & 2x-y+t \\ 0 & 0 & 0 & 0 & 0 \end{pmatrix}$$

Set the entries of the third row equal to 0 to obtain the homogeneous system whose solution set is W:

$$-9x + 3y + z = 0, \quad 4x - 2y + s = 0, \quad 2x - y + t = 0$$

Combining both systems, we obtain the homogeneous system whose solution set is $U \cap W$:

$$\begin{cases} -x + y + z & = 0 \\ 4x - 2y + s & = 0 \\ -6x + y + t & = 0 \\ -9x + 3y + z & = 0 \\ 4x - 2y + s & = 0 \\ 2x - y + t & = 0 \end{cases} \text{ or } \begin{cases} -x + y + z & = 0 \\ 2y + 4z + s & = 0 \\ -5y - 6z + t & = 0 \\ -6y - 8z & = 0 \\ 2y + 4z + s & = 0 \\ y + 2z + t & = 0 \end{cases}$$

$$\begin{cases} -x + y + z & = 0 \\ 2y + 4z + s & = 0 \\ 8z + 5s + 2t & = 0 \\ 4z + 3s & = 0 \\ s - 2t & = 0 \end{cases} \text{ or } \begin{cases} -x + y + z & = 0 \\ 2y + 4z + s & = 0 \\ 8z + 5s + 2t & = 0 \\ s - 2t & = 0 \end{cases}$$

There is one free variable, which is t; hence $\dim(U \cap W) = 1$. Setting $t = 2$, we obtain the solution $x = 1$, $y = 4$, $z = -3$, $s = 4$, $t = 2$. Thus $\{(1, 4, -3, 4, 2)\}$ is a basis of $U \cap W$.

COORDINATE VECTORS

5.36. Find the coordinate vector of v relative to the basis $\{(1, 1, 1), (1, 1, 0), (1, 0, 0)\}$ of $\mathbf{R}^3$ where (i) $v = (4, -3, 2)$, (ii) $v = (a, b, c)$.

In each case set v as a linear combination of the basis vectors using unknown scalars x, y and z:

$$v = x(1, 1, 1) + y(1, 1, 0) + z(1, 0, 0)$$

and then solve for the solution vector (x, y, z). (The solution is unique since the basis vectors are linearly independent.)

(i) $(4, -3, 2) = x(1, 1, 1) + y(1, 1, 0) + z(1, 0, 0)$
$= (x, x, x) + (y, y, 0) + (z, 0, 0)$
$= (x+y+z, x+y, x)$

Set corresponding components equal to each other to obtain the system

$$x + y + z = 4, \quad x + y = -3, \quad x = 2$$

Substitute $x = 2$ into the second equation to obtain $y = -5$; then put $x = 2$, $y = -5$ into the first equation to obtain $z = 7$. Thus $x = 2$, $y = -5$, $z = 7$ is the unique solution to the system and so the coordinate vector of v relative to the given basis is $[v] = (2, -5, 7)$.

(ii) $(a, b, c) = x(1, 1, 1) + y(1, 1, 0) + z(1, 0, 0) = (x + y + z, x + y, x)$

Then
$$x + y + z = a, \quad x + y = b, \quad x = c$$

from which $x = c$, $y = b - c$, $z = a - b$. Thus $[v] = (c, b - c, a - b)$, that is, $[(a, b, c)] = (c, b - c, a - b)$.

5.37. Let V be the vector space of 2×2 matrices over **R**. Find the coordinate vector of the matrix $A \in V$ relative to the basis
$$\left\{ \begin{pmatrix} 1 & 1 \\ 1 & 1 \end{pmatrix}, \begin{pmatrix} 0 & -1 \\ 1 & 0 \end{pmatrix}, \begin{pmatrix} 1 & -1 \\ 0 & 0 \end{pmatrix}, \begin{pmatrix} 1 & 0 \\ 0 & 0 \end{pmatrix} \right\} \quad \text{where} \quad A = \begin{pmatrix} 2 & 3 \\ 4 & -7 \end{pmatrix}$$

Set A as a linear combination of the matrices in the basis using unknown scalars x, y, z, w:
$$A = \begin{pmatrix} 2 & 3 \\ 4 & -7 \end{pmatrix} = x \begin{pmatrix} 1 & 1 \\ 1 & 1 \end{pmatrix} + y \begin{pmatrix} 0 & -1 \\ 1 & 0 \end{pmatrix} + z \begin{pmatrix} 1 & -1 \\ 0 & 0 \end{pmatrix} + w \begin{pmatrix} 1 & 0 \\ 0 & 0 \end{pmatrix}$$
$$= \begin{pmatrix} x & x \\ x & x \end{pmatrix} + \begin{pmatrix} 0 & -y \\ y & 0 \end{pmatrix} + \begin{pmatrix} z & -z \\ 0 & 0 \end{pmatrix} + \begin{pmatrix} w & 0 \\ 0 & 0 \end{pmatrix}$$
$$= \begin{pmatrix} x + z + w & x - y - z \\ x + y & x \end{pmatrix}$$

Set corresponding entries equal to each other to obtain the system
$$x + z + w = 2, \quad x - y - z = 3, \quad x + y = 4, \quad x = -7$$

from which $x = -7$, $y = 11$, $z = -21$, $w = 30$. Thus $[A] = (-7, 11, -21, 30)$. (Note that the coordinate vector of A must be a vector in **R**^{4} since $\dim V = 4$.)

5.38. Let W be the vector space of 2×2 symmetric matrices over **R**. (See Problem 5.29.) Find the coordinate vector of the matrix $A = \begin{pmatrix} 4 & -11 \\ -11 & -7 \end{pmatrix}$ relative to the basis
$$\left\{ \begin{pmatrix} 1 & -2 \\ -2 & 1 \end{pmatrix}, \begin{pmatrix} 2 & 1 \\ 1 & 3 \end{pmatrix}, \begin{pmatrix} 4 & -1 \\ -1 & -5 \end{pmatrix} \right\}.$$

Set A as a linear combination of the matrices in the basis using unknown scalars x, y and z:
$$A = \begin{pmatrix} 4 & -11 \\ -11 & -7 \end{pmatrix} = x \begin{pmatrix} 1 & -2 \\ -2 & 1 \end{pmatrix} + y \begin{pmatrix} 2 & 1 \\ 1 & 3 \end{pmatrix} + z \begin{pmatrix} 4 & -1 \\ -1 & -5 \end{pmatrix} = \begin{pmatrix} x + 2y + 4z & -2x + y - z \\ -2x + y - z & x + 3y - 5z \end{pmatrix}$$

Set corresponding entries equal to each other to obtain the equivalent system of linear equations and reduce to echelon form:

$$\begin{array}{l} x + 2y + 4z = 4 \\ -2x + y - z = -11 \\ -2x + y - z = -11 \\ x + 3y - 5z = -7 \end{array} \quad \text{or} \quad \begin{array}{l} x + 2y + 4z = 4 \\ 5y + 7z = -3 \\ y - 9z = -11 \end{array} \quad \text{or} \quad \begin{array}{l} x + 2y + 4z = 4 \\ 5y + 7z = -3 \\ 52z = 52 \end{array}$$

We obtain $z = 1$ from the third equation, then $y = -2$ from the second equation, and then $x = 4$ from the first equation. Thus the solution of the system is $x = 4$, $y = -2$, $z = 1$; hence $[A] = (4, -2, 1)$. (Since $\dim W = 3$ by Problem 5.29, the coordinate vector of A must be a vector in **R**^{3}.)

5.39. Let $\{e_1, e_2, e_3\}$ and $\{f_1, f_2, f_3\}$ be bases of a vector space V (of dimension 3). Suppose
$$\begin{array}{l} e_1 = a_1 f_1 + a_2 f_2 + a_3 f_3 \\ e_2 = b_1 f_1 + b_2 f_2 + b_3 f_3 \\ e_3 = c_1 f_1 + c_2 f_2 + c_3 f_3 \end{array} \tag{1}$$

Let P be the matrix whose rows are the coordinate vectors of e_1, e_2 and e_3 respectively, relative to the basis $\{f_i\}$:

$$P = \begin{pmatrix} a_1 & a_2 & a_3 \\ b_1 & b_2 & b_3 \\ c_1 & c_2 & c_3 \end{pmatrix}$$

Show that, for any vector $v \in V$, $[v]_e P = [v]_f$. That is, multiplying the coordinate vector of v relative to the basis $\{e_i\}$ by the matrix P, we obtain the coordinate vector of v relative to the basis $\{f_i\}$. (The matrix P is frequently called the change of basis matrix.)

Suppose $v = re_1 + se_2 + te_3$; then $[v]_e = (r, s, t)$. Using (1), we have

$$\begin{aligned} v &= r(a_1 f_1 + a_2 f_2 + a_3 f_3) + s(b_1 f_1 + b_2 f_2 + b_3 f_3) + t(c_1 f_1 + c_2 f_2 + c_3 f_3) \\ &= (ra_1 + sb_1 + tc_1)f_1 + (ra_2 + sb_2 + tc_2)f_2 + (ra_3 + sb_3 + tc_3)f_3 \end{aligned}$$

Hence $\qquad [v]_f = (ra_1 + sb_1 + tc_1, \ ra_2 + sb_2 + tc_2, \ ra_3 + sb_3 + tc_3)$

On the other hand,

$$[v]_e P = (r, s, t) \begin{pmatrix} a_1 & a_2 & a_3 \\ b_1 & b_2 & b_3 \\ c_1 & c_2 & c_3 \end{pmatrix}$$
$$= (ra_1 + sb_1 + tc_1, \ ra_2 + sb_2 + tc_2, \ ra_3 + sb_3 + tc_3)$$

Accordingly, $[v]_e P = [v]_f$.

Remark: In Chapter 8 we shall write coordinate vectors as column vectors rather than row vectors. Then, by above,

$$Q[v]_e = \begin{pmatrix} a_1 & b_1 & c_1 \\ a_2 & b_2 & c_2 \\ a_3 & b_3 & c_3 \end{pmatrix} \begin{pmatrix} r \\ s \\ t \end{pmatrix} = \begin{pmatrix} ra_1 + sb_1 + tc_1 \\ ra_2 + sb_2 + tc_2 \\ ra_3 + sb_3 + tc_3 \end{pmatrix} = [v]_f$$

where Q is the matrix whose columns are the coordinate vectors of e_1, e_2 and e_3 respectively, relative to the basis $\{f_i\}$. Note that Q is the transpose of P and that Q appears on the left of the column vector $[v]_e$ whereas P appears on the right of the row vector $[v]_e$.

RANK OF A MATRIX

5.40. Find the rank of the matrix A where:

(i) $A = \begin{pmatrix} 1 & 3 & 1 & -2 & -3 \\ 1 & 4 & 3 & -1 & -4 \\ 2 & 3 & -4 & -7 & -3 \\ 3 & 8 & 1 & -7 & -8 \end{pmatrix}$ (ii) $A = \begin{pmatrix} 1 & 2 & -3 \\ 2 & 1 & 0 \\ -2 & -1 & 3 \\ -1 & 4 & -2 \end{pmatrix}$ (iii) $A = \begin{pmatrix} 1 & 3 \\ 0 & -2 \\ 5 & -1 \\ -2 & 3 \end{pmatrix}$

(i) Row reduce to echelon form:

$$\begin{pmatrix} 1 & 3 & 1 & -2 & -3 \\ 1 & 4 & 3 & -1 & -4 \\ 2 & 3 & -4 & -7 & -3 \\ 3 & 8 & 1 & -7 & -8 \end{pmatrix} \text{ to } \begin{pmatrix} 1 & 3 & 1 & -2 & -3 \\ 0 & 1 & 2 & 1 & -1 \\ 0 & -3 & -6 & -3 & 3 \\ 0 & -1 & -2 & -1 & 1 \end{pmatrix} \text{ to } \begin{pmatrix} 1 & 3 & 1 & -2 & -3 \\ 0 & 1 & 2 & 1 & -1 \\ 0 & 0 & 0 & 0 & 0 \\ 0 & 0 & 0 & 0 & 0 \end{pmatrix}$$

Since the echelon matrix has two nonzero rows, rank $(A) = 2$.

(ii) Since row rank equals column rank, it is easier to form the transpose of A and then row reduce to echelon form:

$$\begin{pmatrix} 1 & 2 & -2 & -1 \\ 2 & 1 & -1 & 4 \\ -3 & 0 & 3 & -2 \end{pmatrix} \text{ to } \begin{pmatrix} 1 & 2 & -2 & -1 \\ 0 & -3 & 3 & 6 \\ 0 & 6 & -3 & -5 \end{pmatrix} \text{ to } \begin{pmatrix} 1 & 2 & -2 & -1 \\ 0 & -3 & 3 & 6 \\ 0 & 0 & 3 & 7 \end{pmatrix}$$

Thus rank $(A) = 3$.

(iii) The two columns are linearly independent since one is not a multiple of the other. Hence rank $(A) = 2$.

5.41. Let A and B be arbitrary matrices for which the product AB is defined. Show that rank $(AB) \leqq$ rank (B) and rank $(AB) \leqq$ rank (A).

By Problem 4.33, page 80, the row space of AB is contained in the row space of B; hence rank $(AB) \leqq$ rank (B). Furthermore, by Problem 4.71, page 84, the column space of AB is contained in the column space of A; hence rank $(AB) \leqq$ rank (A).

5.42. Let A be an n-square matrix. Show that A is invertible if and only if rank $(A) = n$.

Note that the rows of the n-square identity matrix I_n are linearly independent since I_n is in echelon form; hence rank $(I_n) = n$. Now if A is invertible then, by Problem 3.36, page 57, A is row equivalent to I_n; hence rank $(A) = n$. But if A is not invertible then A is row equivalent to a matrix with a zero row; hence rank $(A) < n$. That is, A is invertible if and only if rank $(A) = n$.

5.43. Let $x_{i_1}, x_{i_2}, \ldots, x_{i_k}$ be the free variables of a homogeneous system of linear equations with n unknowns. Let v_j be the solution for which $x_{i_j} = 1$, and all other free variables $= 0$. Show that the solutions $v_1, v_2, \ldots, v_k$ are linearly independent.

Let A be the matrix whose rows are the v_i respectively. We interchange column 1 and column i_1, then column 2 and column $i_2, \ldots$, and then column k and column i_k; and obtain the $k \times n$ matrix

$$
B = (I, C) = \begin{pmatrix} 1 & 0 & 0 & \ldots & 0 & 0 & 0 & c_{1,k+1} & \ldots & c_{1n} \\ 0 & 1 & 0 & \ldots & 0 & 0 & 0 & c_{2,k+1} & \ldots & c_{2n} \\ \multicolumn{10}{c}{\dotfill} \\ 0 & 0 & 0 & \ldots & 0 & 0 & 1 & c_{k,k+1} & \ldots & c_{kn} \end{pmatrix}
$$

The above matrix B is in echelon form and so its rows are independent; hence rank $(B) = k$. Since A and B are column equivalent, they have the same rank, i.e. rank $(A) = k$. But A has k rows; hence these rows, i.e. the v_i, are linearly independent as claimed.

MISCELLANEOUS PROBLEMS

5.44. The concept of linear dependence is extended to every set of vectors, finite or infinite, as follows: the set of vectors $A = \{v_i\}$ is linearly dependent iff there exist vectors $v_{i_1}, \ldots, v_{i_n} \in A$ and scalars $a_1, \ldots, a_n \in K$, not all of them 0, such that

$$a_1 v_{i_1} + a_2 v_{i_2} + \cdots + a_n v_{i_n} = 0$$

Otherwise A is said to be linearly independent. Suppose that $A_1, A_2, \ldots$ are linearly independent sets of vectors, and that $A_1 \subset A_2 \subset \cdots$. Show that the union $A = A_1 \cup A_2 \cup \cdots$ is also linearly independent.

Suppose A is linearly dependent. Then there exist vectors $v_1, \ldots, v_n \in A$ and scalars $a_1, \ldots, a_n \in K$, not all of them 0, such that

$$a_1 v_1 + a_2 v_2 + \cdots + a_n v_n = 0 \tag{1}$$

Since $A = \cup A_i$ and the $v_i \in A$, there exist sets $A_{i_1}, \ldots, A_{i_n}$ such that

$$v_1 \in A_{i_1}, \quad v_2 \in A_{i_2}, \quad \ldots, \quad v_n \in A_{i_n}$$

Let k be the maximum index of the sets A_{i_j}: $k = \max (i_1, \ldots, i_n)$. It follows then, since $A_1 \subset A_2 \subset \cdots$, that each A_{i_j} is contained in A_k. Hence $v_1, v_2, \ldots, v_n \in A_k$ and so, by (1), A_k is linearly dependent, which contradicts our hypothesis. Thus A is linearly independent.

5.45. Consider a finite sequence of vectors $S = \{v_1, v_2, \ldots, v_n\}$. Let T be the sequence of vectors obtained from S by one of the following "elementary operations": (i) interchange two vectors, (ii) multiply a vector by a nonzero scalar, (iii) add a multiple of one vector to another. Show that S and T generate the same space W. Also show that T is independent if and only if S is independent.

Observe that, for each operation, the vectors in T are linear combinations of vectors in S. On the other hand, each operation has an inverse of the same type (Prove!); hence the vectors in S are linear combinations of vectors in T. Thus S and T generate the same space W. Also, T is independent if and only if $\dim W = n$, and this is true iff S is also independent.

5.46. Let $A = (a_{ij})$ and $B = (b_{ij})$ be row equivalent $m \times n$ matrices over a field K, and let $v_1, \ldots, v_n$ be any vectors in a vector space V over K. Let

$$
\begin{aligned}
u_1 &= a_{11}v_1 + a_{12}v_2 + \cdots + a_{1n}v_n & \qquad w_1 &= b_{11}v_1 + b_{12}v_2 + \cdots + b_{1n}v_n \\
u_2 &= a_{21}v_1 + a_{22}v_2 + \cdots + a_{2n}v_n & \qquad w_2 &= b_{21}v_1 + b_{22}v_2 + \cdots + b_{2n}v_n \\
&\cdots\cdots\cdots\cdots\cdots\cdots\cdots\cdots\cdots & &\cdots\cdots\cdots\cdots\cdots\cdots\cdots\cdots\cdots \\
u_m &= a_{m1}v_1 + a_{m2}v_2 + \cdots + a_{mn}v_n & \qquad w_m &= b_{m1}v_1 + b_{m2}v_2 + \cdots + b_{mn}v_n
\end{aligned}
$$

Show that $\{u_i\}$ and $\{w_i\}$ generate the same space.

Applying an "elementary operation" of the preceding problem to $\{u_i\}$ is equivalent to applying an elementary row operation to the matrix A. Since A and B are row equivalent, B can be obtained from A by a sequence of elementary row operations; hence $\{w_i\}$ can be obtained from $\{u_i\}$ by the corresponding sequence of operations. Accordingly, $\{u_i\}$ and $\{w_i\}$ generate the same space.

5.47. Let $v_1, \ldots, v_n$ belong to a vector space V over a field K. Let

$$
\begin{aligned}
w_1 &= a_{11}v_1 + a_{12}v_2 + \cdots + a_{1n}v_n \\
w_2 &= a_{21}v_1 + a_{22}v_2 + \cdots + a_{2n}v_n \\
&\cdots\cdots\cdots\cdots\cdots\cdots\cdots\cdots\cdots \\
w_n &= a_{n1}v_1 + a_{n2}v_2 + \cdots + a_{nn}v_n
\end{aligned}
$$

where $a_{ij} \in K$. Let P be the n-square matrix of coefficients, i.e. let $P = (a_{ij})$.

(i) Suppose P is invertible. Show that $\{w_i\}$ and $\{v_i\}$ generate the same space; hence $\{w_i\}$ is independent if and only if $\{v_i\}$ is independent.

(ii) Suppose P is not invertible. Show that $\{w_i\}$ is dependent.

(iii) Suppose $\{w_i\}$ is independent. Show that P is invertible.

(i) Since P is invertible, it is row equivalent to the identity matrix I. Hence by the preceding problem $\{w_i\}$ and $\{v_i\}$ generate the same space. Thus one is independent if and only if the other is.

(ii) Since P is not invertible, it is row equivalent to a matrix with a zero row. This means that $\{w_i\}$ generates a space which has a generating set of less than n elements. Thus $\{w_i\}$ is dependent.

(iii) This is the contrapositive of the statement of (ii), and so it follows from (ii).

5.48. Suppose V is the direct sum of its subspaces U and W, i.e. $V = U \oplus W$. Show that: (i) if $\{u_1, \ldots, u_m\} \subset U$ and $\{w_1, \ldots, w_n\} \subset W$ are independent, then $\{u_i, w_j\}$ is also independent; (ii) $\dim V = \dim U + \dim W$.

(i) Suppose $a_1u_1 + \cdots + a_mu_m + b_1w_1 + \cdots + b_nw_n = 0$, where a_i, b_j are scalars. Then

$$0 = (a_1u_1 + \cdots + a_mu_m) + (b_1w_1 + \cdots + b_nw_n) = 0 + 0$$

where $\quad 0, a_1u_1 + \cdots + a_mu_m \in U \quad$ and $\quad 0, b_1w_1 + \cdots + b_nw_n \in W$. Since such a sum for 0 is unique, this leads to

$$a_1u_1 + \cdots + a_mu_m = 0, \qquad b_1w_1 + \cdots + b_nw_n = 0$$

The independence of the u_i implies that the a_i are all 0, and the independence of the w_j implies that the b_j are all 0. Consequently, $\{u_i, w_j\}$ is independent.

(ii) **Method 1.** Since $V = U \oplus W$, we have $V = U + W$ and $U \cap W = \{0\}$. Thus, by Theorem 5.8, page 90,

$$\dim V = \dim U + \dim W - \dim(U \cap W) = \dim U + \dim W - 0 = \dim U + \dim W$$

Method 2. Suppose $\{u_1, \ldots, u_r\}$ and $\{w_1, \ldots, w_s\}$ are bases of U and W respectively. Since they generate U and W respectively, $\{u_i, w_j\}$ generates $V = U + W$. On the other hand, by (i), $\{u_i, w_j\}$ is independent. Thus $\{u_i, w_j\}$ is a basis of V; hence $\dim V = \dim U + \dim W$.

5.49. Let U be a subspace of a vector space V of finite dimension. Show that there exists a subspace W of V such that $V = U \oplus W$.

Let $\{u_1, \ldots, u_r\}$ be a basis of U. Since $\{u_i\}$ is linearly independent, it can be extended to a basis of V, say, $\{u_1, \ldots, u_r, w_1, \ldots, w_s\}$. Let W be the space generated by $\{w_1, \ldots, w_s\}$. Since $\{u_i, w_i\}$ generates V, $V = U + W$. On the other hand, $U \cap W = \{0\}$ (Problem 5.62). Accordingly, $V = U \oplus W$.

5.50. Recall (page 65) that if K is a subfield of a field E (or: E is an extension of K), then E may be viewed as a vector space over K. (i) Show that the complex field $\mathbf{C}$ is a vector space of dimension 2 over the real field $\mathbf{R}$. (ii) Show that the real field $\mathbf{R}$ is a vector space of infinite dimension over the rational field $\mathbf{Q}$.

(i) We claim that $\{1, i\}$ is a basis of $\mathbf{C}$ over $\mathbf{R}$. For if $v \in \mathbf{C}$, then $v = a + bi = a \cdot 1 + b \cdot i$ where $a, b \in \mathbf{R}$; that is, $\{1, i\}$ generates $\mathbf{C}$ over $\mathbf{R}$. Furthermore, if $x \cdot 1 + y \cdot i = 0$ or $x + yi = 0$, where $x, y \in \mathbf{R}$, then $x = 0$ and $y = 0$; that is, $\{1, i\}$ is linearly independent over $\mathbf{R}$. Thus $\{1, i\}$ is a basis of $\mathbf{C}$ over $\mathbf{R}$, and so $\mathbf{C}$ is of dimension 2 over $\mathbf{R}$.

(ii) We claim that, for any n, $\{1, \pi, \pi^2, \ldots, \pi^n\}$ is linearly independent over $\mathbf{Q}$. For suppose $a_0 1 + a_1\pi + a_2\pi^2 + \cdots + a_n\pi^n = 0$, where the $a_i \in \mathbf{Q}$, and not all the a_i are 0. Then π is a root of the following nonzero polynomial over $\mathbf{Q}$: $a_0 + a_1x + a_2x^2 + \cdots + a_nx^n$. But it can be shown that π is a transcendental number, i.e. that π is not a root of any nonzero polynomial over $\mathbf{Q}$. Accordingly, the $n + 1$ real numbers $1, \pi, \pi^2, \ldots, \pi^n$ are linearly independent over $\mathbf{Q}$. Thus for any finite n, $\mathbf{R}$ cannot be of dimension n over $\mathbf{Q}$, i.e. $\mathbf{R}$ is of infinite dimension over $\mathbf{Q}$.

5.51. Let K be a subfield of a field L and L a subfield of a field E: $K \subset L \subset E$. (Hence K is a subfield of E.) Suppose that E is of dimension n over L and L is of dimension m over K. Show that E is of dimension mn over K.

Suppose $\{v_1, \ldots, v_n\}$ is a basis of E over L and $\{a_1, \ldots, a_m\}$ is a basis of L over K. We claim that $\{a_iv_j : i = 1, \ldots, m, j = 1, \ldots, n\}$ is a basis of E over K. Note that $\{a_iv_j\}$ contains mn elements.

Let w be any arbitrary element in E. Since $\{v_1, \ldots, v_n\}$ generates E over L, w is a linear combination of the v_i with coefficients in L:

$$w = b_1v_1 + b_2v_2 + \cdots + b_nv_n, \qquad b_i \in L \tag{1}$$

Since $\{a_1, \ldots, a_m\}$ generates L over K, each $b_i \in L$ is a linear combination of the a_j with coefficients in K:

$$b_1 = k_{11}a_1 + k_{12}a_2 + \cdots + k_{1m}a_m$$
$$b_2 = k_{21}a_1 + k_{22}a_2 + \cdots + k_{2m}a_m$$
$$\cdots\cdots\cdots\cdots\cdots\cdots\cdots\cdots\cdots\cdots\cdots\cdots$$
$$b_n = k_{n1}a_1 + k_{n2}a_2 + \cdots + k_{nm}a_m$$

where $k_{ij} \in K$. Substituting in (1), we obtain

$$w = (k_{11}a_1 + \cdots + k_{1m}a_m)v_1 + (k_{21}a_1 + \cdots + k_{2m}a_m)v_2 + \cdots + (k_{n1}a_1 + \cdots + k_{nm}a_m)v_n$$

$$= k_{11}a_1v_1 + \cdots + k_{1m}a_mv_1 + k_{21}a_1v_2 + \cdots + k_{2m}a_mv_2 + \cdots + k_{n1}a_1v_n + \cdots + k_{nm}a_mv_n$$

$$= \sum_{i,j} k_{ji}(a_iv_j)$$

where $k_{ji} \in K$. Thus w is a linear combination of the a_iv_j with coefficients in K; hence $\{a_iv_j\}$ generates E over K.

The proof is complete if we show that $\{a_iv_j\}$ is linearly independent over K. Suppose, for scalars $x_{ji} \in K$, $\sum_{i,j} x_{ji}(a_iv_j) = 0$; that is,

$$(x_{11}a_1v_1 + x_{12}a_2v_1 + \cdots + x_{1m}a_mv_1) + \cdots + (x_{n1}a_1v_n + x_{n2}a_2v_n + \cdots + x_{nm}a_mv_n) = 0$$

or

$$(x_{11}a_1 + x_{12}a_2 + \cdots + x_{1m}a_m)v_1 + \cdots + (x_{n1}a_1 + x_{n2}a_2 + \cdots + x_{nm}a_m)v_n = 0$$

Since $\{v_1, \ldots, v_n\}$ is linearly independent over L and since the above coefficients of the v_i belong to L, each coefficient must be 0:

$$x_{11}a_1 + x_{12}a_2 + \cdots + x_{1m}a_m = 0, \quad \ldots, \quad x_{n1}a_1 + x_{n2}a_2 + \cdots + x_{nm}a_m = 0$$

But $\{a_1, \ldots, a_m\}$ is linearly independent over K; hence since the $x_{ji} \in K$,

$$x_{11} = 0, \quad x_{12} = 0, \quad \ldots, \quad x_{1m} = 0, \quad \ldots, \quad x_{n1} = 0, \quad x_{n2} = 0, \quad \ldots, \quad x_{nm} = 0$$

Accordingly, $\{a_iv_j\}$ is linearly independent over K and the theorem is proved.

Supplementary Problems

LINEAR DEPENDENCE

5.52. Determine whether u and v are linearly dependent where:

(i) $u = (1, 2, 3, 4)$, $v = (4, 3, 2, 1)$ (iii) $u = (0, 1)$, $v = (0, -3)$

(ii) $u = (-1, 6, -12)$, $v = (\frac{1}{2}, -3, 6)$ (iv) $u = (1, 0, 0)$, $v = (0, 0, -3)$

(v) $u = \begin{pmatrix} 4 & -2 \\ 0 & -1 \end{pmatrix}$, $v = \begin{pmatrix} -2 & 1 \\ 0 & \frac{1}{2} \end{pmatrix}$ (vi) $u = \begin{pmatrix} 1 & 0 \\ 0 & 1 \end{pmatrix}$, $v = \begin{pmatrix} 0 & -1 \\ -1 & 0 \end{pmatrix}$

(vii) $u = -t^3 + \frac{1}{2}t^2 - 16$, $v = \frac{1}{2}t^3 - \frac{1}{4}t^2 + 8$ (viii) $u = t^3 + 3t + 4$, $v = t^3 + 4t + 3$

5.53. Determine whether the following vectors in $\mathbf{R}^4$ are linearly dependent or independent: (i) $(1, 3, -1, 4)$, $(3, 8, -5, 7)$, $(2, 9, 4, 23)$; (ii) $(1, -2, 4, 1)$, $(2, 1, 0, -3)$, $(3, -6, 1, 4)$.

5.54. Let V be the vector space of 2×3 matrices over $\mathbf{R}$. Determine whether the matrices $A, B, C \in V$ are linearly dependent or independent where:

(i) $A = \begin{pmatrix} 1 & -2 & 3 \\ 2 & 4 & -1 \end{pmatrix}$, $B = \begin{pmatrix} 1 & -1 & 4 \\ 4 & 5 & -2 \end{pmatrix}$, $C = \begin{pmatrix} 3 & -8 & 7 \\ 2 & 10 & -1 \end{pmatrix}$

(ii) $A = \begin{pmatrix} 2 & 1 & -1 \\ 3 & -2 & 4 \end{pmatrix}$, $B = \begin{pmatrix} 1 & 1 & -3 \\ -2 & 0 & 5 \end{pmatrix}$, $C = \begin{pmatrix} 4 & -1 & 2 \\ 1 & -2 & -3 \end{pmatrix}$

5.55. Let V be the vector space of polynomials of degree ≤ 3 over $\mathbf{R}$. Determine whether $u, v, w \in V$ are linearly dependent or independent where:

(i) $u = t^3 - 4t^2 + 2t + 3$, $v = t^3 + 2t^2 + 4t - 1$, $w = 2t^3 - t^2 - 3t + 5$

(ii) $u = t^3 - 5t^2 - 2t + 3$, $v = t^3 - 4t^2 - 3t + 4$, $w = 2t^3 - 7t^2 - 7t + 9$

5.56. Let V be the vector space of functions from $\mathbf{R}$ into $\mathbf{R}$. Show that $f, g, h \in V$ are linearly independent where: (i) $f(t) = e^t$, $g(t) = \sin t$, $h(t) = t^2$; (ii) $f(t) = e^t$, $g(t) = e^{2t}$, $h(t) = t$; (iii) $f(t) = e^t$, $g(t) = \sin t$, $h(t) = \cos t$.

5.57. Show that: (i) the vectors $(1 - i, i)$ and $(2, -1 + i)$ in $\mathbf{C}^2$ are linearly dependent over the complex field $\mathbf{C}$ but are linearly independent over the real field $\mathbf{R}$; (ii) the vectors $(3 + \sqrt{2}, 1 + \sqrt{2})$ and $(7, 1 + 2\sqrt{2})$ in $\mathbf{R}^2$ are linearly dependent over the real field $\mathbf{R}$ but are linearly independent over the rational field $\mathbf{Q}$.

5.58. Suppose u, v and w are linearly independent vectors. Show that:

(i) $u + v - 2w$, $u - v - w$ and $u + w$ are linearly independent;

(ii) $u + v - 3w$, $u + 3v - w$ and $v + w$ are linearly dependent.

5.59. Prove or show a counterexample: If the nonzero vectors u, v and w are linearly dependent, then w is a linear combination of u and v.

5.60. Suppose $v_1, v_2, \ldots, v_n$ are linearly independent vectors. Prove the following:

(i) $\{a_1 v_1, a_2 v_2, \ldots, a_n v_n\}$ is linearly independent where each $a_i \neq 0$.

(ii) $\{v_1, \ldots, v_{i-1}, w, v_{i+1}, \ldots, v_n\}$ is linearly independent where $w = b_1 v_1 + \cdots + b_i v_i + \cdots + b_n v_n$ and $b_i \neq 0$.

5.61. Let $v = (a, b)$ and $w = (c, d)$ belong to K^2. Show that $\{v, w\}$ is linearly dependent if and only if $ad - bc = 0$.

5.62. Suppose $\{u_1, \ldots, u_r, w_1, \ldots, w_s\}$ is a linearly independent subset of a vector space V. Show that $L(u_i) \cap L(w_j) = \{0\}$. (Recall that $L(u_i)$ is the linear span, i.e. the space generated by the u_i.)

5.63. Suppose $(a_{11}, \ldots, a_{1n}), \ldots, (a_{m1}, \ldots, a_{mn})$ are linearly independent vectors in K^n, and suppose $v_1, \ldots, v_n$ are linearly independent vectors in a vector space V over K. Show that the vectors

$$w_1 = a_{11} v_1 + \cdots + a_{1n} v_n, \quad \ldots, \quad w_m = a_{m1} v_1 + \cdots + a_{mn} v_n$$

are also linearly independent.

BASIS AND DIMENSION

5.64. Determine whether or not each of the following forms a basis of $\mathbf{R}^2$:

(i) $(1, 1)$ and $(3, 1)$ (iii) $(0, 1)$ and $(0, -3)$

(ii) $(2, 1)$, $(1, -1)$ and $(0, 2)$ (iv) $(2, 1)$ and $(-3, 87)$

5.65. Determine whether or not each of the following forms a basis of $\mathbf{R}^3$:

(i) $(1, 2, -1)$ and $(0, 3, 1)$

(ii) $(2, 4, -3)$, $(0, 1, 1)$ and $(0, 1, -1)$

(iii) $(1, 5, -6)$, $(2, 1, 8)$, $(3, -1, 4)$ and $(2, 1, 1)$

(iv) $(1, 3, -4)$, $(1, 4, -3)$ and $(2, 3, -11)$

5.66. Find a basis and the dimension of the subspace W of $\mathbf{R}^4$ generated by:

(i) $(1, 4, -1, 3)$, $(2, 1, -3, -1)$ and $(0, 2, 1, -5)$

(ii) $(1, -4, -2, 1)$, $(1, -3, -1, 2)$ and $(3, -8, -2, 7)$

5.67. Let V be the space of 2×2 matrices over $\mathbf{R}$ and let W be the subspace generated by

$$\begin{pmatrix} 1 & -5 \\ -4 & 2 \end{pmatrix}, \quad \begin{pmatrix} 1 & 1 \\ -1 & 5 \end{pmatrix}, \quad \begin{pmatrix} 2 & -4 \\ -5 & 7 \end{pmatrix} \quad \text{and} \quad \begin{pmatrix} 1 & -7 \\ -5 & 1 \end{pmatrix}$$

Find a basis and the dimension of W.

5.68. Let W be the space generated by the polynomials

$$u = t^3 + 2t^2 - 2t + 1, \quad v = t^3 + 3t^2 - t + 4 \quad \text{and} \quad w = 2t^3 + t^2 - 7t - 7$$

Find a basis and the dimension of W.

5.69. Find a basis and the dimension of the solution space W of each homogeneous system:

$$
\begin{array}{lll}
x + 3y + 2z = 0 & \quad x - 2y + 7z = 0 & \\
x + 5y + \ z = 0 & \quad 2x + 3y - 2z = 0 & \quad x + 4y + 2z = 0 \\
3x + 5y + 8z = 0 & \quad 2x - \ y + \ z = 0 & \quad 2x + \ y + 5z = 0
\end{array}
$$

$$
\text{(i)} \qquad\qquad\qquad \text{(ii)} \qquad\qquad\qquad \text{(iii)}
$$

5.70. Find a basis and the dimension of the solution space W of each homogeneous system:

$$
\begin{array}{ll}
x + 2y - 2z + 2s - \ t = 0 & \quad x + 2y - \ z + 3s - 4t = 0 \\
x + 2y - \ z + 3s - 2t = 0 & \quad 2x + 4y - 2z - \ s + 5t = 0 \\
2x + 4y - 7z + \ s + \ t = 0 & \quad 2x + 4y - 2z + 4s - 2t = 0
\end{array}
$$

$$
\text{(i)} \qquad\qquad\qquad\qquad \text{(ii)}
$$

5.71. Find a homogeneous system whose solution set W is generated by

$$
\{(1, -2, 0, 3, -1), (2, -3, 2, 5, -3), (1, -2, 1, 2, -2)\}
$$

5.72. Let V and W be the following subspaces of $\mathbf{R}^4$:

$$
V = \{(a, b, c, d): \ b - 2c + d = 0\}, \qquad W = \{(a, b, c, d): \ a = d, \ b = 2c\}
$$

Find a basis and the dimension of (i) V, (ii) W, (iii) $V \cap W$.

5.73. Let V be the vector space of polynomials in t of degree $\leq n$. Determine whether or not each of the following is a basis of V:

(i) $\{1, \ 1 + t, \ 1 + t + t^2, \ 1 + t + t^2 + t^3, \ \ldots, \ 1 + t + t^2 + \cdots + t^{n-1} + t^n\}$

(ii) $\{1 + t, \ t + t^2, \ t^2 + t^3, \ \ldots, \ t^{n-2} + t^{n-1}, \ t^{n-1} + t^n\}$.

SUMS AND INTERSECTIONS

5.74. Suppose U and W are 2-dimensional subspaces of $\mathbf{R}^3$. Show that $U \cap W \neq \{0\}$.

5.75. Suppose U and W are subspaces of V and that $\dim U = 4$, $\dim W = 5$ and $\dim V = 7$. Find the possible dimensions of $U \cap W$.

5.76. Let U and W be subspaces of $\mathbf{R}^3$ for which $\dim U = 1$, $\dim W = 2$ and $U \not\subset W$. Show that $\mathbf{R}^3 = U \oplus W$.

5.77. Let U be the subspace of $\mathbf{R}^5$ generated by

$$
\{(1, 3, -3, -1, -4), (1, 4, -1, -2, -2), (2, 9, 0, -5, -2)\}
$$

and let W be the subspace generated by

$$
\{(1, 6, 2, -2, 3), (2, 8, -1, -6, -5), (1, 3, -1, -5, -6)\}
$$

Find (i) $\dim(U + W)$, (ii) $\dim(U \cap W)$.

5.78. Let V be the vector space of polynomials over $\mathbf{R}$. Let U and W be the subspaces generated by

$\{t^3 + 4t^2 - t + 3, \ t^3 + 5t^2 + 5, \ 3t^3 + 10t^2 - 5t + 5\}$ and $\{t^3 + 4t^2 + 6, \ t^3 + 2t^2 - t + 5, \ 2t^3 + 2t^2 - 3t + 9\}$

respectively. Find (i) $\dim(U + W)$, (ii) $\dim(U \cap W)$.

5.79. Let U be the subspace of $\mathbf{R}^5$ generated by

$$
\{(1, -1, -1, -2, 0), (1, -2, -2, 0, -3), (1, -1, -2, -2, 1)\}
$$

and let W be the subspace generated by

$$
\{(1, -2, -3, 0, -2), (1, -1, -3, 2, -4), (1, -1, -2, 2, -5)\}
$$

(i) Find two homogeneous systems whose solution spaces are U and W, respectively.

(ii) Find a basis and the dimension of $U \cap W$.

COORDINATE VECTORS

5.80. Consider the following basis of $\mathbf{R}^2$: $\{(2,1), (1,-1)\}$. Find the coordinate vector of $v \in \mathbf{R}^2$ relative to the above basis where: (i) $v = (2,3)$; (ii) $v = (4,-1)$, (iii) $(3,-3)$; (iv) $v = (a,b)$.

5.81. In the vector space V of polynomials in t of degree ≤ 3, consider the following basis: $\{1, 1-t, (1-t)^2, (1-t)^3\}$. Find the coordinate vector of $v \in V$ relative to the above basis if: (i) $v = 2 - 3t + t^2 + 2t^3$; (ii) $v = 3 - 2t - t^2$; (iii) $v = a + bt + ct^2 + dt^3$.

5.82. In the vector space W of 2×2 symmetric matrices over $\mathbf{R}$, consider the following basis:

$$\left\{ \begin{pmatrix} 1 & -1 \\ -1 & 2 \end{pmatrix}, \begin{pmatrix} 4 & 1 \\ 1 & 0 \end{pmatrix}, \begin{pmatrix} 3 & -2 \\ -2 & 1 \end{pmatrix} \right\}$$

Find the coordinate vector of the matrix $A \in W$ relative to the above basis if:

(i) $A = \begin{pmatrix} 1 & -5 \\ -5 & 5 \end{pmatrix}$ (ii) $A = \begin{pmatrix} 1 & 2 \\ 2 & 4 \end{pmatrix}$

5.83. Consider the following two bases of $\mathbf{R}^3$:

$\{e_1 = (1,1,1), e_2 = (0,2,3), e_3 = (0,2,-1)\}$ and $\{f_1 = (1,1,0), f_2 = (1,-1,0), f_3 = (0,0,1)\}$

(i) Find the coordinate vector of $v = (3,5,-2)$ relative to each basis: $[v]_e$ and $[v]_f$.

(ii) Find the matrix P whose rows are respectively the coordinate vectors of the e_i relative to the basis $\{f_1, f_2, f_3\}$.

(iii) Verify that $[v]_e P = [v]_f$.

5.84. Suppose $\{e_1, \ldots, e_n\}$ and $\{f_1, \ldots, f_n\}$ are bases of a vector space V (of dimension n). Let P be the matrix whose rows are respectively the coordinate vectors of the e's relative to the basis $\{f_i\}$. Prove that for any vector $v \in V$, $[v]_e P = [v]_f$. (This result is proved in Problem 5.39 in the case $n = 3$.)

5.85. Show that the coordinate vector of $0 \in V$ relative to any basis of V is always the zero n-tuple $(0, 0, \ldots, 0)$.

RANK OF A MATRIX

5.86. Find the rank of each matrix:

$$\begin{pmatrix} 1 & 3 & -2 & 5 & 4 \\ 1 & 4 & 1 & 3 & 5 \\ 1 & 4 & 2 & 4 & 3 \\ 2 & 7 & -3 & 6 & 13 \end{pmatrix} \quad \begin{pmatrix} 1 & 2 & -3 & -2 & -3 \\ 1 & 3 & -2 & 0 & -4 \\ 3 & 8 & -7 & -2 & -11 \\ 2 & 1 & -9 & -10 & -3 \end{pmatrix} \quad \begin{pmatrix} 1 & 1 & 2 \\ 4 & 5 & 5 \\ 5 & 8 & 1 \\ -1 & -2 & 2 \end{pmatrix} \quad \begin{pmatrix} 2 & 1 \\ 3 & -7 \\ -6 & 1 \\ 5 & -8 \end{pmatrix}$$

(i) (ii) (iii) (iv)

5.87. Let A and B be arbitrary $m \times n$ matrices. Show that $\text{rank}(A + B) \leq \text{rank}(A) + \text{rank}(B)$.

5.88. Give examples of 2×2 matrices A and B such that:

(i) $\text{rank}(A + B) < \text{rank}(A), \text{rank}(B)$ (ii) $\text{rank}(A + B) = \text{rank}(A) = \text{rank}(B)$

(iii) $\text{rank}(A + B) > \text{rank}(A), \text{rank}(B)$

MISCELLANEOUS PROBLEMS

5.89. Let W be the vector space of 3×3 symmetric matrices over K. Show that $\dim W = 6$ by exhibiting a basis of W. (Recall that $A = (a_{ij})$ is symmetric iff $a_{ij} = a_{ji}$.)

5.90. Let W be the vector space of 3×3 antisymmetric matrices over K. Show that $\dim W = 3$ by exhibiting a basis of W. (Recall that $A = (a_{ij})$ is antisymmetric iff $a_{ij} = -a_{ji}$.)

5.91. Suppose $\dim V = n$. Show that a generating set with n elements is a basis. (Compare with Theorem 5.6(iii), page 89).

5.92. Let $t_1, t_2, \ldots, t_n$ be symbols, and let K be any field. Let V be the set of expressions $a_1 t_1 + a_2 t_2 + \cdots + a_n t_n$ where $a_i \in K$. Define addition in V by

$$(a_1 t_1 + a_2 t_2 + \cdots + a_n t_n) + (b_1 t_1 + b_2 t_2 + \cdots + b_n t_n)$$
$$= (a_1 + b_1)t_1 + (a_2 + b_2)t_2 + \cdots + (a_n + b_n)t_n$$

Define scalar multiplication on V by

$$k(a_1 t_1 + a_2 t_2 + \cdots + a_n t_n) = ka_1 t_1 + ka_2 t_2 + \cdots + ka_n t_n$$

Show that V is a vector space over K with the above operations. Also show that $\{t_1, \ldots, t_n\}$ is a basis of V where, for $i = 1, \ldots, n$,

$$t_i = 0t_1 + \cdots + 0t_{i-1} + 1t_i + 0t_{i+1} + \cdots + 0t_n$$

5.93. Let V be a vector space of dimension n over a field K, and let K be a vector space of dimension m over a subfield F. (Hence V may also be viewed as a vector space over the subfield F.) Prove that the dimension of V over F is mn.

5.94. Let U and W be vector spaces over the same field K, and let V be the external direct sum of U and W (see Problem 4.45). Let $\hat{U}$ and $\hat{W}$ be the subspaces of V defined by $\hat{U} = \{(u, 0) : u \in U\}$ and $\hat{W} = \{(0, w) : w \in W\}$.

    (i)   Show that U is isomorphic to $\hat{U}$ under the correspondence $u \leftrightarrow (u, 0)$, and that W is isomorphic to $\hat{W}$ under the correspondence $w \leftrightarrow (0, w)$.

    (ii) Show that $\dim V = \dim U + \dim W$.

5.95. Suppose $V = U \oplus W$. Let $\hat{V}$ be the external direct product of U and W. Show that V is isomorphic to $\hat{V}$ under the correspondence $v = u + w \leftrightarrow (u, w)$.

Answers to Supplementary Problems

5.52. (i) no, (ii) yes, (iii) yes, (iv) no, (v) yes, (vi) no, (vii) yes, (viii) no.

5.53. (i) dependent, (ii) independent.

5.54. (i) dependent, (ii) independent.

5.55. (i) independent, (ii) dependent.

5.57. (i) $(2, -1 + i) = (1 + i)(1 - i, i)$;   (ii) $(7, 1 + 2\sqrt{2}) = (3 - \sqrt{2})(3 + \sqrt{2}, 1 + \sqrt{2})$.

5.59. The statement is false. Counterexample: $u = (1, 0)$, $v = (2, 0)$ and $w = (1, 1)$ in $\mathbf{R}^2$. Lemma 5.2 requires that one of the nonzero vectors u, v, w is a linear combination of the preceding ones. In this case, $v = 2u$.

5.64. (i) yes, (ii) no, (iii) no, (iv) yes.

5.65. (i) no, (ii) yes, (iii) no, (iv) no.

5.66. (i) $\dim W = 3$, (ii) $\dim W = 2$.

5.67. $\dim W = 2$.

5.68. $\dim W = 2$.

5.69. (i) basis, $\{(7, -1, -2)\}$; $\dim W = 1$.   (ii) $\dim W = 0$.   (iii) basis, $\{(18, -1, -7)\}$; $\dim W = 1$.

5.70. (i)   basis, $\{(2, -1, 0, 0, 0), (4, 0, 1, -1, 0), (3, 0, 1, 0, 1)\}$; $\dim W = 3$.

    (ii) basis, $\{(2, -1, 0, 0, 0), (1, 0, 1, 0, 0)\}$; $\dim W = 2$.

5.71. $\begin{cases} 5x + y - z - s = 0 \\ x + y - z - t = 0 \end{cases}$

5.72. (i) basis, $\{(1, 0, 0, 0), (0, 2, 1, 0), (0, -1, 0, 1)\}$; dim $V = 3$.

     (ii) basis, $\{(1, 0, 0, 1), (0, 2, 1, 0)\}$; dim $W = 2$.

     (iii) basis, $\{(0, 2, 1, 0)\}$; dim $(V \cap W) = 1$. *Hint.* $V \cap W$ must satisfy all three conditions on a, b, c and d.

5.73. (i) yes, (ii) no. For dim $V = n + 1$, but the set contains only n elements.

5.75. dim $(U \cap W) = 2, 3$ or 4.

5.77. dim $(U + W) = 3$, dim $(U \cap W) = 2$.

5.78. dim $(U + W) = 3$, dim $(U \cap W) = 1$.

5.79. (i) $\begin{cases} 3x + 4y - z \quad - t = 0 \\ 4x + 2y \qquad + s \quad = 0 \end{cases}$, $\begin{cases} 4x + 2y \qquad - s \quad = 0 \\ 9x + 2y + z \quad + t = 0 \end{cases}$

     (ii) $\{(1, -2, -5, 0, 0), (0, 0, 1, 0, -1)\}$. dim $(U \cap W) = 2$.

5.80. (i) $[v] = (5/3, -4/3)$, (ii) $[v] = (1, 2)$, (iii) $[v] = (0, 3)$, (iv) $[v] = ((a + b)/3, (a - 2b)/3)$.

5.81. (i) $[v] = (2, -5, 7, -2)$, (ii) $[v] = (0, 4, -1, 0)$, (iii) $[v] = (a + b + c + d, -b - 2c - 3d, c + 3d, -d)$.

5.82. (i) $[A] = (2, -1, 1)$, (ii) $[A] = (3, 1, -2)$.

5.83. (i) $[v]_e = (3, -1, 2)$, $[v]_f = (4, -1, -2)$; (ii) $P = \begin{pmatrix} 1 & 0 & 1 \\ 1 & -1 & 3 \\ 1 & -1 & -1 \end{pmatrix}$.

5.86. (i) 3, (ii) 2, (iii) 3, (iv) 2.

5.88. (i) $A = \begin{pmatrix} 1 & 1 \\ 0 & 0 \end{pmatrix}$, $B = \begin{pmatrix} -1 & -1 \\ 0 & 0 \end{pmatrix}$ (iii) $A = \begin{pmatrix} 1 & 0 \\ 0 & 0 \end{pmatrix}$, $B = \begin{pmatrix} 0 & 0 \\ 0 & 1 \end{pmatrix}$

     (ii) $A = \begin{pmatrix} 1 & 0 \\ 0 & 0 \end{pmatrix}$, $B = \begin{pmatrix} 0 & 2 \\ 0 & 0 \end{pmatrix}$

5.89. $\left\{ \begin{pmatrix} 1 & 0 & 0 \\ 0 & 0 & 0 \\ 0 & 0 & 0 \end{pmatrix}, \begin{pmatrix} 0 & 1 & 0 \\ 1 & 0 & 0 \\ 0 & 0 & 0 \end{pmatrix}, \begin{pmatrix} 0 & 0 & 1 \\ 0 & 0 & 0 \\ 1 & 0 & 0 \end{pmatrix}, \begin{pmatrix} 0 & 0 & 0 \\ 0 & 1 & 0 \\ 0 & 0 & 0 \end{pmatrix}, \begin{pmatrix} 0 & 0 & 0 \\ 0 & 0 & 1 \\ 0 & 1 & 0 \end{pmatrix}, \begin{pmatrix} 0 & 0 & 0 \\ 0 & 0 & 0 \\ 0 & 0 & 1 \end{pmatrix} \right\}$

5.90. $\left\{ \begin{pmatrix} 0 & 1 & 0 \\ -1 & 0 & 0 \\ 0 & 0 & 0 \end{pmatrix}, \begin{pmatrix} 0 & 0 & 1 \\ 0 & 0 & 0 \\ -1 & 0 & 0 \end{pmatrix}, \begin{pmatrix} 0 & 0 & 0 \\ 0 & 0 & 1 \\ 0 & -1 & 0 \end{pmatrix} \right\}$

5.93. *Hint.* The proof is identical to that given in Problem 5.48, page 113, for a special case (when V is an extension field of K).

Chapter 6

Linear Mappings

MAPPINGS

Let A and B be arbitrary sets. Suppose to each $a \in A$ there is assigned a unique element of B; the collection, f, of such assignments is called a *function* or *mapping* (or: *map*) from A into B, and is written

$$f : A \to B \quad \text{or} \quad A \overset{f}{\to} B$$

We write $f(a)$, read "f of a", for the element of B that f assigns to $a \in A$; it is called the *value* of f at a or the *image* of a under f. If A' is any subset of A, then $f(A')$ denotes the set of images of elements of A'; and if B' is any subset of B, then $f^{-1}(B')$ denotes the set of elements of A each of whose image lies in B':

$$f(A') = \{f(a) : a \in A'\} \quad \text{and} \quad f^{-1}(B') = \{a \in A : f(a) \in B'\}$$

We call $f(A')$ the *image* of A' and $f^{-1}(B')$ the *inverse image* or *preimage* of B'. In particular, the set of all images, i.e. $f(A)$, is called the *image* (or: *range*) of f. Furthermore, A is called the *domain* of the mapping $f : A \to B$, and B is called its *co-domain*.

To each mapping $f : A \to B$ there corresponds the subset of $A \times B$ given by $\{(a, f(a)) : a \in A\}$. We call this set the *graph* of f. Two mappings $f : A \to B$ and $g : A \to B$ are defined to be *equal*, written $f = g$, if $f(a) = g(a)$ for every $a \in A$, that is, if they have the same graph. Thus we do not distinguish between a function and its graph. The negation of $f = g$ is written $f \neq g$ and is the statement: there exists an $a \in A$ for which $f(a) \neq g(a)$.

Example 6.1: Let $A = \{a, b, c, d\}$ and $B = \{x, y, z, w\}$. The following diagram defines a mapping f from A into B:

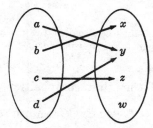

Here $f(a) = y$, $f(b) = x$, $f(c) = z$, and $f(d) = y$. Also,

$$f(\{a, b, d\}) = \{f(a), f(b), f(d)\} = \{y, x, y\} = \{x, y\}$$

The image (or: range) of f is the set $\{x, y, z\}$: $f(A) = \{x, y, z\}$.

Example 6.2: Let $f : \mathbf{R} \to \mathbf{R}$ be the mapping which assigns to each real number x its square x^2:

$$x \mapsto x^2 \quad \text{or} \quad f(x) = x^2$$

Here the image of -3 is 9 so we may write $f(-3) = 9$.

We use the arrow $\mapsto$ to denote the image of an arbitrary element $x \in A$ under a mapping $f : A \to B$ by writing

$$x \mapsto f(x)$$

as illustrated in the preceding example.

Example 6.3: Consider the 2×3 matrix $A = \begin{pmatrix} 1 & -3 & 5 \\ 2 & 4 & -1 \end{pmatrix}$. If we write the vectors in $\mathbf{R}^3$ and $\mathbf{R}^2$ as column vectors, then A determines the mapping $T : \mathbf{R}^3 \to \mathbf{R}^2$ defined by

$$v \mapsto Av, \quad \text{that is,} \quad T(v) = Av, \quad\quad v \in \mathbf{R}^3$$

Thus if $v = \begin{pmatrix} 3 \\ 1 \\ -2 \end{pmatrix}$, then $T(v) = Av = \begin{pmatrix} 1 & -3 & 5 \\ 2 & 4 & -1 \end{pmatrix} \begin{pmatrix} 3 \\ 1 \\ -2 \end{pmatrix} = \begin{pmatrix} -10 \\ 12 \end{pmatrix}$.

Remark: Every $m \times n$ matrix A over a field K determines the mapping $T : K^n \to K^m$ defined by

$$v \mapsto Av$$

where the vectors in K^n and K^m are written as column vectors. For convenience we shall usually denote the above mapping by A, the same symbol used for the matrix.

Example 6.4: Let V be the vector space of polynomials in the variable t over the real field $\mathbf{R}$. Then the derivative defines a mapping $D : V \to V$ where, for any polynomial $f \in V$, we let $D(f) = df/dt$. For example, $D(3t^2 - 5t + 2) = 6t - 5$.

Example 6.5: Let V be the vector space of polynomials in t over $\mathbf{R}$ (as in the preceding example). Then the integral from, say, 0 to 1 defines a mapping $\mathcal{G} : V \to \mathbf{R}$ where, for any polynomial $f \in V$, we let $\mathcal{G}(f) = \int_0^1 f(t)\, dt$. For example,

$$\mathcal{G}(3t^2 - 5t + 2) = \int_0^1 (3t^2 - 5t + 2)\, dt = \tfrac{1}{2}$$

Note that this map is from the vector space V into the scalar field $\mathbf{R}$, whereas the map in the preceding example is from V into itself.

Example 6.6: Consider two mappings $f : A \to B$ and $g : B \to C$ illustrated below:

$$\boxed{A} \xrightarrow{\;f\;} \boxed{B} \xrightarrow{\;g\;} \boxed{C}$$

Let $a \in A$; then $f(a) \in B$, the domain of g. Hence we can obtain the image of $f(a)$ under the mapping g, that is, $g(f(a))$. This map

$$a \mapsto g(f(a))$$

from A into C is called the *composition* or *product* of f and g, and is denoted by $g \circ f$. In other words, $(g \circ f) : A \to C$ is the mapping defined by

$$(g \circ f)(a) = g(f(a))$$

Our first theorem tells us that composition of mappings satisfies the associative law.

Theorem 6.1: Let $f : A \to B$, $g : B \to C$ and $h : C \to D$. Then $h \circ (g \circ f) = (h \circ g) \circ f$.

We prove this theorem now. If $a \in A$, then

$$(h \circ (g \circ f))(a) = h((g \circ f)(a)) = h(g(f(a)))$$

and

$$((h \circ g) \circ f)(a) = (h \circ g)(f(a)) = h(g(f(a)))$$

Thus $(h \circ (g \circ f))(a) = ((h \circ g) \circ f)(a)$ for every $a \in A$, and so $h \circ (g \circ f) = (h \circ g) \circ f$.

Remark: Let $F : A \to B$. Some texts write aF instead of $F(a)$ for the image of $a \in A$ under F. With this notation, the composition of functions $F : A \to B$ and $G : B \to C$ is denoted by $F \circ G$ and not by $G \circ F$ as used in this text.

We next introduce some special types of mappings.

Definition: A mapping $f : A \to B$ is said to be *one-to-one* (or one-one or 1-1) or *injective* if different elements of A have distinct images; that is,

$$\text{if } a \neq a' \quad \text{implies} \quad f(a) \neq f(a')$$

or, equivalently,   if $f(a) = f(a')$ implies $a = a'$

Definition: A mapping $f : A \to B$ is said to be *onto* (or: f maps A onto B) or *surjective* if every $b \in B$ is the image of at least one $a \in A$.

A mapping which is both one-one and onto is said to be *bijective*.

Example 6.7: Let $f : \mathbf{R} \to \mathbf{R}$, $g : \mathbf{R} \to \mathbf{R}$ and $h : \mathbf{R} \to \mathbf{R}$ be defined by $f(x) = 2^x$, $g(x) = x^3 - x$ and $h(x) = x^2$. The graphs of these mappings follow:

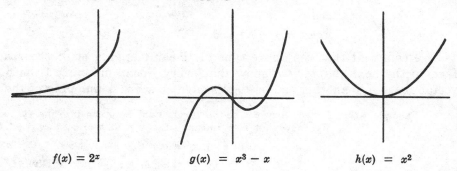

$$f(x) = 2^x \qquad\qquad g(x) = x^3 - x \qquad\qquad h(x) = x^2$$

The mapping f is one-one; geometrically, this means that each horizontal line does not contain more than one point of f. The mapping g is onto; geometrically, this means that each horizontal line contains at least one point of g. The mapping h is neither one-one nor onto; for example, 2 and -2 have the same image 4, and -16 is not the image of any element of $\mathbf{R}$.

Example 6.8: Let A be any set. The mapping $f : A \to A$ defined by $f(a) = a$, i.e. which assigns to each element in A itself, is called the *identity mapping* on A and is denoted by 1_A or 1 or I.

Example 6.9: Let $f : A \to B$. We call $g : B \to A$ the *inverse* of f, written f^{-1}, if

$$f \circ g = 1_B \quad \text{and} \quad g \circ f = 1_A$$

We emphasize that f has an inverse if and only if f is both one-to-one and onto (Problem 6.9). Also, if $b \in B$ then $f^{-1}(b) = a$ where a is the unique element of A for which $f(a) = b$.

LINEAR MAPPINGS

Let V and U be vector spaces over the same field K. A mapping $F : V \to U$ is called a *linear mapping* (or *linear transformation* or *vector space homomorphism*) if it satisfies the following two conditions:

   (1) For any $v, w \in V$, $F(v + w) = F(v) + F(w)$.

   (2) For any $k \in K$ and any $v \in V$, $F(kv) = kF(v)$.

In other words, $F : V \to U$ is linear if it "preserves" the two basic operations of a vector space, that of vector addition and that of scalar multiplication.

Substituting $k = 0$ into (2) we obtain $F(0) = 0$. That is, every linear mapping takes the zero vector into the zero vector.

Now for any scalars $a, b \in K$ and any vectors $v, w \in V$ we obtain, by applying both conditions of linearity,

$$F(av + bw) = F(av) + F(bw) = aF(v) + bF(w)$$

More generally, for any scalars $a_i \in K$ and any vectors $v_i \in V$ we obtain the basic property of linear mappings:

$$F(a_1 v_1 + a_2 v_2 + \cdots + a_n v_n) = a_1 F(v_1) + a_2 F(v_2) + \cdots + a_n F(v_n)$$

We remark that the condition $F(av + bw) = aF(v) + bF(w)$ completely characterizes linear mappings and is sometimes used as its definition.

Example 6.10: Let A be any $m \times n$ matrix over a field K. As noted previously, A determines a mapping $T : K^n \to K^m$ by the assignment $v \mapsto Av$. (Here the vectors in K^n and K^m are written as columns.) We claim that T is linear. For, by properties of matrices,

$$T(v + w) = A(v + w) = Av + Aw = T(v) + T(w)$$

and

$$T(kv) = A(kv) = kAv = kT(v)$$

where $v, w \in K^n$ and $k \in K$.

We comment that the above type of linear mapping shall occur again and again. In fact, in the next chapter we show that every linear mapping from one finite-dimensional vector space into another can be represented as a linear mapping of the above type.

Example 6.11: Let $F : \mathbf{R}^3 \to \mathbf{R}^3$ be the "projection" mapping into the xy plane: $F(x, y, z) = (x, y, 0)$. We show that F is linear. Let $v = (a, b, c)$ and $w = (a', b', c')$. Then

$$F(v + w) = F(a + a', b + b', c + c') = (a + a', b + b', 0)$$
$$= (a, b, 0) + (a', b', 0) = F(v) + F(w)$$

and, for any $k \in \mathbf{R}$,

$$F(kv) = F(ka, kb, kc) = (ka, kb, 0) = k(a, b, 0) = kF(v)$$

That is, F is linear.

Example 6.12: Let $F : \mathbf{R}^2 \to \mathbf{R}^2$ be the "translation" mapping defined by $F(x, y) = (x + 1, y + 2)$. Observe that $F(0) = F(0, 0) = (1, 2) \neq 0$. That is, the zero vector is not mapped onto the zero vector. Hence F is not linear.

Example 6.13: Let $F : V \to U$ be the mapping which assigns $0 \in U$ to every $v \in V$. Then, for any $v, w \in V$ and any $k \in K$, we have

$$F(v + w) = 0 = 0 + 0 = F(v) + F(w) \quad \text{and} \quad F(kv) = 0 = k0 = kF(v)$$

Thus F is linear. We call F the *zero mapping* and shall usually denote it by 0.

Example 6.14: Consider the identity mapping $I : V \to V$ which maps each $v \in V$ into itself. Then, for any $v, w \in V$ and any $a, b \in K$, we have

$$I(av + bw) = av + bw = aI(v) + bI(w)$$

Thus I is linear.

Example 6.15: Let V be the vector space of polynomials in the variable t over the real field $\mathbf{R}$. Then the differential mapping $D : V \to V$ and the integral mapping $\mathcal{J} : V \to \mathbf{R}$ defined in Examples 6.4 and 6.5 are linear. For it is proven in calculus that for any $u, v \in V$ and $k \in \mathbf{R}$,

$$\frac{d(u + v)}{dt} = \frac{du}{dt} + \frac{dv}{dt} \quad \text{and} \quad \frac{d(ku)}{dt} = k\frac{du}{dt}$$

that is, $D(u + v) = D(u) + D(v)$ and $D(ku) = k\,D(u)$; and also,

$$\int_0^1 (u(t) + v(t))\, dt = \int_0^1 u(t)\, dt + \int_0^1 v(t)\, dt$$

and

$$\int_0^1 k\, u(t)\, dt = k \int_0^1 u(t)\, dt$$

that is, $\mathcal{J}(u + v) = \mathcal{J}(u) + \mathcal{J}(v)$ and $\mathcal{J}(ku) = k\,\mathcal{J}(u)$.

Example 6.16: Let $F : V \to U$ be a linear mapping which is both one-one and onto. Then an inverse mapping $F^{-1} : U \to V$ exists. We will show (Problem 6.17) that this inverse mapping is also linear.

When we investigated the coordinates of a vector relative to a basis, we also introduced the notion of two spaces being isomorphic. We now give a formal definition.

Definition: A linear mapping $F : V \to U$ is called an *isomorphism* if it is one-to-one. The vector spaces V, U are said to be *isomorphic* if there is an isomorphism of V onto U.

Example 6.17: Let V be a vector space over K of dimension n and let $\{e_1, \ldots, e_n\}$ be a basis of V. Then as noted previously the mapping $v \mapsto [v]_e$, i.e. which maps each $v \in V$ into its coordinate vector relative to the basis $\{e_i\}$, is an isomorphism of V onto K^n.

Our next theorem gives us an abundance of examples of linear mappings; in particular, it tells us that a linear mapping is completely determined by its values on the elements of a basis.

Theorem 6.2: Let V and U be vector spaces over a field K. Let $\{v_1, v_2, \ldots, v_n\}$ be a basis of V and let $u_1, u_2, \ldots, u_n$ be any vectors in U. Then there exists a unique linear mapping $F : V \to U$ such that $F(v_1) = u_1$, $F(v_2) = u_2$, $\ldots$, $F(v_n) = u_n$.

We emphasize that the vectors $u_1, \ldots, u_n$ in the preceding theorem are completely arbitrary; they may be linearly dependent or they may even be equal to each other.

KERNEL AND IMAGE OF A LINEAR MAPPING

We begin by defining two concepts.

Definition: Let $F : V \to U$ be a linear mapping. The *image* of F, written $\operatorname{Im} F$, is the set of image points in U:

$$\operatorname{Im} F \;=\; \{u \in U : F(v) = u \text{ for some } v \in V\}$$

The *kernel* of F, written $\operatorname{Ker} F$, is the set of elements in V which map into $0 \in U$:

$$\operatorname{Ker} F \;=\; \{v \in V : F(v) = 0\}$$

The following theorem is easily proven (Problem 6.22).

Theorem 6.3: Let $F : V \to U$ be a linear mapping. Then the image of F is a subspace of U and the kernel of F is a subspace of V.

Example 6.18: Let $F : \mathbf{R}^3 \to \mathbf{R}^3$ be the projection mapping into the xy plane: $F(x, y, z) = (x, y, 0)$. Clearly the image of F is the entire xy plane:

$$\operatorname{Im} F \;=\; \{(a, b, 0) : a, b \in \mathbf{R}\}$$

Note that the kernel of F is the z axis:

$$\operatorname{Ker} F \;=\; \{(0, 0, c) : c \in \mathbf{R}\}$$

since these points and only these points map into the zero vector $0 = (0, 0, 0)$.

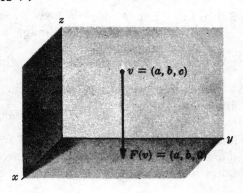

Now suppose that the vectors $v_1, \ldots, v_n$ generate V and that $F : V \to U$ is linear. We show that the vectors $F(v_1), \ldots, F(v_n) \in U$ generate $\operatorname{Im} F$. For suppose $u \in \operatorname{Im} F$; then $F(v) = u$ for some vector $v \in V$. Since the v_i generate V and since $v \in V$, there exist scalars $a_1, \ldots, a_n$ for which $v = a_1 v_1 + a_2 v_2 + \cdots + a_n v_n$. Accordingly,

$$u = F(v) = F(a_1 v_1 + a_2 v_2 + \cdots + a_n v_n) = a_1 F(v_1) + a_2 F(v_2) + \cdots + a_n F(v_n)$$

and hence the vectors $F(v_1), \ldots, F(v_n)$ generate $\operatorname{Im} F$.

Example 6.19:   Consider an arbitrary 4×3 matrix A over a field K:

$$A = \begin{pmatrix} a_1 & a_2 & a_3 \\ b_1 & b_2 & b_3 \\ c_1 & c_2 & c_3 \\ d_1 & d_2 & d_3 \end{pmatrix}$$

which we view as a linear mapping $A : K^3 \to K^4$. Now the usual basis $\{e_1, e_2, e_3\}$ of K^3 generates K^3 and so their values Ae_1, Ae_2, Ae_3 under A generate the image of A. But the vectors $Ae_1, Ae_2,$ and Ae_3 are the columns of A:

$$Ae_1 = \begin{pmatrix} a_1 & a_2 & a_3 \\ b_1 & b_2 & b_3 \\ c_1 & c_2 & c_3 \\ d_1 & d_2 & d_3 \end{pmatrix} \begin{pmatrix} 1 \\ 0 \\ 0 \end{pmatrix} = \begin{pmatrix} a_1 \\ b_1 \\ c_1 \\ d_1 \end{pmatrix}, \qquad Ae_2 = \begin{pmatrix} a_1 & a_2 & a_3 \\ b_1 & b_2 & b_3 \\ c_1 & c_2 & c_3 \\ d_1 & d_2 & d_3 \end{pmatrix} \begin{pmatrix} 0 \\ 1 \\ 0 \end{pmatrix} = \begin{pmatrix} a_2 \\ b_2 \\ c_2 \\ d_2 \end{pmatrix}$$

$$Ae_3 = \begin{pmatrix} a_1 & a_2 & a_3 \\ b_1 & b_2 & b_3 \\ c_1 & c_2 & c_3 \\ d_1 & d_2 & d_3 \end{pmatrix} \begin{pmatrix} 0 \\ 0 \\ 1 \end{pmatrix} = \begin{pmatrix} a_3 \\ b_3 \\ c_3 \\ d_3 \end{pmatrix}$$

thus the image of A is precisely the column space of A.

We emphasize that if A is any $m \times n$ matrix over K viewed as a linear mapping $A : K^n \to K^m$, then the image of A is precisely the column space of A.

So far we have not related the notion of dimension to that of a linear mapping $F : V \to U$. In the case that V is of finite dimension, we have the following fundamental relationship.

Theorem 6.4:   Let V be of finite dimension and let $F : V \to U$ be a linear mapping. Then

$$\dim V = \dim (\operatorname{Ker} F) + \dim (\operatorname{Im} F)$$

That is, the sum of the dimensions of the image and kernel of a linear mapping is equal to the dimension of its domain. This formula is easily seen to hold for the projection mapping F in Example 6.18. There the image (xy plane) and the kernel (z axis) of F have dimensions 2 and 1 respectively, whereas the domain $\mathbf{R}^3$ of F has dimension 3.

Remark: Let $F : V \to U$ be a linear mapping. Then the *rank* of F is defined to be the dimension of its image, and the *nullity* of F is defined to be the dimension of its kernel:

$$\operatorname{rank} (F) = \dim (\operatorname{Im} F) \qquad \text{and} \qquad \operatorname{nullity} (F) = \dim (\operatorname{Ker} F)$$

Thus the preceding theorem yields the following formula for F when V has finite dimension:

$$\operatorname{rank} (F) + \operatorname{nullity} (F) = \dim V$$

Recall that the rank of a matrix A was originally defined to be the dimension of its column space and of its row space. Observe that if we now view A as a linear mapping, then both definitions correspond since the image of A is precisely its column space.

SINGULAR AND NONSINGULAR MAPPINGS

A linear mapping $F:V \to U$ is said to be *singular* if the image of some nonzero vector under F is 0, i.e. if there exists $v \in V$ for which $v \neq 0$ but $F(v) = 0$. Thus $F:V \to U$ is *nonsingular* if only $0 \in V$ maps into $0 \in U$ or, equivalently, if its kernel consists only of the zero vector: $\text{Ker}\, F = \{0\}$.

> **Example 6.20:** Let $F:\mathbf{R}^3 \to \mathbf{R}^3$ be the linear mapping which rotates a vector about the z axis through an angle θ:
>
> $$F(x, y, z) = (x \cos\theta - y \sin\theta,\ x \sin\theta + y \cos\theta,\ z)$$

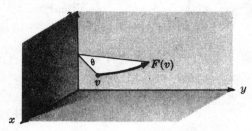

> Observe that only the zero vector is mapped into the zero vector; hence F is nonsingular.

Now if the linear mapping $F:V \to U$ is one-to-one, then only $0 \in V$ can map into $0 \in U$ and so F is nonsingular. The converse is also true. For suppose F is nonsingular and $F(v) = F(w)$; then $F(v-w) = F(v) - F(w) = 0$ and hence $v - w = 0$ or $v = w$. Thus $F(v) = F(w)$ implies $v = w$, that is, F is one-to-one. By definition (page 125), a one-to-one linear mapping is called an isomorphism. Thus we have proven

Theorem 6.5:   A linear mapping $F:V \to U$ is an isomorphism if and only if it is non-singular.

We remark that nonsingular mappings can also be characterized as those mappings which carry independent sets into independent sets (Problem 6.26).

LINEAR MAPPINGS AND SYSTEMS OF LINEAR EQUATIONS

Consider a system of m linear equations in n unknowns over a field K:

$$a_{11}x_1 + a_{12}x_2 + \cdots + a_{1n}x_n = b_1$$
$$a_{21}x_1 + a_{22}x_2 + \cdots + a_{2n}x_n = b_2$$
$$\cdots\cdots\cdots\cdots\cdots\cdots\cdots\cdots\cdots\cdots\cdots\cdots$$
$$a_{m1}x_1 + a_{m2}x_2 + \cdots + a_{mn}x_n = b_m$$

which is equivalent to the matrix equation

$$Ax = b$$

where $A = (a_{ij})$ is the coefficient matrix, and $x = (x_i)$ and $b = (b_i)$ are the column vectors of the unknowns and of the constants, respectively. Now the matrix A may also be viewed as the linear mapping

$$A : K^n \to K^m$$

Thus the solution of the equation $Ax = b$ may be viewed as the preimage of $b \in K^m$ under the linear mapping $A:K^n \to K^m$. Furthermore, the solution of the associated homogeneous equation $Ax = 0$ may be viewed as the kernel of the linear mapping $A:K^n \to K^m$.

By Theorem 6.4,

$$\dim(\text{Ker}\, A) = \dim K^n - \dim(\text{Im}\, A) = n - \text{rank}\, A$$

But n is exactly the number of unknowns in the homogeneous system $Ax = 0$. Thus we have the following theorem on linear equations appearing in Chapter 5.

Theorem 5.11: The dimension of the solution space W of the homogeneous system of linear equations $AX = 0$ is $n - r$ where n is the number of unknowns and r is the rank of the coefficient matrix A.

OPERATIONS WITH LINEAR MAPPINGS

We are able to combine linear mappings in various ways to obtain new linear mappings. These operations are very important and shall be used throughout the text.

Suppose $F : V \to U$ and $G : V \to U$ are linear mappings of vector spaces over a field K. We define the sum $F + G$ to be the mapping from V into U which assigns $F(v) + G(v)$ to $v \in V$:

$$(F + G)(v) = F(v) + G(v)$$

Furthermore, for any scalar $k \in K$, we define the product kF to be the mapping from V into U which assigns $k\,F(v)$ to $v \in V$:

$$(kF)(v) = k\,F(v)$$

We show that if F and G are linear, then $F + G$ and kF are also linear. We have, for any vectors $v, w \in V$ and any scalars $a, b \in K$,

$$
\begin{aligned}
(F + G)(av + bw) &= F(av + bw) + G(av + bw) \\
&= aF(v) + bF(w) + aG(v) + bG(w) \\
&= a(F(v) + G(v)) + b(F(w) + G(w)) \\
&= a(F + G)(v) + b(F + G)(w)
\end{aligned}
$$

and

$$
\begin{aligned}
(kF)(av + bw) &= kF(av + bw) = k(aF(v) + bF(w)) \\
&= akF(v) + bkF(w) = a(kF)(v) + b(kF)(w)
\end{aligned}
$$

Thus $F + G$ and kF are linear.

The following theorem applies.

Theorem 6.6: Let V and U be vector spaces over a field K. Then the collection of all linear mappings from V into U with the above operations of addition and scalar multiplication form a vector space over K.

The space in the above theorem is usually denoted by

$$\text{Hom}\,(V, U)$$

Here Hom comes from the word homomorphism. In the case that V and U are of finite dimension, we have the following theorem.

Theorem 6.7: Suppose $\dim V = m$ and $\dim U = n$. Then $\dim \text{Hom}(V, U) = mn$.

Now suppose that V, U and W are vector spaces over the same field K, and that $F : V \to U$ and $G : U \to W$ are linear mappings:

$$V \xrightarrow{\ F\ } U \xrightarrow{\ G\ } W$$

Recall that the composition function $G \circ F$ is the mapping from V into W defined by $(G \circ F)(v) = G(F(v))$. We show that $G \circ F$ is linear whenever F and G are linear. We have, for any vectors $v, w \in V$ and any scalars $a, b \in K$,

$$
\begin{aligned}
(G \circ F)(av + bw) &= G(F(av + bw)) = G(aF(v) + bF(w)) \\
&= aG(F(v)) + bG(F(w)) = a(G \circ F)(v) + b(G \circ F)(w)
\end{aligned}
$$

That is, $G \circ F$ is linear.

The composition of linear mappings and that of addition and scalar multiplication are related as follows:

Theorem 6.8: Let V, U and W be vector spaces over K. Let F, F' be linear mappings from V into U and G, G' linear mappings from U into W, and let $k \in K$. Then:

(i) $G \circ (F + F') = G \circ F + G \circ F'$

(ii) $(G + G') \circ F = G \circ F + G' \circ F$

(iii) $k(G \circ F) = (kG) \circ F = G \circ (kF)$.

ALGEBRA OF LINEAR OPERATORS

Let V be a vector space over a field K. We now consider the special case of linear mappings $T : V \to V$, i.e. from V into itself. They are also called *linear operators* or *linear transformations* on V. We will write $A(V)$, instead of Hom (V, V), for the space of all such mappings.

By Theorem 6.6, $A(V)$ is a vector space over K; it is of dimension n^2 if V is of dimension n. Now if $T, S \in A(V)$, then the composition $S \circ T$ exists and is also a linear mapping from V into itself, i.e. $S \circ T \in A(V)$. Thus we have a "multiplication" defined in $A(V)$. (We shall write ST for $S \circ T$ in the space $A(V)$.)

We remark that an *algebra* A over a field K is a vector space over K in which an operation of multiplication is defined satisfying, for every $F, G, H \in A$ and every $k \in K$,

(i) $F(G + H) = FG + FH$

(ii) $(G + H)F = GF + HF$

(iii) $k(GF) = (kG)F = G(kF)$.

If the associative law also holds for the multiplication, i.e. if for every $F, G, H \in A$,

(iv) $(FG)H = F(GH)$

then the algebra A is said to be *associative*. Thus by Theorems 6.8 and 6.1, $A(V)$ is an associative algebra over K with respect to composition of mappings; hence it is frequently called the *algebra of linear operators* on V.

Observe that the identity mapping $I : V \to V$ belongs to $A(V)$. Also, for any $T \in A(V)$, we have $TI = IT = T$. We note that we can also form "powers" of T; we use the notation $T^2 = T \circ T$, $T^3 = T \circ T \circ T$, ... Furthermore, for any polynomial

$$p(x) = a_0 + a_1 x + a_2 x^2 + \cdots + a_n x^n, \qquad a_i \in K$$

we can form the operator $p(T)$ defined by

$$p(T) = a_0 I + a_1 T + a_2 T^2 + \cdots + a_n T^n$$

(For a scalar $k \in K$, the operator kI is frequently denoted by simply k.) In particular, if $p(T) = 0$, the zero mapping, then T is said to be a *zero* of the polynomial $p(x)$.

Example 6.21: Let $T : \mathbf{R}^3 \to \mathbf{R}^3$ be defined by $T(x, y, z) = (0, x, y)$. Now if (a, b, c) is any element of $\mathbf{R}^3$, then:

$$(T + I)(a, b, c) = (0, a, b) + (a, b, c) = (a, a + b, b + c)$$

and

$$T^3(a, b, c) = T^2(0, a, b) = T(0, 0, a) = (0, 0, 0)$$

Thus we see that $T^3 = 0$, the zero mapping from V into itself. In other words, T is a zero of the polynomial $p(x) = x^3$.

INVERTIBLE OPERATORS

A linear operator $T : V \to V$ is said to be *invertible* if it has an inverse, i.e. if there exists $T^{-1} \in A(V)$ such that $TT^{-1} = T^{-1}T = I$.

Now T is invertible if and only if it is one-one and onto. Thus in particular, if T is invertible then only $0 \in V$ can map into itself, i.e. T is nonsingular. On the other hand, suppose T is nonsingular, i.e. $\operatorname{Ker} T = \{0\}$. Recall (page 127) that T is also one-one. Moreover, assuming V has finite dimension, we have, by Theorem 6.4,

$$\dim V = \dim(\operatorname{Im} T) + \dim(\operatorname{Ker} T) = \dim(\operatorname{Im} T) + \dim(\{0\})$$
$$= \dim(\operatorname{Im} T) + 0 = \dim(\operatorname{Im} T)$$

Then $\operatorname{Im} T = V$, i.e. the image of T is V; thus T is onto. Hence T is both one-one and onto and so is invertible. We have just proven

Theorem 6.9: A linear operator $T : V \to V$ on a vector space of finite dimension is invertible if and only if it is nonsingular.

> **Example 6.22:** Let T be the operator on $\mathbf{R}^2$ defined by $T(x, y) = (y, 2x - y)$. The kernel of T is $\{(0, 0)\}$; hence T is nonsingular and, by the preceding theorem, invertible. We now find a formula for T^{-1}. Suppose (s, t) is the image of (x, y) under T; hence (x, y) is the image of (s, t) under T^{-1}: $T(x, y) = (s, t)$ and $T^{-1}(s, t) = (x, y)$. We have
> $$T(x, y) = (y, 2x - y) = (s, t) \quad \text{and so} \quad y = s, \; 2x - y = t$$
> Solving for x and y in terms of s and t, we obtain $x = \frac{1}{2}s + \frac{1}{2}t$, $y = s$. Thus T^{-1} is given by the formula $T^{-1}(s, t) = (\frac{1}{2}s + \frac{1}{2}t, s)$.

The finiteness of the dimensionality of V in the preceding theorem is necessary as seen in the next example.

> **Example 6.23:** Let V be the vector space of polynomials over K, and let T be the operator on V defined by
> $$T(a_0 + a_1 t + \cdots + a_n t^n) = a_0 t + a_1 t^2 + \cdots + a_n t^{n+1}$$
> i.e. T increases the exponent of t in each term by 1. Now T is a linear mapping and is nonsingular. However, T is not onto and so is not invertible.

We now give an important application of the above theorem to systems of linear equations over K. Consider a system with the same number of equations as unknowns, say n. We can represent this system by the matrix equation

$$Ax = b \tag{$*$}$$

where A is an n-square matrix over K which we view as a linear operator on K^n. Suppose the matrix A is *nonsingular*, i.e. the matrix equation $Ax = 0$ has only the zero solution. Then, by Theorem 6.9, the linear mapping A is one-to-one and onto. This means that the system $(*)$ has a unique solution for any $b \in K^n$. On the other hand, suppose the matrix A is *singular*, i.e. the matrix equation $Ax = 0$ has a nonzero solution. Then the linear mapping A is not onto. This means that there exist $b \in K^n$ for which $(*)$ does not have a solution. Furthermore, if a solution exists it is not unique. Thus we have proven the following fundamental result:

Theorem 6.10: Consider the following system of linear equations:

$$a_{11}x_1 + a_{12}x_2 + \cdots + a_{1n}x_n = b_1$$
$$a_{21}x_1 + a_{22}x_2 + \cdots + a_{2n}x_n = b_2$$
$$\cdots\cdots\cdots\cdots\cdots\cdots\cdots\cdots\cdots\cdots$$
$$a_{n1}x_1 + a_{n2}x_2 + \cdots + a_{nn}x_n = b_n$$

(i)   If the corresponding homogeneous system has only the zero solution, then the above system has a unique solution for any values of the b_i.

(ii) If the corresponding homogeneous system has a nonzero solution, then: (i) there are values for the b_i for which the above system does not have a solution; (ii) whenever a solution of the above system exists, it is not unique.

Solved Problems

MAPPINGS

6.1. State whether or not each diagram defines a mapping from $A = \{a, b, c\}$ into $B = \{x, y, z\}$.

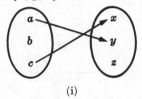   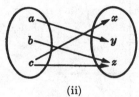   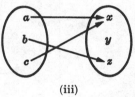

      (i)   (ii)   (iii)

(i)   No. There is nothing assigned to the element $b \in A$.

(ii) No. Two elements, x and z, are assigned to $c \in A$.

(iii) Yes.

6.2. Use a formula to define each of the following functions from $\mathbf{R}$ into $\mathbf{R}$.

(i)   To each number let f assign its cube.

(ii) To each number let g assign the number 5.

(iii) To each positive number let h assign its square, and to each nonpositive number let h assign the number 6.

Also, find the value of each function at 4, -2 and 0.

(i)   Since f assigns to any number x its cube x^3, we can define f by $f(x) = x^3$. Also:
$$f(4) = 4^3 = 64, \quad f(-2) = (-2)^3 = -8, \quad f(0) = 0^3 = 0$$

(ii) Since g assigns 5 to any number x, we can define g by $g(x) = 5$. Thus the value of g at each number 4, -2 and 0 is 5:
$$g(4) = 5, \quad g(-2) = 5, \quad g(0) = 5$$

(iii) Two different rules are used to define h as follows:
$$h(x) = \begin{cases} x^2 & \text{if } x > 0 \\ 6 & \text{if } x \leq 0 \end{cases}$$

Since $4 > 0$, $h(4) = 4^2 = 16$. On the other hand, $-2, 0 \leq 0$ and so $h(-2) = 6$, $h(0) = 6$.

6.3.   Let $A = \{1, 2, 3, 4, 5\}$ and let $f : A \to A$ be the mapping defined by the diagram on the right. (i) Find the image of f. (ii) Find the graph of f.

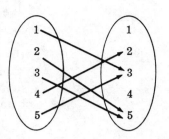

(i)   The image $f(A)$ of the mapping f consists of all the points assigned to elements of A. Now only 2, 3 and 5 appear as the image of any elements of A; hence $f(A) = \{2, 3, 5\}$.

(ii)   The graph of f consists of the ordered pairs $(a, f(a))$, where $a \in A$. Now $f(1) = 3$, $f(2) = 5$, $f(3) = 5$, $f(4) = 2$, $f(5) = 3$; hence the graph of

$$f = \{(1, 3), (2, 5), (3, 5), (4, 2), (5, 3)\}$$

6.4.   Sketch the graph of (i) $f(x) = x^2 + x - 6$, (ii) $g(x) = x^3 - 3x^2 - x + 3$.

Note that these are "polynomial functions". In each case set up a table of values for x and then find the corresponding values of $f(x)$. Plot the points in a coordinate diagram and then draw a smooth continuous curve through the points.

(i)

x	$f(x)$
-4	6
-3	0
-2	-4
-1	-6
0	-6
1	-4
2	0
3	6

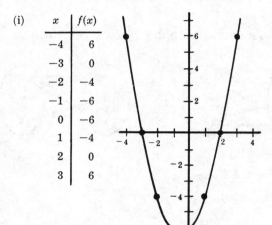

(ii)

x	$g(x)$
-2	-15
-1	0
0	3
1	0
2	-3
3	0
4	15

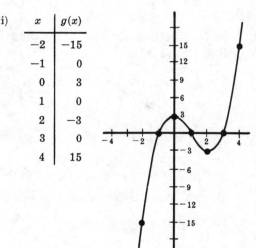

6.5.   Let the mappings $f : A \to B$ and $g : B \to C$ be defined by the diagram

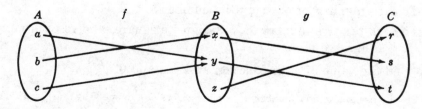

(i)   Find the composition mapping $(g \circ f) : A \to C$. (ii) Find the image of each mapping: f, g and $g \circ f$.

(i)   We use the definition of the composition mapping to compute:

$$(g \circ f)(a) = g(f(a)) = g(y) = t$$
$$(g \circ f)(b) = g(f(b)) = g(x) = s$$
$$(g \circ f)(c) = g(f(c)) = g(y) = t$$

Observe that we arrive at the same answer if we "follow the arrows" in the diagram:

$$a \to y \to t, \quad b \to x \to s, \quad c \to y \to t$$

(ii) By the diagram, the image values under the mapping f are x and y, and the image values under g are r, s and t; hence

$$\text{image of } f = \{x, y\} \qquad \text{and} \qquad \text{image of } g = \{r, s, t\}$$

By (i), the image values under the composition mapping $g \circ f$ are t and s; hence image of $g \circ f = \{s, t\}$. Note that the images of g and $g \circ f$ are different.

6.6. Let the mappings f and g be defined by $f(x) = 2x + 1$ and $g(x) = x^2 - 2$. (i) Find $(g \circ f)(4)$ and $(f \circ g)(4)$. (ii) Find formulae defining the composition mappings $g \circ f$ and $f \circ g$.

(i) $f(4) = 2 \cdot 4 + 1 = 9$. Hence $(g \circ f)(4) = g(f(4)) = g(9) = 9^2 - 2 = 79$.

$g(4) = 4^2 - 2 = 14$. Hence $(f \circ g)(4) = f(g(4)) = f(14) = 2 \cdot 14 + 1 = 29$.

(ii) Compute the formula for $g \circ f$ as follows:

$$(g \circ f)(x) = g(f(x)) = g(2x + 1) = (2x + 1)^2 - 2 = 4x^2 + 4x - 1$$

Observe that the same answer can be found by writing $y = f(x) = 2x + 1$ and $z = g(y) = y^2 - 2$, and then eliminating y: $z = y^2 - 2 = (2x + 1)^2 - 2 = 4x^2 + 4x - 1$.

$(f \circ g)(x) = f(g(x)) = f(x^2 - 2) = 2(x^2 - 2) + 1 = 2x^2 - 3$. Observe that $f \circ g \neq g \circ f$.

6.7. Let the mappings $f : A \to B$, $g : B \to C$ and $h : C \to D$ be defined by the diagram

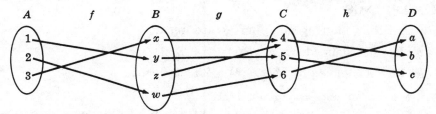

Determine if each mapping (i) is one-one, (ii) is onto, (iii) has an inverse.

(i)   The mapping $f : A \to B$ is one-one since each element of A has a different image. The mapping $g : B \to C$ is not one-one since x and z both map into the same element 4. The mapping $h : C \to D$ is one-one.

(ii) The mapping $f : A \to B$ is not onto since $z \in B$ is not the image of any element of A. The mapping $g : B \to C$ is onto since each element of C is the image of some element of B. The mapping $h : C \to D$ is also onto.

(iii) A mapping has an inverse if and only if it is both one-one and onto. Hence only h has an inverse.

6.8. Suppose $f : A \to B$ and $g : B \to C$; hence the composition mapping $(g \circ f) : A \to C$ exists. Prove the following. (i) If f and g are one-one, then $g \circ f$ is one-one. (ii) If f and g are onto, then $g \circ f$ is onto. (iii) If $g \circ f$ is one-one, then f is one-one. (iv) If $g \circ f$ is onto, then g is onto.

(i)   Suppose $(g \circ f)(x) = (g \circ f)(y)$. Then $g(f(x)) = g(f(y))$. Since g is one-one, $f(x) = f(y)$. Since f is one-one, $x = y$. We have proven that $(g \circ f)(x) = (g \circ f)(y)$ implies $x = y$; hence $g \circ f$ is one-one.

(ii) Suppose $c \in C$. Since g is onto, there exists $b \in B$ for which $g(b) = c$. Since f is onto, there exists $a \in A$ for which $f(a) = b$. Thus $(g \circ f)(a) = g(f(a)) = g(b) = c$; hence $g \circ f$ is onto.

(iii) Suppose f is not one-one. Then there exists distinct elements $x, y \in A$ for which $f(x) = f(y)$. Thus $(g \circ f)(x) = g(f(x)) = g(f(y)) = (g \circ f)(y)$; hence $g \circ f$ is not one-one. Accordingly if $g \circ f$ is one-one, then f must be one-one.

(iv) If $a \in A$, then $(g \circ f)(a) = g(f(a)) \in g(B)$; hence $(g \circ f)(A) \subset g(B)$. Suppose g is not onto. Then $g(B)$ is properly contained in C and so $(g \circ f)(A)$ is properly contained in C; thus $g \circ f$ is not onto. Accordingly if $g \circ f$ is onto, then g must be onto.

6.9. Prove that a mapping $f : A \to B$ has an inverse if and only if it is one-to-one and onto.

Suppose f has an inverse, i.e. there exists a function $f^{-1} : B \to A$ for which $f^{-1} \circ f = 1_A$ and $f \circ f^{-1} = 1_B$. Since 1_A is one-to-one, f is one-to-one by Problem 6.8(iii); and since 1_B is onto, f is onto by Problem 6.8(iv). That is, f is both one-to-one and onto.

Now suppose f is both one-to-one and onto. Then each $b \in B$ is the image of a unique element in A, say $\hat{b}$. Thus if $f(a) = b$, then $a = \hat{b}$; hence $f(\hat{b}) = b$. Now let g denote the mapping from B to A defined by $b \mapsto \hat{b}$. We have:

(i) $(g \circ f)(a) = g(f(a)) = g(b) = \hat{b} = a$, for every $a \in A$; hence $g \circ f = 1_A$.

(ii) $(f \circ g)(b) = f(g(b)) = f(\hat{b}) = b$, for every $b \in B$; hence $f \circ g = 1_B$.

Accordingly, f has an inverse. Its inverse is the mapping g.

6.10. Let $f : \mathbf{R} \to \mathbf{R}$ be defined by $f(x) = 2x - 3$. Now f is one-to-one and onto; hence f has an inverse mapping f^{-1}. Find a formula for f^{-1}.

Let y be the image of x under the mapping f: $y = f(x) = 2x - 3$. Consequently x will be the image of y under the inverse mapping f^{-1}. Thus solve for x in terms of y in the above equation: $x = (y + 3)/2$. Then the formula defining the inverse function is $f^{-1}(y) = (y + 3)/2$.

LINEAR MAPPINGS

6.11. Show that the following mappings F are linear:

(i) $F : \mathbf{R}^2 \to \mathbf{R}^2$ defined by $F(x, y) = (x + y, x)$.

(ii) $F : \mathbf{R}^3 \to \mathbf{R}$ defined by $F(x, y, z) = 2x - 3y + 4z$.

(i)   Let $v = (a, b)$ and $w = (a', b')$; hence
$$v + w = (a + a', b + b') \quad \text{and} \quad kv = (ka, kb), \quad k \in \mathbf{R}$$
We have $F(v) = (a + b, a)$ and $F(w) = (a' + b', a')$. Thus
$$F(v + w) = F(a + a', b + b') = (a + a' + b + b', a + a')$$
$$= (a + b, a) + (a' + b', a') = F(v) + F(w)$$
and
$$F(kv) = F(ka, kb) = (ka + kb, ka) = k(a + b, a) = kF(v)$$
Since v, w and k were arbitrary, F is linear.

(ii) Let $v = (a, b, c)$ and $w = (a', b', c')$; hence
$$v + w = (a + a', b + b', c + c') \quad \text{and} \quad kv = (ka, kb, kc), \quad k \in \mathbf{R}$$
We have $F(v) = 2a - 3b + 4c$ and $F(w) = 2a' - 3b' + 4c'$. Thus
$$F(v + w) = F(a + a', b + b', c + c') = 2(a + a') - 3(b + b') + 4(c + c')$$
$$= (2a - 3b + 4c) + (2a' - 3b' + 4c') = F(v) + F(w)$$
and $\quad F(kv) = F(ka, kb, kc) = 2ka - 3kb + 4kc = k(2a - 3b + 4c) = kF(v)$

Accordingly, F is linear.

6.12. Show that the following mappings F are not linear:

(i) $F : \mathbf{R}^2 \to \mathbf{R}$ defined by $F(x, y) = xy$.

(ii) $F : \mathbf{R}^2 \to \mathbf{R}^3$ defined by $F(x, y) = (x + 1, 2y, x + y)$.

(iii) $F : \mathbf{R}^3 \to \mathbf{R}^2$ defined by $F(x, y, z) = (|x|, 0)$.

(i)   Let $v = (1, 2)$ and $w = (3, 4)$; then $v + w = (4, 6)$.
We have $F(v) = 1 \cdot 2 = 2$ and $F(w) = 3 \cdot 4 = 12$. Hence

$$F(v + w) \ = \ F(4, 6) \ = \ 4 \cdot 6 \ = \ 24 \ \neq \ F(v) + F(w)$$

Accordingly, F is not linear.

(ii)   Since $F(0, 0) = (1, 0, 0) \neq (0, 0, 0)$, F cannot be linear.

(iii) Let $v = (1, 2, 3)$ and $k = -3$; hence $kv = (-3, -6, -9)$.

We have $F(v) = (1, 0)$ and so $kF(v) = -3(1, 0) = (-3, 0)$. Then

$$F(kv) \ = \ F(-3, -6, -9) \ = \ (3, 0) \ \neq \ kF(v)$$

and hence F is not linear.

6.13. Let V be the vector space of n-square matrices over K. Let M be an arbitrary matrix in V. Let $T : V \to V$ be defined by $T(A) = AM + MA$, where $A \in V$. Show that T is linear.

For any $A, B \in V$ and any $k \in K$, we have

$$\begin{aligned}
T(A + B) \ &= \ (A + B)M + M(A + B) \ = \ AM + BM + MA + MB \\
&= \ (AM + MA) + (BM + MB) \ = \ T(A) + T(B)
\end{aligned}$$

and $$T(kA) \ = \ (kA)M + M(kA) \ = \ k(AM) + k(MA) \ = \ k(AM + MA) \ = \ kT(A)$$

Accordingly, T is linear.

6.14. Prove Theorem 6.2: Let V and U be vector spaces over a field K. Let $\{v_1, \ldots, v_n\}$ be a basis of V and let $u_1, \ldots, u_n$ be any arbitrary vectors in U. Then there exists a unique linear mapping $F : V \to U$ such that $F(v_1) = u_1$, $F(v_2) = u_2$, $\ldots$, $F(v_n) = u_n$.

There are three steps to the proof of the theorem: (1) Define a mapping $F : V \to U$ such that $F(v_i) = u_i$, $i = 1, \ldots, n$.   (2) Show that F is linear.   (3) Show that F is unique.

Step (1). Let $v \in V$. Since $\{v_1, \ldots, v_n\}$ is a basis of V, there exist unique scalars $a_1, \ldots, a_n \in K$ for which $v = a_1 v_1 + a_2 v_2 + \cdots + a_n v_n$. We define $F : V \to U$ by $F(v) = a_1 u_1 + a_2 u_2 + \cdots + a_n u_n$. (Since the a_i are unique, the mapping F is well-defined.) Now, for $i = 1, \ldots, n$,

$$v_i \ = \ 0v_1 + \cdots + 1v_i + \cdots + 0v_n$$

Hence $$F(v_i) \ = \ 0u_1 + \cdots + 1u_i + \cdots + 0u_n \ = \ u_i$$

Thus the first step of the proof is complete.

Step (2). Suppose $v = a_1 v_1 + a_2 v_2 + \cdots + a_n v_n$ and $w = b_1 v_1 + b_2 v_2 + \cdots + b_n v_n$. Then

$$v + w \ = \ (a_1 + b_1)v_1 + (a_2 + b_2)v_2 + \cdots + (a_n + b_n)v_n$$

and, for any $k \in K$, $kv = ka_1 v_1 + ka_2 v_2 + \cdots + ka_n v_n$. By definition of the mapping F,

$$F(v) \ = \ a_1 u_1 + a_2 u_2 + \cdots + a_n u_n \qquad \text{and} \qquad F(w) \ = \ b_1 u_1 + b_2 u_2 + \cdots + b_n u_n$$

Hence $$\begin{aligned}
F(v + w) \ &= \ (a_1 + b_1)u_1 + (a_2 + b_2)u_2 + \cdots + (a_n + b_n)u_n \\
&= \ (a_1 u_1 + a_2 u_2 + \cdots + a_n u_n) + (b_1 u_1 + b_2 u_2 + \cdots + b_n u_n) \\
&= \ F(v) + F(w)
\end{aligned}$$

and $$F(kv) \ = \ k(a_1 u_1 + a_2 u_2 + \cdots + a_n u_n) \ = \ kF(v)$$

Thus F is linear.

Step (3). Now suppose $G : V \to U$ is linear and $G(v_i) = u_i$, $i = 1, \ldots, n$. If $v = a_1 v_1 + a_2 v_2 + \cdots + a_n v_n$, then

$$\begin{aligned}
G(v) \ &= \ G(a_1 v_1 + a_2 v_2 + \cdots + a_n v_n) \ = \ a_1 G(v_1) + a_2 G(v_2) + \cdots + a_n G(v_n) \\
&= \ a_1 u_1 + a_2 u_2 + \cdots + a_n u_n \ = \ F(v)
\end{aligned}$$

Since $G(v) = F(v)$ for every $v \in V$, $G = F$. Thus F is unique and the theorem is proved.

6.15. Let $T: \mathbf{R}^2 \to \mathbf{R}$ be the linear mapping for which

$$T(1, 1) = 3 \quad \text{and} \quad T(0, 1) = -2 \tag{1}$$

(Since $\{(1, 1), (0, 1)\}$ is a basis of $\mathbf{R}^2$, such a linear mapping exists and is unique by Theorem 6.2.) Find $T(a, b)$.

First we write (a, b) as a linear combination of $(1, 1)$ and $(0, 1)$ using unknown scalars x and y:

$$(a, b) = x(1, 1) + y(0, 1) \tag{2}$$

Then $(a, b) = (x, x) + (0, y) = (x, x+y)$ and so $x = a, \ x + y = b$

Solving for x and y in terms of a and b, we obtain

$$x = a \quad \text{and} \quad y = b - a \tag{3}$$

Now using (1) and (2) we have

$$T(a, b) = T(x(1, 1) + y(0, 1)) = xT(1, 1) + yT(0, 1) = 3x - 2y$$

Finally, using (3) we have $T(a, b) = 3x - 2y = 3(a) - 2(b - a) = 5a - 2b$.

6.16. Let $T: V \to U$ be linear, and suppose $v_1, \ldots, v_n \in V$ have the property that their images $T(v_1), \ldots, T(v_n)$ are linearly independent. Show that the vectors $v_1, \ldots, v_n$ are also linearly independent.

Suppose that, for scalars $a_1, \ldots, a_n$, $a_1 v_1 + a_2 v_2 + \cdots + a_n v_n = 0$. Then

$$0 = T(0) = T(a_1 v_1 + a_2 v_2 + \cdots + a_n v_n) = a_1 T(v_1) + a_2 T(v_2) + \cdots + a_n T(v_n)$$

Since the $T(v_i)$ are linearly independent, all the $a_i = 0$. Thus the vectors $v_1, \ldots, v_n$ are linearly independent.

6.17. Suppose the linear mapping $F: V \to U$ is one-to-one and onto. Show that the inverse mapping $F^{-1}: U \to V$ is also linear.

Suppose $u, u' \in U$. Since F is one-to-one and onto, there exist unique vectors $v, v' \in V$ for which $F(v) = u$ and $F(v') = u'$. Since F is linear, we also have

$$F(v + v') = F(v) + F(v') = u + u' \quad \text{and} \quad F(kv) = kF(v) = ku$$

By definition of the inverse mapping, $F^{-1}(u) = v$, $F^{-1}(u') = v'$, $F^{-1}(u + u') = v + v'$ and $F^{-1}(ku) = kv$. Then

$$F^{-1}(u + u') = v + v' = F^{-1}(u) + F^{-1}(u') \quad \text{and} \quad F^{-1}(ku) = kv = kF^{-1}(u)$$

and thus F^{-1} is linear.

IMAGE AND KERNEL OF LINEAR MAPPINGS

6.18. Let $F: \mathbf{R}^4 \to \mathbf{R}^3$ be the linear mapping defined by

$$F(x, y, s, t) = (x - y + s + t, \ x + 2s - t, \ x + y + 3s - 3t)$$

Find a basis and the dimension of the (i) image U of F, (ii) kernel W of F.

(i)   The images of the following generators of $\mathbf{R}^4$ generate the image U of F:

$$F(1, 0, 0, 0) = (1, 1, 1) \qquad F(0, 0, 1, 0) = (1, 2, 3)$$
$$F(0, 1, 0, 0) = (-1, 0, 1) \qquad F(0, 0, 0, 1) = (1, -1, -3)$$

Form the matrix whose rows are the generators of U and row reduce to echelon form:

$$\begin{pmatrix} 1 & 1 & 1 \\ -1 & 0 & 1 \\ 1 & 2 & 3 \\ 1 & -1 & -3 \end{pmatrix} \quad \text{to} \quad \begin{pmatrix} 1 & 1 & 1 \\ 0 & 1 & 2 \\ 0 & 1 & 2 \\ 0 & -2 & -4 \end{pmatrix} \quad \text{to} \quad \begin{pmatrix} 1 & 1 & 1 \\ 0 & 1 & 2 \\ 0 & 0 & 0 \\ 0 & 0 & 0 \end{pmatrix}$$

Thus $\{(1, 1, 1), (0, 1, 2)\}$ is a basis of U; hence $\dim U = 2$.

(ii) We seek the set of (x, y, s, t) such that $F(x, y, s, t) = (0, 0, 0)$, i.e.,

$$F(x, y, s, t) = (x - y + s + t, \; x + 2s - t, \; x + y + 3s - 3t) = (0, 0, 0)$$

Set corresponding components equal to each other to form the following homogeneous system whose solution space is the kernel W of F:

$$
\begin{array}{lllll}
x - y + s + t = 0 & & x - y + s + t = 0 & & x - y + s + t = 0 \\
x \quad + 2s - t = 0 & \text{or} & y + s - 2t = 0 & \text{or} & y + s - 2t = 0 \\
x + y + 3s - 3t = 0 & & 2y + 2s - 4t = 0 & &
\end{array}
$$

The free variables are s and t; hence $\dim W = 2$. Set

      (a) $s = -1$, $t = 0$ to obtain the solution $(2, 1, -1, 0)$,

      (b) $s = 0$, $t = 1$ to obtain the solution $(1, 2, 0, 1)$.

Thus $\{(2, 1, -1, 0), (1, 2, 0, 1)\}$ is a basis of W. (Observe that $\dim U + \dim W = 2 + 2 = 4$, which is the dimension of the domain $\mathbf{R}^4$ of F.)

6.19. Let $T : \mathbf{R}^3 \to \mathbf{R}^3$ be the linear mapping defined by

$$T(x, y, z) = (x + 2y - z, \; y + z, \; x + y - 2z)$$

Find a basis and the dimension of the (i) image U of T, (ii) kernel W of T.

(i) The images of generators of $\mathbf{R}^3$ generate the image U of T:

$$T(1, 0, 0) = (1, 0, 1), \quad T(0, 1, 0) = (2, 1, 1), \quad T(0, 0, 1) = (-1, 1, -2)$$

Form the matrix whose rows are the generators of U and row reduce to echelon form:

$$
\begin{pmatrix} 1 & 0 & 1 \\ 2 & 1 & 1 \\ -1 & 1 & -2 \end{pmatrix}
\quad \text{to} \quad
\begin{pmatrix} 1 & 0 & 1 \\ 0 & 1 & -1 \\ 0 & 1 & -1 \end{pmatrix}
\quad \text{to} \quad
\begin{pmatrix} 1 & 0 & 1 \\ 0 & 1 & -1 \\ 0 & 0 & 0 \end{pmatrix}
$$

Thus $\{(1, 0, 1), (0, 1, -1)\}$ is a basis of U, and so $\dim U = 2$.

(ii) We seek the set of (x, y, z) such that $T(x, y, z) = (0, 0, 0)$, i.e.,

$$T(x, y, z) = (x + 2y - z, \; y + z, \; x + y - 2z) = (0, 0, 0)$$

Set corresponding components equal to each other to form the homogeneous system whose solution space is the kernel W of T:

$$
\begin{array}{lllll}
x + 2y - z = 0 & & x + 2y - z = 0 & & x + 2y - z = 0 \\
y + z = 0 & \text{or} & y + z = 0 & \text{or} & y + z = 0 \\
x + y - 2z = 0 & & -y - z = 0 & &
\end{array}
$$

The only free variable is z; hence $\dim W = 1$. Let $z = 1$; then $y = -1$ and $x = 3$. Thus $\{(3, -1, 1)\}$ is a basis of W. (Observe that $\dim U + \dim W = 2 + 1 = 3$, which is the dimension of the domain $\mathbf{R}^3$ of T.)

6.20. Find a linear map $F : \mathbf{R}^3 \to \mathbf{R}^4$ whose image is generated by $(1, 2, 0, -4)$ and $(2, 0, -1, -3)$.

Method 1.

    Consider the usual basis of $\mathbf{R}^3$: $e_1 = (1, 0, 0)$, $e_2 = (0, 1, 0)$, $e_3 = (0, 0, 1)$. Set $F(e_1) = (1, 2, 0, -4)$, $F(e_2) = (2, 0, -1, -3)$ and $F(e_3) = (0, 0, 0, 0)$. By Theorem 6.2, such a linear map F exists and is unique. Furthermore, the image of F is generated by the $F(e_i)$; hence F has the required property. We find a general formula for $F(x, y, z)$:

$$
\begin{aligned}
F(x, y, z) &= F(x e_1 + y e_2 + z e_3) = x F(e_1) + y F(e_2) + z F(e_3) \\
&= x(1, 2, 0, -4) + y(2, 0, -1, -3) + z(0, 0, 0, 0) \\
&= (x + 2y, \; 2x, \; -y, \; -4x - 3y)
\end{aligned}
$$

Method 2.

Form a 4×3 matrix A whose columns consist only of the given vectors; say,

$$A = \begin{pmatrix} 1 & 2 & 2 \\ 2 & 0 & 0 \\ 0 & -1 & -1 \\ -4 & -3 & -3 \end{pmatrix}$$

Recall that A determines a linear map $A : \mathbf{R}^3 \to \mathbf{R}^4$ whose image is generated by the columns of A. Thus A satisfies the required condition.

6.21. Let V be the vector space of 2 by 2 matrices over $\mathbf{R}$ and let $M = \begin{pmatrix} 1 & 2 \\ 0 & 3 \end{pmatrix}$. Let $F : V \to V$ be the linear map defined by $F(A) = AM - MA$. Find a basis and the dimension of the kernel W of F.

We seek the set of $\begin{pmatrix} x & y \\ s & t \end{pmatrix}$ such that $F\begin{pmatrix} x & y \\ s & t \end{pmatrix} = \begin{pmatrix} 0 & 0 \\ 0 & 0 \end{pmatrix}$.

$$
\begin{aligned}
F\begin{pmatrix} x & y \\ s & t \end{pmatrix} &= \begin{pmatrix} x & y \\ s & t \end{pmatrix}\begin{pmatrix} 1 & 2 \\ 0 & 3 \end{pmatrix} - \begin{pmatrix} 1 & 2 \\ 0 & 3 \end{pmatrix}\begin{pmatrix} x & y \\ s & t \end{pmatrix} \\
&= \begin{pmatrix} x & 2x + 3y \\ s & 2s + 3t \end{pmatrix} - \begin{pmatrix} x + 2s & y + 2t \\ 3s & 3t \end{pmatrix} \\
&= \begin{pmatrix} -2s & 2x + 2y - 2t \\ -2s & 2s \end{pmatrix} = \begin{pmatrix} 0 & 0 \\ 0 & 0 \end{pmatrix}
\end{aligned}
$$

Thus
$$
\begin{array}{ccc}
2x + 2y - 2t = 0 & & x + y - t = 0 \\
2s = 0 & \text{or} & s = 0
\end{array}
$$

The free variables are y and t; hence $\dim W = 2$. To obtain a basis of W set

(a) $y = -1$, $t = 0$ to obtain the solution $x = 1$, $y = -1$, $s = 0$, $t = 0$;

(b) $y = 0$, $t = 1$ to obtain the solution $x = 1$, $y = 0$, $s = 0$, $t = 1$.

Thus $\left\{ \begin{pmatrix} 1 & -1 \\ 0 & 0 \end{pmatrix}, \begin{pmatrix} 1 & 0 \\ 0 & 1 \end{pmatrix} \right\}$ is a basis of W.

6.22. Prove Theorem 6.3: Let $F : V \to U$ be a linear mapping. Then (i) the image of F is a subspace of U and (ii) the kernel of F is a subspace of V.

(i) Since $F(0) = 0$, $0 \in \operatorname{Im} F$. Now suppose $u, u' \in \operatorname{Im} F$ and $a, b \in K$. Since u and u' belong to the image of F, there exist vectors $v, v' \in V$ such that $F(v) = u$ and $F(v') = u'$. Then

$$F(av + bv') = aF(v) + bF(v') = au + bu' \in \operatorname{Im} F$$

Thus the image of F is a subspace of U.

(ii) Since $F(0) = 0$, $0 \in \operatorname{Ker} F$. Now suppose $v, w \in \operatorname{Ker} F$ and $a, b \in K$. Since v and w belong to the kernel of F, $F(v) = 0$ and $F(w) = 0$. Thus

$$F(av + bw) = aF(v) + bF(w) = a0 + b0 = 0 \quad \text{and so} \quad av + bw \in \operatorname{Ker} F$$

Thus the kernel of F is a subspace of V.

6.23. Prove Theorem 6.4: Let V be of finite dimension, and let $F : V \to U$ be a linear mapping with image U' and kernel W. Then $\dim U' + \dim W = \dim V$.

Suppose $\dim V = n$. Since W is a subspace of V, its dimension is finite; say, $\dim W = r \leq n$. Thus we need prove that $\dim U' = n - r$.

Let $\{w_1, \ldots, w_r\}$ be a basis of W. We extend $\{w_i\}$ to a basis of V:

$$\{w_1, \ldots, w_r, v_1, \ldots, v_{n-r}\}$$

Let

$$B = \{F(v_1), F(v_2), \ldots, F(v_{n-r})\}$$

The theorem is proved if we show that B is a basis of the image U' of F.

Proof that B generates U'. Let $u \in U'$. Then there exists $v \in V$ such that $F(v) = u$. Since $\{w_i, v_i\}$ generates V and since $v \in V$,

$$v = a_1 w_1 + \cdots + a_r w_r + b_1 v_1 + \cdots + b_{n-r} v_{n-r}$$

where the a_i, b_i are scalars. Note that $F(w_i) = 0$ since the w_i belong to the kernel of F. Thus

$$\begin{aligned} u = F(v) &= F(a_1 w_1 + \cdots + a_r w_r + b_1 v_1 + \cdots + b_{n-r} v_{n-r}) \\ &= a_1 F(w_1) + \cdots + a_r F(w_r) + b_1 F(v_1) + \cdots + b_{n-r} F(v_{n-r}) \\ &= a_1 0 + \cdots + a_r 0 + b_1 F(v_1) + \cdots + b_{n-r} F(v_{n-r}) \\ &= b_1 F(v_1) + \cdots + b_{n-r} F(v_{n-r}) \end{aligned}$$

Accordingly, the $F(v_i)$ generate the image of F.

Proof that B is linearly independent. Suppose

$$a_1 F(v_1) + a_2 F(v_2) + \cdots + a_{n-r} F(v_{n-r}) = 0$$

Then $F(a_1 v_1 + a_2 v_2 + \cdots + a_{n-r} v_{n-r}) = 0$ and so $a_1 v_1 + \cdots + a_{n-r} v_{n-r}$ belongs to the kernel W of F. Since $\{w_i\}$ generates W, there exist scalars $b_1, \ldots, b_r$ such that

$$a_1 v_1 + a_2 v_2 + \cdots + a_{n-r} v_{n-r} = b_1 w_1 + b_2 w_2 + \cdots + b_r w_r$$

or

$$a_1 v_1 + \cdots + a_{n-r} v_{n-r} - b_1 w_1 - \cdots - b_r w_r = 0 \qquad (*)$$

Since $\{w_i, v_i\}$ is a basis of V, it is linearly independent; hence the coefficients of the w_i and v_i in $(*)$ are all 0. In particular, $a_1 = 0, \ldots, a_{n-r} = 0$. Accordingly, the $F(v_i)$ are linearly independent.

Thus B is a basis of U', and so $\dim U' = n - r$ and the theorem is proved.

6.24. Suppose $f : V \to U$ is linear with kernel W, and that $f(v) = u$. Show that the "coset" $v + W = \{v + w : w \in W\}$ is the preimage of u, that is, $f^{-1}(u) = v + W$.

We must prove that (i) $f^{-1}(u) \subset v + W$ and (ii) $v + W \subset f^{-1}(u)$. We first prove (i). Suppose $v' \in f^{-1}(u)$. Then $f(v') = u$ and so $f(v' - v) = f(v') - f(v) = u - u = 0$, that is, $v' - v \in W$. Thus $v' = v + (v' - v) \in v + W$ and hence $f^{-1}(u) \subset v + W$.

Now we prove (ii). Suppose $v' \in v + W$. Then $v' = v + w$ where $w \in W$. Since W is the kernel of f, $f(w) = 0$. Accordingly, $f(v') = f(v + w) = f(v) + f(w) = f(v) + 0 = f(v) = u$. Thus $v' \in f^{-1}(u)$ and so $v + W \subset f^{-1}(u)$.

SINGULAR AND NONSINGULAR MAPPINGS

6.25. Suppose $F : V \to U$ is linear and that V is of finite dimension. Show that V and the image of F have the same dimension if and only if F is nonsingular. Determine all nonsingular mappings $T : \mathbf{R}^4 \to \mathbf{R}^3$.

By Theorem 6.4, $\dim V = \dim(\operatorname{Im} F) + \dim(\operatorname{Ker} F)$. Hence V and $\operatorname{Im} F$ have the same dimension if and only if $\dim(\operatorname{Ker} F) = 0$ or $\operatorname{Ker} F = \{0\}$, i.e. if and only if F is nonsingular.

Since the dimension of $\mathbf{R}^3$ is less than the dimension of $\mathbf{R}^4$, so is the dimension of the image of T. Accordingly, no linear mapping $T : \mathbf{R}^4 \to \mathbf{R}^3$ can be nonsingular.

6.26. Prove that a linear mapping $F : V \to U$ is nonsingular if and only if the image of any independent set is independent.

Suppose F is nonsingular and suppose $\{v_1, \ldots, v_n\}$ is an independent subset of V. We claim that the vectors $F(v_1), \ldots, F(v_n)$ are independent. Suppose $a_1 F(v_1) + a_2 F(v_2) + \cdots + a_n F(v_n) = 0$, where $a_i \in K$. Since F is linear, $F(a_1 v_1 + a_2 v_2 + \cdots + a_n v_n) = 0$; hence

$$a_1 v_1 + a_2 v_2 + \cdots + a_n v_n \in \operatorname{Ker} F$$

But F is nonsingular, i.e. $\text{Ker } F = \{0\}$; hence $a_1v_1 + a_2v_2 + \cdots + a_nv_n = 0$. Since the v_i are linearly independent, all the a_i are 0. Accordingly, the $F(v_i)$ are linearly independent. In other words, the image of the independent set $\{v_1, \ldots, v_n\}$ is independent.

On the other hand, suppose the image of any independent set is independent. If $v \in V$ is nonzero, then $\{v\}$ is independent. Then $\{F(v)\}$ is independent and so $F(v) \neq 0$. Accordingly, F is nonsingular.

OPERATIONS WITH LINEAR MAPPINGS

6.27. Let $F : \mathbf{R}^3 \to \mathbf{R}^2$ and $G : \mathbf{R}^3 \to \mathbf{R}^2$ be defined by $F(x, y, z) = (2x, y + z)$ and $G(x, y, z) = (x - z, y)$. Find formulae defining the mappings $F + G$, $3F$ and $2F - 5G$.

$$(F + G)(x, y, z) = F(x, y, z) + G(x, y, z)$$
$$= (2x, y + z) + (x - z, y) = (3x - z, 2y + z)$$

$$(3F)(x, y, z) = 3F(x, y, z) = 3(2x, y + z) = (6x, 3y + 3z)$$

$$(2F - 5G)(x, y, z) = 2F(x, y, z) - 5G(x, y, z) = 2(2x, y + z) - 5(x - z, y)$$
$$= (4x, 2y + 2z) + (-5x + 5z, -5y) = (-x + 5z, -3y + 2z)$$

6.28. Let $F : \mathbf{R}^3 \to \mathbf{R}^2$ and $G : \mathbf{R}^2 \to \mathbf{R}^2$ be defined by $F(x, y, z) = (2x, y + z)$ and $G(x, y) = (y, x)$. Derive formulae defining the mappings $G \circ F$ and $F \circ G$.

$$(G \circ F)(x, y, z) = G(F(x, y, z)) = G(2x, y + z) = (y + z, 2x)$$

The mapping $F \circ G$ is not defined since the image of G is not contained in the domain of F.

6.29. Show: (i) the zero mapping 0, defined by $0(v) = 0$ for every $v \in V$, is the zero element of $\text{Hom}(V, U)$; (ii) the negative of $F \in \text{Hom}(V, U)$ is the mapping $(-1)F$, i.e. $-F = (-1)F$.

(i)   Let $F \in \text{Hom}(V, U)$. Then, for every $v \in V$,
$$(F + 0)(v) = F(v) + 0(v) = F(v) + 0 = F(v)$$

Since $(F + 0)(v) = F(v)$ for every $v \in V$, $F + 0 = F$.

(ii)   For every $v \in V$,
$$(F + (-1)F)(v) = F(v) + (-1)F(v) = F(v) - F(v) = 0 = 0(v)$$

Since $(F + (-1)F)(v) = 0(v)$ for every $v \in V$, $F + (-1)F = 0$. Thus $(-1)F$ is the negative of F.

6.30. Show that for $F_1, \ldots, F_n \in \text{Hom}(V, U)$ and $a_1, \ldots, a_n \in K$, and for any $v \in V$,
$$(a_1F_1 + a_2F_2 + \cdots + a_nF_n)(v) = a_1F_1(v) + a_2F_2(v) + \cdots + a_nF_n(v)$$

By definition of the mapping a_1F_1, $(a_1F_1)(v) = a_1F_1(v)$; hence the theorem holds for $n = 1$. Thus by induction,
$$(a_1F_1 + a_2F_2 + \cdots + a_nF_n)(v) = (a_1F_1)(v) + (a_2F_2 + \cdots + a_nF_n)(v)$$
$$= a_1F_1(v) + a_2F_2(v) + \cdots + a_nF_n(v)$$

6.31. Let $F : \mathbf{R}^3 \to \mathbf{R}^2$, $G : \mathbf{R}^3 \to \mathbf{R}^2$ and $H : \mathbf{R}^3 \to \mathbf{R}^2$ be defined by $F(x, y, z) = (x + y + z, x + y)$, $G(x, y, z) = (2x + z, x + y)$ and $H(x, y, z) = (2y, x)$. Show that $F, G, H \in \text{Hom}(\mathbf{R}^3, \mathbf{R}^2)$ are linearly independent.

Suppose, for scalars $a, b, c \in K$,
$$aF + bG + cH = 0 \qquad (1)$$

(Here 0 is the zero mapping.)   For $e_1 = (1, 0, 0) \in \mathbf{R}^3$, we have
$$(aF + bG + cH)(e_1) = aF(1, 0, 0) + bG(1, 0, 0) + cH(1, 0, 0)$$
$$= a(1, 1) + b(2, 1) + c(0, 1) = (a + 2b, a + b + c)$$

and $\;0(e_1) = (0, 0)$. Thus by (1), $\;(a + 2b, a + b + c) = (0, 0)\;$ and so

$$a + 2b = 0 \quad \text{and} \quad a + b + c = 0 \tag{2}$$

Similarly for $\;e_2 = (0, 1, 0) \in \mathbf{R}^3$, we have

$$
\begin{aligned}
(aF + bG + cH)(e_2) &= aF(0, 1, 0) + bG(0, 1, 0) + cH(0, 1, 0) \\
&= a(1, 1) + b(0, 1) + c(2, 0) \;=\; (a + 2c, a + b) \;=\; 0(e_2) \;=\; (0, 0)
\end{aligned}
$$

Thus $$a + 2c = 0 \quad \text{and} \quad a + b = 0 \tag{3}$$

Using (2) and (3) we obtain $$a = 0, \;\; b = 0, \;\; c = 0 \tag{4}$$

Since (1) implies (4), the mappings F, G and H are linearly independent.

6.32. Prove Theorem 6.7: Suppose $\dim V = m$ and $\dim U = n$. Then $\dim \operatorname{Hom}(V, U) = mn$.

Suppose $\{v_1, \ldots, v_m\}$ is a basis of V and $\{u_1, \ldots, u_n\}$ is a basis of U. By Theorem 6.2, a linear mapping in $\operatorname{Hom}(V, U)$ is uniquely determined by arbitrarily assigning elements of U to the basis elements v_i of V. We define

$$F_{ij} \in \operatorname{Hom}(V, U), \quad i = 1, \ldots, m, \;\; j = 1, \ldots, n$$

to be the linear mapping for which $F_{ij}(v_i) = u_j$, and $F_{ij}(v_k) = 0$ for $k \neq i$. That is, F_{ij} maps v_i into u_j and the other v's into 0. Observe that $\{F_{ij}\}$ contains exactly mn elements; hence the theorem is proved if we show that it is a basis of $\operatorname{Hom}(V, U)$.

Proof that $\{F_{ij}\}$ generates $\operatorname{Hom}(V, U)$. Let $F \in \operatorname{Hom}(V, U)$. Suppose $F(v_1) = w_1$, $F(v_2) = w_2$, $\ldots$, $F(v_m) = w_m$. Since $w_k \in U$, it is a linear combination of the u's; say,

$$w_k = a_{k1}u_1 + a_{k2}u_2 + \cdots + a_{kn}u_n, \quad k = 1, \ldots, m, \;\; a_{ij} \in K \tag{1}$$

Consider the linear mapping $G = \displaystyle\sum_{i=1}^{m}\sum_{j=1}^{n} a_{ij}F_{ij}$. Since G is a linear combination of the F_{ij}, the proof that $\{F_{ij}\}$ generates $\operatorname{Hom}(V, U)$ is complete if we show that $F = G$.

We now compute $G(v_k)$, $k = 1, \ldots, m$. Since $F_{ij}(v_k) = 0$ for $k \neq i$ and $F_{ki}(v_k) = u_i$,

$$
\begin{aligned}
G(v_k) &= \sum_{i=1}^{m}\sum_{j=1}^{n} a_{ij}F_{ij}(v_k) \;=\; \sum_{j=1}^{n} a_{kj}F_{kj}(v_k) \;=\; \sum_{j=1}^{n} a_{kj}u_j \\
&= a_{k1}u_1 + a_{k2}u_2 + \cdots + a_{kn}u_n
\end{aligned}
$$

Thus by (1), $G(v_k) = w_k$ for each k. But $F(v_k) = w_k$ for each k. Accordingly, by Theorem 6.2, $F = G$; hence $\{F_{ij}\}$ generates $\operatorname{Hom}(V, U)$.

Proof that $\{F_{ij}\}$ is linearly independent. Suppose, for scalars $a_{ij} \in K$,

$$\sum_{i=1}^{m}\sum_{j=1}^{n} a_{ij}F_{ij} = 0$$

For v_k, $k = 1, \ldots, m$,

$$
\begin{aligned}
0 = 0(v_k) &= \sum_{i=1}^{m}\sum_{j=1}^{n} a_{ij}F_{ij}(v_k) \;=\; \sum_{j=1}^{n} a_{kj}F_{kj}(v_k) \;=\; \sum_{j=1}^{n} a_{kj}u_j \\
&= a_{k1}u_1 + a_{k2}u_2 + \cdots + a_{kn}u_n
\end{aligned}
$$

But the u_i are linearly independent; hence for $k = 1, \ldots, m$, we have $a_{k1} = 0$, $a_{k2} = 0$, $\ldots$, $a_{kn} = 0$. In other words, all the $a_{ij} = 0$ and so $\{F_{ij}\}$ is linearly independent.

Thus $\{F_{ij}\}$ is a basis of $\operatorname{Hom}(V, U)$; hence $\dim \operatorname{Hom}(V, U) = mn$.

6.33. Prove Theorem 6.8: Let V, U and W be vector spaces over K. Let F, F' be linear mappings from V into U and let G, G' be linear mappings from U into W; and let $k \in K$. Then: (i) $G \circ (F + F') = G \circ F + G \circ F'$; (ii) $(G + G') \circ F = G \circ F + G' \circ F$; (iii) $k(G \circ F) = (kG) \circ F = G \circ (kF)$.

(i) For every $v \in V$,

$$(G \circ (F + F'))(v) = G((F + F')(v)) = G(F(v) + F'(v))$$
$$= G(F(v)) + G(F'(v)) = (G \circ F)(v) + (G \circ F')(v) = (G \circ F + G \circ F')(v)$$

Since $(G \circ (F + F'))(v) = (G \circ F + G \circ F')(v)$ for every $v \in V$, $G \circ (F + F') = G \circ F + G \circ F'$.

(ii) For every $v \in V$,
$$((G + G') \circ F)(v) = (G + G')(F(v)) = G(F(v)) + G'(F(v))$$
$$= (G \circ F)(v) + (G' \circ F)(v) = (G \circ F + G' \circ F)(v)$$

Since $((G + G') \circ F)(v) = (G \circ F + G \circ F')(v)$ for every $v \in V$, $(G + G') \circ F = G \circ F + G' \circ F$.

(iii) For every $v \in V$,
$$(k(G \circ F))(v) = k(G \circ F)(v) = k(G(F(v))) = (kG)(F(v)) = (kG \circ F)(v)$$

and
$$(k(G \circ F))(v) = k(G \circ F)(v) = k(G(F(v))) = G(kF(v)) = G((kF)(v)) = (G \circ kF)(v)$$

Accordingly, $k(G \circ F) = (kG) \circ F = G \circ (kF)$. (We emphasize that two mappings are shown to be equal by showing that they assign the same image to each point in the domain.)

6.34. Let $F : V \to U$ and $G : U \to W$ be linear. Hence $(G \circ F) : V \to W$ is linear. Show that (i) rank $(G \circ F) \leq$ rank G, (ii) rank $(G \circ F) \leq$ rank F.

(i) Since $F(V) \subset U$, we also have $G(F(V)) \subset G(U)$ and so $\dim G(F(V)) \leq \dim G(U)$. Then
$$\text{rank } (G \circ F) = \dim ((G \circ F)(V)) = \dim (G(F(V))) \leq \dim G(U) = \text{rank } G$$

(ii) By Theorem 6.4, $\dim (G(F(V))) \leq \dim F(V)$. Hence
$$\text{rank } (G \circ F) = \dim ((G \circ F)(V)) = \dim (G(F(V))) \leq \dim F(V) = \text{rank } F$$

ALGEBRA OF LINEAR OPERATORS

6.35. Let S and T be the linear operators on $\mathbf{R}^2$ defined by $S(x, y) = (y, x)$ and $T(x, y) = (0, x)$. Find formulae defining the operators $S + T$, $2S - 3T$, ST, TS, S^2 and T^2.

$(S + T)(x, y) = S(x, y) + T(x, y) = (y, x) + (0, x) = (y, 2x)$.
$(2S - 3T)(x, y) = 2S(x, y) - 3T(x, y) = 2(y, x) - 3(0, x) = (2y, -x)$.
$(ST)(x, y) = S(T(x, y)) = S(0, x) = (x, 0)$.
$(TS)(x, y) = T(S(x, y)) = T(y, x) = (0, y)$.
$S^2(x, y) = S(S(x, y)) = S(y, x) = (x, y)$. Note $S^2 = I$, the identity mapping.
$T^2(x, y) = T(T(x, y)) = T(0, x) = (0, 0)$. Note $T^2 = 0$, the zero mapping.

6.36. Let T be the linear operator on $\mathbf{R}^2$ defined by
$$T(3, 1) = (2, -4) \quad \text{and} \quad T(1, 1) = (0, 2) \qquad (1)$$
(By Theorem 6.2, such a linear operator exists and is unique.) Find $T(a, b)$. In particular, find $T(7, 4)$.

First write (a, b) as a linear combination of $(3, 1)$ and $(1, 1)$ using unknown scalars x and y:
$$(a, b) = x(3, 1) + y(1, 1) \qquad (2)$$

Hence $(a, b) = (3x, x) + (y, y) = (3x + y, x + y)$ and so $\begin{cases} 3x + y = a \\ x + y = b \end{cases}$

Solving for x and y in terms of a and b,
$$x = \tfrac{1}{2}a - \tfrac{1}{2}b \quad \text{and} \quad y = -\tfrac{1}{2}a + \tfrac{3}{2}b \qquad (3)$$

Now using (2), (1) and (3),
$$T(a, b) = xT(3, 1) + yT(1, 1) = x(2, -4) + y(0, 2)$$
$$= (2x, -4x) + (0, 2y) = (2x, -4x + 2y) = (a - b, 5b - 3a)$$

Thus $T(7, 4) = (7 - 4, 20 - 21) = (3, -1)$.

6.37. Let T be the operator on $\mathbf{R}^3$ defined by $T(x, y, z) = (2x, 4x - y, 2x + 3y - z)$. (i) Show that T is invertible. (ii) Find a formula for T^{-1}.

(i) The kernel W of T is the set of all (x, y, z) such that $T(x, y, z) = (0, 0, 0)$, i.e.,

$$T(x, y, z) = (2x, 4x - y, 2x + 3y - z) = (0, 0, 0)$$

Thus W is the solution space of the homogeneous system

$$2x = 0, \quad 4x - y = 0, \quad 2x + 3y - z = 0$$

which has only the trivial solution $(0, 0, 0)$. Thus $W = \{0\}$; hence T is nonsingular and so by Theorem 6.9 is invertible.

(ii) Let (r, s, t) be the image of (x, y, z) under T; then (x, y, z) is the image of (r, s, t) under T^{-1}: $T(x, y, z) = (r, s, t)$ and $T^{-1}(r, s, t) = (x, y, z)$. We will find the values of x, y and z in terms of r, s and t, and then substitute in the above formula for T^{-1}. From

$$T(x, y, z) = (2x, 4x - y, 2x + 3y - z) = (r, s, t)$$

we find $x = \frac{1}{2}r$, $y = 2r - s$, $z = 7r - 3s - t$. Thus T^{-1} is given by

$$T^{-1}(r, s, t) = (\tfrac{1}{2}r, 2r - s, 7r - 3s - t)$$

6.38. Let V be of finite dimension and let T be a linear operator on V. Recall that T is invertible if and only if T is nonsingular or one-to-one. Show that T is invertible if and only if T is onto.

By Theorem 6.4, $\dim V = \dim(\text{Im } T) + \dim(\text{Ker } T)$. Hence the following statements are equivalent: (i) T is onto, (ii) $\text{Im } T = V$, (iii) $\dim(\text{Im } T) = \dim V$, (iv) $\dim(\text{Ker } T) = 0$, (v) $\text{Ker } T = \{0\}$, (vi) T is nonsingular, (vii) T is invertible.

6.39. Let V be of finite dimension and let T be a linear operator on V for which $TS = I$, for some operator S on V. (We call S a right inverse of T.) (i) Show that T is invertible. (ii) Show that $S = T^{-1}$. (iii) Give an example showing that the above need not hold if V is of infinite dimension.

(i) Let $\dim V = n$. By the preceding problem, T is invertible if and only if T is onto; hence T is invertible if and only if $\text{rank } T = n$. We have $n = \text{rank } I = \text{rank } TS \leq \text{rank } T \leq n$. Hence $\text{rank } T = n$ and T is invertible.

(ii) $TT^{-1} = T^{-1}T = I$. Then $S = IS = (T^{-1}T)S = T^{-1}(TS) = T^{-1}I = T^{-1}$.

(iii) Let V be the space of polynomials in t over K; say, $p(t) = a_0 + a_1t + a_2t^2 + \cdots + a_nt^n$. Let T and S be the operators on V defined by

$$T(p(t)) = 0 + a_1 + a_2t + \cdots + a_nt^{n-1} \quad \text{and} \quad S(p(t)) = a_0t + a_1t^2 + \cdots + a_nt^{n+1}$$

We have $\quad (TS)(p(t)) = T(S(p(t))) = T(a_0t + a_1t^2 + \cdots + a_nt^{n+1})$

$$= a_0 + a_1t + \cdots + a_nt^n = p(t)$$

and so $TS = I$, the identity mapping. On the other hand, if $k \in K$ and $k \neq 0$, then $(ST)(k) = S(T(k)) = S(0) = 0 \neq k$. Accordingly, $ST \neq I$.

6.40. Let S and T be the linear operators on $\mathbf{R}^2$ defined by $S(x, y) = (0, x)$ and $T(x, y) = (x, 0)$. Show that $TS = 0$ but $ST \neq 0$. Also show that $T^2 = T$.

$(TS)(x, y) = T(S(x, y)) = T(0, x) = (0, 0)$. Since TS assigns $0 = (0, 0)$ to every $(x, y) \in \mathbf{R}^2$, it is the zero mapping: $TS = 0$.

$(ST)(x, y) = S(T(x, y)) = S(x, 0) = (0, x)$. For example, $(ST)(4, 2) = (0, 4)$. Thus $ST \neq 0$, since it does not assign $0 = (0, 0)$ to every element of $\mathbf{R}^2$.

For any $(x, y) \in \mathbf{R}^2$, $T^2(x, y) = T(T(x, y)) = T(x, 0) = (x, 0) = T(x, y)$. Hence $T^2 = T$.

MISCELLANEOUS PROBLEMS

6.41. Let $\{e_1, e_2, e_3\}$ be a basis of V and $\{f_1, f_2\}$ a basis of U. Let $T : V \to U$ be linear. Furthermore, suppose

$$
\begin{aligned}
T(e_1) &= a_1 f_1 + a_2 f_2 \\
T(e_2) &= b_1 f_1 + b_2 f_2 \\
T(e_3) &= c_1 f_1 + c_2 f_2
\end{aligned}
\qquad \text{and} \qquad
A = \begin{pmatrix} a_1 & b_1 & c_1 \\ a_2 & b_2 & c_2 \end{pmatrix}
$$

Show that, for any $v \in V$, $A[v]_e = [T(v)]_f$ where the vectors in K^2 and K^3 are written as column vectors.

Suppose $v = k_1 e_1 + k_2 e_2 + k_3 e_3$; then $[v]_e = \begin{pmatrix} k_1 \\ k_2 \\ k_3 \end{pmatrix}$. Also,

$$
\begin{aligned}
T(v) &= k_1 T(e_1) + k_2 T(e_2) + k_3 T(e_3) \\
&= k_1(a_1 f_1 + a_2 f_2) + k_2(b_1 f_1 + b_2 f_2) + k_3(c_1 f_1 + c_2 f_2) \\
&= (a_1 k_1 + b_1 k_2 + c_1 k_3) f_1 + (a_2 k_1 + b_2 k_2 + c_2 k_3) f_2
\end{aligned}
$$

Accordingly,
$$
[T(v)]_f = \begin{pmatrix} a_1 k_1 + b_1 k_2 + c_1 k_3 \\ a_2 k_1 + b_2 k_2 + c_2 k_3 \end{pmatrix}
$$

Computing, we obtain

$$
A[v]_e = \begin{pmatrix} a_1 & b_1 & c_1 \\ a_2 & b_2 & c_2 \end{pmatrix} \begin{pmatrix} k_1 \\ k_2 \\ k_3 \end{pmatrix} = \begin{pmatrix} a_1 k_1 + b_1 k_2 + c_1 k_3 \\ a_2 k_1 + b_2 k_2 + c_2 k_3 \end{pmatrix} = [T(v)]_f
$$

6.42. Let k be a nonzero scalar. Show that a linear map T is singular if and only if kT is singular. Hence T is singular if and only if $-T$ is singular.

Suppose T is singular. Then $T(v) = 0$ for some vector $v \neq 0$. Hence $(kT)(v) = kT(v) = k0 = 0$ and so kT is singular.

Now suppose kT is singular. Then $(kT)(w) = 0$ for some vector $w \neq 0$; hence $T(kw) = kT(w) = (kT)(w) = 0$. But $k \neq 0$ and $w \neq 0$ implies $kw \neq 0$; thus T is also singular.

6.43. Let E be a linear operator on V for which $E^2 = E$. (Such an operator is termed a projection.) Let U be the image of E and W the kernel. Show that: (i) if $u \in U$, then $E(u) = u$, i.e. E is the identity map on U; (ii) if $E \neq I$, then E is singular, i.e. $E(v) = 0$ for some $v \neq 0$; (iii) $V = U \oplus W$.

(i)   If $u \in U$, the image of E, then $E(v) = u$ for some $v \in V$. Hence using $E^2 = E$, we have
$$
u = E(v) = E^2(v) = E(E(v)) = E(u)
$$

(ii) If $E \neq I$ then, for some $v \in V$, $E(v) = u$ where $v \neq u$. By (i), $E(u) = u$. Thus
$$
E(v - u) = E(v) - E(u) = u - u = 0 \qquad \text{where} \quad v - u \neq 0
$$

(iii) We first show that $V = U + W$. Let $v \in V$. Set $u = E(v)$ and $w = v - E(v)$. Then
$$
v = E(v) + v - E(v) = u + w
$$

By definition, $u = E(v) \in U$, the image of E. We now show that $w \in W$, the kernel of E:
$$
E(w) = E(v - E(v)) = E(v) - E^2(v) = E(v) - E(v) = 0
$$

and thus $w \in W$. Hence $V = U + W$.

We next show that $U \cap W = \{0\}$. Let $v \in U \cap W$. Since $v \in U$, $E(v) = v$ by (i). Since $v \in W$, $E(v) = 0$. Thus $v = E(v) = 0$ and so $U \cap W = \{0\}$.

The above two properties imply that $V = U \oplus W$.

6.44. Show that a square matrix A is invertible if and only if it is nonsingular. (Compare with Theorem 6.9, page 130.)

Recall that A is invertible if and only if A is row equivalent to the identity matrix I. Thus the following statements are equivalent: (i) A is invertible. (ii) A and I are row equivalent. (iii) The equations $AX = 0$ and $IX = 0$ have the same solution space. (iv) $AX = 0$ has only the zero solution. (v) A is nonsingular.

Supplementary Problems

MAPPINGS

6.45. State whether each diagram defines a mapping from $\{1, 2, 3\}$ into $\{4, 5, 6\}$.

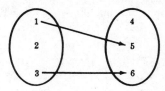 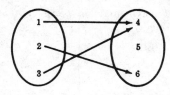 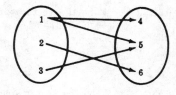

6.46. Define each of the following mappings $f : \mathbf{R} \to \mathbf{R}$ by a formula:

(i)   To each number let f assign its square plus 3.

(ii) To each number let f assign its cube plus twice the number.

(iii) To each number $\geqq 3$ let f assign the number squared, and to each number < 3 let f assign the number -2.

6.47. Let $f : \mathbf{R} \to \mathbf{R}$ be defined by $f(x) = x^2 - 4x + 3$. Find (i) $f(4)$, (ii) $f(-3)$, (iii) $f(y - 2x)$, (iv) $f(x - 2)$.

6.48. Determine the number of different mappings from $\{a, b\}$ into $\{1, 2, 3\}$.

6.49. Let the mapping g assign to each name in the set {Betty, Martin, David, Alan, Rebecca} the number of different letters needed to spell the name. Find (i) the graph of g, (ii) the image of g.

6.50. Sketch the graph of each mapping: (i) $f(x) = \frac{1}{2}x - 1$, (ii) $g(x) = 2x^2 - 4x - 3$.

6.51. The mappings $f : A \to B$, $g : B \to A$, $h : C \to B$, $F : B \to C$ and $G : A \to C$ are illustrated in the diagram below.

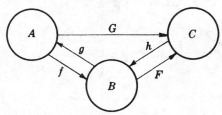

Determine whether each of the following defines a composition mapping and, if it does, find its domain and co-domain: (i) $g \circ f$, (ii) $h \circ f$, (iii) $F \circ f$, (iv) $G \circ f$, (v) $g \circ h$, (vi) $h \circ G \circ g$.

6.52. Let $f : \mathbf{R} \to \mathbf{R}$ and $g : \mathbf{R} \to \mathbf{R}$ be defined by $f(x) = x^2 + 3x + 1$ and $g(x) = 2x - 3$. Find formulae defining the composition mappings (i) $f \circ g$, (ii) $g \circ f$, (iii) $g \circ g$, (iv) $f \circ f$.

6.53. For any mapping $f : A \to B$, show that $1_B \circ f = f = f \circ 1_A$.

6.54. For each of the following mappings $f : \mathbf{R} \to \mathbf{R}$ find a formula for the inverse mapping: (i) $f(x) = 3x - 7$, (ii) $f(x) = x^3 + 2$.

LINEAR MAPPINGS

6.55. Show that the following mappings F are linear:
  (i) $F : \mathbf{R}^2 \to \mathbf{R}^2$ defined by $F(x, y) = (2x - y, x)$.
  (ii) $F : \mathbf{R}^3 \to \mathbf{R}^2$ defined by $F(x, y, z) = (z, x + y)$.
  (iii) $F : \mathbf{R} \to \mathbf{R}^2$ defined by $F(x) = (2x, 3x)$.
  (iv) $F : \mathbf{R}^2 \to \mathbf{R}^2$ defined by $F(x, y) = (ax + by, cx + dy)$ where $a, b, c, d \in \mathbf{R}$.

6.56. Show that the following mappings F are not linear:
  (i) $F : \mathbf{R}^2 \to \mathbf{R}^2$ defined by $F(x, y) = (x^2, y^2)$.
  (ii) $F : \mathbf{R}^3 \to \mathbf{R}^2$ defined by $F(x, y, z) = (x + 1, y + z)$.
  (iii) $F : \mathbf{R} \to \mathbf{R}^2$ defined by $F(x) = (x, 1)$.
  (iv) $F : \mathbf{R}^2 \to \mathbf{R}$ defined by $F(x, y) = |x - y|$.

6.57. Let V be the vector space of polynomials in t over K. Show that the mappings $T : V \to V$ and $S : V \to V$ defined below are linear:
$$T(a_0 + a_1 t + \cdots + a_n t^n) = a_0 t + a_1 t^2 + \cdots + a_n t^{n+1}$$
$$S(a_0 + a_1 t + \cdots + a_n t^n) = 0 + a_1 + a_2 t + \cdots + a_n t^{n-1}$$

6.58. Let V be the vector space of $n \times n$ matrices over K; and let M be an arbitrary matrix in V. Show that the first two mappings $T : V \to V$ are linear, but the third is not linear (unless $M = 0$):
(i) $T(A) = MA$, (ii) $T(A) = MA - AM$, (iii) $T(A) = M + A$.

6.59. Find $T(a, b)$ where $T : \mathbf{R}^2 \to \mathbf{R}^3$ is defined by $T(1, 2) = (3, -1, 5)$ and $T(0, 1) = (2, 1, -1)$.

6.60. Find $T(a, b, c)$ where $T : \mathbf{R}^3 \to \mathbf{R}$ is defined by
$$T(1, 1, 1) = 3, \qquad T(0, 1, -2) = 1 \quad \text{and} \quad T(0, 0, 1) = -2$$

6.61. Suppose $F : V \to U$ is linear. Show that, for any $v \in V$, $F(-v) = -F(v)$.

6.62. Let W be a subspace of V. Show that the *inclusion map of W into V*, denoted by $i : W \subset V$ and defined by $i(w) = w$, is linear.

KERNEL AND IMAGE OF LINEAR MAPPINGS

6.63. For each of the following linear mappings F, find a basis and the dimension of (a) its image U and (b) its kernel W:
  (i) $F : \mathbf{R}^3 \to \mathbf{R}^3$ defined by $F(x, y, z) = (x + 2y, y - z, x + 2z)$.
  (ii) $F : \mathbf{R}^2 \to \mathbf{R}^2$ defined by $F(x, y) = (x + y, x + y)$.
  (iii) $F : \mathbf{R}^3 \to \mathbf{R}^2$ defined by $F(x, y, z) = (x + y, y + z)$.

6.64. Let V be the vector space of 2×2 matrices over $\mathbf{R}$ and let $M = \begin{pmatrix} 1 & -1 \\ -2 & 2 \end{pmatrix}$. Let $F : V \to V$ be the linear map defined by $F(A) = MA$. Find a basis and the dimension of (i) the kernel W of F and (ii) the image U of F.

6.65. Find a linear mapping $F : \mathbf{R}^3 \to \mathbf{R}^3$ whose image is generated by $(1, 2, 3)$ and $(4, 5, 6)$.

6.66. Find a linear mapping $F : \mathbf{R}^4 \to \mathbf{R}^3$ whose kernel is generated by $(1, 2, 3, 4)$ and $(0, 1, 1, 1)$.

6.67. Let V be the vector space of polynomials in t over $\mathbf{R}$. Let $D : V \to V$ be the differential operator: $D(f) = df/dt$. Find the kernel and image of D.

6.68. Let $F : V \to U$ be linear. Show that (i) the image of any subspace of V is a subspace of U and (ii) the preimage of any subspace of U is a subspace of V.

6.69. Each of the following matrices determines a linear map from $\mathbf{R}^4$ into $\mathbf{R}^3$:

$$\text{(i)} \quad A = \begin{pmatrix} 1 & 2 & 0 & 1 \\ 2 & -1 & 2 & -1 \\ 1 & -3 & 2 & -2 \end{pmatrix} \qquad \text{(ii)} \quad B = \begin{pmatrix} 1 & 0 & 2 & -1 \\ 2 & 3 & -1 & 1 \\ -2 & 0 & -5 & 3 \end{pmatrix}$$

Find a basis and the dimension of the image U and the kernel W of each map.

6.70. Let $T : \mathbf{C} \to \mathbf{C}$ be the conjugate mapping on the complex field $\mathbf{C}$. That is, $T(z) = \bar{z}$ where $z \in C$, or $T(a + bi) = a - bi$ where $a, b \in \mathbf{R}$. (i) Show that T is not linear if $\mathbf{C}$ is viewed as a vector space over itself. (ii) Show that T is linear if $\mathbf{C}$ is viewed as a vector space over the real field $\mathbf{R}$.

OPERATIONS WITH LINEAR MAPPINGS

6.71. Let $F : \mathbf{R}^3 \to \mathbf{R}^2$ and $G : \mathbf{R}^3 \to \mathbf{R}^2$ be defined by $F(x, y, z) = (y, x + z)$ and $G(x, y, z) = (2z, x - y)$. Find formulae defining the mappings $F + G$ and $3F - 2G$.

6.72. Let $H : \mathbf{R}^2 \to \mathbf{R}^2$ be defined by $H(x, y) = (y, 2x)$. Using the mappings F and G in the preceding problem, find formulae defining the mappings: (i) $H \circ F$ and $H \circ G$, (ii) $F \circ H$ and $G \circ H$, (iii) $H \circ (F + G)$ and $H \circ F + H \circ G$.

6.73. Show that the following mappings F, G and H are linearly independent:

(i) $F, G, H \in \text{Hom}\,(\mathbf{R}^2, \mathbf{R}^2)$ defined by
$$F(x, y) = (x, 2y), \quad G(x, y) = (y, x + y), \quad H(x, y) = (0, x).$$

(ii) $F, G, H \in \text{Hom}\,(\mathbf{R}^3, \mathbf{R})$ defined by
$$F(x, y, z) = x + y + z, \quad G(x, y, z) = y + z, \quad H(x, y, z) = x - z.$$

6.74. For $F, G \in \text{Hom}\,(V, U)$, show that $\text{rank}\,(F + G) \leq \text{rank}\,F + \text{rank}\,G$. (Here V has finite dimension.)

6.75. Let $F : V \to U$ and $G : U \to V$ be linear. Show that if F and G are nonsingular then $G \circ F$ is nonsingular. Give an example where $G \circ F$ is nonsingular but G is not.

6.76. Prove that $\text{Hom}\,(V, U)$ does satisfy all the required axioms of a vector space. That is, prove Theorem 6.6, page 128.

ALGEBRA OF LINEAR OPERATORS

6.77. Let S and T be the linear operators on $\mathbf{R}^2$ defined by $S(x, y) = (x + y, 0)$ and $T(x, y) = (-y, x)$. Find formulae defining the operators $S + T$, $5S - 3T$, ST, TS, S^2 and T^2.

6.78. Let T be the linear operator on $\mathbf{R}^2$ defined by $T(x, y) = (x + 2y, 3x + 4y)$. Find $p(T)$ where $p(t) = t^2 - 5t - 2$.

6.79. Show that each of the following operators T on $\mathbf{R}^3$ is invertible, and find a formula for T^{-1}: (i) $T(x, y, z) = (x - 3y - 2z, y - 4z, z)$, (ii) $T(x, y, z) = (x + z, x - z, y)$.

6.80. Suppose S and T are linear operators on V and that S is nonsingular. Assume V has finite dimension. Show that $\text{rank}\,(ST) = \text{rank}\,(TS) = \text{rank}\,T$.

6.81. Suppose $V = U \oplus W$. Let E_1 and E_2 be the linear operators on V defined by $E_1(v) = u$, $E_2(v) = w$, where $v = u + w$, $u \in U$, $w \in W$. Show that: (i) $E_1^2 = E_1$ and $E_2^2 = E_2$, i.e. that E_1 and E_2 are "projections"; (ii) $E_1 + E_2 = I$, the identity mapping; (iii) $E_1 E_2 = 0$ and $E_2 E_1 = 0$.

6.82. Let E_1 and E_2 be linear operators on V satisfying (i), (ii) and (iii) of Problem 6.81. Show that V is the direct sum of the image of E_1 and the image of E_2: $V = \text{Im}\,E_1 \oplus \text{Im}\,E_2$.

6.83. Show that if the linear operators S and T are invertible, then ST is invertible and $(ST)^{-1} = T^{-1} S^{-1}$.

6.84. Let V have finite dimension, and let T be a linear operator on V such that rank (T^2) = rank T. Show that Ker $T \cap$ Im $T = \{0\}$.

MISCELLANEOUS PROBLEMS

6.85. Suppose $T : K^n \to K^m$ is a linear mapping. Let $\{e_1, \ldots, e_n\}$ be the usual basis of K^n and let A be the $m \times n$ matrix whose columns are the vectors $T(e_1), \ldots, T(e_n)$ respectively. Show that, for every vector $v \in K^n$, $T(v) = Av$, where v is written as a column vector.

6.86. Suppose $F : V \to U$ is linear and k is a nonzero scalar. Show that the maps F and kF have the same kernel and the same image.

6.87. Show that if $F : V \to U$ is onto, then dim $U \leq$ dim V. Determine all linear maps $T : \mathbf{R}^3 \to \mathbf{R}^4$ which are onto.

6.88. Find those theorems of Chapter 3 which prove that the space of n-square matrices over K is an associative algebra over K.

6.89. Let $T : V \to U$ be linear and let W be a subspace of V. The *restriction of T to W* is the map $T_W : W \to U$ defined by $T_W(w) = T(w)$, for every $w \in W$. Prove the following. (i) T_W is linear. (ii) Ker T_W = Ker $T \cap W$. (iii) Im $T_W = T(W)$.

6.90. Two operators $S, T \in A(V)$ are said to be *similar* if there exists an invertible operator $P \in A(V)$ for which $S = P^{-1}TP$. Prove the following. (i) Similarity of operators is an equivalence relation. (ii) Similar operators have the same rank (when V has finite dimension).

Answers to Supplementary Problems

6.45. (i) No, (ii) Yes, (iii) No.

6.46. (i) $f(x) = x^2 + 3$, (ii) $f(x) = x^3 + 2x$, (iii) $f(x) = \begin{cases} x^2 & \text{if } x \geq 3 \\ -2 & \text{if } x < 3 \end{cases}$

6.47. (i) 3, (ii) 24, (iii) $y^2 - 4xy + 4x^2 - 4y + 8x + 3$, (iv) $x^2 - 8x + 15$.

6.48. Nine.

6.49. (i) $\{(\text{Betty}, 4), (\text{Martin}, 6), (\text{David}, 4), (\text{Alan}, 3), (\text{Rebecca}, 5)\}$.

  (ii) Image of $g = \{3, 4, 5, 6\}$.

6.51. (i) $(g \circ f) : A \to A$, (ii) No, (iii) $(F \circ f) : A \to C$, (iv) No, (v) $(g \circ h) : C \to A$, (vi) $(h \circ G \circ g) : B \to B$.

6.52. (i) $(f \circ g)(x) = 4x^2 - 6x + 1$ (iii) $(g \circ g)(x) = 4x - 9$

  (ii) $(g \circ f)(x) = 2x^2 + 6x - 1$ (iv) $(f \circ f)(x) = x^4 + 6x^3 + 14x^2 + 15x + 5$

6.54. (i) $f^{-1}(x) = (x + 7)/3$, (ii) $f^{-1}(x) = \sqrt[3]{x - 2}$.

6.59. $T(a, b) = (-a + 2b, -3a + b, 7a - b)$.

6.60. $T(a, b, c) = 8a - 3b - 2c$.

6.61. $F(v) + F(-v) = F(v + (-v)) = F(0) = 0$; hence $F(-v) = -F(v)$.

6.63. (i) (a) $\{(1, 0, 1), (0, 1, -2)\}$, dim $U = 2$; (b) $\{(2, -1, -1)\}$, dim $W = 1$.

  (ii) (a) $\{(1, 1)\}$, dim $U = 1$; (b) $\{(1, -1)\}$, dim $W = 1$.

  (iii) (a) $\{(1, 0), (0, 1)\}$, dim $U = 2$; (b) $\{(1, -1, 1)\}$, dim $W = 1$.

6.64. (i) $\left\{ \begin{pmatrix} 1 & 0 \\ 1 & 0 \end{pmatrix}, \begin{pmatrix} 0 & 1 \\ 0 & 1 \end{pmatrix} \right\}$ basis of Ker F; dim (Ker F) = 2.

  (ii) $\left\{ \begin{pmatrix} 1 & 0 \\ -2 & 0 \end{pmatrix}, \begin{pmatrix} 0 & 1 \\ 0 & -2 \end{pmatrix} \right\}$ basis of Im F; dim (Im F) = 2.

6.65. $F(x, y, z) = (x + 4y, 2x + 5y, 3x + 6y)$.

6.66. $F(x, y, z, w) = (x + y - z, 2x + y - w, 0)$.

6.67. The kernel of D is the set of constant polynomials. The image of D is the entire space V.

6.69. (i) (a) $\{(1, 2, 1), (0, 1, 1)\}$ basis of Im A; dim (Im A) = 2.
              (b) $\{(4, -2, -5, 0), (1, -3, 0, 5)\}$ basis of Ker A; dim (Ker A) = 2.

  (ii) (a) Im $B = \mathbf{R}^3$; (b) $\{(-1, 2/3, 1, 1)\}$ basis of Ker B; dim (Ker B) = 1.

6.71. $(F + G)(x, y, z) = (y + 2z, 2x - y + z)$, $(3F - 2G)(x, y, z) = (3y - 4z, x + 2y + 3z)$.

6.72. (i) $(H \circ F)(x, y, z) = (x + z, 2y)$, $(H \circ G)(x, y, z) = (x - y, 4z)$. (ii) Not defined.
  (iii) $(H \circ (F + G))(x, y, z) = (H \circ F + H \circ G)(x, y, z) = (2x - y + z, 2y + 4z)$.

6.77. $(S + T)(x, y) = (x, x)$ $(ST)(x, y) = (x - y, 0)$
  $(5S - 3T)(x, y) = (5x + 8y, -3x)$ $(TS)(x, y) = (0, x + y)$

  $S^2(x, y) = (x + y, 0)$; note that $S^2 = S$.

  $T^2(x, y) = (-x, -y)$; note that $T^2 + I = 0$, hence T is a zero of $x^2 + 1$.

6.78. $p(T) = 0$.

6.79. (i) $T^{-1}(r, s, t) = (14t + 3s + r, 4t + s, t)$, (ii) $T^{-1}(r, s, t) = (\frac{1}{2}r + \frac{1}{2}s, t, \frac{1}{2}r - \frac{1}{2}s)$.

6.87. There are no linear maps from $\mathbf{R}^3$ into $\mathbf{R}^4$ which are onto.

Chapter 7

Matrices and Linear Operators

INTRODUCTION

Suppose $\{e_1, \ldots, e_n\}$ is a basis of a vector space V over a field K and, for $v \in V$, suppose $v = a_1 e_1 + a_2 e_2 + \cdots + a_n e_n$. Then the coordinate vector of v relative to $\{e_i\}$, which we write as a column vector unless otherwise specified or implied, is

$$[v]_e = \begin{pmatrix} a_1 \\ a_2 \\ .. \\ a_n \end{pmatrix}$$

Recall that the mapping $v \mapsto [v]_e$, determined by the basis $\{e_i\}$, is an isomorphism from V onto the space K^n.

In this chapter we show that there is also an isomorphism, determined by the basis $\{e_i\}$, from the algebra $A(V)$ of linear operators on V onto the algebra $\mathcal{A}$ of n-square matrices over K.

A similar result also holds for linear mappings $F : V \to U$, from one space into another.

MATRIX REPRESENTATION OF A LINEAR OPERATOR

Let T be a linear operator on a vector space V over a field K and suppose $\{e_1, \ldots, e_n\}$ is a basis of V. Now $T(e_1), \ldots, T(e_n)$ are vectors in V and so each is a linear combination of the elements of the basis $\{e_i\}$:

$$T(e_1) = a_{11}e_1 + a_{12}e_2 + \cdots + a_{1n}e_n$$
$$T(e_2) = a_{21}e_1 + a_{22}e_2 + \cdots + a_{2n}e_n$$
$$\cdots\cdots\cdots\cdots\cdots\cdots\cdots\cdots\cdots\cdots\cdots$$
$$T(e_n) = a_{n1}e_1 + a_{n2}e_2 + \cdots + a_{nn}e_n$$

The following definition applies.

Definition: The transpose of the above matrix of coefficients, denoted by $[T]_e$ or $[T]$, is called the *matrix representation of T relative to the basis* $\{e_i\}$ or simply the *matrix of T in the basis* $\{e_i\}$:

$$[T]_e = \begin{pmatrix} a_{11} & a_{21} & \ldots & a_{n1} \\ a_{12} & a_{22} & \ldots & a_{n2} \\ \ldots\ldots\ldots\ldots\ldots\ldots \\ a_{1n} & a_{2n} & \ldots & a_{nn} \end{pmatrix}$$

Example 7.1: Let V be the vector space of polynomials in t over $\mathbf{R}$ of degree ≤ 3, and let $D : V \to V$ be the differential operator defined by $D(p(t)) = d(p(t))/dt$. We compute the matrix of D in the basis $\{1, t, t^2, t^3\}$. We have:

$$D(1) = 0 = 0 + 0t + 0t^2 + 0t^3$$
$$D(t) = 1 = 1 + 0t + 0t^2 + 0t^3$$
$$D(t^2) = 2t = 0 + 2t + 0t^2 + 0t^3$$
$$D(t^3) = 3t^2 = 0 + 0t + 3t^2 + 0t^3$$

Accordingly,

$$[D] \;=\; \begin{pmatrix} 0 & 1 & 0 & 0 \\ 0 & 0 & 2 & 0 \\ 0 & 0 & 0 & 3 \\ 0 & 0 & 0 & 0 \end{pmatrix}$$

Example 7.2: Let T be the linear operator on $\mathbf{R}^2$ defined by $T(x, y) = (4x - 2y, 2x + y)$. We compute the matrix of T in the basis $\{f_1 = (1, 1),\ f_2 = (-1, 0)\}$. We have

$$T(f_1) \;=\; T(1, 1) \;=\; (2, 3) \;=\; 3(1, 1) + (-1, 0) \;=\; 3f_1 + f_2$$

$$T(f_2) \;=\; T(-1, 0) \;=\; (-4, -2) \;=\; -2(1, 1) + 2(-1, 0) \;=\; -2f_1 + 2f_2$$

Accordingly, $\quad [T]_f = \begin{pmatrix} 3 & -2 \\ 1 & 2 \end{pmatrix}.$

Remark: Recall that any n-square matrix A over K defines a linear operator on K^n by the map $v \mapsto Av$ (where v is written as a column vector). We show (Problem 7.7) that the matrix representation of this operator is precisely the matrix A if we use the usual basis of K^n.

Our first theorem tells us that the "action" of an operator T on a vector v is preserved by its matrix representation:

Theorem 7.1: Let $\{e_1, \ldots, e_n\}$ be a basis of V and let T be any operator on V. Then, for any vector $v \in V$, $[T]_e\,[v]_e = [T(v)]_e$.

That is, if we multiply the coordinate vector of v by the matrix representation of T, then we obtain the coordinate vector of $T(v)$.

Example 7.3: Consider the differential operator $D : V \to V$ in Example 7.1. Let

$$p(t) \;=\; a + bt + ct^2 + dt^3 \quad \text{and so} \quad D(p(t)) \;=\; b + 2ct + 3dt^2$$

Hence, relative to the basis $\{1, t, t^2, t^3\}$,

$$[p(t)] \;=\; \begin{pmatrix} a \\ b \\ c \\ d \end{pmatrix} \quad \text{and} \quad [D(p(t))] \;=\; \begin{pmatrix} b \\ 2c \\ 3d \\ 0 \end{pmatrix}$$

We show that Theorem 7.1 does hold here:

$$[D][p(t)] \;=\; \begin{pmatrix} 0 & 1 & 0 & 0 \\ 0 & 0 & 2 & 0 \\ 0 & 0 & 0 & 3 \\ 0 & 0 & 0 & 0 \end{pmatrix}\begin{pmatrix} a \\ b \\ c \\ d \end{pmatrix} \;=\; \begin{pmatrix} b \\ 2c \\ 3d \\ 0 \end{pmatrix} \;=\; [D(p(t))]$$

Example 7.4: Consider the linear operator $T : \mathbf{R}^2 \to \mathbf{R}^2$ in Example 7.2: $T(x, y) = (4x - 2y, 2x + y)$. Let $v = (5, 7)$. Then

$$v \;=\; (5, 7) \;=\; 7(1, 1) + 2(-1, 0) \;=\; 7f_1 + 2f_2$$

$$T(v) \;=\; (6, 17) \;=\; 17(1, 1) + 11(-1, 0) \;=\; 17f_1 + 11f_2$$

where $f_1 = (1, 1)$ and $f_2 = (-1, 0)$. Hence, relative to the basis $\{f_1, f_2\}$,

$$[v]_f \;=\; \begin{pmatrix} 7 \\ 2 \end{pmatrix} \quad \text{and} \quad [T(v)]_f \;=\; \begin{pmatrix} 17 \\ 11 \end{pmatrix}$$

Using the matrix $[T]_f$ in Example 7.2, we verify that Theorem 7.1 holds here:

$$[T]_f\,[v]_f \;=\; \begin{pmatrix} 3 & -2 \\ 1 & 2 \end{pmatrix}\begin{pmatrix} 7 \\ 2 \end{pmatrix} \;=\; \begin{pmatrix} 17 \\ 11 \end{pmatrix} \;=\; [T(v)]_f$$

Now we have associated a matrix $[T]_e$ to each T in $A(V)$, the algebra of linear operators on V. By our first theorem the action of an individual operator T is preserved by this representation. The next two theorems tell us that the three basic operations with these operators

$$\text{(i) addition, \quad (ii) scalar multiplication, \quad (iii) composition}$$

are also preserved.

Theorem 7.2: Let $\{e_1, \ldots, e_n\}$ be a basis of V over K, and let $\mathcal{A}$ be the algebra of n-square matrices over K. Then the mapping $T \mapsto [T]_e$ is a vector space isomorphism from $A(V)$ onto $\mathcal{A}$. That is, the mapping is one-one and onto and, for any $S, T \in A(V)$ and any $k \in K$,

$$[T + S]_e = [T]_e + [S]_e \quad \text{and} \quad [kT]_e = k[T]_e$$

Theorem 7.3: For any operators $S, T \in A(V)$, $[ST]_e = [S]_e [T]_e$.

We illustrate the above theorems in the case $\dim V = 2$. Suppose $\{e_1, e_2\}$ is a basis of V, and T and S are operators on V for which

$$\begin{array}{ll} T(e_1) = a_1 e_1 + a_2 e_2 & S(e_1) = c_1 e_1 + c_2 e_2 \\ T(e_2) = b_1 e_1 + b_2 e_2 & S(e_2) = d_1 e_1 + d_2 e_2 \end{array}$$

Then

$$[T]_e = \begin{pmatrix} a_1 & b_1 \\ a_2 & b_2 \end{pmatrix} \quad \text{and} \quad [S]_e = \begin{pmatrix} c_1 & d_1 \\ c_2 & d_2 \end{pmatrix}$$

Now we have

$$\begin{aligned} (T + S)(e_1) = T(e_1) + S(e_1) &= a_1 e_1 + a_2 e_2 + c_1 e_1 + c_2 e_2 \\ &= (a_1 + c_1)e_1 + (a_2 + c_2)e_2 \end{aligned}$$

$$\begin{aligned} (T + S)(e_2) = T(e_2) + S(e_2) &= b_1 e_1 + b_2 e_2 + d_1 e_1 + d_2 e_2 \\ &= (b_1 + d_1)e_1 + (b_2 + d_2)e_2 \end{aligned}$$

Thus

$$[T + S]_e = \begin{pmatrix} a_1 + c_1 & b_1 + d_1 \\ a_2 + c_2 & b_2 + d_2 \end{pmatrix} = \begin{pmatrix} a_1 & b_1 \\ a_2 & b_2 \end{pmatrix} + \begin{pmatrix} c_1 & d_1 \\ c_2 & d_2 \end{pmatrix} = [T]_e + [S]_e$$

Also, for $k \in K$, we have

$$\begin{aligned} (kT)(e_1) &= kT(e_1) = k(a_1 e_1 + a_2 e_2) = ka_1 e_1 + ka_2 e_2 \\ (kT)(e_2) &= kT(e_2) = k(b_1 e_1 + b_2 e_2) = kb_1 e_1 + kb_2 e_2 \end{aligned}$$

Hence

$$[kT]_e = \begin{pmatrix} ka_1 & kb_1 \\ ka_2 & kb_2 \end{pmatrix} = k\begin{pmatrix} a_1 & b_1 \\ a_2 & b_2 \end{pmatrix} = k[T]_e$$

Finally, we have

$$\begin{aligned} (ST)(e_1) = S(T(e_1)) = S(a_1 e_1 + a_2 e_2) &= a_1 S(e_1) + a_2 S(e_2) \\ &= a_1(c_1 e_1 + c_2 e_2) + a_2(d_1 e_1 + d_2 e_2) \\ &= (a_1 c_1 + a_2 d_1)e_1 + (a_1 c_2 + a_2 d_2)e_2 \end{aligned}$$

$$\begin{aligned} (ST)(e_2) = S(T(e_2)) = S(b_1 e_1 + b_2 e_2) &= b_1 S(e_1) + b_2 S(e_2) \\ &= b_1(c_1 e_1 + c_2 e_2) + b_2(d_1 e_1 + d_2 e_2) \\ &= (b_1 c_1 + b_2 d_1)e_1 + (b_1 c_2 + b_2 d_2)e_2 \end{aligned}$$

Accordingly,

$$[ST]_e = \begin{pmatrix} a_1 c_1 + a_2 d_1 & b_1 c_1 + b_2 d_1 \\ a_1 c_2 + a_2 d_2 & b_1 c_2 + b_2 d_2 \end{pmatrix} = \begin{pmatrix} c_1 & d_1 \\ c_2 & d_2 \end{pmatrix}\begin{pmatrix} a_1 & b_1 \\ a_2 & b_2 \end{pmatrix} = [S]_e [T]_e$$

CHANGE OF BASIS

We have shown that we can represent vectors by n-tuples (column vectors) and linear operators by matrices once we have selected a basis. We ask the following natural question: How does our representation change if we select another basis? In order to answer this question, we first need a definition.

Definition: Let $\{e_1, \ldots, e_n\}$ be a basis of V and let $\{f_1, \ldots, f_n\}$ be another basis. Suppose

$$f_1 = a_{11}e_1 + a_{12}e_2 + \cdots + a_{1n}e_n$$

$$f_2 = a_{21}e_1 + a_{22}e_2 + \cdots + a_{2n}e_n$$

$$\cdots\cdots\cdots\cdots\cdots\cdots\cdots\cdots\cdots\cdots$$

$$f_n = a_{n1}e_1 + a_{n2}e_2 + \cdots + a_{nn}e_n$$

Then the transpose P of the above matrix of coefficients is termed the *transition matrix* from the "old" basis $\{e_i\}$ to the "new" basis $\{f_i\}$:

$$P = \begin{pmatrix} a_{11} & a_{21} & \ldots & a_{n1} \\ a_{12} & a_{22} & \ldots & a_{n2} \\ \cdots\cdots\cdots\cdots\cdots\cdots \\ a_{1n} & a_{2n} & \ldots & a_{nn} \end{pmatrix}$$

We comment that since the vectors $f_1, \ldots, f_n$ are linearly independent, the matrix P is invertible (Problem 5.47). In fact, its inverse P^{-1} is the transition matrix from the basis $\{f_i\}$ back to the basis $\{e_i\}$.

Example 7.5:   Consider the following two bases of $\mathbf{R}^2$:

$$\{e_1 = (1, 0),\ e_2 = (0, 1)\} \quad \text{and} \quad \{f_1 = (1, 1),\ f_2 = (-1, 0)\}$$

Then

$$f_1 = (1, 1) = (1, 0) + (0, 1) = e_1 + e_2$$

$$f_2 = (-1, 0) = -(1, 0) + 0(0, 1) = -e_1 + 0e_2$$

Hence the transition matrix P from the basis $\{e_i\}$ to the basis $\{f_i\}$ is

$$P = \begin{pmatrix} 1 & -1 \\ 1 & 0 \end{pmatrix}$$

We also have

$$e_1 = (1, 0) = 0(1, 1) - (-1, 0) = 0f_1 - f_2$$

$$e_2 = (0, 1) = (1, 1) + (-1, 0) = f_1 + f_2$$

Hence the transition matrix Q from the basis $\{f_i\}$ back to the basis $\{e_i\}$ is

$$Q = \begin{pmatrix} 0 & 1 \\ -1 & 1 \end{pmatrix}$$

Observe that P and Q are inverses:

$$PQ = \begin{pmatrix} 1 & -1 \\ 1 & 0 \end{pmatrix}\begin{pmatrix} 0 & 1 \\ -1 & 1 \end{pmatrix} = \begin{pmatrix} 1 & 0 \\ 0 & 1 \end{pmatrix} = I$$

We now show how coordinate vectors are affected by a change of basis.

Theorem 7.4:   Let P be the transition matrix from a basis $\{e_i\}$ to a basis $\{f_i\}$ in a vector space V. Then, for any vector $v \in V$, $P[v]_f = [v]_e$. Hence $[v]_f = P^{-1}[v]_e$.

We emphasize that even though P is called the transition matrix from the old basis $\{e_i\}$ to the new basis $\{f_i\}$, its effect is to transform the coordinates of a vector in the new basis $\{f_i\}$ back to the coordinates in the old basis $\{e_i\}$.

We illustrate the above theorem in the case $\dim V = 3$. Suppose P is the transition matrix from a basis $\{e_1, e_2, e_3\}$ of V to a basis $\{f_1, f_2, f_3\}$ of V; say,

$$
\begin{aligned}
f_1 &= a_1 e_1 + a_2 e_2 + a_3 e_3 \\
f_2 &= b_1 e_1 + b_2 e_2 + b_3 e_3 . \qquad \text{Hence} \quad P = \begin{pmatrix} a_1 & b_1 & c_1 \\ a_2 & b_2 & c_2 \\ a_3 & b_3 & c_3 \end{pmatrix} \\
f_3 &= c_1 e_1 + c_2 e_2 + c_3 e_3
\end{aligned}
$$

Now suppose $v \in V$ and, say, $v = k_1 f_1 + k_2 f_2 + k_3 f_3$. Then, substituting for the f_i from above, we obtain

$$
\begin{aligned}
v &= k_1(a_1 e_1 + a_2 e_2 + a_3 e_3) + k_2(b_1 e_1 + b_2 e_2 + b_3 e_3) + k_3(c_1 e_1 + c_2 e_2 + c_3 e_3) \\
&= (a_1 k_1 + b_1 k_2 + c_1 k_3)e_1 + (a_2 k_1 + b_2 k_2 + c_2 k_3)e_2 + (a_3 k_1 + b_3 k_2 + c_3 k_3)e_3
\end{aligned}
$$

Thus

$$
[v]_f = \begin{pmatrix} k_1 \\ k_2 \\ k_3 \end{pmatrix} \qquad \text{and} \qquad [v]_e = \begin{pmatrix} a_1 k_1 + b_1 k_2 + c_1 k_3 \\ a_2 k_1 + b_2 k_2 + c_2 k_3 \\ a_3 k_1 + b_3 k_2 + c_3 k_3 \end{pmatrix}
$$

Accordingly,

$$
P[v]_f = \begin{pmatrix} a_1 & b_1 & c_1 \\ a_2 & b_2 & c_2 \\ a_3 & b_3 & c_3 \end{pmatrix} \begin{pmatrix} k_1 \\ k_2 \\ k_3 \end{pmatrix} = \begin{pmatrix} a_1 k_1 + b_1 k_2 + c_1 k_3 \\ a_2 k_1 + b_2 k_2 + c_2 k_3 \\ a_3 k_1 + b_3 k_2 + c_3 k_3 \end{pmatrix} = [v]_e
$$

Also, multiplying the above equation by P^{-1}, we have

$$
P^{-1}[v]_e = P^{-1}P[v]_f = I[v]_f = [v]_f
$$

Example 7.6:   Let $v = (a, b) \in \mathbf{R}^2$. Then, for the bases of $\mathbf{R}^2$ in the preceding example,

$$
v = (a, b) = a(1, 0) + b(0, 1) = ae_1 + be_2
$$

$$
v = (a, b) = b(1, 1) + (b - a)(-1, 0) = bf_1 + (b - a)f_2
$$

Hence $\qquad\qquad [v]_e = \begin{pmatrix} a \\ b \end{pmatrix} \quad$ and $\quad [v]_f = \begin{pmatrix} b \\ b - a \end{pmatrix}$

By the preceding example, the transition matrix P from $\{e_i\}$ to $\{f_i\}$ and its inverse P^{-1} are given by

$$
P = \begin{pmatrix} 1 & -1 \\ 1 & 0 \end{pmatrix} \quad \text{and} \quad P^{-1} = \begin{pmatrix} 0 & 1 \\ -1 & 1 \end{pmatrix}
$$

We verify the result of Theorem 7.4:

$$
P[v]_f = \begin{pmatrix} 1 & -1 \\ 1 & 0 \end{pmatrix}\begin{pmatrix} b \\ b - a \end{pmatrix} = \begin{pmatrix} a \\ b \end{pmatrix} = [v]_e
$$

$$
P^{-1}[v]_e = \begin{pmatrix} 0 & 1 \\ -1 & 1 \end{pmatrix}\begin{pmatrix} a \\ b \end{pmatrix} = \begin{pmatrix} b \\ b - a \end{pmatrix} = [v]_f
$$

The next theorem shows how matrix representations of linear operators are affected by a change of basis.

Theorem 7.5:   Let P be the transition matrix from a basis $\{e_i\}$ to a basis $\{f_i\}$ in a vector space V. Then for any linear operator T on V, $[T]_f = P^{-1}[T]_e P$.

Example 7.7:   Let T be the linear operator on $\mathbf{R}^2$ defined by $T(x, y) = (4x - 2y, 2x + y)$. Then for the bases of $\mathbf{R}^2$ in Example 7.5, we have

$$
T(e_1) = T(1, 0) = (4, 2) = 4(1, 0) + 2(0, 1) = 4e_1 + 2e_2
$$

$$
T(e_2) = T(0, 1) = (-2, 1) = -2(1, 0) + (0, 1) = -2e_1 + e_2
$$

Accordingly, $\qquad\qquad\qquad [T]_e = \begin{pmatrix} 4 & -2 \\ 2 & 1 \end{pmatrix}$

We compute $[T]_f$ using Theorem 7.5:

$$[T]_f = P^{-1}[T]_e P = \begin{pmatrix} 0 & 1 \\ -1 & 1 \end{pmatrix}\begin{pmatrix} 4 & -2 \\ 2 & 1 \end{pmatrix}\begin{pmatrix} 1 & -1 \\ 1 & 0 \end{pmatrix} = \begin{pmatrix} 3 & -2 \\ 1 & 2 \end{pmatrix}$$

Note that this agrees with the derivation of $[T]_f$ in Example 7.2.

Remark: Suppose $P = (a_{ij})$ is any n-square invertible matrix over a field K. Now if $\{e_1, \ldots, e_n\}$ is a basis of a vector space V over K, then the n vectors

$$f_i = a_{1i}e_1 + a_{2i}e_2 + \cdots + a_{ni}e_n, \qquad i = 1, \ldots, n$$

are linearly independent (Problem 5.47) and so form another basis of V. Furthermore, P is the transition matrix from the basis $\{e_i\}$ to the basis $\{f_i\}$. Accordingly, if A is any matrix representation of a linear operator T on V, then the matrix $B = P^{-1}AP$ is also a matrix representation of T.

SIMILARITY

Suppose A and B are square matrices for which there exists an invertible matrix P such that $B = P^{-1}AP$. Then B is said to be *similar* to A or is said to be obtained from A by a *similarity transformation*. We show (Problem 7.16) that similarity of matrices is an equivalence relation. Thus by Theorem 7.5 and the above remark, we have the following basic result.

Theorem 7.6: Two matrices A and B represent the same linear operator T if and only if they are similar to each other.

That is, all the matrix representations of the linear operator T form an equivalence class of similar matrices.

A linear operator T is said to be *diagonalizable* if for some basis $\{e_i\}$ it is represented by a diagonal matrix; the basis $\{e_i\}$ is then said to *diagonalize* T. The preceding theorem gives us the following result.

Theorem 7.7: Let A be a matrix representation of a linear operator T. Then T is diagonalizable if and only if there exists an invertible matrix P such that $P^{-1}AP$ is a diagonal matrix.

That is, T is diagonalizable if and only if its matrix representation can be diagonalized by a similarity transformation.

We emphasize that not every operator is diagonalizable. However, we will show (Chapter 10) that every operator T can be represented by certain "standard" matrices called its *normal* or *canonical* forms. We comment now that that discussion will require some theory of fields, polynomials and determinants.

Now suppose f is a function on square matrices which assigns the same value to similar matrices; that is, $f(A) = f(B)$ whenever A is similar to B. Then f induces a function, also denoted by f, on linear operators T in the following natural way: $f(T) = f([T]_e)$, where $\{e_i\}$ is any basis. The function is well-defined by the preceding theorem.

The *determinant* is perhaps the most important example of the above type of functions. Another important example follows.

Example 7.8: The *trace* of a square matrix $A = (a_{ij})$, written tr (A), is defined to be the sum of its diagonal elements:

$$\text{tr}\,(A) = a_{11} + a_{22} + \cdots + a_{nn}$$

We show (Problem 7.17) that similar matrices have the same trace. Thus we can speak of the trace of a linear operator T; it is the trace of any one of its matrix representations: tr (T) = tr $([T]_e)$.

MATRICES AND LINEAR MAPPINGS

We now consider the general case of linear mappings from one space into another. Let V and U be vector spaces over the same field K and, say, $\dim V = m$ and $\dim U = n$. Furthermore, let $\{e_1, \ldots, e_m\}$ and $\{f_1, \ldots, f_n\}$ be arbitrary but fixed bases of V and U respectively.

Suppose $F : V \to U$ is a linear mapping. Then the vectors $F(e_1), \ldots, F(e_m)$ belong to U and so each is a linear combination of the f_i:

$$
\begin{aligned}
F(e_1) &= a_{11}f_1 + a_{12}f_2 + \cdots + a_{1n}f_n \\
F(e_2) &= a_{21}f_1 + a_{22}f_2 + \cdots + a_{2n}f_n \\
&\cdots\cdots\cdots\cdots\cdots\cdots\cdots\cdots\cdots\cdots\cdots \\
F(e_m) &= a_{m1}f_1 + a_{m2}f_2 + \cdots + a_{mn}f_n
\end{aligned}
$$

The transpose of the above matrix of coefficients, denoted by $[F]_e^f$ is called the *matrix representation* of F relative to the bases $\{e_i\}$ and $\{f_i\}$, or the matrix of F in the bases $\{e_i\}$ and $\{f_i\}$:

$$
[F]_e^f = \begin{pmatrix}
a_{11} & a_{21} & \ldots & a_{m1} \\
a_{12} & a_{22} & \ldots & a_{m2} \\
\multicolumn{4}{c}{\cdots\cdots\cdots\cdots\cdots\cdots} \\
a_{1n} & a_{2n} & \ldots & a_{mn}
\end{pmatrix}
$$

The following theorems apply.

Theorem 7.8:   For any vector $v \in V$, $[F]_e^f [v]_e = [F(v)]_f$.

That is, multiplying the coordinate vector of v in the basis $\{e_i\}$ by the matrix $[F]_e^f$, we obtain the coordinate vector of $F(v)$ in the basis $\{f_i\}$.

Theorem 7.9:   The mapping $F \mapsto [F]_e^f$ is an isomorphism from $\mathrm{Hom}\,(V, U)$ onto the vector space of $n \times m$ matrices over K. That is, the mapping is one-one and onto and, for any $F, G \in \mathrm{Hom}\,(V, U)$ and any $k \in K$,

$$
[F + G]_e^f = [F]_e^f + [G]_e^f \qquad \text{and} \qquad [kF]_e^f = k[F]_e^f
$$

Remark: Recall that any $n \times m$ matrix A over K has been identified with the linear mapping from K^m into K^n given by $v \mapsto Av$. Now suppose V and U are vector spaces over K of dimensions m and n respectively, and suppose $\{e_i\}$ is a basis of V and $\{f_i\}$ is a basis of U. Then in view of the preceding theorem, we shall also identify A with the linear mapping $F : V \to U$ given by $[F(v)]_f = A[v]_e$. We comment that if other bases of V and U are given, then A is identified with another linear mapping from V into U.

Theorem 7.10:   Let $\{e_i\}$, $\{f_i\}$ and $\{g_i\}$ be bases of V, U and W respectively. Let $F : V \to U$ and $G : U \to W$ be linear mappings. Then

$$
[G \circ F]_e^g = [G]_f^g [F]_e^f
$$

That is, relative to the appropriate bases, the matrix representation of the composition of two linear mappings is equal to the product of the matrix representations of the individual mappings.

We lastly show how the matrix representation of a linear mapping $F : V \to U$ is affected when new bases are selected.

Theorem 7.11:   Let P be the transition matrix from a basis $\{e_i\}$ to a basis $\{e_i'\}$ in V, and let Q be the transition matrix from a basis $\{f_i\}$ to a basis $\{f_i'\}$ in U. Then for any linear mapping $F : V \to U$,

$$
[F]_{e'}^{f'} = Q^{-1} [F]_e^f P
$$

Thus in particular,

$$[F]^{f'}_e = Q^{-1}[F]^f_e$$

i.e. when the change of basis only takes place in U; and

$$[F]^f_{e'} = [F]^f_e P$$

i.e. when the change of basis only takes place in V.

Note that Theorems 7.1, 7.2, 7.3 and 7.5 are special cases of Theorems 7.8, 7.9, 7.10 and 7.11 respectively.

The next theorem shows that every linear mapping from one space into another can be represented by a very simple matrix.

Theorem 7.12: Let $F: V \to U$ be linear and, say, rank $F = r$. Then there exist bases of V and of U such that the matrix representation of F has the form

$$A = \begin{pmatrix} I & 0 \\ 0 & 0 \end{pmatrix}$$

where I is the r-square identity matrix. We call A the *normal* or *canonical* form of F.

WARNING

As noted previously, some texts write the operator symbol T to the right of the vector v on which it acts, that is,

$$vT \quad \text{instead of} \quad T(v)$$

In such texts, vectors and operators are represented by n-tuples and matrices which are the transposes of those appearing here. That is, if

$$v = k_1e_1 + k_2e_2 + \cdots + k_ne_n$$

then they write

$$[v]_e = (k_1, k_2, \ldots, k_n) \quad \text{instead of} \quad [v]_e = \begin{pmatrix} k_1 \\ k_2 \\ \cdot\cdot \\ k_n \end{pmatrix}$$

And if

$$T(e_1) = a_1e_1 + a_2e_2 + \cdots + a_ne_n$$
$$T(e_2) = b_1e_1 + b_2e_2 + \cdots + b_ne_n$$
$$\ldots\ldots\ldots\ldots\ldots\ldots\ldots\ldots\ldots\ldots$$
$$T(e_n) = c_1e_1 + c_2e_2 + \cdots + c_ne_n$$

then they write

$$[T]_e = \begin{pmatrix} a_1 & a_2 & \ldots & a_n \\ b_1 & b_2 & \ldots & b_n \\ \ldots\ldots\ldots\ldots\ldots \\ c_1 & c_2 & \ldots & c_n \end{pmatrix} \quad \text{instead of} \quad [T]_e = \begin{pmatrix} a_1 & b_1 & \ldots & c_1 \\ a_2 & b_2 & \ldots & c_2 \\ \ldots\ldots\ldots\ldots\ldots \\ a_n & b_n & \ldots & c_n \end{pmatrix}$$

This is also true for the transition matrix from one basis to another and for matrix representations of linear mappings $F: V \to U$. We comment that such texts have theorems which are analogous to the ones appearing here.

Solved Problems

MATRIX REPRESENTATIONS OF LINEAR OPERATORS

7.1. Find the matrix representation of each of the following operators T on $\mathbf{R}^2$ relative to the usual basis $\{e_1 = (1, 0),\ e_2 = (0, 1)\}$:

(i) $T(x, y) = (2y, 3x - y)$,   (ii) $T(x, y) = (3x - 4y, x + 5y)$.

Note first that if $(a, b) \in \mathbf{R}^2$, then $(a, b) = ae_1 + be_2$.

(i) $T(e_1) = T(1, 0) = (0, 3) = 0e_1 + 3e_2$
      $T(e_2) = T(0, 1) = (2, -1) = 2e_1 - e_2$ and $[T]_e = \begin{pmatrix} 0 & 2 \\ 3 & -1 \end{pmatrix}$.

(ii) $T(e_1) = T(1, 0) = (3, 1) = 3e_1 + e_2$
      $T(e_2) = T(0, 1) = (-4, 5) = -4e_1 + 5e_2$ and $[T]_e = \begin{pmatrix} 3 & -4 \\ 1 & 5 \end{pmatrix}$.

7.2. Find the matrix representation of each operator T in the preceding problem relative to the basis $\{f_1 = (1, 3),\ f_2 = (2, 5)\}$.

We must first find the coordinates of an arbitrary vector $(a, b) \in \mathbf{R}^2$ with respect to the basis $\{f_i\}$. We have

$$(a, b) = x(1, 3) + y(2, 5) = (x + 2y, 3x + 5y)$$

or $x + 2y = a$ and $3x + 5y = b$

or $x = 2b - 5a$ and $y = 3a - b$

Thus $(a, b) = (2b - 5a)f_1 + (3a - b)f_2$

(i)   We have $T(x, y) = (2y, 3x - y)$. Hence
      $T(f_1) = T(1, 3) = (6, 0) = -30f_1 + 18f_2$
      $T(f_2) = T(2, 5) = (10, 1) = -48f_1 + 29f_2$ and $[T]_f = \begin{pmatrix} -30 & -48 \\ 18 & 29 \end{pmatrix}$

(ii) We have $T(x, y) = (3x - 4y, x + 5y)$. Hence
      $T(f_1) = T(1, 3) = (-9, 16) = 77f_1 - 43f_2$
      $T(f_2) = T(2, 5) = (-14, 27) = 124f_1 - 69f_2$ and $[T]_f = \begin{pmatrix} 77 & 124 \\ -43 & -69 \end{pmatrix}$

7.3. Suppose that T is the linear operator on $\mathbf{R}^3$ defined by

$$T(x, y, z) = (a_1x + a_2y + a_3z,\ b_1x + b_2y + b_3z,\ c_1x + c_2y + c_3z)$$

Show that the matrix of T in the usual basis $\{e_i\}$ is given by

$$[T]_e = \begin{pmatrix} a_1 & a_2 & a_3 \\ b_1 & b_2 & b_3 \\ c_1 & c_2 & c_3 \end{pmatrix}$$

That is, the rows of $[T]_e$ are obtained from the coefficients of x, y and z in the components of $T(x, y, z)$.

$$T(e_1) = T(1, 0, 0) = (a_1, b_1, c_1) = a_1e_1 + b_1e_2 + c_1e_3$$
$$T(e_2) = T(0, 1, 0) = (a_2, b_2, c_2) = a_2e_1 + b_2e_2 + c_2e_3$$
$$T(e_3) = T(0, 0, 1) = (a_3, b_3, c_3) = a_3e_1 + b_3e_2 + c_3e_3$$

Accordingly,
$$[T]_e = \begin{pmatrix} a_1 & a_2 & a_3 \\ b_1 & b_2 & b_3 \\ c_1 & c_2 & c_3 \end{pmatrix}$$

Remark: This property holds for any space K^n but only relative to the usual basis

$$\{e_1 = (1, 0, \ldots, 0),\ e_2 = (0, 1, 0, \ldots, 0),\ \ldots,\ e_n = (0, \ldots, 0, 1)\}$$

7.4. Find the matrix representation of each of the following linear operators T on $\mathbf{R}^3$ relative to the usual basis $\{e_1 = (1, 0, 0),\ e_2 = (0, 1, 0),\ e_3 = (0, 0, 1)\}$:

(i) $T(x, y, z) = (2x - 3y + 4z,\ 5x - y + 2z,\ 4x + 7y)$,

(ii) $T(x, y, z) = (2y + z,\ x - 4y,\ 3x)$.

By Problem 7.3:   (i) $[T]_e = \begin{pmatrix} 2 & -3 & 4 \\ 5 & -1 & 2 \\ 4 & 7 & 0 \end{pmatrix}$,   (ii) $[T]_e = \begin{pmatrix} 0 & 2 & 1 \\ 1 & -4 & 0 \\ 3 & 0 & 0 \end{pmatrix}$.

7.5. Let T be the linear operator on $\mathbf{R}^3$ defined by $T(x, y, z) = (2y + z,\ x - 4y,\ 3x)$.

(i) Find the matrix of T in the basis $\{f_1 = (1, 1, 1),\ f_2 = (1, 1, 0),\ f_3 = (1, 0, 0)\}$

(ii) Verify that $[T]_f [v]_f = [T(v)]_f$ for any vector $v \in \mathbf{R}^3$.

We must first find the coordinates of an arbitrary vector $(a, b, c) \in \mathbf{R}^3$ with respect to the basis $\{f_1, f_2, f_3\}$. Write (a, b, c) as a linear combination of the f_i using unknown scalars x, y and z:

$$(a, b, c) = x(1, 1, 1) + y(1, 1, 0) + z(1, 0, 0)$$
$$= (x + y + z,\ x + y,\ x)$$

Set corresponding components equal to each other to obtain the system of equations

$$x + y + z = a, \qquad x + y = b, \qquad x = c$$

Solve the system for x, y and z in terms of a, b and c to find $x = c$, $y = b - c$, $z = a - b$. Thus

$$(a, b, c) = cf_1 + (b - c)f_2 + (a - b)f_3$$

(i) Since $T(x, y, z) = (2y + z,\ x - 4y,\ 3x)$

$$\begin{aligned} T(f_1) &= T(1, 1, 1) = (3, -3, 3) = 3f_1 - 6f_2 + 6f_3 \\ T(f_2) &= T(1, 1, 0) = (2, -3, 3) = 3f_1 - 6f_2 + 5f_3 \\ T(f_3) &= T(1, 0, 0) = (0, 1, 3) = 3f_1 - 2f_2 - f_3 \end{aligned} \qquad \text{and} \qquad [T]_f = \begin{pmatrix} 3 & 3 & 3 \\ -6 & -6 & -2 \\ 6 & 5 & -1 \end{pmatrix}$$

(ii) Suppose $v = (a, b, c)$; then

$$v = (a, b, c) = cf_1 + (b - c)f_2 + (a - b)f_3 \qquad \text{and so} \qquad [v]_f = \begin{pmatrix} c \\ b - c \\ a - b \end{pmatrix}$$

Also,

$$\begin{aligned} T(v) &= T(a, b, c) = (2b + c,\ a - 4b,\ 3a) \\ &= 3af_1 + (-2a - 4b)f_2 + (-a + 6b + c)f_3 \end{aligned} \qquad \text{and so} \qquad [T(v)]_f = \begin{pmatrix} 3a \\ -2a - 4b \\ -a + 6b + c \end{pmatrix}$$

Thus

$$[T]_f [v]_f = \begin{pmatrix} 3 & 3 & 3 \\ -6 & -6 & -2 \\ 6 & 5 & -1 \end{pmatrix} \begin{pmatrix} c \\ b - c \\ a - b \end{pmatrix} = \begin{pmatrix} 3a \\ -2a - 4b \\ -a + 6b + c \end{pmatrix} = [T(v)]_f$$

7.6. Let $A = \begin{pmatrix} 1 & 2 \\ 3 & 4 \end{pmatrix}$ and let T be the linear operator on $\mathbf{R}^2$ defined by $T(v) = Av$ (where v is written as a column vector). Find the matrix of T in each of the following bases:

(i) $\{e_1 = (1, 0),\ e_2 = (0, 1)\}$, i.e. the usual basis;

(ii) $\{f_1 = (1, 3),\ f_2 = (2, 5)\}$.

(i) $T(e_1) = \begin{pmatrix} 1 & 2 \\ 3 & 4 \end{pmatrix}\begin{pmatrix} 1 \\ 0 \end{pmatrix} = \begin{pmatrix} 1 \\ 3 \end{pmatrix} = 1e_1 + 3e_2$

$T(e_2) = \begin{pmatrix} 1 & 2 \\ 3 & 4 \end{pmatrix}\begin{pmatrix} 0 \\ 1 \end{pmatrix} = \begin{pmatrix} 2 \\ 4 \end{pmatrix} = 2e_1 + 4e_2$

and thus $[T]_e = \begin{pmatrix} 1 & 2 \\ 3 & 4 \end{pmatrix}$.

Observe that the matrix of T in the usual basis is precisely the original matrix A which defined T. This is not unusual. In fact, we show in the next problem that this is true for any matrix A when using the usual basis.

(ii) By Problem 7.2, $(a, b) = (2b - 5a)f_1 + (3a - b)f_2$. Hence

$$T(f_1) = \begin{pmatrix} 1 & 2 \\ 3 & 4 \end{pmatrix}\begin{pmatrix} 1 \\ 3 \end{pmatrix} = \begin{pmatrix} 7 \\ 15 \end{pmatrix} = -5f_1 + 6f_2$$

$$T(f_2) = \begin{pmatrix} 1 & 2 \\ 3 & 4 \end{pmatrix}\begin{pmatrix} 2 \\ 5 \end{pmatrix} = \begin{pmatrix} 12 \\ 26 \end{pmatrix} = -8f_1 + 10f_2$$

and thus $\quad [T]_f = \begin{pmatrix} -5 & -8 \\ 6 & 10 \end{pmatrix}$

7.7. Recall that any n-square matrix $A = (a_{ij})$ may be viewed as the linear operator T on K^n defined by $T(v) = Av$, where v is written as a column vector. Show that the matrix representation of T relative to the usual basis $\{e_i\}$ of K^n is the matrix A, that is, $[T]_e = A$.

$$T(e_1) = Ae_1 = \begin{pmatrix} a_{11} & a_{12} & \cdots & a_{1n} \\ a_{21} & a_{22} & \cdots & a_{2n} \\ \cdots\cdots\cdots\cdots\cdots \\ a_{n1} & a_{n2} & \cdots & a_{nn} \end{pmatrix}\begin{pmatrix} 1 \\ 0 \\ \cdot\cdot \\ 0 \end{pmatrix} = \begin{pmatrix} a_{11} \\ a_{21} \\ \cdot\cdot \\ a_{n1} \end{pmatrix} = a_{11}e_1 + a_{21}e_2 + \cdots + a_{n1}e_n$$

$$T(e_2) = Ae_2 = \begin{pmatrix} a_{11} & a_{12} & \cdots & a_{1n} \\ a_{21} & a_{22} & \cdots & a_{2n} \\ \cdots\cdots\cdots\cdots\cdots \\ a_{n1} & a_{n2} & \cdots & a_{nn} \end{pmatrix}\begin{pmatrix} 0 \\ 1 \\ \cdot\cdot \\ 0 \end{pmatrix} = \begin{pmatrix} a_{12} \\ a_{22} \\ \cdot\cdot \\ a_{n2} \end{pmatrix} = a_{12}e_1 + a_{22}e_2 + \cdots + a_{n2}e_n$$

$$\cdots\cdots\cdots\cdots\cdots\cdots\cdots\cdots\cdots\cdots\cdots\cdots\cdots$$

$$T(e_n) = Ae_n = \begin{pmatrix} a_{11} & a_{12} & \cdots & a_{1n} \\ a_{21} & a_{22} & \cdots & a_{2n} \\ \cdots\cdots\cdots\cdots\cdots \\ a_{n1} & a_{n2} & \cdots & a_{nn} \end{pmatrix}\begin{pmatrix} 0 \\ 0 \\ \cdot\cdot \\ 1 \end{pmatrix} = \begin{pmatrix} a_{1n} \\ a_{2n} \\ \cdot\cdot \\ a_{nn} \end{pmatrix} = a_{1n}e_1 + a_{2n}e_2 + \cdots + a_{nn}e_n$$

(That is, $T(e_i) = Ae_i$ is the ith column of A.) Accordingly,

$$[T]_e = \begin{pmatrix} a_{11} & a_{12} & \cdots & a_{1n} \\ a_{21} & a_{22} & \cdots & a_{2n} \\ \cdots\cdots\cdots\cdots\cdots \\ a_{n1} & a_{n2} & \cdots & a_{nn} \end{pmatrix} = A$$

7.8. Each of the sets (i) $\{1, t, e^t, te^t\}$ and (ii) $\{e^{3t}, te^{3t}, t^2e^{3t}\}$ is a basis of a vector space V of functions $f : \mathbf{R} \to \mathbf{R}$. Let D be the differential operator on V, that is, $D(f) = df/dt$. Find the matrix of D in the given basis.

(i)
$$\begin{aligned}
D(1) &= 0 &&= 0(1) + 0(t) + 0(e^t) + 0(te^t) \\
D(t) &= 1 &&= 1(1) + 0(t) + 0(e^t) + 0(te^t) \\
D(e^t) &= e^t &&= 0(1) + 0(t) + 1(e^t) + 0(te^t) \\
D(te^t) &= e^t + te^t &&= 0(1) + 0(t) + 1(e^t) + 1(te^t)
\end{aligned}$$
and $\quad [D] = \begin{pmatrix} 0 & 1 & 0 & 0 \\ 0 & 0 & 0 & 0 \\ 0 & 0 & 1 & 1 \\ 0 & 0 & 0 & 1 \end{pmatrix}$

(ii)
$$\begin{aligned}
D(e^{3t}) &= 3e^{3t} &&= 3(e^{3t}) + 0(te^{3t}) + 0(t^2e^{3t}) \\
D(te^{3t}) &= e^{3t} + 3te^{3t} &&= 1(e^{3t}) + 3(te^{3t}) + 0(t^2e^{3t}) \\
D(t^2e^{3t}) &= 2te^{3t} + 3t^2e^{3t} &&= 0(e^{3t}) + 2(te^{3t}) + 3(t^2e^{3t})
\end{aligned}$$
and $\quad [D] = \begin{pmatrix} 3 & 1 & 0 \\ 0 & 3 & 2 \\ 0 & 0 & 3 \end{pmatrix}$

7.9. Prove Theorem 7.1: Suppose $\{e_1, \ldots, e_n\}$ is a basis of V and T is a linear operator on V. Then for any $v \in V$, $[T]_e\,[v]_e = [T(v)]_e$.

Suppose, for $i = 1, \ldots, n$,

$$T(e_i) \;=\; a_{i1}e_1 + a_{i2}e_2 + \cdots + a_{in}e_n \;=\; \sum_{j=1}^{n} a_{ij}e_j$$

Then $[T]_e$ is the n-square matrix whose jth row is

$$(a_{1j}, a_{2j}, \ldots, a_{nj}) \tag{1}$$

Now suppose $v \;=\; k_1e_1 + k_2e_2 + \cdots + k_ne_n \;=\; \sum_{i=1}^{n} k_ie_i$

Writing a column vector as the transpose of a row vector,

$$[v]_e \;=\; (k_1, k_2, \ldots, k_n)^t \tag{2}$$

Furthermore, using the linearity of T,

$$T(v) \;=\; T\left(\sum_{i=1}^{n} k_ie_i\right) \;=\; \sum_{i=1}^{n} k_iT(e_i) \;=\; \sum_{i=1}^{n} k_i\left(\sum_{j=1}^{n} a_{ij}e_j\right)$$

$$=\; \sum_{j=1}^{n}\left(\sum_{i=1}^{n} a_{ij}k_i\right)e_j \;=\; \sum_{j=1}^{n} (a_{1j}k_1 + a_{2j}k_2 + \cdots + a_{nj}k_n)e_j$$

Thus $[T(v)]_e$ is the column vector whose jth entry is

$$a_{1j}k_1 + a_{2j}k_2 + \cdots + a_{nj}k_n \tag{3}$$

On the other hand, the jth entry of $[T]_e[v]_e$ is obtained by multiplying the jth row of $[T]_e$ by $[v]_e$, i.e. (1) by (2). But the product of (1) and (2) is (3); hence $[T]_e[v]_e$ and $[T(v)]_e$ have the same entries. Thus $[T]_e\,[v]_e = [T(v)]_e$.

7.10. Prove Theorem 7.2: Let $\{e_1, \ldots, e_n\}$ be a basis of V over K, and let $\mathcal{A}$ be the algebra of n-square matrices over K. Then the mapping $T \mapsto [T]_e$ is a vector space isomorphism from $A(V)$ onto $\mathcal{A}$. That is, the mapping is one-one and onto and, for any $S, T \in A(V)$ and any $k \in K$, $[T + S]_e = [T]_e + [S]_e$ and $[kT]_e = k[T]_e$.

The mapping is one-one since, by Theorem 8.1, a linear mapping is completely determined by its values on a basis. The mapping is onto since each matrix $M \in \mathcal{A}$ is the image of the linear operator

$$F(e_i) \;=\; \sum_{j=1}^{n} m_{ij}\,e_j \qquad i = 1, \ldots, n$$

where (m_{ij}) is the transpose of the matrix M.

Now suppose, for $i = 1, \ldots, n$,

$$T(e_i) \;=\; \sum_{j=1}^{n} a_{ij}e_j \quad \text{and} \quad S(e_i) \;=\; \sum_{j=1}^{n} b_{ij}e_j$$

Let A and B be the matrices $A = (a_{ij})$ and $B = (b_{ij})$. Then $[T]_e = A^t$ and $[S]_e = B^t$. We have, for $i = 1, \ldots, n$,

$$(T + S)(e_i) \;=\; T(e_i) + S(e_i) \;=\; \sum_{j=1}^{n} (a_{ij} + b_{ij})e_j$$

Observe that $A + B$ is the matrix $(a_{ij} + b_{ij})$. Accordingly,

$$[T + S]_e \;=\; (A + B)^t \;=\; A^t + B^t \;=\; [T]_e + [S]_e$$

We also have, for $i = 1, \ldots, n$,

$$(kT)(e_i) \;=\; k\,T(e_i) \;=\; k\sum_{j=1}^{n} a_{ij}e_j \;=\; \sum_{j=1}^{n} (ka_{ij})e_j$$

Observe that kA is the matrix (ka_{ij}). Accordingly,

$$[kT]_e \;=\; (kA)^t \;=\; kA^t \;=\; k[T]_e$$

Thus the theorem is proved.

7.11. Prove Theorem 7.3: Let $\{e_1, \ldots, e_n\}$ be a basis of V. Then for any linear operators $S, T \in A(V)$, $[ST]_e = [S]_e [T]_e$.

Suppose $T(e_i) = \sum_{j=1}^{n} a_{ij} e_j$ and $S(e_j) = \sum_{k=1}^{n} b_{jk} e_k$. Let A and B be the matrices $A = (a_{ij})$ and $B = (b_{jk})$. Then $[T]_e = A^t$ and $[S]_e = B^t$. We have

$$(ST)(e_i) = S(T(e_i)) = S\left(\sum_{j=1}^{n} a_{ij} e_j\right) = \sum_{j=1}^{n} a_{ij} S(e_j)$$

$$= \sum_{j=1}^{n} a_{ij}\left(\sum_{k=1}^{n} b_{jk} e_k\right) = \sum_{k=1}^{n}\left(\sum_{j=1}^{n} a_{ij} b_{jk}\right) e_k$$

Recall that AB is the matrix $AB = (c_{ik})$ where $c_{ik} = \sum_{j=1}^{n} a_{ij} b_{jk}$. Accordingly,

$$[ST]_e = (AB)^t = B^t A^t = [S]_e [T]_e$$

CHANGE OF BASIS, SIMILAR MATRICES

7.12. Consider these bases of $\mathbf{R}^2$: $\{e_1 = (1,0),\ e_2 = (0,1)\}$ and $\{f_1 = (1,3),\ f_2 = (2,5)\}$. (i) Find the transition matrix P from $\{e_i\}$ to $\{f_i\}$. (ii) Find the transition matrix Q from $\{f_i\}$ to $\{e_i\}$. (iii) Verify that $Q = P^{-1}$. (iv) Show that $[v]_f = P^{-1}[v]_e$ for any vector $v \in \mathbf{R}^2$. (v) Show that $[T]_f = P^{-1}[T]_e P$ for the operator T on $\mathbf{R}^2$ defined by $T(x, y) = (2y, 3x - y)$. (See Problems 7.1 and 7.2.)

(i)
$$f_1 = (1,3) = 1e_1 + 3e_2 \qquad \text{and} \qquad P = \begin{pmatrix} 1 & 2 \\ 3 & 5 \end{pmatrix}$$
$$f_2 = (2,5) = 2e_1 + 5e_2$$

(ii) By Problem 7.2, $(a, b) = (2b - 5a)f_1 + (3a - b)f_2$. Thus

$$e_1 = (1,0) = -5f_1 + 3f_2 \qquad \text{and} \qquad Q = \begin{pmatrix} -5 & 2 \\ 3 & -1 \end{pmatrix}$$
$$e_2 = (0,1) = 2f_1 - f_2$$

(iii)
$$PQ = \begin{pmatrix} 1 & 2 \\ 3 & 5 \end{pmatrix}\begin{pmatrix} -5 & 2 \\ 3 & -1 \end{pmatrix} = \begin{pmatrix} 1 & 0 \\ 0 & 1 \end{pmatrix} = I$$

(iv) If $v = (a, b)$, then $[v]_e = \begin{pmatrix} a \\ b \end{pmatrix}$ and $[v]_f = \begin{pmatrix} 2b - 5a \\ 3a - b \end{pmatrix}$. Hence

$$P^{-1}[v]_e = \begin{pmatrix} -5 & 2 \\ 3 & -1 \end{pmatrix}\begin{pmatrix} a \\ b \end{pmatrix} = \begin{pmatrix} -5a + 2b \\ 3a - b \end{pmatrix} = [v]_f$$

(v) By Problems 7.1 and 7.2; $[T]_e = \begin{pmatrix} 0 & 2 \\ 3 & -1 \end{pmatrix}$ and $[T]_f = \begin{pmatrix} -30 & -48 \\ 18 & 29 \end{pmatrix}$. Hence

$$P^{-1}[T]_e P = \begin{pmatrix} -5 & 2 \\ 3 & -1 \end{pmatrix}\begin{pmatrix} 0 & 2 \\ 3 & -1 \end{pmatrix}\begin{pmatrix} 1 & 2 \\ 3 & 5 \end{pmatrix} = \begin{pmatrix} -30 & -48 \\ 18 & 29 \end{pmatrix} = [T]_f$$

7.13. Consider the following bases of $\mathbf{R}^3$: $\{e_1 = (1,0,0),\ e_2 = (0,1,0),\ e_3 = (0,0,1)\}$ and $\{f_1 = (1,1,1),\ f_2 = (1,1,0),\ f_3 = (1,0,0)\}$. (i) Find the transition matrix P from $\{e_i\}$ to $\{f_i\}$. (ii) Find the transition matrix Q from $\{f_i\}$ to $\{e_i\}$. (iii) Verify that $Q = P^{-1}$. (iv) Show that $[v]_f = P^{-1}[v]_e$ for any vector $v \in \mathbf{R}^3$. (v) Show that $[T]_f = P^{-1}[T]_e P$ for the T defined by $T(x, y, z) = (2y + z, x - 4y, 3x)$. (See Problems 7.4 and 7.5.)

(i)
$$\begin{aligned} f_1 &= (1,1,1) = 1e_1 + 1e_2 + 1e_3 \\ f_2 &= (1,1,0) = 1e_1 + 1e_2 + 0e_3 \qquad \text{and} \qquad P = \begin{pmatrix} 1 & 1 & 1 \\ 1 & 1 & 0 \\ 1 & 0 & 0 \end{pmatrix} \\ f_3 &= (1,0,0) = 1e_1 + 0e_2 + 0e_3 \end{aligned}$$

(ii)   By Problem 7.5, $(a, b, c) = cf_1 + (b - c)f_2 + (a - b)f_3$. Thus

$$e_1 = (1, 0, 0) = 0f_1 + 0f_2 + 1f_3$$
$$e_2 = (0, 1, 0) = 0f_1 + 1f_2 - 1f_3 \qquad \text{and} \qquad Q = \begin{pmatrix} 0 & 0 & 1 \\ 0 & 1 & -1 \\ 1 & -1 & 0 \end{pmatrix}$$
$$e_3 = (0, 0, 1) = 1f_1 - 1f_2 + 0f_3$$

(iii)

$$PQ = \begin{pmatrix} 1 & 1 & 1 \\ 1 & 1 & 0 \\ 1 & 0 & 0 \end{pmatrix} \begin{pmatrix} 0 & 0 & 1 \\ 0 & 1 & -1 \\ 1 & -1 & 0 \end{pmatrix} = \begin{pmatrix} 1 & 0 & 0 \\ 0 & 1 & 0 \\ 0 & 0 & 1 \end{pmatrix} = I$$

(iv)   If $v = (a, b, c)$, then $[v]_e = \begin{pmatrix} a \\ b \\ c \end{pmatrix}$ and $[v]_f = \begin{pmatrix} c \\ b - c \\ a - b \end{pmatrix}$. Thus

$$P^{-1}[v]_e = \begin{pmatrix} 0 & 0 & 1 \\ 0 & 1 & -1 \\ 1 & -1 & 0 \end{pmatrix} \begin{pmatrix} a \\ b \\ c \end{pmatrix} = \begin{pmatrix} c \\ b - c \\ a - b \end{pmatrix} = [v]_f$$

(v)   By Problems 7.4(ii) and 7.5, $[T]_e = \begin{pmatrix} 0 & 2 & 1 \\ 1 & -4 & 0 \\ 3 & 0 & 0 \end{pmatrix}$ and $[T]_f = \begin{pmatrix} 3 & 3 & 3 \\ -6 & -6 & -2 \\ 6 & 5 & -1 \end{pmatrix}$. Thus

$$P^{-1}[T]_e P = \begin{pmatrix} 0 & 0 & 1 \\ 0 & 1 & -1 \\ 1 & -1 & 0 \end{pmatrix} \begin{pmatrix} 0 & 2 & 1 \\ 1 & -4 & 0 \\ 3 & 0 & 0 \end{pmatrix} \begin{pmatrix} 1 & 1 & 1 \\ 1 & 1 & 0 \\ 1 & 0 & 0 \end{pmatrix} = \begin{pmatrix} 3 & 3 & 3 \\ -6 & -6 & -2 \\ 6 & 5 & -1 \end{pmatrix} = [T]_f$$

7.14. Prove Theorem 7.4: Let P be the transition matrix from a basis $\{e_i\}$ to a basis $\{f_i\}$ in a vector space V. Then for any $v \in V$, $P[v]_f = [v]_e$. Also, $[v]_f = P^{-1}[v]_e$.

Suppose, for $i = 1, \ldots, n$, $f_i = a_{i1}e_1 + a_{i2}e_2 + \cdots + a_{in}e_n = \sum_{j=1}^{n} a_{ij}e_j$. Then P is the n-square matrix whose jth row is

$$(a_{1j}, a_{2j}, \ldots, a_{nj}) \tag{1}$$

Also suppose $v = k_1 f_1 + k_2 f_2 + \cdots + k_n f_n = \sum_{i=1}^{n} k_i f_i$. Then writing a column vector as the transpose of a row vector,

$$[v]_f = (k_1, k_2, \ldots, k_n)^t \tag{2}$$

Substituting for f_i in the equation for v,

$$v = \sum_{i=1}^{n} k_i f_i = \sum_{i=1}^{n} k_i \left(\sum_{j=1}^{n} a_{ij}e_j \right) = \sum_{j=1}^{n} \left(\sum_{i=1}^{n} a_{ij}k_i \right) e_j$$
$$= \sum_{j=1}^{n} (a_{1j}k_1 + a_{2j}k_2 + \cdots + a_{nj}k_n)e_j$$

Accordingly, $[v]_e$ is the column vector whose jth entry is

$$a_{1j}k_1 + a_{2j}k_2 + \cdots + a_{nj}k_n \tag{3}$$

On the other hand, the jth entry of $P[v]_f$ is obtained by multiplying the jth row of P by $[v]_f$, i.e. (1) by (2). But the product of (1) and (2) is (3); hence $P[v]_f$ and $[v]_e$ have the same entries and thus $P[v]_f = [v]_e$.

Furthermore, multiplying the above by P^{-1} gives $P^{-1}[v]_e = P^{-1}P[v]_f = [v]_f$.

7.15. Prove Theorem 7.5: Let P be the transition matrix from a basis $\{e_i\}$ to a basis $\{f_i\}$ in a vector space V. Then, for any linear operator T on V, $[T]_f = P^{-1}[T]_e P$.

For any vector $v \in V$, $P^{-1}[T]_e P[v]_f = P^{-1}[T]_e [v]_e = P^{-1}[T(v)]_e = [T(v)]_f$.

But $[T]_f[v]_f = [T(v)]_f$; hence $P^{-1}[T]_e P[v]_f = [T]_f[v]_f$.

Since the mapping $v \mapsto [v]_f$ is onto K^n, $P^{-1}[T]_e PX = [T]_f X$ for every $X \in K^n$.

Accordingly, $P^{-1}[T]_e P = [T]_f$.

7.16. Show that similarity of matrices is an equivalence relation, that is: (i) A is similar to A; (ii) if A is similar to B, then B is similar to A; (iii) if A is similar to B and B is similar to C then A is similar to C.

(i)   The identity matrix I is invertible and $I = I^{-1}$. Since $A = I^{-1}AI$, A is similar to A.

(ii) Since A is similar to B there exists an invertible matrix P such that $A = P^{-1}BP$. Hence $B = PAP^{-1} = (P^{-1})^{-1}AP^{-1}$ and P^{-1} is invertible. Thus B is similar to A.

(iii) Since A is similar to B there exists an invertible matrix P such that $A = P^{-1}BP$, and since B is similar to C there exists an invertible matrix Q such that $B = Q^{-1}CQ$. Hence $A = P^{-1}BP = P^{-1}(Q^{-1}CQ)P = (QP)^{-1}C(QP)$ and QP is invertible. Thus A is similar to C.

TRACE

7.17. The *trace* of a square matrix $A = (a_{ij})$, written $\operatorname{tr}(A)$, is the sum of its diagonal elements: $\operatorname{tr}(A) = a_{11} + a_{22} + \cdots + a_{nn}$. Show that (i) $\operatorname{tr}(AB) = \operatorname{tr}(BA)$, (ii) if A is similar to B then $\operatorname{tr}(A) = \operatorname{tr}(B)$.

(i)   Suppose $A = (a_{ij})$ and $B = (b_{ij})$. Then $AB = (c_{ik})$ where $c_{ik} = \sum_{j=1}^{n} a_{ij}b_{jk}$. Thus

$$\operatorname{tr}(AB) = \sum_{i=1}^{n} c_{ii} = \sum_{i=1}^{n} \sum_{j=1}^{n} a_{ij}b_{ji}$$

On the other hand, $BA = (d_{jk})$ where $d_{jk} = \sum_{i=1}^{n} b_{ji}a_{ik}$. Thus

$$\operatorname{tr}(BA) = \sum_{j=1}^{n} d_{jj} = \sum_{j=1}^{n} \sum_{i=1}^{n} b_{ji}a_{ij} = \sum_{i=1}^{n} \sum_{j=1}^{n} a_{ij}b_{ji} = \operatorname{tr}(AB)$$

(ii) If A is similar to B, there exists an invertible matrix P such that $A = P^{-1}BP$. Using (i),

$$\operatorname{tr}(A) = \operatorname{tr}(P^{-1}BP) = \operatorname{tr}(BPP^{-1}) = \operatorname{tr}(B)$$

7.18. Find the trace of the following operator on $\mathbf{R}^3$:
$$T(x, y, z) = (a_1 x + a_2 y + a_3 z,\ b_1 x + b_2 y + b_3 z,\ c_1 x + c_2 y + c_3 z)$$

We first must find a matrix representation of T. Choosing the usual basis $\{e_i\}$,

$$[T]_e = \begin{pmatrix} a_1 & a_2 & a_3 \\ b_1 & b_2 & b_3 \\ c_1 & c_2 & c_3 \end{pmatrix}$$

and $\operatorname{tr}(T) = \operatorname{tr}([T]_e) = a_1 + b_2 + c_3$.

7.19. Let V be the space of 2×2 matrices over $\mathbf{R}$, and let $M = \begin{pmatrix} 1 & 2 \\ 3 & 4 \end{pmatrix}$. Let T be the linear operator on V defined by $T(A) = MA$. Find the trace of T.

We must first find a matrix representation of T. Choose the usual basis of V:

$$\left\{ E_1 = \begin{pmatrix} 1 & 0 \\ 0 & 0 \end{pmatrix},\ E_2 = \begin{pmatrix} 0 & 1 \\ 0 & 0 \end{pmatrix},\ E_3 = \begin{pmatrix} 0 & 0 \\ 1 & 0 \end{pmatrix},\ E_4 = \begin{pmatrix} 0 & 0 \\ 0 & 1 \end{pmatrix} \right\}$$

Then

$$T(E_1) = ME_1 = \begin{pmatrix} 1 & 2 \\ 3 & 4 \end{pmatrix}\begin{pmatrix} 1 & 0 \\ 0 & 0 \end{pmatrix} = \begin{pmatrix} 1 & 0 \\ 3 & 0 \end{pmatrix} = 1E_1 + 0E_2 + 3E_3 + 0E_4$$

$$T(E_2) = ME_2 = \begin{pmatrix} 1 & 2 \\ 3 & 4 \end{pmatrix}\begin{pmatrix} 0 & 1 \\ 0 & 0 \end{pmatrix} = \begin{pmatrix} 0 & 1 \\ 0 & 3 \end{pmatrix} = 0E_1 + 1E_2 + 0E_3 + 3E_4$$

$$T(E_3) = ME_3 = \begin{pmatrix} 1 & 2 \\ 3 & 4 \end{pmatrix}\begin{pmatrix} 0 & 0 \\ 1 & 0 \end{pmatrix} = \begin{pmatrix} 2 & 0 \\ 4 & 0 \end{pmatrix} = 2E_1 + 0E_2 + 4E_3 + 0E_4$$

$$T(E_4) = ME_4 = \begin{pmatrix} 1 & 2 \\ 3 & 4 \end{pmatrix}\begin{pmatrix} 0 & 0 \\ 0 & 1 \end{pmatrix} = \begin{pmatrix} 0 & 2 \\ 0 & 4 \end{pmatrix} = 0E_1 + 2E_2 + 0E_3 + 4E_4$$

Hence

$$[T]_E = \begin{pmatrix} 1 & 0 & 2 & 0 \\ 0 & 1 & 0 & 2 \\ 3 & 0 & 4 & 0 \\ 0 & 3 & 0 & 4 \end{pmatrix}$$

and $\operatorname{tr}(T) = 1 + 1 + 4 + 4 = 10$.

MATRIX REPRESENTATIONS OF LINEAR MAPPINGS

7.20.   Let $F : \mathbf{R}^3 \to \mathbf{R}^2$ be the linear mapping defined by $F(x, y, z) = (3x + 2y - 4z,\ x - 5y + 3z)$.

(i)   Find the matrix of F in the following bases of $\mathbf{R}^3$ and $\mathbf{R}^2$:

$$\{f_1 = (1, 1, 1),\ f_2 = (1, 1, 0),\ f_3 = (1, 0, 0)\}, \quad \{g_1 = (1, 3),\ g_2 = (2, 5)\}$$

(ii)   Verify that the action of F is preserved by its matrix representation; that is, for any $v \in \mathbf{R}^3$, $[F]_f^g [v]_f = [F(v)]_g$.

(i)   By Problem 7.2, $(a, b) = (2b - 5a)g_1 + (3a - b)g_2$. Hence

$$\begin{aligned} F(f_1) &= F(1, 1, 1) = (1, -1) = -7g_1 + 4g_2 \\ F(f_2) &= F(1, 1, 0) = (5, -4) = -33g_1 + 19g_2 \qquad \text{and} \qquad [F]_f^g = \begin{pmatrix} -7 & -33 & -13 \\ 4 & 19 & 8 \end{pmatrix} \\ F(f_3) &= F(1, 0, 0) = (3, 1) = -12g_1 + 8g_2 \end{aligned}$$

(ii)   If $v = (x, y, z)$ then, by Problem 7.5, $v = zf_1 + (y - z)f_2 + (x - y)f_3$. Also,

$$F(v) = (3x + 2y - 4z,\ x - 5y + 3z) = (-13x - 20y + 26z)g_1 + (8x + 11y - 15z)g_2$$

Hence $[v]_f = \begin{pmatrix} z \\ y - z \\ x - y \end{pmatrix}$ and $[F(v)]_g = \begin{pmatrix} -13x - 20y + 26z \\ 8x + 11y - 15z \end{pmatrix}$.   Thus

$$[F]_f^g [v]_f = \begin{pmatrix} -7 & -33 & -13 \\ 4 & 19 & 8 \end{pmatrix}\begin{pmatrix} z \\ y - z \\ x - y \end{pmatrix} = \begin{pmatrix} -13x - 20y + 26z \\ 8x + 11y - 15z \end{pmatrix} = [F(v)]_g$$

7.21.   Let $F : K^n \to K^m$ be the linear mapping defined by

$$F(x_1, x_2, \ldots, x_n) = (a_{11}x_1 + \cdots + a_{1n}x_n,\ a_{21}x_1 + \cdots + a_{2n}x_n,\ \ldots,\ a_{m1}x_1 + \cdots + a_{mn}x_n)$$

Show that the matrix representation of F relative to the usual bases of K^n and of K^m is given by

$$[F] = \begin{pmatrix} a_{11} & a_{12} & \ldots & a_{1n} \\ a_{21} & a_{22} & \ldots & a_{2n} \\ \multicolumn{4}{c}{\dotfill} \\ a_{m1} & a_{m2} & \ldots & a_{mn} \end{pmatrix}$$

That is, the rows of $[F]$ are obtained from the coefficients of the x_i in the components of $F(x_1, \ldots, x_n)$, respectively.

$$
\begin{aligned}
F(1, 0, \ldots, 0) &= (a_{11}, a_{21}, \ldots, a_{m1}) \\
F(0, 1, \ldots, 0) &= (a_{12}, a_{22}, \ldots, a_{m2}) \\
&\cdots\cdots\cdots\cdots\cdots\cdots\cdots\cdots \\
F(0, 0, \ldots, 1) &= (a_{1n}, a_{2n}, \ldots, a_{mn})
\end{aligned}
\qquad \text{and} \qquad
[F] = \begin{pmatrix} a_{11} & a_{12} & \cdots & a_{1n} \\ a_{21} & a_{22} & \cdots & a_{2n} \\ \multicolumn{4}{c}{\cdots\cdots\cdots\cdots\cdots} \\ a_{m1} & a_{m2} & \cdots & a_{mn} \end{pmatrix}
$$

7.22. Find the matrix representation of each of the following linear mappings relative to the usual bases of $\mathbf{R}^n$:

(i) $F : \mathbf{R}^2 \to \mathbf{R}^3$ defined by $F(x, y) = (3x - y, 2x + 4y, 5x - 6y)$

(ii) $F : \mathbf{R}^4 \to \mathbf{R}^2$ defined by $F(x, y, s, t) = (3x - 4y + 2s - 5t, 5x + 7y - s - 2t)$

(iii) $F : \mathbf{R}^3 \to \mathbf{R}^4$ defined by $F(x, y, z) = (2x + 3y - 8z, x + y + z, 4x - 5z, 6y)$

By Problem 7.21, we need only look at the coefficients of the unknowns in $F(x, y, \ldots)$. Thus

(i) $[F] = \begin{pmatrix} 3 & -1 \\ 2 & 4 \\ 5 & -6 \end{pmatrix}$ (ii) $[F] = \begin{pmatrix} 3 & -4 & 2 & -5 \\ 5 & 7 & -1 & -2 \end{pmatrix}$ (iii) $[F] = \begin{pmatrix} 2 & 3 & -8 \\ 1 & 1 & 1 \\ 4 & 0 & -5 \\ 0 & 6 & 0 \end{pmatrix}$

7.23. Let $T : \mathbf{R}^2 \to \mathbf{R}^2$ be defined by $T(x, y) = (2x - 3y, x + 4y)$. Find the matrix of T in the bases $\{e_1 = (1, 0),\ e_2 = (0, 1)\}$ and $\{f_1 = (1, 3),\ f_2 = (2, 5)\}$ of $\mathbf{R}^2$ respectively. (We can view T as a linear mapping from one space into another, each having its own basis.)

By Problem 7.2, $(a, b) = (2b - 5a)f_1 + (3a - b)f_2$. Then

$$
\begin{aligned}
T(e_1) &= T(1, 0) = (2, 1) &= -8f_1 + 5f_2 \\
T(e_2) &= T(0, 1) = (-3, 4) &= 23f_1 - 13f_2
\end{aligned}
\qquad \text{and} \qquad
[T]_e^f = \begin{pmatrix} -8 & 23 \\ 5 & -13 \end{pmatrix}
$$

7.24. Let $A = \begin{pmatrix} 2 & 5 & -3 \\ 1 & -4 & 7 \end{pmatrix}$. Recall that A determines a linear mapping $F : \mathbf{R}^3 \to \mathbf{R}^2$ defined by $F(v) = Av$ where v is written as a column vector.

(i) Show that the matrix representation of F relative to the usual basis of $\mathbf{R}^3$ and of $\mathbf{R}^2$ is the matrix A itself: $[F] = A$.

(ii) Find the matrix representation of F relative to the following bases of $\mathbf{R}^3$ and $\mathbf{R}^2$.

$$\{f_1 = (1, 1, 1),\ f_2 = (1, 1, 0),\ f_3 = (1, 0, 0)\}, \quad \{g_1 = (1, 3),\ g_2 = (2, 5)\}$$

(i)

$$F(1, 0, 0) = \begin{pmatrix} 2 & 5 & -3 \\ 1 & -4 & 7 \end{pmatrix} \begin{pmatrix} 1 \\ 0 \\ 0 \end{pmatrix} = \begin{pmatrix} 2 \\ 1 \end{pmatrix} = 2e_1 + 1e_2$$

$$F(0, 1, 0) = \begin{pmatrix} 2 & 5 & -3 \\ 1 & -4 & 7 \end{pmatrix} \begin{pmatrix} 0 \\ 1 \\ 0 \end{pmatrix} = \begin{pmatrix} 5 \\ -4 \end{pmatrix} = 5e_1 - 4e_2$$

$$F(0, 0, 1) = \begin{pmatrix} 2 & 5 & -3 \\ 1 & -4 & 7 \end{pmatrix} \begin{pmatrix} 0 \\ 0 \\ 1 \end{pmatrix} = \begin{pmatrix} -3 \\ 7 \end{pmatrix} = -3e_1 + 7e_2$$

from which $[F] = \begin{pmatrix} 2 & 5 & -3 \\ 1 & -4 & 7 \end{pmatrix} = A$. (Compare with Problem 7.7.)

(ii) By Problem 7.2, $(a, b) = (2b - 5a)g_1 + (3a - b)g_2$. Then

$$F(f_1) \;=\; \begin{pmatrix} 2 & 5 & -3 \\ 1 & -4 & 7 \end{pmatrix} \begin{pmatrix} 1 \\ 1 \\ 1 \end{pmatrix} \;=\; \begin{pmatrix} 4 \\ 4 \end{pmatrix} \;=\; -12g_1 + 8g_2$$

$$F(f_2) \;=\; \begin{pmatrix} 2 & 5 & -3 \\ 1 & -4 & 7 \end{pmatrix} \begin{pmatrix} 1 \\ 1 \\ 0 \end{pmatrix} \;=\; \begin{pmatrix} 7 \\ -3 \end{pmatrix} \;=\; -41g_1 + 24g_2$$

$$F(f_3) \;=\; \begin{pmatrix} 2 & 5 & -3 \\ 1 & -4 & 7 \end{pmatrix} \begin{pmatrix} 1 \\ 0 \\ 0 \end{pmatrix} \;=\; \begin{pmatrix} 2 \\ 1 \end{pmatrix} \;=\; -8g_1 + 5g_2$$

and $\quad [F]_f^g \;=\; \begin{pmatrix} -12 & -41 & -8 \\ 8 & 24 & 5 \end{pmatrix}.$

7.25. Prove Theorem 7.12: Let $F : V \to U$ be linear. Then there exists a basis of V and a basis of U such that the matrix representation A of F has the form $A = \begin{pmatrix} I & 0 \\ 0 & 0 \end{pmatrix}$ where I is the r-square identity matrix and r is the rank of F.

Suppose $\dim V = m$ and $\dim U = n$. Let W be the kernel of F and U' the image of F. We are given that rank $F = r$; hence the dimension of the kernel of F is $m - r$. Let $\{w_1, \ldots, w_{m-r}\}$ be a basis of the kernel of F and extend this to a basis of V:

$$\{v_1, \ldots, v_r, \; w_1, \ldots, w_{m-r}\}$$

Set $\qquad\qquad u_1 = F(v_1), \;\; u_2 = F(v_2), \;\; \ldots, \;\; u_r = F(v_r)$

We note that $\{u_1, \ldots, u_r\}$ is a basis of U', the image of F. Extend this to a basis

$$\{u_1, \ldots, u_r, \; u_{r+1}, \ldots, u_n\}$$

of U. Observe that

$$F(v_1) \;=\; u_1 \;=\; 1u_1 + 0u_2 + \cdots + 0u_r + 0u_{r+1} + \cdots + 0u_n$$
$$F(v_2) \;=\; u_2 \;=\; 0u_1 + 1u_2 + \cdots + 0u_r + 0u_{r+1} + \cdots + 0u_n$$
$$\cdots\cdots\cdots\cdots\cdots\cdots\cdots\cdots\cdots\cdots\cdots\cdots\cdots\cdots$$
$$F(v_r) \;=\; u_r \;=\; 0u_1 + 0u_2 + \cdots + 1u_r + 0u_{r+1} + \cdots + 0u_n$$
$$F(w_1) \;=\; 0 \;=\; 0u_1 + 0u_2 + \cdots + 0u_r + 0u_{r+1} + \cdots + 0u_n$$
$$\cdots\cdots\cdots\cdots\cdots\cdots\cdots\cdots\cdots\cdots\cdots\cdots\cdots\cdots$$
$$F(w_{m-r}) \;=\; 0 \;=\; 0u_1 + 0u_2 + \cdots + 0u_r + 0u_{r+1} + \cdots + 0u_n$$

Thus the matrix of F in the above bases has the required form.

Supplementary Problems

MATRIX REPRESENTATIONS OF LINEAR OPERATORS

7.26. Find the matrix of each of the following linear operators T on $\mathbf{R}^2$ with respect to the usual basis $\{e_1 = (1, 0), \; e_2 = (0, 1)\}$: (i) $T(x, y) = (2x - 3y, \; x + y)$, (ii) $T(x, y) = (5x + y, \; 3x - 2y)$.

7.27. Find the matrix of each operator T in the preceding problem with respect to the basis $\{f_1 = (1, 2), \; f_2 = (2, 3)\}$. In each case, verify that $[T]_f [v]_f = [T(v)]_f$ for any $v \in \mathbf{R}^2$.

7.28. Find the matrix of each operator T in Problem 7.26 in the basis $\{g_1 = (1, 3), \; g_2 = (1, 4)\}$.

7.29. Find the matrix representation of each of the following linear operators T on $\mathbf{R}^3$ relative to the usual basis:

(i) $T(x, y, z) = (x, y, 0)$

(ii) $T(x, y, z) = (2x - 7y - 4z, 3x + y + 4z, 6x - 8y + z)$

(iii) $T(x, y, z) = (z, y + z, x + y + z)$

7.30. Let D be the differential operator, i.e. $D(f) = df/dt$. Each of the following sets is a basis of a vector space V of functions $f : \mathbf{R} \to \mathbf{R}$. Find the matrix of D in each basis: (i) $\{e^t, e^{2t}, te^{2t}\}$, (ii) $\{\sin t, \cos t\}$, (iii) $\{e^{5t}, te^{5t}, t^2 e^{5t}\}$, (iv) $\{1, t, \sin 3t, \cos 3t\}$.

7.31. Consider the complex field $\mathbf{C}$ as a vector space over the real field $\mathbf{R}$. Let T be the conjugation operator on $\mathbf{C}$, i.e. $T(z) = \bar{z}$. Find the matrix of T in each basis: (i) $\{1, i\}$, (ii) $\{1 + i, 1 + 2i\}$.

7.32. Let V be the vector space of 2×2 matrices over $\mathbf{R}$ and let $M = \begin{pmatrix} a & b \\ c & d \end{pmatrix}$. Find the matrix of each of the following linear operators T on V in the usual basis (see Problem 7.19) of V: (i) $T(A) = MA$, (ii) $T(A) = AM$, (iii) $T(A) = MA - AM$.

7.33. Let 1_V and 0_V denote the identity and zero operators, respectively, on a vector space V. Show that, for any basis $\{e_i\}$ of V, (i) $[1_V]_e = I$, the identity matrix, (ii) $[0_V]_e = 0$, the zero matrix.

CHANGE OF BASIS, SIMILAR MATRICES

7.34. Consider the following bases of $\mathbf{R}^2$: $\{e_1 = (1, 0),\ e_2 = (0, 1)\}$ and $\{f_1 = (1, 2),\ f_2 = (2, 3)\}$.

(i) Find the transition matrices P and Q from $\{e_i\}$ to $\{f_i\}$ and from $\{f_i\}$ to $\{e_i\}$, respectively. Verify $Q = P^{-1}$.

(ii) Show that $[v]_e = P[v]_f$ for any vector $v \in \mathbf{R}^2$.

(iii) Show that $[T]_f = P^{-1}[T]_e P$ for each operator T in Problem 7.26.

7.35. Repeat Problem 7.34 for the bases $\{f_1 = (1, 2),\ f_2 = (2, 3)\}$ and $\{g_1 = (1, 3),\ g_2 = (1, 4)\}$.

7.36. Suppose $\{e_1, e_2\}$ is a basis of V and $T : V \to V$ is the linear operator for which $T(e_1) = 3e_1 - 2e_2$ and $T(e_2) = e_1 + 4e_2$. Suppose $\{f_1, f_2\}$ is the basis of V for which $f_1 = e_1 + e_2$ and $f_2 = 2e_1 + 3e_2$. Find the matrix of T in the basis $\{f_1, f_2\}$.

7.37. Consider the bases $B = \{1, i\}$ and $B' = \{1 + i, 1 + 2i\}$ of the complex field $\mathbf{C}$ over the real field $\mathbf{R}$. (i) Find the transition matrices P and Q from B to B' and from B' to B, respectively. Verify that $Q = P^{-1}$. (ii) Show that $[T]_{B'} = P^{-1}[T]_B P$ for the conjugation operator T in Problem 7.31.

7.38. Suppose $\{e_i\}$, $\{f_i\}$ and $\{g_i\}$ are bases of V, and that P and Q are the transition matrices from $\{e_i\}$ to $\{f_i\}$ and from $\{f_i\}$ to $\{g_i\}$, respectively. Show that PQ is the transition matrix from $\{e_i\}$ to $\{g_i\}$.

7.39. Let A be a 2 by 2 matrix such that only A is similar to itself. Show that A has the form

$$A = \begin{pmatrix} a & 0 \\ 0 & a \end{pmatrix}$$

Generalize to $n \times n$ matrices.

7.40. Show that all the matrices similar to an invertible matrix are invertible. More generally, show that similar matrices have the same rank.

MATRIX REPRESENTATIONS OF LINEAR MAPPINGS

7.41. Find the matrix representation of the linear mappings relative to the usual bases for $\mathbf{R}^n$:

(i) $F : \mathbf{R}^3 \to \mathbf{R}^2$ defined by $F(x, y, z) = (2x - 4y + 9z, 5x + 3y - 2z)$

(ii) $F : \mathbf{R}^2 \to \mathbf{R}^4$ defined by $F(x, y) = (3x + 4y, 5x - 2y, x + 7y, 4x)$

(iii) $F : \mathbf{R}^4 \to \mathbf{R}$ defined by $F(x, y, s, t) = 2x + 3y - 7s - t$

(iv) $F : \mathbf{R} \to \mathbf{R}^2$ defined by $F(x) = (3x, 5x)$

7.42. Let $F : \mathbf{R}^3 \to \mathbf{R}^2$ be the linear mapping defined by $F(x, y, z) = (2x + y - z, \, 3x - 2y + 4z)$.

 (i) Find the matrix of F in the following bases of $\mathbf{R}^3$ and $\mathbf{R}^2$:

$$\{f_1 = (1, 1, 1), \; f_2 = (1, 1, 0), \; f_3 = (1, 0, 0)\} \quad \text{and} \quad \{g_1 = (1, 3), \; g_2 = (1, 4)\}$$

 (ii) Verify that, for any vector $v \in \mathbf{R}^3$, $[F]_f^g [v]_f = [F(v)]_g$.

7.43. Let $\{e_i\}$ and $\{f_i\}$ be bases of V, and let 1_V be the identity mapping on V. Show that the matrix of 1_V in the bases $\{e_i\}$ and $\{f_i\}$ is the inverse of the transition matrix P from $\{e_i\}$ to $\{f_i\}$; that is, $[1_V]_e^f = P^{-1}$.

7.44. Prove Theorem 7.7, page 155.   (*Hint.* See Problem 7.9, page 161.)

7.45. Prove Theorem 7.8.   (*Hint.* See Problem 7.10.)

7.46. Prove Theorem 7.9.   (*Hint.* See Problem 7.11.)

7.47. Prove Theorem 7.10.   (*Hint.* See Problem 7.15.)

MISCELLANEOUS PROBLEMS

7.48. Let T be a linear operator on V and let W be a subspace of V *invariant* under T, that is, $T(W) \subset W$. Suppose $\dim W = m$. Show that T has a matrix representation of the form $\begin{pmatrix} A & B \\ 0 & C \end{pmatrix}$ where A is an $m \times m$ submatrix.

7.49. Let $V = U \oplus W$, and let U and W each be invariant under a linear operator $T : V \to V$. Suppose $\dim U = m$ and $\dim V = n$. Show that T has a matrix representation of the form $\begin{pmatrix} A & 0 \\ 0 & B \end{pmatrix}$ where A and B are $m \times m$ and $n \times n$ submatrices, respectively.

7.50. Recall that two linear operators F and G on V are said to be *similar* if there exists an invertible operator T on V such that $G = T^{-1}FT$.

 (i) Show that linear operators F and G are similar if and only if, for any basis $\{e_i\}$ of V, the matrix representations $[F]_e$ and $[G]_e$ are similar matrices.

 (ii) Show that if an operator F is diagonalizable, then any similar operator G is also diagonalizable.

7.51. Two $m \times n$ matrices A and B over K are said to be *equivalent* if there exists an m-square invertible matrix Q and an n-square invertible matrix P such that $B = QAP$.

 (i) Show that equivalence of matrices is an equivalence relation.

 (ii) Show that A and B can be matrix representations of the same linear operator $F : V \to U$ if and only if A and B are equivalent.

 (iii) Show that every matrix A is equivalent to a matrix of the form $\begin{pmatrix} I & 0 \\ 0 & 0 \end{pmatrix}$ where I is the r-square identity matrix and $r = \operatorname{rank} A$.

7.52. Two algebras $\mathbf{A}$ and $\mathbf{B}$ over a field K are said to be *isomorphic* (as algebras) if there exists a bijective mapping $f : \mathbf{A} \to \mathbf{B}$ such that for $u, v \in \mathbf{A}$ and $k \in K$, (i) $f(u + v) = f(u) + f(v)$, (ii) $f(ku) = kf(u)$, (iii) $f(uv) = f(u)f(v)$. (That is, f preserves the three operations of an algebra: vector addition, scalar multiplication, and vector multiplication.) The mapping f is then called an *isomorphism* of $\mathbf{A}$ onto $\mathbf{B}$. Show that the relation of algebra isomorphism is an equivalence relation.

7.53. Let $\mathcal{A}$ be the algebra of n-square matrices over K, and let P be an invertible matrix in $\mathcal{A}$. Show that the map $A \mapsto P^{-1}AP$, where $A \in \mathcal{A}$, is an algebra isomorphism of $\mathcal{A}$ onto itself.

Answers to Supplementary Problems

7.26.   (i) $\begin{pmatrix} 2 & -3 \\ 1 & 1 \end{pmatrix}$ (ii) $\begin{pmatrix} 5 & 1 \\ 3 & -2 \end{pmatrix}$

7.27.   Here $(a, b) = (2b - 3a)f_1 + (2a - b)f_2$.   (i) $\begin{pmatrix} 18 & 25 \\ -11 & -15 \end{pmatrix}$ (ii) $\begin{pmatrix} -23 & -39 \\ 15 & 26 \end{pmatrix}$

7.28.   Here $(a, b) = (4a - b)g_1 + (b - 3a)g_2$.   (i) $\begin{pmatrix} -32 & -45 \\ 25 & 35 \end{pmatrix}$ (ii) $\begin{pmatrix} 35 & 41 \\ -27 & -32 \end{pmatrix}$

7.29.   (i) $\begin{pmatrix} 1 & 0 & 0 \\ 0 & 1 & 0 \\ 0 & 0 & 0 \end{pmatrix}$ (ii) $\begin{pmatrix} 2 & -7 & -4 \\ 3 & 1 & 4 \\ 6 & -8 & 1 \end{pmatrix}$ (iii) $\begin{pmatrix} 0 & 0 & 1 \\ 0 & 1 & 1 \\ 1 & 1 & 1 \end{pmatrix}$

7.30.   (i) $\begin{pmatrix} 1 & 0 & 0 \\ 0 & 2 & 1 \\ 0 & 0 & 2 \end{pmatrix}$ (ii) $\begin{pmatrix} 0 & -1 \\ 1 & 0 \end{pmatrix}$ (iii) $\begin{pmatrix} 5 & 1 & 0 \\ 0 & 5 & 2 \\ 0 & 0 & 5 \end{pmatrix}$ (iv) $\begin{pmatrix} 0 & 1 & 0 & 0 \\ 0 & 0 & 0 & 0 \\ 0 & 0 & 0 & -3 \\ 0 & 0 & 3 & 0 \end{pmatrix}$

7.31.   (i) $\begin{pmatrix} 1 & 0 \\ 0 & -1 \end{pmatrix}$ (ii) $\begin{pmatrix} -3 & 4 \\ -2 & -3 \end{pmatrix}$

7.32.   (i) $\begin{pmatrix} a & 0 & b & 0 \\ 0 & a & 0 & b \\ c & 0 & d & 0 \\ 0 & c & 0 & d \end{pmatrix}$ (ii) $\begin{pmatrix} a & c & 0 & 0 \\ b & d & 0 & 0 \\ 0 & 0 & a & c \\ 0 & 0 & b & d \end{pmatrix}$ (iii) $\begin{pmatrix} 0 & -c & b & 0 \\ -b & a-d & 0 & b \\ c & 0 & d-a & -c \\ 0 & c & -b & 0 \end{pmatrix}$

7.34. $P = \begin{pmatrix} 1 & 2 \\ 2 & 3 \end{pmatrix}$, $Q = \begin{pmatrix} -3 & 2 \\ 2 & -1 \end{pmatrix}$

7.35. $P = \begin{pmatrix} 3 & 5 \\ -1 & -2 \end{pmatrix}$, $Q = \begin{pmatrix} 2 & 5 \\ -1 & -3 \end{pmatrix}$

7.36. $\begin{pmatrix} 8 & 11 \\ -2 & -1 \end{pmatrix}$

7.37. $P = \begin{pmatrix} 1 & 1 \\ 1 & 2 \end{pmatrix}$, $Q = \begin{pmatrix} 2 & -1 \\ -1 & 1 \end{pmatrix}$

7.41.   (i) $\begin{pmatrix} 2 & -4 & 9 \\ 5 & 3 & -2 \end{pmatrix}$ (ii) $\begin{pmatrix} 3 & 4 \\ 5 & -2 \\ 1 & 7 \\ 4 & 0 \end{pmatrix}$ (iii) $(2, 3, -7, -1)$ (iv) $\begin{pmatrix} 3 \\ 5 \end{pmatrix}$

7.42.   (i) $\begin{pmatrix} 3 & 11 & 5 \\ -1 & -8 & -3 \end{pmatrix}$

Chapter 8

Determinants

INTRODUCTION

To every square matrix A over a field K there is assigned a specific scalar called the determinant of A; it is usually denoted by

$$\det(A) \quad \text{or} \quad |A|$$

This determinant function was first discovered in the investigation of systems of linear equations. We shall see in the succeeding chapters that the determinant is an indispensable tool in investigating and obtaining properties of a linear operator.

We comment that the definition of the determinant and most of its properties also apply in the case where the entries of a matrix come from a ring (see Appendix B).

We shall begin the chapter with a discussion of *permutations*, which is necessary for the definition of the determinant.

PERMUTATIONS

A one-to-one mapping σ of the set $\{1, 2, \ldots, n\}$ onto itself is called a *permutation*. We denote the permutation σ by

$$\sigma = \begin{pmatrix} 1 & 2 & \ldots & n \\ j_1 & j_2 & \ldots & j_n \end{pmatrix} \quad \text{or} \quad \sigma = j_1 j_2 \ldots j_n, \qquad \text{where} \quad j_i = \sigma(i)$$

Observe that since σ is one-to-one and onto, the sequence $j_1 j_2 \ldots j_n$ is simply a rearrangement of the numbers $1, 2, \ldots, n$. We remark that the number of such permutations is $n!$, and that the set of them is usually denoted by S_n. We also remark that if $\sigma \in S_n$, then the inverse mapping $\sigma^{-1} \in S_n$; and if $\sigma, \tau \in S_n$, then the composition mapping $\sigma \circ \tau \in S_n$. In particular, the identity mapping

$$\epsilon = \sigma \circ \sigma^{-1} = \sigma^{-1} \circ \sigma$$

belongs to S_n. (In fact, $\epsilon = 1 2 \ldots n$.)

> **Example 8.1:** There are $2! = 2 \cdot 1 = 2$ permutations in S_2: 12 and 21.

> **Example 8.2:** There are $3! = 3 \cdot 2 \cdot 1 = 6$ permutations in S_3: 123, 132, 213, 231, 312, 321.

Consider an arbitrary permutation σ in S_n: $\sigma = j_1 j_2 \ldots j_n$. We say σ is *even* or *odd* according as to whether there is an even or odd number of pairs (i, k) for which

$$i > k \quad \text{but} \quad i \text{ precedes } k \text{ in } \sigma \tag{*}$$

We then define the *sign* or *parity* of σ, written sgn σ, by

$$\text{sgn } \sigma = \begin{cases} 1 & \text{if } \sigma \text{ is even} \\ -1 & \text{if } \sigma \text{ is odd} \end{cases}$$

Example 8.3:   Consider the permutation $\sigma = 35142$ in S_5.

3 and 5 precede and are greater than 1; hence (3, 1) and (5, 1) satisfy (*).

3, 5 and 4 precede and are greater than 2; hence (3, 2), (5, 2) and (4, 2) satisfy (*).

5 precedes and is greater than 4; hence (5, 4) satisfies (*).

Since exactly six pairs satisfy (*), σ is even and sgn $\sigma = 1$.

Example 8.4:   The *identity permutation* $\epsilon = 1\,2\,\ldots\,n$ is even since no pair can satisfy (*).

Example 8.5:   In S_2, 12 is even, and 21 is odd.

In S_3, 123, 231 and 312 are even, and 132, 213 and 321 are odd.

Example 8.6:   Let τ be the permutation which interchanges two numbers i and j and leaves the other numbers fixed:

$$\tau(i) = j, \quad \tau(j) = i, \quad \tau(k) = k, \quad k \neq i, j$$

We call τ a *transposition*.   If $i < j$, then

$$\tau = 1\,2\,\ldots\,(i-1)\,j\,(i+1)\,\ldots\,(j-1)\,i\,(j+1)\,\ldots\,n$$

There are $2(j - i - 1) + 1$ pairs satisfying (*):

$$(j, i),\ (j, x),\ (x, i), \quad \text{where } x = i{+}1, \ldots, j{-}1$$

Thus the transposition τ is odd.

DETERMINANT

Let $A = (a_{ij})$ be an n-square matrix over a field K:

$$A \;=\; \begin{pmatrix} a_{11} & a_{12} & \ldots & a_{1n} \\ a_{21} & a_{22} & \ldots & a_{2n} \\ \cdots\cdots\cdots\cdots\cdots\cdots \\ a_{n1} & a_{n2} & \ldots & a_{nn} \end{pmatrix}$$

Consider a product of n elements of A such that one and only one element comes from each row and one and only one element comes from each column.   Such a product can be written in the form

$$a_{1j_1}\, a_{2j_2}\, \ldots\, a_{nj_n}$$

that is, where the factors come from successive rows and so the first subscripts are in the natural order $1, 2, \ldots, n$.   Now since the factors come from different columns, the sequence of second subscripts form a permutation $\sigma = j_1 j_2 \ldots j_n$ in S_n.   Conversely, each permutation in S_n determines a product of the above form.   Thus the matrix A contains $n!$ such products.

Definition: The determinant of the n-square matrix $A = (a_{ij})$, denoted by $\det(A)$ or $|A|$, is the following sum which is summed over all permutations $\sigma = j_1 j_2 \ldots j_n$ in S_n:

$$|A| \;=\; \sum_{\sigma} (\text{sgn } \sigma)\, a_{1j_1}\, a_{2j_2}\, \ldots\, a_{nj_n}$$

That is,
$$|A| \;=\; \sum_{\sigma \in S_n} (\text{sgn } \sigma)\, a_{1\sigma(1)}\, a_{2\sigma(2)}\, \ldots\, a_{n\sigma(n)}$$

The determinant of the n-square matrix A is said to be of *order n* and is frequently denoted by

$$\begin{vmatrix} a_{11} & a_{12} & \ldots & a_{1n} \\ a_{21} & a_{22} & \ldots & a_{2n} \\ \cdots\cdots\cdots\cdots\cdots\cdots \\ a_{n1} & a_{n2} & \ldots & a_{nn} \end{vmatrix}$$

We emphasize that a square array of scalars enclosed by straight lines is not a matrix but rather the scalar that the determinant assigns to the matrix formed by the array of scalars.

Example 8.7: The determinant of a 1×1 matrix $A = (a_{11})$ is the scalar a_{11} itself: $|A| = a_{11}$. (We note that the one permutation in S_1 is even.)

Example 8.8: In S_2, the permutation 12 is even and the permutation 21 is odd. Hence

$$\begin{vmatrix} a_{11} & a_{12} \\ a_{21} & a_{22} \end{vmatrix} = a_{11}a_{22} - a_{12}a_{21}$$

Thus $\begin{vmatrix} 4 & -5 \\ -1 & -2 \end{vmatrix} = 4(-2) - (-5)(-1) = -13$ and $\begin{vmatrix} a & b \\ c & d \end{vmatrix} = ad - bc$.

Example 8.9: In S_3, the permutations 123, 231 and 312 are even, and the permutations 321, 213 and 132 are odd. Hence

$$\begin{vmatrix} a_{11} & a_{12} & a_{13} \\ a_{21} & a_{22} & a_{23} \\ a_{31} & a_{32} & a_{33} \end{vmatrix} = \begin{matrix} a_{11}a_{22}a_{33} + a_{12}a_{23}a_{31} + a_{13}a_{21}a_{32} \\ - a_{13}a_{22}a_{31} - a_{12}a_{21}a_{33} - a_{11}a_{23}a_{32} \end{matrix}$$

This may be written as:

$$a_{11}(a_{22}a_{33} - a_{23}a_{32}) - a_{12}(a_{21}a_{33} - a_{23}a_{31}) + a_{13}(a_{21}a_{32} - a_{22}a_{31})$$

or

$$a_{11}\begin{vmatrix} a_{22} & a_{23} \\ a_{32} & a_{33} \end{vmatrix} - a_{12}\begin{vmatrix} a_{21} & a_{23} \\ a_{31} & a_{33} \end{vmatrix} + a_{13}\begin{vmatrix} a_{21} & a_{22} \\ a_{31} & a_{32} \end{vmatrix}$$

which is a linear combination of three determinants of order two whose coefficients (with alternating signs) form the first row of the given matrix. Note that each 2×2 matrix can be obtained by deleting, in the original matrix, the row and column containing its coefficient:

$$a_{11}\begin{vmatrix} a_{11} & a_{12} & a_{13} \\ a_{21} & a_{22} & a_{23} \\ a_{31} & a_{32} & a_{33} \end{vmatrix} - a_{12}\begin{vmatrix} a_{11} & a_{12} & a_{13} \\ a_{21} & a_{22} & a_{23} \\ a_{31} & a_{32} & a_{33} \end{vmatrix} + a_{13}\begin{vmatrix} a_{11} & a_{12} & a_{13} \\ a_{21} & a_{22} & a_{23} \\ a_{31} & a_{32} & a_{33} \end{vmatrix}$$

Example 8.10: (i) $\begin{vmatrix} 2 & 3 & 4 \\ 5 & 6 & 7 \\ 8 & 9 & 1 \end{vmatrix} = 2\begin{vmatrix} 6 & 7 \\ 9 & 1 \end{vmatrix} - 3\begin{vmatrix} 5 & 7 \\ 8 & 1 \end{vmatrix} + 4\begin{vmatrix} 5 & 6 \\ 8 & 9 \end{vmatrix}$

$$= 2(6 - 63) - 3(5 - 56) + 4(45 - 48) = 27$$

(ii) $\begin{vmatrix} 2 & 3 & -4 \\ 0 & -4 & 2 \\ 1 & -1 & 5 \end{vmatrix} = 2\begin{vmatrix} -4 & 2 \\ -1 & 5 \end{vmatrix} - 3\begin{vmatrix} 0 & 2 \\ 1 & 5 \end{vmatrix} + (-4)\begin{vmatrix} 0 & -4 \\ 1 & -1 \end{vmatrix}$

$$= 2(-20 + 2) - 3(0 - 2) - 4(0 + 4) = -46$$

As n increases, the number of terms in the determinant becomes astronomical. Accordingly, we use indirect methods to evaluate determinants rather than its definition. In fact we prove a number of properties about determinants which will permit us to shorten the computation considerably. In particular, we show that a determinant of order n is equal to a linear combination of determinants of order $n - 1$ as in case $n = 3$ above.

PROPERTIES OF DETERMINANTS

We now list basic properties of the determinant.

Theorem 8.1: The determinant of a matrix A and its transpose A^t are equal: $|A| = |A^t|$.

By this theorem, any theorem about the determinant of a matrix A which concerns the rows of A will have an analogous theorem concerning the columns of A.

The next theorem gives certain cases for which the determinant can be obtained immediately.

Theorem 8.2:   Let A be a square matrix.
  (i)   If A has a row (column) of zeros, then $|A| = 0$.
  (ii) If A has two identical rows (columns), then $|A| = 0$.
  (iii) If A is triangular, i.e. A has zeros above or below the diagonal, then $|A| = $ product of diagonal elements. Thus in particular, $|I| = 1$ where I is the identity matrix.

The next theorem shows how the determinant of a matrix is affected by the "elementary" operations.

Theorem 8.3:   Let B be the matrix obtained from a matrix A by
  (i)   multiplying a row (column) of A by a scalar k; then $|B| = k|A|$.
  (ii) interchanging two rows (columns) of $|A|$; then $|B| = -|A|$.
  (iii) adding a multiple of a row (column) of A to another; then $|B| = |A|$.

We now state two of the most important and useful theorems on determinants.

Theorem 8.4:   Let A be any n-square matrix. Then the following are equivalent:
  (i) A is invertible, i.e. A has an inverse A^{-1}.
  (ii) A is nonsingular, i.e. $AX = 0$ has only the zero solution, or rank $A = n$, or the rows (columns) of A are linearly independent.
  (iii) The determinant of A is not zero: $|A| \neq 0$.

Theorem 8.5:   The determinant is a multiplicative function. That is, the determinant of a product of two matrices A and B is equal to the product of their determinants: $|AB| = |A||B|$.

We shall prove the above two theorems using the theory of elementary matrices (see page 56) and the following lemma.

Lemma 8.6:   Let E be an elementary matrix. Then, for any matrix A, $|EA| = |E||A|$.

We comment that one can also prove the preceding two theorems directly without resorting to the theory of elementary matrices.

MINORS AND COFACTORS

Consider an n-square matrix $A = (a_{ij})$. Let M_{ij} denote the $(n-1)$-square submatrix of A obtained by deleting its ith row and jth column. The determinant $|M_{ij}|$ is called the *minor* of the element a_{ij} of A, and we define the *cofactor* of a_{ij}, denoted by A_{ij}, to be the "signed" minor:

$$A_{ij} = (-1)^{i+j}|M_{ij}|$$

Note that the "signs" $(-1)^{i+j}$ accompanying the minors form a chessboard pattern with +'s on the main diagonal:

$$\begin{pmatrix} + & - & + & - & \cdots \\ - & + & - & + & \cdots \\ + & - & + & - & \cdots \\ \cdots\cdots\cdots\cdots\cdots\cdots \end{pmatrix}$$

We emphasize that M_{ij} denotes a matrix whereas A_{ij} denotes a scalar.

Example 8.11: Let $A = \begin{pmatrix} 2 & 3 & 4 \\ 5 & 6 & 7 \\ 8 & 9 & 1 \end{pmatrix}$. Then $M_{23} = \begin{pmatrix} 2 & 3 & 4 \\ 5 & 6 & 7 \\ 8 & 9 & 1 \end{pmatrix} = \begin{pmatrix} 2 & 3 \\ 8 & 9 \end{pmatrix}$ and

$$A_{23} = (-1)^{2+3} \begin{vmatrix} 2 & 3 \\ 8 & 9 \end{vmatrix} = -(18-24) = 6$$

The following theorem applies.

Theorem 8.7: The determinant of the matrix $A = (a_{ij})$ is equal to the sum of the products obtained by multiplying the elements of any row (column) by their respective cofactors:

$$|A| = a_{i1}A_{i1} + a_{i2}A_{i2} + \cdots + a_{in}A_{in} = \sum_{j=1}^{n} a_{ij}A_{ij}$$

and

$$|A| = a_{1j}A_{1j} + a_{2j}A_{2j} + \cdots + a_{nj}A_{nj} = \sum_{i=1}^{n} a_{ij}A_{ij}$$

The above formulae, called the Laplace expansions of the determinant of A by the ith row and the jth column respectively, offer a method of simplifying the computation of $|A|$. That is, by adding a multiple of a row (column) to another row (column) we can reduce A to a matrix containing a row or column with one entry 1 and the others 0. Expanding by this row or column reduces the computation of $|A|$ to the computation of a determinant of order one less than that of $|A|$.

Example 8.12: Compute the determinant of $A = \begin{pmatrix} 5 & 4 & 2 & 1 \\ 2 & 3 & 1 & -2 \\ -5 & -7 & -3 & 9 \\ 1 & -2 & -1 & 4 \end{pmatrix}$.

Note that a 1 appears in the second row, third column. Perform the following operations on A, where R_i denotes the ith row:

(i) add $-2R_2$ to R_1,   (ii) add $3R_2$ to R_3,   (iii) add $1R_2$ to R_4.

By Theorem 8.3(iii), the value of the determinant does not change by these operations; that is,

$$|A| = \begin{vmatrix} 5 & 4 & 2 & 1 \\ 2 & 3 & 1 & -2 \\ -5 & -7 & -3 & 9 \\ 1 & -2 & -1 & 4 \end{vmatrix} = \begin{vmatrix} 1 & -2 & 0 & 5 \\ 2 & 3 & 1 & -2 \\ 1 & 2 & 0 & 3 \\ 3 & 1 & 0 & 2 \end{vmatrix}$$

Now if we expand by the third column, we may neglect all terms which contain 0. Thus

$$|A| = (-1)^{2+3} \begin{vmatrix} 1 & -2 & 0 & 5 \\ 2 & 3 & 1 & -2 \\ 1 & 2 & 0 & 3 \\ 3 & 1 & 0 & 2 \end{vmatrix} = -\begin{vmatrix} 1 & -2 & 5 \\ 1 & 2 & 3 \\ 3 & 1 & 2 \end{vmatrix}$$

$$= -\left\{ \begin{vmatrix} 2 & 3 \\ 1 & 2 \end{vmatrix} - (-2)\begin{vmatrix} 1 & 3 \\ 3 & 2 \end{vmatrix} + 5\begin{vmatrix} 1 & 2 \\ 3 & 1 \end{vmatrix} \right\} = 38$$

CLASSICAL ADJOINT

Consider an n-square matrix $A = (a_{ij})$ over a field K:

$$A = \begin{pmatrix} a_{11} & a_{12} & \ldots & a_{1n} \\ a_{21} & a_{22} & \ldots & a_{2n} \\ \cdots\cdots\cdots\cdots\cdots\cdots \\ a_{n1} & a_{n2} & \ldots & a_{nn} \end{pmatrix}$$

The transpose of the matrix of cofactors of the elements a_{ij} of A, denoted by adj A, is called the *classical adjoint* of A:

$$\text{adj } A \;=\; \begin{pmatrix} A_{11} & A_{21} & \dots & A_{n1} \\ A_{12} & A_{22} & \dots & A_{n1} \\ \multicolumn{4}{c}{\dotfill} \\ A_{1n} & A_{2n} & \dots & A_{nn} \end{pmatrix}$$

We say "classical adjoint" instead of simply "adjoint" because the term adjoint will be used in Chapter 13 for an entirely different concept.

Example 8.13: Let $A = \begin{pmatrix} 2 & 3 & -4 \\ 0 & -4 & 2 \\ 1 & -1 & 5 \end{pmatrix}$. The cofactors of the nine elements of A are

$$A_{11} = + \begin{vmatrix} -4 & 2 \\ -1 & 5 \end{vmatrix} = -18, \quad A_{12} = - \begin{vmatrix} 0 & 2 \\ 1 & 5 \end{vmatrix} = 2, \quad A_{13} = + \begin{vmatrix} 0 & -4 \\ 1 & -1 \end{vmatrix} = 4$$

$$A_{21} = - \begin{vmatrix} 3 & -4 \\ -1 & 5 \end{vmatrix} = -11, \quad A_{22} = + \begin{vmatrix} 2 & -4 \\ 1 & 5 \end{vmatrix} = 14, \quad A_{23} = - \begin{vmatrix} 2 & 3 \\ 1 & -1 \end{vmatrix} = 5$$

$$A_{31} = + \begin{vmatrix} 3 & -4 \\ -4 & 2 \end{vmatrix} = -10, \quad A_{32} = - \begin{vmatrix} 2 & -4 \\ 0 & 2 \end{vmatrix} = -4, \quad A_{33} = + \begin{vmatrix} 2 & 3 \\ 0 & -4 \end{vmatrix} = -8$$

We form the transpose of the above matrix of cofactors to obtain the classical adjoint of A:

$$\text{adj } A \;=\; \begin{pmatrix} -18 & -11 & -10 \\ 2 & 14 & -4 \\ 4 & 5 & -8 \end{pmatrix}$$

Theorem 8.8: For any square matrix A,

$$A \cdot (\text{adj } A) = (\text{adj } A) \cdot A = |A| I$$

where I is the identity matrix. Thus, if $|A| \neq 0$,

$$A^{-1} = \frac{1}{|A|} (\text{adj } A)$$

Observe that the above theorem gives us an important method of obtaining the inverse of a given matrix.

Example 8.14: Consider the matrix A of the preceding example for which $|A| = -46$. We have

$$A\,(\text{adj } A) = \begin{pmatrix} 2 & 3 & -4 \\ 0 & -4 & 2 \\ 1 & -1 & 5 \end{pmatrix} \begin{pmatrix} -18 & -11 & -10 \\ 2 & 14 & -4 \\ 4 & 5 & -8 \end{pmatrix} = \begin{pmatrix} -46 & 0 & 0 \\ 0 & -46 & 0 \\ 0 & 0 & -46 \end{pmatrix} = -46 \begin{pmatrix} 1 & 0 & 0 \\ 0 & 1 & 0 \\ 0 & 0 & 1 \end{pmatrix}$$

$$= -46I = |A|\,I$$

We also have, by Theorem 8.8,

$$A^{-1} = \frac{1}{|A|} (\text{adj } A) = \begin{pmatrix} -18/-46 & -11/-46 & -10/-46 \\ 2/-46 & 14/-46 & -4/-46 \\ 4/-46 & 5/-46 & -8/-46 \end{pmatrix} = \begin{pmatrix} 9/23 & 11/46 & 5/23 \\ -1/23 & -7/23 & 2/23 \\ -2/23 & -5/46 & 4/23 \end{pmatrix}$$

APPLICATIONS TO LINEAR EQUATIONS

Consider a system of n linear equations in n unknowns:

$$a_{11}x_1 + a_{12}x_2 + \cdots + a_{1n}x_n = b_1$$
$$a_{21}x_1 + a_{22}x_2 + \cdots + a_{2n}x_n = b_2$$
$$\dotfill$$
$$a_{n1}x_1 + a_{n2}x_2 + \cdots + a_{nn}x_n = b_n$$

Let Δ denote the determinant of the matrix $A = (a_{ij})$ of coefficients: $\Delta = |A|$. Also, let Δ_i denote the determinant of the matrix obtained by replacing the ith column of A by the column of constant terms. The fundamental relationship between determinants and the solution of the above system follows.

Theorem 8.9:   The above system has a unique solution if and only if $\Delta \neq 0$. In this case the unique solution is given by

$$x_1 = \frac{\Delta_1}{\Delta}, \quad x_2 = \frac{\Delta_2}{\Delta}, \quad \ldots, \quad x_n = \frac{\Delta_n}{\Delta}$$

The above theorem is known as "Cramer's rule" for solving systems of linear equations. We emphasize that the theorem only refers to a system with the same number of equations as unknowns, and that it only gives the solution when $\Delta \neq 0$. In fact, if $\Delta = 0$ the theorem does not tell whether or not the system has a solution. However, in the case of a homogeneous system we have the following useful result.

Theorem 8.10:   The homogeneous system $Ax = 0$ has a nonzero solution if and only if $\Delta = |A| = 0$.

Example 8.15:   Solve, using determinants: $\begin{cases} 2x - 3y = 7 \\ 3x + 5y = 1 \end{cases}$.

First compute the determinant Δ of the matrix of coefficients:

$$\Delta = \begin{vmatrix} 2 & -3 \\ 3 & 5 \end{vmatrix} = 10 + 9 = 19$$

Since $\Delta \neq 0$, the system has a unique solution. We also have

$$\Delta_x = \begin{vmatrix} 7 & -3 \\ 1 & 5 \end{vmatrix} = 38, \quad \Delta_y = \begin{vmatrix} 2 & 7 \\ 3 & 1 \end{vmatrix} = -19$$

Accordingly, the unique solution of the system is

$$x = \frac{\Delta_x}{\Delta} = \frac{38}{19} = 2, \quad y = \frac{\Delta_y}{\Delta} = \frac{-19}{19} = -1$$

We remark that the preceding theorem is of interest more for theoretical and historical reasons than for practical reasons. The previous method of solving systems of linear equations, i.e. by reducing a system to echelon form, is usually much more efficient than by using determinants.

DETERMINANT OF A LINEAR OPERATOR

Using the multiplicative property of the determinant (Theorem 8.5), we obtain

Theorem 8.11:   Suppose A and B are similar matrices. Then $|A| = |B|$.

Now suppose T is an arbitrary linear operator on a vector space V. We define the determinant of T, written $\det(T)$, by

$$\det(T) = |[T]_e|$$

where $[T]_e$ is the matrix of T in a basis $\{e_i\}$. By the above theorem this definition is independent of the particular basis that is chosen.

The next theorem follows from the analogous theorems on matrices.

Theorem 8.12:   Let T and S be linear operators on a vector space V. Then

  (i) $\det(S \circ T) = \det(S) \cdot \det(T)$,

  (ii) T is invertible if and only if $\det(T) \neq 0$.

We also remark that $\det(1_V) = 1$ where 1_V is the identity mapping, and that $\det(T^{-1}) = \det(T)^{-1}$ if T is invertible.

Example 8.16:   Let T be the linear operator on $\mathbf{R}^3$ defined by

$$T(x, y, z) = (2x - 4y + z, \; x - 2y + 3z, \; 5x + y - z)$$

The matrix of T in the usual basis of $\mathbf{R}^3$ is $[T] = \begin{pmatrix} 2 & -4 & 1 \\ 1 & -2 & 3 \\ 5 & 1 & -1 \end{pmatrix}$.   Then

$$\det(T) = \begin{vmatrix} 2 & -4 & 1 \\ 1 & -2 & 3 \\ 5 & 1 & -1 \end{vmatrix} = 2(2-3) + 4(-1-15) + 1(1+10) = -55$$

MULTILINEARITY AND DETERMINANTS

Let $\mathcal{A}$ denote the set of all n-square matrices A over a field K. We may view A as an n-tuple consisting of its row vectors $A_1, A_2, \ldots, A_n$:

$$A = (A_1, A_2, \ldots, A_n)$$

Hence $\mathcal{A}$ may be viewed as the set of n-tuples of n-tuples in K:

$$\mathcal{A} = (K^n)^n$$

The following definitions apply.

Definition: A function $D: \mathcal{A} \to K$ is said to be *multilinear* if it is linear in each of the components; that is:

(i)   if row $A_i = B + C$, then

$$D(A) = D(\ldots, B+C, \ldots) = D(\ldots, B, \ldots) + D(\ldots, C, \ldots);$$

(ii)   if row $A_i = kB$ where $k \in K$, then

$$D(A) = D(\ldots, kB, \ldots) = k\, D(\ldots, B, \ldots).$$

We also say *n-linear* for multilinear if there are n components.

Definition: A function $D: \mathcal{A} \to K$ is said to be *alternating* if $D(A) = 0$ whenever A has two identical rows:

$$D(A_1, A_2, \ldots, A_n) = 0 \qquad \text{whenever} \quad A_i = A_j, \; i \neq j$$

We have the following basic result; here I denotes the identity matrix.

Theorem 8.13:   There exists a unique function $D: \mathcal{A} \to K$ such that:

(i) D is multilinear,   (ii) D is alternating,   (iii) $D(I) = 1$.

This function D is none other than the determinant function; that is, for any matrix $A \in \mathcal{A}$, $D(A) = |A|$.

Solved Problems

COMPUTATION OF DETERMINANTS

8.1. Evaluate the determinant of each matrix: (i) $\begin{pmatrix} 3 & -2 \\ 4 & 5 \end{pmatrix}$,   (ii) $\begin{pmatrix} a-b & a \\ a & a+b \end{pmatrix}$.

(i) $\begin{vmatrix} 3 & -2 \\ 4 & 5 \end{vmatrix} = 3 \cdot 5 - (-2) \cdot 4 = 23$.   (ii) $\begin{vmatrix} a-b & a \\ a & a+b \end{vmatrix} = (a-b)(a+b) - a \cdot a = -b^2$.

8.2. Determine those values of k for which $\begin{vmatrix} k & k \\ 4 & 2k \end{vmatrix} = 0$.

$\begin{vmatrix} k & k \\ 4 & 2k \end{vmatrix} = 2k^2 - 4k = 0$, or $2k(k-2) = 0$. Hence $k = 0$; and $k = 2$. That is, if $k = 0$ or $k = 2$, the determinant is zero.

8.3. Compute the determinant of each matrix:

(i) $\begin{pmatrix} 1 & 2 & 3 \\ 4 & -2 & 3 \\ 2 & 5 & -1 \end{pmatrix}$,   (ii) $\begin{pmatrix} 2 & 0 & 1 \\ 4 & 2 & -3 \\ 5 & 3 & 1 \end{pmatrix}$,   (iii) $\begin{pmatrix} 2 & 0 & 1 \\ 3 & 2 & -3 \\ -1 & -3 & 5 \end{pmatrix}$,   (iv) $\begin{pmatrix} 1 & 0 & 0 \\ 3 & 2 & -4 \\ 4 & 1 & 3 \end{pmatrix}$.

(i) $\begin{vmatrix} 1 & 2 & 3 \\ 4 & -2 & 3 \\ 2 & 5 & -1 \end{vmatrix} = 1 \begin{vmatrix} -2 & 3 \\ 5 & -1 \end{vmatrix} - 2 \begin{vmatrix} 4 & 3 \\ 2 & -1 \end{vmatrix} + 3 \begin{vmatrix} 4 & -2 \\ 2 & 5 \end{vmatrix}$

$\qquad = 1(2 - 15) - 2(-4 - 6) + 3(20 + 4) = 79$

(ii) $\begin{vmatrix} 2 & 0 & 1 \\ 4 & 2 & -3 \\ 5 & 3 & 1 \end{vmatrix} = 2 \begin{vmatrix} 2 & -3 \\ 3 & 1 \end{vmatrix} - 0 \begin{vmatrix} 4 & -3 \\ 5 & 1 \end{vmatrix} + 1 \begin{vmatrix} 4 & 2 \\ 5 & 3 \end{vmatrix} = 24$

(iii) $\begin{vmatrix} 2 & 0 & 1 \\ 3 & 2 & -3 \\ -1 & -3 & 5 \end{vmatrix} = 2(10 - 9) + 1(-9 + 2) = -5$

(iv) $\begin{vmatrix} 1 & 0 & 0 \\ 3 & 2 & -4 \\ 4 & 1 & 3 \end{vmatrix} = 1(6 + 4) = 10$

8.4. Consider the 3-square matrix $A = \begin{pmatrix} a_1 & b_1 & c_1 \\ a_2 & b_2 & c_2 \\ a_3 & b_3 & c_3 \end{pmatrix}$. Show that the diagrams below can

be used to obtain the determinant of A:

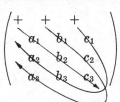 ,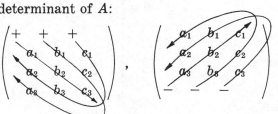

Form the product of each of the three numbers joined by an arrow in the diagram on the left, and precede each product by a plus sign as follows:

$$+\ a_1 b_2 c_3\ +\ b_1 c_2 a_3\ +\ c_1 a_2 b_3$$

Now form the product of each of the three numbers joined by an arrow in the diagram on the right, and precede each product by a minus sign as follows:

$$- a_3 b_2 c_1 - b_3 c_2 a_1 - c_3 a_2 b_1$$

Then the determinant of A is precisely the sum of the above two expressions:

$$|A| = \begin{vmatrix} a_1 & b_1 & c_1 \\ a_2 & b_2 & c_2 \\ a_3 & b_3 & c_3 \end{vmatrix} = a_1 b_2 c_3 + b_1 c_2 a_3 + c_1 a_2 b_3 - a_3 b_2 c_1 - b_3 c_2 a_1 - c_3 a_2 b_1$$

The above method of computing $|A|$ does not hold for determinants of order greater than 3.

8.5. Evaluate the determinant of each matrix:

(i) $\begin{pmatrix} 2 & 0 & -1 \\ 3 & 0 & 2 \\ 4 & -3 & 7 \end{pmatrix}$,   (ii) $\begin{pmatrix} a & b & c \\ c & a & b \\ b & c & a \end{pmatrix}$,   (iii) $\begin{pmatrix} 3 & 2 & -4 \\ 1 & 0 & -2 \\ -2 & 3 & 3 \end{pmatrix}$

(i)   Expand the determinant by the second column, neglecting terms containing a 0:

$$\begin{vmatrix} 2 & 0 & -1 \\ 3 & 0 & 2 \\ 4 & -3 & 7 \end{vmatrix} = -(-3)\begin{vmatrix} 2 & -1 \\ 3 & 2 \end{vmatrix} = 3(4+3) = 21$$

(ii)   Use the method of the preceding problem:

$$\begin{vmatrix} a & b & c \\ c & a & b \\ b & c & a \end{vmatrix} = a^3 + b^3 + c^3 - abc - abc - abc = a^3 + b^3 + c^3 - 3abc$$

(iii)   Add twice the first column to the third column, and then expand by the second row:

$$\begin{vmatrix} 3 & 2 & -4 \\ 1 & 0 & -2 \\ -2 & 3 & 3 \end{vmatrix} = \begin{vmatrix} 3 & 2 & -4+2(3) \\ 1 & 0 & -2+2(1) \\ -2 & 3 & 3+2(-2) \end{vmatrix} = \begin{vmatrix} 3 & 2 & 2 \\ 1 & 0 & 0 \\ -2 & 3 & -1 \end{vmatrix} = -1\begin{vmatrix} 2 & 2 \\ 3 & -1 \end{vmatrix} = 8$$

8.6. Evaluate the determinant of $A = \begin{pmatrix} \frac{1}{2} & -1 & -\frac{1}{3} \\ \frac{3}{4} & \frac{1}{2} & -1 \\ 1 & -4 & 1 \end{pmatrix}$.

First multiply the first row by 6 and the second row by 4.   Then

$$6 \cdot 4 |A| = 24|A| = \begin{vmatrix} 3 & -6 & -2 \\ 3 & 2 & -4 \\ 1 & -4 & 1 \end{vmatrix} = \begin{vmatrix} 3 & -6+4(3) & -2-(3) \\ 1 & 2+4(3) & -4-(3) \\ 1 & -4+4(1) & 1-(1) \end{vmatrix} = \begin{vmatrix} 3 & 6 & -5 \\ 1 & 14 & -7 \\ 1 & 0 & 0 \end{vmatrix}$$

$$= +\begin{vmatrix} 6 & -5 \\ 14 & -7 \end{vmatrix} = 28, \quad \text{and } |A| = 28/24 = 7/6.$$

8.7. Evaluate the determinant of $A = \begin{pmatrix} 2 & 5 & -3 & -2 \\ -2 & -3 & 2 & -5 \\ 1 & 3 & -2 & 2 \\ -1 & -6 & 4 & 3 \end{pmatrix}$.

Note that a 1 appears in the third row, first column. Apply the following operations on A (where R_i denotes the ith row): (i) add $-2R_3$ to R_1, (ii) add $2R_3$ to R_2, (iii) add $1R_3$ to R_4. Thus

$$|A| \;=\; \begin{vmatrix} 2 & 5 & -3 & -2 \\ -2 & -3 & 2 & -5 \\ 1 & 3 & -2 & 2 \\ -1 & -6 & 4 & 3 \end{vmatrix} \;=\; \begin{vmatrix} 0 & -1 & 1 & -6 \\ 0 & 3 & -2 & -1 \\ 1 & 3 & -2 & 2 \\ 0 & -3 & 2 & 5 \end{vmatrix} \;=\; + \begin{vmatrix} -1 & 1 & -6 \\ 3 & -2 & -1 \\ -3 & 2 & 5 \end{vmatrix}$$

$$=\; \begin{vmatrix} -1+1 & 1 & -6+6(1) \\ 3-2 & -2 & -1+6(-2) \\ -3+2 & 2 & 5+6(2) \end{vmatrix} \;=\; \begin{vmatrix} 0 & 1 & 0 \\ 1 & -2 & -13 \\ -1 & 2 & 17 \end{vmatrix} \;=\; - \begin{vmatrix} 1 & -13 \\ -1 & 17 \end{vmatrix} \;=\; -4$$

8.8. Evaluate the determinant of $A \;=\; \begin{pmatrix} 3 & -2 & -5 & 4 \\ -5 & 2 & 8 & -5 \\ -2 & 4 & 7 & -3 \\ 2 & -3 & -5 & 8 \end{pmatrix}$.

First reduce A to a matrix which has 1 as an entry, such as adding twice the first row to the second row, and then proceed as in the preceding problem.

$$|A| \;=\; \begin{vmatrix} 3 & -2 & -5 & 4 \\ -5 & 2 & 8 & -5 \\ -2 & 4 & 7 & -3 \\ 2 & -3 & -5 & 8 \end{vmatrix} \;=\; \begin{vmatrix} 3 & -2 & -5 & 4 \\ -5+2(3) & 2+2(-2) & 8+2(-5) & -5+2(4) \\ -2 & 4 & 7 & -3 \\ 2 & -3 & -5 & 8 \end{vmatrix}$$

$$=\; \begin{vmatrix} 3 & -2 & -5 & 4 \\ 1 & -2 & -2 & 3 \\ -2 & 4 & 7 & -3 \\ 2 & -3 & -5 & 8 \end{vmatrix} \;=\; \begin{vmatrix} 3 & -2+2(3) & -5+2(3) & 4-3(3) \\ 1 & -2+2(1) & -2+2(1) & 3-3(1) \\ -2 & 4+2(-2) & 7+2(-2) & -3-3(-2) \\ 2 & -3+2(2) & -5+2(2) & 8-3(2) \end{vmatrix}$$

$$=\; \begin{vmatrix} 3 & 4 & 1 & -5 \\ 1 & 0 & 0 & 0 \\ -2 & 0 & 3 & 3 \\ 2 & 1 & -1 & 2 \end{vmatrix} \;=\; - \begin{vmatrix} 4 & 1 & -5 \\ 0 & 3 & 3 \\ 1 & -1 & 2 \end{vmatrix} \;=\; - \begin{vmatrix} 4 & 1 & -5-(1) \\ 0 & 3 & 3-(3) \\ 1 & -1 & 2-(-1) \end{vmatrix}$$

$$=\; - \begin{vmatrix} 4 & 1 & -6 \\ 0 & 3 & 0 \\ 1 & -1 & 3 \end{vmatrix} \;=\; -3 \begin{vmatrix} 4 & -6 \\ 1 & 3 \end{vmatrix} \;=\; -3(12+6) \;=\; -54$$

8.9. Evaluate the determinant of $A \;=\; \begin{pmatrix} t+3 & -1 & 1 \\ 5 & t-3 & 1 \\ 6 & -6 & t+4 \end{pmatrix}$.

Add the second column to the first column, and then add the third column to the second column to obtain

$$|A| \;=\; \begin{vmatrix} t+2 & 0 & 1 \\ t+2 & t-2 & 1 \\ 0 & t-2 & t+4 \end{vmatrix}$$

Now factor $t+2$ from the first column and $t-2$ from the second column to get

$$|A| \;=\; (t+2)(t-2) \begin{vmatrix} 1 & 0 & 1 \\ 1 & 1 & 1 \\ 0 & 1 & t+4 \end{vmatrix}$$

Finally subtract the first column from the third column to obtain

$$|A| \;=\; (t+2)(t-2) \begin{vmatrix} 1 & 0 & 0 \\ 1 & 1 & 0 \\ 0 & 1 & t+4 \end{vmatrix} \;=\; (t+2)(t-2)(t+4)$$

COFACTORS

8.10. Find the cofactor of the 7 in the matrix $\begin{pmatrix} 2 & 1 & -3 & 4 \\ 5 & -4 & 7 & -2 \\ 4 & 0 & 6 & -3 \\ 3 & -2 & 5 & 2 \end{pmatrix}$.

$$(-1)^{2+3} \begin{vmatrix} 2 & 1 & -3 & 4 \\ 5 & -4 & 7 & -2 \\ 4 & 0 & 6 & -3 \\ 3 & -2 & 5 & 2 \end{vmatrix} = - \begin{vmatrix} 2 & 1 & 4 \\ 4 & 0 & -3 \\ 3 & -2 & 2 \end{vmatrix} = - \begin{vmatrix} 2 & 1 & 4 \\ 4 & 0 & -3 \\ 7 & 0 & 10 \end{vmatrix} = - \left(- \begin{vmatrix} 4 & -3 \\ 7 & 10 \end{vmatrix} \right) = 61$$

The exponent $2+3$ comes from the fact that 7 appears in the second row, third column.

8.11. Consider the matrix $A = \begin{pmatrix} 1 & 2 & 3 \\ 2 & 3 & 4 \\ 1 & 5 & 7 \end{pmatrix}$. (i) Compute $|A|$. (ii) Find $\operatorname{adj} A$. (iii) Verify $A \cdot (\operatorname{adj} A) = |A| I$. (iv) Find A^{-1}.

(i) $|A| = 1 \begin{vmatrix} 3 & 4 \\ 5 & 7 \end{vmatrix} - 2 \begin{vmatrix} 2 & 4 \\ 1 & 7 \end{vmatrix} + 3 \begin{vmatrix} 2 & 3 \\ 1 & 5 \end{vmatrix} = 1 - 20 + 21 = 2$

(ii) $\operatorname{adj} A = \begin{pmatrix} +\begin{vmatrix} 3 & 4 \\ 5 & 7 \end{vmatrix} & -\begin{vmatrix} 2 & 4 \\ 1 & 7 \end{vmatrix} & +\begin{vmatrix} 2 & 3 \\ 1 & 5 \end{vmatrix} \\ -\begin{vmatrix} 2 & 3 \\ 5 & 7 \end{vmatrix} & +\begin{vmatrix} 1 & 3 \\ 1 & 7 \end{vmatrix} & -\begin{vmatrix} 1 & 2 \\ 1 & 5 \end{vmatrix} \\ +\begin{vmatrix} 2 & 3 \\ 3 & 4 \end{vmatrix} & -\begin{vmatrix} 1 & 3 \\ 2 & 4 \end{vmatrix} & +\begin{vmatrix} 1 & 2 \\ 2 & 3 \end{vmatrix} \end{pmatrix}^t = \begin{pmatrix} 1 & -10 & 7 \\ 1 & 4 & -3 \\ -1 & 2 & -1 \end{pmatrix}^t = \begin{pmatrix} 1 & 1 & -1 \\ -10 & 4 & 2 \\ 7 & -3 & -1 \end{pmatrix}$

That is, $\operatorname{adj} A$ is the transpose of the matrix of cofactors. Observe that the "signs" in the matrix of cofactors form the chessboard pattern $\begin{pmatrix} + & - & + \\ - & + & - \\ + & - & + \end{pmatrix}$.

(iii) $A \cdot (\operatorname{adj} A) = \begin{pmatrix} 1 & 2 & 3 \\ 2 & 3 & 4 \\ 1 & 5 & 7 \end{pmatrix} \begin{pmatrix} 1 & 1 & -1 \\ -10 & 4 & 2 \\ 7 & -3 & -1 \end{pmatrix} = \begin{pmatrix} 2 & 0 & 0 \\ 0 & 2 & 0 \\ 0 & 0 & 2 \end{pmatrix} = 2 \begin{pmatrix} 1 & 0 & 0 \\ 0 & 1 & 0 \\ 0 & 0 & 1 \end{pmatrix} = |A| I$

(iv) $A^{-1} = \dfrac{1}{|A|} (\operatorname{adj} A) = \dfrac{1}{2} \begin{pmatrix} 1 & 1 & -1 \\ -10 & 4 & 2 \\ 7 & -3 & -1 \end{pmatrix} = \begin{pmatrix} \frac{1}{2} & \frac{1}{2} & -\frac{1}{2} \\ -5 & 2 & 1 \\ \frac{7}{2} & -\frac{3}{2} & -\frac{1}{2} \end{pmatrix}$

8.12. Consider an arbitrary 2 by 2 matrix $A = \begin{pmatrix} a & b \\ c & d \end{pmatrix}$.

(i) Find $\operatorname{adj} A$. (ii) Show that $\operatorname{adj}(\operatorname{adj} A) = A$.

(i) $\operatorname{adj} A = \begin{pmatrix} +|d| & -|c| \\ -|b| & +|a| \end{pmatrix}^t = \begin{pmatrix} d & -c \\ -b & a \end{pmatrix}^t = \begin{pmatrix} d & -b \\ -c & a \end{pmatrix}$

(ii) $\operatorname{adj}(\operatorname{adj} A) = \operatorname{adj} \begin{pmatrix} d & -b \\ -c & a \end{pmatrix} = \begin{pmatrix} +|a| & -|-c| \\ -|-b| & +|d| \end{pmatrix}^t = \begin{pmatrix} a & c \\ b & d \end{pmatrix}^t = \begin{pmatrix} a & b \\ c & d \end{pmatrix} = A$

DETERMINANTS AND SYSTEMS OF LINEAR EQUATIONS

8.13. Solve for x and y, using determinants:

(i) $\begin{array}{l} 2x + y = 7 \\ 3x - 5y = 4 \end{array}$ (ii) $\begin{array}{l} ax - 2by = c \\ 3ax - 5by = 2c \end{array}$, where $ab \neq 0$.

(i) $\Delta = \begin{vmatrix} 2 & 1 \\ 3 & -5 \end{vmatrix} = -13$, $\Delta_x = \begin{vmatrix} 7 & 1 \\ 4 & -5 \end{vmatrix} = -39$, $\Delta_y = \begin{vmatrix} 2 & 7 \\ 3 & -4 \end{vmatrix} = -13$. Then $x = \Delta_x/\Delta = 3$, $y = \Delta_y/\Delta = 1$.

(ii) $\Delta = \begin{vmatrix} a & -2b \\ 3a & -5b \end{vmatrix} = ab$, $\Delta_x = \begin{vmatrix} c & -2b \\ 2c & -5b \end{vmatrix} = -bc$, $\Delta_y = \begin{vmatrix} a & c \\ 3a & 2c \end{vmatrix} = -ac$. Then $x = \Delta_x/\Delta = -c/a$, $y = \Delta_y/\Delta = -c/b$.

8.14. Solve using determinants: $\begin{cases} 3y + 2x = z + 1 \\ 3x + 2z = 8 - 5y \\ 3z - 1 = x - 2y \end{cases}$.

First arrange the system in standard form with the unknowns appearing in columns:
$$\begin{array}{r} 2x + 3y - z = 1 \\ 3x + 5y + 2z = 8 \\ x - 2y - 3z = -1 \end{array}$$

Compute the determinant Δ of the matrix A of coefficients:
$$\Delta = \begin{vmatrix} 2 & 3 & -1 \\ 3 & 5 & 2 \\ 1 & -2 & -3 \end{vmatrix} = 2(-15+4) - 3(-9-2) - 1(-6-5) = 22$$

Since $\Delta \neq 0$, the system has a unique solution. To obtain Δ_x, Δ_y and Δ_z, replace the coefficients of the unknown in the matrix A by the column of constants. Thus
$$\Delta_x = \begin{vmatrix} 1 & 3 & -1 \\ 8 & 5 & 2 \\ -1 & -2 & -3 \end{vmatrix} = 66, \quad \Delta_y = \begin{vmatrix} 2 & 1 & -1 \\ 3 & 8 & 2 \\ 1 & -1 & -3 \end{vmatrix} = -22, \quad \Delta_z = \begin{vmatrix} 2 & 3 & 1 \\ 3 & 5 & 8 \\ 1 & -2 & -1 \end{vmatrix} = 44$$
and $x = \Delta_x/\Delta = 3$, $y = \Delta_y/\Delta = -1$, $z = \Delta_z/\Delta = 2$.

PROOF OF THEOREMS

8.15. Prove Theorem 8.1: $|A^t| = |A|$.

Suppose $A = (a_{ij})$. Then $A^t = (b_{ij})$ where $b_{ij} = a_{ji}$. Hence
$$|A^t| = \sum_{\sigma \in S_n} (\text{sgn } \sigma)\, b_{1\sigma(1)} b_{2\sigma(2)} \ldots b_{n\sigma(n)}$$
$$= \sum_{\sigma \in S_n} (\text{sgn } \sigma)\, a_{\sigma(1),1} a_{\sigma(2),2} \ldots a_{\sigma(n),n}$$

Let $\tau = \sigma^{-1}$. By Problem 8.36, $\text{sgn } \tau = \text{sgn } \sigma$, and
$$a_{\sigma(1),1} a_{\sigma(2),2} \ldots a_{\sigma(n),n} = a_{1\tau(1)} a_{2\tau(2)} \ldots a_{n\tau(n)}$$

Hence $$|A^t| = \sum_{\sigma \in S_n} (\text{sgn } \tau)\, a_{1\tau(1)} a_{2\tau(2)} \ldots a_{n\tau(n)}$$

However, as σ runs through all the elements of S_n, $\tau = \sigma^{-1}$ also runs through all the elements of S_n. Thus $|A^t| = |A|$.

8.16. Prove Theorem 8.3(ii): Let B be obtained from a square matrix A by interchanging two rows (columns) of A. Then $|B| = -|A|$.

We prove the theorem for the case that two columns are interchanged. Let τ be the transposition which interchanges the two numbers corresponding to the two columns of A that are interchanged. If $A = (a_{ij})$ and $B = (b_{ij})$, then $b_{ij} = a_{i\tau(j)}$. Hence, for any permutation σ,

$$b_{1\sigma(1)}\, b_{2\sigma(2)} \ldots b_{n\sigma(n)} \;=\; a_{1\tau\sigma(1)}\, a_{2\tau\sigma(2)} \ldots a_{n\tau\sigma(n)}$$

Thus
$$|B| \;=\; \sum_{\sigma \in S_n} (\operatorname{sgn} \sigma)\, b_{1\sigma(1)}\, b_{2\sigma(2)} \ldots b_{n\sigma(n)}$$

$$=\; \sum_{\sigma \in S_n} (\operatorname{sgn} \sigma)\, a_{1\tau\sigma(1)}\, a_{2\tau\sigma(2)} \ldots a_{n\tau\sigma(n)}$$

Since the transposition τ is an odd permutation, $\operatorname{sgn} \tau\sigma = \operatorname{sgn} \tau \cdot \operatorname{sgn} \sigma = -\operatorname{sgn} \sigma$. Thus $\operatorname{sgn} \sigma = -\operatorname{sgn} \tau\sigma$, and so

$$|B| \;=\; -\sum_{\sigma \in S_n} (\operatorname{sgn} \tau\sigma)\, a_{1\tau\sigma(1)}\, a_{2\tau\sigma(2)} \ldots a_{n\tau\sigma(n)}$$

But as σ runs through all the elements of S_n, $\tau\sigma$ also runs through all the elements of S_n; hence $|B| = -|A|$.

8.17. Prove Theorem 8.2: (i) If A has a row (column) of zeros, then $|A| = 0$. (ii) If A has two identical rows (columns), then $|A| = 0$. (iii) If A is triangular, then $|A| =$ product of diagonal elements. Thus in particular, $|I| = 1$ where I is the identity matrix.

(i) Each term in $|A|$ contains a factor from every row and so from the row of zeros. Thus each term of $|A|$ is zero and so $|A| = 0$.

(ii) Suppose $1 + 1 \neq 0$ in K. If we interchange the two identical rows of A, we still obtain the matrix A. Hence by the preceding problem, $|A| = -|A|$ and so $|A| = 0$.

Now suppose $1 + 1 = 0$ in K. Then $\operatorname{sgn} \sigma = 1$ for every $\sigma \in S_n$. Since A has two identical rows, we can arrange the terms of A into pairs of equal terms. Since each pair is 0, the determinant of A is zero.

(iii) Suppose $A = (a_{ij})$ is lower triangular, that is, the entries above the diagonal are all zero: $a_{ij} = 0$ whenever $i < j$. Consider a term t of the determinant of A:

$$t \;=\; (\operatorname{sgn} \sigma)\, a_{1i_1}\, a_{2i_2} \ldots a_{ni_n}, \qquad \text{where} \quad \sigma = i_1 i_2 \ldots i_n$$

Suppose $i_1 \neq 1$. Then $1 < i_1$ and so $a_{1i_1} = 0$; hence $t = 0$. That is, each term for which $i_1 \neq 1$ is zero.

Now suppose $i_1 = 1$ but $i_2 \neq 2$. Then $2 < i_2$ and so $a_{2i_2} = 0$; hence $t = 0$. Thus each term for which $i_1 \neq 1$ or $i_2 \neq 2$ is zero.

Similarly we obtain that each term for which $i_1 \neq 1$ or $i_2 \neq 2$ or $\ldots$ or $i_n \neq n$ is zero. Accordingly, $|A| = a_{11} a_{22} \ldots a_{nn} =$ product of diagonal elements.

8.18. Prove Theorem 8.3: Let B be obtained from A by

(i) multiplying a row (column) of A by a scalar k; then $|B| = k\,|A|$.

(ii) interchanging two rows (columns) of A; then $|B| = -|A|$.

(iii) adding a multiple of a row (column) of A to another; then $|B| = |A|$.

(i) If the jth row of A is multiplied by k, then every term in $|A|$ is multiplied by k and so $|B| = k\,|A|$. That is,

$$|B| \;=\; \sum_{\sigma} (\operatorname{sgn} \sigma)\, a_{1i_1}\, a_{2i_2} \ldots (k a_{ji_j}) \ldots a_{ni_n}$$

$$=\; k \sum_{\sigma} (\operatorname{sgn} \sigma)\, a_{1i_1}\, a_{2i_2} \ldots a_{ni_n} \;=\; k\,|A|$$

(ii) Proved in Problem 8.16.

(iii) Suppose c times the kth row is added to the jth row of A. Using the symbol $\wedge$ to denote the jth position in a determinant term, we have

$$|B| \;=\; \sum_{\sigma} (\operatorname{sgn} \sigma)\, a_{1i_1}\, a_{2i_2} \ldots \overset{\frown}{(c a_{ki_k} + a_{ji_j})} \ldots a_{ni_n}$$

$$=\; c \sum_{\sigma} (\operatorname{sgn} \sigma)\, a_{1i_1}\, a_{2i_2} \ldots \overset{\frown}{a_{ki_k}} \ldots a_{ni_n} \;+\; \sum_{\sigma} (\operatorname{sgn} \sigma)\, a_{1i_1}\, a_{2i_2} \ldots \overset{\frown}{a_{ji_j}} \ldots a_{ni_n}$$

The first sum is the determinant of a matrix whose kth and jth rows are identical; hence by Theorem 8.2(ii) the sum is zero. The second sum is the determinant of A. Thus $|B| = c \cdot 0 + |A| = A$.

8.19.   Prove Lemma 8.6: For any elementary matrix E, $|EA| = |E|\,|A|$.

Consider the following elementary row operations: (i) multiply a row by a constant $k \neq 0$; (ii) interchange two rows; (iii) add a multiple of one row to another. Let E_1, E_2 and E_3 be the corresponding elementary matrices. That is, E_1, E_2 and E_3 are obtained by applying the above operations, respectively, to the identity matrix I. By the preceding problem,

$$|E_1| = k\,|I| = k, \qquad |E_2| = -|I| = -1, \qquad |E_3| = |I| = 1$$

Recall (page 56) that $E_i A$ is identical to the matrix obtained by applying the corresponding operation to A. Thus by the preceding problem,

$$|E_1 A| = k\,|A| = |E_1|\,|A|, \qquad |E_2 A| = -|A| = |E_2|\,|A|, \qquad |E_3 A| = |A| = 1\,|A| = |E_3|\,|A|$$

and the lemma is proved.

8.20.   Suppose B is row equivalent to A; say $B = E_n E_{n-1} \ldots E_2 E_1 A$ where the E_i are elementary matrices. Show that:

(i) $|B| = |E_n|\,|E_{n-1}| \ldots |E_2|\,|E_1|\,|A|$,   (ii) $|B| \neq 0$ if and only if $|A| \neq 0$.

(i)   By the preceding problem, $|E_1 A| = |E_1|\,|A|$. Hence by induction,

$$|B| = |E_n|\,|E_{n-1} \ldots E_2 E_1 A| = |E_n|\,|E_{n-1}| \ldots |E_2|\,|E_1|\,|A|$$

(ii)   By the preceding problem, $E_i \neq 0$ for each i. Hence $|B| \neq 0$ if and only if $|A| \neq 0$.

8.21.   Prove Theorem 8.4: Let A be an n-square matrix. Then the following are equivalent: (i) A is invertible, (ii) A is nonsingular, (iii) $|A| \neq 0$.

By Problem 6.44, (i) and (ii) are equivalent. Hence it suffices to show that (i) and (iii) are equivalent.

Suppose A is invertible. Then A is row equivalent to the identity matrix I. But $|I| \neq 0$; hence by the preceding problem, $|A| \neq 0$. On the other hand, suppose A is not invertible. Then A is row equivalent to a matrix B which has a zero row. By Theorem 8.2(i), $|B| = 0$; then by the preceding problem, $|A| = 0$. Thus (i) and (iii) are equivalent.

8.22.   Prove Theorem 8.5: $|AB| = |A|\,|B|$.

If A is singular, then AB is also singular and so $|AB| = 0 = |A|\,|B|$. On the other hand if A is nonsingular, then $A = E_n \ldots E_2 E_1$, a product of elementary matrices. Thus, by Problem 8.20,

$$|A| = |E_n \ldots E_2 E_1 I| = |E_n| \ldots |E_2|\,|E_1|\,|I| = |E_n| \ldots |E_2|\,|E_1|$$

and so

$$|AB| = |E_n \ldots E_2 E_1 B| = |E_n| \ldots |E_2|\,|E_1|\,|B| = |A|\,|B|$$

8.23.   Prove Theorem 8.7: Let $A = (a_{ij})$; then $|A| = a_{i1} A_{i1} + a_{i2} A_{i2} + \cdots + a_{in} A_{in}$, where A_{ij} is the cofactor of a_{ij}.

Each term in $|A|$ contains one and only one entry of the ith row $(a_{i1}, a_{i2}, \ldots, a_{in})$ of A. Hence we can write $|A|$ in the form

$$|A| = a_{i1} A_{i1}^{*} + a_{i2} A_{i2}^{*} + \cdots + a_{in} A_{in}^{*}$$

(Note A_{ij}^{*} is a sum of terms involving no entry of the ith row of A.) Thus the theorem is proved if we can show that

$$A_{ij}^{*} = A_{ij} = (-1)^{i+j}\,|M_{ij}|$$

where M_{ij} is the matrix obtained by deleting the row and column containing the entry a_{ij}. (Historically, the expression A_{ij}^{*} was defined as the cofactor of a_{ij}, and so the theorem reduces to showing that the two definitions of the cofactor are equivalent.)

First we consider the case that $i = n$, $j = n$. Then the sum of terms in $|A|$ containing a_{nn} is

$$a_{nn}A_{nn}^* = a_{nn}\sum_\sigma (\text{sgn } \sigma)\, a_{1\sigma(1)}\, a_{2\sigma(2)}\, \cdots\, a_{n-1, \sigma(n-1)}$$

where we sum over all permutations $\sigma \in S_n$ for which $\sigma(n) = n$. However, this is equivalent (Problem 8.63) to summing over all permutations of $\{1, \ldots, n-1\}$. Thus $A_{nn}^* = |M_{nn}| = (-1)^{n+n}|M_{nn}|$.

Now we consider any i and j. We interchange the ith row with each succeeding row until it is last, and we interchange the jth column with each succeeding column until it is last. Note that the determinant $|M_{ij}|$ is not affected since the relative positions of the other rows and columns are not affected by these interchanges. However, the "sign" of $|A|$ and of A_{ij}^* is changed $n-i$ and then $n-j$ times. Accordingly,

$$A_{ij}^* = (-1)^{n-i+n-j}|M_{ij}| = (-1)^{i+j}|M_{ij}|$$

8.24. Let $A = (a_{ij})$ and let B be the matrix obtained from A by replacing the ith row of A by the row vector $(b_{i1}, \ldots, b_{in})$. Show that

$$|B| = b_{i1}A_{i1} + b_{i2}A_{i2} + \cdots + b_{in}A_{in}$$

Furthermore, show that, for $j \neq i$,

$$a_{j1}A_{i1} + a_{j2}A_{i2} + \cdots + a_{jn}A_{in} = 0$$

and

$$a_{1j}A_{1i} + a_{2j}A_{2i} + \cdots + a_{nj}A_{ni} = 0$$

Let $B = (b_{ij})$. By the preceding problem,

$$|B| = b_{i1}B_{i1} + b_{i2}B_{i2} + \cdots + b_{in}B_{in}$$

Since B_{ij} does not depend upon the ith row of B, $B_{ij} = A_{ij}$ for $j = 1, \ldots, n$. Hence

$$|B| = b_{i1}A_{i1} + b_{i2}A_{i2} + \cdots + b_{in}A_{in}$$

Now let A' be obtained from A by replacing the ith row of A by the jth row of A. Since A' has two identical rows, $|A'| = 0$. Thus by the above result,

$$|A'| = a_{j1}A_{i1} + a_{j2}A_{i2} + \cdots + a_{jn}A_{in} = 0$$

Using $|A^t| = |A|$, we also obtain that $a_{1j}A_{1i} + a_{2j}A_{2i} + \cdots + a_{nj}A_{ni} = 0$.

8.25. Prove Theorem 8.8: $A \cdot (\text{adj } A) = (\text{adj } A) \cdot A = |A| I$. Thus if $|A| \neq 0$, $A^{-1} = (1/|A|)(\text{adj } A)$.

Let $A = (a_{ij})$ and let $A \cdot (\text{adj } A) = (b_{ij})$. The ith row of A is

$$(a_{i1}, a_{i2}, \ldots, a_{in}) \tag{1}$$

Since $\text{adj } A$ is the transpose of the matrix of cofactors, the jth column of $\text{adj } A$ is the transpose of the cofactors of the jth row of A:

$$(A_{j1}, A_{j2}, \ldots, A_{jn})^t \tag{2}$$

Now b_{ij}, the ij-entry in $A \cdot (\text{adj } A)$, is obtained by multiplying (1) and (2):

$$b_{ij} = a_{i1}A_{j1} + a_{i2}A_{j2} + \cdots + a_{in}A_{jn}$$

Thus by Theorem 8.7 and the preceding problem,

$$b_{ij} = \begin{cases} |A| & \text{if } i = j \\ 0 & \text{if } i \neq j \end{cases}$$

Accordingly, $A \cdot (\text{adj } A)$ is the diagonal matrix with each diagonal element $|A|$. In other words, $A \cdot (\text{adj } A) = |A| I$. Similarly, $(\text{adj } A) \cdot A = |A| I$.

8.26. Prove Theorem 8.9: The system of linear equations $Ax = b$ has a unique solution if and only if $\Delta = |A| \neq 0$. In this case the unique solution is given by $x_1 = \Delta_1/\Delta$, $x_2 = \Delta_2/\Delta$, ..., $x_n = \Delta_n/\Delta$.

By preceding results, $Ax = b$ has a unique solution if and only if A is invertible, and A is invertible if and only if $\Delta = |A| \neq 0$.

Now suppose $\Delta \neq 0$. By Problem 8.25, $A^{-1} = (1/\Delta)(\operatorname{adj} A)$. Multiplying $Ax = b$ by A^{-1}, we obtain

$$x = A^{-1}Ax = (1/\Delta)(\operatorname{adj} A)b \tag{1}$$

Note that the ith row of $(1/\Delta)(\operatorname{adj} A)$ is $(1/\Delta)(A_{1i}, A_{2i}, \ldots, A_{ni})$. If $b = (b_1, b_2, \ldots, b_n)^t$ then, by (1),

$$x_i = (1/\Delta)(b_1 A_{1i} + b_2 A_{2i} + \cdots + b_n A_{ni})$$

However, as in Problem 8.24;

$$b_1 A_{1i} + b_2 A_{2i} + \cdots + b_n A_{ni} = \Delta_i$$

the determinant of the matrix obtained by replacing the ith column of A by the column vector b. Thus $x_i = (1/\Delta)\Delta_i$, as required.

8.27. Suppose P is invertible. Show that $|P^{-1}| = |P|^{-1}$.

$P^{-1}P = I$. Hence $1 = |I| = |P^{-1}P| = |P^{-1}| \, |P|$, and so $|P^{-1}| = |P|^{-1}$.

8.28. Prove Theorem 8.11: Suppose A and B are similar matrices. Then $|A| = |B|$.

Since A and B are similar, there exists an invertible matrix P such that $B = P^{-1}AP$. Then by the preceding problem, $|B| = |P^{-1}AP| = |P^{-1}| \, |A| \, |P| = |A| \, |P^{-1}| \, |P| = |A|$.

We remark that although the matrices P^{-1} and A may not commute, their determinants $|P^{-1}|$ and $|A|$ do commute since they are scalars in the field K.

8.29. Prove Theorem 8.13: There exists a unique function $D : \mathcal{A} \to K$ such that (i) D is multilinear, (ii) D is alternating, (iii) $D(I) = 1$. This function D is the determinant function, i.e. $D(A) = |A|$.

Let D be the determinant function: $D(A) = |A|$. We must show that D satisfies (i), (ii) and (iii), and that D is the only function satisfying (i), (ii) and (iii).

By preceding results, D satisfies (ii) and (iii); hence we need show that it is multilinear. Suppose $A = (a_{ij}) = (A_1, A_2, \ldots, A_n)$ where A_k is the kth row of A. Furthermore, suppose for a fixed i,

$$A_i = B_i + C_i, \qquad \text{where } B_i = (b_1, \ldots, b_n) \text{ and } C_i = (c_1, \ldots, c_n)$$

Accordingly, $\qquad a_{i1} = b_1 + c_1, \quad a_{i2} = b_2 + c_2, \quad \ldots, \quad a_{in} = b_n + c_n$

Expanding $D(A) = |A|$ by the ith row,

$$D(A) = D(A_1, \ldots, B_i + C_i, \ldots, A_n) = a_{i1}A_{i1} + a_{i2}A_{i2} + \cdots + a_{in}A_{in}$$
$$= (b_1 + c_1)A_{i1} + (b_2 + c_2)A_{i2} + \cdots + (b_n + c_n)A_{in}$$
$$= (b_1 A_{i1} + b_2 A_{i2} + \cdots + b_n A_{in}) + (c_1 A_{i1} + c_2 A_{i2} + \cdots + c_n A_{in})$$

However, by Problem 8.24, the two sums above are the determinants of the matrices obtained from A by replacing the ith row by B_i and C_i respectively. That is,

$$D(A) = D(A_1, \ldots, B_i + C_i, \ldots, A_n)$$
$$= D(A_1, \ldots, B_i, \ldots, A_n) + D(A_1, \ldots, C_i, \ldots, A_n)$$

Furthermore, by Theorem 8.3(i),

$$D(A_1, \ldots, kA_i, \ldots, A_n) = k\,D(A_1, \ldots, A_i, \ldots, A_n)$$

Thus D is multilinear, i.e. D satisfies (iii).

We next must prove the uniqueness of D. Suppose D satisfies (i), (ii) and (iii). If $\{e_1, \ldots, e_n\}$ is the usual basis of K^n, then by (iii), $D(e_1, e_2, \ldots, e_n) = D(I) = 1$. Using (ii) we also have (Problem 8.73) that

$$D(e_{i_1}, e_{i_2}, \ldots, e_{i_n}) = \text{sgn } \sigma, \qquad \text{where } \sigma = i_1 i_2 \ldots i_n \tag{1}$$

Now suppose $A = (a_{ij})$. Observe that the kth row A_k of A is

$$A_k = (a_{k1}, a_{k2}, \ldots, a_{kn}) = a_{k1}e_1 + a_{k2}e_2 + \cdots + a_{kn}e_n$$

Thus $\qquad D(A) = D(a_{11}e_1 + \cdots + a_{1n}e_n, a_{21}e_1 + \cdots + a_{2n}e_n, \ldots, a_{n1}e_1 + \cdots + a_{nn}e_n)$

Using the multilinearity of D, we can write $D(A)$ as a sum of terms of the form

$$\begin{aligned} D(A) &= \sum D(a_{1i_1}e_{i_1}, a_{2i_2}e_{i_2}, \ldots, a_{ni_n}e_{i_n}) \\ &= \sum (a_{1i_1} a_{2i_2} \ldots a_{ni_n}) D(e_{i_1}, e_{i_2}, \ldots, e_{i_n}) \end{aligned} \tag{2}$$

where the sum is summed over all sequences $i_1 i_2 \ldots i_n$ where $i_k \in \{1, \ldots, n\}$. If two of the indices are equal, say $i_j = i_k$ but $j \neq k$, then by (ii),

$$D(e_{i_1}, e_{i_2}, \ldots, e_{i_n}) = 0$$

Accordingly, the sum in (2) need only be summed over all permutations $\sigma = i_1 i_2 \ldots i_n$. Using (1), we finally have that

$$\begin{aligned} D(A) &= \sum_\sigma (a_{1i_1} a_{2i_2} \ldots a_{ni_n}) D(e_{i_1}, e_{i_2}, \ldots, e_{i_n}) \\ &= \sum_\sigma (\text{sgn } \sigma) a_{1i_1} a_{2i_2} \ldots a_{ni_n}, \qquad \text{where } \sigma = i_1 i_2 \ldots i_n \end{aligned}$$

Hence D is the determinant function and so the theorem is proved.

PERMUTATIONS

8.30. Determine the parity of $\sigma = 542163$.

Method 1.

We need to obtain the number of pairs (i, j) for which $i > j$ and i precedes j in σ. There are:

3 numbers (5, 4 and 2) greater than and preceding 1,

2 numbers (5 and 4) greater than and preceding 2,

3 numbers (5, 4 and 6) greater than and preceding 3,

1 number (5) greater than and preceding 4,

0 numbers greater than and preceding 5,

0 numbers greater than and preceding 6.

Since $3 + 2 + 3 + 1 + 0 + 0 = 9$ is odd, σ is an odd permutation and so sgn $\sigma = -1$.

Method 2.

Transpose 1 to the first position as follows:

$$5 \ 4 \ 2 \ 1 \ 6 \ 3 \qquad \text{to} \qquad 1 \ 5 \ 4 \ 2 \ 6 \ 3$$

Transpose 2 to the second position:

$$1 \ 5 \ 4 \ 2 \ 6 \ 3 \qquad \text{to} \qquad 1 \ 2 \ 5 \ 4 \ 6 \ 3$$

Transpose 3 to the third position:

$$1 \ 2 \ 5 \ 4 \ 6 \ 3 \qquad \text{to} \qquad 1 \ 2 \ 3 \ 5 \ 4 \ 6$$

Transpose 4 to the fourth position:

$$1 \ 2 \ 3 \ 5 \ 4 \ 6 \qquad \text{to} \qquad 1 \ 2 \ 3 \ 4 \ 5 \ 6$$

Note that 5 and 6 are in the "correct" positions. Count the number of numbers "jumped": $3 + 2 + 3 + 1 = 9$. Since 9 is odd, σ is an odd permutation. (Remark: This method is essentially the same as the preceding method.)

Method 3.

An interchange of two numbers in a permutation is equivalent to multiplying the permutation by a transposition. Hence transform σ to the identity permutation using transpositions; such as,

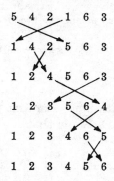

Since an odd number, 5, of transpositions was used, σ is an odd permutation.

8.31. Let $\sigma = 24513$ and $\tau = 41352$ be permutations in S_5. Find (i) the composition permutations $\tau \circ \sigma$ and $\sigma \circ \tau$, (ii) σ^{-1}.

Recall that $\sigma = 24513$ and $\tau = 41352$ are short ways of writing

$$\sigma = \begin{pmatrix} 1 & 2 & 3 & 4 & 5 \\ 2 & 4 & 5 & 1 & 3 \end{pmatrix} \quad \text{and} \quad \tau = \begin{pmatrix} 1 & 2 & 3 & 4 & 5 \\ 4 & 1 & 3 & 5 & 2 \end{pmatrix}$$

which means

$$\sigma(1) = 2, \quad \sigma(2) = 4, \quad \sigma(3) = 5, \quad \sigma(4) = 1 \quad \text{and} \quad \sigma(5) = 3$$

and

$$\tau(1) = 4, \quad \tau(2) = 1, \quad \tau(3) = 3, \quad \tau(4) = 5 \quad \text{and} \quad \tau(5) = 2$$

(i)

$$\begin{array}{ccccc} 1 & 2 & 3 & 4 & 5 \\ \sigma \downarrow & \downarrow & \downarrow & \downarrow & \downarrow \\ 2 & 4 & 5 & 1 & 3 \\ \tau \downarrow & \downarrow & \downarrow & \downarrow & \downarrow \\ 1 & 5 & 2 & 4 & 3 \end{array} \quad \text{and} \quad \begin{array}{ccccc} 1 & 2 & 3 & 4 & 5 \\ \tau \downarrow & \downarrow & \downarrow & \downarrow & \downarrow \\ 4 & 1 & 3 & 5 & 2 \\ \sigma \downarrow & \downarrow & \downarrow & \downarrow & \downarrow \\ 1 & 2 & 5 & 3 & 4 \end{array}$$

Thus $\tau \circ \sigma = 15243$ and $\sigma \circ \tau = 12534$.

(ii)

$$\sigma^{-1} = \begin{pmatrix} 2 & 4 & 5 & 1 & 3 \\ 1 & 2 & 3 & 4 & 5 \end{pmatrix} = \begin{pmatrix} 1 & 2 & 3 & 4 & 5 \\ 4 & 1 & 5 & 2 & 3 \end{pmatrix}$$

That is, $\sigma^{-1} = 41523$.

8.32. Consider any permutation $\sigma = j_1 j_2 \ldots j_n$. Show that for each pair (i, k) such that

$$i > k \quad \text{and} \quad i \text{ precedes } k \text{ in } \sigma$$

there is a pair (i^*, k^*) such that

$$i^* < k^* \quad \text{and} \quad \sigma(i^*) > \sigma(k^*) \tag{1}$$

and vice versa. Thus σ is even or odd according as to whether there is an even or odd number of pairs satisfying (1).

Choose i^* and k^* so that $\sigma(i^*) = i$ and $\sigma(k^*) = k$. Then $i > k$ if and only if $\sigma(i^*) > \sigma(k^*)$, and i precedes k in σ if and only if $i^* < k^*$.

8.33. Consider the polynomial $g = g(x_1, \ldots, x_n) = \prod_{i<j} (x_i - x_j)$. Write out explicitly the polynomial $g = g(x_1, x_2, x_3, x_4)$.

The symbol $\prod$ is used for a product of terms in the same way that the symbol $\sum$ is used for a sum of terms. That is, $\prod_{i<j} (x_i - x_j)$ means the product of all terms $(x_i - x_j)$ for which $i < j$. Hence

$$g = g(x_1, \ldots, x_4) = (x_1 - x_2)(x_1 - x_3)(x_1 - x_4)(x_2 - x_3)(x_2 - x_4)(x_3 - x_4)$$

8.34. Let σ be an arbitrary permutation. For the polynomial g in the preceding problem, define $\sigma(g) = \prod_{i<j} (x_{\sigma(i)} - x_{\sigma(j)})$. Show that

$$\sigma(g) = \begin{cases} g & \text{if } \sigma \text{ is even} \\ -g & \text{if } \sigma \text{ is odd} \end{cases}$$

Accordingly, $\sigma(g) = (\text{sgn } \sigma)g$.

Since σ is one-one and onto,

$$\sigma(g) = \prod_{i<j} (x_{\sigma(i)} - x_{\sigma(j)}) = \prod_{i<j \text{ or } i>j} (x_i - x_j)$$

Thus $\sigma(g) = g$ or $\sigma(g) = -g$ according as to whether there is an even or an odd number of terms of the form $(x_i - x_j)$ where $i > j$. Note that for each pair (i, j) for which

$$i < j \quad \text{and} \quad \sigma(i) > \sigma(j) \tag{1}$$

there is a term $(x_{\sigma(i)} - x_{\sigma(j)})$ in $\sigma(g)$ for which $\sigma(i) > \sigma(j)$. Since σ is even if and only if there is an even number of pairs satisfying (1), we have $\sigma(g) = g$ if and only if σ is even; hence $\sigma(g) = -g$ if and only if σ is odd.

8.35. Let $\sigma, \tau \in S_n$. Show that $\text{sgn } (\tau \circ \sigma) = (\text{sgn } \tau)(\text{sgn } \sigma)$. Thus the product of two even or two odd permutations is even, and the product of an odd and an even permutation is odd.

Using the preceding problem, we have

$$\text{sgn } (\tau \circ \sigma)g = (\tau \circ \sigma)(g) = \tau(\sigma(g)) = \tau((\text{sgn } \sigma)g) = (\text{sgn } \tau)(\text{sgn } \sigma)g$$

Accordingly, $\text{sgn } (\tau \circ \sigma) = (\text{sgn } \tau)(\text{sgn } \sigma)$.

8.36. Consider the permutation $\sigma = j_1 j_2 \ldots j_n$. Show that $\text{sgn } \sigma^{-1} = \text{sgn } \sigma$ and, for scalars a_{ij},

$$a_{j_1 1} a_{j_2 2} \ldots a_{j_n n} = a_{1k_1} a_{2k_2} \ldots a_{nk_n} \quad \text{where } \sigma^{-1} = k_1 k_2 \ldots k_n$$

We have $\sigma^{-1} \circ \sigma = \epsilon$, the identity permutation. Since ϵ is even, σ^{-1} and σ are both even or both odd. Hence $\text{sgn } \sigma^{-1} = \text{sgn } \sigma$.

Since $\sigma = j_1 j_2 \ldots j_n$ is a permutation, $a_{j_1 1} a_{j_2 2} \ldots a_{j_n n} = a_{1k_1} a_{2k_2} \ldots a_{nk_n}$. Then $k_1, k_2, \ldots, k_n$ have the property that

$$\sigma(k_1) = 1, \quad \sigma(k_2) = 2, \quad \ldots, \quad \sigma(k_n) = n$$

Let $\tau = k_1 k_2 \ldots k_n$. Then for $i = 1, \ldots, n$,

$$(\sigma \circ \tau)(i) = \sigma(\tau(i)) = \sigma(k_i) = i$$

Thus $\sigma \circ \tau = \epsilon$, the identity permutation; hence $\tau = \sigma^{-1}$.

MISCELLANEOUS PROBLEMS

8.37. Find $\det(T)$ for each linear operator T:

(i) T is the operator on $\mathbf{R}^3$ defined by

$$T(x, y, z) = (2x - z,\ x + 2y - 4z,\ 3x - 3y + z)$$

(ii) T is the operator on the vector space V of 2-square matrices over K defined by

$$T(A) = MA \quad \text{where} \quad M = \begin{pmatrix} a & b \\ c & d \end{pmatrix}.$$

(i) Find the matrix representation of T relative to, say, the usual basis: $[T] = \begin{pmatrix} 2 & 0 & -1 \\ 1 & 2 & -4 \\ 3 & -3 & 1 \end{pmatrix}$

Then

$$\det(T) = \begin{vmatrix} 2 & 0 & -1 \\ 1 & 2 & -4 \\ 3 & -3 & 1 \end{vmatrix} = 2(2 - 12) - 1(-3 - 6) = -11$$

(ii) Find a matrix representation of T in some basis of V, say,

$$\left\{ E_1 = \begin{pmatrix} 1 & 0 \\ 0 & 0 \end{pmatrix},\ E_2 = \begin{pmatrix} 0 & 1 \\ 0 & 0 \end{pmatrix},\ E_3 = \begin{pmatrix} 0 & 0 \\ 1 & 0 \end{pmatrix},\ E_4 = \begin{pmatrix} 0 & 0 \\ 0 & 1 \end{pmatrix} \right\}$$

Then

$$T(E_1) = \begin{pmatrix} a & b \\ c & d \end{pmatrix}\begin{pmatrix} 1 & 0 \\ 0 & 0 \end{pmatrix} = \begin{pmatrix} a & 0 \\ c & 0 \end{pmatrix} = aE_1 + 0E_2 + cE_3 + 0E_4$$

$$T(E_2) = \begin{pmatrix} a & b \\ c & d \end{pmatrix}\begin{pmatrix} 0 & 1 \\ 0 & 0 \end{pmatrix} = \begin{pmatrix} 0 & a \\ 0 & c \end{pmatrix} = 0E_1 + aE_2 + 0E_3 + cE_4$$

$$T(E_3) = \begin{pmatrix} a & b \\ c & d \end{pmatrix}\begin{pmatrix} 0 & 0 \\ 1 & 0 \end{pmatrix} = \begin{pmatrix} b & 0 \\ d & 0 \end{pmatrix} = bE_1 + 0E_2 + dE_3 + 0E_4$$

$$T(E_4) = \begin{pmatrix} a & b \\ c & d \end{pmatrix}\begin{pmatrix} 0 & 0 \\ 0 & 1 \end{pmatrix} = \begin{pmatrix} 0 & b \\ 0 & d \end{pmatrix} = 0E_1 + bE_2 + 0E_3 + dE_4$$

Thus $[T]_E = \begin{pmatrix} a & 0 & c & 0 \\ 0 & a & 0 & c \\ b & 0 & d & 0 \\ 0 & b & 0 & d \end{pmatrix}$ and

$$\det(T) = \begin{vmatrix} a & 0 & c & 0 \\ 0 & a & 0 & c \\ b & 0 & d & 0 \\ 0 & b & 0 & d \end{vmatrix} = a\begin{vmatrix} a & 0 & c \\ 0 & d & 0 \\ b & 0 & d \end{vmatrix} + c\begin{vmatrix} 0 & a & c \\ b & 0 & 0 \\ 0 & b & d \end{vmatrix} = a^2d^2 + b^2c^2 - 2abcd$$

8.38. Find the inverse of $A = \begin{pmatrix} 1 & 1 & 1 \\ 0 & 1 & 1 \\ 0 & 0 & 1 \end{pmatrix}$.

The inverse of A is of the form (Problem 8.53): $A^{-1} = \begin{pmatrix} 1 & x & y \\ 0 & 1 & z \\ 0 & 0 & 1 \end{pmatrix}$.

Set $AA^{-1} = I$, the identity matrix:

$$AA^{-1} = \begin{pmatrix} 1 & 1 & 1 \\ 0 & 1 & 1 \\ 0 & 0 & 1 \end{pmatrix}\begin{pmatrix} 1 & x & y \\ 0 & 1 & z \\ 0 & 0 & 1 \end{pmatrix} = \begin{pmatrix} 1 & x+1 & y+z+1 \\ 0 & 1 & z+1 \\ 0 & 0 & 1 \end{pmatrix} = \begin{pmatrix} 1 & 0 & 0 \\ 0 & 1 & 0 \\ 0 & 0 & 1 \end{pmatrix} = I$$

Set corresponding entries equal to each other to obtain the system

$$x + 1 = 0, \quad y + z + 1 = 0, \quad z + 1 = 0$$

The solution of the system is $x = -1$, $y = 0$, $z = -1$. Hence $A^{-1} = \begin{pmatrix} 1 & -1 & 0 \\ 0 & 1 & -1 \\ 0 & 0 & 1 \end{pmatrix}$.

A^{-1} could also be found by the formula $A^{-1} = (\text{adj } A)/|A|$.

8.39. Let D be a 2-linear, alternating function. Show that $D(A, B) = -D(B, A)$. More generally, show that if D is multilinear and alternating, then
$$D(\dots, A, \dots, B, \dots) = -D(\dots, B, \dots, A, \dots)$$
that is, the sign is changed whenever two components are interchanged.

Since D is alternating, $D(A + B, A + B) = 0$. Furthermore, since D is multilinear,
$$0 = D(A + B, A + B) = D(A, A + B) + D(B, A + B)$$
$$= D(A, A) + D(A, B) + D(B, A) + D(B, B)$$

But $D(A, A) = 0$ and $D(B, B) = 0$. Hence
$$0 = D(A, B) + D(B, A) \quad \text{or} \quad D(A, B) = -D(B, A)$$

Similarly,
$$0 = D(\dots, A + B, \dots, A + B, \dots)$$
$$= D(\dots, A, \dots, A, \dots) + D(\dots, A, \dots, B, \dots)$$
$$+ D(\dots, B, \dots, A, \dots) + D(\dots, B, \dots, B, \dots)$$
$$= D(\dots, A, \dots, B, \dots) + D(\dots, B, \dots, A, \dots)$$

and thus $D(\dots, A, \dots, B, \dots) = -D(\dots, B, \dots, A, \dots)$.

8.40. Let V be the vector space of 2 by 2 matrices $M = \begin{pmatrix} a & b \\ c & d \end{pmatrix}$ over $\mathbf{R}$. Determine whether or not $D : V \to \mathbf{R}$ is 2-linear (with respect to the rows) if (i) $D(M) = a + d$, (ii) $D(M) = ad$.

(i) No. For example, suppose $A = (1, 1)$ and $B = (3, 3)$. Then
$$D(A, B) = D \begin{pmatrix} 1 & 1 \\ 3 & 3 \end{pmatrix} = 4 \quad \text{and} \quad D(2A, B) = D \begin{pmatrix} 2 & 2 \\ 3 & 3 \end{pmatrix} = 5 \neq 2D(A, B)$$

(ii) Yes. Let $A = (a_1, a_2)$, $B = (b_1, b_2)$ and $C = (c_1, c_2)$; then
$$D(A, C) = D \begin{pmatrix} a_1 & a_2 \\ c_1 & c_2 \end{pmatrix} = a_1 c_2 \quad \text{and} \quad D(B, C) = D \begin{pmatrix} b_1 & b_2 \\ c_1 & c_2 \end{pmatrix} = b_1 c_2$$

Hence for any scalars $s, t \in \mathbf{R}$,
$$D(sA + tB, C) = D \begin{pmatrix} sa_1 + tb_1 & sa_2 + tb_2 \\ c_1 & c_2 \end{pmatrix} = (sa_1 + tb_1)c_2$$
$$= s(a_1 c_2) + t(b_1 c_2) = s\,D(A, C) + t\,D(B, C)$$

That is, D is linear with respect to the first row.

Furthermore,
$$D(C, A) = D \begin{pmatrix} c_1 & c_2 \\ a_1 & a_2 \end{pmatrix} = c_1 a_2 \quad \text{and} \quad D(C, B) = D \begin{pmatrix} c_1 & c_2 \\ b_1 & b_2 \end{pmatrix} = c_1 b_2$$

Hence for any scalars $s, t \in \mathbf{R}$,
$$D(C, sA + tB) = D \begin{pmatrix} c_1 & c_2 \\ sa_1 + tb_1 & sa_2 + tb_2 \end{pmatrix} = c_1(sa_2 + tb_2)$$
$$= s(c_1 a_2) + t(c_1 b_2) = s\,D(C, A) + t\,D(C, B)$$

That is, D is linear with respect to the second row.

Both linearity conditions imply that D is 2-linear.

Supplementary Problems

COMPUTATION OF DETERMINANTS

8.41. Evaluate the determinant of each matrix: (i) $\begin{pmatrix} 2 & 5 \\ 4 & 1 \end{pmatrix}$, (ii) $\begin{pmatrix} 6 & 1 \\ 3 & -2 \end{pmatrix}$.

8.42. Compute the determinant of each matrix: (i) $\begin{pmatrix} t-2 & -3 \\ -4 & t-1 \end{pmatrix}$, (ii) $\begin{pmatrix} t-5 & 7 \\ -1 & t+3 \end{pmatrix}$.

8.43. For each matrix in the preceding problem, find those values of t for which the determinant is zero.

8.44. Compute the determinant of each matrix:

(i) $\begin{pmatrix} 2 & 1 & 1 \\ 0 & 5 & -2 \\ 1 & -3 & 4 \end{pmatrix}$, (ii) $\begin{pmatrix} 3 & -2 & -4 \\ 2 & 5 & -1 \\ 0 & 6 & 1 \end{pmatrix}$, (iii) $\begin{pmatrix} -2 & -1 & 4 \\ 6 & -3 & -2 \\ 4 & 1 & 2 \end{pmatrix}$, (iv) $\begin{pmatrix} 7 & 6 & 5 \\ 1 & 2 & 1 \\ 3 & -2 & 1 \end{pmatrix}$.

8.45. Evaluate the determinant of each matrix:

(i) $\begin{pmatrix} t-2 & 4 & 3 \\ 1 & t+1 & -2 \\ 0 & 0 & t-4 \end{pmatrix}$, (ii) $\begin{pmatrix} t-1 & 3 & -3 \\ -3 & t+5 & -3 \\ -6 & 6 & t-4 \end{pmatrix}$, (iii) $\begin{pmatrix} t+3 & -1 & 1 \\ 7 & t-5 & 1 \\ 6 & -6 & t+2 \end{pmatrix}$.

8.46. For each matrix in the preceding problem, determine those values of t for which the determinant is zero.

8.47. Evaluate the determinant of each matrix: (i) $\begin{pmatrix} 1 & 2 & 2 & 3 \\ 1 & 0 & -2 & 0 \\ 3 & -1 & 1 & -2 \\ 4 & -3 & 0 & 2 \end{pmatrix}$, (ii) $\begin{pmatrix} 2 & 1 & 3 & 2 \\ 3 & 0 & 1 & -2 \\ 1 & -1 & 4 & 3 \\ 2 & 2 & -1 & 1 \end{pmatrix}$.

COFACTORS, CLASSICAL ADJOINTS, INVERSES

8.48. For the matrix $\begin{pmatrix} 1 & 2 & -2 & 3 \\ 3 & -1 & 5 & 0 \\ 4 & 0 & 2 & 1 \\ 1 & 7 & 2 & -3 \end{pmatrix}$, find the cofactor of:

(i) the entry 4, (ii) the entry 5, (iii) the entry 7.

8.49. Let $A = \begin{pmatrix} 1 & 1 & 0 \\ 1 & 1 & 1 \\ 0 & 2 & 1 \end{pmatrix}$. Find (i) adj A, (ii) A^{-1}.

8.50. Let $A = \begin{pmatrix} 1 & 2 & 2 \\ 3 & 1 & 0 \\ 1 & 1 & 1 \end{pmatrix}$. Find (i) adj A, (ii) A^{-1}.

8.51. Find the classical adjoint of each matrix in Problem 8.47.

8.52. Determine the general 2 by 2 matrix A for which $A = \text{adj } A$.

8.53. Suppose A is diagonal and B is triangular; say,

$$A = \begin{pmatrix} a_1 & 0 & \dots & 0 \\ 0 & a_2 & \dots & 0 \\ \multicolumn{4}{c}{\dotfill} \\ 0 & 0 & \dots & a_n \end{pmatrix} \quad \text{and} \quad B = \begin{pmatrix} b_1 & c_{12} & \dots & c_{1n} \\ 0 & b_2 & \dots & c_{2n} \\ \multicolumn{4}{c}{\dotfill} \\ 0 & 0 & \dots & b_n \end{pmatrix}$$

(i)   Show that adj A is diagonal and adj B is triangular.

(ii)   Show that B is invertible iff all $b_i \neq 0$; hence A is invertible iff all $a_i \neq 0$.

(iii)   Show that the inverses of A and B (if either exists) are of the form

$$A^{-1} = \begin{pmatrix} a_1^{-1} & 0 & \dots & 0 \\ 0 & a_2^{-1} & \dots & 0 \\ \dotfill \\ 0 & 0 & \dots & a_n^{-1} \end{pmatrix}, \quad B^{-1} = \begin{pmatrix} b_1^{-1} & d_{12} & \dots & d_{1n} \\ 0 & b_2^{-1} & \dots & d_{2n} \\ \dotfill \\ 0 & 0 & \dots & b_n^{-1} \end{pmatrix}$$

That is, the diagonal elements of A^{-1} and B^{-1} are the inverses of the corresponding diagonal elements of A and B.

DETERMINANT OF A LINEAR OPERATOR

8.54. Let T be the linear operator on $\mathbf{R}^3$ defined by

$$T(x, y, z) = (3x - 2z, 5y + 7z, x + y + z)$$

Find det (T).

8.55. Let $D: V \to V$ be the differential operator, i.e. $D(v) = dv/dt$. Find det (D) if V is the space generated by (i) $\{1, t, \dots, t^n\}$, (ii) $\{e^t, e^{2t}, e^{3t}\}$, (iii) $\{\sin t, \cos t\}$.

8.56. Prove Theorem 8.12: Let T and S be linear operators on V. Then:
(i) det $(S \circ T) = $ det $(S) \cdot $ det (T); (ii) T is invertible if and only if det $(T) \neq 0$.

8.57. Show that: (i) det $(1_V) = 1$ where 1_V is the identity operator; (ii) det $(T^{-1}) = $ det $(T)^{-1}$ if T is invertible.

DETERMINANTS AND LINEAR EQUATIONS

8.58. Solve by determinants: (i) $\begin{cases} 3x + 5y = 8 \\ 4x - 2y = 1 \end{cases}$ (ii) $\begin{cases} 2x - 3y = -1 \\ 4x + 7y = -1 \end{cases}$.

8.59. Solve by determinants: (i) $\begin{cases} 2x - 5y + 2z = 7 \\ x + 2y - 4z = 3 \\ 3x - 4y - 6z = 5 \end{cases}$ (ii) $\begin{cases} 2z + 3 = y + 3x \\ x - 3z = 2y + 1 \\ 3y + z = 2 - 2x \end{cases}$.

8.60. Prove Theorem 8.10: The homogeneous system $Ax = 0$ has a nonzero solution if and only if $\Delta = |A| = 0$.

PERMUTATIONS

8.61. Determine the parity of these permutations in S_5: (i) $\sigma = 3\,2\,1\,5\,4$, (ii) $\tau = 1\,3\,5\,2\,4$, (iii) $\pi = 4\,2\,5\,3\,1$.

8.62. For the permutations σ, τ and π in Problem 8.61, find (i) $\tau \circ \sigma$, (ii) $\pi \circ \sigma$, (iii) σ^{-1}, (iv) τ^{-1}.

8.63. Let $\tau \in S_n$. Show that $\tau \circ \sigma$ runs through S_n as σ runs through S_n; that is, $S_n = \{\tau \circ \sigma : \sigma \in S_n\}$.

8.64. Let $\sigma \in S_n$ have the property that $\sigma(n) = n$. Let $\sigma^* \in S_{n-1}$ be defined by $\sigma^*(x) = \sigma(x)$. (i) Show that sgn $\sigma^* = $ sgn σ. (ii) Show that as σ runs through S_n, where $\sigma(n) = n$, σ^* runs through S_{n-1}; that is, $S_{n-1} = \{\sigma^* : \sigma \in S_n, \sigma(n) = n\}$.

MULTILINEARITY

8.65. Let $V = (K^m)^m$, i.e. V is the space of m-square matrices viewed as m-tuples of row vectors. Let $D : V \to K$.

(i)   Show that the following weaker statement is equivalent to D being alternating:

$$D(A_1, A_2, \dots, A_n) = 0$$

whenever $A_i = A_{i+1}$ for some i.

(ii)   Suppose D is m-linear and alternating. Show that if $A_1, A_2, \dots, A_m$ are linearly dependent, then $D(A_1, \dots, A_m) = 0$.

8.66. Let V be the space of 2 by 2 matrices $M = \begin{pmatrix} a & b \\ c & d \end{pmatrix}$ over **R**. Determine whether or not $D : V \to \mathbf{R}$ is 2-linear (with respect to the rows) if (i) $D(M) = ac - bd$, (ii) $D(M) = ab - cd$, (iii) $D(M) = 0$, (iv) $D(M) = 1$.

8.67. Let V be the space of n-square matrices over K. Suppose $B \in V$ is invertible and so $\det(B) \neq 0$. Define $D : V \to K$ by $D(A) = \det(AB)/\det(B)$ where $A \in V$. Hence

$$D(A_1, A_2, \ldots, A_n) = \det(A_1 B, A_2 B, \ldots, A_n B)/\det(B)$$

where A_i is the ith row of A and so $A_i B$ is the ith row of AB. Show that D is multilinear and alternating, and that $D(I) = 1$. (Thus by Theorem 8.13, $D(A) = \det(A)$ and so $\det(AB) = \det(A)\det(B)$. This method is used by some texts to prove Theorem 8.5, i.e. $|AB| = |A|\,|B|$.)

MISCELLANEOUS PROBLEMS

8.68. Let A be an n-square matrix. Prove $|kA| = k^n\,|A|$.

8.69. Prove:

$$\begin{vmatrix} 1 & x_1 & x_1^2 & \ldots & x_1^{n-1} \\ 1 & x_2 & x_2^2 & \ldots & x_2^{n-1} \\ \cdots\cdots\cdots\cdots\cdots\cdots \\ 1 & x_n & x_n^2 & \ldots & x_n^{n-1} \end{vmatrix} = (-1)^n \prod_{i<j} (x_i - x_j)$$

The above is called the Vandermonde determinant of order n.

8.70. Consider the block matrix $M = \begin{pmatrix} A & B \\ 0 & C \end{pmatrix}$ where A and C are square matrices. Prove $|M| = |A|\,|C|$. More generally, prove that if M is a triangular block matrix with square matrices $A_1, \ldots, A_m$ on the diagonal, then $|M| = |A_1|\,|A_2| \cdots |A_m|$.

8.71. Let A, B, C and D be commuting n-square matrices. Consider the $2n$-square block matrix $M = \begin{pmatrix} A & B \\ C & D \end{pmatrix}$. Prove that $|M| = |A|\,|D| - |B|\,|C|$.

8.72. Suppose A is *orthogonal*, that is, $A^t A = I$. Show that $|A| = \pm 1$.

8.73. Consider a permutation $\sigma = j_1 j_2 \ldots j_n$. Let $\{e_i\}$ be the usual basis of K^n, and let A be the matrix whose ith row is e_{j_i}, i.e. $A = (e_{j_1}, e_{j_2}, \ldots, e_{j_n})$. Show that $|A| = \operatorname{sgn}\sigma$.

8.74. Let A be an n-square matrix. The *determinantal rank* of A is the order of the largest submatrix of A (obtained by deleting rows and columns of A) whose determinant is not zero. Show that the determinantal rank of A is equal to its rank, i.e. the maximum number of linearly independent rows (or columns).

Answers to Supplementary Problems

8.41. (i) -18, (ii) -15.

8.42. (i) $t^2 - 3t - 10$, (ii) $t^2 - 2t - 8$.

8.43. (i) $t = 5$, $t = -2$; (ii) $t = 4$, $t = -2$.

8.44. (i) 21, (ii) -11, (iii) 100, (iv) 0.

8.45. (i) $(t+2)(t-3)(t-4)$, (ii) $(t+2)^2(t-4)$, (iii) $(t+2)^2(t-4)$.

8.46. (i) 3, 4, -2; (ii) 4, -2; (iii) 4, -2.

8.47. (i) -131, (ii) -55.

8.48. (i) -135, (ii) -103, (iii) -31.

8.49. $\text{adj } A = \begin{pmatrix} -1 & -1 & 1 \\ -1 & 1 & -1 \\ 2 & -2 & 0 \end{pmatrix}$, $A^{-1} = (\text{adj } A)/|A| = \begin{pmatrix} \frac{1}{2} & \frac{1}{2} & -\frac{1}{2} \\ \frac{1}{2} & -\frac{1}{2} & \frac{1}{2} \\ -1 & 1 & 0 \end{pmatrix}$.

8.50. $\text{adj } A = \begin{pmatrix} 1 & 0 & -2 \\ -3 & -1 & 6 \\ 2 & 1 & -5 \end{pmatrix}$, $A^{-1} = \begin{pmatrix} -1 & 0 & 2 \\ 3 & 1 & -6 \\ -2 & -1 & 5 \end{pmatrix}$.

8.51. (i) $\begin{pmatrix} -16 & -29 & -26 & -2 \\ -30 & -38 & -16 & 29 \\ -8 & 51 & -13 & -1 \\ -13 & 1 & 28 & -18 \end{pmatrix}$ (ii) $\begin{pmatrix} 21 & -14 & -17 & -19 \\ -44 & 11 & 33 & 11 \\ -29 & 1 & 13 & 21 \\ 17 & 7 & -19 & -18 \end{pmatrix}$

8.52. $A = \begin{pmatrix} k & 0 \\ 0 & k \end{pmatrix}$

8.54. $\det(T) = 4$.

8.55. (i) 0, (ii) 6, (iii) 1.

8.58. (i) $x = 21/26$, $y = 29/26$; (ii) $x = -5/13$, $y = 1/13$.

8.59. (i) $x = 5$, $y = 1$, $z = 1$.   (ii) Since $\Delta = 0$, the system cannot be solved by determinants.

8.61. $\text{sgn } \sigma = 1$, $\text{sgn } \tau = -1$, $\text{sgn } \pi = -1$.

8.62. (i) $\tau \circ \sigma = 53142$, (ii) $\pi \circ \sigma = 52413$, (iii) $\sigma^{-1} = 32154$, (iv) $\tau^{-1} = 14253$.

8.66. (i) Yes, (ii) No, (iii) Yes, (iv) No.

Chapter 9

Eigenvalues and Eigenvectors

INTRODUCTION

In this chapter we investigate the theory of a single linear operator T on a vector space V of finite dimension. In particular, we find conditions under which T is diagonalizable. As was seen in Chapter 7, this question is closely related to the theory of similarity transformations for matrices.

We shall also associate certain polynomials with an operator T: its characteristic polynomial and its minimum polynomial. These polynomials and their roots play a major role in the investigation of T. We comment that the particular field K also plays an important part in the theory since the existence of roots of a polynomial depends on K.

POLYNOMIALS OF MATRICES AND LINEAR OPERATORS

Consider a polynomial $f(t)$ over a field K: $f(t) = a_n t^n + \cdots + a_1 t + a_0$. If A is a square matrix over K, then we define

$$f(A) = a_n A^n + \cdots + a_1 A + a_0 I$$

where I is the identity matrix. In particular, we say that A is a *root* or *zero* of the polynomial $f(t)$ if $f(A) = 0$.

Example 9.1: Let $A = \begin{pmatrix} 1 & 2 \\ 3 & 4 \end{pmatrix}$, and let $f(t) = 2t^2 - 3t + 7$, $g(t) = t^2 - 5t - 2$. Then

$$f(A) = 2\begin{pmatrix} 1 & 2 \\ 3 & 4 \end{pmatrix}^2 - 3\begin{pmatrix} 1 & 2 \\ 3 & 4 \end{pmatrix} + 7\begin{pmatrix} 1 & 0 \\ 0 & 1 \end{pmatrix} = \begin{pmatrix} 18 & 14 \\ 21 & 39 \end{pmatrix}$$

and

$$g(A) = \begin{pmatrix} 1 & 2 \\ 3 & 4 \end{pmatrix}^2 - 5\begin{pmatrix} 1 & 2 \\ 3 & 4 \end{pmatrix} - 2\begin{pmatrix} 1 & 0 \\ 0 & 1 \end{pmatrix} = \begin{pmatrix} 0 & 0 \\ 0 & 0 \end{pmatrix}$$

Thus A is a zero of $g(t)$.

The following theorem applies.

Theorem 9.1: Let f and g be polynomials over K, and let A be an n-square matrix over K. Then

    (i) $(f + g)(A) = f(A) + g(A)$

    (ii) $(fg)(A) = f(A)\,g(A)$

and, for any scalar $k \in K$,

    (iii) $(kf)(A) = k\,f(A)$

Furthermore, since $f(t)\,g(t) = g(t)\,f(t)$ for any polynomials $f(t)$ and $g(t)$,

$$f(A)\,g(A) = g(A)\,f(A)$$

That is, any two polynomials in the matrix A commute.

Now suppose $T : V \to V$ is a linear operator on a vector space V over K. If $f(t) = a_n t^n + \cdots + a_1 t + a_0$, then we define $f(T)$ in the same way as we did for matrices:

$$f(T) = a_n T^n + \cdots + a_1 T + a_0 I$$

where I is now the identity mapping. We also say that T is a *zero* or *root* of $f(t)$ if $f(T) = 0$. We remark that the relations in Theorem 9.1 hold for operators as they do for matrices; hence any two polynomials in T commute.

Furthermore, if A is a matrix representation of T, then $f(A)$ is the matrix representation of $f(T)$. In particular, $f(T) = 0$ if and only if $f(A) = 0$.

EIGENVALUES AND EIGENVECTORS

Let $T : V \to V$ be a linear operator on a vector space V over a field K. A scalar $\lambda \in K$ is called an *eigenvalue* of T if there exists a nonzero vector $v \in V$ for which

$$T(v) = \lambda v$$

Every vector satisfying this relation is then called an *eigenvector* of T belonging to the eigenvalue λ. Note that each scalar multiple kv is such an eigenvector:

$$T(kv) = k\,T(v) = k(\lambda v) = \lambda(kv)$$

The set of all such vectors is a subspace of V (Problem 9.6) called the *eigenspace* of λ.

The terms *characteristic value* and *characteristic vector* (or: *proper value* and *proper vector*) are frequently used instead of eigenvalue and eigenvector.

Example 9.2: Let $I : V \to V$ be the identity mapping. Then, for every $v \in V$, $I(v) = v = 1v$. Hence 1 is an eigenvalue of I, and every vector in V is an eigenvector belonging to 1.

Example 9.3: Let $T : \mathbf{R}^2 \to \mathbf{R}^2$ be the linear operator which rotates each vector $v \in \mathbf{R}^2$ by an angle $\theta = 90°$. Note that no nonzero vector is a multiple of itself. Hence T has no eigenvalues and so no eigenvectors.

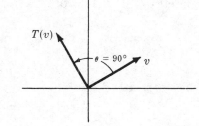

Example 9.4: Let D be the differential operator on the vector space V of differentiable functions. We have $D(e^{5t}) = 5e^{5t}$. Hence 5 is an eigenvalue of D with eigenvector e^{5t}.

If A is an n-square matrix over K, then an eigenvalue of A means an eigenvalue of A viewed as an operator on K^n. That is, $\lambda \in K$ is an eigenvalue of A if, for some nonzero (column) vector $v \in K^n$,

$$Av = \lambda v$$

In this case v is an eigenvector of A belonging to λ.

Example 9.5: Find eigenvalues and associated nonzero eigenvectors of the matrix $A = \begin{pmatrix} 1 & 2 \\ 3 & 2 \end{pmatrix}$.

We seek a scalar t and a nonzero vector $X = \begin{pmatrix} x \\ y \end{pmatrix}$ such that $AX = tX$:

$$\begin{pmatrix} 1 & 2 \\ 3 & 2 \end{pmatrix} \begin{pmatrix} x \\ y \end{pmatrix} = t \begin{pmatrix} x \\ y \end{pmatrix}$$

The above matrix equation is equivalent to the homogeneous system

$$\begin{cases} x + 2y = tx \\ 3x + 2y = ty \end{cases} \quad \text{or} \quad \begin{cases} (t-1)x - 2y = 0 \\ -3x + (t-2)y = 0 \end{cases} \qquad (1)$$

Recall that the homogeneous system has a nonzero solution if and only if the determinant of the matrix of coefficients is 0:

$$\begin{vmatrix} t-1 & -2 \\ -3 & t-2 \end{vmatrix} = t^2 - 3t - 4 = (t-4)(t+1) = 0$$

Thus t is an eigenvalue of A if and only if $t = 4$ **or** $t = -1$.

Setting $t = 4$ in (1),

$$\begin{cases} 3x - 2y = 0 \\ -3x + 2y = 0 \end{cases} \qquad \text{or simply} \qquad 3x - 2y = 0$$

Thus $v = \begin{pmatrix} x \\ y \end{pmatrix} = \begin{pmatrix} 2 \\ 3 \end{pmatrix}$ is a nonzero eigenvector belonging to the eigenvalue $t = 4$, and every other eigenvector belonging to $t = 4$ is a multiple of v.

Setting $t = -1$ in (1),

$$\begin{cases} -2x - 2y = 0 \\ -3x - 3y = 0 \end{cases} \qquad \text{or simply} \qquad x + y = 0$$

Thus $w = \begin{pmatrix} x \\ y \end{pmatrix} = \begin{pmatrix} 1 \\ -1 \end{pmatrix}$ is a nonzero eigenvector belonging to the eigenvalue $t = -1$, and every other eigenvector belonging to $t = -1$ is a multiple of w.

The next theorem gives an important characterization of eigenvalues which is frequently used as its definition.

Theorem 9.2: Let $T : V \to V$ be a linear operator on a vector space over K. Then $\lambda \in K$ is an eigenvalue of T if and only if the operator $\lambda I - T$ is singular. The eigenspace of λ is then the kernel of $\lambda I - T$.

Proof. λ is an eigenvalue of T if and only if there exists a nonzero vector v such that

$$T(v) = \lambda v \qquad \text{or} \qquad (\lambda I)(v) - T(v) = 0 \qquad \text{or} \qquad (\lambda I - T)(v) = 0$$

i.e. $\lambda I - T$ is singular. We also have that v is in the eigenspace of λ if and only if the above relations hold; hence v is in the kernel of $\lambda I - T$.

We now state a very useful theorem which we prove (Problem 9.14) by induction:

Theorem 9.3: Nonzero eigenvectors belonging to distinct eigenvalues are linearly independent.

Example 9.6: Consider the functions $e^{a_1 t}, e^{a_2 t}, \ldots, e^{a_n t}$ where $a_1, \ldots, a_n$ are distinct real numbers. If D is the differential operator then $D(e^{a_k t}) = a_k e^{a_k t}$. Accordingly, $e^{a_1 t}, \ldots, e^{a_n t}$ are eigenvectors of D belonging to the distinct eigenvalues $a_1, \ldots, a_n$, and so, by Theorem 9.3, are linearly independent.

We remark that independent eigenvectors can belong to the same eigenvalue (see Problem 9.7).

DIAGONALIZATION AND EIGENVECTORS

Let $T : V \to V$ be a linear operator on a vector space V with finite dimension n. Note that T can be represented by a diagonal matrix

$$\begin{pmatrix} k_1 & 0 & \ldots & 0 \\ 0 & k_2 & \ldots & 0 \\ \multicolumn{4}{c}{\dotfill} \\ 0 & 0 & \ldots & k_n \end{pmatrix}$$

if and only if there exists a basis $\{v_1, \ldots, v_n\}$ of V for which

$$
\begin{aligned}
T(v_1) &= k_1 v_1 \\
T(v_2) &= \quad\;\; k_2 v_2 \\
&\cdots\cdots\cdots\cdots\cdots\cdots \\
T(v_n) &= \qquad\qquad k_n v_n
\end{aligned}
$$

that is, such that the vectors $v_1, \ldots, v_n$ are eigenvectors of T belonging respectively to eigenvalues $k_1, \ldots, k_n$. In other words:

Theorem 9.4:   A linear operator $T : V \to V$ can be represented by a diagonal matrix B if and only if V has a basis consisting of eigenvectors of T. In this case the diagonal elements of B are the corresponding eigenvalues.

We have the following equivalent statement.

Alternative Form of Theorem 9.4:   An n-square matrix A is similar to a diagonal matrix B if and only if A has n linearly independent eigenvectors. In this case the diagonal elements of B are the corresponding eigenvalues.

In the above theorem, if we let P be the matrix whose columns are the n independent eigenvectors of A, then $B = P^{-1}AP$.

Example 9.7:   Consider the matrix $A = \begin{pmatrix} 1 & 2 \\ 3 & 2 \end{pmatrix}$. By Example 9.5, A has two independent eigenvectors $\begin{pmatrix} 2 \\ 3 \end{pmatrix}$ and $\begin{pmatrix} 1 \\ -1 \end{pmatrix}$. Set $P = \begin{pmatrix} 2 & 1 \\ 3 & -1 \end{pmatrix}$, and so $P^{-1} = \begin{pmatrix} 1/5 & 1/5 \\ 3/5 & -2/5 \end{pmatrix}$.

Then A is similar to the diagonal matrix

$$
B = P^{-1}AP = \begin{pmatrix} 1/5 & 1/5 \\ 3/5 & -2/5 \end{pmatrix}\begin{pmatrix} 1 & 2 \\ 3 & 2 \end{pmatrix}\begin{pmatrix} 2 & 1 \\ 3 & -1 \end{pmatrix} = \begin{pmatrix} 4 & 0 \\ 0 & -1 \end{pmatrix}
$$

As expected, the diagonal elements 4 and -1 of the diagonal matrix B are the eigenvalues corresponding to the given eigenvectors.

CHARACTERISTIC POLYNOMIAL, CAYLEY-HAMILTON THEOREM

Consider an n-square matrix A over a field K:

$$
A = \begin{pmatrix} a_{11} & a_{12} & \ldots & a_{1n} \\ a_{21} & a_{22} & \ldots & a_{2n} \\ \cdots\cdots\cdots\cdots\cdots\cdots \\ a_{n1} & a_{n2} & \ldots & a_{nn} \end{pmatrix}
$$

The matrix $tI_n - A$, where I_n is the n-square identity matrix and t is an indeterminant, is called the *characteristic matrix* of A:

$$
tI_n - A = \begin{pmatrix} t - a_{11} & -a_{12} & \ldots & -a_{1n} \\ -a_{21} & t - a_{22} & \ldots & -a_{2n} \\ \cdots\cdots\cdots\cdots\cdots\cdots\cdots\cdots \\ -a_{n1} & -a_{n2} & \ldots & t - a_{nn} \end{pmatrix}
$$

Its determinant $\Delta_A(t) = \det(tI_n - A)$

which is a polynomial in t, is called the *characteristic polynomial* of A. We also call

$$
\Delta_A(t) = \det(tI_n - A) = 0
$$

the *characteristic equation* of A.

Now each term in the determinant contains one and only one entry from each row and from each column; hence the above characteristic polynomial is of the form

$$\Delta_A(t) \;=\; (t - a_{11})(t - a_{22}) \cdots (t - a_{nn})$$
$$+ \text{ terms with at most } n-2 \text{ factors of the form } t - a_{ii}$$

Accordingly,

$$\Delta_A(t) \;=\; t^n - (a_{11} + a_{22} + \cdots + a_{nn})t^{n-1} + \text{ terms of lower degree}$$

Recall that the trace of A is the sum of its diagonal elements. Thus the characteristic polynomial $\Delta_A(t) = \det(tI_n - A)$ of A is a monic polynomial of degree n, and the coefficient of t^{n-1} is the negative of the trace of A. (A polynomial is *monic* if its leading coefficient is 1.)

Furthermore, if we set $t = 0$ in $\Delta_A(t)$, we obtain

$$\Delta_A(0) \;=\; |-A| \;=\; (-1)^n |A|$$

But $\Delta_A(0)$ is the constant term of the polynomial $\Delta_A(t)$. Thus the constant term of the characteristic polynomial of the matrix A is $(-1)^n |A|$ where n is the order of A.

Example 9.8: The characteristic polynomial of the matrix $A = \begin{pmatrix} 1 & 3 & 0 \\ -2 & 2 & -1 \\ 4 & 0 & -2 \end{pmatrix}$ is

$$\Delta(t) \;=\; |tI - A| \;=\; \begin{vmatrix} t-1 & -3 & 0 \\ 2 & t-2 & 1 \\ -4 & 0 & t+2 \end{vmatrix} \;=\; t^3 - t^2 + 2t + 28$$

As expected, $\Delta(t)$ is a monic polynomial of degree 3.

We now state one of the most important theorems in linear algebra.

Cayley-Hamilton Theorem 9.5: Every matrix is a zero of its characteristic polynomial.

Example 9.9: The characteristic polynomial of the matrix $A = \begin{pmatrix} 1 & 2 \\ 3 & 2 \end{pmatrix}$ is

$$\Delta(t) \;=\; |tI - A| \;=\; \begin{vmatrix} t-1 & -2 \\ -3 & t-2 \end{vmatrix} \;=\; t^2 - 3t - 4$$

As expected from the Cayley-Hamilton theorem, A is a zero of $\Delta(t)$:

$$\Delta(A) \;=\; \begin{pmatrix} 1 & 2 \\ 3 & 2 \end{pmatrix}^2 - 3\begin{pmatrix} 1 & 2 \\ 3 & 2 \end{pmatrix} - 4\begin{pmatrix} 1 & 0 \\ 0 & 1 \end{pmatrix} \;=\; \begin{pmatrix} 0 & 0 \\ 0 & 0 \end{pmatrix}$$

The next theorem shows the intimate relationship between characteristic polynomials and eigenvalues.

Theorem 9.6: Let A be an n-square matrix over a field K. A scalar $\lambda \in K$ is an eigenvalue of A if and only if λ is a root of the characteristic polynomial $\Delta(t)$ of A.

Proof. By Theorem 9.2, λ is an eigenvalue of A if and only if $\lambda I - A$ is singular. Furthermore, by Theorem 8.4, $\lambda I - A$ is singular if and only if $|\lambda I - A| = 0$, i.e. λ is a root of $\Delta(t)$. Thus the theorem is proved.

Using Theorems 9.3, 9.4 and 9.6, we obtain

Corollary 9.7: If the characteristic polynomial $\Delta(t)$ of an n-square matrix A is a product of distinct linear factors:

$$\Delta(t) \;=\; (t - a_1)(t - a_2) \cdots (t - a_n)$$

i.e. if $a_1, \ldots, a_n$ are distinct roots of $\Delta(t)$, then A is similar to a diagonal matrix whose diagonal elements are the a_i.

Furthermore, using the Fundamental Theorem of Algebra (every polynomial over **C** has a root) and the above theorem, we obtain

Corollary 9.8:   Let A be an n-square matrix over the complex field **C**. Then A has at least one eigenvalue.

Example 9.10:   Let $A = \begin{pmatrix} 3 & 0 & 0 \\ 0 & 2 & -5 \\ 0 & 1 & -2 \end{pmatrix}$.   Its characteristic polynomial is

$$\Delta(t) \;=\; \begin{vmatrix} t-3 & 0 & 0 \\ 0 & t-2 & 5 \\ 0 & -1 & t+2 \end{vmatrix} \;=\; (t-3)(t^2+1)$$

We consider two cases:

(i) A is a matrix over the real field **R**. Then A has only the one eigenvalue 3. Since 3 has only one independent eigenvector, A is not diagonalizable.

(ii) A is a matrix over the complex field **C**. Then A has three distinct eigenvalues: 3, i and $-i$. Thus there exists an invertible matrix P over the complex field **C** for which

$$P^{-1}AP \;=\; \begin{pmatrix} 3 & 0 & 0 \\ 0 & i & 0 \\ 0 & 0 & -i \end{pmatrix}$$

i.e. A is diagonalizable.

Now suppose A and B are similar matrices, say $B = P^{-1}AP$ where P is invertible. We show that A and B have the same characteristic polynomial. Using $tI = P^{-1}tIP$,

$$|tI - B| \;=\; |tI - P^{-1}AP| \;=\; |P^{-1}tIP - P^{-1}AP|$$
$$=\; |P^{-1}(tI - A)P| \;=\; |P^{-1}|\,|tI - A|\,|P|$$

Since determinants are scalars and commute, and since $|P^{-1}|\,|P| = 1$, we finally obtain

$$|tI - B| \;=\; |tI - A|$$

Thus we have proved

Theorem 9.9:   Similar matrices have the same characteristic polynomial.

MINIMUM POLYNOMIAL

Let A be an n-square matrix over a field K. Observe that there are nonzero polynomials $f(t)$ for which $f(A) = 0$; for example, the characteristic polynomial of A. Among these polynomials we consider those of lowest degree and from them we select one whose leading coefficient is 1, i.e. which is monic. Such a polynomial $m(t)$ exists and is unique (Problem 9.25); we call it the *minimum polynomial* of A.

Theorem 9.10:   The minimum polynomial $m(t)$ of A divides every polynomial which has A as a zero. In particular, $m(t)$ divides the characteristic polynomial $\Delta(t)$ of A.

There is an even stronger relationship between $m(t)$ and $\Delta(t)$.

Theorem 9.11: The characteristic and minimum polynomials of a matrix A have the same irreducible factors.

This theorem does not say that $m(t) = \Delta(t)$; only that any irreducible factor of one must divide the other. In particular, since a linear factor is irreducible, $m(t)$ and $\Delta(t)$ have the same linear factors; hence they have the same roots. Thus from Theorem 9.6 we obtain

Theorem 9.12: A scalar λ is an eigenvalue for a matrix A if and only if λ is a root of the minimum polynomial of A.

Example 9.11: Find the minimum polynomial $m(t)$ of the matrix $A = \begin{pmatrix} 2 & 1 & 0 & 0 \\ 0 & 2 & 0 & 0 \\ 0 & 0 & 2 & 0 \\ 0 & 0 & 0 & 5 \end{pmatrix}$.

The characteristic polynomial of A is $\Delta(t) = |tI - A| = (t-2)^3(t-5)$. By Theorem 9.11, both $t-2$ and $t-5$ must be factors of $m(t)$. But by Theorem 9.10, $m(t)$ must divide $\Delta(t)$; hence $m(t)$ must be one of the following three polynomials:

$$m_1(t) = (t-2)(t-5), \qquad m_2(t) = (t-2)^2(t-5), \qquad m_3(t) = (t-2)^3(t-5)$$

We know from the Cayley-Hamilton theorem that $m_3(A) = \Delta(A) = 0$. The reader can verify that $m_1(A) \neq 0$ but $m_2(A) = 0$. Accordingly, $m_2(t) = (t-2)^2(t-5)$ is the minimum polynomial of A.

Example 9.12: Let A be a 3 by 3 matrix over the real field $\mathbf{R}$. We show that A cannot be a zero of the polynomial $f(t) = t^2 + 1$. By the Cayley-Hamilton theorem, A is a zero of its characteristic polynomial $\Delta(t)$. Note that $\Delta(t)$ is of degree 3; hence it has at least one real root.

Now suppose A is a zero of $f(t)$. Since $f(t)$ is irreducible over $\mathbf{R}$, $f(t)$ must be the minimal polynomial of A. But $f(t)$ has no real root. This contradicts the fact that the characteristic and minimal polynomials have the same roots. Thus A is not a zero of $f(t)$.

The reader can verify that the following 3 by 3 matrix over the complex field $\mathbf{C}$ is a zero of $f(t)$:

$$\begin{pmatrix} 0 & -1 & 0 \\ 1 & 0 & 0 \\ 0 & 0 & i \end{pmatrix}$$

CHARACTERISTIC AND MINIMUM POLYNOMIALS OF LINEAR OPERATORS

Now suppose $T : V \to V$ is a linear operator on a vector space V with finite dimension. We define the *characteristic polynomial* $\Delta(t)$ of T to be the characteristic polynomial of any matrix representation of T. By Theorem 9.9, $\Delta(t)$ is independent of the particular basis in which the matrix representation is computed. Note that the degree of $\Delta(t)$ is equal to the dimension of V. We have theorems for T which are similar to the ones we had for matrices:

Theorem 9.5′: T is a zero of its characteristic polynomial.

Theorem 9.6′: The scalar $\lambda \in K$ is an eigenvalue of T if and only if λ is a root of the characteristic polynomial of T.

The *algebraic multiplicity* of an eigenvalue $\lambda \in K$ of T is defined to be the multiplicity of λ as a root of the characteristic polynomial of T. The *geometric multiplicity* of the eigenvalue λ is defined to be the dimension of its eigenspace.

Theorem 9.13: The geometric multiplicity of an eigenvalue λ does not exceed its algebraic multiplicity.

Example 9.13: Let V be the vector space of functions which has $\{\sin\theta, \cos\theta\}$ as a basis, and let D be the differential operator on V. Then

$$D(\sin\theta) \;=\; \cos\theta \;=\; 0(\sin\theta) + 1(\cos\theta)$$

$$D(\cos\theta) \;=\; -\sin\theta \;=\; -1(\sin\theta) + 0(\cos\theta)$$

The matrix A of D in the above basis is therefore $A = [D] = \begin{pmatrix} 0 & 1 \\ -1 & 0 \end{pmatrix}$. Thus

$$\det(tI - A) \;=\; \begin{vmatrix} t & -1 \\ 1 & t \end{vmatrix} \;=\; t^2 + 1$$

and the characteristic polynomial of D is $\Delta(t) = t^2 + 1$.

On the other hand, the *minimum polynomial* $m(t)$ of the operator T is defined independently of the theory of matrices, as the polynomial of lowest degree and leading coefficient 1 which has T as a zero. However, for any polynomial $f(t)$,

$$f(T) = 0 \quad \text{if and only if} \quad f(A) = 0$$

where A is any matrix representation of T. Accordingly, T and A have the same minimum polynomial. We remark that all the theorems in this chapter on the minimum polynomial of a matrix also hold for the minimum polynomial of the operator T.

Solved Problems

POLYNOMIALS OF MATRICES AND LINEAR OPERATORS

9.1. Find $f(A)$ where $A = \begin{pmatrix} 1 & -2 \\ 4 & 5 \end{pmatrix}$ and $f(t) = t^2 - 3t + 7$.

$$f(A) \;=\; A^2 - 3A + 7I \;=\; \begin{pmatrix} 1 & -2 \\ 4 & 5 \end{pmatrix}^2 - 3\begin{pmatrix} 1 & -2 \\ 4 & 5 \end{pmatrix} + 7\begin{pmatrix} 1 & 0 \\ 0 & 1 \end{pmatrix} = \begin{pmatrix} -3 & -6 \\ 12 & 9 \end{pmatrix}$$

9.2. Show that $A = \begin{pmatrix} 1 & 4 \\ 2 & 3 \end{pmatrix}$ is a zero of $f(t) = t^2 - 4t - 5$.

$$f(A) \;=\; A^2 - 4A - 5I \;=\; \begin{pmatrix} 1 & 4 \\ 2 & 3 \end{pmatrix}^2 - 4\begin{pmatrix} 1 & 4 \\ 2 & 3 \end{pmatrix} - 5\begin{pmatrix} 1 & 0 \\ 0 & 1 \end{pmatrix} = \begin{pmatrix} 0 & 0 \\ 0 & 0 \end{pmatrix}$$

9.3. Let V be the vector space of functions which has $\{\sin\theta, \cos\theta\}$ as a basis, and let D be the differential operator on V. Show that D is a zero of $f(t) = t^2 + 1$.

Apply $f(D)$ to each basis vector:

$$f(D)(\sin\theta) \;=\; (D^2 + I)(\sin\theta) \;=\; D^2(\sin\theta) + I(\sin\theta) \;=\; -\sin\theta + \sin\theta \;=\; 0$$

$$f(D)(\cos\theta) \;=\; (D^2 + I)(\cos\theta) \;=\; D^2(\cos\theta) + I(\cos\theta) \;=\; -\cos\theta + \cos\theta \;=\; 0$$

Since each basis vector is mapped into 0, every vector $v \in V$ is also mapped into 0 by $f(D)$. Thus $f(D) = 0$.

This result is expected since, by Example 9.13, $f(t)$ is the characteristic polynomial of D.

9.4. Let A be a matrix representation of an operator T. Show that $f(A)$ is the matrix representation of $f(T)$, for any polynomial $f(t)$.

Let ϕ be the mapping $T \mapsto A$, i.e. which sends the operator T into its matrix representation A. We need to prove that $\phi(f(T)) = f(A)$. Suppose $f(t) = a_n t^n + \cdots + a_1 t + a_0$. The proof is by induction on n, the degree of $f(t)$.

Suppose $n = 0$. Recall that $\phi(I') = I$ where I' is the identity mapping and I is the identity matrix. Thus

$$\phi(f(T)) = \phi(a_0 I') = a_0 \phi(I') = a_0 I = f(A)$$

and so the theorem holds for $n = 0$.

Now assume the theorem holds for polynomials of degree less than n. Then since ϕ is an algebra isomorphism,

$$\phi(f(T)) = \phi(a_n T^n + a_{n-1} T^{n-1} + \cdots + a_1 T + a_0 I')$$
$$= a_n \phi(T) \phi(T^{n-1}) + \phi(a_{n-1} T^{n-1} + \cdots + a_1 T + a_0 I')$$
$$= a_n A A^{n-1} + (a_{n-1} A^{n-1} + \cdots + a_1 A + a_0 I) = f(A)$$

and the theorem is proved.

9.5. Prove Theorem 9.1: Let f and g be polynomials over K. Let A be a square matrix over K. Then: (i) $(f + g)(A) = f(A) + g(A)$; (ii) $(fg)(A) = f(A) g(A)$; and (iii) $(kf)(A) = k f(A)$ where $k \in K$.

Suppose $f = a_n t^n + \cdots + a_1 t + a_0$ and $g = b_m t^m + \cdots + b_1 t + b_0$. Then by definition,

$$f(A) = a_n A^n + \cdots + a_1 A + a_0 I \quad \text{and} \quad g(A) = b_m A^m + \cdots + b_1 A + b_0 I$$

(i) Suppose $m \le n$ and let $b_i = 0$ if $i > m$. Then

$$f + g = (a_n + b_n) t^n + \cdots + (a_1 + b_1) t + (a_0 + b_0)$$

Hence

$$(f + g)(A) = (a_n + b_n) A^n + \cdots + (a_1 + b_1) A + (a_0 + b_0) I$$
$$= a_n A^n + b_n A^n + \cdots + a_1 A + b_1 A + a_0 I + b_0 I = f(A) + g(A)$$

(ii) By definition, $fg = c_{n+m} t^{n+m} + \cdots + c_1 t + c_0 = \sum_{k=0}^{n+m} c_k t^k$ where $c_k = a_0 b_k + a_1 b_{k-1} + \cdots + a_k b_0 = \sum_{i=0}^{k} a_i b_{k-i}$. Hence $(fg)(A) = \sum_{k=0}^{n+m} c_k A^k$ and

$$f(A) g(A) = \left(\sum_{i=0}^{n} a_i A^i \right) \left(\sum_{j=0}^{m} b_j A^j \right) = \sum_{i=0}^{n} \sum_{j=0}^{m} a_i b_j A^{i+j} = \sum_{k=0}^{n+m} c_k A^k = (fg)(A)$$

(iii) By definition, $kf = k a_n t^n + \cdots + k a_1 t + k a_0$, and so

$$(kf)(A) = k a_n A^n + \cdots + k a_1 A + k a_0 I = k(a_n A^n + \cdots + a_1 A + a_0 I) = k f(A)$$

EIGENVALUES AND EIGENVECTORS

9.6. Let λ be an eigenvalue of an operator $T : V \to V$. Let V_λ denote the set of all eigenvectors of T belonging to the eigenvalue λ (called the *eigenspace* of λ). Show that V_λ is a subspace of V.

Suppose $v, w \in V_\lambda$; that is, $T(v) = \lambda v$ and $T(w) = \lambda w$. Then for any scalars $a, b \in K$,

$$T(av + bw) = a T(v) + b T(w) = a(\lambda v) + b(\lambda w) = \lambda(av + bw)$$

Thus $av + bw$ is an eigenvector belonging to λ, i.e. $av + bw \in V_\lambda$. Hence V_λ is a subspace of V.

9.7. Let $A = \begin{pmatrix} 1 & 4 \\ 2 & 3 \end{pmatrix}$. (i) Find all eigenvalues of A and the corresponding eigenvectors. (ii) Find an invertible matrix P such that $P^{-1}AP$ is diagonal.

(i) Form the characteristic matrix $tI - A$ of A:

$$tI - A = \begin{pmatrix} t & 0 \\ 0 & t \end{pmatrix} - \begin{pmatrix} 1 & 4 \\ 2 & 3 \end{pmatrix} = \begin{pmatrix} t-1 & -4 \\ -2 & t-3 \end{pmatrix} \tag{1}$$

The characteristic polynomial $\Delta(t)$ of A is its determinant:

$$\Delta(t) = |tI - A| = \begin{vmatrix} t-1 & -4 \\ -2 & t-3 \end{vmatrix} = t^2 - 4t - 5 = (t-5)(t+1)$$

The roots of $\Delta(t)$ are 5 and -1, and so these numbers are the eigenvalues of A.

We obtain the eigenvectors belonging to the eigenvalue 5. First substitute $t = 5$ into the characteristic matrix (1) to obtain the matrix $\begin{pmatrix} 4 & -4 \\ -2 & 2 \end{pmatrix}$. The eigenvectors belonging to 5 form the solution of the homogeneous system determined by the above matrix, i.e.,

$$\begin{pmatrix} 4 & -4 \\ -2 & 2 \end{pmatrix}\begin{pmatrix} x \\ y \end{pmatrix} = \begin{pmatrix} 0 \\ 0 \end{pmatrix} \quad \text{or} \quad \begin{cases} 4x - 4y = 0 \\ -2x + 2y = 0 \end{cases} \quad \text{or} \quad x - y = 0$$

(In other words, the eigenvectors belonging to 5 form the kernel of the operator $tI - A$ for $t = 5$.) The above system has only one independent solution; for example, $x = 1$, $y = 1$. Thus $v = (1, 1)$ is an eigenvector which generates the eigenspace of 5, i.e. every eigenvector belonging to 5 is a multiple of v.

We obtain the eigenvectors belonging to the eigenvalue -1. Substitute $t = -1$ into (1) to obtain the homogeneous system

$$\begin{pmatrix} -2 & -4 \\ -2 & -4 \end{pmatrix}\begin{pmatrix} x \\ y \end{pmatrix} = \begin{pmatrix} 0 \\ 0 \end{pmatrix} \quad \text{or} \quad \begin{cases} -2x - 4y = 0 \\ -2x - 4y = 0 \end{cases} \quad \text{or} \quad x + 2y = 0$$

The system has only one independent solution; for example, $x = 2$, $y = -1$. Thus $w = (2, -1)$ is an eigenvector which generates the eigenspace of -1.

(ii) Let P be the matrix whose columns are the above eigenvectors: $P = \begin{pmatrix} 1 & 2 \\ 1 & -1 \end{pmatrix}$. Then $B = P^{-1}AP$ is the diagonal matrix whose diagonal entries are the respective eigenvalues:

$$B = P^{-1}AP = \begin{pmatrix} 1/3 & 2/3 \\ 1/3 & -1/3 \end{pmatrix}\begin{pmatrix} 1 & 4 \\ 2 & 3 \end{pmatrix}\begin{pmatrix} 1 & 2 \\ 1 & -1 \end{pmatrix} = \begin{pmatrix} 5 & 0 \\ 0 & -1 \end{pmatrix}$$

(*Remark.* Here P is the transition matrix from the usual basis of $\mathbf{R}^2$ to the basis of eigenvectors $\{v, w\}$. Hence B is the matrix representation of the operator A in this new basis.)

9.8. For each matrix, find all eigenvalues and a basis of each eigenspace:

$$\text{(i)} \quad A = \begin{pmatrix} 1 & -3 & 3 \\ 3 & -5 & 3 \\ 6 & -6 & 4 \end{pmatrix}, \qquad \text{(ii)} \quad B = \begin{pmatrix} -3 & 1 & -1 \\ -7 & 5 & -1 \\ -6 & 6 & -2 \end{pmatrix}$$

Which matrix can be diagonalized, and why?

(i) Form the characteristic matrix $tI - A$ and compute its determinant to obtain the characteristic polynomial $\Delta(t)$ of A:

$$\Delta(t) = |tI - A| = \begin{vmatrix} t-1 & 3 & -3 \\ -3 & t+5 & -3 \\ -6 & 6 & t-4 \end{vmatrix} = (t+2)^2(t-4)$$

The roots of $\Delta(t)$ are -2 and 4; hence these numbers are the eigenvalues of A.

We find a basis of the eigenspace of the eigenvalue -2. Substitute $t = -2$ into the characteristic matrix $tI - A$ to obtain the homogeneous system

$$\begin{pmatrix} -3 & 3 & -3 \\ -3 & 3 & -3 \\ -6 & 6 & -6 \end{pmatrix} \begin{pmatrix} x \\ y \\ z \end{pmatrix} = \begin{pmatrix} 0 \\ 0 \\ 0 \end{pmatrix} \quad \text{or} \quad \begin{cases} -3x + 3y - 3z = 0 \\ -3x + 3y - 3z = 0 \\ -6x + 6y - 6z = 0 \end{cases} \quad \text{or} \quad x - y + z = 0$$

The system has two independent solutions, e.g. $x = 1$, $y = 1$, $z = 0$ and $x = 1$, $y = 0$, $z = -1$. Thus $u = (1, 1, 0)$ and $v = (1, 0, -1)$ are independent eigenvectors which generate the eigenspace of -2. That is, u and v form a basis of the eigenspace of -2. This means that every eigenvector belonging to -2 is a linear combination of u and v.

We find a basis of the eigenspace of the eigenvalue 4. Substitute $t = 4$ into the characteristic matrix $tI - A$ to obtain the homogeneous system

$$\begin{pmatrix} 3 & 3 & -3 \\ -3 & 9 & -3 \\ -6 & 6 & 0 \end{pmatrix} \begin{pmatrix} x \\ y \\ z \end{pmatrix} = \begin{pmatrix} 0 \\ 0 \\ 0 \end{pmatrix} \quad \text{or} \quad \begin{cases} 3x + 3y - 3z = 0 \\ -3x + 9y - 3z = 0 \\ -6x + 6y \quad\quad = 0 \end{cases} \quad \text{or} \quad \begin{cases} x + y - z = 0 \\ 2y - z = 0 \end{cases}$$

The system has only one free variable; hence any particular nonzero solution, e.g. $x = 1$, $y = 1$, $z = 2$, generates its solution space. Thus $w = (1, 1, 2)$ is an eigenvector which generates, and so forms a basis, of the eigenspace of 4.

Since A has three linearly independent eigenvectors, A is diagonalizable. In fact, let P be the matrix whose columns are the three independent eigenvectors:

$$P = \begin{pmatrix} 1 & 1 & 1 \\ 1 & 0 & 1 \\ 0 & -1 & 2 \end{pmatrix}. \quad \text{Then} \quad P^{-1}AP = \begin{pmatrix} -2 & 0 & 0 \\ 0 & -2 & 0 \\ 0 & 0 & 4 \end{pmatrix}$$

As expected, the diagonal elements of $P^{-1}AP$ are the eigenvalues of A corresponding to the columns of P.

(ii) $$\Delta(t) = |tI - B| = \begin{vmatrix} t + 3 & -1 & 1 \\ 7 & t - 5 & 1 \\ 6 & -6 & t + 2 \end{vmatrix} = (t + 2)^2(t - 4)$$

The eigenvalues of B are therefore -2 and 4.

We find a basis of the eigenspace of the eigenvalue -2. Substitute $t = -2$ into $tI - B$ to obtain the homogeneous system

$$\begin{pmatrix} 1 & -1 & 1 \\ 7 & -7 & 1 \\ 6 & -6 & 0 \end{pmatrix} \begin{pmatrix} x \\ y \\ z \end{pmatrix} = \begin{pmatrix} 0 \\ 0 \\ 0 \end{pmatrix} \quad \text{or} \quad \begin{cases} x - y + z = 0 \\ 7x - 7y + z = 0 \\ 6x - 6y \quad\quad = 0 \end{cases} \quad \text{or} \quad \begin{cases} x - y + z = 0 \\ x - y \quad\quad = 0 \end{cases}$$

The system has only one independent solution, e.g. $x = 1$, $y = 1$, $z = 0$. Thus $u = (1, 1, 0)$ forms a basis of the eigenspace of -2.

We find a basis of the eigenspace of the eigenvalue 4. Substitute $t = 4$ into $tI - B$ to obtain the homogeneous system

$$\begin{pmatrix} 7 & -1 & 1 \\ 7 & -1 & 1 \\ 6 & -6 & 6 \end{pmatrix} \begin{pmatrix} x \\ y \\ z \end{pmatrix} = \begin{pmatrix} 0 \\ 0 \\ 0 \end{pmatrix} \quad \text{or} \quad \begin{cases} 7x - y + z = 0 \\ 7x - y + z = 0 \\ 6x - 6y + 6z = 0 \end{cases} \quad \text{or} \quad \begin{cases} 7x - y + z = 0 \\ x = 0 \end{cases}$$

The system has only one independent solution, e.g. $x = 0$, $y = 1$, $z = 1$. Thus $v = (0, 1, 1)$ forms a basis of the eigenspace of 4.

Observe that B is not similar to a diagonal matrix since B has only two independent eigenvectors. Furthermore, since A can be diagonalized but B cannot, A and B are not similar matrices, even though they have the same characteristic polynomial.

9.9. Let $A = \begin{pmatrix} 3 & -1 \\ 1 & 1 \end{pmatrix}$ and $B = \begin{pmatrix} 1 & -1 \\ 2 & -1 \end{pmatrix}$. Find all eigenvalues and the corresponding eigenvectors of A and B viewed as matrices over (i) the real field **R**, (ii) the complex field **C**.

(i)
$$\Delta_A(t) = |tI - A| = \begin{vmatrix} t-3 & 1 \\ -1 & t-1 \end{vmatrix} = t^2 - 4t + 4 = (t-2)^2$$

Hence only 2 is an eigenvalue. Put $t = 2$ into $tI - A$ and obtain the homogeneous system

$$\begin{pmatrix} -1 & 1 \\ -1 & 1 \end{pmatrix}\begin{pmatrix} x \\ y \end{pmatrix} = \begin{pmatrix} 0 \\ 0 \end{pmatrix} \quad \text{or} \quad \begin{cases} -x + y = 0 \\ -x + y = 0 \end{cases} \quad \text{or} \quad x - y = 0$$

The system has only one independent solution, e.g. $x = 1$, $y = 1$. Thus $v = (1, 1)$ is an eigenvector which generates the eigenspace of 2, i.e. every eigenvector belonging to 2 is a multiple of v.

We also have
$$\Delta_B(t) = |tI - B| = \begin{vmatrix} t-1 & 1 \\ -2 & t+1 \end{vmatrix} = t^2 + 1$$

Since $t^2 + 1$ has no solution in **R**, B has no eigenvalue as a matrix over **R**.

(ii) Since $\Delta_A(t) = (t-2)^2$ has only the real root 2, the results are the same as in (i). That is, 2 is an eigenvalue of A, and $v = (1, 1)$ is an eigenvector which generates the eigenspace of 2, i.e. every eigenvector of 2 is a (complex) multiple of v.

The characteristic matrix of B is $\Delta_B(t) = |tI - B| = t^2 + 1$. Hence i and $-i$ are the eigenvalues of B.

We find the eigenvectors associated with $t = i$. Substitute $t = i$ in $tI - B$ to obtain the homogeneous system

$$\begin{pmatrix} i-1 & 1 \\ -2 & i+1 \end{pmatrix}\begin{pmatrix} x \\ y \end{pmatrix} = \begin{pmatrix} 0 \\ 0 \end{pmatrix} \quad \text{or} \quad \begin{cases} (i-1)x + y = 0 \\ -2x + (i+1)y = 0 \end{cases} \quad \text{or} \quad (i-1)x + y = 0$$

The system has only one independent solution, e.g. $x = 1$, $y = 1 - i$. Thus $w = (1, 1-i)$ is an eigenvector which generates the eigenspace of i.

Now substitute $t = -i$ into $tI - B$ to obtain the homogeneous system

$$\begin{pmatrix} -i-1 & 1 \\ -2 & -i-1 \end{pmatrix}\begin{pmatrix} x \\ y \end{pmatrix} = \begin{pmatrix} 0 \\ 0 \end{pmatrix} \quad \text{or} \quad \begin{cases} (-i-1)x + y = 0 \\ -2x + (-i-1)y = 0 \end{cases} \quad \text{or} \quad (-i-1)x + y = 0$$

The system has only one independent solution, e.g. $x = 1$, $y = 1 + i$. Thus $w' = (1, 1+i)$ is an eigenvector which generates the eigenspace of $-i$.

9.10. Find all eigenvalues and a basis of each eigenspace of the operator $T : \mathbf{R}^3 \to \mathbf{R}^3$ defined by $T(x, y, z) = (2x + y, y - z, 2y + 4z)$.

First find a matrix representation of T, say relative to the usual basis of $\mathbf{R}^3$:

$$A = [T] = \begin{pmatrix} 2 & 1 & 0 \\ 0 & 1 & -1 \\ 0 & 2 & 4 \end{pmatrix}$$

The characteristic polynomial $\Delta(t)$ of T is then

$$\Delta(t) = |tI - A| = \begin{vmatrix} t-2 & -1 & 0 \\ 0 & t-1 & 1 \\ 0 & -2 & t-4 \end{vmatrix} = (t-2)^2(t-3)$$

Thus 2 and 3 are the eigenvalues of T.

We find a basis of the eigenspace of the eigenvalue 2. Substitute $t = 2$ into $tI - A$ to obtain the homogeneous system

$$\begin{pmatrix} 0 & -1 & 0 \\ 0 & 1 & 1 \\ 0 & -2 & -2 \end{pmatrix}\begin{pmatrix} x \\ y \\ z \end{pmatrix} = \begin{pmatrix} 0 \\ 0 \\ 0 \end{pmatrix} \quad \text{or} \quad \begin{cases} -y = 0 \\ y + z = 0 \\ -2y - 2z = 0 \end{cases} \quad \text{or} \quad \begin{cases} y = 0 \\ y + z = 0 \end{cases}$$

The system has only one independent solution, e.g. $x = 1$, $y = 0$, $z = 0$. Thus $u = (1, 0, 0)$ forms a basis of the eigenspace of 2.

We find a basis of the eigenspace of the eigenvalue 3. Substitute $t = 3$ into $tI - A$ to obtain the homogeneous system

$$\begin{pmatrix} 1 & -1 & 0 \\ 0 & 2 & 1 \\ 0 & -2 & -1 \end{pmatrix}\begin{pmatrix} x \\ y \\ z \end{pmatrix} = \begin{pmatrix} 0 \\ 0 \\ 0 \end{pmatrix} \quad \text{or} \quad \begin{cases} x - y = 0 \\ 2y + z = 0 \\ -2y - z = 0 \end{cases} \quad \text{or} \quad \begin{cases} x - y = 0 \\ 2y + z = 0 \end{cases}$$

The system has only one independent solution, e.g. $x = 1$, $y = 1$, $z = -2$. Thus $v = (1, 1, -2)$ forms a basis of the eigenspace of 3.

Observe that T is not diagonalizable, since T has only two linearly independent eigenvectors.

9.11. Show that 0 is an eigenvalue of T if and only if T is singular.

We have that 0 is an eigenvalue of T if and only if there exists a nonzero vector v such that $T(v) = 0v = 0$, i.e. that T is singular.

9.12. Let A and B be n-square matrices. Show that AB and BA have the same eigenvalues.

By Problem 9.11 and the fact that the product of nonsingular matrices is nonsingular, the following statements are equivalent: (i) 0 is an eigenvalue of AB, (ii) AB is singular, (iii) A or B is singular, (iv) BA is singular, (v) 0 is an eigenvalue of BA.

Now suppose λ is a nonzero eigenvalue of AB. Then there exists a nonzero vector v such that $ABv = \lambda v$. Set $w = Bv$. Since $\lambda \neq 0$ and $v \neq 0$,

$$Aw = ABv = \lambda v \neq 0 \quad \text{and so} \quad w \neq 0$$

But w is an eigenvector of BA belonging to the eigenvalue λ since

$$BAw = BABv = B\lambda v = \lambda Bv = \lambda w$$

Hence λ is an eigenvalue of BA. Similarly, any nonzero eigenvalue of BA is also an eigenvalue of AB.

Thus AB and BA have the same eigenvalues.

9.13. Suppose λ is an eigenvalue of an invertible operator T. Show that λ^{-1} is an eigenvalue of T^{-1}.

Since T is invertible, it is also nonsingular; hence by Problem 9.11, $\lambda \neq 0$.

By definition of an eigenvalue, there exists a nonzero vector v for which $T(v) = \lambda v$. Applying T^{-1} to both sides, we obtain $v = T^{-1}(\lambda v) = \lambda T^{-1}(v)$. Hence $T^{-1}(v) = \lambda^{-1}v$; that is, λ^{-1} is an eigenvalue of T^{-1}.

9.14. Prove Theorem 9.3: Let $v_1, \ldots, v_n$ be nonzero eigenvectors of an operator $T : V \to V$ belonging to distinct eigenvalues $\lambda_1, \ldots, \lambda_n$. Then $v_1, \ldots, v_n$ are linearly independent.

The proof is by induction on n. If $n = 1$, then v_1 is linearly independent since $v_1 \neq 0$. Assume $n > 1$. Suppose

$$a_1v_1 + a_2v_2 + \cdots + a_nv_n = 0 \tag{1}$$

where the a_i are scalars. Applying T to the above relation, we obtain by linearity

$$a_1T(v_1) + a_2T(v_2) + \cdots + a_nT(v_n) = T(0) = 0$$

But by hypothesis $T(v_i) = \lambda_i v_i$; hence

$$a_1\lambda_1 v_1 + a_2\lambda_2 v_2 + \cdots + a_n\lambda_n v_n = 0 \tag{2}$$

On the other hand, multiplying (1) by λ_n,

$$a_1\lambda_n v_1 + a_2\lambda_n v_2 + \cdots + a_n\lambda_n v_n = 0 \qquad (3)$$

Now subtracting (3) from (2),

$$a_1(\lambda_1 - \lambda_n)v_1 + a_2(\lambda_2 - \lambda_n)v_2 + \cdots + a_{n-1}(\lambda_{n-1} - \lambda_n)v_{n-1} = 0$$

By induction, each of the above coefficients is 0. Since the λ_i are distinct, $\lambda_i - \lambda_n \neq 0$ for $i \neq n$. Hence $a_1 = \cdots = a_{n-1} = 0$. Substituting this into (1) we get $a_n v_n = 0$, and hence $a_n = 0$. Thus the v_i are linearly independent.

CHARACTERISTIC POLYNOMIAL, CAYLEY-HAMILTON THEOREM

9.15. Consider a triangular matrix

$$A = \begin{pmatrix} a_{11} & a_{12} & \ldots & a_{1n} \\ 0 & a_{22} & \ldots & a_{2n} \\ \cdots\cdots\cdots\cdots\cdots\cdots \\ 0 & 0 & \ldots & a_{nn} \end{pmatrix}$$

Find its characteristic polynomial $\Delta(t)$ and its eigenvalues.

Since A is triangular and tI is diagonal, $tI - A$ is also triangular with diagonal elements $t - a_{ii}$:

$$tI - A = \begin{pmatrix} t - a_{11} & -a_{12} & \ldots & -a_{1n} \\ 0 & t - a_{22} & \ldots & -a_{2n} \\ \cdots\cdots\cdots\cdots\cdots\cdots\cdots\cdots \\ 0 & 0 & \ldots & t - a_{nn} \end{pmatrix}$$

Then $\Delta(t) = |tI - A|$ is the product of the diagonal elements $t - a_{ii}$:

$$\Delta(t) = (t - a_{11})(t - a_{22})\cdots(t - a_{nn})$$

Hence the eigenvalues of A are $a_{11}, a_{22}, \ldots, a_{nn}$, i.e. its diagonal elements.

9.16. Let $A = \begin{pmatrix} 1 & 2 & 3 \\ 0 & 2 & 3 \\ 0 & 0 & 3 \end{pmatrix}$. Is A similar to a diagonal matrix? If so, find one such matrix.

Since A is triangular, the eigenvalues of A are the diagonal elements 1, 2 and 3. Since they are distinct, A is similar to a diagonal matrix whose diagonal elements are 1, 2 and 3; for example,

$$\begin{pmatrix} 1 & 0 & 0 \\ 0 & 2 & 0 \\ 0 & 0 & 3 \end{pmatrix}$$

9.17. For each matrix find a polynomial having the matrix as a root:

(i) $A = \begin{pmatrix} 2 & 5 \\ 1 & -3 \end{pmatrix}$, (ii) $B = \begin{pmatrix} 2 & -3 \\ 7 & -4 \end{pmatrix}$, (iii) $C = \begin{pmatrix} 1 & 4 & -3 \\ 0 & 3 & 1 \\ 0 & 2 & -1 \end{pmatrix}$.

By the Cayley-Hamilton theorem every matrix is a root of its characteristic polynomial. Therefore we find the characteristic polynomial $\Delta(t)$ in each case.

(i) $\Delta(t) = |tI - A| = \begin{vmatrix} t - 2 & -5 \\ -1 & t + 3 \end{vmatrix} = t^2 + t - 11$

(ii) $\Delta(t) = |tI - B| = \begin{vmatrix} t - 2 & 3 \\ -7 & t + 4 \end{vmatrix} = t^2 + 2t + 13$

(iii) $\Delta(t) = |tI - C| = \begin{vmatrix} t - 1 & -4 & 3 \\ 0 & t - 3 & -1 \\ 0 & -2 & t + 1 \end{vmatrix} = (t - 1)(t^2 - 2t - 5)$

9.18. Prove the Cayley-Hamilton Theorem 9.5: Every matrix is a zero of its characteristic polynomial.

Let A be an arbitrary n-square matrix and let $\Delta(t)$ be its characteristic polynomial; say,

$$\Delta(t) \;=\; |tI - A| \;=\; t^n + a_{n-1}t^{n-1} + \cdots + a_1 t + a_0$$

Now let $B(t)$ denote the classical adjoint of the matrix $tI - A$. The elements of $B(t)$ are cofactors of the matrix $tI - A$ and hence are polynomials in t of degree not exceeding $n-1$. Thus

$$B(t) \;=\; B_{n-1}t^{n-1} + \cdots + B_1 t + B_0$$

where the B_i are n-square matrices over K which are independent of t. By the fundamental property of the classical adjoint (Theorem 8.8),

$$(tI - A)B(t) \;=\; |tI - A|I$$

or $\qquad (tI - A)(B_{n-1}t^{n-1} + \cdots + B_1 t + B_0) \;=\; (t^n + a_{n-1}t^{n-1} + \cdots + a_1 t + a_0)I$

Removing parentheses and equating the coefficients of corresponding powers of t,

$$B_{n-1} = I$$
$$B_{n-2} - AB_{n-1} = a_{n-1}I$$
$$B_{n-3} - AB_{n-2} = a_{n-2}I$$
$$\cdots\cdots\cdots\cdots\cdots\cdots\cdots$$
$$B_0 - AB_1 = a_1 I$$
$$-AB_0 = a_0 I$$

Multiplying the above matrix equations by $A^n, A^{n-1}, \ldots, A, I$ respectively,

$$A^n B_{n-1} \;=\; A^n$$
$$A^{n-1}B_{n-2} - A^n B_{n-1} \;=\; a_{n-1}A^{n-1}$$
$$A^{n-2}B_{n-3} - A^{n-1}B_{n-2} \;=\; a_{n-2}A^{n-2}$$
$$\cdots\cdots\cdots\cdots\cdots\cdots\cdots\cdots\cdots$$
$$AB_0 - A^2 B_1 \;=\; a_1 A$$
$$-AB_0 \;=\; a_0 I$$

Adding the above matrix equations,

$$0 \;=\; A^n + a_{n-1}A^{n-1} + \cdots + a_1 A + a_0 I$$

In other words, $\Delta(A) = 0$. That is, A is a zero of its characteristic polynomial.

9.19. Show that a matrix A and its transpose A^t have the same characteristic polynomial.

By the transpose operation, $(tI - A)^t = tI^t - A^t = tI - A^t$. Since a matrix and its transpose have the same determinant, $|tI - A| = |(tI - A)^t| = |tI - A^t|$. Hence A and A^t have the same characteristic polynomial.

9.20. Suppose $M = \begin{pmatrix} A_1 & B \\ 0 & A_2 \end{pmatrix}$ where A_1 and A_2 are square matrices. Show that the characteristic polynomial of M is the product of the characteristic polynomials of A_1 and A_2. Generalize.

$tI - M = \begin{pmatrix} tI - A_1 & -B \\ 0 & tI - A_2 \end{pmatrix}$. Hence by Problem 8.70, $|tI - M| = \begin{vmatrix} tI - A_1 & -B \\ 0 & tI - A_2 \end{vmatrix} =$ $|tI - A| \, |tI - B|$, as required.

By induction, the characteristic polynomial of the triangular block matrix

$$M = \begin{pmatrix} A_1 & B & \dots & C \\ 0 & A_2 & \dots & D \\ \hdotsfor{4} \\ 0 & 0 & \dots & A_n \end{pmatrix}$$

where the A_i are square matrices, is the product of the characteristic polynomials of the A_i.

MINIMUM POLYNOMIAL

9.21. Find the minimum polynomial $m(t)$ of $\quad A = \begin{pmatrix} 2 & 1 & 0 & 0 \\ 0 & 2 & 0 & 0 \\ 0 & 0 & 1 & 1 \\ 0 & 0 & -2 & 4 \end{pmatrix}$.

The characteristic polynomial of A is

$$\Delta(t) = \begin{vmatrix} t-2 & -1 & 0 & 0 \\ 0 & t-2 & 0 & 0 \\ 0 & 0 & t-1 & -1 \\ 0 & 0 & 2 & t-4 \end{vmatrix} = \begin{vmatrix} t-2 & -1 \\ 0 & t-2 \end{vmatrix} \begin{vmatrix} t-1 & -1 \\ 2 & t-4 \end{vmatrix} = (t-3)(t-2)^3$$

The minimum polynomial $m(t)$ must divide $\Delta(t)$. Also, each irreducible factor of $\Delta(t)$, i.e. $t-2$ and $t-3$, must be a factor of $m(t)$. Thus $m(t)$ is exactly one of the following:

$$f(t) = (t-3)(t-2), \quad g(t) = (t-3)(t-2)^2, \quad h(t) = (t-3)(t-2)^3$$

We have

$$f(A) = (A-3I)(A-2I) = \begin{pmatrix} -1 & 1 & 0 & 0 \\ 0 & -1 & 0 & 0 \\ 0 & 0 & -2 & 1 \\ 0 & 0 & -2 & 1 \end{pmatrix}\begin{pmatrix} 0 & 1 & 0 & 0 \\ 0 & 0 & 0 & 0 \\ 0 & 0 & -1 & 1 \\ 0 & 0 & -2 & 2 \end{pmatrix} \neq 0$$

$$g(A) = (A-3I)(A-2I)^2 = \begin{pmatrix} -1 & 1 & 0 & 0 \\ 0 & -1 & 0 & 0 \\ 0 & 0 & -2 & 1 \\ 0 & 0 & -2 & 1 \end{pmatrix}\begin{pmatrix} 0 & 1 & 0 & 0 \\ 0 & 0 & 0 & 0 \\ 0 & 0 & -1 & 1 \\ 0 & 0 & -2 & 2 \end{pmatrix}^2 = 0$$

Thus $g(t) = (t-3)(t-2)^2$ is the minimum polynomial of A.

Remark. We know that $h(A) = \Delta(A) = 0$ by the Cayley-Hamilton theorem. However, the degree of $g(t)$ is less than the degree of $h(t)$; hence $g(t)$, and not $h(t)$, is the minimum polynomial of A.

9.22. Find the minimal polynomial $m(t)$ of each matrix (where $a \neq 0$):

(i) $A = \begin{pmatrix} \lambda & a \\ 0 & \lambda \end{pmatrix}$, (ii) $B = \begin{pmatrix} \lambda & a & 0 \\ 0 & \lambda & a \\ 0 & 0 & \lambda \end{pmatrix}$, (iii) $C = \begin{pmatrix} \lambda & a & 0 & 0 \\ 0 & \lambda & a & 0 \\ 0 & 0 & \lambda & a \\ 0 & 0 & 0 & \lambda \end{pmatrix}$.

(i)   The characteristic polynomial of A is $\Delta(t) = (t-\lambda)^2$. We find $A - \lambda I \neq 0$; hence $m(t) = \Delta(t) = (t-\lambda)^2$.

(ii) The characteristic polynomial of B is $\Delta(t) = (t-\lambda)^3$. (Note $m(t)$ is exactly one of $t-\lambda$, $(t-\lambda)^2$ or $(t-\lambda)^3$.) We find $(B-\lambda I)^2 \neq 0$; thus $m(t) = \Delta(t) = (t-\lambda)^3$.

(iii) The characteristic polynomial of C is $\Delta(t) = (t-\lambda)^4$. We find $(C-\lambda I)^3 \neq 0$; hence $m(t) = \Delta(t) = (t-\lambda)^4$.

9.23. Let $M = \begin{pmatrix} A & 0 \\ 0 & B \end{pmatrix}$ where A and B are square matrices. Show that the minimum polynomial $m(t)$ of M is the least common multiple of the minimum polynomials $g(t)$ and $h(t)$ of A and B respectively. Generalize.

Since $m(t)$ is the minimum polynomial of M, $m(M) = \begin{pmatrix} m(A) & 0 \\ 0 & m(B) \end{pmatrix} = 0$ and hence $m(A) = 0$ and $m(B) = 0$. Since $g(t)$ is the minimum polynomial of A, $g(t)$ divides $m(t)$. Similarly, $h(t)$ divides $m(t)$. Thus $m(t)$ is a multiple of $g(t)$ and $h(t)$.

Now let $f(t)$ be another multiple of $g(t)$ and $h(t)$; then $f(M) = \begin{pmatrix} f(A) & 0 \\ 0 & f(B) \end{pmatrix} = \begin{pmatrix} 0 & 0 \\ 0 & 0 \end{pmatrix} = 0$.

But $m(t)$ is the minimum polynomial of M; hence $m(t)$ divides $f(t)$. Thus $m(t)$ is the least common multiple of $g(t)$ and $h(t)$.

We then have, by induction, that the minimum polynomial of

$$M = \begin{pmatrix} A_1 & 0 & \dots & 0 \\ 0 & A_2 & \dots & 0 \\ \multicolumn{4}{c}{\dotfill} \\ 0 & 0 & \dots & A_n \end{pmatrix}$$

where the A_i are square matrices, is the least common multiple of the minimum polynomials of the A_i.

9.24. Find the minimum polynomial $m(t)$ of

$$M = \begin{pmatrix} 2 & 8 & 0 & 0 & 0 & 0 & 0 \\ 0 & 2 & 0 & 0 & 0 & 0 & 0 \\ 0 & 0 & 4 & 2 & 0 & 0 & 0 \\ 0 & 0 & 1 & 3 & 0 & 0 & 0 \\ 0 & 0 & 0 & 0 & 0 & 3 & 0 \\ 0 & 0 & 0 & 0 & 0 & 0 & 0 \\ 0 & 0 & 0 & 0 & 0 & 0 & 5 \end{pmatrix}$$

Let $A = \begin{pmatrix} 2 & 8 \\ 0 & 2 \end{pmatrix}$, $B = \begin{pmatrix} 4 & 2 \\ 1 & 3 \end{pmatrix}$, $C = \begin{pmatrix} 0 & 3 \\ 0 & 0 \end{pmatrix}$, $D = (5)$. The minimum polynomials of A, C and D are $(t-2)^2$, t^2 and $t-5$ respectively. The characteristic polynomial of B is

$$|tI - B| = \begin{vmatrix} t-4 & -2 \\ -1 & t-3 \end{vmatrix} = t^2 - 7t + 10 = (t-2)(t-5)$$

and so it is also the minimum polynomial of B.

Observe that $M = \begin{pmatrix} A & 0 & 0 & 0 \\ 0 & B & 0 & 0 \\ 0 & 0 & C & 0 \\ 0 & 0 & 0 & D \end{pmatrix}$. Thus $m(t)$ is the least common multiple of the minimum polynomials of A, B, C and D. Accordingly, $m(t) = t^2(t-2)^2(t-5)$.

9.25. Show that the minimum polynomial of a matrix (operator) A exists and is unique.

By the Cayley-Hamilton theorem, A is a zero of some nonzero polynomial (see also Problem 9.31). Let n be the lowest degree for which a polynomial $f(t)$ exists such that $f(A) = 0$. Dividing $f(t)$ by its leading coefficient, we obtain a monic polynomial $m(t)$ of degree n which has A as a zero. Suppose $m'(t)$ is another monic polynomial of degree n for which $m'(A) = 0$. Then the difference $m(t) - m'(t)$ is a nonzero polynomial of degree less than n which has A as a zero. This contradicts the original assumption on n; hence $m(t)$ is a unique minimum polynomial.

9.26. Prove Theorem 9.10: The minimum polynomial $m(t)$ of a matrix (operator) A divides every polynomial which has A as a zero. In particular, $m(t)$ divides the characteristic polynomial of A.

Suppose $f(t)$ is a polynomial for which $f(A) = 0$. By the division algorithm there exist polynomials $q(t)$ and $r(t)$ for which $f(t) = m(t)q(t) + r(t)$ and $r(t) = 0$ or $\deg r(t) < \deg m(t)$. Substituting $t = A$ in this equation, and using that $f(A) = 0$ and $m(A) = 0$, we obtain $r(A) = 0$. If $r(t) \neq 0$, then $r(t)$ is a polynomial of degree less than $m(t)$ which has A as a zero; this contradicts the definition of the minimum polynomial. Thus $r(t) = 0$ and so $f(t) = m(t)q(t)$, i.e. $m(t)$ divides $f(t)$.

9.27. Let $m(t)$ be the minimum polynomial of an n-square matrix A. Show that the characteristic polynomial of A divides $(m(t))^n$.

Suppose $m(t) = t^r + c_1 t^{r-1} + \cdots + c_{r-1}t + c_r$. Consider the following matrices:

$$B_0 = I$$
$$B_1 = A + c_1 I$$
$$B_2 = A^2 + c_1 A + c_2 I$$
$$\cdots\cdots\cdots\cdots\cdots\cdots\cdots\cdots$$
$$B_{r-1} = A^{r-1} + c_1 A^{r-2} + \cdots + c_{r-1}I$$

Then

$$B_0 = I$$
$$B_1 - AB_0 = c_1 I$$
$$B_2 - AB_1 = c_2 I$$
$$\cdots\cdots\cdots\cdots\cdots\cdots$$
$$B_{r-1} - AB_{r-2} = c_{r-1}I$$

Also,

$$\begin{aligned} -AB_{r-1} &= c_r I - (A^r + c_1 A^{r-1} + \cdots + c_{r-1}A + c_r I) \\ &= c_r I - m(A) \\ &= c_r I \end{aligned}$$

Set

$$B(t) = t^{r-1}B_0 + t^{r-2}B_1 + \cdots + tB_{r-2} + B_{r-1}$$

Then

$$\begin{aligned} (tI - A) \cdot B(t) &= (t^r B_0 + t^{r-1}B_1 + \cdots + tB_{r-1}) - (t^{r-1}AB_0 + t^{r-2}AB_1 + \cdots + AB_{r-1}) \\ &= t^r B_0 + t^{r-1}(B_1 - AB_0) + t^{r-2}(B_2 - AB_1) + \cdots + t(B_{r-1} - AB_{r-2}) - AB_{r-1} \\ &= t^r I + c_1 t^{r-1}I + c_2 t^{r-2}I + \cdots + c_{r-1}tI + c_r I \\ &= m(t)I \end{aligned}$$

The determinant of both sides gives $|tI - A|\,|B(t)| = |m(t)\,I| = (m(t))^n$. Since $|B(t)|$ is a polynomial, $|tI - A|$ divides $(m(t))^n$; that is, the characteristic polynomial of A divides $(m(t))^n$.

9.28. Prove Theorem 9.11: The characteristic polynomial $\Delta(t)$ and the minimum polynomial $m(t)$ of a matrix A have the same irreducible factors.

Suppose $f(t)$ is an irreducible polynomial. If $f(t)$ divides $m(t)$ then, since $m(t)$ divides $\Delta(t)$, $f(t)$ divides $\Delta(t)$. On the other hand, if $f(t)$ divides $\Delta(t)$ then, by the preceding problem, $f(t)$ divides $(m(t))^n$. But $f(t)$ is irreducible; hence $f(t)$ also divides $m(t)$. Thus $m(t)$ and $\Delta(t)$ have the same irreducible factors.

9.29. Let T be a linear operator on a vector space V of finite dimension. Show that T is invertible if and only if the constant term of the minimal (characteristic) polynomial of T is not zero.

Suppose the minimal (characteristic) polynomial of T is $f(t) = t^r + a_{n-1}t^{r-1} + \cdots + a_1 t + a_0$. Each of the following statements is equivalent to the succeeding one by preceding results: (i) T is invertible; (ii) T is nonsingular; (iii) 0 is not an eigenvalue of T; (iv) 0 is not a root of $m(t)$; (v) the constant term a_0 is not zero. Thus the theorem is proved.

9.30. Suppose $\dim V = n$. Let $T : V \to V$ be an invertible operator. Show that T^{-1} is equal to a polynomial in T of degree not exceeding n.

Let $m(t)$ be the minimal polynomial of T. Then $m(t) = t^r + a_{r-1}t^{r-1} + \cdots + a_1 t + a_0$, where $r \leq n$. Since T is invertible, $a_0 \neq 0$. We have

$$m(T) = T^r + a_{r-1}T^{r-1} + \cdots + a_1 T + a_0 I = 0$$

Hence

$$-\frac{1}{a_0}(T^{r-1} + a_{r-1}T^{r-2} + \cdots + a_1 I)T = I \quad \text{and} \quad T^{-1} = -\frac{1}{a_0}(T^{r-1} + a_{r-1}T^{r-2} + \cdots + a_1 I)$$

MISCELLANEOUS PROBLEMS

9.31. Let T be a linear operator on a vector space V of dimension n. Without using the Cayley-Hamilton theorem, show that T is a zero of a nonzero polynomial.

Let $N = n^2$. Consider the following $N+1$ operators on V: $I, T, T^2, \ldots, T^N$. Recall that the vector space $A(V)$ of operators on V has dimension $N = n^2$. Thus the above $N+1$ operators are linearly dependent. Hence there exist scalars $a_0, a_1, \ldots, a_N$ for which $a_N T^N + \cdots + a_1 T + a_0 I = 0$. Accordingly, T is a zero of the polynomial $f(t) = a_N t^N + \cdots + a_1 t + a_0$.

9.32. Prove Theorem 9.13: Let λ be an eigenvalue of an operator $T : V \to V$. The geometric multiplicity of λ does not exceed its algebraic multiplicity.

Suppose the geometric multiplicity of λ is r. Then λ contains r linearly independent eigenvectors $v_1, \ldots, v_r$. Extend the set $\{v_i\}$ to a basis of V: $\{v_1, \ldots, v_r, w_1, \ldots, w_s\}$. We have

$$
\begin{aligned}
T(v_1) &= \lambda v_1 \\
T(v_2) &= \lambda v_2 \\
&\cdots\cdots\cdots\cdots \\
T(v_r) &= \lambda v_r \\
T(w_1) &= a_{11}v_1 + \cdots + a_{1r}v_r + b_{11}w_1 + \cdots + b_{1s}w_s \\
T(w_2) &= a_{21}v_1 + \cdots + a_{2r}v_r + b_{21}w_1 + \cdots + b_{2s}w_s \\
&\cdots\cdots\cdots\cdots \\
T(w_s) &= a_{s1}v_1 + \cdots + a_{sr}v_r + b_{s1}w_1 + \cdots + b_{ss}w_s
\end{aligned}
$$

The matrix of T in the above basis is

$$
M = \left(\begin{array}{cccc|cccc}
\lambda & 0 & \ldots & 0 & a_{11} & a_{21} & \ldots & a_{s1} \\
0 & \lambda & \ldots & 0 & a_{12} & a_{22} & \ldots & a_{s2} \\
\hline
\multicolumn{8}{c}{\cdots\cdots\cdots\cdots} \\
0 & 0 & \ldots & \lambda & a_{1r} & a_{2r} & \ldots & a_{sr} \\
\hline
0 & 0 & \ldots & 0 & b_{11} & b_{21} & \ldots & b_{r1} \\
0 & 0 & \ldots & 0 & b_{12} & b_{22} & \ldots & b_{r2} \\
\multicolumn{8}{c}{\cdots\cdots\cdots\cdots} \\
0 & 0 & \ldots & 0 & b_{1s} & b_{2s} & \ldots & b_{ss}
\end{array}\right) = \left(\begin{array}{c|c} \lambda I_r & A \\ \hline 0 & B \end{array}\right)
$$

where $A = (a_{ij})^t$ and $B = (b_{ij})^t$.

By Problem 9.20 the characteristic polynomial of λI_r, which is $(t-\lambda)^r$, must divide the characteristic polynomial of M and hence T. Thus the algebraic multiplicity of λ for the operator T is at least r, as required.

9.33. Show that $A = \begin{pmatrix} 1 & 1 \\ 0 & 1 \end{pmatrix}$ is not diagonalizable.

The characteristic polynomial of A is $\Delta(t) = (t-1)^2$; hence 1 is the only eigenvalue of A. We find a basis of the eigenspace of the eigenvalue 1. Substitute $t = 1$ into the matrix $tI - A$ to obtain the homogeneous system

$$\begin{pmatrix} 0 & -1 \\ 0 & 0 \end{pmatrix} \begin{pmatrix} x \\ y \end{pmatrix} = \begin{pmatrix} 0 \\ 0 \end{pmatrix} \quad \text{or} \quad \begin{cases} -y = 0 \\ 0 = 0 \end{cases} \quad \text{or} \quad y = 0$$

The system has only one independent solution, e.g. $x = 1$, $y = 0$. Hence $u = (1, 0)$ forms a basis of the eigenspace of 1.

Since A has at most one independent eigenvector, A cannot be diagonalized.

9.34. Let F be an extension of a field K. Let A be an n-square matrix over K. Note that A may also be viewed as a matrix $\hat{A}$ over F. Clearly $|tI - A| = |tI - \hat{A}|$, that is, A and $\hat{A}$ have the same characteristic polynomial. Show that A and $\hat{A}$ also have the same minimum polynomial.

Let $m(t)$ and $m'(t)$ be the minimum polynomials of A and $\hat{A}$ respectively. Now $m'(t)$ divides every polynomial over F which has A as a zero. Since $m(t)$ has A as a zero and since $m(t)$ may be viewed as a polynomial over F, $m'(t)$ divides $m(t)$. We show now that $m(t)$ divides $m'(t)$.

Since $m'(t)$ is a polynomial over F which is an extension of K, we may write

$$m'(t) = f_1(t) b_1 + f_2(t) b_2 + \cdots + f_n(t) b_n$$

where $f_i(t)$ are polynomials over K, and $b_1, \ldots, b_n$ belong to F and are linearly independent over K. We have

$$m'(A) = f_1(A) b_1 + f_2(A) b_2 + \cdots + f_n(A) b_n = 0 \tag{1}$$

Let $a_{ij}^{(k)}$ denote the ij-entry of $f_k(A)$. The above matrix equation implies that, for each pair (i, j),

$$a_{ij}^{(1)} b_1 + a_{ij}^{(2)} b_2 + \cdots + a_{ij}^{(n)} b_n = 0$$

Since the b_i are linearly independent over K and since the $a_{ij}^{(k)} \in K$, every $a_{ij}^{(k)} = 0$. Then

$$f_1(A) = 0, \quad f_2(A) = 0, \quad \ldots, \quad f_n(A) = 0$$

Since the $f_i(t)$ are polynomials over K which have A as a zero and since $m(t)$ is the minimum polynomial of A as a matrix over K, $m(t)$ divides each of the $f_i(t)$. Accordingly, by *(1)*, $m(t)$ must also divide $m'(t)$. But monic polynomials which divide each other are necessarily equal. That is, $m(t) = m'(t)$, as required.

9.35. Let $\{v_1, \ldots, v_n\}$ be a basis of V. Let $T : V \to V$ be an operator for which $T(v_1) = 0$, $T(v_2) = a_{21} v_1$, $T(v_3) = a_{31} v_1 + a_{32} v_2$, $\ldots$, $T(v_n) = a_{n1} v_1 + \cdots + a_{n, n-1} v_{n-1}$. Show that $T^n = 0$.

It suffices to show that

$$T^j(v_j) = 0 \tag{*}$$

for $j = 1, \ldots, n$. For then it follows that

$$T^n(v_j) = T^{n-j}(T^j(v_j)) = T^{n-j}(0) = 0, \quad \text{for } j = 1, \ldots, n$$

and, since $\{v_1, \ldots, v_n\}$ is a basis, $T^n = 0$.

We prove *(*)* by induction on j. The case $j = 1$ is true by hypothesis. The inductive step follows (for $j = 2, \ldots, n$) from

$$T^j(v_j) = T^{j-1}(T(v_j)) = T^{j-1}(a_{j1} v_1 + \cdots + a_{j, j-1} v_{j-1})$$
$$= a_{j1} T^{j-1}(v_1) + \cdots + a_{j, j-1} T^{j-1}(v_{j-1})$$
$$= a_{j1} 0 + \cdots + a_{j, j-1} 0 = 0$$

Remark. Observe that the matrix representation of T in the above basis is triangular with diagonal elements 0:

$$\begin{pmatrix} 0 & a_{21} & a_{31} & \ldots & a_{n1} \\ 0 & 0 & a_{32} & \ldots & a_{n2} \\ \cdots\cdots\cdots\cdots\cdots\cdots\cdots\cdots \\ 0 & 0 & 0 & \ldots & a_{n, n-1} \\ 0 & 0 & 0 & \ldots & 0 \end{pmatrix}$$

Supplementary Problems

POLYNOMIALS OF MATRICES AND LINEAR OPERATORS

9.36. Let $f(t) = 2t^2 - 5t + 6$ and $g(t) = t^3 - 2t^2 + t + 3$. Find $f(A), g(A), f(B)$ and $g(B)$ where $A = \begin{pmatrix} 2 & -3 \\ 5 & 1 \end{pmatrix}$ and $B = \begin{pmatrix} 1 & 2 \\ 0 & 3 \end{pmatrix}$.

9.37. Let $T : \mathbf{R}^2 \to \mathbf{R}^2$ be defined by $T(x, y) = (x + y, 2x)$. Let $f(t) = t^2 - 2t + 3$. Find $f(T)(x, y)$.

9.38. Let V be the vector space of polynomials $v(x) = ax^2 + bx + c$. Let $D : V \to V$ be the differential operator. Let $f(t) = t^2 + 2t - 5$. Find $f(D)(v(x))$.

9.39. Let $A = \begin{pmatrix} 1 & 1 \\ 0 & 1 \end{pmatrix}$. Find A^2, A^3, A^n.

9.40. Let $B = \begin{pmatrix} 8 & 12 & 0 \\ 0 & 8 & 12 \\ 0 & 0 & 8 \end{pmatrix}$. Find a real matrix A such that $B = A^3$.

9.41. Consider a diagonal matrix M and a triangular matrix N:

$$M = \begin{pmatrix} a_1 & 0 & \dots & 0 \\ 0 & a_2 & \dots & 0 \\ \multicolumn{4}{c}{\dotfill} \\ 0 & 0 & \dots & a_n \end{pmatrix} \quad \text{and} \quad N = \begin{pmatrix} a_1 & b & \dots & c \\ 0 & a_2 & \dots & d \\ \multicolumn{4}{c}{\dotfill} \\ 0 & 0 & \dots & a_n \end{pmatrix}$$

Show that, for any polynomial $f(t)$, $f(M)$ and $f(N)$ are of the form

$$f(M) = \begin{pmatrix} f(a_1) & 0 & \dots & 0 \\ 0 & f(a_2) & \dots & 0 \\ \multicolumn{4}{c}{\dotfill} \\ 0 & 0 & \dots & f(a_n) \end{pmatrix} \quad \text{and} \quad f(N) = \begin{pmatrix} f(a_1) & x & \dots & y \\ 0 & f(a_2) & \dots & z \\ \multicolumn{4}{c}{\dotfill} \\ 0 & 0 & \dots & f(a_n) \end{pmatrix}$$

9.42. Consider a block diagonal matrix M and a block triangular matrix N:

$$M = \begin{pmatrix} A_1 & 0 & \dots & 0 \\ 0 & A_2 & \dots & 0 \\ \multicolumn{4}{c}{\dotfill} \\ 0 & 0 & \dots & A_n \end{pmatrix} \quad \text{and} \quad N = \begin{pmatrix} A_1 & B & \dots & C \\ 0 & A_2 & \dots & D \\ \multicolumn{4}{c}{\dotfill} \\ 0 & 0 & \dots & A_n \end{pmatrix}$$

where the A_i are square matrices. Show that, for any polynomial $f(t)$, $f(M)$ and $f(N)$ are of the form

$$f(M) = \begin{pmatrix} f(A_1) & 0 & \dots & 0 \\ 0 & f(A_2) & \dots & 0 \\ \multicolumn{4}{c}{\dotfill} \\ 0 & 0 & \dots & f(A_n) \end{pmatrix} \quad \text{and} \quad f(N) = \begin{pmatrix} f(A_1) & X & \dots & Y \\ 0 & f(A_2) & \dots & Z \\ \multicolumn{4}{c}{\dotfill} \\ 0 & 0 & \dots & f(A_n) \end{pmatrix}$$

9.43. Show that for any square matrix (or operator) A, $(P^{-1}AP)^n = P^{-1}A^nP$ where P is invertible. More generally, show that $f(P^{-1}AP) = P^{-1}f(A)P$ for any polynomial $f(t)$.

9.44. Let $f(t)$ be any polynomial. Show that: (i) $f(A^t) = (f(A))^t$; (ii) if A is symmetric, i.e. $A^t = A$, then $f(A)$ is symmetric.

EIGENVALUES AND EIGENVECTORS

9.45. For each matrix, find all eigenvalues and linearly independent eigenvectors:

$$\text{(i)} \quad A = \begin{pmatrix} 2 & 2 \\ 1 & 3 \end{pmatrix}, \quad \text{(ii)} \quad B = \begin{pmatrix} 4 & 2 \\ 3 & 3 \end{pmatrix}, \quad \text{(iii)} \quad C = \begin{pmatrix} 5 & -1 \\ 1 & 3 \end{pmatrix}$$

Find invertible matrices P_1, P_2 and P_3 such that $P_1^{-1}AP_1, P_2^{-1}BP_2$ and $P_3^{-1}CP_3$ are diagonal.

9.46. For each matrix, find all eigenvalues and a basis for each eigenspace:

$$\text{(i)} \quad A = \begin{pmatrix} 3 & 1 & 1 \\ 2 & 4 & 2 \\ 1 & 1 & 3 \end{pmatrix}, \quad \text{(ii)} \quad B = \begin{pmatrix} 1 & 2 & 2 \\ 1 & 2 & -1 \\ -1 & 1 & 4 \end{pmatrix}, \quad \text{(iii)} \quad C = \begin{pmatrix} 1 & 1 & 0 \\ 0 & 1 & 0 \\ 0 & 0 & 1 \end{pmatrix}$$

When possible, find invertible matrices P_1, P_2 and P_3 such that $P_1^{-1}AP_1, P_2^{-1}BP_2$ and $P_3^{-1}CP_3$ are diagonal.

9.47. Consider $A = \begin{pmatrix} 2 & -1 \\ 1 & 4 \end{pmatrix}$ and $B = \begin{pmatrix} 3 & -1 \\ 13 & -3 \end{pmatrix}$ as matrices over the real field **R**. Find all eigenvalues and linearly independent eigenvectors.

9.48. Consider A and B in the preceding problem as matrices over the complex field **C**. Find all eigenvalues and linearly independent eigenvectors.

9.49. For each of the following operators $T : \mathbf{R}^2 \to \mathbf{R}^2$, find all eigenvalues and a basis for each eigenspace: (i) $T(x, y) = (3x + 3y, x + 5y)$; (ii) $T(x, y) = (y, x)$; (iii) $T(x, y) = (y, -x)$.

9.50. For each of the following operators $T : \mathbf{R}^3 \to \mathbf{R}^3$, find all eigenvalues and a basis for each eigenspace: (i) $T(x, y, z) = (x + y + z, 2y + z, 2y + 3z)$; (ii) $T(x, y, z) = (x + y, y + z, -2y - z)$; (iii) $T(x, y, z) = (x - y, 2x + 3y + 2z, x + y + 2z)$.

9.51. For each of the following matrices over the complex field **C**, find all eigenvalues and linearly independent eigenvectors:

$$\text{(i)} \begin{pmatrix} 1 & i \\ 0 & i \end{pmatrix}, \quad \text{(ii)} \begin{pmatrix} 1 & 3 \\ 0 & 1 \end{pmatrix}, \quad \text{(iii)} \begin{pmatrix} 1 & -3i \\ i & -1 \end{pmatrix}, \quad \text{(iv)} \begin{pmatrix} 1 & -2 \\ 1 & -1 \end{pmatrix}.$$

9.52. Suppose v is an eigenvector of operators S and T. Show that v is also an eigenvector of the operator $aS + bT$ where a and b are any scalars.

9.53. Suppose v is an eigenvector of an operator T belonging to the eigenvalue λ. Show that for $n > 0$, v is also an eigenvector of T^n belonging to λ^n.

9.54. Suppose λ is an eigenvalue of an operator T. Show that $f(\lambda)$ is an eigenvalue of $f(T)$.

9.55. Show that similar matrices have the same eigenvalues.

9.56. Show that matrices A and A^t have the same eigenvalues. Give an example where A and A^t have different eigenvectors.

9.57. Let S and T be linear operators such that $ST = TS$. Let λ be an eigenvalue of T and let W be its eigenspace. Show that W is invariant under S, i.e. $S(W) \subset W$.

9.58. Let V be a vector space of finite dimension over the complex field **C**. Let $W \neq \{0\}$ be a subspace of V invariant under a linear operator $T : V \to V$. Show that W contains a nonzero eigenvector of T.

9.59. Let A be an n-square matrix over K. Let $v_1, \ldots, v_n \in K^n$ be linearly independent eigenvectors of A belonging to the eigenvalues $\lambda_1, \ldots, \lambda_n$ respectively. Let P be the matrix whose columns are the vectors $v_1, \ldots, v_n$. Show that $P^{-1}AP$ is the diagonal matrix whose diagonal elements are the eigenvalues $\lambda_1, \ldots, \lambda_n$.

CHARACTERISTIC AND MINIMUM POLYNOMIALS

9.60. For each matrix, find a polynomial for which the matrix is a root:

$$\text{(i)} \quad A = \begin{pmatrix} 3 & -7 \\ 4 & 5 \end{pmatrix}, \quad \text{(ii)} \quad B = \begin{pmatrix} 5 & -1 \\ 8 & 3 \end{pmatrix}, \quad \text{(iii)} \quad C = \begin{pmatrix} 2 & 3 & -2 \\ 0 & 5 & 4 \\ 1 & 0 & -1 \end{pmatrix}.$$

9.61. Consider the n-square matrix

$$A = \begin{pmatrix} \lambda & 1 & 0 & \ldots & 0 & 0 \\ 0 & \lambda & 1 & \ldots & 0 & 0 \\ \multicolumn{6}{c}{\ldots\ldots\ldots\ldots\ldots\ldots} \\ 0 & 0 & 0 & \ldots & \lambda & 1 \\ 0 & 0 & 0 & \ldots & 0 & \lambda \end{pmatrix}$$

Show that $f(t) = (t-\lambda)^n$ is both the characteristic and minimum polynomial of A.

9.62. Find the characteristic and minimum polynomials of each matrix:

$$A = \begin{pmatrix} 2 & 5 & 0 & 0 & 0 \\ 0 & 2 & 0 & 0 & 0 \\ 0 & 0 & 4 & 2 & 0 \\ 0 & 0 & 3 & 5 & 0 \\ 0 & 0 & 0 & 0 & 7 \end{pmatrix}, \quad B = \begin{pmatrix} 3 & 1 & 0 & 0 & 0 \\ 0 & 3 & 0 & 0 & 0 \\ 0 & 0 & 3 & 1 & 0 \\ 0 & 0 & 0 & 3 & 1 \\ 0 & 0 & 0 & 0 & 3 \end{pmatrix}, \quad C = \begin{pmatrix} \lambda & 0 & 0 & 0 & 0 \\ 0 & \lambda & 0 & 0 & 0 \\ 0 & 0 & \lambda & 0 & 0 \\ 0 & 0 & 0 & \lambda & 0 \\ 0 & 0 & 0 & 0 & \lambda \end{pmatrix}$$

9.63. Let $A = \begin{pmatrix} 1 & 1 & 0 \\ 0 & 2 & 0 \\ 0 & 0 & 1 \end{pmatrix}$ and $B = \begin{pmatrix} 2 & 0 & 0 \\ 0 & 2 & 2 \\ 0 & 0 & 1 \end{pmatrix}$. Show that A and B have different characteristic

polynomials (and so are not similar), but have the same minimum polynomial. Thus nonsimilar matrices may have the same minimum polynomial.

9.64. The mapping $T: V \to V$ defined by $T(v) = kv$ is called the *scalar mapping* belonging to $k \in K$. Show that T is the scalar mapping belonging to $k \in K$ if and only if the minimal polynomial of T is $m(t) = t - k$.

9.65. Let A be an n-square matrix for which $A^k = 0$ for some $k > n$. Show that $A^n = 0$.

9.66. Show that a matrix A and its transpose A^t have the same minimum polynomial.

9.67. Suppose $f(t)$ is an irreducible monic polynomial for which $f(T) = 0$ where T is a linear operator $T: V \to V$. Show that $f(t)$ is the minimal polynomial of T.

9.68. Consider a block matrix $M = \begin{pmatrix} A & B \\ C & D \end{pmatrix}$. Show that $tI - M = \begin{pmatrix} tI - A & -B \\ -C & tI - D \end{pmatrix}$ is the characteristic matrix of M.

9.69. Let T be a linear operator on a vector space V of finite dimension. Let W be a subspace of V invariant under T, i.e. $T(W) \subset W$. Let $T_W: W \to W$ be the restriction of T to W. (i) Show that the characteristic polynomial of T_W divides the characteristic polynomial of T. (ii) Show that the minimum polynomial of T_W divides the minimum polynomial of T.

9.70. Let $A = \begin{pmatrix} a_{11} & a_{12} & a_{13} \\ a_{21} & a_{22} & a_{23} \\ a_{31} & a_{32} & a_{33} \end{pmatrix}$. Show that the characteristic polynomial of A is

$$\Delta(t) = t^3 - (a_{11} + a_{22} + a_{33})t^2 + \left(\begin{vmatrix} a_{11} & a_{12} \\ a_{21} & a_{22} \end{vmatrix} + \begin{vmatrix} a_{11} & a_{13} \\ a_{31} & a_{33} \end{vmatrix} + \begin{vmatrix} a_{22} & a_{23} \\ a_{32} & a_{33} \end{vmatrix} \right) t - \begin{vmatrix} a_{11} & a_{12} & a_{13} \\ a_{21} & a_{22} & a_{23} \\ a_{31} & a_{32} & a_{33} \end{vmatrix}$$

9.71. Let A be an n-square matrix. The determinant of the matrix of order $n - m$ obtained by deleting the rows and columns passing through m diagonal elements of A is called a *principal minor* of degree $n - m$. Show that the coefficient of t^m in the characteristic polynomial $\Delta(t) = |tI - A|$ is the sum of all principal minors of A of degree $n - m$ multiplied by $(-1)^{n-m}$. (Observe that the preceding problem is a special case of this result.)

9.72. Consider an arbitrary monic polynomial $f(t) = t^n + a_{n-1}t^{n-1} + \cdots + a_1 t + a_0$. The following n-square matrix A is called the *companion matrix* of $f(t)$:

$$A = \begin{pmatrix} 0 & 0 & \ldots & 0 & -a_0 \\ 1 & 0 & \ldots & 0 & -a_1 \\ 0 & 1 & \ldots & 0 & -a_2 \\ \cdots\cdots\cdots\cdots\cdots\cdots \\ 0 & 0 & \ldots & 1 & -a_{n-1} \end{pmatrix}$$

Show that $f(t)$ is the minimum polynomial of A.

9.73. Find a matrix A whose minimum polynomial is (i) $t^3 - 5t^2 + 6t + 8$, (ii) $t^4 - 5t^3 - 2t + 7t + 4$.

DIAGONALIZATION

9.74. Let $A = \begin{pmatrix} a & b \\ c & d \end{pmatrix}$ be a matrix over the real field **R**. Find necessary and sufficient conditions on a, b, c and d so that A is diagonalizable, i.e. has two linearly independent eigenvectors.

9.75. Repeat the preceding problem for the case that A is a matrix over the complex field **C**.

9.76. Show that a matrix (operator) is diagonalizable if and only if its minimal polynomial is a product of distinct linear factors.

9.77. Let A and B be n-square matrices over K such that (i) $AB = BA$ and (ii) A and B are both diagonalizable. Show that A and B can be simultaneously diagonalized, i.e. there exists a basis of K^n in which both A and B are represented by diagonal matrices. (See Problem 9.57.)

9.78. Let $E : V \to V$ be a projection operator, i.e. $E^2 = E$. Show that E is diagonalizable and, in fact, can be represented by the diagonal matrix $A = \begin{pmatrix} I_r & 0 \\ 0 & 0 \end{pmatrix}$ where r is the rank of E.

Answers to Supplementary Problems

9.36. $f(A) = \begin{pmatrix} -26 & -3 \\ 5 & -27 \end{pmatrix}$, $g(A) = \begin{pmatrix} -40 & 39 \\ -65 & -27 \end{pmatrix}$, $f(B) = \begin{pmatrix} 3 & 6 \\ 0 & 9 \end{pmatrix}$, $g(B) = \begin{pmatrix} 3 & 12 \\ 0 & 15 \end{pmatrix}$.

9.37. $f(T)(x, y) = (4x - y, -2x + 5y)$.

9.38. $f(D)(v(x)) = -5ax^2 + (4a - 5b)x + (2a + 2b - 5c)$.

9.39. $A^2 = \begin{pmatrix} 1 & 2 \\ 0 & 1 \end{pmatrix}$, $A^3 = \begin{pmatrix} 1 & 3 \\ 0 & 1 \end{pmatrix}$, $A^n = \begin{pmatrix} 1 & n \\ 0 & 1 \end{pmatrix}$.

9.40. *Hint.* Let $A = \begin{pmatrix} 2 & a & b \\ 0 & 2 & c \\ 0 & 0 & 2 \end{pmatrix}$. Set $B = A^3$ and then obtain conditions on a, b and c.

9.44. (ii) Using (i), we have $(f(A))^t = f(A^t) = f(A)$.

9.45. (i) $\lambda_1 = 1$, $u = (2, -1)$; $\lambda_2 = 4$, $v = (1, 1)$.
  (ii) $\lambda_1 = 1$, $u = (2, -3)$; $\lambda_2 = 6$, $v = (1, 1)$.
  (iii) $\lambda = 4$, $u = (1, 1)$.

Let $P_1 = \begin{pmatrix} 2 & 1 \\ -1 & 1 \end{pmatrix}$ and $P_2 = \begin{pmatrix} 2 & 1 \\ -3 & 1 \end{pmatrix}$. P_3 does not exist since C has only one independent eigenvector, and so cannot be diagonalized.

9.46. (i) $\lambda_1 = 2$, $u = (1, -1, 0)$, $v = (1, 0, -1)$; $\lambda_2 = 6$, $w = (1, 2, 1)$.

  (ii) $\lambda_1 = 3$, $u = (1, 1, 0)$, $v = (1, 0, 1)$; $\lambda_2 = 1$, $w = (2, -1, 1)$.

  (iii) $\lambda = 1$, $u = (1, 0, 0)$, $v = (0, 0, 1)$.

Let $P_1 = \begin{pmatrix} 1 & 1 & 1 \\ -1 & 0 & 2 \\ 0 & -1 & 1 \end{pmatrix}$ and $P_2 = \begin{pmatrix} 1 & 1 & 2 \\ 1 & 0 & -1 \\ 0 & 1 & 1 \end{pmatrix}$. P_3 does not exist since C has at most two

linearly independent eigenvectors, and so cannot be diagonalized.

9.47. (i) $\lambda = 3$, $u = (1, -1)$;   (ii) B has no eigenvalues (in **R**).

9.48. (i) $\lambda = 3$, $u = (1, -1)$.   (ii) $\lambda_1 = 2i$, $u = (1, 3 - 2i)$; $\lambda_2 = -2i$, $v = (1, 3 + 2i)$.

9.49. (i) $\lambda_1 = 2$, $u = (3, -1)$; $\lambda_2 = 6$, $v = (1, 1)$.   (ii) $\lambda_1 = 1$, $u = (1, 1)$; $\lambda_2 = -1$, $v = (1, -1)$.   (iii) **There** are no eigenvalues (in **R**).

9.50. (i) $\lambda_1 = 1$, $u = (1, 0, 0)$; $\lambda_2 = 4$, $v = (1, 1, 2)$.

  (ii) $\lambda = 1$, $u = (1, 0, 0)$. There are no other eigenvalues (in **R**).

  (iii) $\lambda_1 = 1$, $u = (1, 0, -1)$; $\lambda_2 = 2$, $v = (2, -2, -1)$; $\lambda_3 = 3$, $w = (1, -2, -1)$.

9.51. (i) $\lambda_1 = 1$, $u = (1, 0)$; $\lambda_2 = i$, $v = (1, 1 + i)$. (ii) $\lambda = 1$, $u = (1, 0)$. (iii) $\lambda_1 = 2$, $u = (3, i)$; $\lambda_2 = -2$, $v = (1, -i)$. (iv) $\lambda_1 = i$, $u = (2, 1 - i)$; $\lambda_2 = -i$, $v = (2, 1 + i)$.

9.56. Let $A = \begin{pmatrix} 1 & 1 \\ 0 & 1 \end{pmatrix}$. Then $\lambda = 1$ is the only eigenvalue and $v = (1, 0)$ generates the eigenspace of $\lambda = 1$. On the other hand, for $A^t = \begin{pmatrix} 1 & 0 \\ 1 & 1 \end{pmatrix}$, $\lambda = 1$ is still the only eigenvalue, but $w = (0, 1)$ generates the eigenspace of $\lambda = 1$.

9.57. Let $v \in W$, and so $T(v) = \lambda v$. Then $T(Sv) = S(Tv) = S(\lambda v) = \lambda(Sv)$, that is, Sv is an eigenvector of T belonging to the eigenvalue λ. In other words, $Sv \in W$ and thus $S(W) \subset W$.

9.58. Let $\widehat{T} : W \to W$ be the restriction of T to W. The characteristic polynomial of $\widehat{T}$ is a polynomial over the complex field **C** which, by the fundamental theorem of algebra, has a root λ. Then λ is an eigenvalue of $\widehat{T}$, and so $\widehat{T}$ has a nonzero eigenvector in W which is also an eigenvector of T.

9.59. Suppose $T(v) = \lambda v$. Then $(kT)(v) = kT(v) = k(\lambda v) = (k\lambda)v$.

9.60. (i) $f(t) = t^2 - 8t + 43$, (ii) $g(t) = t^2 - 8t + 23$, (iii) $h(t) = t^3 - 6t^2 + 5t - 12$.

9.62. (i) $\Delta(t) = (t - 2)^3(t - 7)^2$; $m(t) = (t - 2)^2(t - 7)$.   (ii) $\Delta(t) = (t - 3)^5$; $m(t) = (t - 3)^3$.   (iii) $\Delta(t) = (t - \lambda)^5$; $m(t) = t - \lambda$.

9.73. Use the result of Problem 9.72.   (i) $A = \begin{pmatrix} 0 & 0 & -8 \\ 1 & 0 & -6 \\ 0 & 1 & 5 \end{pmatrix}$, (ii) $A = \begin{pmatrix} 0 & 0 & 0 & -4 \\ 1 & 0 & 0 & -7 \\ 0 & 1 & 0 & 2 \\ 0 & 0 & 1 & 5 \end{pmatrix}$.

9.77. *Hint.* Use the result of Problem 9.57.

Chapter 10

Canonical Forms

INTRODUCTION

Let T be a linear operator on a vector space of finite dimension. As seen in the preceding chapter, T may not have a diagonal matrix representation. However, it is still possible to "simplify" the matrix representation of T in a number of ways. This is the main topic of this chapter. In particular, we obtain the *primary decomposition theorem*, and the *triangular, Jordan* and *rational* canonical forms.

We comment that the triangular and Jordan canonical forms exist for T if and only if the characteristic polynomial $\Delta(t)$ of T has all its roots in the base field K. This is always true if K is the complex field $\mathbf{C}$ but may not be true if K is the real field $\mathbf{R}$.

We also introduce the idea of a quotient space. This is a very powerful tool and will be used in the proof of the existence of the triangular and rational canonical forms.

TRIANGULAR FORM

Let T be a linear operator on an n-dimensional vector space V. Suppose T can be represented by the triangular matrix

$$A = \begin{pmatrix} a_{11} & a_{12} & \ldots & a_{1n} \\ & a_{22} & \ldots & a_{2n} \\ & & \cdots\cdots\cdots \\ & & & a_{nn} \end{pmatrix}$$

Then the characteristic polynomial of T,

$$\Delta(t) = |tI - A| = (t - a_{11})(t - a_{22}) \ldots (t - a_{nn})$$

is a product of linear factors. The converse is also true and is an important theorem; namely,

Theorem 10.1: Let $T : V \to V$ be a linear operator whose characteristic polynomial factors into linear polynomials. Then there exists a basis of V in which T is represented by a triangular matrix.

Alternative Form of Theorem 10.1: Let A be a square matrix whose characteristic polynomial factors into linear polynomials. Then A is similar to a triangular matrix, i.e. there exists an invertible matrix P such that $P^{-1}AP$ is triangular.

We say that an operator T *can be brought into triangular form* if it can be represented by a triangular matrix. Note that in this case the eigenvalues of T are precisely those entries appearing on the main diagonal. We give an application of this remark.

Example 10.1: Let A be a square matrix over the complex field $\mathbf{C}$. Suppose λ is an eigenvalue of A^2. Show that $\sqrt{\lambda}$ or $-\sqrt{\lambda}$ is an eigenvalue of A. We know by the above theorem that A is similar to a triangular matrix

$$B = \begin{pmatrix} \mu_1 & * & \cdots & * \\ & \mu_2 & \cdots & * \\ & & \cdots\cdots\cdots \\ & & & \mu_n \end{pmatrix}$$

Hence A^2 is similar to the matrix

$$B^2 = \begin{pmatrix} \mu_1^2 & * & \cdots & * \\ & \mu_2^2 & \cdots & * \\ & & \cdots\cdots\cdots \\ & & & \mu_n^2 \end{pmatrix}$$

Since similar matrices have the same eigenvalues, $\lambda = \mu_i^2$ for some i. Hence $\mu_i = \sqrt{\lambda}$ or $\mu_i = -\sqrt{\lambda}$; that is, $\sqrt{\lambda}$ or $-\sqrt{\lambda}$ is an eigenvalue of A.

INVARIANCE

Let $T:V \to V$ be linear. A subspace W of V is said to be *invariant under T* or *T-invariant* if T maps W into itself, i.e. if $v \in W$ implies $T(v) \in W$. In this case T restricted to W defines a linear operator on W; that is, T induces a linear operator $\hat{T}:W \to W$ defined by $\hat{T}(w) = T(w)$ for every $w \in W$.

Example 10.2: Let $T:\mathbf{R}^3 \to \mathbf{R}^3$ be the linear operator which rotates each vector about the z axis by an angle θ:

$$T(x, y, z) = (x\cos\theta - y\sin\theta,\ x\sin\theta + y\cos\theta,\ z)$$

Observe that each vector $w = (a, b, 0)$ in the xy plane W remains in W under the mapping T, i.e. W is T-invariant. Observe also that the z axis U is invariant under T. Furthermore, the restriction of T to W rotates each vector about the origin O, and the restriction of T to U is the identity mapping on U.

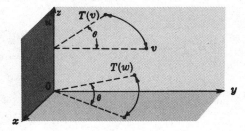

Example 10.3: Nonzero eigenvectors of a linear operator $T:V \to V$ may be characterized as generators of T-invariant 1-dimensional subspaces. For suppose $T(v) = \lambda v$, $v \neq 0$. Then $W = \{kv,\ k \in K\}$, the 1-dimensional subspace generated by v, is invariant under T because

$$T(kv) = k\,T(v) = k(\lambda v) = k\lambda v \in W$$

Conversely, suppose $\dim U = 1$ and $u \neq 0$ generates U, and U is invariant under T. Then $T(u) \in U$ and so $T(u)$ is a multiple of u, i.e. $T(u) = \mu u$. Hence u is an eigenvector of T.

The next theorem gives us an important class of invariant subspaces.

Theorem 10.2: Let $T:V \to V$ be linear, and let $f(t)$ be any polynomial. Then the kernel of $f(T)$ is invariant under T.

The notion of invariance is related to matrix representations as follows.

Theorem 10.3: Suppose W is an invariant subspace of $T:V \to V$. Then T has a block matrix representation $\begin{pmatrix} A & B \\ 0 & C \end{pmatrix}$ where A is a matrix representation of the restriction of T to W.

INVARIANT DIRECT-SUM DECOMPOSITIONS

A vector space V is termed the *direct sum* of its subspaces $W_1, \ldots, W_r$, written

$$V = W_1 \oplus W_2 \oplus \cdots \oplus W_r$$

if every vector $v \in V$ can be written uniquely in the form

$$v = w_1 + w_2 + \cdots + w_r \qquad \text{with } w_i \in W_i$$

The following theorem applies.

Theorem 10.4:   Suppose $W_1, \ldots, W_r$ are subspaces of V, and suppose

$$\{w_{11}, \ldots, w_{1n_1}\}, \ \ldots, \ \{w_{r1}, \ldots, w_{rn_r}\}$$

are bases of $W_1, \ldots, W_r$ respectively. Then V is the direct sum of the W_i if and only if the union $\{w_{11}, \ldots, w_{1n_1}, \ldots, w_{r1}, \ldots, w_{rn_r}\}$ is a basis of V.

Now suppose $T : V \to V$ is linear and V is the direct sum of (nonzero) T-invariant subspaces $W_1, \ldots, W_r$:

$$V = W_1 \oplus \cdots \oplus W_r \qquad \text{and} \qquad T(W_i) \subset W_i, \quad i = 1, \ldots, r$$

Let T_i denote the restriction of T to W_i. Then T is said to be *decomposable* into the operators T_i or T is said to be the *direct sum* of the T_i, written $T = T_1 \oplus \cdots \oplus T_r$. Also, the subspaces $W_1, \ldots, W_r$ are said to *reduce* T or to form a *T-invariant direct-sum decomposition* of V.

Consider the special case where two subspaces U and W reduce an operator $T : V \to V$; say, $\dim U = 2$ and $\dim W = 3$ and suppose $\{u_1, u_2\}$ and $\{w_1, w_2, w_3\}$ are bases of U and W respectively. If T_1 and T_2 denote the restrictions of T to U and W respectively, then

$$
\begin{aligned}
T_1(u_1) &= a_{11}u_1 + a_{12}u_2 \\
T_1(u_2) &= a_{21}u_1 + a_{22}u_2
\end{aligned}
\qquad
\begin{aligned}
T_2(w_1) &= b_{11}w_1 + b_{12}w_2 + b_{13}w_3 \\
T_2(w_2) &= b_{21}w_1 + b_{22}w_2 + b_{23}w_3 \\
T_2(w_3) &= b_{31}w_1 + b_{32}w_2 + b_{33}w_3
\end{aligned}
$$

Hence

$$A = \begin{pmatrix} a_{11} & a_{21} \\ a_{12} & a_{22} \end{pmatrix} \qquad \text{and} \qquad B = \begin{pmatrix} b_{11} & b_{21} & b_{31} \\ b_{12} & b_{22} & b_{32} \\ b_{13} & b_{23} & b_{33} \end{pmatrix}$$

are matrix representations of T_1 and T_2 respectively. By the above theorem $\{u_1, u_2, w_1, w_2, w_3\}$ is a basis of V. Since $T(u_i) = T_1(u_i)$ and $T(w_j) = T_2(w_j)$, the matrix of T in this basis is the block diagonal matrix $\begin{pmatrix} A & 0 \\ 0 & B \end{pmatrix}$.

A generalization of the above argument gives us the following theorem.

Theorem 10.5:   Suppose $T : V \to V$ is linear and V is the direct sum of T-invariant subspaces $W_1, \ldots, W_r$. If A_i is a matrix representation of the restriction of T to W_i, then T can be represented by the block diagonal matrix

$$M = \begin{pmatrix} A_1 & 0 & \ldots & 0 \\ 0 & A_2 & \ldots & 0 \\ \multicolumn{4}{c}{\dotfill} \\ 0 & 0 & \ldots & A_r \end{pmatrix}$$

The block diagonal matrix M with diagonal entries $A_1, \ldots, A_r$ is sometimes called the *direct sum* of the matrices $A_1, \ldots, A_r$ and denoted by $M = A_1 \oplus \cdots \oplus A_r$.

PRIMARY DECOMPOSITION

The following theorem shows that any operator $T : V \to V$ is decomposable into operators whose minimal polynomials are powers of irreducible polynomials. This is the first step in obtaining a canonical form for T,

Primary Decomposition Theorem 10.6:   Let $T : V \to V$ be a linear operator with minimal polynomial

$$m(t) = f_1(t)^{n_1} f_2(t)^{n_2} \ldots f_r(t)^{n_r}$$

where the $f_i(t)$ are distinct monic irreducible polynomials. Then V is the direct sum of T-invariant subspaces $W_1, \ldots, W_r$ where W_i is the kernel of $f_i(T)^{n_i}$. Moreover, $f_i(t)^{n_i}$ is the minimal polynomial of the restriction of T to W_i.

Since the polynomials $f_i(t)^{n_i}$ are relatively prime, the above fundamental result follows (Problem 10.11) from the next two theorems.

Theorem 10.7:   Suppose $T : V \to V$ is linear, and suppose $f(t) = g(t) h(t)$ are polynomials such that $f(T) = 0$ and $g(t)$ and $h(t)$ are relatively prime. Then V is the direct sum of the T-invariant subspaces U and W, where $U = \operatorname{Ker} g(T)$ and $W = \operatorname{Ker} h(T)$.

Theorem 10.8:   In Theorem 10.7, if $f(t)$ is the minimal polynomial of T [and $g(t)$ and $h(t)$ are monic], then $g(t)$ and $h(t)$ are the minimal polynomials of the restrictions of T to U and W respectively.

We will also use the primary decomposition theorem to prove the following useful characterization of diagonalizable operators.

Theorem 10.9:   A linear operator $T : V \to V$ has a diagonal matrix representation if and only if its minimal polynomial $m(t)$ is a product of distinct linear polynomials.

Alternative Form of Theorem 10.9:   A matrix A is similar to a diagonal matrix if and only if its minimal polynomial is a product of distinct linear polynomials.

> **Example 10.4:**   Suppose $A \neq I$ is a square matrix for which $A^3 = I$. Determine whether or not A is similar to a diagonal matrix if A is a matrix over (i) the real field **R**, (ii) the complex field **C**.
>
> Since $A^3 = I$, A is a zero of the polynomial $f(t) = t^3 - 1 = (t-1)(t^2 + t + 1)$. The minimal polynomial $m(t)$ of A cannot be $t - 1$, since $A \neq I$. Hence
>
> $$m(t) = t^2 + t + 1 \quad \text{or} \quad m(t) = t^3 - 1$$
>
> Since neither polynomial is a product of linear polynomials over **R**, A is not diagonalizable over **R**. On the other hand, each of the polynomials is a product of distinct linear polynomials over **C**. Hence A is diagonalizable over **C**.

NILPOTENT OPERATORS

A linear operator $T : V \to V$ is termed *nilpotent* if $T^n = 0$ for some positive integer n; we call k the *index of nilpotency* of T if $T^k = 0$ but $T^{k-1} \neq 0$. Analogously, a square matrix A is termed *nilpotent* if $A^n = 0$ for some positive integer n, and of *index* k if $A^k = 0$ but $A^{k-1} \neq 0$. Clearly the minimum polynomial of a nilpotent operator (matrix) of index k is $m(t) = t^k$; hence 0 is its only eigenvalue.

The fundamental result on nilpotent operators follows.

Theorem 10.10:   Let $T : V \to V$ be a nilpotent operator of index k. Then T has a block diagonal matrix representation whose diagonal entries are of the form

$$N = \begin{pmatrix} 0 & 1 & 0 & \ldots & 0 & 0 \\ 0 & 0 & 1 & \ldots & 0 & 0 \\ \multicolumn{6}{c}{\cdots\cdots\cdots\cdots\cdots} \\ 0 & 0 & 0 & \ldots & 0 & 1 \\ 0 & 0 & 0 & \ldots & 0 & 0 \end{pmatrix}$$

(i.e. all entries of N are 0 except those just above the main diagonal where they are 1). There is at least one N of order k and all other N are of orders $\leq k$. The number of N of each possible order is uniquely determined by T. Moreover, the total number of N of all orders is equal to the nullity of T.

In the proof of the above theorem, we shall show that the number of N of order i is $2m_i - m_{i+1} - m_{i-1}$, where m_i is the nullity of T^i.

We remark that the above matrix N is itself nilpotent and that its index of nilpotency is equal to its order (Problem 10.13). Note that the matrix N of order 1 is just the 1×1 zero matrix (0).

JORDAN CANONICAL FORM

An operator T can be put into Jordan canonical form if its characteristic and minimal polynomials factor into linear polynomials. This is always true if K is the complex field $\mathbf{C}$. In any case, we can always extend the base field K to a field in which the characteristic and minimum polynomials do factor into linear factors; thus in a broad sense every operator has a Jordan canonical form. Analogously, every matrix is similar to a matrix in Jordan canonical form.

Theorem 10.11: Let $T:V \to V$ be a linear operator whose characteristic and minimum polynomials are respectively

$$\Delta(t) = (t-\lambda_1)^{n_1} \ldots (t-\lambda_r)^{n_r} \quad \text{and} \quad m(t) = (t-\lambda_1)^{m_1} \ldots (t-\lambda_r)^{m_r}$$

where the λ_i are distinct scalars. Then T has a block diagonal matrix representation J whose diagonal entries are of the form

$$J_{ij} = \begin{pmatrix} \lambda_i & 1 & 0 & \ldots & 0 & 0 \\ 0 & \lambda_i & 1 & \ldots & 0 & 0 \\ \multicolumn{6}{c}{\cdots\cdots\cdots\cdots\cdots} \\ 0 & 0 & 0 & \ldots & \lambda_i & 1 \\ 0 & 0 & 0 & \ldots & 0 & \lambda_i \end{pmatrix}$$

For each λ_i the corresponding blocks J_{ij} have the following properties:

(i)   There is at least one J_{ij} of order m_i; all other J_{ij} are of order $\leq m_i$.

(ii) The sum of the orders of the J_{ij} is n_i.

(iii) The number of J_{ij} equals the geometric multiplicity of λ_i.

(iv) The number of J_{ij} of each possible order is uniquely determined by T.

The matrix J appearing in the above theorem is called the *Jordan canonical form* of the operator T. A diagonal block J_{ij} is called a *Jordan block* belonging to the eigenvalue λ_i. Observe that

$$\begin{pmatrix} \lambda_i & 1 & 0 & \ldots & 0 & 0 \\ 0 & \lambda_i & 1 & \ldots & 0 & 0 \\ \multicolumn{6}{c}{\cdots\cdots\cdots\cdots\cdots} \\ 0 & 0 & 0 & \ldots & \lambda_i & 1 \\ 0 & 0 & 0 & \ldots & 0 & \lambda_i \end{pmatrix} = \begin{pmatrix} \lambda_i & 0 & \ldots & 0 & 0 \\ 0 & \lambda_i & \ldots & 0 & 0 \\ \multicolumn{5}{c}{\cdots\cdots\cdots\cdots} \\ 0 & 0 & \ldots & \lambda_i & 0 \\ 0 & 0 & \ldots & 0 & \lambda_i \end{pmatrix} + \begin{pmatrix} 0 & 1 & 0 & \ldots & 0 & 0 \\ 0 & 0 & 1 & \ldots & 0 & 0 \\ \multicolumn{6}{c}{\cdots\cdots\cdots\cdots\cdots} \\ 0 & 0 & 0 & \ldots & 0 & 1 \\ 0 & 0 & 0 & \ldots & 0 & 0 \end{pmatrix}$$

That is,

$$J_{ij} = \lambda_i I + N$$

where N is the nilpotent block appearing in Theorem 10.10. In fact, we prove the above theorem (Problem 10.18) by showing that T can be decomposed into operators, each the sum of a scalar and a nilpotent operator.

Example 10.5: Suppose the characteristic and minimum polynomials of an operator T are respectively

$$\Delta(t) = (t-2)^4(t-3)^3 \quad \text{and} \quad m(t) = (t-2)^2(t-3)^2$$

Then the Jordan canonical form of T is one of the following matrices:

$$\begin{pmatrix} 2 & 1 & & & & & \\ 0 & 2 & & & & & \\ & & 2 & 1 & & & \\ & & 0 & 2 & & & \\ & & & & 3 & 1 & \\ & & & & 0 & 3 & \\ & & & & & & 3 \end{pmatrix} \quad \text{or} \quad \begin{pmatrix} 2 & 1 & & & & & \\ 0 & 2 & & & & & \\ & & 2 & & & & \\ & & & 2 & & & \\ & & & & 3 & 1 & \\ & & & & 0 & 3 & \\ & & & & & & 3 \end{pmatrix}$$

The first matrix occurs if T has two independent eigenvectors belonging to its eigenvalue 2; and the second matrix occurs if T has three independent eigenvectors belonging to 2.

CYCLIC SUBSPACES

Let T be a linear operator on a vector space V of finite dimension over K. Suppose $v \in V$ and $v \neq 0$. The set of all vectors of the form $f(T)(v)$, where $f(t)$ ranges over all polynomials over K, is a T-invariant subspace of V called the *T-cyclic subspace of V generated by v*; we denote it by $Z(v, T)$ and denote the restriction of T to $Z(v, T)$ by T_v. We could equivalently define $Z(v, T)$ as the intersection of all T-invariant subspaces of V containing v.

Now consider the sequence

$$v, \ T(v), \ T^2(v), \ T^3(v), \ \ldots$$

of powers of T acting on v. Let k be the lowest integer such that $T^k(v)$ is a linear combination of those vectors which precede it in the sequence; say,

$$T^k(v) = -a_{k-1} T^{k-1}(v) - \cdots - a_1 T(v) - a_0 v$$

Then

$$m_v(t) = t^k + a_{k-1} t^{k-1} + \cdots + a_1 t + a_0$$

is the unique monic polynomial of lowest degree for which $m_v(T)(v) = 0$. We call $m_v(t)$ the *T-annihilator* of v and $Z(v, T)$.

The following theorem applies.

Theorem 10.12: Let $Z(v, T)$, T_v and $m_v(t)$ be defined as above. Then:

(i) The set $\{v, T(v), \ldots, T^{k-1}(v)\}$ is a basis of $Z(v, T)$; hence $\dim Z(v, T) = k$.

(ii) The minimal polynomial of T_v is $m_v(t)$.

(iii) The matrix representation of T_v in the above basis is

$$C = \begin{pmatrix} 0 & 0 & 0 & \ldots & 0 & -a_0 \\ 1 & 0 & 0 & \ldots & 0 & -a_1 \\ 0 & 1 & 0 & \ldots & 0 & -a_2 \\ \multicolumn{6}{c}{\dotfill} \\ 0 & 0 & 0 & \ldots & 0 & -a_{k-2} \\ 0 & 0 & 0 & \ldots & 1 & -a_{k-1} \end{pmatrix}$$

The above matrix C is called the *companion matrix* of the polynomial $m_v(t)$.

RATIONAL CANONICAL FORM

In this section we present the rational canonical form for a linear operator $T : V \to V$. We emphasize that this form exists even when the minimal polynomial cannot be factored into linear polynomials. (Recall that this is not the case for the Jordan canonical form.)

Lemma 10.13: Let $T : V \to V$ be a linear operator whose minimal polynomial is $f(t)^n$ where $f(t)$ is a monic irreducible polynomial. Then V is the direct sum

$$V = Z(v_1, T) \oplus \cdots \oplus Z(v_r, T)$$

of T-cyclic subspaces $Z(v_i, T)$ with corresponding T-annihilators

$$f(t)^{n_1}, f(t)^{n_2}, \ldots, f(t)^{n_r}, \qquad n = n_1 \geq n_2 \geq \cdots \geq n_r$$

Any other decomposition of V into T-cyclic subspaces has the same number of components and the same set of T-annihilators.

We emphasize that the above lemma does not say that the vectors v_i or the T-cyclic subspaces $Z(v_i, T)$ are uniquely determined by T; but it does say that the set of T-annihilators are uniquely determined by T. Thus T has a unique matrix representation

$$\begin{pmatrix} C_1 & & & \\ & C_2 & & \\ & & \ddots & \\ & & & C_r \end{pmatrix}$$

where the C_i are companion matrices. In fact, the C_i are the companion matrices to the polynomials $f(t)^{n_i}$.

Using the primary decomposition theorem and the above lemma, we obtain the following fundamental result.

Theorem 10.14: Let $T : V \to V$ be a linear operator with minimal polynomial

$$m(t) = f_1(t)^{m_1} f_2(t)^{m_2} \ldots f_s(t)^{m_s}$$

where the $f_i(t)$ are distinct monic irreducible polynomials. Then T has a unique block diagonal matrix representation

$$\begin{pmatrix} C_{11} & & & & & \\ & \ddots & & & & \\ & & C_{1r_1} & & & \\ & & & \ddots & & \\ & & & & C_{s1} & \\ & & & & & \ddots \\ & & & & & & C_{sr_s} \end{pmatrix}$$

where the C_{ij} are companion matrices. In particular, the C_{ij} are the companion matrices of the polynomials $f_i(t)^{n_{ij}}$ where

$$m_1 = n_{11} \geq n_{12} \geq \cdots \geq n_{1r_1}, \quad \ldots, \quad m_s = n_{s1} \geq n_{s2} \geq \cdots \geq n_{sr_s}$$

The above matrix representation of T is called its *rational canonical form*. The polynomials $f_i(t)^{n_{ij}}$ are called the *elementary divisors* of T.

Example 10.6:   Let V be a vector space of dimension 6 over **R**, and let T be a linear operator whose minimal polynomial is $m(t) = (t^2 - t + 3)(t - 2)^2$. Then the rational canonical form of T is one of the following direct sums of companion matrices:

(i) $C(t^2 - t + 3) \oplus C(t^2 - t + 3) \oplus C((t - 2)^2)$

(ii) $C(t^2 - t + 3) \oplus C((t - 2)^2) \oplus C((t - 2)^2)$

(iii) $C(t^2 - t + 3) \oplus C((t - 2)^2) \oplus C(t - 2) \oplus C(t - 2)$

where $C(f(t))$ is the companion matrix of $f(t)$; that is,

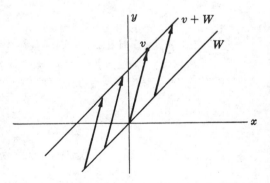

(i)   (ii)   (iii)

QUOTIENT SPACES

Let V be a vector space over a field K and let W be a subspace of V. If v is any vector in V, we write $v + W$ for the set of sums $v + w$ with $w \in W$:

$$v + W = \{v + w : w \in W\}$$

These sets are called the *cosets* of W in V. We show (Problem 10.22) that these cosets partition V into mutually disjoint subsets.

Example 10.7:   Let W be the subspace of **R**^{2} defined by

$$W = \{(a, b) : a = b\}$$

That is, W is the line given by the equation $x - y = 0$. We can view $v + W$ as a translation of the line, obtained by adding the vector v to each point in W. As noted in the diagram on the right, $v + W$ is also a line and is parallel to W. Thus the cosets of W in **R**^{2} are precisely all the lines parallel to W.

In the next theorem we use the cosets of a subspace W of a vector space V to define a new vector space; it is called the *quotient space* of V by W and is denoted by V/W.

Theorem 10.15:   Let W be a subspace of a vector space over a field K. Then the cosets of W in V form a vector space over K with the following operations of addition and scalar multiplication:

(i) $(u + W) + (v + W) = (u + v) + W$

(ii) $k(u + W) = ku + W$, where $k \in K$.

We note that, in the proof of the above theorem, it is first necessary to show that the operations are well defined; that is, whenever $u + W = u' + W$ and $v + W = v' + W$, then

(i) $(u + v) + W = (u' + v') + W$ and   (ii) $ku + W = ku' + W$, for any $k \in K$

In the case of an invariant subspace, we have the following useful result.

Theorem 10.16: Suppose W is a subspace invariant under a linear operator $T : V \to V$. Then T induces a linear operator $\bar{T}$ on V/W defined by $\bar{T}(v + W) = T(v) + W$. Moreover, if T is a zero of any polynomial, then so is $\bar{T}$. Thus the minimum polynomial of $\bar{T}$ divides the minimum polynomial of T.

Solved Problems

INVARIANT SUBSPACES

10.1. Suppose $T : V \to V$ is linear. Show that each of the following is invariant under T: (i) $\{0\}$, (ii) V, (iii) kernel of T, (iv) image of T.

    (i)   We have $T(0) = 0 \in \{0\}$; hence $\{0\}$ is invariant under T.

    (ii)   For every $v \in V$, $T(v) \in V$; hence V is invariant under T.

    (iii)   Let $u \in \operatorname{Ker} T$. Then $T(u) = 0 \in \operatorname{Ker} T$ since the kernel of T is a subspace of V. Thus $\operatorname{Ker} T$ is invariant under T.

    (iv)   Since $T(v) \in \operatorname{Im} T$ for every $v \in V$, it is certainly true if $v \in \operatorname{Im} T$. Hence the image of T is invariant under T.

10.2. Suppose $\{W_i\}$ is a collection of T-invariant subspaces of a vector space V. Show that the intersection $W = \cap_i W_i$ is also T-invariant.

    Suppose $v \in W$; then $v \in W_i$ for every i. Since W_i is T-invariant, $T(v) \in W_i$ for every i. Thus $T(v) \in W = \cap_i W_i$ and so W is T-invariant.

10.3. Prove Theorem 10.2: Let $T : V \to V$ be any linear operator and let $f(t)$ be any polynomial. Then the kernel of $f(T)$ is invariant under T.

    Suppose $v \in \operatorname{Ker} f(T)$, i.e. $f(T)(v) = 0$. We need to show that $T(v)$ also belongs to the kernel of $f(T)$, i.e. $f(T)(T(v)) = 0$. Since $f(t)\, t = t\, f(t)$, we have $f(T)\, T = T\, f(T)$. Thus

$$f(T)T(v) \;=\; Tf(T)(v) \;=\; T(0) \;=\; 0$$

as required.

10.4. Find all invariant subspaces of $A = \begin{pmatrix} 2 & -5 \\ 1 & -2 \end{pmatrix}$ viewed as an operator on $\mathbf{R}^2$.

    First of all, we have that $\mathbf{R}^2$ and $\{0\}$ are invariant under A. Now if A has any other invariant subspaces, then it must be 1-dimensional. However, the characteristic polynomial of A is

$$\Delta(t) \;=\; |tI - A| \;=\; \begin{vmatrix} t-2 & 5 \\ -1 & t+2 \end{vmatrix} \;=\; t^2 + 1$$

Hence A has no eigenvalues (in $\mathbf{R}$) and so A has no eigenvectors. But the 1-dimensional invariant subspaces correspond to the eigenvectors; thus $\mathbf{R}^2$ and $\{0\}$ are the only subspaces invariant under A.

10.5. Prove Theorem 10.3: Suppose W is an invariant subspace of $T : V \to V$. Then T has a block diagonal matrix representation $\begin{pmatrix} A & B \\ 0 & C \end{pmatrix}$ where A is a matrix representation of the restriction $\hat{T}$ of T to W.

    We choose a basis $\{w_1, \ldots, w_r\}$ of W and extend it to a basis $\{w_1, \ldots, w_r, v_1, \ldots, v_s\}$ of V. We have

$$\widehat{T}(w_1) = T(w_1) = a_{11}w_1 + \cdots + a_{1r}w_r$$
$$\widehat{T}(w_2) = T(w_2) = a_{21}w_1 + \cdots + a_{2r}w_r$$
$$\cdots\cdots\cdots\cdots\cdots\cdots\cdots\cdots\cdots\cdots\cdots\cdots\cdots\cdots\cdots$$
$$\widehat{T}(w_r) = T(w_r) = a_{r1}w_1 + \cdots + a_{rr}w_r$$
$$T(v_1) = b_{11}w_1 + \cdots + b_{1r}w_r + c_{11}v_1 + \cdots + c_{1s}v_s$$
$$T(v_2) = b_{21}w_1 + \cdots + b_{2r}w_r + c_{21}v_1 + \cdots + c_{2s}v_s$$
$$\cdots\cdots\cdots\cdots\cdots\cdots\cdots\cdots\cdots\cdots\cdots\cdots\cdots\cdots\cdots$$
$$T(v_s) = b_{s1}w_1 + \cdots + b_{sr}w_r + c_{s1}v_1 + \cdots + c_{ss}v_s$$

But the matrix of T in this basis is the transpose of the matrix of coefficients in the above system of equations. (See page 150.) Therefore it has the form $\begin{pmatrix} A & B \\ 0 & C \end{pmatrix}$ where A is the transpose of the matrix of coefficients for the obvious subsystem. By the same argument, A is the matrix of $\widehat{T}$ relative to the basis $\{w_i\}$ of W.

10.6. Let $\widehat{T}$ denote the restriction of an operator T to an invariant subspace W, i.e. $\widehat{T}(w) = T(w)$ for every $w \in W$. Prove:

(i) For any polynomial $f(t)$, $f(\widehat{T})(w) = f(T)(w)$.

(ii) The minimum polynomial of $\widehat{T}$ divides the minimum polynomial of T.

(i) If $f(t) = 0$ or if $f(t)$ is a constant, i.e. of degree 1, then the result clearly holds. Assume $\deg f = n > 1$ and that the result holds for polynomials of degree less than n. Suppose that

$$f(t) = a_n t^n + a_{n-1} t^{n-1} + \cdots + a_1 t + a_0$$

Then
$$f(\widehat{T})(w) = (a_n \widehat{T}^n + a_{n-1} \widehat{T}^{n-1} + \cdots + a_0 I)(w)$$
$$= (a_n \widehat{T}^{n-1})(\widehat{T}(w)) + (a_{n-1} \widehat{T}^{n-1} + \cdots + a_0 I)(w)$$
$$= (a_n T^{n-1})(T(w)) + (a_{n-1} T^{n-1} + \cdots + a_0 I)(w)$$
$$= f(T)(w)$$

(ii) Let $m(t)$ denote the minimum polynomial of T. Then by (i), $m(\widehat{T})(w) = m(T)(w) = 0(w) = 0$ for every $w \in W$; that is, $\widehat{T}$ is a zero of the polynomial $m(t)$. Hence the minimum polynomial of $\widehat{T}$ divides $m(t)$.

INVARIANT DIRECT-SUM DECOMPOSITIONS

10.7. Prove Theorem 10.4: Suppose $W_1, \ldots, W_r$ are subspaces of V and suppose, for $i = 1, \ldots, r$, $\{w_{i1}, \ldots, w_{in_i}\}$ is a basis of W_i. Then V is the direct sum of the W_i if and only if the union

$$B = \{w_{11}, \ldots, w_{1n_1}, \ldots, w_{r1}, \ldots, w_{rn_r}\}$$

is a basis of V.

Suppose B is a basis of V. Then, for any $v \in V$,
$$v = a_{11}w_{11} + \cdots + a_{1n_1}w_{1n_1} + \cdots + a_{r1}w_{r1} + \cdots + a_{rn_r}w_{rn_r} = w_1 + w_2 + \cdots + w_r$$
where $w_i = a_{i1}w_{i1} + \cdots + a_{in_i}w_{in_i} \in W_i$. We next show that such a sum is unique. Suppose
$$v = w_1' + w_2' + \cdots + w_r' \qquad \text{where } w_i' \in W_i$$
Since $\{w_{i1}, \ldots, w_{in_i}\}$ is a basis of W_i, $w_i' = b_{i1}w_{i1} + \cdots + b_{in_i}w_{in_i}$ and so
$$v = b_{11}w_{11} + \cdots + b_{1n_1}w_{1n_1} + \cdots + b_{r1}w_{r1} + \cdots + b_{rn_r}w_{rn_r}$$
Since B is a basis of V, $a_{ij} = b_{ij}$, for each i and each j. Hence $w_i = w_i'$ and so the sum for v is unique. Accordingly, V is the direct sum of the W_i.

Conversely, suppose V is the direct sum of the W_i. Then for any $v \in V$, $v = w_1 + \cdots + w_r$ where $w_i \in W_i$. Since $\{w_{ij_i}\}$ is a basis of W_i, each w_i is a linear combination of the w_{ij_i} and so v is a linear combination of the elements of B. Thus B spans V. We now show that B is linearly independent. Suppose

$$a_{11}w_{11} + \cdots + a_{1n_1}w_{1n_1} + \cdots + a_{r1}w_{r1} + \cdots + a_{rn_r}w_{rn_r} = 0$$

Note that $a_{i1}w_{i1} + \cdots + a_{in_i}w_{in_i} \in W_i$. We also have that $0 = 0 + 0 + \cdots + 0$ where $0 \in W_i$. Since such a sum for 0 is unique,

$$a_{i1}w_{i1} + \cdots + a_{in_i}w_{in_i} = 0 \qquad \text{for } i = 1, \ldots, r$$

The independence of the bases $\{w_{ij_i}\}$ imply that all the a's are 0. Thus B is linearly independent and hence is a basis of V.

10.8. Suppose $T : V \to V$ is linear and suppose $T = T_1 \oplus T_2$ with respect to a T-invariant direct-sum decomposition $V = U \oplus W$. Show that:

(i) $m(t)$ is the least common multiple of $m_1(t)$ and $m_2(t)$ where $m(t)$, $m_1(t)$ and $m_2(t)$ are the minimum polynomials of T, T_1 and T_2 respectively;

(ii) $\Delta(t) = \Delta_1(t)\,\Delta_2(t)$, where $\Delta(t)$, $\Delta_1(t)$ and $\Delta_2(t)$ are the characteristic polynomials of T, T_1 and T_2 respectively.

(i)   By Problem 10.6, each of $m_1(t)$ and $m_2(t)$ divides $m(t)$. Now suppose $f(t)$ is a multiple of both $m_1(t)$ and $m_2(t)$; then $f(T_1)(U) = 0$ and $f(T_2)(W) = 0$. Let $v \in V$; then $v = u + w$ with $u \in U$ and $w \in W$. Now

$$f(T)\,v \;=\; f(T)\,u + f(T)\,w \;=\; f(T_1)\,u + f(T_2)\,w \;=\; 0 + 0 \;=\; 0$$

That is, T is a zero of $f(t)$. Hence $m(t)$ divides $f(t)$, and so $m(t)$ is the least common multiple of $m_1(t)$ and $m_2(t)$.

(ii) By Theorem 10.5, T has a matrix representation $M = \begin{pmatrix} A & 0 \\ 0 & B \end{pmatrix}$ where A and B are matrix representations of T_1 and T_2 respectively. Then, by Problem 9.66,

$$\Delta(t) \;=\; |tI - M| \;=\; \begin{vmatrix} tI - A & 0 \\ 0 & tI - B \end{vmatrix} \;=\; |tI - A|\,|tI - B| \;=\; \Delta_1(t)\,\Delta_2(t)$$

as required.

10.9. Prove Theorem 10.7: Suppose $T : V \to V$ is linear, and suppose $f(t) = g(t)\,h(t)$ are polynomials such that $f(T) = 0$ and $g(t)$ and $h(t)$ are relatively prime. Then V is the direct sum of the T-invariant subspaces U and W where $U = \operatorname{Ker} g(T)$ and $W = \operatorname{Ker} h(T)$.

Note first that U and W are T-invariant by Theorem 10.2. Now since $g(t)$ and $h(t)$ are relatively prime, there exist polynomials $r(t)$ and $s(t)$ such that

$$r(t)\,g(t) + s(t)\,h(t) = 1$$

Hence for the operator T, $\qquad r(T)\,g(T) + s(T)\,h(T) = I \qquad\qquad\qquad\qquad (*)$

Let $v \in V$; then by $(*)$, $\qquad v = r(T)\,g(T)\,v + s(T)\,h(T)\,v$

But the first term in this sum belongs to $W = \operatorname{Ker} h(T)$ since

$$h(T)\,r(T)\,g(T)\,v \;=\; r(T)\,g(T)\,h(T)\,v \;=\; r(T)\,f(T)\,v \;=\; r(T)\,0\,v \;=\; 0$$

Similarly, the second term belongs to U. Hence V is the sum of U and W.

To prove that $V = U \oplus W$, we must show that a sum $v = u + w$ with $u \in U$, $w \in W$, is uniquely determined by v. Applying the operator $r(T)g(T)$ to $v = u + w$ and using $g(T)u = 0$, we obtain

$$r(T)\,g(T)\,v \;=\; r(T)\,g(T)\,u + r(T)\,g(T)\,w \;=\; r(T)\,g(T)\,w$$

Also, applying $(*)$ to w alone and using $h(T)\,w = 0$, we obtain

$$w \;=\; r(T)\,g(T)\,w + s(T)\,h(T)\,w \;=\; r(T)\,g(T)\,w$$

Both of the above formulae give us $w = r(T)\,g(T)\,v$ and so w is uniquely determined by v. Similarly u is uniquely determined by v. Hence $V = U \oplus W$, as required.

10.10. Prove Theorem 10.8: In Theorem 10.7 (Problem 10.9), if $f(t)$ is the minimal polynomial of T (and $g(t)$ and $h(t)$ are monic), then $g(t)$ is the minimal polynomial of the restriction T_1 of T to U and $h(t)$ is the minimal polynomial of the restriction T_2 of T to W.

Let $m_1(t)$ and $m_2(t)$ be the minimal polynomials of T_1 and T_2 respectively. Note that $g(T_1) = 0$ and $h(T_2) = 0$ because $U = \operatorname{Ker} g(T)$ and $W = \operatorname{Ker} h(T)$. Thus

$$m_1(t) \text{ divides } g(t) \quad \text{and} \quad m_2(t) \text{ divides } h(t) \tag{1}$$

By Problem 10.9, $f(t)$ is the least common multiple of $m_1(t)$ and $m_2(t)$. But $m_1(t)$ and $m_2(t)$ are relatively prime since $g(t)$ and $h(t)$ are relatively prime. Accordingly, $f(t) = m_1(t)\, m_2(t)$. We also have that $f(t) = g(t)\, h(t)$. These two equations together with (1) and the fact that all the polynomials are monic, imply that $g(t) = m_1(t)$ and $h(t) = m_2(t)$, as required.

10.11. Prove the Primary Decomposition Theorem 10.6: Let $T : V \to V$ be a linear operator with minimal polynomial

$$m(t) \;=\; f_1(t)^{n_1} f_2(t)^{n_2} \ldots f_r(t)^{n_r}$$

where the $f_i(t)$ are distinct monic irreducible polynomials. Then V is the direct sum of T-invariant subspaces $W_1, \ldots, W_r$ where W_i is the kernel of $f_i(T)^{n_i}$. Moreover, $f_i(t)^{n_i}$ is the minimal polynomial of the restriction of T to W_i.

The proof is by induction on r. The case $r = 1$ is trivial. Suppose that the theorem has been proved for $r - 1$. By Theorem 10.7 we can write V as the direct sum of T-invariant subspaces W_1 and V_1 where W_1 is the kernel of $f_1(T)^{n_1}$ and where V_1 is the kernel of $f_2(T)^{n_2} \ldots f_r(T)^{n_r}$. By Theorem 10.8, the minimal polynomial of the restrictions of T to W_1 and V_1 are respectively $f_1(t)^{n_1}$ and $f_2(t)^{n_2} \ldots f_r(t)^{n_r}$.

Denote the restriction of T to V_1 by T_1. By the inductive hypothesis, V_1 is the direct sum of subspaces $W_2, \ldots, W_r$ such that W_i is the kernel of $f_i(T_1)^{n_i}$ and such that $f_i(t)^{n_i}$ is the minimal polynomial for the restriction of T_1 to W_i. But the kernel of $f_i(T)^{n_i}$, for $i = 2, \ldots, r$ is necessarily contained in V_1 since $f_i(t)^{n_i}$ divides $f_2(t)^{n_2} \ldots f_r(t)^{n_r}$. Thus the kernel of $f_i(T)^{n_i}$ is the same as the kernel of $f_i(T_1)^{n_i}$, which is W_i. Also, the restriction of T to W_i is the same as the restriction of T_1 to W_i (for $i = 2, \ldots, r$); hence $f_i(t)^{n_i}$ is also the minimal polynomial for the restriction of T to W_i. Thus $V = W_1 \oplus W_2 \oplus \cdots \oplus W_r$ is the desired decomposition of T.

10.12. Prove Theorem 10.9: A linear operator $T : V \to V$ has a diagonal matrix representation if and only if its minimal polynomial $m(t)$ is a product of distinct linear polynomials.

Suppose $m(t)$ is a product of distinct linear polynomials; say,

$$m(t) \;=\; (t - \lambda_1)(t - \lambda_2) \ldots (t - \lambda_r)$$

where the λ_i are distinct scalars. By the primary decomposition theorem, V is the direct sum of subspaces $W_1, \ldots, W_r$ where $W_i = \operatorname{Ker}(T - \lambda_i I)$. Thus if $v \in W_i$, then $(T - \lambda_i I)(v) = 0$ or $T(v) = \lambda_i v$. In other words, every vector in W_i is an eigenvector belonging to the eigenvalue λ_i. By Theorem 10.4, the union of bases for $W_1, \ldots, W_r$ is a basis of V. This basis consists of eigenvectors and so T is diagonalizable.

Conversely, suppose T is diagonalizable, i.e. V has a basis consisting of eigenvectors of T. Let $\lambda_1, \ldots, \lambda_s$ be the distinct eigenvalues of T. Then the operator

$$f(T) \;=\; (T - \lambda_1 I)(T - \lambda_2 I) \ldots (T - \lambda_s I)$$

maps each basis vector into 0. Thus $f(T) = 0$ and hence the minimum polynomial $m(t)$ of T divides the polynomial

$$f(t) \;=\; (t - \lambda_1)(t - \lambda_2) \ldots (t - \lambda_s I)$$

Accordingly, $m(t)$ is a product of distinct linear polynomials.

NILPOTENT OPERATORS, JORDAN CANONICAL FORM

10.13. Let $T : V \to V$ be linear. Suppose, for $v \in V$, $T^k(v) = 0$ but $T^{k-1}(v) \neq 0$. Prove:

(i)   The set $S = \{v, T(v), \ldots, T^{k-1}(v)\}$ is linearly independent.

(ii) The subspace W generated by S is T-invariant.

(iii) The restriction $\widehat{T}$ of T to W is nilpotent of index k.

(iv) Relative to the basis $\{T^{k-1}(v), \ldots, T(v), v\}$ of W, the matrix of T is of the form

$$\begin{pmatrix} 0 & 1 & 0 & \ldots & 0 & 0 \\ 0 & 0 & 1 & \ldots & 0 & 0 \\ \multicolumn{6}{c}{\dotfill} \\ 0 & 0 & 0 & \ldots & 0 & 1 \\ 0 & 0 & 0 & \ldots & 0 & 0 \end{pmatrix}$$

Hence the above k-square matrix is nilpotent of index k.

(i)   **Suppose**
$$av + a_1 T(v) + a_2 T^2(v) + \cdots + a_{k-1} T^{k-1}(v) = 0 \qquad (*)$$

Applying T^{k-1} to $(*)$ and using $T^k(v) = 0$, we obtain $aT^{k-1}(v) = 0$; since $T^{k-1}(v) \neq 0$, $a = 0$. Now applying T^{k-2} to $(*)$ and using $T^k(v) = 0$ and $a = 0$, we find $a_1 T^{k-1}(v) = 0$; hence $a_1 = 0$. Next applying T^{k-3} to $(*)$ and using $T^k(v) = 0$ and $a = a_1 = 0$, we obtain $a_2 T^{k-1}(v) = 0$; hence $a_2 = 0$. Continuing this process, we find that all the a's are 0; hence S is independent.

(ii) **Let** $v \in W$. Then
$$v = bv + b_1 T(v) + b_2 T^2(v) + \cdots + b_{k-1} T^{k-1}(v)$$
Using $T^k(v) = 0$, we have that
$$T(v) = b\, T(v) + b_1 T^2(v) + \cdots + b_{k-2} T^{k-1}(v) \in W$$
Thus W is T-invariant.

(iii) By hypothesis $T^k(v) = 0$. Hence, for $i = 0, \ldots, k-1$,
$$\widehat{T}^k(T^i(v)) = T^{k+i}(v) = 0$$

That is, applying $\widehat{T}^k$ to each generator of W, we obtain 0; hence $\widehat{T}^k = 0$ and so $\widehat{T}$ is nilpotent of index at most k. On the other hand, $\widehat{T}^{k-1}(v) = T^{k-1}(v) \neq 0$; hence T is nilpotent of index exactly k.

(iv) For the basis $\{T^{k-1}(v), T^{k-2}(v), \ldots, T(v), v\}$ of W,
$$\widehat{T}(T^{k-1}(v)) = T^k(v) = 0$$
$$\widehat{T}(T^{k-2}(v)) = T^{k-1}(v)$$
$$\widehat{T}(T^{k-3}(v)) = T^{k-2}(v)$$
$$\dotfill$$
$$\widehat{T}(T(v)) = T^2(v)$$
$$\widehat{T}(v) = T(v)$$

Hence the matrix of T in this basis is

$$\begin{pmatrix} 0 & 1 & 0 & \ldots & 0 & 0 \\ 0 & 0 & 1 & \ldots & 0 & 0 \\ \multicolumn{6}{c}{\dotfill} \\ 0 & 0 & 0 & \ldots & 0 & 1 \\ 0 & 0 & 0 & \ldots & 0 & 0 \end{pmatrix}$$

10.14. Let $T : V \to V$ be linear. Let $U = \operatorname{Ker} T^i$ and $W = \operatorname{Ker} T^{i+1}$. Show that (i) $U \subset W$, (ii) $T(W) \subset U$.

(i) Suppose $u \in U = \operatorname{Ker} T^i$. Then $T^i(u) = 0$ and so $T^{i+1}(u) = T(T^i(u)) = T(0) = 0$. Thus $u \in \operatorname{Ker} T^{i+1} = W$. But this is true for every $u \in U$; hence $U \subset W$.

(ii) Similarly, if $w \in W = \operatorname{Ker} T^{i+1}$, then $T^{i+1}(w) = 0$. Thus $T^{i+1}(w) = T^i(T(w)) = T^i(0) = 0$ and so $T(W) \subset U$.

10.15. Let $T : V \to V$ be linear. Let $X = \operatorname{Ker} T^{i-2}$, $Y = \operatorname{Ker} T^{i-1}$ and $Z = \operatorname{Ker} T^i$. By the preceding problem, $X \subset Y \subset Z$. Suppose

$$\{u_1, \ldots, u_r\}, \quad \{u_1, \ldots, u_r, v_1, \ldots, v_s\}, \quad \{u_1, \ldots, u_r, v_1, \ldots, v_s, w_1, \ldots, w_t\}$$

are bases of X, Y and Z respectively. Show that

$$S = \{u_1, \ldots, u_r, T(w_1), \ldots, T(w_t)\}$$

is contained in Y and is linearly independent.

By the preceding problem, $T(Z) \subset Y$ and hence $S \subset Y$. Now suppose S is linearly dependent. Then there exists a relation

$$a_1 u_1 + \cdots + a_r u_r + b_1 T(w_1) + \cdots + b_t T(w_t) = 0$$

where at least one coefficient is not zero. Furthermore, since $\{u_i\}$ is independent, at least one of the b_k must be nonzero. Transposing, we find

$$b_1 T(w_1) + \cdots + b_t T(w_t) = -a_1 u_1 - \cdots - a_r u_r \in X = \operatorname{Ker} T^{i-2}$$

Hence
$$T^{i-2}(b_1 T(w_1) + \cdots + b_t T(w_t)) = 0$$

Thus
$$T^{i-1}(b_1 w_1 + \cdots + b_t w_t) = 0 \quad \text{and so} \quad b_1 w_1 + \cdots + b_t w_t \in Y = \operatorname{Ker} T^{i-1}$$

Since $\{u_i, v_j\}$ generates Y, we obtain a relation among the u_i, v_j and w_k where one of the coefficients, i.e. one of the b_k, is not zero. This contradicts the fact that $\{u_i, v_j, w_k\}$ is independent. Hence S must also be independent.

10.16. Prove Theorem 10.10: Let $T : V \to V$ be a nilpotent operator of index k. Then T has a block diagonal matrix representation whose diagonal entries are of the form

$$N = \begin{pmatrix} 0 & 1 & 0 & \ldots & 0 & 0 \\ 0 & 0 & 1 & \ldots & 0 & 0 \\ \hdotsfor{6} \\ 0 & 0 & 0 & \ldots & 0 & 1 \\ 0 & 0 & 0 & \ldots & 0 & 0 \end{pmatrix}$$

There is at least one N of order k and all other N are of orders $\leq k$. The number of N of each possible order is uniquely determined by T. Moreover, the total number of N of all orders is the nullity of T.

Suppose $\dim V = n$. Let $W_1 = \operatorname{Ker} T$, $W_2 = \operatorname{Ker} T^2$, $\ldots$, $W_k = \operatorname{Ker} T^k$. Set $m_i = \dim W_i$, for $i = 1, \ldots, k$. Since T is of index k, $W_k = V$ and $W_{k-1} \neq V$ and so $m_{k-1} < m_k = n$. By Problem 10.17,

$$W_1 \subset W_2 \subset \cdots \subset W_k = V$$

Thus, by induction, we can choose a basis $\{u_1, \ldots, u_n\}$ of V such that $\{u_1, \ldots, u_{m_i}\}$ is a basis of W_i.

We now choose a new basis for V with respect to which T has the desired form. It will be convenient to label the members of this new basis by pairs of indices. We begin by setting

$$v(1, k) = u_{m_{k-1}+1}, \quad v(2, k) = u_{m_{k-1}+2}, \quad \ldots, \quad v(m_k - m_{k-1}, k) = u_{m_k}$$

and setting
$$v(1, k-1) = Tv(1, k), \quad v(2, k-1) = Tv(2, k), \quad \ldots, \quad v(m_k - m_{k-1}, k-1) = Tv(m_k - m_{k-1}, k)$$

By the preceding problem,
$$S_1 = \{u_1 \ldots, u_{m_{k-2}}, v(1, k-1), \ldots, v(m_k - m_{k-1}, k-1)\}$$

is a linearly independent subset of W_{k-1}. We extend S_1 to a basis of W_{k-1} by adjoining new elements (if necessary) which we denote by
$$v(m_k - m_{k-1} + 1, k-1), \quad v(m_k - m_{k-1} + 2, k-1), \quad \ldots, \quad v(m_{k-1} - m_{k-2}, k-1)$$

Next we set
$$v(1, k-2) = Tv(1, k-1), \quad v(2, k-2) = Tv(2, k-1), \ldots,$$
$$v(m_{k-1} - m_{k-2}, k-2) = Tv(m_{k-1} - m_{k-2}, k-1)$$

Again by the preceding problem,
$$S_2 = \{u_1, \ldots, u_{m_{k-3}}, v(1, k-2), \ldots, v(m_{k-1} - m_{k-2}, k-2)\}$$

is a linearly independent subset of W_{k-2} which we can extend to a basis of W_{k-2} by adjoining elements
$$v(m_{k-1} - m_{k-2} + 1, k-2), \quad v(m_{k-1} - m_{k-2} + 2, k-2), \quad \ldots, \quad v(m_{k-2} - m_{k-3}, k-2)$$

Continuing in this manner we get a new basis for V which for convenient reference we arrange as follows:

$v(1, k), \qquad \ldots, \quad v(m_k - m_{k-1}, k)$

$v(1, k-1), \ldots, \quad v(m_k - m_{k-1}, k-1), \ldots, \quad v(m_{k-1} - m_{k-2}, k-1)$

. . . .

$v(1, 2), \qquad \ldots, \quad v(m_k - m_{k-1}, 2), \qquad \ldots, \quad v(m_{k-1} - m_{k-2}, 2), \ldots, \quad v(m_2 - m_1, 2)$

$v(1, 1), \qquad \ldots, \quad v(m_k - m_{k-1}, 1), \qquad \ldots, \quad v(m_{k-1} - m_{k-2}, 1), \ldots, \quad v(m_2 - m_1, 1), \ldots, \quad v(m_1, 1)$

The bottom row forms a basis of W_1, the bottom two rows form a basis of W_2, etc. But what is important for us is that T maps each vector into the vector immediately below it in the table or into 0 if the vector is in the bottom row. That is,
$$Tv(i, j) = \begin{cases} v(i, j-1) & \text{for } j > 1 \\ 0 & \text{for } j = 1 \end{cases}$$

Now it is clear (see Problem 10.13(iv)) that T will have the desired form if the $v(i, j)$ are ordered lexicographically: beginning with $v(1, 1)$ and moving up the first column to $v(1, k)$, then jumping to $v(2, 1)$ and moving up the second column as far as possible, etc.

Moreover, there will be exactly

$$\begin{array}{ll} m_k - m_{k-1} & \text{diagonal entries of order } k \\ (m_{k-1} - m_{k-2}) - (m_k - m_{k-1}) = 2m_{k-1} - m_k - m_{k-2} & \text{diagonal entries of order } k-1 \\ \cdots\cdots\cdots\cdots\cdots\cdots\cdots\cdots\cdots\cdots\cdots\cdots\cdots & \\ 2m_2 - m_1 - m_3 & \text{diagonal entries of order } 2 \\ 2m_1 - m_2 & \text{diagonal entries of order } 1 \end{array}$$

as can be read off directly from the table. In particular, since the numbers $m_1, \ldots, m_k$ are uniquely determined by T, the number of diagonal entries of each order is uniquely determined by T. Finally, the identity
$$m_1 = (m_k - m_{k-1}) + (2m_{k-1} - m_k - m_{k-2}) + \cdots + (2m_2 - m_1 - m_3) + (2m_1 - m_2)$$

shows that the nullity m_1 of T is the total number of diagonal entries of T.

10.17. Let $\quad A = \begin{pmatrix} 0 & 1 & 1 & 0 & 1 \\ 0 & 0 & 1 & 1 & 1 \\ 0 & 0 & 0 & 0 & 0 \\ 0 & 0 & 0 & 0 & 0 \\ 0 & 0 & 0 & 0 & 0 \end{pmatrix}$. Then $\quad A^2 = \begin{pmatrix} 0 & 0 & 1 & 1 & 1 \\ 0 & 0 & 0 & 0 & 0 \\ 0 & 0 & 0 & 0 & 0 \\ 0 & 0 & 0 & 0 & 0 \\ 0 & 0 & 0 & 0 & 0 \end{pmatrix}$ and $\quad A^3 = 0$;

hence A is nilpotent of index 2. Find the nilpotent matrix M in canonical form which is similar to A.

Since A is nilpotent of index 2, M contains a diagonal block of order 2 and none greater than 2. Note that rank $A = 2$; hence nullity of $A = 5 - 2 = 3$. Thus M contains 3 diagonal blocks. Accordingly M must contain 2 diagonal blocks of order 2 and 1 of order 1; that is,

$$M = \begin{pmatrix} 0 & 1 & 0 & 0 & 0 \\ 0 & 0 & 0 & 0 & 0 \\ 0 & 0 & 0 & 1 & 0 \\ 0 & 0 & 0 & 0 & 0 \\ 0 & 0 & 0 & 0 & 0 \end{pmatrix}$$

10.18. Prove Theorem 10.11, page 226, on the Jordan canonical form for an operator T.

By the primary decomposition theorem, T is decomposable into operators $T_1, \ldots, T_r$, i.e. $T = T_1 \oplus \cdots \oplus T_r$, where $(t - \lambda_i)^{m_i}$ is the minimal polynomial of T_i. Thus in particular,

$$(T_1 - \lambda_1 I)^{m_1} = 0, \quad \ldots, \quad (T_r - \lambda_r I)^{m_r} = 0$$

Set $N_i = T_i - \lambda_i I$. Then for $i = 1, \ldots, r$,

$$T_i = N_i + \lambda_i I, \qquad \text{where } N_i^{m_i} = 0$$

That is, T_i is the sum of the scalar operator $\lambda_i I$ and a nilpotent operator N_i, which is of index m_i since $(t - \lambda_i)^{m_i}$ is the minimal polynomial of T_i.

Now by Theorem 10.10 on nilpotent operators, we can choose a basis so that N_i is in canonical form. In this basis, $T_i = N_i + \lambda_i I$ is represented by a block diagonal matrix M_i whose diagonal entries are the matrices J_{ij}. The direct sum J of the matrices M_i is in Jordan canonical form and, by Theorem 10.5, is a matrix representation of T.

Lastly we must show that the blocks J_{ij} satisfy the required properties. Property (i) follows from the fact that N_i is of index m_i. Property (ii) is true since T and J have the same characteristic polynomial. Property (iii) is true since the nullity of $N_i = T_i - \lambda_i I$ is equal to the geometric multiplicity of the eigenvalue λ_i. Property (iv) follows from the fact that the T_i and hence the N_i are uniquely determined by T.

10.19. Determine all possible Jordan canonical forms for a linear operator $T : V \to V$ whose characteristic polynomial is $\Delta(t) = (t - 2)^3 (t - 5)^2$.

Since $t - 2$ has exponent 3 in $\Delta(t)$, 2 must appear three times on the main diagonal. Similarly 5 must appear twice. Thus the possible Jordan canonical forms are

$$\begin{pmatrix} 2 & 1 & & & \\ & 2 & 1 & & \\ & & 2 & & \\ & & & 5 & 1 \\ & & & & 5 \end{pmatrix}$$

(i)

$$\begin{pmatrix} 2 & 1 & & & \\ & 2 & & & \\ & & 2 & & \\ & & & 5 & 1 \\ & & & & 5 \end{pmatrix}$$

(ii)

$$\begin{pmatrix} 2 & & & & \\ & 2 & & & \\ & & 2 & & \\ & & & 5 & 1 \\ & & & & 5 \end{pmatrix}$$

(iii)

$$\begin{pmatrix} 2 & 1 & & & \\ & 2 & 1 & & \\ & & 2 & & \\ & & & 5 & \\ & & & & 5 \end{pmatrix}$$

(iv)

$$\begin{pmatrix} 2 & 1 & & & \\ & 2 & & & \\ & & 2 & & \\ & & & 5 & \\ & & & & 5 \end{pmatrix}$$

(v)

$$\begin{pmatrix} 2 & & & & \\ & 2 & & & \\ & & 2 & & \\ & & & 5 & \\ & & & & 5 \end{pmatrix}$$

(vi)

10.20. Determine all possible Jordan canonical forms J for a matrix of order 5 whose minimal polynomial is $m(t) = (t-2)^2$.

J must have one Jordan block of order 2 and the others must be of order 2 or 1. Thus there are only two possibilities:

$$J = \begin{pmatrix} 2 & 1 & & & \\ & 2 & & & \\ & & 2 & 1 & \\ & & & 2 & \\ & & & & 2 \end{pmatrix} \quad \text{or} \quad J = \begin{pmatrix} 2 & 1 & & & \\ & 2 & & & \\ & & 2 & & \\ & & & 2 & \\ & & & & 2 \end{pmatrix}$$

Note that all the diagonal entries must be 2 since 2 is the only eigenvalue.

QUOTIENT SPACE AND TRIANGULAR FORM

10.21. Let W be a subspace of a vector space V. Show that the following are equivalent: (i) $u \in v + W$, (ii) $u - v \in W$, (iii) $v \in u + W$.

Suppose $u \in v + W$. Then there exists $w_0 \in W$ such that $u = v + w_0$. Hence $u - v = w_0 \in W$. Conversely, suppose $u - v \in W$. Then $u - v = w_0$ where $w_0 \in W$. Hence $u = v + w_0 \in v + W$. Thus (i) and (ii) are equivalent.

We also have: $u - v \in W$ iff $-(u-v) = v - u \in W$ iff $v \in u + W$. Thus (ii) and (iii) are also equivalent.

10.22. Prove: The cosets of W in V partition V into mutually disjoint sets. That is:

(i)   any two cosets $u + W$ and $v + W$ are either identical or disjoint; and

(ii)   each $v \in V$ belongs to a coset; in fact, $v \in v + W$.

Furthermore, $u + W = v + W$ if and only if $u - v \in W$, and so $(v + w) + W = v + W$ for any $w \in W$.

Let $v \in V$. Since $0 \in W$, we have $v = v + 0 \in v + W$ which proves (ii).

Now suppose the cosets $u + W$ and $v + W$ are not disjoint; say, the vector x belongs to both $u + W$ and $v + W$. Then $u - x \in W$ and $x - v \in W$. The proof of (i) is complete if we show that $u + W = v + W$. Let $u + w_0$ be any element in the coset $u + W$. Since $u - x, x - v$ and w_0 belong to W,

$$(u + w_0) - v = (u - x) + (x - v) + w_0 \in W$$

Thus $u + w_0 \in v + W$ and hence the coset $u + W$ is contained in the coset $v + W$. Similarly $v + W$ is contained in $u + W$ and so $u + W = v + W$.

The last statement follows from the fact that $u + W = v + W$ if and only if $u \in v + W$, and by the preceding problem this is equivalent to $u - v \in W$.

10.23. Let W be the solution space of the homogeneous equation $2x + 3y + 4z = 0$. Describe the cosets of W in $\mathbf{R}^3$.

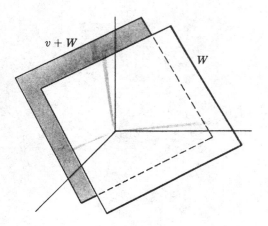

W is a plane through the origin $O = (0,0,0)$, and the cosets of W are the planes parallel to W. Equivalently, the cosets of W are the solution sets of the family of equations

$$2x + 3y + 4z = k, \quad k \in \mathbf{R}$$

In particular the coset $v + W$, where $v = (a, b, c)$, is the solution set of the linear equation

$$2x + 3y + 4z = 2a + 3b + 4c$$

or $\quad 2(x - a) + 3(y - b) + 4(z - c) = 0$

10.24. Suppose W is a subspace of a vector space V. Show that the operations in Theorem 10.15, page 229, are well defined; namely, show that if $u + W = u' + W$ and $v + W = v' + W$, then

$$\text{(i)} \quad (u + v) + W = (u' + v') + W \quad \text{and} \quad \text{(ii)} \quad ku + W = ku' + W, \quad \text{for any } k \in K$$

(i)   Since $u + W = u' + W$ and $v + W = v' + W$, both $u - u'$ and $v - v'$ belong to W. But then $(u + v) - (u' + v') = (u - u') + (v - v') \in W$. Hence $(u + v) + W = (u' + v') + W$.

(ii)   Also, since $u - u' \in W$ implies $k(u - u') \in W$, then $ku - ku' = k(u - u') \in W$; hence $ku + W = ku' + W$.

10.25. Let V be a vector space and W a subspace of V. Show that the natural map $\eta : V \to V/W$, defined by $\eta(v) = v + W$, is linear.

For any $u, v \in V$ and any $k \in K$, we have

$$\eta(u + v) = u + v + W = u + W + v + W = \eta(u) + \eta(v)$$

and

$$\eta(kv) = kv + W = k(v + W) = k\,\eta(v)$$

Accordingly, η is linear.

10.26. Let W be a subspace of a vector space V. Suppose $\{w_1, \ldots, w_r\}$ is a basis of W and the set of cosets $\{\bar{v}_1, \ldots, \bar{v}_s\}$, where $\bar{v}_j = v_j + W$, is a basis of the quotient space. Show that $B = \{v_1, \ldots, v_s, w_1, \ldots, w_r\}$ is a basis of V. Thus $\dim V = \dim W + \dim (V/W)$.

Suppose $u \in V$. Since $\{\bar{v}_j\}$ is a basis of V/W,

$$\bar{u} = u + W = a_1\bar{v}_1 + a_2\bar{v}_2 + \cdots + a_s\bar{v}_s$$

Hence $u = a_1 v_1 + \cdots + a_s v_s + w$ where $w \in W$. Since $\{w_i\}$ is a basis of W,

$$u = a_1 v_1 + \cdots + a_s v_s + b_1 w_1 + \cdots + b_r w_r$$

Accordingly, B generates V.

We now show that B is linearly independent. Suppose

$$c_1 v_1 + \cdots + c_s v_s + d_1 w_1 + \cdots + d_r w_r = 0 \tag{1}$$

Then

$$c_1 \bar{v}_1 + \cdots + c_s \bar{v}_s = \bar{0} = W$$

Since $\{\bar{v}_j\}$ is independent, the c's are all 0. Substituting into (1), we find $d_1 w_1 + \cdots + d_r w_r = 0$. Since $\{w_i\}$ is independent, the d's are all 0. Thus B is linearly independent and therefore a basis of V.

10.27. Prove Theorem 10.16: Suppose W is a subspace invariant under a linear operator $T : V \to V$. Then T induces a linear operator $\bar{T}$ on V/W defined by $\bar{T}(v + W) = T(v) + W$. Moreover, if T is a zero of any polynomial, then so is $\bar{T}$. Thus the minimum polynomial of $\bar{T}$ divides the minimum polynomial of T.

We first show that $\bar{T}$ is well defined, i.e. if $u + W = v + W$ then $\bar{T}(u + W) = \bar{T}(v + W)$. If $u + W = v + W$ then $u - v \in W$ and, since W is T-invariant, $T(u - v) = T(u) - T(v) \in W$. Accordingly,

$$\bar{T}(u + W) = T(u) + W = T(v) + W = \bar{T}(v + W)$$

as required.

We next show that $\bar{T}$ is linear. We have

$$\bar{T}((u + W) + (v + W)) = \bar{T}(u + v + W) = T(u + v) + W = T(u) + T(v) + W$$
$$= T(u) + W + T(v) + W = \bar{T}(u + W) + \bar{T}(v + W)$$

and

$$\bar{T}(k(u + W)) = \bar{T}(ku + W) = T(ku) + W = kT(u) + W = k(T(u) + W) = k\,\bar{T}(u + W)$$

Thus $\bar{T}$ is linear.

Now, for any coset $u + W$ in V/W,

$$\overline{T^2}(u + W) \ = \ T^2(u) + W \ = \ T(T(u)) + W \ = \ \bar{T}(T(u) + W) \ = \ \bar{T}(\bar{T}(u + W)) \ = \ \bar{T}^2(u + W)$$

Hence $\overline{T^2} = \bar{T}^2$. Similarly $\overline{T^n} = \bar{T}^n$ for any n. Thus for any polynomial

$$f(t) = a_n t^n + \cdots + a_0 \ = \ \sum a_i t^i,$$

$$\overline{f(T)}(u + W) \ = \ f(T)(u) + W \ = \ \sum a_i T^i(u) + W \ = \ \sum a_i (T^i(u) + W)$$

$$= \ \sum a_i \overline{T^i}(u + W) \ = \ \sum a_i \bar{T}^i(u + W) \ = \ \left(\sum a_i \bar{T}^i\right)(u + W) \ = \ f(\bar{T})(u + W)$$

and so $\overline{f(T)} = f(\bar{T})$. Accordingly, if T is a root of $f(t)$ then $\overline{f(T)} = \bar{0} = W = f(\bar{T})$, i.e. $\bar{T}$ is also a root of $f(t)$. Thus the theorem is proved.

10.28. Prove Theorem 10.1: Let $T : V \to V$ be a linear operator whose characteristic polynomial factors into linear polynomials. Then V has a basis in which T is represented by a triangular matrix.

The proof is by induction on the dimension of V. If $\dim V = 1$, then every matrix representation of T is a 1 by 1 matrix which is triangular.

Now suppose $\dim V = n > 1$ and that the theorem holds for spaces of dimension less than n. Since the characteristic polynomial of T factors into linear polynomials, T has at least one eigenvalue and so at least one nonzero eigenvector v, say $T(v) = a_{11}v$. Let W be the 1-dimensional subspace spanned by v. Set $\bar{V} = V/W$. Then (Problem 10.26) $\dim \bar{V} = \dim V - \dim W = n - 1$. Note also that W is invariant under T. By Theorem 10.16, T induces a linear operator $\bar{T}$ on $\bar{V}$ whose minimum polynomial divides the minimum polynomial of T. Since the characteristic polynomial of T is a product of linear polynomials, so is its minimum polynomial; hence so are the minimum and characteristic polynomials of $\bar{T}$. Thus $\bar{V}$ and $\bar{T}$ satisfy the hypothesis of the theorem. Hence, by induction, there exists a basis $\{\bar{v}_2, \ldots, \bar{v}_n\}$ of $\bar{V}$ such that

$$\bar{T}(\bar{v}_2) \ = \ a_{22}\bar{v}_2$$
$$\bar{T}(\bar{v}_3) \ = \ a_{32}\bar{v}_2 + a_{33}\bar{v}_3$$
$$\dotsi\dotsi\dotsi\dotsi\dotsi\dotsi\dotsi\dotsi\dotsi\dotsi\dotsi\dotsi\dotsi\dotsi$$
$$\bar{T}(\bar{v}_n) \ = \ a_{n2}\bar{v}_2 + a_{n3}\bar{v}_3 + \cdots + a_{nn}\bar{v}_n$$

Now let $v_2, \ldots, v_n$ be elements of V which belong to the cosets $\bar{v}_2, \ldots, \bar{v}_n$ respectively. Then $\{v, v_2, \ldots, v_n\}$ is a basis of V (Problem 10.26). Since $\bar{T}(\bar{v}_2) = a_{22}\bar{v}_2$, we have

$$\bar{T}(\bar{v}_2) - a_{22}\bar{v}_2 = 0 \quad \text{and so} \quad T(v_2) - a_{22}v_2 \in W$$

But W is spanned by v; hence $T(v_2) - a_{22}v_2$ is a multiple of v, say

$$T(v_2) - a_{22}v_2 \ = \ a_{21}v \quad \text{and so} \quad T(v_2) \ = \ a_{21}v + a_{22}v_2$$

Similarly, for $i = 3, \ldots, n$,

$$T(v_i) - a_{i2}v_2 - a_{i3}v_3 - \cdots - a_{ii}v_i \in W \quad \text{and so} \quad T(v_i) \ = \ a_{i1}v + a_{i2}v_2 + \cdots + a_{ii}v_i$$

Thus
$$T(v) \ = \ a_{11}v$$
$$T(v_2) \ = \ a_{21}v + a_{22}v_2$$
$$\dotsi\dotsi\dotsi\dotsi\dotsi\dotsi\dotsi\dotsi\dotsi\dotsi\dotsi\dotsi\dotsi\dotsi$$
$$T(v_n) \ = \ a_{n1}v + a_{n2}v_2 + \cdots + a_{nn}v_n$$

and hence the matrix of T in this basis is triangular.

CYCLIC SUBSPACES, RATIONAL CANONICAL FORM

10.29. Prove Theorem 10.12: Let $Z(v, T)$ be a T-cyclic subspace, T_v the restriction of T to $Z(v, T)$, and $m_v(t) = t^k + a_{k-1}t^{k-1} + \cdots + a_0$ the T-annihilator of v. Then:

(i)   The set $\{v, T(v), \ldots, T^{k-1}(v)\}$ is a basis of $Z(v, T)$; hence $\dim Z(v, T) = k$.

(ii) The minimal polynomial of T_v is $m_v(t)$.

(iii) The matrix of T_v in the above basis is

$$C \;=\; \begin{pmatrix} 0 & 0 & 0 & \ldots & 0 & -a_0 \\ 1 & 0 & 0 & \ldots & 0 & -a_1 \\ \multicolumn{6}{c}{\dotfill} \\ 0 & 0 & 0 & \ldots & 0 & -a_{k-2} \\ 0 & 0 & 0 & \ldots & 1 & -a_{k-1} \end{pmatrix}$$

(i) By definition of $m_v(t)$, $T^k(v)$ is the first vector in the sequence $v, T(v), T^2(v), \ldots$ which is a linear combination of those vectors which precede it in the sequence; hence the set $B = \{v, T(v), \ldots, T^{k-1}(v)\}$ is linearly independent. We now only have to show that $Z(v, T) = L(B)$, the linear span of B. By the above, $T^k(v) \in L(B)$. We prove by induction that $T^n(v) \in L(B)$ for every n. Suppose $n > k$ and $T^{n-1}(v) \in L(B)$, i.e. $T^{n-1}(v)$ is a linear combination of $v, \ldots, T^{k-1}(v)$. Then $T^n(v) = T(T^{n-1}(v))$ is a linear combination of $T(v), \ldots, T^k(v)$. But $T^k(v) \in L(B)$; hence $T^n(v) \in L(B)$ for every n. Consequently $f(T)(v) \in L(B)$ for any polynomial $f(t)$. Thus $Z(v, T) = L(B)$ and so B is a basis as claimed.

(ii) Suppose $m(t) = t^s + b_{s-1}t^{s-1} + \cdots + b_0$ is the minimal polynomial of T_v. Then, since $v \in Z(v, T)$,
$$0 = m(T_v)(v) = m(T)(v) = T^s(v) + b_{s-1}T^{s-1}(v) + \cdots + b_0 v$$
Thus $T^s(v)$ is a linear combination of $v, T(v), \ldots, T^{s-1}(v)$, and therefore $k \leqq s$. However, $m_v(T) = 0$ and so $m_v(T_v) = 0$. Then $m(t)$ divides $m_v(t)$ and so $s \leqq k$. Accordingly $k = s$ and hence $m_v(t) = m(t)$.

(iii)
$$\begin{aligned} T_v(v) &= & T(v) \\ T_v(T(v)) &= & T^2(v) \\ &\multicolumn{2}{c}{\dotfill} \\ T_v(T^{k-2}(v)) &= & T^{k-1}(v) \\ T_v(T^{k-1}(v)) &= T^k(v) = -a_0 v - a_1 T(v) - a_2 T^2(v) - \cdots - a_{k-1}T^{k-1}(v) \end{aligned}$$

By definition, the matrix of T_v in this basis is the transpose of the matrix of coefficients of the above system of equations; hence it is C, as required.

10.30. Let $T : V \to V$ be linear. Let W be a T-invariant subspace of V and $\bar{T}$ the induced operator on V/W. Prove: (i) The T-annihilator of $v \in V$ divides the minimal polynomial of T. (ii) The $\bar{T}$-annihilator of $\bar{v} \in V/W$ divides the minimal polynomial of T.

(i) The T-annihilator of $v \in V$ is the minimal polynomial of the restriction of T to $Z(v, T)$ and therefore, by Problem 10.6, it divides the minimal polynomial of T.

(ii) The $\bar{T}$-annihilator of $\bar{v} \in V/W$ divides the minimal polynomial of $\bar{T}$, which divides the minimal polynomial of T by Theorem 10.16.

Remark. In case the minimal polynomial of T is $f(t)^n$ where $f(t)$ is a monic irreducible polynomial, then the T-annihilator of $v \in V$ and the $\bar{T}$-annihilator of $\bar{v} \in V/W$ are of the form $f(t)^m$ where $m \leqq n$.

10.31. Prove Lemma 10.13: Let $T : V \to V$ be a linear operator whose minimal polynomial is $f(t)^n$ where $f(t)$ is a monic irreducible polynomial. Then V is the direct sum of T-cyclic subspaces $Z_i = Z(v_i, T)$, $i = 1, \ldots, r$, with corresponding T-annihilators
$$f(t)^{n_1}, \ f(t)^{n_2}, \ \ldots, \ f(t)^{n_r}, \quad n = n_1 \geqq n_2 \geqq \cdots \geqq n_r$$

Any other decomposition of V into the direct sum of T-cyclic subspaces has the same number of components and the same set of T-annihilators.

The proof is by induction on the dimension of V. If $\dim V = 1$, then V is itself T-cyclic and the lemma holds. Now suppose $\dim V > 1$ and that the lemma holds for those vector spaces of dimension less than that of V.

Since the minimal polynomial of T is $f(t)^n$, there exists $v_1 \in V$ such that $f(T)^{n-1}(v_1) \neq 0$; hence the T-annihilator of v_1 is $f(t)^n$. Let $Z_1 = Z(v_1, T)$ and recall that Z_1 is T-invariant. Let $\bar{V} = V/Z_1$ and let $\bar{T}$ be the linear operator on $\bar{V}$ induced by T. By Theorem 10.16, the minimal polynomial of $\bar{T}$ divides $f(t)^n$; hence the hypothesis holds for $\bar{V}$ and $\bar{T}$. Consequently, by induction, $\bar{V}$ is the direct sum of $\bar{T}$-cyclic subspaces; say,

$$\bar{V} = Z(\bar{v}_2, \bar{T}) \oplus \cdots \oplus Z(\bar{v}_r, \bar{T})$$

where the corresponding $\bar{T}$-annihilators are $f(t)^{n_2}, \ldots, f(t)^{n_r}$, $n \geq n_2 \geq \cdots \geq n_r$.

We claim that there is a vector v_2 in the coset $\bar{v}_2$ whose T-annihilator is $f(t)^{n_2}$, the $\bar{T}$-annihilator of $\bar{v}_2$. Let w be any vector in $\bar{v}_2$. Then $f(T)^{n_2}(w) \in Z_1$. Hence there exists a polynomial $g(t)$ for which

$$f(T)^{n_2}(w) = g(T)(v_1) \tag{1}$$

Since $f(t)^n$ is the minimal polynomial of T, we have by (1),

$$0 = f(T)^n(w) = f(T)^{n-n_2} g(T)(v_1)$$

But $f(t)^n$ is the T-annihilator of v_1; hence $f(t)^n$ divides $f(t)^{n-n_2} g(t)$ and so $g(t) = f(t)^{n_2} h(t)$ for some polynomial $h(t)$. We set
$$v_2 = w - h(T)(v_1)$$

Since $w - v_2 = h(T)(v_1) \in Z_1$, v_2 also belongs to the coset $\bar{v}_2$. Thus the T-annihilator of v_2 is a multiple of the $\bar{T}$-annihilator of $\bar{v}_2$. On the other hand, by (1),

$$f(T)^{n_2}(v_2) = f(T)^{n_2}(w - h(T)(v_1)) = f(T)^{n_2}(w) - g(T)(v_1) = 0$$

Consequently the T-annihilator of v_2 is $f(t)^{n_2}$ as claimed.

Similarly, there exist vectors $v_3, \ldots, v_r \in V$ such that $v_i \in \bar{v}_i$ and that the T-annihilator of v_i is $f(t)^{n_i}$, the $\bar{T}$-annihilator of $\bar{v}_i$. We set

$$Z_2 = Z(v_2, T), \quad \ldots, \quad Z_r = Z(v_r, T)$$

Let d denote the degree of $f(t)$ so that $f(t)^{n_i}$ has degree dn_i. Then since $f(t)^{n_i}$ is both the T-annihilator of v_i and the $\bar{T}$-annihilator of $\bar{v}_i$, we know that

$$\{v_i, T(v_i), \ldots, T^{dn_i-1}(v_i)\} \quad \text{and} \quad \{\bar{v}_i, \bar{T}(\bar{v}_i), \ldots, \bar{T}^{dn_i-1}(\bar{v}_i)\}$$

are bases for $Z(v_i, T)$ and $Z(\bar{v}_i, \bar{T})$ respectively, for $i = 2, \ldots, r$. But $\bar{V} = Z(\bar{v}_2, \bar{T}) \oplus \cdots \oplus Z(\bar{v}_r, \bar{T})$; hence

$$\{\bar{v}_2, \ldots, \bar{T}^{dn_2-1}(\bar{v}_2), \ldots, \bar{v}_r, \ldots, \bar{T}^{dn_r-1}(\bar{v}_r)\}$$

is a basis for $\bar{V}$. Therefore by Problem 10.26 and the relation $\bar{T}^i(\bar{v}) = \overline{T^i(v)}$ (see Problem 10.27),

$$\{v_1, \ldots, T^{dn_1-1}(v_1), v_2, \ldots, T^{dn_2-1}(v_2), \ldots, v_r, \ldots, T^{dn_r-1}(v_r)\}$$

is a basis for V. Thus by Theorem 10.4, $V = Z(v_1, T) \oplus \cdots \oplus Z(v_r, T)$, as required.

It remains to show that the exponents $n_1, \ldots, n_r$ are uniquely determined by T. Since d denotes the degree of $f(t)$,

$$\dim V = d(n_1 + \cdots + n_r) \quad \text{and} \quad \dim Z_i = dn_i, \quad i = 1, \ldots, r$$

Also, if s is any positive integer then (Problem 10.59) $f(T)^s(Z_i)$ is a cyclic subspace generated by $f(T)^s(v_i)$ and it has dimension $d(n_i - s)$ if $n_i > s$ and dimension 0 if $n_i \leq s$.

Now any vector $v \in V$ can be written uniquely in the form $v = w_1 + \cdots + w_r$ where $w_i \in Z_i$. Hence any vector in $f(T)^s(V)$ can be written uniquely in the form

$$f(T)^s(v) = f(T)^s(w_1) + \cdots + f(T)^s(w_r)$$

where $f(T)^s(w_i) \in f(T)^s(Z_i)$. Let t be the integer, dependent on s, for which

$$n_1 > s, \quad \ldots, \quad n_t > s, \quad n_{t+1} \leq s$$

Then
$$f(T)^s(V) = f(T)^s(Z_1) \oplus \cdots \oplus f(T)^s(Z_t)$$

and so
$$\dim(f(T)^s(V)) = d[(n_1 - s) + \cdots + (n_t - s)] \tag{*}$$

The numbers on the left of (*) are uniquely determined by T. Set $s = n - 1$ and (*) determines the number of n_i equal to n. Next set $s = n - 2$ and (*) determines the number of n_i (if any) equal to $n - 1$. We repeat the process until we set $s = 0$ and determine the number of n_i equal to 1. Thus the n_i are uniquely determined by T and V, and the lemma is proved.

10.32. Let V be a vector space of dimension 7 over **R,** and let $T : V \rightarrow V$ be a linear operator with minimal polynomial $m(t) = (t^2 + 2)(t + 3)^3$. Find all the possible rational canonical forms for T.

The sum of the degrees of the companion matrices must add up to 7. Also, one companion matrix must be $t^2 + 2$ and one must be $(t + 3)^3$. Thus the rational canonical form of T is exactly one of the following direct sums of companion matrices:

(i) $C(t^2 + 2) \oplus C(t^2 + 2) \oplus C((t + 3)^3)$

(ii) $C(t^2 + 2) \oplus C((t + 3)^3) \oplus C((t + 3)^2)$

(iii) $C(t^2 + 2) \oplus C((t + 3)^3) \oplus C(t + 3) \oplus C(t + 3)$

That is,

$$
\begin{pmatrix}
0 & -2 & & & & & \\
1 & 0 & & & & & \\
& & 0 & -2 & & & \\
& & 1 & 0 & & & \\
& & & & 0 & 0 & -27 \\
& & & & 1 & 0 & -27 \\
& & & & 0 & 1 & -9
\end{pmatrix}
\quad
\begin{pmatrix}
0 & -2 & & & & \\
1 & 0 & & & & \\
& & 0 & 0 & -27 & \\
& & 1 & 0 & -27 & \\
& & 0 & 1 & -9 & \\
& & & & & 0 & -9 \\
& & & & & 1 & -6
\end{pmatrix}
\quad
\begin{pmatrix}
0 & -2 & & & & \\
1 & 0 & & & & \\
& & 0 & 0 & -27 & \\
& & 1 & 0 & -27 & \\
& & 0 & 1 & -9 & \\
& & & & & -3 & \\
& & & & & & -3
\end{pmatrix}
$$

$\qquad\qquad$ (i) $\qquad\qquad\qquad\qquad\qquad$ (ii) $\qquad\qquad\qquad\qquad\qquad$ (iii)

PROJECTIONS

10.33. Suppose $V = W_1 \oplus \cdots \oplus W_r$. The *projection* of V into its subspace W_k is the mapping $E : V \rightarrow V$ defined by $E(v) = w_k$ where $v = w_1 + \cdots + w_r$, $w_i \in W_i$. Show that (i) E is linear, (ii) $E^2 = E$.

(i) Since the sum $v = w_1 + \cdots + w_r$, $w_i \in W$ is uniquely determined by v, the mapping E is well defined. Suppose, for $u \in V$, $u = w_1' + \cdots + w_r'$, $w_i' \in W_i$. Then

$$v + u = (w_1 + w_1') + \cdots + (w_r + w_r') \quad \text{and} \quad kv = kw_1 + \cdots + kw_r, \quad kw_i, w_i + w_i' \in W_i$$

are the unique sums corresponding to $v + u$ and kv. Hence

$$E(v + u) = w_k + w_k' = E(v) + E(u) \quad \text{and} \quad E(kv) = kw_k = kE(v)$$

and therefore E is linear.

(ii) We have that $\qquad\qquad w_k = 0 + \cdots + 0 + w_k + 0 + \cdots + 0$

is the unique sum corresponding to $w_k \in W_k$; hence $E(w_k) = w_k$. Then for any $v \in V$,

$$E^2(v) = E(E(v)) = E(w_k) = w_k = E(v)$$

Thus $E^2 = E$, as required.

10.34. Suppose $E : V \rightarrow V$ is linear and $E^2 = E$. Show that: (i) $E(u) = u$ for any $u \in \text{Im} E$, i.e. the restriction of E to its image is the identity mapping; (ii) V is the direct sum of the image and kernel of E: $V = \text{Im} E \oplus \text{Ker} E$; (iii) E is the projection of V into $\text{Im} E$, its image. Thus, by the preceding problem, a linear mapping $T : V \rightarrow V$ is a projection if and only if $T^2 = T$; this characterization of a projection is frequently used as its definition.

(i)   If $u \in \text{Im} E$, then there exists $v \in V$ for which $E(v) = u$; hence

$$E(u) = E(E(v)) = E^2(v) = E(v) = u$$

as required.

(ii) Let $v \in V$. We can write v in the form $v = E(v) + v - E(v)$. Now $E(v) \in \text{Im} E$ and, since

$$E(v - E(v)) = E(v) - E^2(v) = E(v) - E(v) = 0$$

$v - E(v) \in \text{Ker} E$. Accordingly, $V = \text{Im} E + \text{Ker} E$.

Now suppose $w \in \operatorname{Im} E \cap \operatorname{Ker} E$. By (i), $E(w) = w$ because $w \in \operatorname{Im} E$. On the other hand, $E(w) = 0$ because $w \in \operatorname{Ker} E$. Thus $w = 0$ and so $\operatorname{Im} E \cap \operatorname{Ker} E = \{0\}$. These two conditions imply that V is the direct sum of the image and kernel of E.

(iii) Let $v \in V$ and suppose $v = u + w$ where $u \in \operatorname{Im} E$ and $w \in \operatorname{Ker} E$. Note that $E(u) = u$ by (i), and $E(w) = 0$ because $w \in \operatorname{Ker} E$. Hence

$$E(v) = E(u + w) = E(u) + E(w) = u + 0 = u$$

That is, E is the projection of V into its image.

10.35. Suppose $V = U \oplus W$ and suppose $T : V \to V$ is linear. Show that U and W are both T-invariant if and only if $TE = ET$ where E is the projection of V into U.

Observe that $E(v) \in U$ for every $v \in V$, and that (i) $E(v) = v$ iff $v \in U$, (ii) $E(v) = 0$ iff $v \in W$.

Suppose $ET = TE$. Let $u \in U$. Since $E(u) = u$,

$$T(u) = T(E(u)) = (TE)(u) = (ET)(u) = E(T(u)) \in U$$

Hence U is T-invariant. Now let $w \in W$. Since $E(w) = 0$,

$$E(T(w)) = (ET)(w) = (TE)(w) = T(E(w)) = T(0) = 0 \quad \text{and so} \quad T(w) \in W$$

Hence W is also T-invariant.

Conversely, suppose U and W are both T-invariant. Let $v \in V$ and suppose $v = u + w$ where $u \in T$ and $w \in W$. Then $T(u) \in U$ and $T(w) \in W$; hence $E(T(u)) = T(u)$ and $E(T(w)) = 0$. Thus

$$(ET)(v) = (ET)(u + w) = (ET)(u) + (ET)(w) = E(T(u)) + E(T(w)) = T(u)$$

and

$$(TE)(v) = (TE)(u + w) = T(E(u + w)) = T(u)$$

That is, $(ET)(v) = (TE)(v)$ for every $v \in V$; therefore $ET = TE$ as required.

Supplementary Problems

INVARIANT SUBSPACES

10.36. Suppose W is invariant under $T : V \to V$. Show that W is invariant under $f(T)$ for any polynomial $f(t)$.

10.37. Show that every subspace of V is invariant under I and 0, the identity and zero operators.

10.38. Suppose W is invariant under $S : V \to V$ and $T : V \to V$. Show that W is also invariant under $S + T$ and ST.

10.39. Let $T : V \to V$ be linear and let W be the eigenspace belonging to an eigenvalue λ of T. Show that W is T-invariant.

10.40. Let V be a vector space of odd dimension (greater than 1) over the real field $\mathbf{R}$. Show that any linear operator on V has an invariant subspace other than V or $\{0\}$.

10.41. Determine the invariant subspaces of $A = \begin{pmatrix} 2 & -4 \\ 5 & -2 \end{pmatrix}$ viewed as a linear operator on (i) $\mathbf{R}^2$, (ii) $\mathbf{C}^2$.

10.42. Suppose $\dim V = n$. Show that $T : V \to V$ has a triangular matrix representation if and only if there exist T-invariant subspaces $W_1 \subset W_2 \subset \cdots \subset W_n = V$ for which $\dim W_k = k$, $k = 1, \ldots, n$.

INVARIANT DIRECT-SUMS

10.43. The subspaces $W_1, \ldots, W_r$ are said to be *independent* if $w_1 + \cdots + w_r = 0$, $w_i \in W_i$, implies that each $w_i = 0$. Show that $L(W_i) = W_1 \oplus \cdots \oplus W_r$ if and only if the W_i are independent. (Here $L(W_i)$ denotes the linear span of the W_i.)

10.44. Show that $V = W_1 \oplus \cdots \oplus W_r$ if and only if (i) $V = L(W_i)$ and (ii) $W_k \cap L(W_1, \ldots, W_{k-1}, W_{k+1}, \ldots, W_r) = \{0\}$, $k = 1, \ldots, r$.

10.45. Show that $L(W_i) = W_1 \oplus \cdots \oplus W_r$ if and only if $\dim L(W_i) = \dim W_1 + \cdots + \dim W_r$.

10.46. Suppose the characteristic polynomial of $T : V \to V$ is $\Delta(t) = f_1(t)^{n_1} f_2(t)^{n_2} \ldots f_r(t)^{n_r}$ where the $f_i(t)$ are distinct monic irreducible polynomials. Let $V = W_1 \oplus \cdots \oplus W_r$ be the primary decomposition of V into T-invariant subspaces. Show that $f_i(t)^{n_i}$ is the characteristic polynomial of the restriction of T to W_i.

NILPOTENT OPERATORS

10.47. Suppose S and T are nilpotent operators which commute, i.e. $ST = TS$. Show that $S + T$ and ST are also nilpotent.

10.48. Suppose A is a supertriangular matrix, i.e. all entries on and below the main diagonal are 0. Show that A is nilpotent.

10.49. Let V be the vector space of polynomials of degree $\le n$. Show that the differential operator on V is nilpotent of index $n + 1$.

10.50. Show that the following nilpotent matrices of order n are similar:

$$\begin{pmatrix} 0 & 1 & 0 & \ldots & 0 \\ 0 & 0 & 1 & \ldots & 0 \\ \cdots\cdots\cdots\cdots\cdots \\ 0 & 0 & 0 & \ldots & 1 \\ 0 & 0 & 0 & \ldots & 0 \end{pmatrix} \quad \text{and} \quad \begin{pmatrix} 0 & 0 & \ldots & 0 & 0 \\ 1 & 0 & \ldots & 0 & 0 \\ 0 & 1 & \ldots & 0 & 0 \\ \cdots\cdots\cdots\cdots\cdots \\ 0 & 0 & \ldots & 1 & 0 \end{pmatrix}$$

10.51. Show that two nilpotent matrices of order 3 are similar if and only if they have the same index of nilpotency. Show by example that the statement is not true for nilpotent matrices of order 4.

JORDAN CANONICAL FORM

10.52. Find all possible Jordan canonical forms for those matrices whose characteristic polynomial $\Delta(t)$ and minimal polynomial $m(t)$ are as follows:

(i) $\Delta(t) = (t-2)^4(t-3)^2$, $m(t) = (t-2)^2(t-3)^2$
(ii) $\Delta(t) = (t-7)^5$, $m(t) = (t-7)^2$
(iii) $\Delta(t) = (t-2)^7$, $m(t) = (t-2)^3$
(iv) $\Delta(t) = (t-3)^4(t-5)^4$, $m(t) = (t-3)^2(t-5)^2$

10.53. Show that every complex matrix is similar to its transpose. (*Hint.* Use Jordan canonical form and Problem 10.50.)

10.54. Show that all complex matrices A of order n for which $A^n = I$ are similar.

10.55. Suppose A is a complex matrix with only real eigenvalues. Show that A is similar to a matrix with only real entries.

CYCLIC SUBSPACES

10.56. Suppose $T : V \to V$ is linear. Prove that $Z(v, T)$ is the intersection of all T-invariant subspaces containing v.

10.57. Let $f(t)$ and $g(t)$ be the T-annihilators of u and v respectively. Show that if $f(t)$ and $g(t)$ are relatively prime, then $f(t)g(t)$ is the T-annihilator of $u + v$.

10.58. Prove that $Z(u, T) = Z(v, T)$ if and only if $g(T)(u) = v$ where $g(t)$ is relatively prime to the T-annihilator of u.

10.59. Let $W = Z(v, T)$, and suppose the T-annihilator of v is $f(t)^n$ where $f(t)$ is a monic irreducible polynomial of degree d. Show that $f(T)^s(W)$ is a cyclic subspace generated by $f(T)^s(v)$ and it has dimension $d(n-s)$ if $n > s$ and dimension 0 if $n \le s$.

RATIONAL CANONICAL FORM

10.60. Find all possible rational canonical forms for:
(i) 6×6 matrices with minimum polynomial $m(t) = (t^2+3)(t+1)^2$
(ii) 6×6 matrices with minimum polynomial $m(t) = (t+1)^3$
(iii) 8×8 matrices with minimum polynomial $m(t) = (t^2+2)^2(t+3)^2$

10.61. Let A be a 4×4 matrix with minimum polynomial $m(t) = (t^2+1)(t^2-3)$. Find the rational canonical form for A if A is a matrix over (i) the rational field $\mathbf{Q}$, (ii) the real field $\mathbf{R}$, (iii) the complex field $\mathbf{C}$.

10.62. Find the rational canonical form for the Jordan block $\begin{pmatrix} \lambda & 1 & 0 & 0 \\ 0 & \lambda & 1 & 0 \\ 0 & 0 & \lambda & 1 \\ 0 & 0 & 0 & \lambda \end{pmatrix}$.

10.63. Prove that the characteristic polynomial of an operator $T : V \to V$ is a product of its elementary divisors.

10.64. Prove that two 3×3 matrices with the same minimum and characteristic polynomials are similar.

10.65. Let $C(f(t))$ denote the companion matrix to an arbitrary polynomial $f(t)$. Show that $f(t)$ is the characteristic polynomial of $C(f(t))$.

PROJECTIONS

10.66. Suppose $V = W_1 \oplus \cdots \oplus W_r$. Let E_i denote the projection of V into W_i. Prove: (i) $E_i E_j = 0$, $i \neq j$; (ii) $I = E_1 + \cdots + E_r$.

10.67. Let $E_1, \ldots, E_r$ be linear operators on V such that: (i) $E_i^2 = E_i$, i.e. the E_i are projections; (ii) $E_i E_j = 0$, $i \neq j$; (iii) $I = E_1 + \cdots + E_r$. Prove that $V = \operatorname{Im} E_1 \oplus \cdots \oplus \operatorname{Im} E_r$.

10.68. Suppose $E : V \to V$ is a projection, i.e. $E^2 = E$. Prove that E has a matrix representation of the form $\begin{pmatrix} I_r & 0 \\ 0 & 0 \end{pmatrix}$ where r is the rank of E and I_r is the r-square identity matrix.

10.69. Prove that any two projections of the same rank are similar. (*Hint.* Use the result of Problem 10.68.)

10.70. Suppose $E : V \to V$ is a projection. Prove:
  (i) $I - E$ is a projection and $V = \operatorname{Im} E \oplus \operatorname{Im}(I - E)$;   (ii) $I + E$ is invertible (if $1 + 1 \neq 0$).

QUOTIENT SPACES

10.71. Let W be a subspace of V. Suppose the set of cosets $\{v_1 + W, v_2 + W, \ldots, v_n + W\}$ in V/W is linearly independent. Show that the set of vectors $\{v_1, v_2, \ldots, v_n\}$ in V is also linearly independent.

10.72. Let W be a subspace of V. Suppose the set of vectors $\{u_1, u_2, \ldots, u_n\}$ in V is linearly independent, and that $L(u_i) \cap W = \{0\}$. Show that the set of cosets $\{u_1 + W, \ldots, u_n + W\}$ in V/W is also linearly independent.

10.73. Suppose $V = U \oplus W$ and that $\{u_1, \ldots, u_n\}$ is a basis of U. Show that $\{u_1 + W, \ldots, u_n + W\}$ is a basis of the quotient space V/W. (Observe that no condition is placed on the dimensionality of V or W.)

10.74. Let W be the solution space of the linear equation
$$a_1 x_1 + a_2 x_2 + \cdots + a_n x_n = 0, \qquad a_i \in K$$
and let $v = (b_1, b_2, \ldots, b_n) \in K^n$. Prove that the coset $v + W$ of W in K^n is the solution set of the linear equation
$$a_1 x_1 + a_2 x_2 + \cdots + a_n x_n = b \qquad \text{where} \qquad b = a_1 b_1 + \cdots + a_n b_n$$

10.75. Let V be the vector space of polynomials over $\mathbf{R}$ and let W be the subspace of polynomials divisible by t^4, i.e. of the form $a_0 t^4 + a_1 t^5 + \cdots + a_{n-4} t^n$. Show that the quotient space V/W is of dimension 4.

10.76. Let U and W be subspaces of V such that $W \subset U \subset V$. Note that any coset $u + W$ of W in U may also be viewed as a coset of W in V since $u \in U$ implies $u \in V$; hence U/W is a subset of V/W. Prove that (i) U/W is a subspace of V/W, (ii) $\dim(V/W) - \dim(U/W) = \dim(V/U)$.

10.77. Let U and W be subspaces of V. Show that the cosets of $U \cap W$ in V can be obtained by intersecting each of the cosets of U in V by each of the cosets of W in V:
$$V/(U \cap W) = \{(v + U) \cap (v' + W) : v, v' \in V\}$$

10.78. Let $T : V \to V'$ be linear with kernel W and image U. Show that the quotient space V/W is isomorphic to U under the mapping $\theta : V/W \to U$ defined by $\theta(v + W) = T(v)$. Furthermore, show that $T = i \circ \theta \circ \eta$ where $\eta : V \to V/W$ is the natural mapping of V into V/W, i.e. $\eta(v) = v + W$, and $i : U \subset V'$ is the inclusion mapping, i.e. $i(u) = u$. (See diagram.)

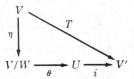

Answers to Supplementary Problems

10.41. (i) $\mathbf{R}^2$ and $\{0\}$ (ii) $\mathbf{C}^2$, $\{0\}$, $W_1 = L((2, 1-2i))$, $W_2 = L((2, 1+2i))$.

10.52. (i)

$$
\begin{pmatrix}
2 & 1 & & & & \\
 & 2 & & & & \\
 & & 2 & 1 & & \\
 & & & 2 & & \\
 & & & & 3 & 1 \\
 & & & & & 3
\end{pmatrix},
\quad
\begin{pmatrix}
2 & 1 & & & & \\
 & 2 & & & & \\
 & & 2 & & & \\
 & & & 2 & & \\
 & & & & 3 & 1 \\
 & & & & & 3
\end{pmatrix}
$$

(ii)

$$
\begin{pmatrix}
7 & 1 & & & \\
 & 7 & & & \\
 & & 7 & 1 & \\
 & & & 7 & \\
 & & & & 7
\end{pmatrix},
\quad
\begin{pmatrix}
7 & 1 & & & \\
 & 7 & & & \\
 & & 7 & & \\
 & & & 7 & \\
 & & & & 7
\end{pmatrix}
$$

(iii)

$$
\begin{pmatrix}
2 & 1 & & & & & \\
 & 2 & 1 & & & & \\
 & & 2 & & & & \\
 & & & 2 & 1 & & \\
 & & & & 2 & 1 & \\
 & & & & & 2 & \\
 & & & & & & 2
\end{pmatrix},
\quad
\begin{pmatrix}
2 & 1 & & & & & \\
 & 2 & 1 & & & & \\
 & & 2 & & & & \\
 & & & 2 & 1 & & \\
 & & & & 2 & & \\
 & & & & & 2 & 1 \\
 & & & & & & 2
\end{pmatrix}
$$

$$
\begin{pmatrix}
2 & 1 & & & & & \\
 & 2 & 1 & & & & \\
 & & 2 & & & & \\
 & & & 2 & 1 & & \\
 & & & & 2 & & \\
 & & & & & 2 & \\
 & & & & & & 2
\end{pmatrix},
\quad
\begin{pmatrix}
2 & 1 & & & & & \\
 & 2 & 1 & & & & \\
 & & 2 & & & & \\
 & & & 2 & & & \\
 & & & & 2 & & \\
 & & & & & 2 & \\
 & & & & & & 2
\end{pmatrix}
$$

(iv)

$$
\begin{pmatrix}
3 & 1 & & & & & & \\
 & 3 & & & & & & \\
 & & 3 & 1 & & & & \\
 & & & 3 & & & & \\
 & & & & 5 & 1 & & \\
 & & & & & 5 & & \\
 & & & & & & 5 & 1 \\
 & & & & & & & 5
\end{pmatrix},
\quad
\begin{pmatrix}
3 & 1 & & & & & & \\
 & 3 & & & & & & \\
 & & 3 & 1 & & & & \\
 & & & 3 & & & & \\
 & & & & 5 & 1 & & \\
 & & & & & 5 & & \\
 & & & & & & 5 & \\
 & & & & & & & 5
\end{pmatrix},
$$

$$
\begin{pmatrix}
3 & 1 & & & & & & \\
 & 3 & & & & & & \\
 & & 3 & & & & & \\
 & & & 3 & & & & \\
 & & & & 5 & 1 & & \\
 & & & & & 5 & & \\
 & & & & & & 5 & 1 \\
 & & & & & & & 5
\end{pmatrix},
\quad
\begin{pmatrix}
3 & 1 & & & & & & \\
 & 3 & & & & & & \\
 & & 3 & & & & & \\
 & & & 3 & & & & \\
 & & & & 5 & 1 & & \\
 & & & & & 5 & & \\
 & & & & & & 5 & \\
 & & & & & & & 5
\end{pmatrix}
$$

10.60. (i)

$$\begin{pmatrix} 0 & -3 & & & & \\ 1 & 0 & & & & \\ & & 0 & -3 & & \\ & & 1 & 0 & & \\ & & & & 0 & -1 \\ & & & & 1 & -2 \end{pmatrix}, \quad \begin{pmatrix} 0 & -3 & & & & \\ 1 & 0 & & & & \\ & & 0 & -1 & & \\ & & 1 & -2 & & \\ & & & & 0 & -1 \\ & & & & 1 & -2 \end{pmatrix}, \quad \begin{pmatrix} 0 & -3 & & & \\ 1 & 0 & & & \\ & & 0 & -1 & & \\ & & 1 & -2 & & \\ & & & & -1 & \\ & & & & & -1 \end{pmatrix}$$

(ii)

$$\begin{pmatrix} 0 & 0 & -1 & & & \\ 1 & 0 & -3 & & & \\ 0 & 1 & -3 & & & \\ & & & 0 & 0 & -1 \\ & & & 1 & 0 & -3 \\ & & & 0 & 1 & -3 \end{pmatrix}, \quad \begin{pmatrix} 0 & 0 & -1 & & & \\ 1 & 0 & -3 & & & \\ 0 & 1 & -3 & & & \\ & & & 0 & -1 & \\ & & & 1 & -2 & \\ & & & & & -1 \end{pmatrix}, \quad \begin{pmatrix} 0 & 0 & -1 & & & \\ 1 & 0 & -3 & & & \\ 0 & 1 & -3 & & & \\ & & & -1 & & \\ & & & & -1 & \\ & & & & & -1 \end{pmatrix}$$

(iii)

$$\begin{pmatrix} 0 & 0 & 0 & 2 & & & & \\ 1 & 0 & 0 & 0 & & & & \\ 0 & 1 & 0 & -4 & & & & \\ 0 & 0 & 1 & 0 & & & & \\ & & & & 0 & -2 & & \\ & & & & 1 & 0 & & \\ & & & & & & 0 & -9 \\ & & & & & & 1 & -6 \end{pmatrix}, \quad \begin{pmatrix} 0 & 0 & 0 & 2 & & & \\ 1 & 0 & 0 & 0 & & & \\ 0 & 1 & 0 & -4 & & & \\ 0 & 0 & 1 & 0 & & & \\ & & & & 0 & -9 & \\ & & & & 1 & -6 & \\ & & & & & & 0 & -9 \\ & & & & & & 1 & -6 \end{pmatrix},$$

$$\begin{pmatrix} 0 & 0 & 0 & 2 & & & & \\ 1 & 0 & 0 & 0 & & & & \\ 0 & 1 & 0 & -4 & & & & \\ 0 & 0 & 1 & 0 & & & & \\ & & & & 0 & -9 & & \\ & & & & 1 & -6 & & \\ & & & & & & -3 & \\ & & & & & & & -3 \end{pmatrix}$$

10.61. (i) $\begin{pmatrix} 0 & -1 & & \\ 1 & 0 & & \\ & & 0 & \sqrt{3} \\ & & 1 & 0 \end{pmatrix}$ (ii) $\begin{pmatrix} 0 & -1 & & \\ 1 & 0 & & \\ & & \sqrt{3} & \\ & & & -\sqrt{3} \end{pmatrix}$ (iii) $\begin{pmatrix} i & & & \\ & -i & & \\ & & \sqrt{3} & \\ & & & -\sqrt{3} \end{pmatrix}$

10.62. $\begin{pmatrix} 0 & 0 & 0 & -\lambda^4 \\ 1 & 0 & 0 & 4\lambda^3 \\ 0 & 1 & 0 & -6\lambda^2 \\ 0 & 0 & 1 & 4\lambda \end{pmatrix}$

Chapter 11

Linear Functionals and the Dual Space

INTRODUCTION

In this chapter we study linear mappings from a vector space V into its field K of scalars. (Unless otherwise stated or implied, we view K as a vector space over itself.) Naturally all the theorems and results for arbitrary linear mappings on V hold for this special case. However, we treat these mappings separately because of their fundamental importance and because the special relationship of V to K gives rise to new notions and results which do not apply in the general case.

LINEAR FUNCTIONALS AND THE DUAL SPACE

Let V be a vector space over a field K. A mapping $\phi : V \to K$ is termed a *linear functional* (or *linear form*) if, for every $u, v \in V$ and every $a, b \in K$,

$$\phi(au + bv) = a\,\phi(u) + b\,\phi(v)$$

In other words, a linear functional on V is a linear mapping from V into K.

> **Example 11.1:** Let $\pi_i : K^n \to K$ be the *i*th *projection mapping*, i.e. $\pi_i(a_1, a_2, \ldots, a_n) = a_i$. Then π_i is linear and so it is a linear functional on K^n.

> **Example 11.2:** Let V be the vector space of polynomials in t over $\mathbf{R}$. Let $\mathcal{J} : V \to \mathbf{R}$ be the integral operator defined by $\mathcal{J}(p(t)) = \displaystyle\int_0^1 p(t)\,dt$. Recall that $\mathcal{J}$ is linear; and hence it is a linear functional on V.

> **Example 11.3:** Let V be the vector space of n-square matrices over K. Let $T : V \to K$ be the *trace* mapping
> $$T(A) = a_{11} + a_{22} + \cdots + a_{nn}, \qquad \text{where } A = (a_{ij})$$
> That is, T assigns to a matrix A the sum of its diagonal elements. This map is linear (Problem 11.27) and so it is a linear functional on V.

By Theorem 6.6, the set of linear functionals on a vector space V over a field K is also a vector space over K with addition and scalar multiplication defined by

$$(\phi + \sigma)(v) = \phi(v) + \sigma(v) \qquad \text{and} \qquad (k\phi)(v) = k\,\phi(v)$$

where ϕ and σ are linear functionals on V and $k \in K$. This space is called the *dual space* of V and is denoted by V^*.

> **Example 11.4:** Let $V = K^n$, the vector space of n-tuples which we write as column vectors. Then the dual space V^* can be identified with the space of row vectors. In particular, any linear functional $\phi = (a_1, \ldots, a_n)$ in V^* has the representation
> $$\phi(x_1, \ldots, x_n) = (a_1, a_2, \ldots, a_n)\begin{pmatrix} x_1 \\ x_2 \\ \cdot\cdot \\ x_n \end{pmatrix}$$

or simply

$$\phi(x_1, \ldots, x_n) = a_1 x_1 + a_2 x_2 + \cdots + a_n x_n$$

Historically, the above formal expression was termed a *linear form*.

DUAL BASIS

Suppose V is a vector space of dimension n over K. By Theorem 6.7, the dimension of the dual space V^* is also n (since K is of dimension 1 over itself.) In fact, each basis of V determines a basis of V^* as follows:

Theorem 11.1: Suppose $\{v_1, \ldots, v_n\}$ is a basis of V over K. Let $\phi_1, \ldots, \phi_n \in V^*$ be the linear functionals defined by

$$\phi_i(v_j) = \delta_{ij} = \begin{cases} 1 & \text{if } i = j \\ 0 & \text{if } i \neq j \end{cases}$$

Then $\{\phi_1, \ldots, \phi_n\}$ is a basis of V^*.

The above basis $\{\phi_i\}$ is termed the basis *dual* to $\{v_i\}$ or the *dual basis*. The above formula which uses the Kronecker delta δ_{ij} is a short way of writing

$$\phi_1(v_1) = 1, \quad \phi_1(v_2) = 0, \quad \phi_1(v_3) = 0, \quad \ldots, \quad \phi_1(v_n) = 0$$
$$\phi_2(v_1) = 0, \quad \phi_2(v_2) = 1, \quad \phi_2(v_3) = 0, \quad \ldots, \quad \phi_2(v_n) = 0$$
$$\cdots\cdots\cdots\cdots\cdots\cdots\cdots\cdots\cdots\cdots\cdots\cdots\cdots\cdots\cdots\cdots$$
$$\phi_n(v_1) = 0, \quad \phi_n(v_2) = 0, \quad \ldots, \quad \phi_n(v_{n-1}) = 0, \quad \phi_n(v_n) = 1$$

By Theorem 6.2, these linear mappings ϕ_i are unique and well defined.

Example 11.5: Consider the following basis of $\mathbf{R}^2$: $\{v_1 = (2, 1), v_2 = (3, 1)\}$. Find the dual basis $\{\phi_1, \phi_2\}$.

We seek linear functionals $\phi_1(x, y) = ax + by$ and $\phi_2(x, y) = cx + dy$ such that

$$\phi_1(v_1) = 1, \quad \phi_1(v_2) = 0, \quad \phi_2(v_1) = 0, \quad \phi_2(v_2) = 1$$

Thus
$$\left.\begin{array}{l} \phi_1(v_1) = \phi_1(2, 1) = 2a + b = 1 \\ \phi_1(v_2) = \phi_1(3, 1) = 3a + b = 0 \end{array}\right\} \quad \text{or} \quad a = -1, \ b = 3$$

$$\left.\begin{array}{l} \phi_2(v_1) = \phi_2(2, 1) = 2c + d = 0 \\ \phi_2(v_2) = \phi_2(3, 1) = 3c + d = 1 \end{array}\right\} \quad \text{or} \quad c = 1, \ d = -2$$

Hence the dual basis is $\{\phi_1(x, y) = -x + 3y, \ \phi_2(x, y) = x - 2y\}$.

The next theorems give relationships between bases and their duals.

Theorem 11.2: Let $\{v_1, \ldots, v_n\}$ be a basis of V and let $\{\phi_1, \ldots, \phi_n\}$ be the dual basis of V^*. Then for any vector $u \in V$,

$$u = \phi_1(u)v_1 + \phi_2(u)v_2 + \cdots + \phi_n(u)v_n$$

and, for any linear functional $\sigma \in V^*$,

$$\sigma = \sigma(v_1)\phi_1 + \sigma(v_2)\phi_2 + \cdots + \sigma(v_n)\phi_n$$

Theorem 11.3: Let $\{v_1, \ldots, v_n\}$ and $\{w_1, \ldots, w_n\}$ be bases of V and let $\{\phi_1, \ldots, \phi_n\}$ and $\{\sigma_1, \ldots, \sigma_n\}$ be the bases of V^* dual to $\{v_i\}$ and $\{w_i\}$ respectively. Suppose P is the transition matrix from $\{v_i\}$ to $\{w_i\}$. Then $(P^{-1})^t$ is the transition matrix from $\{\phi_i\}$ to $\{\sigma_i\}$.

SECOND DUAL SPACE

We repeat: every vector space V has a dual space V^* which consists of all the linear functionals on V. Thus V^* itself has a dual space V^{**}, called the *second dual* of V, which consists of all the linear functionals on V^*.

We now show that each $v \in V$ determines a specific element $\hat{v} \in V^{**}$. First of all, for any $\phi \in V^*$ we define

$$\hat{v}(\phi) = \phi(v)$$

It remains to be shown that this map $\hat{v} : V^* \to K$ is linear. For any scalars $a, b \in K$ and any linear functionals $\phi, \sigma \in V^*$, we have

$$\hat{v}(a\phi + b\sigma) = (a\phi + b\sigma)(v) = a\,\phi(v) + b\,\sigma(v) = a\,\hat{v}(\phi) + b\,\hat{v}(\sigma)$$

That is, $\hat{v}$ is linear and so $\hat{v} \in V^{**}$. The following theorem applies.

Theorem 11.4:   If V has finite dimension, then the mapping $v \mapsto \hat{v}$ is an isomorphism of V onto V^{**}.

The above mapping $v \mapsto \hat{v}$ is called the *natural mapping* of V into V^{**}. We emphasize that this mapping is never onto V^{**} if V is not finite-dimensional. However, it is always linear and, moreover, it is always one-to-one.

Now suppose V does have finite dimension. By the above theorem the natural mapping determines an isomorphism between V and V^{**}. Unless otherwise stated we shall identify V with V^{**} by this mapping. Accordingly we shall view V as the space of linear functionals on V^* and shall write $V = V^{**}$. We remark that if $\{\phi_i\}$ is the basis of V^* dual to a basis $\{v_i\}$ of V, then $\{v_i\}$ is the basis of $V = V^{**}$ which is dual to $\{\phi_i\}$.

ANNIHILATORS

Let W be a subset (not necessarily a subspace) of a vector space V. A linear functional $\phi \in V^*$ is called an *annihilator* of W if $\phi(w) = 0$ for every $w \in W$, i.e. if $\phi(W) = \{0\}$. We show that the set of all such mappings, denoted by W^0 and called the *annihilator* of W, is a subspace of V^*. Clearly $0 \in W^0$. Now suppose $\phi, \sigma \in W^0$. Then, for any scalars $a, b \in K$ and for any $w \in W$,

$$(a\phi + b\sigma)(w) = a\,\phi(w) + b\,\sigma(w) = a0 + b0 = 0$$

Thus $a\phi + b\sigma \in W^0$ and so W^0 is a subspace of V^*.

In the case that W is a subspace of V, we have the following relationship between W and its annihilator W^0.

Theorem 11.5:   Suppose V has finite dimension and W is a subspace of V. Then (i) $\dim W + \dim W^0 = \dim V$ and (ii) $W^{00} = W$.

Here $W^{00} = \{v \in V : \phi(v) = 0 \text{ for every } \phi \in W^0\}$ or, equivalently, $W^{00} = (W^0)^0$ where W^{00} is viewed as a subspace of V under the identification of V and V^{**}.

The concept of an annihilator enables us to give another interpretation of a homogeneous system of linear equations,

$$a_{11}x_1 + a_{12}x_2 + \cdots + a_{1n}x_n = 0$$
$$a_{21}x_1 + a_{22}x_2 + \cdots + a_{2n}x_n = 0$$
$$\cdots\cdots\cdots\cdots\cdots\cdots\cdots\cdots\cdots$$
$$a_{m1}x_1 + a_{m2}x_2 + \cdots + a_{mn}x_n = 0$$

$$(*)$$

Here each row $(a_{i1}, a_{i2}, \ldots, a_{in})$ of the coefficient matrix $A = (a_{ij})$ is viewed as an element of K^n and each solution vector $\phi = (x_1, x_2, \ldots, x_n)$ is viewed as an element of the dual space. In this context, the solution space S of (∗) is the annihilator of the rows of A and hence of the row space of A. Consequently, using Theorem 11.5, we again obtain the following fundamental result on the dimension of the solution space of a homogeneous system of linear equations:

$$\dim S \ = \ \dim K^n - \dim (\text{row space of } A) \ = \ n - \text{rank}(A)$$

TRANSPOSE OF A LINEAR MAPPING

Let $T : V \to U$ be an arbitrary linear mapping from a vector space V into a vector space U. Now for any linear functional $\phi \in U^*$, the composition $\phi \circ T$ is a linear mapping from V into K:

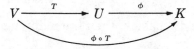

That is, $\phi \circ T \in V^*$. Thus the correspondence

$$\phi \ \mapsto \ \phi \circ T$$

is a mapping from U^* into V^*; we denote it by T^t and call it the *transpose* of T. In other words, $T^t : U^* \to V^*$ is defined by

$$T^t(\phi) \ = \ \phi \circ T$$

Thus $(T^t(\phi))(v) = \phi(T(v))$ for every $v \in V$.

Theorem 11.6:   The transpose mapping T^t defined above is linear.

Proof. For any scalars $a, b \in K$ and any linear functionals $\phi, \sigma \in U^*$,

$$T^t(a\phi + b\sigma) \ = \ (a\phi + b\sigma) \circ T \ = \ a(\phi \circ T) + b(\sigma \circ T)$$
$$= \ a\,T^t(\phi) + b\,T^t(\sigma)$$

That is, T^t is linear as claimed.

We emphasize that if T is a linear mapping from V into U, then T^t is a linear mapping from U^* into V^*:

$$V \xrightarrow{T} U \qquad V^* \xleftarrow{T^t} U^*$$

The name "transpose" for the mapping T^t no doubt derives from the following theorem.

Theorem 11.7:   Let $T : V \to U$ be linear, and let A be the matrix representation of T relative to bases $\{v_i\}$ of V and $\{u_i\}$ of U. Then the transpose matrix A^t is the matrix representation of $T^t : U^* \to V^*$ relative to the bases dual to $\{u_i\}$ and $\{v_i\}$.

Solved Problems

DUAL SPACES AND BASES

11.1. Let $\phi : \mathbf{R}^2 \to \mathbf{R}$ and $\sigma : \mathbf{R}^2 \to \mathbf{R}$ be the linear functionals defined by $\phi(x,y) = x + 2y$ and $\sigma(x,y) = 3x - y$. Find (i) $\phi + \sigma$, (ii) 4ϕ, (iii) $2\phi - 5\sigma$.

(i) $(\phi + \sigma)(x,y) = \phi(x,y) + \sigma(x,y) = x + 2y + 3x - y = 4x + y$

(ii) $(4\phi)(x,y) = 4\,\phi(x,y) = 4(x + 2y) = 4x + 8y$

(iii) $(2\phi - 5\sigma)(x,y) = 2\,\phi(x,y) - 5\,\sigma(x,y) = 2(x + 2y) - 5(3x - y) = -13x + 9y$

11.2. Consider the following basis of $\mathbf{R}^3$: $\{v_1 = (1, -1, 3),\ v_2 = (0, 1, -1),\ v_3 = (0, 3, -2)\}$. Find the dual basis $\{\phi_1, \phi_2, \phi_3\}$.

We seek linear functionals

$$\phi_1(x,y,z) = a_1 x + a_2 y + a_3 z, \quad \phi_2(x,y,z) = b_1 x + b_2 y + b_3 z, \quad \phi_3(x,y,z) = c_1 x + c_2 y + c_3 z$$

such that

$$\begin{array}{ccc}
\phi_1(v_1) = 1 & \phi_1(v_2) = 0 & \phi_1(v_3) = 0 \\
\phi_2(v_1) = 0 & \phi_2(v_2) = 1 & \phi_2(v_3) = 0 \\
\phi_3(v_1) = 0 & \phi_3(v_2) = 0 & \phi_3(v_3) = 1
\end{array}$$

We find ϕ_1 as follows:

$$\begin{aligned}
\phi_1(v_1) &= \phi_1(1, -1, 3) = a_1 - a_2 + 3a_3 = 1 \\
\phi_1(v_2) &= \phi_1(0, 1, -1) = \ a_2 - a_3 = 0 \\
\phi_1(v_3) &= \phi_1(0, 3, -2) = \ 3a_2 - 2a_3 = 0
\end{aligned}$$

Solving the system of equations, we obtain $a_1 = 1$, $a_2 = 0$, $a_3 = 0$. Thus $\phi_1(x,y,z) = x$.

We next find ϕ_2:

$$\begin{aligned}
\phi_2(v_1) &= \phi_2(1, -1, 3) = b_1 - b_2 + 3b_3 = 0 \\
\phi_2(v_2) &= \phi_2(0, 1, -1) = \ b_2 - b_3 = 1 \\
\phi_2(v_3) &= \phi_2(0, 3, -2) = \ 3b_2 - 2b_3 = 0
\end{aligned}$$

Solving the system, we obtain $b_1 = 7$, $b_2 = -2$, $b_3 = -3$. Hence $\phi_2(x,y,z) = 7x - 2y - 3z$.

Finally, we find ϕ_3:

$$\begin{aligned}
\phi_3(v_1) &= \phi_3(1, -1, 3) = c_1 - c_2 + 3c_3 = 0 \\
\phi_3(v_2) &= \phi_3(0, 1, -1) = \ c_2 - c_3 = 0 \\
\phi_3(v_3) &= \phi_3(0, 3, -2) = \ 3c_2 - 2c_3 = 1
\end{aligned}$$

Solving the system, we obtain $c_1 = -2$, $c_2 = 1$, $c_3 = 1$. Thus $\phi_3(x,y,z) = -2x + y + z$.

11.3. Let V be the vector space of polynomials over $\mathbf{R}$ of degree ≤ 1, i.e. $V = \{a + bt : a, b \in \mathbf{R}\}$. Let $\phi_1 : V \to \mathbf{R}$ and $\phi_2 : V \to \mathbf{R}$ be defined by

$$\phi_1(f(t)) = \int_0^1 f(t)\,dt \quad \text{and} \quad \phi_2(f(t)) = \int_0^2 f(t)\,dt$$

(We remark that ϕ_1 and ϕ_2 are linear and so belong to the dual space V^*.) Find the basis $\{v_1, v_2\}$ of V which is dual to $\{\phi_1, \phi_2\}$.

Let $v_1 = a + bt$ and $v_2 = c + dt$. By definition of the dual basis,

$$\phi_1(v_1) = 1, \ \phi_2(v_1) = 0 \quad \text{and} \quad \phi_1(v_2) = 0, \ \phi_2(v_2) = 1$$

Thus

$$\left.\begin{aligned}
\phi_1(v_1) &= \int_0^1 (a + bt)\,dt = a + \tfrac{1}{2}b = 1 \\
\phi_2(v_1) &= \int_0^2 (a + bt)\,dt = 2a + 2b = 0
\end{aligned}\right\} \quad \text{or} \quad a = 2,\ b = -2$$

$$
\left.\begin{aligned}
\phi_1(v_2) &= \int_0^1 (c+dt)\,dt = c + \tfrac{1}{2}d = 0 \\
\phi_2(v_2) &= \int_0^2 (c+dt)\,dt = 2c + 2d = 1
\end{aligned}\right\} \quad \text{or} \quad c = -\tfrac{1}{2},\ d = 1
$$

In other words, $\{2 - 2t,\ -\tfrac{1}{2} + t\}$ is the basis of V which is dual to $\{\phi_1, \phi_2\}$.

11.4. **Prove Theorem 11.1:** Suppose $\{v_1, \ldots, v_n\}$ is a basis of V over K. Let $\phi_1, \ldots, \phi_n \in V^*$ be the linear functionals defined by

$$
\phi_i(v_j) = \delta_{ij} = \begin{cases} 1 & \text{if } i = j \\ 0 & \text{if } i \neq j \end{cases}
$$

Then $\{\phi_1, \ldots, \phi_n\}$ is a basis of V^*.

    We first show that $\{\phi_1, \ldots, \phi_n\}$ spans V^*. Let ϕ be an arbitrary element of V^*, and suppose

$$
\phi(v_1) = k_1,\ \phi(v_2) = k_2,\ \ldots,\ \phi(v_n) = k_n
$$

Set $\sigma = k_1\phi_1 + \cdots + k_n\phi_n$. Then

$$
\begin{aligned}
\sigma(v_1) &= (k_1\phi_1 + \cdots + k_n\phi_n)(v_1) \\
&= k_1\,\phi_1(v_1) + k_2\,\phi_2(v_1) + \cdots + k_n\,\phi_n(v_1) \\
&= k_1 \cdot 1 + k_2 \cdot 0 + \cdots + k_n \cdot 0 = k_1
\end{aligned}
$$

Similarly, for $i = 2, \ldots, n$,

$$
\begin{aligned}
\sigma(v_i) &= (k_1\phi_1 + \cdots + k_n\phi_n)(v_i) \\
&= k_1\,\phi_1(v_i) + \cdots + k_i\,\phi_i(v_i) + \cdots + k_n\,\phi_n(v_i) = k_i
\end{aligned}
$$

Thus $\phi(v_i) = \sigma(v_i)$ for $i = 1, \ldots, n$. Since ϕ and σ agree on the basis vectors, $\phi = \sigma = k_1\phi_1 + \cdots + k_n\phi_n$. Accordingly, $\{\phi_1, \ldots, \phi_n\}$ spans V^*.

    It remains to be shown that $\{\phi_1, \ldots, \phi_n\}$ is linearly independent. Suppose

$$
a_1\phi_1 + a_2\phi_2 + \cdots + a_n\phi_n = 0
$$

Applying both sides to v_1, we obtain

$$
\begin{aligned}
0 = 0(v_1) &= (a_1\phi_1 + \cdots + a_n\phi_n)(v_1) \\
&= a_1\,\phi_1(v_1) + a_2\,\phi_2(v_1) + \cdots + a_n\,\phi_n(v_1) \\
&= a_1 \cdot 1 + a_2 \cdot 0 + \cdots + a_n \cdot 0 = a_1
\end{aligned}
$$

Similarly, for $i = 2, \ldots, n$,

$$
\begin{aligned}
0 = 0(v_i) &= (a_1\phi_1 + \cdots + a_n\phi_n)(v_i) \\
&= a_1\,\phi_1(v_i) + \cdots + a_i\,\phi_i(v_i) + \cdots + a_n\,\phi_n(v_i) = a_i
\end{aligned}
$$

That is, $a_1 = 0, \ldots, a_n = 0$. Hence $\{\phi_1, \ldots, \phi_n\}$ is linearly independent and so it is a basis of V^*.

11.5. **Prove Theorem 11.2:** Let $\{v_1, \ldots, v_n\}$ be a basis of V and let $\{\phi_1, \ldots, \phi_n\}$ be the dual basis of V^*. Then, for any vector $u \in V$,

$$
u = \phi_1(u)v_1 + \phi_2(u)v_2 + \cdots + \phi_n(u)v_n \tag{1}
$$

and, for any linear functional $\sigma \in V^*$,

$$
\sigma = \sigma(v_1)\phi_1 + \sigma(v_2)\phi_2 + \cdots + \sigma(v_n)\phi_n \tag{2}
$$

    Suppose $u = a_1v_1 + a_2v_2 + \cdots + a_nv_n$ (3)

Then

$$
\phi_1(u) = a_1\,\phi_1(v_1) + a_2\,\phi_1(v_2) + \cdots + a_n\,\phi_1(v_n) = a_1 \cdot 1 + a_2 \cdot 0 + \cdots + a_n \cdot 0 = a_1
$$

Similarly, for $i = 2, \ldots, n$,

$$\phi_i(u) = a_1\,\phi_i(v_1) + \cdots + a_i\,\phi_i(v_i) + \cdots + a_n\,\phi_i(v_n) = a_i$$

That is, $\phi_1(u) = a_1$, $\phi_2(u) = a_2$, $\ldots$, $\phi_n(u) = a_n$. Substituting these results into *(3)*, we obtain *(1)*.

Next we prove *(2)*. Applying the linear functional σ to both sides of *(1)*,

$$\begin{aligned}
\sigma(u) &= \phi_1(u)\,\sigma(v_1) + \phi_2(u)\,\sigma(v_2) + \cdots + \phi_n(u)\,\sigma(v_n) \\
&= \sigma(v_1)\,\phi_1(u) + \sigma(v_2)\,\phi_2(u) + \cdots + \sigma(v_n)\,\phi_n(u) \\
&= (\sigma(v_1)\phi_1 + \sigma(v_2)\phi_2 + \cdots + \sigma(v_n)\phi_n)(u)
\end{aligned}$$

Since the above holds for every $u \in V$, $\sigma = \sigma(v_1)\phi_1 + \sigma(v_2)\phi_2 + \cdots + \sigma(v_n)\phi_n$ as claimed.

11.6. Prove Theorem 11.3: Let $\{v_1, \ldots, v_n\}$ and $\{w_1, \ldots, w_n\}$ be bases of V and let $\{\phi_1, \ldots, \phi_n\}$ and $\{\sigma_1, \ldots, \sigma_n\}$ be the bases of V^* dual to $\{v_i\}$ and $\{w_i\}$ respectively. Suppose P is the transition matrix from $\{v_i\}$ to $\{w_i\}$. Then $(P^{-1})^t$ is the transition matrix from $\{\phi_i\}$ to $\{\sigma_i\}$.

Suppose

$$\begin{aligned}
w_1 &= a_{11}v_1 + a_{12}v_2 + \cdots + a_{1n}v_n & \sigma_1 &= b_{11}\phi_1 + b_{12}\phi_2 + \cdots + b_{1n}\phi_n \\
w_2 &= a_{21}v_1 + a_{22}v_2 + \cdots + a_{2n}v_n & \sigma_2 &= b_{21}\phi_1 + b_{22}\phi_2 + \cdots + b_{2n}\phi_n \\
&\cdots\cdots\cdots\cdots\cdots\cdots\cdots\cdots\cdots & &\cdots\cdots\cdots\cdots\cdots\cdots\cdots\cdots\cdots \\
w_n &= a_{n1}v_1 + a_{n2}v_2 + \cdots + a_{nn}v_n & \sigma_n &= b_{n1}\phi_1 + b_{n2}\phi_2 + \cdots + b_{nn}\phi_n
\end{aligned}$$

where $P = (a_{ij})$ and $Q = (b_{ij})$. We seek to prove that $Q = (P^{-1})^t$.

Let R_i denote the ith row of Q and let C_j denote the jth column of P^t. Then

$$R_i = (b_{i1}, b_{i2}, \ldots, b_{in}) \quad \text{and} \quad C_j = (a_{j1}, a_{j2}, \ldots, a_{jn})^t$$

By definition of the dual basis,

$$\begin{aligned}
\sigma_i(w_j) &= (b_{i1}\phi_1 + b_{i2}\phi_2 + \cdots + b_{in}\phi_n)(a_{j1}v_1 + a_{j2}v_2 + \cdots + a_{jn}v_n) \\
&= b_{i1}a_{j1} + b_{i2}a_{j2} + \cdots + b_{in}a_{jn} = R_iC_j = \delta_{ij}
\end{aligned}$$

where δ_{ij} is the Kronecker delta. Thus

$$QP^t = \begin{pmatrix} R_1C_1 & R_1C_2 & \ldots & R_nC_n \\ R_2C_1 & R_2C_2 & \ldots & R_2C_n \\ \cdots\cdots\cdots\cdots\cdots\cdots\cdots \\ R_nC_1 & R_nC_2 & \ldots & R_nC_n \end{pmatrix} = \begin{pmatrix} 1 & 0 & \ldots & 0 \\ 0 & 1 & \ldots & 0 \\ \cdots\cdots\cdots\cdots \\ 0 & 0 & \ldots & 1 \end{pmatrix} = I$$

and hence $Q = (P^t)^{-1} = (P^{-1})^t$ as claimed.

11.7. Suppose V has finite dimension. Show that if $v \in V$, $v \neq 0$, then there exists $\phi \in V^*$ such that $\phi(v) \neq 0$.

We extend $\{v\}$ to a basis $\{v, v_2, \ldots, v_n\}$ of V. By Theorem 6.1, there exists a unique linear mapping $\phi : V \to K$ such that $\phi(v) = 1$ and $\phi(v_i) = 0$, $i = 2, \ldots, n$. Hence ϕ has the desired property.

11.8. Prove Theorem 11.4: If V has finite dimension, then the mapping $v \mapsto \hat{v}$ is an isomorphism of V onto V^{**}. (Here $\hat{v} : V^* \to K$ is defined by $\hat{v}(\phi) = \phi(v)$.)

We first prove that the map $v \mapsto \hat{v}$ is linear, i.e. for any vectors $v, w \in V$ and any scalars $a, b \in K$, $\widehat{av + bw} = a\hat{v} + b\hat{w}$. For any linear functional $\phi \in V^*$,

$$\begin{aligned}
\widehat{av + bw}\,(\phi) &= \phi(av + bw) = a\,\phi(v) + b\,\phi(w) \\
&= a\,\hat{v}(\phi) + b\,\hat{w}(\phi) = (a\hat{v} + b\hat{w})(\phi)
\end{aligned}$$

Since $\widehat{av + bw}\,(\phi) = (a\hat{v} + b\hat{w})(\phi)$ for every $\phi \in V^*$, we have $\widehat{av + bw} = a\hat{v} + b\hat{w}$. Thus the map $v \mapsto \hat{v}$ is linear.

Now suppose $v \in V$, $v \neq 0$. Then, by the preceding problem, there exists $\phi \in V^*$ for which $\phi(v) \neq 0$. Hence $\hat{v}(\phi) = \phi(v) \neq 0$ and thus $\hat{v} \neq 0$. Since $v \neq 0$ implies $\hat{v} \neq 0$, the map $v \mapsto \hat{v}$ is nonsingular and hence an isomorphism (Theorem 6.5).

Now $\dim V = \dim V^* = \dim V^{**}$ because V has finite dimension. Accordingly, mapping $v \mapsto \hat{v}$ is an isomorphism of V onto V^{**}.

ANNIHILATORS

11.9. Show that if $\phi \in V^*$ annihilates a subset S of V, then ϕ annihilates the linear span $L(S)$ of S. Hence $S^0 = (L(S))^0$.

Suppose $v \in L(S)$. Then there exist $w_1, \ldots, w_r \in S$ for which $v = a_1 w_1 + a_2 w_2 + \cdots + a_r w_r$.

$$\phi(v) = a_1 \phi(w_1) + a_2 \phi(w_2) + \cdots + a_r \phi(w_r) = a_1 0 + a_2 0 + \cdots + a_r 0 = 0$$

Since v was an arbitrary element of $L(S)$, ϕ annihilates $L(S)$ as claimed.

11.10. Let W be the subspace of $\mathbf{R}^4$ spanned by $v_1 = (1, 2, -3, 4)$ and $v_2 = (0, 1, 4, -1)$. Find a basis of the annihilator of W.

By the preceding problem, it suffices to find a basis of the set of linear functionals $\phi(x, y, z, w) = ax + by + cz + dw$ for which $\phi(v_1) = 0$ and $\phi(v_2) = 0$:

$$\phi(1, 2, -3, 4) = a + 2b - 3c + 4d = 0$$
$$\phi(0, 1, 4, -1) = \qquad b + 4c - d = 0$$

The system of equations in unknowns a, b, c, d is in echelon form with free variables c and d.

Set $c = 1$, $d = 0$ to obtain the solution $a = 11$, $b = -4$, $c = 1$, $d = 0$ and hence the linear functional $\phi_1(x, y, z, w) = 11x - 4y + z$.

Set $c = 0$, $d = -1$ to obtain the solution $a = 6$, $b = -1$, $c = 0$, $d = -1$ and hence the linear functional $\phi_2(x, y, z, w) = 6x - y - w$.

The set of linear functionals $\{\phi_1, \phi_2\}$ is a basis of W^0, the annihilator of W.

11.11. Show that: (i) for any subset S of V, $S \subset S^{00}$; (ii) if $S_1 \subset S_2$, then $S_2^0 \subset S_1^0$.

(i)   Let $v \in S$. Then for every linear functional $\phi \in S^0$, $\hat{v}(\phi) = \phi(v) = 0$. Hence $\hat{v} \in (S^0)^0$. Therefore, under the identification of V and V^{**}, $v \in S^{00}$. Accordingly, $S \subset S^{00}$.

(ii)   Let $\phi \in S_2^0$. Then $\phi(v) = 0$ for every $v \in S_2$. But $S_1 \subset S_2$; hence ϕ annihilates every element of S_1, i.e. $\phi \in S_1^0$. Therefore $S_2^0 \subset S_1^0$.

11.12. Prove Theorem 11.5: Suppose V has finite dimension and W is a subspace of V. Then (i) $\dim W + \dim W^0 = \dim V$ and (ii) $W^{00} = W$.

(i)   Suppose $\dim V = n$ and $\dim W = r \leq n$. We want to show that $\dim W^0 = n - r$. We choose a basis $\{w_1, \ldots, w_r\}$ of W and extend it to the following basis of V: $\{w_1, \ldots, w_r, v_1, \ldots, v_{n-r}\}$. Consider the dual basis

$$\{\phi_1, \ldots, \phi_r, \sigma_1, \ldots, \sigma_{n-r}\}$$

By definition of the dual basis, each of the above σ's annihilates each w_i; hence $\sigma_1, \ldots, \sigma_{n-r} \in W^0$. We claim that $\{\sigma_j\}$ is a basis of W^0. Now $\{\sigma_j\}$ is part of a basis of V^* and so it is linearly independent.

We next show that $\{\sigma_j\}$ spans W^0. Let $\sigma \in W^0$. By Theorem 11.2,

$$\sigma = \sigma(w_1)\phi_1 + \cdots + \sigma(w_r)\phi_r + \sigma(v_1)\sigma_1 + \cdots + \sigma(v_{n-r})\sigma_{n-r}$$
$$= 0\phi_1 + \cdots + 0\phi_r + \sigma(v_1)\sigma_1 + \cdots + \sigma(v_{n-r})\sigma_{n-r}$$
$$= \sigma(v_1)\sigma_1 + \cdots + \sigma(v_{n-r})\sigma_{n-r}$$

Thus $\{\sigma_1, \ldots, \sigma_{n-r}\}$ spans W^0 and so it is a basis of W^0. Accordingly, $\dim W^0 = n - r = \dim V - \dim W$ as required.

(ii)   Suppose $\dim V = n$ and $\dim W = r$. Then $\dim V^* = n$ and, by (i), $\dim W^0 = n - r$. Thus by (i), $\dim W^{00} = n - (n - r) = r$; therefore $\dim W = \dim W^{00}$. By the preceding problem, $W \subset W^{00}$. Accordingly, $W = W^{00}$.

11.13. Let U and W be subspaces of V. Prove: $(U + W)^0 = U^0 \cap W^0$.

Let $\phi \in (U + W)^0$. Then ϕ annihilates $U + W$ and so, in particular, ϕ annihilates U and V. That is, $\phi \in U^0$ and $\phi \in W^0$; hence $\phi \in U^0 \cap W^0$. Thus $(U + W)^0 \subset U^0 \cap W^0$.

On the other hand, suppose $\sigma \in U^0 \cap W^0$. Then σ annihilates U and also W. If $v \in U + W$, then $v = u + w$ where $u \in U$ and $w \in W$. Hence $\sigma(v) = \sigma(u) + \sigma(w) = 0 + 0 = 0$. Thus σ annihilates $U + W$, i.e. $\sigma \in (U + W)^0$. Accordingly, $U^0 + W^0 \subset (U + W)^0$.

Both inclusion relations give us the desired equality.

Remark: Observe that no dimension argument is employed in the proof; hence the result holds for spaces of finite or infinite dimension.

TRANSPOSE OF A LINEAR MAPPING

11.14. Let ϕ be the linear functional on $\mathbf{R}^2$ defined by $\phi(x, y) = x - 2y$. For each of the following linear operators T on $\mathbf{R}^2$, find $(T^t(\phi))(x, y)$: (i) $T(x, y) = (x, 0)$; (ii) $T(x, y) = (y, x + y)$; (iii) $T(x, y) = (2x - 3y, 5x + 2y)$.

By definition of the transpose mapping, $T^t(\phi) = \phi \circ T$, i.e. $(T^t(\phi))(v) = \phi(T(v))$ for every vector v. Hence

(i) $(T^t(\phi))(x, y) = \phi(T(x, y)) = \phi(x, 0) = x$

(ii) $(T^t(\phi))(x, y) = \phi(T(x, y)) = \phi(y, x + y) = y - 2(x + y) = -2x - y$

(iii) $(T^t(\phi))(x, y) = \phi(T(x, y)) = \phi(2x - 3y, 5x + 2y) = (2x - 3y) - 2(5x + 2y) = -8x - 7y$.

11.15. Let $T : V \to U$ be linear and let $T^t : U^* \to V^*$ be its transpose. Show that the kernel of T^t is the annihilator of the image of T, i.e. $\operatorname{Ker} T^t = (\operatorname{Im} T)^0$.

Suppose $\phi \in \operatorname{Ker} T^t$; that is, $T^t(\phi) = \phi \circ T = 0$. If $u \in \operatorname{Im} T$, then $u = T(v)$ for some $v \in V$; hence

$$\phi(u) = \phi(T(v)) = (\phi \circ T)(v) = 0(v) = 0$$

We have that $\phi(u) = 0$ for every $u \in \operatorname{Im} T$; hence $\phi \in (\operatorname{Im} T)^0$. Thus $\operatorname{Ker} T^t \subset (\operatorname{Im} T)^0$.

On the other hand, suppose $\sigma \in (\operatorname{Im} T)^0$; that is, $\sigma(\operatorname{Im} T) = \{0\}$. Then, for every $v \in V$,

$$(T^t(\sigma))(v) = (\sigma \circ T)(v) = \sigma(T(v)) = 0 = 0(v)$$

We have that $(T^t(\sigma))(v) = 0(v)$ for every $v \in V$; hence $T^t(\sigma) = 0$. Therefore $\sigma \in \operatorname{Ker} T^t$ and so $(\operatorname{Im} T)^0 \subset \operatorname{Ker} T^t$.

Both inclusion relations give us the required equality.

11.16. Suppose V and U have finite dimension and suppose $T : V \to U$ is linear. Prove: $\operatorname{rank}(T) = \operatorname{rank}(T^t)$.

Suppose $\dim V = n$ and $\dim U = m$. Also suppose $\operatorname{rank}(T) = r$. Then, by Theorem 11.5,

$$\dim((\operatorname{Im} T)^0) = \dim U - \dim(\operatorname{Im} T) = m - \operatorname{rank}(T) = m - r$$

By the preceding problem, $\operatorname{Ker} T^t = (\operatorname{Im} T)^0$. Hence $\operatorname{nullity}(T^t) = m - r$. It then follows that, as claimed,

$$\operatorname{rank}(T^t) = \dim U^* - \operatorname{nullity}(T^t) = m - (m - r) = r = \operatorname{rank}(T)$$

11.17. Prove Theorem 11.7: Let $T : V \to U$ be linear and let A be the matrix representation of T relative to bases $\{v_1, \ldots, v_m\}$ of V and $\{u_1, \ldots, u_n\}$ of U. Then the transpose matrix A^t is the matrix representation of $T^t : U^* \to V^*$ relative to the bases dual to $\{u_i\}$ and $\{v_j\}$.

Suppose

$$\begin{aligned}
T(v_1) &= a_{11}u_1 + a_{12}u_2 + \cdots + a_{1n}u_n \\
T(v_2) &= a_{21}u_1 + a_{22}u_2 + \cdots + a_{2n}u_n \\
&\cdots\cdots\cdots\cdots\cdots\cdots\cdots\cdots\cdots \\
T(v_m) &= a_{m1}u_1 + a_{m2}u_2 + \cdots + a_{mn}u_n
\end{aligned} \qquad (1)$$

We want to prove that

$$T^t(\sigma_1) = a_{11}\phi_1 + a_{21}\phi_2 + \cdots + a_{m1}\phi_m$$
$$T^t(\sigma_2) = a_{12}\phi_1 + a_{22}\phi_2 + \cdots + a_{m2}\phi_m$$
$$\cdots\cdots\cdots\cdots\cdots\cdots\cdots\cdots\cdots\cdots\cdots\cdots\cdots$$
$$T^t(\sigma_n) = a_{1n}\phi_1 + a_{2n}\phi_2 + \cdots + a_{mn}\phi_m$$

(2)

where $\{\sigma_i\}$ and $\{\phi_j\}$ are the bases dual to $\{u_i\}$ and $\{v_j\}$ respectively.

Let $v \in V$ and suppose $v = k_1 v_1 + k_2 v_2 + \cdots + k_m v_m$. Then, by (1),

$$
\begin{aligned}
T(v) &= k_1 T(v_1) + k_2 T(v_2) + \cdots + k_m T(v_m) \\
&= k_1(a_{11}u_1 + \cdots + a_{1n}u_n) + k_2(a_{21}u_1 + \cdots + a_{2n}u_n) + \cdots + k_m(a_{m1}u_1 + \cdots + a_{mn}u_n) \\
&= (k_1 a_{11} + k_2 a_{21} + \cdots + k_m a_{m1})u_1 + \cdots + (k_1 a_{1n} + k_2 a_{2n} + \cdots + k_m a_{mn})u_n \\
&= \sum_{i=1}^{n} (k_1 a_{1i} + k_2 a_{2i} + \cdots + k_m a_{mi})u_i
\end{aligned}
$$

Hence for $j = 1, \ldots, n$,

$$
\begin{aligned}
(T^t(\sigma_j)(v)) = \sigma_j(T(v)) &= \sigma_j\left(\sum_{i=1}^{n} (k_1 a_{1i} + k_2 a_{2i} + \cdots + k_m a_{mi})u_i \right) \\
&= k_1 a_{1j} + k_2 a_{2j} + \cdots + k_m a_{mj}
\end{aligned}
$$

(3)

On the other hand, for $j = 1, \ldots, n$,

$$
\begin{aligned}
(a_{1j}\phi_1 + a_{2j}\phi_2 + \cdots + a_{mj}\phi_m)(v) &= (a_{1j}\phi_1 + a_{2j}\phi_2 + \cdots + a_{mj}\phi_m)(k_1 v_1 + k_2 v_2 + \cdots + k_m v_m) \\
&= k_1 a_{1j} + k_2 a_{2j} + \cdots + k_m a_{mj}
\end{aligned}
$$

(4)

Since $v \in V$ was arbitrary, (3) and (4) imply that

$$T^t(\sigma_j) = a_{1j}\phi_1 + a_{2j}\phi_2 + \cdots + a_{mj}\phi_m, \qquad j = 1, \ldots, n$$

which is (2). Thus the theorem is proved.

11.18. Let A be an arbitrary $m \times n$ matrix over a field K. Prove that the row rank and the column rank of A are equal.

Let $T : K^n \to K^m$ be the linear map defined by $T(v) = Av$, where the elements of K^n and K^m are written as column vectors. Then A is the matrix representation of T relative to the usual bases of K^n and K^m, and the image of T is the column space of A. Hence

$$\text{rank}\,(T) = \text{column rank of } A$$

By Theorem 11.7, A^t is the matrix representation of T^t relative to the dual bases. Hence

$$\text{rank}\,(T^t) = \text{column rank of } A^t = \text{row rank of } A$$

But by Problem 11.16, $\text{rank}\,(T) = \text{rank}\,(T^t)$; hence the row rank and the column rank of A are equal. (This result was stated earlier as Theorem 5.9, page 90, and was proved in a direct way in Problem 5.21.)

Supplementary Problems

DUAL SPACES AND DUAL BASES

11.19. Let $\phi : \mathbf{R}^3 \to \mathbf{R}$ and $\sigma : \mathbf{R}^3 \to \mathbf{R}$ be the linear functionals defined by $\phi(x, y, z) = 2x - 3y + z$ and $\sigma(x, y, z) = 4x - 2y + 3z$. Find (i) $\phi + \sigma$, (ii) 3ϕ, (iii) $2\phi - 5\sigma$.

11.20. Let ϕ be the linear functional on $\mathbf{R}^2$ defined by $\phi(2, 1) = 15$ and $\phi(1, -2) = -10$. Find $\phi(x, y)$ and, in particular, find $\phi(-2, 7)$.

11.21. Find the dual basis of each of the following bases of $\mathbf{R}^3$:

(i) $\{(1, 0, 0), (0, 1, 0), (0, 0, 1)\}$, (ii) $\{(1, -2, 3), (1, -1, 1), (2, -4, 7)\}$.

11.22. Let V be the vector space of polynomials over $\mathbf{R}$ of degree $\leqq 2$. Let ϕ_1, ϕ_2 and ϕ_3 be the linear functionals on V defined by

$$\phi_1(f(t)) \ = \ \int_0^1 f(t)\, dt, \quad \phi_2(f(t)) \ = \ f'(1), \quad \phi_3(f(t)) \ = \ f(0)$$

Here $f(t) = a + bt + ct^2 \in V$ and $f'(t)$ denotes the derivative of $f(t)$. Find the basis $\{f_1(t), f_2(t), f_3(t)\}$ of V which is dual to $\{\phi_1, \phi_2, \phi_3\}$.

11.23. Suppose $u, v \in V$ and that $\phi(u) = 0$ implies $\phi(v) = 0$ for all $\phi \in V^*$. Show that $v = ku$ for some scalar k.

11.24. Suppose $\phi, \sigma \in V^*$ and that $\phi(v) = 0$ implies $\sigma(v) = 0$ for all $v \in V$. Show that $\sigma = k\phi$ for some scalar k.

11.25. Let V be the vector space of polynomials over K. For $a \in K$, define $\phi_a : V \to K$ by $\phi_a(f(t)) = f(a)$. Show that: (i) ϕ_a is linear; (ii) if $a \neq b$, then $\phi_a \neq \phi_b$.

11.26. Let V be the vector space of polynomials of degree $\leqq 2$. Let $a, b, c \in K$ be distinct scalars. Let ϕ_a, ϕ_b and ϕ_c be the linear functionals defined by $\phi_a(f(t)) = f(a)$, $\phi_b(f(t)) = f(b)$, $\phi_c(f(t)) = f(c)$. Show that $\{\phi_a, \phi_b, \phi_c\}$ is linearly independent, and find the basis $\{f_1(t), f_2(t), f_3(t)\}$ of V which is its dual.

11.27. Let V be the vector space of square matrices of order n. Let $T : V \to K$ be the trace mapping: $T(A) = a_{11} + a_{22} + \cdots + a_{nn}$, where $A = (a_{ij})$. Show that T is linear.

11.28. Let W be a subspace of V. For any linear functional ϕ on W, show that there is a linear functional σ on V such that $\sigma(w) = \phi(w)$ for any $w \in W$, i.e. ϕ is the restriction of σ to W.

11.29. Let $\{e_1, \ldots, e_n\}$ be the usual basis of K^n. Show that the dual basis is $\{\pi_1, \ldots, \pi_n\}$ where π_i is the ith projection mapping: $\pi_i(a_1, \ldots, a_n) = a_i$.

11.30. Let V be a vector space over $\mathbf{R}$. Let $\phi_1, \phi_2 \in V^*$ and suppose $\sigma : V \to \mathbf{R}$ defined by $\sigma(v) = \phi_1(v)\, \phi_2(v)$ also belongs to V^*. Show that either $\phi_1 = 0$ or $\phi_2 = 0$.

ANNIHILATORS

11.31. Let W be the subspace of $\mathbf{R}^4$ spanned by $(1, 2, -3, 4)$, $(1, 3, -2, 6)$ and $(1, 4, -1, 8)$. Find a basis of the annihilator of W.

11.32. Let W be the subspace of $\mathbf{R}^3$ spanned by $(1, 1, 0)$ and $(0, 1, 1)$. Find a basis of the annihilator of W.

11.33. Show that, for any subset S of V, $L(S) = S^{00}$ where $L(S)$ is the linear span of S.

11.34. Let U and W be subspaces of a vector space V of finite dimension. Prove: $(U \cap W)^0 = U^0 + W^0$.

11.35. Suppose $V = U \oplus W$. Prove that $V^* = U^0 \oplus W^0$.

TRANSPOSE OF A LINEAR MAPPING

11.36. Let ϕ be the linear functional on $\mathbf{R}^2$ defined by $\phi(x, y) = 3x - 2y$. For each linear mapping $T : \mathbf{R}^3 \to \mathbf{R}^2$, find $(T^t(\phi))(x, y, z)$:
(i) $T(x, y, z) = (x + y, y + z)$; (ii) $T(x, y, z) = (x + y + z, 2x - y)$.

11.37. Suppose $S : U \to V$ and $T : V \to W$ are linear. Prove that $(T \circ S)^t = S^t \circ T^t$.

11.38. Suppose $T : V \to U$ is linear and V has finite dimension. Prove that $\operatorname{Im} T^t = (\operatorname{Ker} T)^0$.

11.39. Suppose $T : V \to U$ is linear and $u \in U$. Prove that $u \in \operatorname{Im} T$ or there exists $\phi \in V^*$ such that $T^t(\phi) = 0$ and $\phi(u) = 1$.

11.40. Let V be of finite dimension. Show that the mapping $T \mapsto T^t$ is an isomorphism from $\operatorname{Hom}(V, V)$ onto $\operatorname{Hom}(V^*, V^*)$. (Here T is any linear operator on V.)

MISCELLANEOUS PROBLEMS

11.41. Let V be a vector space over **R**. The line segment $\overline{uv}$ joining points $u, v \in V$ is defined by $\overline{uv} = \{tu + (1-t)v : 0 \leq t \leq 1\}$. A subset S of V is termed *convex* if $u, v \in S$ implies $\overline{uv} \subset S$. Let $\phi \in V^*$ and let

$$W^+ = \{v \in V : \phi(v) > 0\}, \quad W = \{v \in V : \phi(v) = 0\}, \quad W^- = \{v \in V : \phi(v) < 0\}$$

Prove that W^+, W and W^- are convex.

11.42. Let V be a vector space of finite dimension. A *hyperplane* H of V is defined to be the kernel of a nonzero linear functional ϕ on V. Show that every subspace of V is the intersection of a finite number of hyperplanes.

Answers to Supplementary Problems

11.19. (i) $6x - 5y + 4z$, (ii) $6x - 9y + 3z$, (iii) $-16x + 4y - 13z$

11.20. $\phi(x, y) = 4x + 7y$, $\phi(-2, 7) = 41$

11.21. (i) $\{\phi_1(x, y, z) = x, \ \phi_2(x, y, z) = y, \ \phi_3(x, y, z) = z\}$
(ii) $\{\phi_1(x, y, z) = -3x - 5y - 2z, \ \phi_2(x, y, z) = 2x + y, \ \phi_3(x, y, z) = x + 2y + z\}$

11.25. (ii) Let $f(t) = t$. Then $\phi_a(f(t)) = a \neq b = \phi_b(f(t))$, and therefore $\phi_a \neq \phi_b$.

11.26. $\left\{ f_1(t) = \dfrac{t^2 - (b+c)t + bc}{(a-b)(a-c)}, \quad f_2(t) = \dfrac{t^2 - (a+c)t + ac}{(b-a)(b-c)}, \quad f_3(t) = \dfrac{t^2 - (a+b)t + ab}{(c-a)(c-b)} \right\}$

11.31. $\{\phi_1(x, y, z, t) = 5x - y + z, \ \phi_2(x, y, z, t) = 2y - t\}$

11.32. $\{\phi(x, y, z) = x - y + z\}$

11.36. (i) $(T^t(\phi))(x, y, z) = 3x + y - 2z$, (ii) $(T^t(\phi))(x, y, z) = -x + 5y + 3z$.

Chapter 12

Bilinear, Quadratic and Hermitian Forms

BILINEAR FORMS

Let V be a vector space of finite dimension over a field K. A *bilinear form* on V is a mapping $f: V \times V \to K$ which satisfies

(i) $f(au_1 + bu_2, v) = af(u_1, v) + bf(u_2, v)$

(ii) $f(u, av_1 + bv_2) = af(u, v_1) + bf(u, v_2)$

for all $a, b \in K$ and all $u_i, v_i \in V$. We express condition (i) by saying f is linear in the first variable, and condition (ii) by saying f is linear in the second variable.

Example 12.1: Let ϕ and σ be arbitrary linear functionals on V. Let $f: V \times V \to K$ be defined by $f(u, v) = \phi(u) \sigma(v)$. Then f is bilinear because ϕ and σ are each linear. (Such a bilinear form f turns out to be the "tensor product" of ϕ and σ and so is sometimes written $f = \phi \otimes \sigma$.)

Example 12.2: Let f be the dot product on $\mathbf{R}^n$; that is,
$$f(u, v) = u \cdot v = a_1 b_1 + a_2 b_2 + \cdots + a_n b_n$$
where $u = (a_i)$ and $v = (b_i)$. Then f is a bilinear form on $\mathbf{R}^n$.

Example 12.3: Let $A = (a_{ij})$ be any $n \times n$ matrix over K. Then A may be viewed as a bilinear form f on K^n by defining
$$f(X, Y) = X^t A Y = (x_1, x_2, \ldots, x_n) \begin{pmatrix} a_{11} & a_{12} & \cdots & a_{1n} \\ a_{21} & a_{22} & \cdots & a_{2n} \\ \cdots\cdots\cdots\cdots\cdots \\ a_{n1} & a_{n2} & \cdots & a_{nn} \end{pmatrix} \begin{pmatrix} y_1 \\ y_2 \\ \cdots \\ y_n \end{pmatrix}$$
$$= \sum_{i,j=1}^{n} a_{ij} x_i y_j = a_{11} x_1 y_1 + a_{12} x_1 y_2 + \cdots + a_{nn} x_n y_n$$

The above formal expression in variables x_i, y_i is termed the *bilinear polynomial* corresponding to the matrix A. Formula (1) below shows that, in a certain sense, every bilinear form is of this type.

We will let $B(V)$ denote the set of bilinear forms on V. A vector space structure is placed on $B(V)$ by defining $f + g$ and kf by:
$$(f + g)(u, v) = f(u, v) + g(u, v)$$
$$(kf)(u, v) = k f(u, v)$$
for any $f, g \in B(V)$ and any $k \in K$. In fact,

Theorem 12.1: Let V be a vector space of dimension n over K. Let $\{\phi_1, \ldots, \phi_n\}$ be a basis of the dual space V^*. Then $\{f_{ij} : i,j = 1, \ldots, n\}$ is a basis of $B(V)$ where f_{ij} is defined by $f_{ij}(u, v) = \phi_i(u) \phi_j(v)$. Thus, in particular, $\dim B(V) = n^2$.

BILINEAR FORMS AND MATRICES

Let f be a bilinear form on V, and let $\{e_1, \ldots, e_n\}$ be a basis of V. Suppose $u, v \in V$ and suppose

$$u = a_1 e_1 + \cdots + a_n e_n, \quad v = b_1 e_1 + \cdots + b_n e_n$$

Then

$$
\begin{aligned}
f(u, v) &= f(a_1 e_1 + \cdots + a_n e_n, \, b_1 e_1 + \cdots + b_n e_n) \\
&= a_1 b_1 f(e_1, e_1) + a_1 b_2 f(e_1, e_2) + \cdots + a_n b_n f(e_n, e_n) = \sum_{i,j=1}^{n} a_i b_j f(e_i, e_j)
\end{aligned}
$$

Thus f is completely determined by the n^2 values $f(e_i, e_j)$.

The matrix $A = (a_{ij})$ where $a_{ij} = f(e_i, e_j)$ is called the *matrix representation of f relative to* the basis $\{e_i\}$ or, simply, the *matrix of f in* $\{e_i\}$. It "represents" f in the sense that

$$f(u, v) = \sum a_i b_j f(e_i, e_j) = (a_1, \ldots, a_n) A \begin{pmatrix} b_1 \\ b_2 \\ \cdot\cdot \\ b_n \end{pmatrix} = [u]_e^t \, A \, [v]_e \tag{1}$$

for all $u, v \in V$. (As usual, $[u]_e$ denotes the coordinate (column) vector of $u \in V$ in the basis $\{e_i\}$.)

We next ask, how does a matrix representing a bilinear form transform when a new basis is selected? The answer is given in the following theorem. (Recall Theorem 7.4 that the transition matrix P from one basis $\{e_i\}$ to another $\{e_i'\}$ has the property that $[u]_e = P[u]_{e'}$ for every $u \in V$.)

Theorem 12.2: Let P be the transition matrix from one basis to another. If A is the matrix of f in the original basis, then

$$B = P^t A P$$

is the matrix of f in the new basis.

The above theorem motivates the following definition.

Definition: A matrix B is said to be *congruent* to a matrix A if there exists an invertible (or nonsingular) matrix P such that $B = P^t A P$.

Thus by the above theorem matrices representing the same bilinear form are congruent. We remark that congruent matrices have the same rank because P and P^t are nonsingular; hence the following definition is well defined.

Definition: The *rank* of a bilinear form f on V, written rank (f), is defined to be the rank of any matrix representation. We say that f is *degenerate* or *nondegenerate* according as to whether rank $(f) < \dim V$ or rank $(f) = \dim V$.

ALTERNATING BILINEAR FORMS

A bilinear form f on V is said to be *alternating* if

$$\text{(i)} \quad f(v, v) = 0$$

for every $v \in V$. If f is alternating, then

$$0 = f(u + v, u + v) = f(u, u) + f(u, v) + f(v, u) + f(v, v)$$

and so

$$\text{(ii)} \quad f(u, v) = -f(v, u)$$

for every $u, v \in V$. A bilinear form which satisfies condition (ii) is said to be *skew symmetric* (or: *anti-symmetric*). If $1 + 1 \neq 0$ in K, then condition (ii) implies $f(v, v) = -f(v, v)$ which implies condition (i). In other words, alternating and skew symmetric are equivalent when $1 + 1 \neq 0$.

The main structure theorem of alternating bilinear forms follows.

Theorem 12.3: Let f be an alternating bilinear form on V. Then there exists a basis of V in which f is represented by a matrix of the form

$$\begin{pmatrix} 0 & 1 & & & & & & & \\ -1 & 0 & & & & & & & \\ & & 0 & 1 & & & & & \\ & & -1 & 0 & & & & & \\ & & & & \ddots & & & & \\ & & & & & 0 & 1 & & \\ & & & & & -1 & 0 & & \\ & & & & & & & 0 & \\ & & & & & & & & 0 \\ & & & & & & & & & \ddots \\ & & & & & & & & & & 0 \end{pmatrix}$$

Moreover, the number of $\begin{pmatrix} 0 & 1 \\ -1 & 0 \end{pmatrix}$ is uniquely determined by f (because it is equal to $\frac{1}{2}$ rank (f)).

In particular, the above theorem shows that an alternating bilinear form must have even rank.

SYMMETRIC BILINEAR FORMS, QUADRATIC FORMS

A bilinear form f on V is said to be *symmetric* if

$$f(u, v) = f(v, u)$$

for every $u, v \in V$. If A is a matrix representation of f, we can write

$$f(X, Y) = X^t A Y = (X^t A Y)^t = Y^t A^t X$$

(We use the fact that $X^t A Y$ is a scalar and therefore equals its transpose.) Thus if f is symmetric,

$$Y^t A^t X = f(X, Y) = f(Y, X) = Y^t A X$$

and since this is true for all vectors X, Y it follows that $A = A^t$ or A is symmetric. Conversely if A is symmetric, then f is symmetric.

The main result for symmetric bilinear forms is given in

Theorem 12.4: Let f be a symmetric bilinear form on V over K (in which $1 + 1 \neq 0$). Then V has a basis $\{v_1, \ldots, v_n\}$ in which f is represented by a diagonal matrix, i.e. $f(v_i, v_j) = 0$ for $i \neq j$.

Alternative Form of Theorem 12.4: Let A be a symmetric matrix over K (in which $1 + 1 \neq 0$). Then there exists an invertible (or: nonsingular) matrix P such that $P^t A P$ is diagonal. That is, A is congruent to a diagonal matrix.

Since an invertible matrix P is a product of elementary matrices (Problem 3.36), one way of obtaining the diagonal form P^tAP is by a sequence of elementary row operations and the same sequence of elementary column operations. These same elementary row operations on I will yield P^t. This method is illustrated in the next example.

Example 12.4: Let $A = \begin{pmatrix} 1 & 2 & -3 \\ 2 & 5 & -4 \\ -3 & -4 & 8 \end{pmatrix}$, a symmetric matrix. It is convenient to form the block matrix (A, I):

$$(A, I) = \begin{pmatrix} 1 & 2 & -3 & \vdots & 1 & 0 & 0 \\ 2 & 5 & -4 & \vdots & 0 & 1 & 0 \\ -3 & -4 & 8 & \vdots & 0 & 0 & 1 \end{pmatrix}$$

We apply the operations $R_2 \to -2R_1 + R_2$ and $R_3 \to 3R_1 + R_3$ to (A, I), and then the corresponding operations $C_2 \to -2C_1 + C_2$ and $C_3 \to 3C_1 + C_3$ to A to obtain

$$\begin{pmatrix} 1 & 2 & -3 & \vdots & 1 & 0 & 0 \\ 0 & 1 & 2 & \vdots & -2 & 1 & 0 \\ 0 & 2 & -1 & \vdots & 3 & 0 & 1 \end{pmatrix} \quad \text{and then} \quad \begin{pmatrix} 1 & 0 & 0 & \vdots & 1 & 0 & 0 \\ 0 & 1 & 2 & \vdots & -2 & 1 & 0 \\ 0 & 2 & -1 & \vdots & 3 & 0 & 1 \end{pmatrix}$$

We next apply the operation $R_3 \to -2R_2 + R_3$ and then the corresponding operation $C_3 \to -2C_2 + C_3$ to obtain

$$\begin{pmatrix} 1 & 0 & 0 & \vdots & 1 & 0 & 0 \\ 0 & 1 & 2 & \vdots & -2 & 1 & 0 \\ 0 & 0 & -5 & \vdots & 7 & -2 & 1 \end{pmatrix} \quad \text{and then} \quad \begin{pmatrix} 1 & 0 & 0 & \vdots & 1 & 0 & 0 \\ 0 & 1 & 0 & \vdots & -2 & 1 & 0 \\ 0 & 0 & -5 & \vdots & 7 & -2 & 1 \end{pmatrix}$$

Now A has been diagonalized. We set

$$P = \begin{pmatrix} 1 & -2 & 7 \\ 0 & 1 & -2 \\ 0 & 0 & 1 \end{pmatrix} \quad \text{and then} \quad P^tAP = \begin{pmatrix} 1 & 0 & 0 \\ 0 & 1 & 0 \\ 0 & 0 & -5 \end{pmatrix}$$

Definition: A mapping $q : V \to K$ is called a *quadratic form* if $q(v) = f(v, v)$ for some symmetric bilinear form f on V.

We call q the quadratic form *associated* with the symmetric bilinear form f. If $1 + 1 \neq 0$ in K, then f is obtainable from q according to the identity

$$f(u, v) = \tfrac{1}{2}(q(u + v) - q(u) - q(v))$$

The above formula is called the *polar form* of f.

Now if f is represented by a symmetric matrix $A = (a_{ij})$, then q is represented in the form

$$q(X) = f(X, X) = X^tAX = (x_1, \ldots, x_n) \begin{pmatrix} a_{11} & a_{12} & \ldots & a_{1n} \\ a_{21} & a_{22} & \ldots & a_{2n} \\ \cdots\cdots\cdots\cdots\cdots\cdots \\ a_{n1} & a_{n2} & \ldots & a_{nn} \end{pmatrix} \begin{pmatrix} x_1 \\ x_2 \\ \cdot\cdot \\ x_n \end{pmatrix}$$

$$= \sum_{i,j} a_{ij}x_ix_j = a_{11}x_1^2 + a_{22}x_2^2 + \cdots + a_{nn}x_n^2 + 2\sum_{i<j} a_{ij}x_ix_j$$

The above formal expression in variables x_i is termed the *quadratic polynomial* corresponding to the symmetric matrix A. Observe that if the matrix A is diagonal, then q has the *diagonal representation*

$$q(X) = X^tAX = a_{11}x_1^2 + a_{22}x_2^2 + \cdots + a_{nn}x_n^2$$

that is, the quadratic polynomial representing q will contain no "cross product" terms. By Theorem 12.4, every quadratic form has such a representation (when $1 + 1 \neq 0$).

Example 12.5:   Consider the following quadratic form on $\mathbf{R}^2$:

$$q(x, y) \;=\; 2x^2 - 12xy + 5y^2$$

One way of diagonalizing q is by the method known as "completing the square" which is fully described in Problem 12.35. In this case, we make the substitution $x = s + 3t$, $y = t$ to obtain the diagonal form

$$q(x, y) \;=\; 2(s + 3t)^2 - 12(s + 3t)t + 5t^2 \;=\; 2s^2 - 13t^2$$

REAL SYMMETRIC BILINEAR FORMS. LAW OF INERTIA

In this section we treat symmetric bilinear forms and quadratic forms on vector spaces over the real field $\mathbf{R}$. These forms appear in many branches of mathematics and physics. The special nature of $\mathbf{R}$ permits an independent theory. The main result follows.

Theorem 12.5:   Let f be a symmetric bilinear form on V over $\mathbf{R}$. Then there is a basis of V in which f is represented by a diagonal matrix; every other diagonal representation has the same number P of positive entries and the same number N of negative entries. The difference $S = P - N$ is called the *signature* of f.

A real symmetric bilinear form f is said to be *nonnegative semidefinite* if

$$q(v) \;=\; f(v, v) \;\geqq\; 0$$

for every vector v; and is said to be *positive definite* if

$$q(v) \;=\; f(v, v) \;>\; 0$$

for every vector $v \neq 0$. By the above theorem,

  (i) f is nonnegative semidefinite if and only if $S = \text{rank}\,(f)$
  (ii) f is positive definite if and only if $S = \dim V$

where S is the signature of f.

Example 12.6:   Let f be the dot product on $\mathbf{R}^n$; that is,

$$f(u, v) \;=\; u \cdot v \;=\; a_1 b_1 + a_2 b_2 + \cdots + a_n b_n$$

where $u = (a_i)$ and $v = (b_i)$. Note that f is symmetric since

$$f(u, v) \;=\; u \cdot v \;=\; v \cdot u \;=\; f(v, u)$$

Furthermore, f is positive definite because

$$f(u, u) \;=\; a_1^2 + a_2^2 + \cdots + a_n^2 \;>\; 0$$

when $u \neq 0$.

In the next chapter we will see how a real quadratic form q transforms when the transition matrix P is "orthogonal". If no condition is placed on P, then q can be represented in diagonal form with only 1's and -1's as nonzero coefficients. Specifically,

Corollary 12.6:   Any real quadratic form q has a unique representation in the form

$$q(x_1, \ldots, x_n) \;=\; x_1^2 + \cdots + x_s^2 - x_{s+1}^2 - \cdots - x_r^2$$

The above result for real quadratic forms is sometimes referred to as the Law of Inertia or Sylvester's Theorem.

HERMITIAN FORMS

Let V be a vector space of finite dimension over the complex field $\mathbf{C}$. Let $f: V \times V \to \mathbf{C}$ be such that

$$\text{(i)} \qquad f(au_1 + bu_2, v) = a\, f(u_1, v) + b\, f(u_2, v)$$

$$\text{(ii)} \qquad f(u, v) = \overline{f(v, u)}$$

where $a, b \in \mathbf{C}$ and $u_i, v \in V$. Then f is called a *Hermitian form* on V. (As usual, $\overline{k}$ denotes the complex conjugate of $k \in \mathbf{C}$.) By (i) and (ii),

$$f(u, av_1 + bv_2) = \overline{f(av_1 + bv_2, u)} = \overline{a\, f(v_1, u) + b\, f(v_2, u)}$$
$$= \overline{a}\, \overline{f(v_1, u)} + \overline{b}\, \overline{f(v_2, u)} = \overline{a}\, f(u, v_1) + \overline{b}\, f(u, v_2)$$

That is, $\qquad\qquad$ (iii) $\quad f(u, av_1 + bv_2) = \overline{a}\, f(u, v_1) + \overline{b}\, f(u, v_2)$

As before, we express condition (i) by saying f is linear in the first variable. On the other hand, we express condition (iii) by saying f is *conjugate linear* in the second variable. Note that, by (ii), $f(v, v) = \overline{f(v, v)}$ and so $f(v, v)$ is real for every $v \in V$.

> **Example 12.7:**   Let $A = (a_{ij})$ be an $n \times n$ matrix over $\mathbf{C}$. We write $\bar{A}$ for the matrix obtained by taking the complex conjugate of every entry of A, that is, $\bar{A} = (\overline{a_{ij}})$. We also write A^* for $\bar{A}^t = \overline{A^t}$. The matrix A is said to be Hermitian if $A^* = A$, i.e. if $a_{ij} = \overline{a_{ji}}$. If A is Hermitian, then $f(X, Y) = X^t A\, \bar{Y}$ defines a Hermitian form on $\mathbf{C}^n$ (Problem 12.16).

The mapping $q: V \to \mathbf{R}$ defined by $q(v) = f(v, v)$ is called the *Hermitian quadratic form* or *complex quadratic form* associated with the Hermitian form f. We can obtain f from q according to the following identity called the *polar form* of f:

$$f(u, v) = \tfrac{1}{4}(q(u+v) - q(u-v)) + \tfrac{i}{4}(q(u+iv) - q(u-iv))$$

Now suppose $\{e_1, \ldots, e_n\}$ is a basis of V. The matrix $H = (h_{ij})$ where $h_{ij} = f(e_i, e_j)$ is called the *matrix representation* of f in the basis $\{e_i\}$. By (ii), $f(e_i, e_j) = \overline{f(e_j, e_i)}$; hence H is Hermitian and, in particular, the diagonal entries of H are real. Thus any diagonal representation of f contains only real entries. The next theorem is the complex analogue of Theorem 12.5 on real symmetric bilinear forms.

Theorem 12.7:   Let f be a Hermitian form on V. Then there exists a basis $\{e_1, \ldots, e_n\}$ of V in which f is represented by a diagonal matrix, i.e. $f(e_i, e_j) = 0$ for $i \neq j$. Moreover, every diagonal representation of f has the same number P of positive entries, and the same number N of negative entries. The difference $S = P - N$ is called the *signature* of f.

Analogously, a Hermitian form f is said to be *nonnegative semidefinite* if

$$q(v) = f(v, v) \geqq 0$$

for every $v \in V$, and is said to be *positive definite* if

$$q(v) = f(v, v) > 0$$

for every $v \neq 0$.

> **Example 12.8:**   Let f be the dot product on $\mathbf{C}^n$; that is,
>
> $$f(u, v) = u \cdot v = z_1 \overline{w}_1 + z_2 \overline{w}_2 + \cdots + z_n \overline{w}_n$$
>
> where $u = (z_i)$ and $v = (w_i)$. Then f is a Hermitian form on $\mathbf{C}^n$. Moreover, f is positive definite since, for any $v \neq 0$,
>
> $$f(u, u) = z_1 \bar{z}_1 + z_2 \bar{z}_2 + \cdots + z_n \bar{z}_n = |z_1|^2 + |z_2|^2 + \cdots + |z_n|^2 > 0$$

Solved Problems

BILINEAR FORMS

12.1. Let $u = (x_1, x_2, x_3)$ and $v = (y_1, y_2, y_3)$, and let
$$f(u, v) \;=\; 3x_1y_1 - 2x_1y_2 + 5x_2y_1 + 7x_2y_2 - 8x_2y_3 + 4x_3y_2 - x_3y_3$$
Express f in matrix notation.

Let A be the 3×3 matrix whose ij-entry is the coefficient of x_iy_j. Then
$$f(u, v) \;=\; X^t A Y \;=\; (x_1, x_2, x_3) \begin{pmatrix} 3 & -2 & 0 \\ 5 & 7 & -8 \\ 0 & 4 & -1 \end{pmatrix} \begin{pmatrix} y_1 \\ y_2 \\ y_3 \end{pmatrix}$$

12.2. Let A be an $n \times n$ matrix over K. Show that the following mapping f is a bilinear form on K^n: $f(X, Y) = X^t A Y$.

For any $a, b \in K$ and any $X_i, Y_i \in K^n$,
$$\begin{aligned} f(aX_1 + bX_2, Y) &= (aX_1 + bX_2)^t A Y = (aX_1^t + bX_2^t) A Y \\ &= aX_1^t A Y + b X_2^t A Y = a f(X_1, Y) + b f(X_2, Y) \end{aligned}$$

Hence f is linear in the first variable. Also,
$$f(X, aY_1 + bY_2) \;=\; X^t A(aY_1 + bY_2) \;=\; aX^t A Y_1 + bX^t A Y_2 \;=\; a f(X, Y_1) + b f(X, Y_2)$$

Hence f is linear in the second variable, and so f is a bilinear form on K^n.

12.3. Let f be the bilinear form on $\mathbf{R}^2$ defined by
$$f((x_1, x_2), (y_1, y_2)) \;=\; 2x_1y_1 - 3x_1y_2 + x_2y_2$$

(i)   Find the matrix A of f in the basis $\{u_1 = (1, 0), u_2 = (1, 1)\}$.
(ii) Find the matrix B of f in the basis $\{v_1 = (2, 1), v_2 = (1, -1)\}$.
(iii) Find the transition matrix P from the basis $\{u_i\}$ to the basis $\{v_i\}$, and verify that $B = P^t A P$.

(i)   Set $A = (a_{ij})$ where $a_{ij} = f(u_i, u_j)$:
$$\begin{aligned} a_{11} &= f(u_1, u_1) = f((1, 0), (1, 0)) = 2 - 0 + 0 = 2 \\ a_{12} &= f(u_1, u_2) = f((1, 0), (1, 1)) = 2 - 3 + 0 = -1 \\ a_{21} &= f(u_2, u_1) = f((1, 1), (1, 0)) = 2 - 0 + 0 = 2 \\ a_{22} &= f(u_2, u_2) = f((1, 1), (1, 1)) = 2 - 3 + 1 = 0 \end{aligned}$$

Thus $A = \begin{pmatrix} 2 & -1 \\ 2 & 0 \end{pmatrix}$ is the matrix of f in the basis $\{u_1, u_2\}$.

(ii) Set $B = (b_{ij})$ where $b_{ij} = f(v_i, v_j)$:
$$\begin{aligned} b_{11} &= f(v_1, v_1) = f((2, 1), (2, 1)) &= 8 - 6 + 1 = 3 \\ b_{12} &= f(v_1, v_2) = f((2, 1), (1, -1)) &= 4 + 6 - 1 = 9 \\ b_{21} &= f(v_2, v_1) = f((1, -1), (2, 1)) &= 4 - 3 - 1 = 0 \\ b_{22} &= f(v_2, v_2) = f((1, -1), (1, -1)) &= 2 + 3 + 1 = 6 \end{aligned}$$

Thus $B = \begin{pmatrix} 3 & 9 \\ 0 & 6 \end{pmatrix}$ is the matrix of f in the basis $\{v_1, v_2\}$.

(iii) We must write v_1 and v_2 in terms of the u_i:
$$\begin{aligned} v_1 &= (2, 1) = (1, 0) + (1, 1) &= u_1 + u_2 \\ v_2 &= (1, -1) = 2(1, 0) - (1, 1) &= 2u_1 - u_2 \end{aligned}$$

Then $\quad P = \begin{pmatrix} 1 & 2 \\ 1 & -1 \end{pmatrix}$ and so $\quad P^t = \begin{pmatrix} 1 & 1 \\ 2 & -1 \end{pmatrix}$. Thus

$$P^t A P = \begin{pmatrix} 1 & 1 \\ 2 & -1 \end{pmatrix}\begin{pmatrix} 2 & -1 \\ 2 & 0 \end{pmatrix}\begin{pmatrix} 1 & 2 \\ 1 & -1 \end{pmatrix} = \begin{pmatrix} 3 & 9 \\ 0 & 6 \end{pmatrix} = B$$

12.4. Prove Theorem 12.1: Let V be a vector space of dimension n over K. Let $\{\phi_1, \ldots, \phi_n\}$ be a basis of the dual space V^*. Then $\{f_{ij} : i,j = 1, \ldots, n\}$ is a basis of $B(V)$ where f_{ij} is defined by $f_{ij}(u, v) = \phi_i(u)\,\phi_j(v)$. Thus, in particular, $\dim B(V) = n^2$.

Let $\{e_1, \ldots, e_n\}$ be the basis of V dual to $\{\phi_i\}$. We first show that $\{f_{ij}\}$ spans $B(V)$. Let $f \in B(V)$ and suppose $f(e_i, e_j) = a_{ij}$. We claim that $f = \sum a_{ij} f_{ij}$. It suffices to show that $f(e_s, e_t) = \left(\sum a_{ij} f_{ij}\right)(e_s, e_t)$ for $s,t = 1, \ldots, n$. We have

$$\left(\sum a_{ij} f_{ij}\right)(e_s, e_t) = \sum a_{ij} f_{ij}(e_s, e_t) = \sum a_{ij}\,\phi_i(e_s)\,\phi_j(e_t)$$
$$= \sum a_{ij}\,\delta_{is}\,\delta_{jt} = a_{st} = f(e_s, e_t)$$

as required. Hence $\{f_{ij}\}$ spans $B(V)$.

It remains to show that $\{f_{ij}\}$ is linearly independent. Suppose $\sum a_{ij} f_{ij} = 0$. Then for $s,t = 1, \ldots, n$,

$$0 = 0(e_s, e_t) = \left(\sum a_{ij} f_{ij}\right)(e_s, e_t) = a_{rs}$$

The last step follows as above. Thus $\{f_{ij}\}$ is independent and hence is a basis of $B(V)$.

12.5. Let $[f]$ denote the matrix representation of a bilinear form f on V relative to a basis $\{e_1, \ldots, e_n\}$ of V. Show that the mapping $f \mapsto [f]$ is an isomorphism of $B(V)$ onto the vector space of n-square matrices.

Since f is completely determined by the scalars $f(e_i, e_j)$, the mapping $f \mapsto [f]$ is one-to-one and onto. It suffices to show that the mapping $f \mapsto [f]$ is a homomorphism; that is, that

$$[af + bg] = a[f] + b[g] \tag{*}$$

However, for $i,j = 1, \ldots, n$,

$$(af + bg)(e_i, e_j) = af(e_i, e_j) + bg(e_i, e_j)$$

which is a restatement of (*). Thus the result is proved.

12.6. Prove Theorem 12.2: Let P be the transition matrix from one basis $\{e_i\}$ to another basis $\{e_i'\}$. If A is the matrix of f in the original basis $\{e_i\}$, then $B = P^t A P$ is the matrix of f in the new basis $\{e_i'\}$.

Let $u, v \in V$. Since P is the transition matrix from $\{e_i\}$ to $\{e_i'\}$, we have $P[u]_{e'} = [u]_e$ and $P[v]_{e'} = [v]_e$; hence $[u]_e^t = [u]_{e'}^t\,P^t$. Thus

$$f(u, v) = [u]_e^t\,A\,[v]_e = [u]_{e'}^t\,P^t A P [v]_{e'}$$

Since u and v are arbitrary elements of V, $P^t A P$ is the matrix of f in the basis $\{e_i'\}$.

SYMMETRIC BILINEAR FORMS. QUADRATIC FORMS

12.7. Find the symmetric matrix which corresponds to each of the following quadratic polynomials:

(i) $q(x, y) = 4x^2 - 6xy - 7y^2$ (iii) $q(x, y, z) = 3x^2 + 4xy - y^2 + 8xz - 6yz + z^2$

(ii) $q(x, y) = xy + y^2$ (iv) $q(x, y, z) = x^2 - 2yz + xz$

The symmetric matrix $A = (a_{ij})$ representing $q(x_1, \ldots, x_n)$ has the diagonal entry a_{ii} equal to the coefficient of x_i^2 and has the entries a_{ij} and a_{ji} each equal to half the coefficient of $x_i x_j$. Thus

$$\begin{pmatrix} 4 & -3 \\ -3 & -7 \end{pmatrix} \qquad \begin{pmatrix} 0 & \frac{1}{2} \\ \frac{1}{2} & 1 \end{pmatrix} \qquad \begin{pmatrix} 3 & 2 & 4 \\ 2 & -1 & -3 \\ 4 & -3 & 1 \end{pmatrix} \qquad \begin{pmatrix} 1 & 0 & \frac{1}{2} \\ 0 & 0 & -1 \\ \frac{1}{2} & -1 & 0 \end{pmatrix}$$

$$\text{(i)} \qquad\qquad\quad \text{(ii)} \qquad\qquad\qquad \text{(iii)} \qquad\qquad\qquad \text{(iv)}$$

12.8. For each of the following real symmetric matrices A, find a nonsingular matrix P such that $P^t A P$ is diagonal and also find its signature:

$$\text{(i)} \quad A = \begin{pmatrix} 1 & -3 & 2 \\ -3 & 7 & -5 \\ 2 & -5 & 8 \end{pmatrix} \qquad \text{(ii)} \quad A = \begin{pmatrix} 0 & 1 & 1 \\ 1 & -2 & 2 \\ 1 & 2 & -1 \end{pmatrix}$$

(i) First form the block matrix (A, I):

$$(A, I) = \begin{pmatrix} 1 & -3 & 2 & \vdots & 1 & 0 & 0 \\ -3 & 7 & -5 & \vdots & 0 & 1 & 0 \\ 2 & -5 & 8 & \vdots & 0 & 0 & 1 \end{pmatrix}$$

Apply the row operations $R_2 \to 3R_1 + R_2$ and $R_3 \to -2R_1 + R_3$ to (A, I) and then the corresponding column operations $C_2 \to 3C_1 + C_2$ and $C_3 \to -2C_1 + C_3$ to A to obtain

$$\begin{pmatrix} 1 & -3 & 2 & \vdots & 1 & 0 & 0 \\ 0 & -2 & 1 & \vdots & 3 & 1 & 0 \\ 0 & 1 & 4 & \vdots & -2 & 0 & 1 \end{pmatrix} \quad \text{and then} \quad \begin{pmatrix} 1 & 0 & 0 & \vdots & 1 & 0 & 0 \\ 0 & -2 & 1 & \vdots & 3 & 1 & 0 \\ 0 & 1 & 4 & \vdots & -2 & 0 & 1 \end{pmatrix}$$

Next apply the row operation $R_3 \to R_2 + 2R_3$ and then the corresponding column operation $C_3 \to C_2 + 2C_3$ to obtain

$$\begin{pmatrix} 1 & 0 & 0 & \vdots & 1 & 0 & 0 \\ 0 & -2 & 1 & \vdots & 3 & 1 & 0 \\ 0 & 0 & 9 & \vdots & -1 & 1 & 2 \end{pmatrix} \quad \text{and then} \quad \begin{pmatrix} 1 & 0 & 0 & \vdots & 1 & 0 & 0 \\ 0 & -2 & 0 & \vdots & 3 & 1 & 0 \\ 0 & 0 & 18 & \vdots & -1 & 1 & 2 \end{pmatrix}$$

Now A has been diagonalized. Set $P = \begin{pmatrix} 1 & 3 & -1 \\ 0 & 1 & 1 \\ 0 & 0 & 2 \end{pmatrix}$; then $P^t A P = \begin{pmatrix} 1 & 0 & 0 \\ 0 & -2 & 0 \\ 0 & 0 & 18 \end{pmatrix}$.

The signature S of A is $S = 2 - 1 = 1$.

(ii) First form the block matrix (A, I):

$$(A, I) = \begin{pmatrix} 0 & 1 & 1 & \vdots & 1 & 0 & 0 \\ 1 & -2 & 2 & \vdots & 0 & 1 & 0 \\ 1 & 2 & -1 & \vdots & 0 & 0 & 1 \end{pmatrix}$$

In order to bring the nonzero diagonal entry -1 into the first diagonal position, apply the row operation $R_1 \leftrightarrow R_3$ and then the corresponding column operation $C_1 \leftrightarrow C_3$ to obtain

$$\begin{pmatrix} 1 & 2 & -1 & \vdots & 0 & 0 & 1 \\ 1 & -2 & 2 & \vdots & 0 & 1 & 0 \\ 0 & 1 & 1 & \vdots & 1 & 0 & 0 \end{pmatrix} \quad \text{and then} \quad \begin{pmatrix} -1 & 2 & 1 & \vdots & 0 & 0 & 1 \\ 2 & -2 & 1 & \vdots & 0 & 1 & 0 \\ 1 & 1 & 0 & \vdots & 1 & 0 & 0 \end{pmatrix}$$

Apply the row operations $R_2 \to 2R_1 + R_2$ and $R_3 \to R_1 + R_3$ and then the corresponding column operations $C_2 \to 2C_1 + C_2$ and $C_3 \to C_1 + C_3$ to obtain

$$\begin{pmatrix} -1 & 2 & 1 & \vdots & 0 & 0 & 1 \\ 0 & 2 & 3 & \vdots & 0 & 1 & 2 \\ 0 & 3 & 1 & \vdots & 1 & 0 & 1 \end{pmatrix} \quad \text{and then} \quad \begin{pmatrix} -1 & 0 & 0 & \vdots & 0 & 0 & 1 \\ 0 & 2 & 3 & \vdots & 0 & 1 & 2 \\ 0 & 3 & 1 & \vdots & 1 & 0 & 1 \end{pmatrix}$$

Apply the row operation $R_3 \to -3R_2 + 2R_3$ and then the corresponding column operation $C_3 \to -3C_2 + 2C_3$ to obtain

$$\begin{pmatrix} -1 & 0 & 0 & 0 & 0 & 1 \\ 0 & 2 & 3 & 0 & 1 & 2 \\ 0 & 0 & -7 & 2 & -3 & -4 \end{pmatrix} \quad \text{and then} \quad \begin{pmatrix} -1 & 0 & 0 & 0 & 0 & 1 \\ 0 & 2 & 0 & 0 & 1 & 2 \\ 0 & 0 & -14 & 2 & -3 & -4 \end{pmatrix}$$

Now A has been diagonalized. Set $P = \begin{pmatrix} 0 & 0 & 2 \\ 0 & 1 & -3 \\ 1 & 2 & -4 \end{pmatrix}$; then $P^t A P = \begin{pmatrix} -1 & 0 & 0 \\ 0 & 2 & 0 \\ 0 & 0 & -14 \end{pmatrix}$.

The signature S of A is the difference $S = 1 - 2 = -1$.

12.9. Suppose $1 + 1 \neq 0$ in K. Give a formal algorithm to diagonalize (under congruence) a symmetric matrix $A = (a_{ij})$ over K.

Case I: $a_{11} \neq 0$. Apply the row operations $R_i \to -a_{i1}R_1 + a_{11}R_i$, $i = 2, \ldots, n$, and then the corresponding column operations $C_i \to -a_{i1}C_1 + a_{11}C_i$ to reduce A to the form $\begin{pmatrix} a_{11} & 0 \\ 0 & B \end{pmatrix}$.

Case II: $a_{11} = 0$ but $a_{ii} \neq 0$, for some $i > 1$. Apply the row operation $R_1 \leftrightarrow R_i$ and then the corresponding column operation $C_1 \leftrightarrow C_i$ to bring a_{ii} into the first diagonal position. This reduces the matrix to Case I.

Case III: All diagonal entries $a_{ii} = 0$. Choose i, j such that $a_{ij} \neq 0$, and apply the row operation $R_i \to R_j + R_i$ and the corresponding column operation $C_i \to C_j + C_i$ to bring $2a_{ij} \neq 0$ into the ith diagonal position. This reduces the matrix to Case II.

In each of the cases, we can finally reduce A to the form $\begin{pmatrix} a_{11} & 0 \\ 0 & B \end{pmatrix}$ where B is a symmetric matrix of order less than A. By induction we can finally bring A into diagonal form.

Remark: The hypothesis that $1 + 1 \neq 0$ in K, is used in Case III where we state that $2a_{ij} \neq 0$.

12.10. Let q be the quadratic form associated with the symmetric bilinear form f. Verify the following polar form of f: $f(u, v) = \frac{1}{2}(q(u + v) - q(u) - q(v))$. (Assume that $1 + 1 \neq 0$.)

$$\begin{aligned} q(u + v) - q(u) - q(v) &= f(u + v, u + v) - f(u, u) - f(v, v) \\ &= f(u, u) + f(u, v) + f(v, u) + f(v, v) - f(u, u) - f(v, v) \\ &= 2f(u, v) \end{aligned}$$

If $1 + 1 \neq 0$, we can divide by 2 to obtain the required identity.

12.11. Prove Theorem 12.4: Let f be a symmetric bilinear form on V over K (in which $1 + 1 \neq 0$). Then V has a basis $\{v_1, \ldots, v_n\}$ in which f is represented by a diagonal matrix, i.e. $f(v_i, v_j) = 0$ for $i \neq j$.

Method 1.

If $f = 0$ or if $\dim V = 1$, then the theorem clearly holds. Hence we can suppose $f \neq 0$ and $\dim V = n > 1$. If $q(v) = f(v, v) = 0$ for every $v \in V$, then the polar form of f (see Problem 12.10) implies that $f = 0$. Hence we can assume there is a vector $v_1 \in V$ such that $f(v_1, v_1) \neq 0$. Let U be the subspace spanned by v_1 and let W consist of those vectors $v \in V$ for which $f(v_1, v) = 0$. We claim that $V = U \oplus W$.

(i) Proof that $U \cap W = \{0\}$: Suppose $u \in U \cap W$. Since $u \in U$, $u = kv_1$ for some scalar $k \in K$. Since $u \in W$, $0 = f(u, u) = f(kv_1, kv_1) = k^2 f(v_1, v_1)$. But $f(v_1, v_1) \neq 0$; hence $k = 0$ and therefore $u = kv_1 = 0$. Thus $U \cap W = \{0\}$.

(ii) Proof that $V = U + W$: Let $v \in V$. Set

$$w \;=\; v - \frac{f(v_1, v)}{f(v_1, v_1)}\, v_1 \tag{1}$$

Then
$$f(v_1, w) \;=\; f(v_1, v) - \frac{f(v_1, v)}{f(v_1, v_1)} f(v_1, v_1) \;=\; 0$$

Thus $w \in W$. By (1), v is the sum of an element of U and an element of W. Thus $V = U + W$. By (i) and (ii), $V = U \oplus W$.

Now f restricted to W is a symmetric bilinear form on W. But $\dim W = n - 1$; hence by induction there is a basis $\{v_2, \ldots, v_n\}$ of W such that $f(v_i, v_j) = 0$ for $i \neq j$ and $2 \le i, j \le n$. But by the very definition of W, $f(v_1, v_j) = 0$ for $j = 2, \ldots, n$. Therefore the basis $\{v_1, \ldots, v_n\}$ of V has the required property that $f(v_i, v_j) = 0$ for $i \neq j$.

Method 2.

The algorithm in Problem 12.9 shows that every symmetric matrix over K is congruent to a diagonal matrix. This is equivalent to the statement that f has a diagonal matrix representation.

12.12. Let $A = \begin{pmatrix} a_1 & & & \\ & a_2 & & \\ & & \ddots & \\ & & & a_n \end{pmatrix}$, a diagonal matrix over K.   Show that:

(i) for any nonzero scalars $k_1, \ldots, k_n \in K$, A is congruent to a diagonal matrix with diagonal entries $a_i k_i^2$;

(ii) if K is the complex field **C**, then A is congruent to a diagonal matrix with only 1's and 0's as diagonal entries;

(iii) if K is the real field **R**, then A is congruent to a diagonal matrix with only 1's, -1's and 0's as diagonal entries.

(i) Let P be the diagonal matrix with diagonal entries k_i. Then

$$P^t A P = \begin{pmatrix} k_1 & & & \\ & k_2 & & \\ & & \ddots & \\ & & & k_n \end{pmatrix} \begin{pmatrix} a_1 & & & \\ & a_2 & & \\ & & \ddots & \\ & & & a_n \end{pmatrix} \begin{pmatrix} k_1 & & & \\ & k_2 & & \\ & & \ddots & \\ & & & k_n \end{pmatrix} = \begin{pmatrix} a_1 k_1^2 & & & \\ & a_2 k_2^2 & & \\ & & \ddots & \\ & & & a_n k_n^2 \end{pmatrix}$$

(ii) Let P be the diagonal matrix with diagonal entries $b_i = \begin{cases} 1/\sqrt{a_i} & \text{if } a_i \neq 0 \\ 1 & \text{if } a_i = 0 \end{cases}$. Then $P^t A P$ has the required form.

(iii) Let P be the diagonal matrix with diagonal entries $b_i = \begin{cases} 1/\sqrt{|a_i|} & \text{if } a_i \neq 0 \\ 1 & \text{if } a_i = 0 \end{cases}$. Then $P^t A P$ has the required form.

Remark. We emphasize that (ii) is no longer true if congruence is replaced by Hermitian congruence (see Problems 12.40 and 12.41).

12.13. Prove Theorem 12.5:   Let f be a symmetric bilinear form on V over R.   Then there is a basis of V in which f is represented by a diagonal matrix, and every other diagonal representation of f has the same number of positive entries and the same number of negative entries.

By Theorem 12.4, there is a basis $\{u_1, \ldots, u_n\}$ of V in which f is represented by a diagonal matrix, say, with P positive and N negative entries. Now suppose $\{w_1, \ldots, w_n\}$ is another basis of V in which f is represented by a diagonal matrix, say, with P' positive and N' negative entries. We can assume without loss in generality that the positive entries in each matrix appear first. Since $\operatorname{rank}(f) = P + N = P' + N'$, it suffices to prove that $P = P'$.

Let U be the linear span of $u_1, \ldots, u_P$ and let W be the linear span of $w_{P'+1}, \ldots, w_n$. Then $f(v, v) > 0$ for every nonzero $v \in U$, and $f(v, v) \leq 0$ for every nonzero $v \in W$. Hence $U \cap W = \{0\}$. Note that $\dim U = P$ and $\dim W = n - P'$. Thus

$$\dim(U + W) = \dim U + \dim W - \dim(U \cap W) = P + (n - P') - 0 = P - P' + n$$

But $\dim(U + W) \leq \dim V = n$; hence $P - P' + n \leq n$ or $P \leq P'$. Similarly, $P' \leq P$ and therefore $P = P'$, as required.

Remark. The above theorem and proof depend only on the concept of positivity. Thus the theorem is true for any subfield K of the real field **R**.

12.14. An $n \times n$ real symmetric matrix A is said to be *positive definite* if $X^t A X > 0$ for every nonzero (column) vector $X \in \mathbf{R}^n$, i.e. if A is positive definite viewed as a bilinear form. Let B be any real nonsingular matrix. Show that (i) $B^t B$ is symmetric and (ii) $B^t B$ is positive definite.

(i) $(B^t B)^t = B^t B^{tt} = B^t B$; hence $B^t B$ is symmetric.

(ii)   Since B is nonsingular, $BX \neq 0$ for any nonzero $X \in \mathbf{R}^n$. Hence the dot product of BX with itself, $BX \cdot BX = (BX)^t(BX)$, is positive. Thus $X^t(B^t B)X = (X^t B^t)(BX) = (BX)^t(BX) > 0$ as required.

HERMITIAN FORMS

12.15. Determine which of the following matrices are Hermitian:

$$\begin{pmatrix} 2 & 2+3i & 4-5i \\ 2-3i & 5 & 6+2i \\ 4+5i & 6-2i & -7 \end{pmatrix} \quad \begin{pmatrix} 3 & 2-i & 4+i \\ 2-i & 6 & i \\ 4+i & i & 3 \end{pmatrix} \quad \begin{pmatrix} 4 & -3 & 5 \\ -3 & 2 & 1 \\ 5 & 1 & -6 \end{pmatrix}$$

$$\text{(i)} \qquad\qquad\qquad\qquad \text{(ii)} \qquad\qquad\qquad\qquad \text{(iii)}$$

A matrix $A = (a_{ij})$ is Hermitian iff $A = A^*$, i.e. iff $a_{ij} = \overline{a_{ji}}$.

(i)   The matrix is Hermitian, since it is equal to its conjugate transpose.

(ii)   The matrix is not Hermitian, even though it is symmetric.

(iii) The matrix is Hermitian. In fact, a real matrix is Hermitian if and only if it is symmetric.

12.16. Let A be a Hermitian matrix. Show that f is a Hermitian form on $\mathbf{C}^n$ where f is defined by $f(X, Y) = X^t A \bar{Y}$.

For all $a, b \in \mathbf{C}$ and all $X_1, X_2, Y \in \mathbf{C}^n$,

$$\begin{aligned} f(aX_1 + bX_2, Y) &= (aX_1 + bX_2)^t A \bar{Y} = (aX_1^t + bX_2^t) A \bar{Y} \\ &= a X_1^t A \bar{Y} + b X_2^t A \bar{Y} = a f(X_1, Y) + b f(X_2, Y) \end{aligned}$$

Hence f is linear in the first variable. Also,

$$\overline{f(X, Y)} = \overline{X^t A \bar{Y}} = \overline{(X^t A \bar{Y})^t} = \overline{\bar{Y}^t A^t X} = Y^t A^* \bar{X} = Y^t A \bar{X} = f(Y, X)$$

Hence f is a Hermitian form on $\mathbf{C}^n$. (*Remark.* We use the fact that $X^t A \bar{Y}$ is a scalar and so it is equal to its transpose.)

12.17. Let f be a Hermitian form on V. Let H be the matrix of f in a basis $\{e_1, \ldots, e_n\}$ of V. Show that:

(i) $f(u, v) = [u]_e^t H \overline{[v]_e}$ for all $u, v \in V$;

(ii)   if P is the transition matrix from $\{e_i\}$ to a new basis $\{e_i'\}$ of V, then $B = P^t H \bar{P}$ (or: $B = Q^* H Q$ where $Q = \bar{P}$) is the matrix of f in the new basis $\{e_i'\}$.

Note that (ii) is the complex analogue of Theorem 12.2.

(i)   Let $u, v \in V$ and suppose

$$u = a_1 e_1 + a_2 e_2 + \cdots + a_n e_n \qquad \text{and} \qquad v = b_1 e_1 + b_2 e_2 + \cdots + b_n e_n$$

Then $f(u, v) \;=\; f(a_1 e_1 + \cdots + a_n e_n, \; b_1 e_1 + \cdots + b_n e_n)$

$$= \sum_{i,j} a_i \overline{b_j} f(e_i, e_j) \;=\; (a_1, \ldots, a_n) \, H \begin{pmatrix} \overline{b_1} \\ \overline{b_2} \\ \cdot\cdot \\ \overline{b_n} \end{pmatrix} \;=\; [u]_e^t \, H \, \overline{[v]}_e$$

as required.

(ii) Since P is the transition matrix from $\{e_i\}$ to $\{e_i'\}$, then

$$P[u]_{e'} = [u]_e, \; P[v]_{e'} = [v]_e \quad \text{and so} \quad [u]_e^t = [u]_{e'}^t P^t, \; \overline{[v]}_e = \overline{P} \, \overline{[v]}_{e'}$$

Thus by (i), $f(u, v) = [u]_e^t \, H \, \overline{[v]}_e = [u]_{e'}^t \, P^t \, H \, \overline{P} \, \overline{[v]}_{e'}$. But u and v are arbitrary elements of V; hence $P^t H \overline{P}$ is the matrix of f in the basis $\{e_i'\}$.

12.18. Let $\;H = \begin{pmatrix} 1 & 1+i & 2i \\ 1-i & 4 & 2-3i \\ -2i & 2+3i & 7 \end{pmatrix}$, a Hermitian matrix. Find a nonsingular matrix P such that $P^t H \overline{P}$ is diagonal.

First form the block matrix (H, I):

$$\begin{pmatrix} 1 & 1+i & 2i & \vdots & 1 & 0 & 0 \\ 1-i & 4 & 2-3i & \vdots & 0 & 1 & 0 \\ -2i & 2+3i & 7 & \vdots & 0 & 0 & 1 \end{pmatrix}$$

Apply the row operations $R_2 \to (-1+i)R_1 + R_2$ and $R_3 \to 2iR_1 + R_3$ to (A, I) and then the corresponding "Hermitian column operations" (see Problem 12.42) $C_2 \to (-1-i)C_1 + C_2$ and $C_3 \to -2iC_1 + C_3$ to A to obtain

$$\begin{pmatrix} 1 & 1+i & 2i & \vdots & 1 & 0 & 0 \\ 0 & 2 & -5i & \vdots & -1+i & 1 & 0 \\ 0 & 5i & 3 & \vdots & 2i & 0 & 1 \end{pmatrix} \quad \text{and then} \quad \begin{pmatrix} 1 & 0 & 0 & \vdots & 1 & 0 & 0 \\ 0 & 2 & -5i & \vdots & -1+i & 1 & 0 \\ 0 & 5i & 3 & \vdots & 2i & 0 & 1 \end{pmatrix}$$

Next apply the row operation $R_3 \to -5iR_2 + 2R_3$ and the corresponding Hermitian column operation $C_3 \to 5iC_2 + 2C_3$ to obtain

$$\begin{pmatrix} 1 & 0 & 0 & \vdots & 1 & 0 & 0 \\ 0 & 2 & -5i & \vdots & -1+i & 1 & 0 \\ 0 & 0 & -19 & \vdots & 5+9i & -5i & 2 \end{pmatrix} \quad \text{and then} \quad \begin{pmatrix} 1 & 0 & 0 & \vdots & 1 & 0 & 0 \\ 0 & 2 & 0 & \vdots & -1+i & 1 & 0 \\ 0 & 0 & -38 & \vdots & 5+9i & -5i & 2 \end{pmatrix}$$

Now H has been diagonalized. Set

$$P = \begin{pmatrix} 1 & -1+i & 5+9i \\ 0 & 1 & -5i \\ 0 & 0 & 2 \end{pmatrix} \quad \text{and then} \quad P^t H \overline{P} = \begin{pmatrix} 1 & 0 & 0 \\ 0 & 2 & 0 \\ 0 & 0 & -38 \end{pmatrix}$$

Observe that the signature S of H is $S = 2 - 1 = 1$.

MISCELLANEOUS PROBLEMS

12.19. Show that any bilinear form f on V is the sum of a symmetric bilinear form and a skew symmetric bilinear form.

Set $g(u, v) = \frac{1}{2}[f(u, v) + f(v, u)]$ and $h(u, v) = \frac{1}{2}[f(u, v) - f(v, u)]$. Then g is symmetric because

$$g(u, v) \;=\; \tfrac{1}{2}[f(u, v) + f(v, u)] \;=\; \tfrac{1}{2}[f(v, u) + f(u, v)] \;=\; g(v, u)$$

and h is skew symmetric because

$$h(u, v) \;=\; \tfrac{1}{2}[f(u, v) - f(v, u)] \;=\; -\tfrac{1}{2}[f(v, u) - f(u, v)] \;=\; -h(v, u)$$

Furthermore, $f = g + h$.

12.20. Prove Theorem 12.3:   Let f be an alternating bilinear form on V. Then there exists a basis of V in which f is represented by a matrix of the form

$$\begin{pmatrix} 0 & 1 & & & & & & & \\ -1 & 0 & & & & & & & \\ & & 0 & 1 & & & & & \\ & & -1 & 0 & & & & & \\ & & & & \ddots & & & & \\ & & & & & 0 & 1 & & \\ & & & & & -1 & 0 & & \\ & & & & & & & 0 & \\ & & & & & & & & 0 \\ & & & & & & & & & \ddots \\ & & & & & & & & & & 0 \end{pmatrix}$$

Moreover, the number of $\begin{pmatrix} 0 & 1 \\ -1 & 0 \end{pmatrix}$ is uniquely determined by f (because it is equal to $\frac{1}{2}[\text{rank}(f)]$).

If $f = 0$, then the theorem is obviously true. Also, if $\dim V = 1$, then $f(k_1 u, k_2 u) = k_1 k_2 f(u, u) = 0$ and so $f = 0$. Accordingly we can assume that $\dim V > 1$ and $f \neq 0$.

Since $f \neq 0$, there exist (nonzero) $u_1, u_2 \in V$ such that $f(u_1, u_2) \neq 0$. In fact, multiplying u_1 by an appropriate factor, we can assume that $f(u_1, u_2) = 1$ and so $f(u_2, u_1) = -1$. Now u_1 and u_2 are linearly independent; because if, say, $u_2 = k u_1$, then $f(u_1, u_2) = f(u_1, k u_1) = k f(u_1, u_1) = 0$. Let U be the subspace spanned by u_1 and u_2, i.e. $U = L(u_1, u_2)$. Note:

(i)   the matrix representation of the restriction of f to U in the basis $\{u_1, u_2\}$ is $\begin{pmatrix} 0 & 1 \\ -1 & 0 \end{pmatrix}$;

(ii) if $u \in U$, say $u = a u_1 + b u_2$, then

$$f(u, u_1) = f(a u_1 + b u_2, u_1) = -b$$
$$f(u, u_2) = f(a u_1 + b u_2, u_2) = a$$

Let W consist of those vectors $w \in V$ such that $f(w, u_1) = 0$ and $f(w, u_2) = 0$. Equivalently,

$$W = \{w \in V : f(w, u) = 0 \text{ for every } u \in U\}$$

We claim that $V = U \oplus W$. It is clear that $U \cap W = \{0\}$, and so it remains to show that $V = U + W$. Let $v \in V$. Set

$$u = f(v, u_2) u_1 - f(v, u_1) u_2 \quad \text{and} \quad w = v - u \tag{1}$$

Since u is a linear combination of u_1 and u_2, $u \in U$. We show that $w \in W$. By (1) and (ii), $f(u, u_1) = f(v, u_1)$; hence

$$f(w, u_1) = f(v - u, u_1) = f(v, u_1) - f(u, u_1) = 0$$

Similarly, $f(u, u_2) = f(v, u_2)$ and so

$$f(w, u_2) = f(v - u, u_2) = f(v, u_2) - f(u, u_2) = 0$$

Then $w \in W$ and so, by (1), $v = u + w$ where $u \in U$ and $w \in W$. This shows that $V = U + W$; and therefore $V = U \oplus W$.

Now the restriction of f to W is an alternating bilinear form on W. By induction, there exists a basis $u_3, \ldots, u_n$ of W in which the matrix representing f restricted to W has the desired form. Thus $u_1, u_2, u_3, \ldots, u_n$ is a basis of V in which the matrix representing f has the desired form.

Supplementary Problems

BILINEAR FORMS

12.21. Let $u = (x_1, x_2)$ and $v = (y_1, y_2)$. Determine which of the following are bilinear forms on $\mathbf{R}^2$:

(i) $f(u, v) = 2x_1 y_2 - 3x_2 y_1$ (iv) $f(u, v) = x_1 x_2 + y_1 y_2$

(ii) $f(u, v) = x_1 + y_2$ (v) $f(u, v) = 1$

(iii) $f(u, v) = 3x_2 y_2$ (vi) $f(u, v) = 0.$

12.22. Let f be the bilinear form on $\mathbf{R}^2$ defined by

$$f((x_1, x_2), (y_1, y_2)) = 3x_1 y_1 - 2x_1 y_2 + 4x_2 y_1 - x_2 y_2$$

(i)   Find the matrix A of f in the basis $\{u_1 = (1, 1),\ u_2 = (1, 2)\}$.

(ii) Find the matrix B of f in the basis $\{v_1 = (1, -1),\ v_2 = (3, 1)\}$.

(iii) Find the transition matrix P from $\{u_i\}$ to $\{v_i\}$ and verify that $B = P^t A P$.

12.23. Let V be the vector space of 2×2 matrices over $\mathbf{R}$. Let $M = \begin{pmatrix} 1 & 2 \\ 3 & 5 \end{pmatrix}$, and let $f(A, B) = \operatorname{tr}(A^t M B)$ where $A, B \in V$ and "tr" denotes trace. (i) Show that f is a bilinear form on V.
(ii) Find the matrix of f in the basis $\left\{ \begin{pmatrix} 1 & 0 \\ 0 & 0 \end{pmatrix}, \begin{pmatrix} 0 & 1 \\ 0 & 0 \end{pmatrix}, \begin{pmatrix} 0 & 0 \\ 1 & 0 \end{pmatrix}, \begin{pmatrix} 0 & 0 \\ 0 & 1 \end{pmatrix} \right\}$.

12.24. Let $B(V)$ be the set of bilinear forms on V over K. Prove:

(i)   if $f, g \in B(V)$, then $f + g$ and kf, for $k \in K$, also belong to $B(V)$, and so $B(V)$ is a subspace of the vector space of functions from $V \times V$ into K;

(ii) if ϕ and σ are linear functionals on V, then $f(u, v) = \phi(u)\,\sigma(v)$ belongs to $B(V)$.

12.25. Let f be a bilinear form on V. For any subset S of V, we write

$$S^{\perp} = \{v \in V : f(u, v) = 0 \text{ for every } u \in S\}, \quad S^{\top} = \{v \in V : f(v, u) = 0 \text{ for every } u \in S\}$$

Show that: (i) $S^{\perp}$ and $S^{\top}$ are subspaces of V; (ii) $S_1 \subset S_2$ implies $S_2^{\perp} \subset S_1^{\perp}$ and $S_2^{\top} \subset S_1^{\top}$; (iii) $\{0\}^{\perp} = \{0\}^{\top} = V$.

12.26. Prove: If f is a bilinear form on V, then $\operatorname{rank}(f) = \dim V - \dim V^{\perp} = \dim V - \dim V^{\top}$ and hence $\dim V^{\perp} = \dim V^{\top}$.

12.27. Let f be a bilinear form on V. For each $u \in V$, let $\hat{u} : V \to K$ and $\tilde{u} : V \to K$ be defined by $\hat{u}(x) = f(x, u)$ and $\tilde{u}(x) = f(u, x)$. Prove:

(i) $\hat{u}$ and $\tilde{u}$ are each linear, i.e. $\hat{u}, \tilde{u} \in V^*$;

(ii) $u \mapsto \hat{u}$ and $u \mapsto \tilde{u}$ are each linear mappings from V into V^*;

(iii) $\operatorname{rank}(f) = \operatorname{rank}(u \mapsto \hat{u}) = \operatorname{rank}(u \mapsto \tilde{u})$.

12.28. Show that congruence of matrices is an equivalence relation, i.e. (i) A is congruent to A; (ii) if A is congruent to B, then B is congruent to A; (iii) if A is congruent to B and B is congruent to C, then A is congruent to C.

SYMMETRIC BILINEAR FORMS. QUADRATIC FORMS

12.29. Find the symmetric matrix belonging to each of the following quadratic polynomials:

(i) $q(x, y, z) = 2x^2 - 8xy + y^2 - 16xz + 14yz + 5z^2$

(ii) $q(x, y, z) = x^2 - xz + y^2$

(iii) $q(x, y, z) = xy + y^2 + 4xz + z^2$

(iv) $q(x, y, z) = xy + yz.$

12.30. For each of the following matrices A, find a nonsingular matrix P such that $P^t A P$ is diagonal:

$$\text{(i)} \quad A = \begin{pmatrix} 2 & 3 \\ 3 & 4 \end{pmatrix}, \quad \text{(ii)} \quad A = \begin{pmatrix} 1 & -2 & 3 \\ -2 & 6 & -9 \\ 3 & -9 & 4 \end{pmatrix}, \quad \text{(iii)} \quad A = \begin{pmatrix} 1 & 1 & -2 & -3 \\ 1 & 2 & -5 & -1 \\ -2 & -5 & 6 & 9 \\ -3 & -1 & 9 & 11 \end{pmatrix}$$

In each case find the rank and signature.

12.31. Let q be the quadratic form associated with a symmetric bilinear form f. Verify the following alternative polar form of f: $f(u, v) = \frac{1}{4}[q(u + v) - q(u - v)]$.

12.32. Let $S(V)$ be the set of symmetric bilinear forms on V. Show that:
(i) $S(V)$ is a subspace of $B(V)$; (ii) if $\dim V = n$, then $\dim S(V) = \frac{1}{2}n(n + 1)$.

12.33. Let f be the symmetric bilinear form associated with the real quadratic form $q(x, y) = ax^2 + bxy + cy^2$. Show that:
(i) f is nondegenerate if and only if $b^2 - 4ac \neq 0$;
(ii) f is positive definite if and only if $a > 0$ and $b^2 - 4ac < 0$.

12.34. Suppose A is a real symmetric positive definite matrix. Show that there exists a nonsingular matrix P such that $A = P^t P$.

12.35. Consider a real quadratic polynomial $q(x_1, \ldots, x_n) = \displaystyle\sum_{i,j=1}^{n} a_{ij} x_i x_j$, where $a_{ij} = a_{ji}$.
(i) If $a_{11} \neq 0$, show that the substitution

$$x_1 = y_1 - \frac{1}{a_{11}}(a_{12}y_2 + \cdots + a_{1n}y_n), \quad x_2 = y_2, \quad \ldots, \quad x_n = y_n$$

yields the equation $q(x_1, \ldots, x_n) = a_{11}y_1^2 + q'(y_2, \ldots, y_n)$, where q' is also a quadratic polynomial.

(ii) If $a_{11} = 0$ but, say, $a_{12} \neq 0$, show that the substitution

$$x_1 = y_1 + y_2, \quad x_2 = y_1 - y_2, \quad x_3 = y_3, \quad \ldots, \quad x_n = y_n$$

yields the equation $q(x_1, \ldots, x_n) = \sum b_{ij} y_i y_j$, where $b_{11} \neq 0$, i.e. reduces this case to case (i).

This method of diagonalizing q is known as "completing the square".

12.36. Use steps of the type in the preceding problem to reduce each quadratic polynomial in Problem 12.29 to diagonal form. Find the rank and signature in each case.

HERMITIAN FORMS

12.37. For any complex matrices A, B and any $k \in \mathbf{C}$, show that:
(i) $\overline{A + B} = \bar{A} + \bar{B}$, (ii) $\overline{kA} = \bar{k}\bar{A}$, (iii) $\overline{AB} = \bar{A}\,\bar{B}$, (iv) $\bar{A}^t = \overline{A^t}$.

12.38. For each of the following Hermitian matrices H, find a nonsingular matrix P such that $P^t H \bar{P}$ is diagonal:

$$\text{(i)} \quad H = \begin{pmatrix} 1 & i \\ -i & 2 \end{pmatrix}, \quad \text{(ii)} \quad H = \begin{pmatrix} 1 & 2+3i \\ 2-3i & -1 \end{pmatrix}, \quad \text{(iii)} \quad H = \begin{pmatrix} 1 & i & 2+i \\ -i & 2 & 1-i \\ 2-i & 1+i & 2 \end{pmatrix}$$

Find the rank and signature in each case.

12.39. Let A be any complex nonsingular matrix. Show that $H = A^* A$ is Hermitian and positive definite.

12.40. We say that B is Hermitian congruent to A if there exists a nonsingular matrix Q such that $B = Q^* A Q$. Show that Hermitian congruence is an equivalence relation.

12.41. Prove Theorem 12.7: Let f be a Hermitian form on V. Then there exists a basis $\{e_1, \ldots, e_n\}$ of V in which f is represented by a diagonal matrix, i.e. $f(e_i, e_j) = 0$ for $i \neq j$. Moreover, every diagonal representation of f has the same number P of positive entries and the same number N of negative entries. (Note that the second part of the theorem does not hold for complex symmetric bilinear forms, as seen by Problem 12.12(ii). However, the proof of Theorem 12.5 in Problem 12.13 does carry over to the Hermitian case.)

MISCELLANEOUS PROBLEMS

12.42. Consider the following elementary row operations:

$$[a_1] \quad R_i \leftrightarrow R_j, \qquad [a_2] \quad R_i \to kR_i, \ k \neq 0, \qquad [a_3] \quad R_i \to kR_j + R_i$$

The corresponding elementary column operations are, respectively,

$$[b_1] \quad C_i \leftrightarrow C_j, \qquad [b_2] \quad C_i \to kC_i, \ k \neq 0, \qquad [b_3] \quad C_i \to kC_j + C_i$$

If K is the complex field **C**, then the corresponding *Hermitian column operations* are, respectively,

$$[c_1] \quad C_i \leftrightarrow C_j, \qquad [c_2] \quad C_i \to \bar{k}C_i, \ \bar{k} \neq 0, \qquad [c_3] \quad C_i \to \bar{k}C_j + C_i$$

(i) Show that the elementary matrix corresponding to $[b_i]$ is the transpose of the elementary matrix corresponding to $[a_i]$.

(ii) Show that the elementary matrix corresponding to $[c_i]$ is the conjugate transpose of the elementary matrix corresponding to $[a_i]$.

12.43. Let V and W be vector spaces over K. A mapping $f \colon V \times W \to K$ is called a *bilinear form on V and W* if:

    (i) $f(av_1 + bv_2, w) \;=\; af(v_1, w) + bf(v_2, w)$

    (ii) $f(v, aw_1 + bw_2) \;=\; af(v, w_1) + bf(v, w_2)$

for every $a, b \in K$, $v_i \in V$, $w_j \in W$. Prove the following:

(i) The set $B(V, W)$ of bilinear forms on V and W is a subspace of the vector space of functions from $V \times W$ into K.

(ii) If $\{\phi_1, \ldots, \phi_m\}$ is a basis of V^* and $\{\sigma_1, \ldots, \sigma_n\}$ is a basis of W^*, then $\{f_{ij} : i = 1, \ldots, m,\ j = 1, \ldots, n\}$ is a basis of $B(V, W)$ where f_{ij} is defined by $f_{ij}(v, w) = \phi_i(v)\,\sigma_j(w)$. Thus $\dim B(V, W) = \dim V \cdot \dim W$.

(*Remark.* Observe that if $V = W$, then we obtain the space $B(V)$ investigated in this chapter.)

12.44. Let V be a vector space over K. A mapping $f \colon \overbrace{V \times V \times \cdots \times V}^{m \text{ times}} \to K$ is called a *multilinear* (or: *m-linear*) form on V if f is linear in each variable, i.e. for $i = 1, \ldots, m$,

$$f(\ldots, \overbrace{au + bv}, \ldots) \;=\; a f(\ldots, \hat{u}, \ldots) + b f(\ldots, \hat{v}, \ldots)$$

where $\wedge$ denotes the ith component, and other components are held fixed. An m-linear form f is said to be *alternating* if

$$f(v_1, \ldots, v_m) = 0 \quad \text{whenever} \quad v_i = v_k, \ i \neq k$$

Prove:

(i) The set $B_m(V)$ of m-linear forms on V is a subspace of the vector space of functions from $V \times V \times \cdots \times V$ into K.

(ii) The set $A_m(V)$ of alternating m-linear forms on V is a subspace of $B_m(V)$.

Remark 1. If $m = 2$, then we obtain the space $B(V)$ investigated in this chapter.

Remark 2. If $V = K^m$, then the determinant function is a particular alternating m-linear form on V.

Answers to Supplementary Problems

12.21. (i) Yes   (ii) No   (iii) Yes   (iv) No   (v) No   (vi) Yes

12.22. (i) $A = \begin{pmatrix} 4 & 1 \\ 7 & 3 \end{pmatrix}$ (ii) $B = \begin{pmatrix} 0 & -4 \\ 20 & 32 \end{pmatrix}$ (iii) $P = \begin{pmatrix} 3 & 5 \\ -2 & -2 \end{pmatrix}$

12.23. (ii) $\begin{pmatrix} 1 & 0 & 2 & 0 \\ 0 & 1 & 0 & 2 \\ 3 & 0 & 4 & 0 \\ 0 & 3 & 0 & 4 \end{pmatrix}$

12.29. (i) $\begin{pmatrix} 2 & -4 & -8 \\ -4 & 1 & 7 \\ -8 & 7 & 5 \end{pmatrix}$ (ii) $\begin{pmatrix} 1 & 0 & -\frac{1}{2} \\ 0 & 1 & 0 \\ -\frac{1}{2} & 0 & 0 \end{pmatrix}$ (iii) $\begin{pmatrix} 0 & \frac{1}{2} & 2 \\ \frac{1}{2} & 1 & 0 \\ 2 & 0 & 1 \end{pmatrix}$ (iv) $\begin{pmatrix} 0 & \frac{1}{2} & 0 \\ \frac{1}{2} & 0 & \frac{1}{2} \\ 0 & \frac{1}{2} & 0 \end{pmatrix}$

12.30. (i) $P = \begin{pmatrix} 1 & -3 \\ 0 & 2 \end{pmatrix}$, $P^t A P = \begin{pmatrix} 2 & 0 \\ 0 & -2 \end{pmatrix}$, $S = 0$.

(ii) $P = \begin{pmatrix} 1 & 2 & 0 \\ 0 & 1 & 3 \\ 0 & 0 & 2 \end{pmatrix}$, $P^t A P = \begin{pmatrix} 1 & 0 & 0 \\ 0 & 2 & 0 \\ 0 & 0 & -38 \end{pmatrix}$, $S = 1$.

(iii) $P = \begin{pmatrix} 1 & -1 & -1 & 26 \\ 0 & 1 & 3 & 13 \\ 0 & 0 & 1 & 9 \\ 0 & 0 & 0 & 7 \end{pmatrix}$, $P^t A P = \begin{pmatrix} 1 & 0 & 0 & 0 \\ 0 & 1 & 0 & 0 \\ 0 & 0 & -7 & 0 \\ 0 & 0 & 0 & 469 \end{pmatrix}$, $S = 2$.

12.38. (i) $P = \begin{pmatrix} 1 & i \\ 0 & 1 \end{pmatrix}$, $P^t H \bar{P} = \begin{pmatrix} 1 & 0 \\ 0 & 1 \end{pmatrix}$, $S = 2$.

(ii) $P = \begin{pmatrix} 1 & -2+3i \\ 0 & 1 \end{pmatrix}$, $P^t H \bar{P} = \begin{pmatrix} 1 & 0 \\ 0 & -14 \end{pmatrix}$, $S = 0$.

(iii) $P = \begin{pmatrix} 1 & i & -3+i \\ 0 & 1 & i \\ 0 & 0 & 1 \end{pmatrix}$, $P^t H \bar{P} = \begin{pmatrix} 1 & 0 & 0 \\ 0 & 1 & 0 \\ 0 & 0 & -4 \end{pmatrix}$, $S = 1$.

Chapter 13

Inner Product Spaces

INTRODUCTION

The definition of a vector space V involves an arbitrary field K. In this chapter we restrict K to be either the real field **R** or the complex field **C**. In the first case we call V a *real vector space*, and in the second case a *complex vector space*.

Recall that the concepts of "length" and "orthogonality" did not appear in the investigation of arbitrary vector spaces (although they did appear in Chapter 1 on the spaces **R**^{n} and **C**^{n}). In this chapter we place an additional structure on a vector space V to obtain an *inner product space*, and in this context these concepts are defined.

We emphasize that V shall denote a vector space of finite dimension unless otherwise stated or implied. In fact, many of the theorems in this chapter are not valid for spaces of infinite dimension. This is illustrated by some of the examples and problems.

INNER PRODUCT SPACES

We begin with a definition.

Definition: Let V be a (real or complex) vector space over K. Suppose to each pair of vectors $u, v \in V$ there is assigned a scalar $\langle u, v \rangle \in K$. This mapping is called an *inner product* in V if it satisfies the following axioms:

$[I_1]$ $\langle au_1 + bu_2, v \rangle = a\langle u_1, v \rangle + b\langle u_2, v \rangle$

$[I_2]$ $\langle u, v \rangle = \overline{\langle v, u \rangle}$

$[I_3]$ $\langle u, u \rangle \geqq 0$; and $\langle u, u \rangle = 0$ if and only if $u = 0$.

The vector space V with an inner product is called an *inner product space*.

Observe that $\langle u, u \rangle$ is always real by $[I_2]$, and so the inequality relation in $[I_3]$ makes sense. We also use the notation

$$\|u\| = \sqrt{\langle u, u \rangle}$$

This nonnegative real number $\|u\|$ is called the *norm* or *length* of u. Also, using $[I_1]$ and $[I_2]$ we obtain (Problem 13.1) the relation

$$\langle u, av_1 + bv_2 \rangle = \bar{a}\langle u, v_1 \rangle + \bar{b}\langle u, v_2 \rangle$$

If the base field K is real, the conjugate signs appearing above and in $[I_2]$ may be ignored.

In the language of the preceding chapter, an inner product is a positive definite symmetric bilinear form if the base field is real, and is a positive definite Hermitian form if the base field is complex.

A real inner product space is sometimes called a *Euclidean space*, and a complex inner product space is sometimes called a *unitary space*.

Example 13.1:   Consider the dot product in $\mathbf{R}^n$:

$$u \cdot v = a_1 b_1 + a_2 b_2 + \cdots + a_n b_n$$

where $u = (a_i)$ and $v = (b_i)$. This is an inner product on $\mathbf{R}^n$, and $\mathbf{R}^n$ with this inner product is usually referred to as *Euclidean n-space*. Although there are many different ways to define an inner product on $\mathbf{R}^n$ (see Problem 13.2), we shall assume this inner product on $\mathbf{R}^n$ unless otherwise stated or implied.

Example 13.2:   Consider the dot product on $\mathbf{C}^n$:

$$u \cdot v = z_1 \overline{w}_1 + z_2 \overline{w}_2 + \cdots + z_n \overline{w}_n$$

where $u = (z_i)$ and $v = (w_i)$. As in the real case, this is an inner product on $\mathbf{C}^n$ and we shall assume this inner product on $\mathbf{C}^n$ unless otherwise stated or implied.

Example 13.3:   Let V denote the vector space of $m \times n$ matrices over $\mathbf{R}$. The following is an inner product in V:

$$\langle A, B \rangle = \operatorname{tr}(B^t A)$$

where tr stands for *trace*, the sum of the diagonal elements.

Analogously, if U denotes the vector space of $m \times n$ matrices over $\mathbf{C}$, then the following is an inner product in U:

$$\langle A, B \rangle = \operatorname{tr}(B^* A)$$

As usual, B^* denotes the conjugate transpose of the matrix B.

Example 13.4:   Let V be the vector space of real continuous functions on the interval $a \leqq t \leqq b$. Then the following is an inner product on V:

$$\langle f, g \rangle = \int_a^b f(t)\, g(t)\, dt$$

Analogously, if U denotes the vector space of complex continuous functions on the (real) interval $a \leqq t \leqq b$, then the following is an inner product on U:

$$\langle f, g \rangle = \int_a^b f(t)\, \overline{g(t)}\, dt$$

Example 13.5:   Let V be the vector space of infinite sequences of real numbers $(a_1, a_2, \ldots)$ satisfying

$$\sum_{i=1}^{\infty} a_i^2 = a_1^2 + a_2^2 + \cdots < \infty$$

i.e. the sum converges. Addition and scalar multiplication are defined componentwise:

$$(a_1, a_2, \ldots) + (b_1, b_2, \ldots) = (a_1 + b_1, a_2 + b_2, \ldots)$$

$$k(a_1, a_2, \ldots) = (ka_1, ka_2, \ldots)$$

An inner product is defined in V by

$$\langle (a_1, a_2, \ldots), (b_1, b_2, \ldots) \rangle = a_1 b_1 + a_2 b_2 + \cdots$$

The above sum converges absolutely for any pair of points in V (Problem 13.44); hence the inner product is well defined. This inner product space is called l_2-space (or: Hilbert space).

Remark 1:   If $\|v\| = 1$, i.e. if $\langle v, v \rangle = 1$, then v is called a *unit* vector or is said to be *normalized*. We note that every nonzero vector $u \in V$ can be *normalized* by setting $v = u/\|u\|$.

Remark 2:   The nonnegative real number $d(u, v) = \|v - u\|$ is called the *distance* between u and v; this function does satisfy the axioms of a metric space (see Problem 13.51).

CAUCHY-SCHWARZ INEQUALITY

The following formula, called the Cauchy-Schwarz inequality, is used in many branches of mathematics.

Theorem 13.1: (Cauchy-Schwarz):   For any vectors $u, v \in V$,

$$|\langle u, v \rangle| \leq ||u|| \, ||v||$$

Next we examine this inequality in specific cases.

> **Example 13.6:** Consider any complex numbers $a_1, \ldots, a_n, b_1, \ldots, b_n \in \mathbf{C}$. Then by the Cauchy-Schwarz inequality,
>
> $$(a_1\bar{b}_1 + \cdots + a_n\bar{b}_n)^2 \leq (|a_1|^2 + \cdots + |a_n|^2)(|b_1|^2 + \cdots + |b_n|^2)$$
>
> that is, $(u \cdot v)^2 \leq ||u||^2 \, ||v||^2$
>
> where $u = (a_i)$ and $v = (b_i)$.

> **Example 13.7:** Let f and g be any real continuous functions defined on the unit interval $0 \leq t \leq 1$. Then by the Cauchy-Schwarz inequality,
>
> $$(\langle f, g \rangle)^2 = \left(\int_0^1 f(t)\, g(t)\, dt \right)^2 \leq \int_0^1 f^2(t)\, dt \int_0^1 g^2(t)\, dt = ||f||^2 \, ||g||^2$$
>
> Here V is the inner product space of Example 13.4.

ORTHOGONALITY

Let V be an inner product space. The vectors $u, v \in V$ are said to be *orthogonal* if $\langle u, v \rangle = 0$. The relation is clearly symmetric; that is, if u is orthogonal to v, then $\langle v, u \rangle = \overline{\langle u, v \rangle} = \bar{0} = 0$ and so v is orthogonal to u. We note that $0 \in V$ is orthogonal to every $v \in V$ for

$$\langle 0, v \rangle = \langle 0v, v \rangle = 0 \langle v, v \rangle = 0$$

Conversely, if u is orthogonal to every $v \in V$, then $\langle u, u \rangle = 0$ and hence $u = 0$ by $[I_3]$.

Now suppose W is any subset of V. The *orthogonal complement* of W, denoted by $W^\perp$ (read "W perp") consists of those vectors in V which are orthogonal to every $w \in W$:

$$W^\perp = \{v \in V : \langle v, w \rangle = 0 \text{ for every } w \in W\}$$

We show that $W^\perp$ is a subspace of V. Clearly, $0 \in W^\perp$. Now suppose $u, v \in W^\perp$. Then for any $a, b \in K$ and any $w \in W$,

$$\langle au + bv, w \rangle = a\langle u, w \rangle + b\langle v, w \rangle = a \cdot 0 + b \cdot 0 = 0$$

Thus $au + bv \in W^\perp$ and therefore W is a subspace of V.

Theorem 13.2:   Let W be a subspace of V. Then V is the direct sum of W and $W^\perp$, i.e. $V = W \oplus W^\perp$.

Now if W is a subspace of V, then $V = W \oplus W^\perp$ by the above theorem; hence there is a unique projection $E_W : V \to V$ with image W and kernel $W^\perp$. That is, if $v \in V$ and $v = w + w'$, where $w \in W$, $w' \in W^\perp$, then E_W is defined by $E_W(v) = w$. This mapping E_W is called the *orthogonal projection* of V onto W.

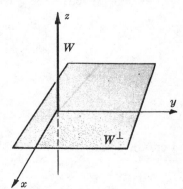

> **Example 13.8:** Let W be the z axis in $\mathbf{R}^3$, i.e.
>
> $$W = \{(0, 0, c) : c \in \mathbf{R}\}$$
>
> Then $W^\perp$ is the xy plane, i.e.
>
> $$W^\perp = \{(a, b, 0) : a, b \in \mathbf{R}\}$$
>
> As noted previously, $\mathbf{R}^3 = W \oplus W^\perp$. The orthogonal projection E of $\mathbf{R}^3$ onto W is given by $E(x, y, z) = (0, 0, z)$.

Example 13.9: Consider a homogeneous system of linear equations over **R**:

$$a_{11}x_1 + a_{12}x_2 + \cdots + a_{1n}x_n = 0$$
$$a_{21}x_1 + a_{22}x_2 + \cdots + a_{2n}x_n = 0$$
$$\cdots\cdots\cdots\cdots\cdots\cdots\cdots\cdots\cdots\cdots\cdots\cdots$$
$$a_{m1}x_1 + a_{m2}x_2 + \cdots + a_{mn}x_n = 0$$

or in matrix notation $AX = 0$. Recall that the solution space W may be viewed as the kernel of the linear operator A. We may also view W as the set of all vectors $v = (x_1, \ldots, x_n)$ which are orthogonal to each row of A. Thus W is the orthogonal complement of the row space of A. Theorem 13.2 then gives another proof of the fundamental result: $\dim W = n - \text{rank}(A)$.

Remark: If V is a real inner product space, then the angle θ between nonzero vectors $u, v \in V$ is defined by

$$\cos \theta = \frac{\langle u, v \rangle}{\|u\| \|v\|}$$

By the Cauchy-Schwarz inequality, $-1 \le \cos\theta \le 1$ and so the angle θ always exists. Observe that u and v are orthogonal if and only if they are "perpendicular", i.e. $\theta = \pi/2$.

ORTHONORMAL SETS

A set $\{u_i\}$ of vectors in V is said to be *orthogonal* if its distinct elements are orthogonal, i.e. if $\langle u_i, u_j \rangle = 0$ for $i \ne j$. In particular, the set $\{u_i\}$ is said to be *orthonormal* if it is orthogonal and if each u_i has length 1, that is, if

$$\langle u_i, u_j \rangle = \delta_{ij} = \begin{cases} 0 \text{ for } i \ne j \\ 1 \text{ for } i = j \end{cases}$$

An orthonormal set can always be obtained from an orthogonal set of nonzero vectors by normalizing each vector.

Example 13.10: Consider the usual basis of Euclidean 3-space $\mathbf{R}^3$:

$$\{e_1 = (1, 0, 0), \ e_2 = (0, 1, 0), \ e_3 = (0, 0, 1)\}$$

It is clear that

$$\langle e_1, e_1 \rangle = \langle e_2, e_2 \rangle = \langle e_3, e_3 \rangle = 1 \quad \text{and} \quad \langle e_i, e_j \rangle = 0 \text{ for } i \ne j$$

That is, $\{e_1, e_2, e_3\}$ is an orthonormal basis of $\mathbf{R}^3$. More generally, the usual basis of $\mathbf{R}^n$ or of $\mathbf{C}^n$ is orthonormal for every n.

Example 13.11: Let V be the vector space of real continuous functions on the interval $-\pi \le t \le \pi$ with inner product defined by $\langle f, g \rangle = \int_{-\pi}^{\pi} f(t) g(t) \, dt$. The following is a classical example of an orthogonal subset of V:

$$\{1, \cos t, \cos 2t, \ldots, \sin t, \sin 2t, \ldots\}$$

The above orthogonal set plays a fundamental role in the theory of Fourier series.

The following properties of an orthonormal set will be used in the next section.

Lemma 13.3: An orthonormal set $\{u_1, \ldots, u_r\}$ is linearly independent and, for any $v \in V$, the vector
$$w = v - \langle v, u_1 \rangle u_1 - \langle v, u_2 \rangle u_2 - \cdots - \langle v, u_r \rangle u_r$$
is orthogonal to each of the u_i.

GRAM-SCHMIDT ORTHOGONALIZATION PROCESS

Orthonormal bases play an important role in inner product spaces. The next theorem shows that such a basis always exists; its proof uses the celebrated Gram-Schmidt orthogonalization process.

Theorem 13.4:   Let $\{v_1, \ldots, v_n\}$ be an arbitrary basis of an inner product space V. Then there exists an orthonormal basis $\{u_1, \ldots, u_n\}$ of V such that the transition matrix from $\{v_i\}$ to $\{u_i\}$ is triangular; that is, for $i = 1, \ldots, n$,

$$u_i = a_{i1}v_1 + a_{i2}v_2 + \cdots + a_{ii}v_i$$

Proof. We set $u_1 = v_1/\|v_1\|$; then $\{u_1\}$ is orthonormal.   We next set

$$w_2 = v_2 - \langle v_2, u_1 \rangle u_1 \quad \text{and} \quad u_2 = w_2/\|w_2\|$$

By Lemma 13.3, w_2 (and hence u_2) is orthogonal to u_1; then $\{u_1, u_2\}$ is orthonormal.   We next set

$$w_3 = v_3 - \langle v_3, u_1 \rangle u_1 - \langle v_3, u_2 \rangle u_2 \quad \text{and} \quad u_3 = w_3/\|w_3\|$$

Again, by Lemma 13.3, w_3 (and hence u_3) is orthogonal to u_1 and u_2; then $\{u_1, u_2, u_3\}$ is orthonormal.   In general, after obtaining $\{u_1, \ldots, u_i\}$ we set

$$w_{i+1} = v_{i+1} - \langle v_{i+1}, u_1 \rangle u_1 - \cdots - \langle v_{i+1}, u_i \rangle u_i \quad \text{and} \quad u_{i+1} = w_{i+1}/\|w_{i+1}\|$$

(Note that $w_{i+1} \neq 0$ because $v_{i+1} \notin L(v_1, \ldots, v_i) = L(u_1, \ldots, u_i)$.)   As above, $\{u_1, \ldots, u_{i+1}\}$ is also orthonormal.   By induction we obtain an orthonormal set $\{u_1, \ldots, u_n\}$ which is independent and hence a basis of V. The specific construction guarantees that the transition matrix is indeed triangular.

Example 13.12:   Consider the following basis of Euclidean space $\mathbf{R}^3$:

$$\{v_1 = (1, 1, 1), \ v_2 = (0, 1, 1), \ v_3 = (0, 0, 1)\}$$

We use the Gram-Schmidt orthogonalization process to transform $\{v_i\}$ into an orthonormal basis $\{u_i\}$.   First we normalize v_1, i.e. we set

$$u_1 = \frac{v_1}{\|v_1\|} = \frac{(1, 1, 1)}{\sqrt{3}} = \left(\frac{1}{\sqrt{3}}, \frac{1}{\sqrt{3}}, \frac{1}{\sqrt{3}}\right)$$

Next we set

$$w_2 = v_2 - \langle v_2, u_1 \rangle u_1 = (0, 1, 1) - \frac{2}{\sqrt{3}}\left(\frac{1}{\sqrt{3}}, \frac{1}{\sqrt{3}}, \frac{1}{\sqrt{3}}\right) = \left(-\frac{2}{3}, \frac{1}{3}, \frac{1}{3}\right)$$

and then we normalize w_2, i.e. we set

$$u_2 = \frac{w_2}{\|w_2\|} = \left(-\frac{2}{\sqrt{6}}, \frac{1}{\sqrt{6}}, \frac{1}{\sqrt{6}}\right)$$

Finally we set

$$w_3 = v_3 - \langle v_3, u_1 \rangle u_1 - \langle v_3, u_2 \rangle u_2$$
$$= (0, 0, 1) - \frac{1}{\sqrt{3}}\left(\frac{1}{\sqrt{3}}, \frac{1}{\sqrt{3}}, \frac{1}{\sqrt{3}}\right) - \frac{1}{\sqrt{6}}\left(-\frac{2}{\sqrt{6}}, \frac{1}{\sqrt{6}}, \frac{1}{\sqrt{6}}\right) = \left(0, -\frac{1}{2}, \frac{1}{2}\right)$$

and then we normalize w_3:

$$u_3 = \frac{w_3}{\|w_3\|} = \left(0, -\frac{1}{\sqrt{2}}, \frac{1}{\sqrt{2}}\right)$$

The required orthonormal basis of $\mathbf{R}^3$ is

$$\left\{u_1 = \left(\frac{1}{\sqrt{3}}, \frac{1}{\sqrt{3}}, \frac{1}{\sqrt{3}}\right), \ u_2 = \left(-\frac{2}{\sqrt{6}}, \frac{1}{\sqrt{6}}, \frac{1}{\sqrt{6}}\right), \ u_3 = \left(0, -\frac{1}{\sqrt{2}}, \frac{1}{\sqrt{2}}\right)\right\}$$

LINEAR FUNCTIONALS AND ADJOINT OPERATORS

Let V be an inner product space.   Each $u \in V$ determines a mapping $\hat{u} : V \to K$ defined by

$$\hat{u}(v) = \langle v, u \rangle$$

Now for any $a, b \in K$ and any $v_1, v_2 \in V$,

$$\hat{u}(av_1 + bv_2) = \langle av_1 + bv_2, u \rangle = a\langle v_1, u \rangle + b\langle v_2, u \rangle = a\hat{u}(v_1) + b\hat{u}(v_2)$$

That is, $\hat{u}$ is a linear functional on V. The converse is also true for spaces of finite dimension and is an important theorem. Namely,

Theorem 13.5: Let ϕ be a linear functional on a finite dimensional inner product space V. Then there exists a unique vector $u \in V$ such that $\phi(v) = \langle v, u \rangle$ for every $v \in V$.

We remark that the above theorem is not valid for spaces of infinite dimension (Problem 13.45), although some general results in this direction are known. (One such famous result is the Riesz representation theorem.)

We use the above theorem to prove

Theorem 13.6: Let T be a linear operator on a finite dimensional inner product space V. Then there exists a unique linear operator T^* on V such that

$$\langle T(u), v \rangle = \langle u, T^*(v) \rangle$$

for every $u, v \in V$. Moreover, if A is the matrix of T relative to an orthonormal basis $\{e_i\}$ of V, then the conjugate transpose A^* of A is the matrix of T^* in the basis $\{e_i\}$.

We emphasize that no such simple relationship exists between the matrices representing T and T^* if the basis is not orthonormal. Thus we see one useful property of orthonormal bases.

Definition: A linear operator T on an inner product space V is said to have an *adjoint* operator T^* on V if $\langle T(u), v \rangle = \langle u, T^*(v) \rangle$ for every $u, v \in V$.

Thus Theorem 13.6 states that every operator T has an adjoint if V has finite dimension. This theorem is not valid if V has infinite dimension (Problem 13.78).

Example 13.13: Let T be the linear operator on $\mathbf{C}^3$ defined by

$$T(x, y, z) = (2x + iy, \ y - 5iz, \ x + (1 - i)y + 3z)$$

We find a similar formula for the adjoint T^* of T. Note (Problem 7.3) that the matrix of T in the usual basis of $\mathbf{C}^3$ is

$$[T] = \begin{pmatrix} 2 & i & 0 \\ 0 & 1 & -5i \\ 1 & 1-i & 3 \end{pmatrix}$$

Recall that the usual basis is orthonormal. Thus by Theorem 13.6, the matrix of T^* in this basis is the conjugate transpose of $[T]$:

$$[T^*] = \begin{pmatrix} 2 & 0 & 1 \\ -i & 1 & 1+i \\ 0 & 5i & 3 \end{pmatrix}$$

Accordingly,

$$T^*(x, y, z) = (2x + z, \ -ix + y + (1 + i)z, \ 5iy + 3z)$$

The following theorem summarizes some of the properties of the adjoint.

Theorem 13.7: Let S and T be linear operators on V and let $k \in K$. Then:

(i) $(S + T)^* = S^* + T^*$ (iii) $(ST)^* = T^*S^*$

(ii) $(kT)^* = \bar{k}T^*$ (iv) $(T^*)^* = T$

ANALOGY BETWEEN $A(V)$ AND C, SPECIAL OPERATORS

Let $A(V)$ denote the algebra of all linear operators on a finite dimensional inner product space V. The adjoint mapping $T \mapsto T^*$ on $A(V)$ is quite analogous to the conjugation mapping $z \mapsto \bar{z}$ on the complex field **C**. To illustrate this analogy we identify in the following table certain classes of operators $T \in A(V)$ whose behaviour under the adjoint map imitates the behaviour under conjugation of familiar classes of complex numbers.

Class of complex numbers	Behaviour under conjugation	Class of operators in $A(V)$	Behaviour under the adjoint map
Unit circle ($|z|=1$)	$\bar{z} = 1/z$	Orthogonal operators (real case) Unitary operators (complex case)	$T^* = T^{-1}$

Real axis	$\bar{z} = z$	Self-adjoint operators
		 Also called:
		     symmetric (real case)
		     Hermitian (complex case)
			$T^* = T$

Imaginary axis	$\bar{z} = -z$	Skew-adjoint operators
		 Also called:
		     skew-symmetric (real case)
		     skew-Hermitian (complex case)
			$T^* = -T$

Positive half axis $(0, \infty)$	$z = \bar{w}w, \ w \neq 0$	Positive definite operators	$T = S^*S$ with S nonsingular

The analogy between these classes of operators T and complex numbers z is reflected in the following theorem.

Theorem 13.8:   Let λ be an eigenvalue of a linear operator T on V.

      (i)   If $T^* = T^{-1}$, then $|\lambda| = 1$.

      (ii) If $T^* = T$, then λ is real.

      (iii) If $T^* = -T$, then λ is pure imaginary.

      (iv) If $T = S^*S$ with S nonsingular, then λ is real and positive.

We now prove the above theorem. In each case let v be a nonzero eigenvector of T belonging to λ, that is, $T(v) = \lambda v$ with $v \neq 0$; hence $\langle v, v \rangle$ is positive.

Proof of (i): We show that $\lambda \bar{\lambda} \langle v, v \rangle = \langle v, v \rangle$:

$$\lambda \bar{\lambda} \langle v, v \rangle = \langle \lambda v, \lambda v \rangle = \langle T(v), T(v) \rangle = \langle v, T^*T(v) \rangle = \langle v, I(v) \rangle = \langle v, v \rangle$$

But $\langle v, v \rangle \neq 0$; hence $\lambda \bar{\lambda} = 1$ and so $|\lambda| = 1$.

Proof of (ii): We show that $\lambda \langle v, v \rangle = \bar{\lambda} \langle v, v \rangle$:

$$\lambda \langle v, v \rangle = \langle \lambda v, v \rangle = \langle T(v), v \rangle = \langle v, T^*(v) \rangle = \langle v, T(v) \rangle = \langle v, \lambda v \rangle = \bar{\lambda} \langle v, v \rangle$$

But $\langle v, v \rangle \neq 0$; hence $\lambda = \bar{\lambda}$ and so λ is real.

Proof of (iii): We show that $\lambda \langle v, v \rangle = -\bar{\lambda} \langle v, v \rangle$:

$$\lambda \langle v, v \rangle = \langle \lambda v, v \rangle = \langle T(v), v \rangle = \langle v, T^*(v) \rangle = \langle v, -T(v) \rangle = \langle v, -\lambda v \rangle = -\bar{\lambda} \langle v, v \rangle$$

But $\langle v, v \rangle \neq 0$; hence $\lambda = -\bar{\lambda}$ or $\bar{\lambda} = -\lambda$, and so λ is pure imaginary.

Proof of (iv): Note first that $S(v) \neq 0$ because S is nonsingular; hence $\langle S(v), S(v) \rangle$ is positive. We show that $\lambda \langle v, v \rangle = \langle S(v), S(v) \rangle$:

$$\lambda \langle v, v \rangle = \langle \lambda v, v \rangle = \langle T(v), v \rangle = \langle S^*S(v), v \rangle = \langle S(v), S(v) \rangle$$

But $\langle v, v \rangle$ and $\langle S(v), S(v) \rangle$ are positive; hence λ is positive.

We remark that all the above operators T commute with their adjoint, that is, $TT^* = T^*T$. Such operators are called *normal* operators.

ORTHOGONAL AND UNITARY OPERATORS

Let U be a linear operator on a finite dimensional inner product space V. As defined above, if

$$U^* = U^{-1} \quad \text{or equivalently} \quad UU^* = U^*U = I$$

then U is said to be *orthogonal* or *unitary* according as the underlying field is real or complex. The next theorem gives alternative characterizations of these operators.

Theorem 13.9:   The following conditions on an operator U are equivalent:

(i) $U^* = U^{-1}$, that is, $UU^* = U^*U = I$.

(ii) U *preserves inner products*, i.e. for every $v, w \in V$,
$$\langle U(v), U(w) \rangle = \langle v, w \rangle$$

(iii) U *preserves lengths*, i.e. for every $v \in V$, $\|U(v)\| = \|v\|$.

Example 13.14: Let $T : \mathbf{R}^3 \to \mathbf{R}^3$ be the linear operator which rotates each vector about the z axis by a fixed angle θ:

$$T(x, y, z) = (x \cos \theta - y \sin \theta,$$
$$x \sin \theta + y \cos \theta,\ z)$$

Observe that lengths (distances from the origin) are preserved under T. Thus T is an orthogonal operator.

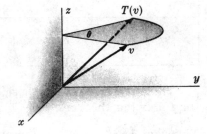

Example 13.15: Let V be the l_2-space of Example 13.5. Let $T : V \to V$ be the linear operator defined by $T(a_1, a_2, \ldots) = (0, a_1, a_2, \ldots)$. Clearly, T preserves inner products and lengths. However, T is not surjective since, for example, $(1, 0, 0, \ldots)$ does not belong to the image of T; hence T is not invertible. Thus we see that Theorem 13.9 is not valid for spaces of infinite dimension.

An *isomorphism* from one inner product space into another is a bijective mapping which preserves the three basic operations of an inner product space: vector addition, scalar multiplication, and inner products. Thus the above mappings (orthogonal and unitary) may also be characterized as the isomorphisms of V into itself. Note that such a mapping U also preserves distances, since

$$\|U(v) - U(w)\| = \|U(v - w)\| = \|v - w\|$$

and so U is also called an *isometry*.

ORTHOGONAL AND UNITARY MATRICES

Let U be a linear operator on an inner product space V. By Theorem 13.6 we obtain the following result when the base field K is complex.

Theorem 13.10A: A matrix A with complex entries represents a unitary operator U (relative to an orthonormal basis) if and only if $A^* = A^{-1}$.

On the other hand, if the base field K is real then $A^* = A^t$; hence we have the following corresponding theorem for real inner product spaces.

Theorem 13.10B: A matrix A with real entries represents an orthogonal operator U (relative to an orthonormal basis) if and only if $A^t = A^{-1}$.

The above theorems motivate the following definitions.

Definition: A complex matrix A for which $A^* = A^{-1}$, or equivalently $AA^* = A^*A = I$, is called a *unitary* matrix.

Definition: A real matrix A for which $A^t = A^{-1}$, or equivalently $AA^t = A^tA = I$, is called an *orthogonal* matrix.

Observe that a unitary matrix with real entries is orthogonal.

Example 13.16: Suppose $A = \begin{pmatrix} a_1 & a_2 \\ b_1 & b_2 \end{pmatrix}$ is a unitary matrix. Then $AA^* = I$ and hence

$$AA^* = \begin{pmatrix} a_1 & a_2 \\ b_1 & b_2 \end{pmatrix}\begin{pmatrix} \bar{a}_1 & \bar{b}_1 \\ \bar{a}_2 & \bar{b}_2 \end{pmatrix} = \begin{pmatrix} |a_1|^2 + |a_2|^2 & a_1\bar{b}_1 + a_2\bar{b}_2 \\ \bar{a}_1 b_1 + \bar{a}_2 b_2 & |b_1|^2 + |b_2|^2 \end{pmatrix} = \begin{pmatrix} 1 & 0 \\ 0 & 1 \end{pmatrix} = I$$

Thus

$$|a_1|^2 + |a_2|^2 = 1, \quad |b_1|^2 + |b_2|^2 = 1 \quad \text{and} \quad a_1\bar{b}_1 + a_2\bar{b}_2 = 0$$

Accordingly, the rows of A form an orthonormal set. Similarly, $A^*A = I$ forces the columns of A to form an orthonormal set.

The result in the above example holds true in general; namely,

Theorem 13.11:   The following conditions for a matrix A are equivalent:
(i) A is unitary (orthogonal).
(ii) The rows of A form an orthonormal set.
(iii) The columns of A form an orthonormal set.

Example 13.17: The matrix A representing the rotation T in Example 13.14 relative to the usual basis of $\mathbf{R}^3$ is

$$A = \begin{pmatrix} \cos\theta & -\sin\theta & 0 \\ \sin\theta & \cos\theta & 0 \\ 0 & 0 & 1 \end{pmatrix}$$

As expected, the rows and the columns of A each form an orthonormal set; that is, A is an orthogonal matrix.

CHANGE OF ORTHONORMAL BASIS

In view of the special role of orthonormal bases in the theory of inner product spaces, we are naturally interested in the properties of the transition matrix from one such basis to another. The following theorem applies.

Theorem 13.12:   Let $\{e_1, \ldots, e_n\}$ be an orthonormal basis of an inner product space V. Then the transition matrix from $\{e_i\}$ into another orthonormal basis is unitary (orthogonal). Conversely, if $P = (a_{ij})$ is a unitary (orthogonal) matrix, then the following is an orthonormal basis:

$$\{e_i' = a_{1i}e_1 + a_{2i}e_2 + \cdots + a_{ni}e_n : \; i = 1, \ldots, n\}$$

Recall that matrices A and B representing the same linear operator T are similar, i.e. $B = P^{-1}AP$ where P is the (nonsingular) transition matrix. On the other hand, if V is an inner product space, we are usually interested in the case when P is unitary (or orthogonal) as suggested by the above theorem. (Recall that P is unitary if $P^* = P^{-1}$, and P is orthogonal if $P^t = P^{-1}$.) This leads to the following definition.

Definition: Complex matrices A and B are *unitarily equivalent* if there is a unitary matrix P for which $B = P^*AP$. Analogously, real matrices A and B are *orthogonally equivalent* if there is an orthogonal matrix P for which $B = P^tAP$.

Observe that orthogonally equivalent matrices are necessarily congruent (see page 262).

POSITIVE OPERATORS

Let P be a linear operator on an inner product space V. P is said to be *positive* (or: *semi-definite*) if
$$P = S^*S \quad \text{for some operator } S$$
and is said to be *positive definite* if S is also nonsingular. The next theorems give alternative characterizations of these operators.

Theorem 13.13A: The following conditions on an operator P are equivalent:

 (i) $P = T^2$ for some self-adjoint operator T.

 (ii) $P = S^*S$ for some operator S.

 (iii) P is self-adjoint and $\langle P(u), u \rangle \geqq 0$ for every $u \in V$.

The corresponding theorem for positive definite operators is

Theorem 13.13B: The following conditions on an operator P are equivalent:

 (i) $P = T^2$ for some nonsingular self-adjoint operator T.

 (ii) $P = S^*S$ for some nonsingular operator S.

 (iii) P is self-adjoint and $\langle P(u), u \rangle > 0$ for every $u \neq 0$ in V.

DIAGONALIZATION AND CANONICAL FORMS IN EUCLIDEAN SPACES

Let T be a linear operator on a finite dimensional inner product space V over K. Representing T by a diagonal matrix depends upon the eigenvectors and eigenvalues of T, and hence upon the roots of the characteristic polynomial $\Delta(t)$ of T (Theorem 9.6). Now $\Delta(t)$ always factors into linear polynomials over the complex field $\mathbf{C}$, but may not have any linear polynomials over the real field $\mathbf{R}$. Thus the situation for Euclidean spaces (where $K = \mathbf{R}$) is inherently different than that for unitary spaces (where $K = \mathbf{C}$); hence we treat them separately. We investigate Euclidean spaces below, and unitary spaces in the next section.

Theorem 13.14:   Let T be a symmetric (self-adjoint) operator on a real finite dimensional inner product space V. Then there exists an orthonormal basis of V consisting of eigenvectors of T; that is, T can be represented by a diagonal matrix relative to an orthonormal basis.

We give the corresponding statement for matrices.

Alternative Form of Theorem 13.14:   Let A be a real symmetric matrix. Then there exists an orthogonal matrix P such that $B = P^{-1}AP = P^tAP$ is diagonal.

We can choose the columns of the above matrix P to be normalized orthogonal eigenvectors of A; then the diagonal entries of B are the corresponding eigenvalues.

Example 13.18: Let $A = \begin{pmatrix} 2 & -2 \\ -2 & 5 \end{pmatrix}$. We find an orthogonal matrix P such that $P^t A P$ is diagonal. The characteristic polynomial $\Delta(t)$ of A is

$$\Delta(t) = |tI - A| = \begin{vmatrix} t-2 & 2 \\ 2 & t-5 \end{vmatrix} = (t-6)(t-1)$$

The eigenvalues of A are 6 and 1. Substitute $t = 6$ into the matrix $tI - A$ to obtain the corresponding homogeneous system of linear equations

$$4x + 2y = 0, \quad 2x + y = 0$$

A nonzero solution is $v_1 = (1, -2)$. Next substitute $t = 1$ into the matrix $tI - A$ to find the corresponding homogeneous system

$$-x + 2y = 0, \quad 2x - 4y = 0$$

A nonzero solution is $(2, 1)$. As expected by Problem 13.31, v_1 and v_2 are orthogonal. Normalize v_1 and v_2 to obtain the orthonormal basis

$$\{u_1 = (1/\sqrt{5}, -2/\sqrt{5}), \ u_2 = (2/\sqrt{5}, 1/\sqrt{5})\}$$

Finally let P be the matrix whose columns are u_1 and u_2 respectively. Then

$$P = \begin{pmatrix} 1/\sqrt{5} & 2/\sqrt{5} \\ -2/\sqrt{5} & 1/\sqrt{5} \end{pmatrix} \quad \text{and} \quad P^{-1}AP = P^t A P = \begin{pmatrix} 6 & 0 \\ 0 & 1 \end{pmatrix}$$

As expected, the diagonal entries of $P^t A P$ are the eigenvalues corresponding to the columns of P.

We observe that the matrix $B = P^{-1}AP = P^t A P$ is also congruent to A. Now if q is a real quadratic form represented by the matrix A, then the above method can be used to diagonalize q under an orthogonal change of coordinates. This is illustrated in the next example.

Example 13.19: Find an orthogonal transformation of coordinates which diagonalizes the quadratic form $q(x, y) = 2x^2 - 4xy + 5y^2$.

The symmetric matrix representing q is $A = \begin{pmatrix} 2 & -2 \\ -2 & 5 \end{pmatrix}$. In the preceding example we obtained the orthogonal matrix

$$P = \begin{pmatrix} 1/\sqrt{5} & 2/\sqrt{5} \\ -2/\sqrt{5} & 1/\sqrt{5} \end{pmatrix} \quad \text{for which} \quad P^t A P = \begin{pmatrix} 6 & 0 \\ 0 & 1 \end{pmatrix}$$

(Here 6 and 1 are the eigenvalues of A.) Thus the required orthogonal transformation of coordinates is

$$\begin{pmatrix} x \\ y \end{pmatrix} = P \begin{pmatrix} x' \\ y' \end{pmatrix} \quad \text{that is,} \quad \begin{aligned} x &= x'/\sqrt{5} + 2y'\sqrt{5} \\ y &= -2x'/\sqrt{5} + y'/\sqrt{5} \end{aligned}$$

Under this change of coordinates q is transformed into the diagonal form

$$q(x', y') = 6x'^2 + y'^2$$

Note that the diagonal entries of q are the eigenvalues of A.

An orthogonal operator T need not be symmetric, and so it may not be represented by a diagonal matrix relative to an orthonormal basis. However, such an operator T does have a simple canonical representation, as described in the next theorem.

Theorem 13.15: Let T be an orthogonal operator on a real inner product space V. Then there is an orthonormal basis with respect to which T has the following form:

$$\begin{pmatrix} 1 & & & & & & & & & & \\ & 1 & & & & & & & & \\ & & \ddots & & & & & & & \\ & & & 1 & & & & & & \\ \hline & & & & -1 & & & & & \\ & & & & & -1 & & & & \\ & & & & & & \ddots & & & \\ & & & & & & & -1 & & \\ \hline & & & & & & & & \cos\theta_1 & -\sin\theta_1 \\ & & & & & & & & \sin\theta_1 & \cos\theta_1 \\ & & & & & & & & & & \ddots \\ & & & & & & & & & & & \cos\theta_r & -\sin\theta_r \\ & & & & & & & & & & & \sin\theta_r & \cos\theta_r \end{pmatrix}$$

The reader may recognize the above 2 by 2 diagonal blocks as representing rotations in the corresponding two-dimensional subspaces.

DIAGONALIZATION AND CANONICAL FORMS IN UNITARY SPACES

We now present the fundamental diagonalization theorem for complex inner product spaces, i.e. for unitary spaces. Recall that an operator T is said to be *normal* if it commutes with its adjoint, i.e. if $TT^* = T^*T$. Analogously, a complex matrix A is said to be *normal* if it commutes with its conjugate transpose, i.e. if $AA^* = A^*A$.

Example 13.20: Let $A = \begin{pmatrix} 1 & 1 \\ i & 3+2i \end{pmatrix}$. Then

$$AA^* = \begin{pmatrix} 1 & 1 \\ i & 3+2i \end{pmatrix}\begin{pmatrix} 1 & -i \\ 1 & 3-2i \end{pmatrix} = \begin{pmatrix} 2 & 3-3i \\ 3+3i & 14 \end{pmatrix}$$

$$A^*A = \begin{pmatrix} 1 & -i \\ 1 & 3-2i \end{pmatrix}\begin{pmatrix} 1 & 1 \\ i & 3+2i \end{pmatrix} = \begin{pmatrix} 2 & 3-3i \\ 3+3i & 14 \end{pmatrix}$$

Thus A is a normal matrix.

The following theorem applies.

Theorem 13.16: Let T be a normal operator on a complex finite dimensional inner product space V. Then there exists an orthonormal basis of V consisting of eigenvectors of T; that is, T can be represented by a diagonal matrix relative to an orthonormal basis.

We give the corresponding statement for matrices.

Alternative Form of Theorem 13.16: Let A be a normal matrix. Then there exists a unitary matrix P such that $B = P^{-1}AP = P^*AP$ is diagonal.

The next theorem shows that even non-normal operators on unitary spaces have a relatively simple form.

Theorem 13.17: Let T be an arbitrary operator on a complex finite dimensional inner product space V. Then T can be represented by a triangular matrix relative to an orthonormal basis of V.

Alternative Form of Theorem 13.17:   Let A be an arbitrary complex matrix.   Then there exists a unitary matrix P such that $B = P^{-1}AP = P*AP$ is triangular.

SPECTRAL THEOREM

The Spectral Theorem is a reformulation of the diagonalization Theorems 13.14 and 13.16.

Theorem 13.18 (Spectral Theorem):   Let T be a normal (symmetric) operator on a complex (real) finite dimensional inner product space V.   Then there exist orthogonal projections $E_1, \ldots, E_r$ on V and scalars $\lambda_1, \ldots, \lambda_r$ such that

(i) $T = \lambda_1 E_1 + \lambda_2 E_2 + \cdots + \lambda_r E_r$

(ii) $E_1 + E_2 + \cdots + E_r = I$

(iii) $E_i E_j = 0$ for $i \neq j$.

The next example shows the relationship between a diagonal matrix representation and the corresponding orthogonal projections.

Example 13.21:   Consider a diagonal matrix, say $A = \begin{pmatrix} 2 & & & \\ & 3 & & \\ & & 3 & \\ & & & 5 \end{pmatrix}$.   Let

$$E_1 = \begin{pmatrix} 1 & & & \\ & 0 & & \\ & & 0 & \\ & & & 0 \end{pmatrix}, \quad E_2 = \begin{pmatrix} 0 & & & \\ & 1 & & \\ & & 1 & \\ & & & 0 \end{pmatrix}, \quad E_3 = \begin{pmatrix} 0 & & & \\ & 0 & & \\ & & 0 & \\ & & & 1 \end{pmatrix}$$

The reader can verify that the E_i are projections, i.e. $E_i^2 = E_i$, and that

(i) $A = 2E_1 + 3E_2 + 5E_3$,   (ii) $E_1 + E_2 + E_3 = I$,   (iii) $E_i E_j = 0$ for $i \neq j$

Solved Problems

INNER PRODUCTS

13.1.   Verify the relation $\langle u, av_1 + bv_2 \rangle = \bar{a} \langle u, v_1 \rangle + \bar{b} \langle u, v_2 \rangle$.

Using $[I_2]$, $[I_1]$ and then $[I_2]$, we find

$$\langle u, av_1 + bv_2 \rangle = \overline{\langle av_1 + bv_2, u \rangle} = \overline{a \langle v_1, u \rangle + b \langle v_2, u \rangle}$$
$$= \bar{a} \overline{\langle v_1, u \rangle} + \bar{b} \overline{\langle v_2, u \rangle} = \bar{a} \langle u, v_1 \rangle + \bar{b} \langle u, v_2 \rangle$$

13.2.   Verify that the following is an inner product in $\mathbf{R}^2$:

$\langle u, v \rangle = x_1 y_1 - x_1 y_2 - x_2 y_1 + 3x_2 y_2$, where $u = (x_1, x_2)$, $v = (y_1, y_2)$.

Method 1.

We verify the three axioms of an inner product.   Letting $w = (z_1, z_2)$, we find

$$au + bw = a(x_1, x_2) + b(z_1, z_2) = (ax_1 + bz_1, ax_2 + bz_2)$$

Thus

$$\langle au + bw, v \rangle = \langle (ax_1 + bz_1, ax_2 + bz_2), (y_1, y_2) \rangle$$

$$= (ax_1 + bz_1)y_1 - (ax_1 + bz_1)y_2 - (ax_2 + bz_2)y_1 + 3(ax_2 + bz_2)y_2$$

$$= a(x_1y_1 - x_1y_2 - x_2y_1 + 3x_2y_2) + b(z_1y_1 - z_1y_2 - z_2y_1 + 3z_2y_2)$$

$$= a\langle u, v \rangle + b\langle w, v \rangle$$

and so axiom $[I_1]$ is satisfied. Also,

$$\langle v, u \rangle = y_1x_1 - y_1x_2 - y_2x_1 + 3y_2x_2 = x_1y_1 - x_1y_2 - x_2y_1 + 3x_2y_2 = \langle u, v \rangle$$

and axiom $[I_2]$ is satisfied. Finally,

$$\langle u, u \rangle = x_1^2 - 2x_1x_2 + 3x_2^2 = x_1^2 - 2x_1x_2 + x_2^2 + 2x_2^2 = (x_1 - x_2)^2 + 2x_2^2 \geq 0$$

Also, $\langle u, u \rangle = 0$ if and only if $x_1 = 0$, $x_2 = 0$, i.e. $u = 0$. Hence the last axiom $[I_3]$ is satisfied.

Method 2.

We argue via matrices. That is, we can write $\langle u, v \rangle$ in matrix notation:

$$\langle u, v \rangle = u^t A v = (x_1, x_2) \begin{pmatrix} 1 & -1 \\ -1 & 3 \end{pmatrix} \begin{pmatrix} y_1 \\ y_2 \end{pmatrix}$$

and so $[I_1]$ holds. Since A is symmetric, $[I_2]$ holds. Thus we need only show that A is positive definite. Applying the elementary row operation $R_2 \to R_1 + R_2$ and then the corresponding elementary column operation $C_2 \to C_1 + C_2$, we transform A into diagonal form $\begin{pmatrix} 1 & 0 \\ 0 & 2 \end{pmatrix}$. Thus A is positive definite and $[I_3]$ holds.

13.3. Find the norm of $v = (3, 4) \in \mathbf{R}^2$ with respect to:

(i) the usual inner product, (ii) the inner product in Problem 13.2.

(i) $||v||^2 = \langle v, v \rangle = \langle (3, 4), (3, 4) \rangle = 9 + 16 = 25$; hence $||v|| = 5$.

(ii) $||v||^2 = \langle v, v \rangle = \langle (3, 4), (3, 4) \rangle = 9 - 12 - 12 + 48 = 33$; hence $||v|| = \sqrt{33}$.

13.4. Normalize each of the following vectors in Euclidean space $\mathbf{R}^3$:

(i) $u = (2, 1, -1)$, (ii) $v = (\frac{1}{2}, \frac{2}{3}, -\frac{1}{4})$.

(i) Note $\langle u, u \rangle$ is the sum of the squares of the entries of u; that is, $\langle u, u \rangle = 2^2 + 1^2 + (-1)^2 = 6$. Hence divide u by $||u|| = \sqrt{\langle u, u \rangle} = \sqrt{6}$ to obtain the required unit vector:

$$u/||u|| = (2/\sqrt{6}, 1/\sqrt{6}, -1/\sqrt{6})$$

(ii) First multiply v by 12 to "clear" of fractions: $12v = (6, 8, -3)$. We have $\langle 12v, 12v \rangle = 6^2 + 8^2 + (-3)^2 = 109$. Then the required unit vector is

$$12v/||12v|| = (6/\sqrt{109}, 8/\sqrt{109}, -3/\sqrt{109})$$

13.5. Let V be the vector space of polynomials with inner product given by $\langle f, g \rangle = \int_0^1 f(t)\, g(t)\, dt$. Let $f(t) = t + 2$ and $g(t) = t^2 - 2t - 3$. Find (i) $\langle f, g \rangle$ and (ii) $||f||$.

(i) $\langle f, g \rangle = \int_0^1 (t + 2)(t^2 - 2t - 3)\, dt = \left[t^4/4 - 7t^2/2 - 6t \right]_0^1 = -37/4$

(ii) $\langle f, f \rangle = \int_0^1 (t + 2)(t + 2)\, dt = 19/3$ and $||f|| = \sqrt{\langle f, f \rangle} = \sqrt{19/3}$

13.6. Prove Theorem 13.1 (Cauchy-Schwarz): $|\langle u, v\rangle| \leq \|u\|\,\|v\|$.

If $v = 0$, the inequality reduces to $0 \leq 0$ and hence is valid. Now suppose $v \neq 0$. Using $z\bar{z} = |z|^2$ (for any complex number z) and $\langle v, u\rangle = \overline{\langle u, v\rangle}$, we expand $\|u - \langle u, v\rangle tv\|^2 \geq 0$ where t is any real value:

$$
\begin{aligned}
0 \;\leq\; \|u - \langle u, v\rangle tv\|^2 \;&=\; \langle u - \langle u, v\rangle tv,\; u - \langle u, v\rangle tv\rangle \\
&=\; \langle u, u\rangle - \overline{\langle u, v\rangle}t\langle u, v\rangle - \langle u, v\rangle t\langle v, u\rangle + \langle u, v\rangle\overline{\langle u, v\rangle}t^2\langle v, v\rangle \\
&=\; \|u\|^2 - 2t\,|\langle u, v\rangle|^2 + |\langle u, v\rangle|^2\,t^2\,\|v\|^2
\end{aligned}
$$

Set $t = 1/\|v\|^2$ to find $0 \leq \|u\|^2 - \dfrac{|\langle u, v\rangle|^2}{\|v\|^2}$, from which $|\langle u, v\rangle|^2 \leq \|u\|^2\,\|v\|^2$. **Taking the square root of both sides, we obtain the required inequality.**

13.7. Prove that the norm in an inner product space satisfies the following axioms:

[N_1]: $\|v\| \geq 0$; and $\|v\| = 0$ if and only if $v = 0$.

[N_2]: $\|kv\| = |k|\,\|v\|$.

[N_3]: $\|u + v\| \leq \|u\| + \|v\|$.

By [I_3], $\langle v, v\rangle \geq 0$; hence $\|v\| = \sqrt{\langle v, v\rangle} \geq 0$. Furthermore, $\|v\| = 0$ if and only if $\langle v, v\rangle = 0$, and this holds if and only if $v = 0$. Thus [N_1] is valid.

We find $\|kv\|^2 = \langle kv, kv\rangle = k\bar{k}\langle v, v\rangle = |k|^2\,\|v\|^2$. Taking the square root of both sides gives [N_2].

Using the Cauchy-Schwarz inequality, we obtain

$$
\begin{aligned}
\|u + v\|^2 \;&=\; \langle u + v, u + v\rangle \;=\; \langle u, u\rangle + \langle u, v\rangle + \overline{\langle u, v\rangle} + \langle v, v\rangle \\
&\leq\; \|u\|^2 + 2\|u\|\,\|v\| + \|v\|^2 \;=\; (\|u\| + \|v\|)^2
\end{aligned}
$$

Taking the square root of both sides yields [N_3].

Remark: [N_3] is frequently called the *triangle inequality* because if we view $u + v$ as the side of the triangle formed with u and v (as illustrated on the right), then [N_3] states that the length of one side of a triangle is less than or equal to the sum of the lengths of the other two sides.

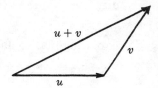

ORTHOGONALITY

13.8. Show that if u is orthogonal to v, then every scalar multiple of u is also orthogonal to v. Find a unit vector orthogonal to $v_1 = (1, 1, 2)$ and $v_2 = (0, 1, 3)$ in $\mathbf{R}^3$.

If $\langle u, v\rangle = 0$ then $\langle ku, v\rangle = k\langle u, v\rangle = k \cdot 0 = 0$, as required. Let $w = (x, y, z)$. We want

$$0 = \langle w, v_1\rangle = x + y + 2z \quad\text{and}\quad 0 = \langle w, v_2\rangle = y + 3z$$

Thus we obtain the homogeneous system

$$x + y + 2z = 0, \quad y + 3z = 0$$

Set $z = 1$ to find $y = -3$ and $x = 1$; then $w = (1, -3, 1)$. Normalize w to obtain the required unit vector w' orthogonal to v_1 and v_2: $w' = w/\|w\| = (1/\sqrt{11}, -3/\sqrt{11}, 1/\sqrt{11})$.

13.9. Let W be the subspace of $\mathbf{R}^5$ spanned by $u = (1, 2, 3, -1, 2)$ and $v = (2, 4, 7, 2, -1)$. Find a basis of the orthogonal complement $W^\perp$ of W.

We seek all vectors $w = (x, y, z, s, t)$ such that

$$
\begin{aligned}
\langle w, u\rangle &= x + 2y + 3z - s + 2t = 0 \\
\langle w, v\rangle &= 2x + 4y + 7z + 2s - t = 0
\end{aligned}
$$

Eliminating x from the second equation, we find the equivalent system

$$
\begin{aligned}
x + 2y + 3z - s + 2t &= 0 \\
z + 4s - 5t &= 0
\end{aligned}
$$

The free variables are y, s and t. Set $y = -1$, $s = 0$, $t = 0$ to obtain the solution $w_1 = (2, -1, 0, 0, 0)$. Set $y = 0$, $s = 1$, $t = 0$ to find the solution $w_2 = (13, 0, -4, 1, 0)$. Set $y = 0$, $s = 0$, $t = 1$ to obtain the solution $w_3 = (-17, 0, 5, 0, 1)$. The set $\{w_1, w_2, w_3\}$ is a basis of $W^\perp$

13.10. Find an orthonormal basis of the subspace W of $\mathbf{C}^3$ spanned by $v_1 = (1, i, 0)$ and $v_2 = (1, 2, 1 - i)$.

Apply the Gram-Schmidt orthogonalization process. First normalize v_1. We find

$$||v_1||^2 = \langle v_1, v_1 \rangle = 1 \cdot 1 + i \cdot (-i) + 0 \cdot 0 = 2 \quad \text{and so} \quad ||v_1|| = \sqrt{2}$$

Thus $u_1 = v_1/||v_1|| = (1/\sqrt{2}, i/\sqrt{2}, 0)$.

To form $w_2 = v_2 - \langle v_2, u_1 \rangle u_1$, first compute

$$\langle v_2, u_1 \rangle = \langle (1, 2, 1-i), (1/\sqrt{2}, i/\sqrt{2}, 0) \rangle = 1/\sqrt{2} - 2i/\sqrt{2} = (1 - 2i)/\sqrt{2}$$

Then $\quad w_2 = (1, 2, 1-i) - \dfrac{1 - 2i}{\sqrt{2}} \left(\dfrac{1}{\sqrt{2}}, \dfrac{i}{\sqrt{2}}, 0 \right) = \left(\dfrac{1 + 2i}{2}, \dfrac{2 - i}{2}, 1 - i \right)$

Next normalize w_2 or, equivalently, $2w_2 = (1 + 2i, 2 - i, 2 - 2i)$. We have

$$||2w_1||^2 = \langle 2w_1, 2w_1 \rangle = (1 + 2i)(1 - 2i) + (2 - i)(2 + i) + (2 - 2i)(2 + 2i) = 18$$

and $||2w_1|| = \sqrt{18}$. Thus the required orthonormal basis of W is

$$\left\{ u_1 = \left(\frac{1}{\sqrt{2}}, \frac{i}{\sqrt{2}}, 0 \right), \quad u_2 = \frac{2w_1}{||2w_1||} = \left(\frac{1 + 2i}{\sqrt{18}}, \frac{2 - i}{\sqrt{18}}, \frac{2 - 2i}{\sqrt{18}} \right) \right\}$$

13.11. Prove Lemma 13.3: An orthonormal set $\{u_1, \ldots, u_r\}$ is linearly independent and, for any $v \in V$, the vector

$$w = v - \langle v, u_1 \rangle u_1 - \langle v, u_2 \rangle u_2 - \cdots - \langle v, u_r \rangle u_r$$

is orthogonal to each of the u_i.

Suppose $a_1 u_1 + \cdots + a_r u_r = 0$. Taking the inner product of both sides with respect to u_1,

$$\begin{aligned} 0 = \langle 0, u_1 \rangle &= \langle a_1 u_1 + \cdots + a_r u_r, u_1 \rangle \\ &= a_1 \langle u_1, u_1 \rangle + a_2 \langle u_2, u_1 \rangle + \cdots + a_r \langle u_r, u_1 \rangle \\ &= a_1 \cdot 1 + a_2 \cdot 0 + \cdots + a_r \cdot 0 = a_1 \end{aligned}$$

or $a_1 = 0$. Similarly, for $i = 2, \ldots, r$,

$$\begin{aligned} 0 = \langle 0, u_i \rangle &= \langle a_1 u_1 + \cdots + a_r u_r, u_i \rangle \\ &= a_1 \langle u_1, u_i \rangle + \cdots + a_i \langle u_i, u_i \rangle + \cdots + a_r \langle u_r, u_i \rangle = a_i \end{aligned}$$

Accordingly, $\{u_1, \ldots, u_r\}$ is linearly independent.

It remains to show that w is orthogonal to each of the u_i. Taking the inner product of w with respect to u_1,

$$\begin{aligned} \langle w, u_1 \rangle &= \langle v, u_1 \rangle - \langle v, u_1 \rangle \langle u_1, u_1 \rangle - \langle v, u_2 \rangle \langle u_2, u_1 \rangle - \cdots - \langle v, u_r \rangle \langle u_r, u_1 \rangle \\ &= \langle v, u_1 \rangle - \langle v, u_1 \rangle \cdot 1 - \langle v, u_2 \rangle \cdot 0 - \cdots - \langle v, u_r \rangle \cdot 0 = 0 \end{aligned}$$

That is, w is orthogonal to u_1. Similarly, for $i = 2, \ldots, r$,

$$\langle w, u_i \rangle = \langle v, u_i \rangle - \langle v, u_1 \rangle \langle u_1, u_i \rangle - \cdots - \langle v, u_i \rangle \langle u_i, u_i \rangle - \cdots - \langle v, u_r \rangle \langle u_r, u_i \rangle = 0$$

Thus w is orthogonal to u_i for $i = 1, \ldots, r$, as claimed.

13.12. Let W be a subspace of an inner product space V. Show that there is an orthonormal basis of W which is part of an orthonormal basis of V.

We choose a basis $\{v_1, \ldots, v_r\}$ of W and extend it to a basis $\{v_1, \ldots, v_n\}$ of V. We then apply the Gram-Schmidt orthogonalization process to $\{v_1, \ldots, v_n\}$ to obtain an orthonormal basis $\{u_1, \ldots, u_n\}$ of V where, for $i = 1, \ldots, n$, $u_i = a_{i1} v_1 + \cdots + a_{ii} v_i$. Thus $u_1, \ldots, u_r \in W$ and therefore $\{u_1, \ldots, u_r\}$ is an orthonormal basis of W.

13.13. Prove Theorem 13.2: Let W be a subspace of V; then $V = W \oplus W^{\perp}$.

By Problem 13.12 there exists an orthonormal basis $\{u_1, \ldots, u_r\}$ of W which is part of an orthonormal basis $\{u_1, \ldots, u_n\}$ of V. Since $\{u_1, \ldots, u_n\}$ is orthonormal, $u_{r+1}, \ldots, u_n \in W^{\perp}$. If $v \in V$,

$$v = a_1 u_1 + \cdots + a_n u_n \quad \text{where} \quad a_1 u_1 + \cdots + a_r u_r \in W, \ a_{r+1}u_{r+1} + \cdots + a_n u_n \in W^{\perp}$$

Accordingly, $V = W + W^{\perp}$.

On the other hand, if $w \in W \cap W^{\perp}$, then $\langle w, w \rangle = 0$. This yields $w = 0$; hence $W \cap W^{\perp} = \{0\}$. The two conditions, $V = W + W^{\perp}$ and $W \cap W^{\perp} = \{0\}$, give the desired result $V = W \oplus W^{\perp}$.

Note that we have proved the theorem only for the case that V has finite dimension; we remark that the theorem also holds for spaces of arbitrary dimension.

13.14. Let W be a subspace of W. Show that $W \subset W^{\perp\perp}$, and that $W = W^{\perp\perp}$ when V has finite dimension.

Let $w \in W$. Then $\langle w, v \rangle = 0$ for every $v \in W^{\perp}$; hence $w \in W^{\perp\perp}$. Accordingly, $W \subset W^{\perp\perp}$.

Now suppose V has finite dimension. By Theorem 13.2, $V = W \oplus W^{\perp}$ and, also, $V = W^{\perp} \oplus W^{\perp\perp}$. Hence

$$\dim W = \dim V - \dim W^{\perp} \quad \text{and} \quad \dim W^{\perp\perp} = \dim V - \dim W^{\perp}$$

This yields $\dim W = \dim W^{\perp\perp}$. But $W \subset W^{\perp\perp}$ by the above; hence $W = W^{\perp\perp}$, as required.

13.15. Let $\{e_1, \ldots, e_n\}$ be an orthonormal basis of V. Prove:

(i)   for any $u \in V$, $u = \langle u, e_1 \rangle e_1 + \langle u, e_2 \rangle e_2 + \cdots + \langle u, e_n \rangle e_n$;

(ii) $\langle a_1 e_1 + \cdots + a_n e_n, \ b_1 e_1 + \cdots + b_n e_n \rangle = a_1 \overline{b_1} + a_2 \overline{b_2} + \cdots + a_n \overline{b_n}$;

(iii) for any $u, v \in V$, $\langle u, v \rangle = \langle u, e_1 \rangle \overline{\langle v, e_1 \rangle} + \cdots + \langle u, e_n \rangle \overline{\langle v, e_n \rangle}$;

(iv) if $T: V \to V$ is linear, then $\langle T(e_j), e_i \rangle$ is the ij-entry of the matrix A representing T in the given basis $\{e_i\}$.

(i)   Suppose $u = k_1 e_1 + k_2 e_2 + \cdots + k_n e_n$. Taking the inner product of u with e_1,

$$\begin{aligned}
\langle u, e_1 \rangle &= \langle k_1 e_1 + k_2 e_2 + \cdots + k_n e_n, \ e_1 \rangle \\
&= k_1 \langle e_1, e_1 \rangle + k_2 \langle e_2, e_1 \rangle + \cdots + k_n \langle e_n, e_1 \rangle \\
&= k_1 \cdot 1 + k_2 \cdot 0 + \cdots + k_n \cdot 0 = k_1
\end{aligned}$$

Similarly, for $i = 2, \ldots, n$,

$$\begin{aligned}
\langle u, e_i \rangle &= \langle k_1 e_1 + \cdots + k_i e_i + \cdots + k_n e_n, \ e_i \rangle \\
&= k_1 \langle e_1, e_i \rangle + \cdots + k_i \langle e_i, e_i \rangle + \cdots + k_n \langle e_n, e_i \rangle \\
&= k_1 \cdot 0 + \cdots + k_i \cdot 1 + \cdots + k_n \cdot 0 = k_i
\end{aligned}$$

Substituting $\langle u, e_i \rangle$ for k_i in the equation $u = k_1 e_1 + \cdots + k_n e_n$, we obtain the desired result.

(ii) We have
$$\left\langle \sum_{i=1}^{n} a_i e_i, \ \sum_{j=1}^{n} b_j e_j \right\rangle = \sum_{i,j=1}^{n} a_i \overline{b_j} \langle e_i, e_j \rangle$$

But $\langle e_i, e_j \rangle = 0$ for $i \neq j$, and $\langle e_i, e_j \rangle = 1$ for $i = j$; hence, as required,

$$\left\langle \sum_{i=1}^{n} a_i e_i, \ \sum_{j=1}^{n} b_j e_j \right\rangle = \sum_{i=1}^{n} a_i \overline{b_i} = a_1 \overline{b_1} + a_2 \overline{b_2} + \cdots + a_n \overline{b_n}$$

(iii) By (i), $u = \langle u, e_1 \rangle e_1 + \cdots + \langle u, e_n \rangle e_n$ and $v = \langle v, e_1 \rangle e_1 + \cdots + \langle v, e_n \rangle e_n$

Then by (ii), $\langle u, v \rangle = \langle u, e_1 \rangle \overline{\langle v, e_1 \rangle} + \langle u, e_2 \rangle \overline{\langle v, e_2 \rangle} + \cdots + \langle u, e_n \rangle \overline{\langle v, e_n \rangle}$

(iv) By (i),

$$T(e_1) \;=\; \langle T(e_1), e_1 \rangle e_1 + \langle T(e_1), e_2 \rangle e_2 + \cdots + \langle T(e_1), e_n \rangle e_n$$

$$T(e_2) \;=\; \langle T(e_2), e_1 \rangle e_1 + \langle T(e_2), e_2 \rangle e_2 + \cdots + \langle T(e_2), e_n \rangle e_n$$

$$\cdots\cdots\cdots\cdots\cdots\cdots\cdots\cdots\cdots\cdots\cdots\cdots\cdots\cdots\cdots\cdots$$

$$T(e_n) \;=\; \langle T(e_n), e_1 \rangle e_1 + \langle T(e_n), e_2 \rangle e_2 + \cdots + \langle T(e_n), e_n \rangle e_n$$

The matrix A representing T in the basis $\{e_i\}$ is the transpose of the above matrix of coefficients; hence the ij-entry of A is $\langle T(e_j), e_i \rangle$.

ADJOINTS

13.16. Let T be the linear operator on $\mathbf{C}^3$ defined by

$$T(x, y, z) \;=\; (2x + (1-i)y, \; (3+2i)x - 4iz, \; 2ix + (4-3i)y - 3z)$$

Find $T^*(x, y, z)$.

First find the matrix A representing T in the usual basis of $\mathbf{C}^3$ (see Problem 7.3):

$$A \;=\; \begin{pmatrix} 2 & 1-i & 0 \\ 3+2i & 0 & -4i \\ 2i & 4-3i & -3 \end{pmatrix}$$

Form the conjugate transpose A^* of A:

$$A^* \;=\; \begin{pmatrix} 2 & 3-2i & -2i \\ 1+i & 0 & 4+3i \\ 0 & 4i & -3 \end{pmatrix}$$

Thus

$$T^*(x, y, z) \;=\; (2x + (3-2i)y - 2iz, \; (1+i)x + (4+3i)z, \; 4iy - 3z)$$

13.17. Prove Theorem 13.5: Let ϕ be a linear functional on a finite dimensional inner product space V. Then there exists a unique $u \in V$ such that $\phi(v) = \langle v, u \rangle$ for every $v \in V$.

Let $\{e_1, \ldots, e_n\}$ be an orthonormal basis of V. Set

$$u \;=\; \overline{\phi(e_1)}e_1 + \overline{\phi(e_2)}e_2 + \cdots + \overline{\phi(e_n)}e_n$$

Let $\hat{u}$ be the linear functional on V defined by $\hat{u}(v) = \langle v, u \rangle$, for every $v \in V$. Then for $i = 1, \ldots, n$,

$$\hat{u}(e_i) \;=\; \langle e_i, u \rangle \;=\; \langle e_i, \overline{\phi(e_1)}e_1 + \cdots + \overline{\phi(e_n)}e_n \rangle \;=\; \phi(e_i)$$

Since $\hat{u}$ and ϕ agree on each basis vector, $\hat{u} = \phi$.

Now suppose u' is another vector in V for which $\phi(v) = \langle v, u' \rangle$ for every $v \in V$. Then $\langle v, u \rangle = \langle v, u' \rangle$ or $\langle v, u - u' \rangle = 0$. In particular this is true for $v = u - u'$ and so $\langle u - u', u - u' \rangle = 0$. This yields $u - u' = 0$ and $u = u'$. Thus such a vector u is unique as claimed.

13.18. Prove Theorem 13.6: Let T be a linear operator on a finite dimensional inner product space V. Then there exists a unique linear operator T^* on V such that $\langle T(u), v \rangle = \langle u, T^*(v) \rangle$, for every $u, v \in V$. Moreover, if A is the matrix representing T in an orthonormal basis $\{e_i\}$ of V, then the conjugate transpose A^* of A is the matrix representing T^* in $\{e_i\}$.

We first define the mapping T^*. Let v be an arbitrary but fixed element of V. The map $u \mapsto \langle T(u), v \rangle$ is a linear functional on V. Hence by Theorem 13.5 there exists a unique element $v' \in V$ such that $\langle T(u), v \rangle = \langle u, v' \rangle$ for every $u \in V$. We define $T^* V \to V$ by $T^*(v) = v'$. Then $\langle T(u), v \rangle = \langle u, T^*(v) \rangle$ for every $u, v \in V$.

We next show that T^* is linear.   For any $u, v_i \in V$, and any $a, b \in K$,

$$\langle u, T^*(av_1 + bv_2) \rangle = \langle T(u), av_1 + bv_2 \rangle = \bar{a}\langle T(u), v_1 \rangle + \bar{b}\langle T(u), v_2 \rangle$$
$$= \bar{a}\langle u, T^*(v_1) \rangle + \bar{b}\langle u, T^*(v_2) \rangle = \langle u, aT^*(v_1) + bT^*(v_2) \rangle$$

But this is true for every $u \in V$; hence $T^*(av_1 + bv_2) = aT^*(v_1) + bT^*(v_2)$. Thus T^* is linear.

By Problem 13.15(iv), the matrices $A = (a_{ij})$ and $B = (b_{ij})$ representing T and T^* respectively in the basis $\{e_i\}$ are given by $a_{ij} = \langle T(e_j), e_i \rangle$ and $b_{ij} = \langle T^*(e_j), e_i \rangle$. Hence

$$b_{ij} = \langle T^*(e_j), e_i \rangle = \overline{\langle e_i, T^*(e_j) \rangle} = \overline{\langle T(e_i), e_j \rangle} = \bar{a}_{ji}$$

Thus $B = A^*$, as claimed.

13.19. Prove Theorem 13.7:   Let S and T be linear operators on a finite dimensional inner product space V and let $k \in K$.   Then:

$$\text{(i)} \quad (S + T)^* = S^* + T^* \qquad \text{(iii)} \quad (ST)^* = T^*S^*$$
$$\text{(ii)} \quad (kT)^* = \bar{k}T^* \qquad\qquad \text{(iv)} \quad (T^*)^* = T$$

(i)   For any $u, v \in V$,

$$\langle (S + T)(u), v \rangle = \langle S(u) + T(u), v \rangle = \langle S(u), v \rangle + \langle T(u), v \rangle = \langle u, S^*(v) \rangle + \langle u, T^*(v) \rangle$$
$$= \langle u, S^*(v) + T^*(v) \rangle = \langle u, (S^* + T^*)(v) \rangle$$

The uniqueness of the adjoint implies $(S + T)^* = S^* + T^*$.

(ii)   For any $u, v \in V$,

$$\langle (kT)(u), v \rangle = \langle kT(u), v \rangle = k\langle T(u), v \rangle = k\langle u, T^*(v) \rangle = \langle u, \bar{k}T^*(v) \rangle = \langle u, (\bar{k}T^*)(v) \rangle$$

The uniqueness of the adjoint implies $(kT)^* = \bar{k}T^*$.

(iii)   For any $u, v \in V$,

$$\langle (ST)(u), v \rangle = \langle S(T(u)), v \rangle = \langle T(u), S^*(v) \rangle = \langle u, T^*(S^*(v)) \rangle = \langle u, (T^*S^*)(v) \rangle$$

The uniqueness of the adjoint implies $(ST)^* = T^*S^*$.

(iv)   For any $u, v \in V$, $\langle T^*(u), v \rangle = \overline{\langle v, T^*(u) \rangle} = \overline{\langle T(v), u \rangle} = \langle u, T(v) \rangle$

The uniqueness of the adjoint implies $(T^*)^* = T$.

13.20. Show that: (i) $I^* = I$; (ii) $0^* = 0$; (iii) if T is invertible, then $(T^{-1})^* = T^{*-1}$.

(i)   For every $u, v \in V$, $\langle I(u), v \rangle = \langle u, v \rangle = \langle u, I(v) \rangle$; hence $I^* = I$.

(ii)   For every $u, v \in V$, $\langle 0(u), v \rangle = \langle 0, v \rangle = 0 = \langle u, 0 \rangle = \langle u, 0(v) \rangle$; hence $0^* = 0$.

(iii) $I = I^* = (TT^{-1})^* = (T^{-1})^*T^*$; hence $(T^{-1})^* = T^{*-1}$.

13.21. Let T be a linear operator on V, and let W be a T-invariant subspace of V.   Show that $W^\perp$ is invariant under T^*.

Let $u \in W^\perp$. If $w \in W$, then $T(w) \in W$ and so $\langle w, T^*(u) \rangle = \langle T(w), u \rangle = 0$. Thus $T^*(u) \in W^\perp$ since it is orthogonal to every $w \in W$. Hence $W^\perp$ is invariant under T^*.

13.22. Let T be a linear operator on V.   Show that each of the following conditions implies $T = 0$:

(i) $\langle T(u), v \rangle = 0$ for every $u, v \in V$;

(ii) V is a complex space, and $\langle T(u), u \rangle = 0$ for every $u \in V$;

(iii) T is self-adjoint and $\langle T(u), u \rangle = 0$ for every $u \in V$.

Give an example of an operator T on a real space V for which $\langle T(u), u \rangle = 0$ for every $u \in V$ but $T \neq 0$.

(i)   Set $v = T(u)$. Then $\langle T(u), T(u) \rangle = 0$ and hence $T(u) = 0$, for every $u \in V$. Accordingly, $T = 0$.

(ii) By hypothesis, $\langle T(v + w),\, v + w \rangle = 0$ for any $v, w \in V$. Expanding and setting $\langle T(v), v \rangle = 0$ and $\langle T(w), w \rangle = 0$,

$$\langle T(v),\, w \rangle + \langle T(w),\, v \rangle = 0 \qquad\qquad (1)$$

Note w is arbitrary in (1). Substituting iw for w, and using $\langle T(v), iw \rangle = \bar{i}\langle T(v), w \rangle = -i\langle T(v), w \rangle$ and $\langle T(iw), v \rangle = \langle iT(w), v \rangle = i\langle T(w), v \rangle$,

$$-i\langle T(v),\, w \rangle + i\langle T(w),\, v \rangle = 0$$

Dividing through by i and adding to (1), we obtain $\langle T(w), v \rangle = 0$ for any $v, w \in V$. By (i), $T = 0$.

(iii) By (ii), the result holds for the complex case; hence we need only consider the real case. Expanding $\langle T(v + w),\, v + w \rangle = 0$, we again obtain (1). Since T is self-adjoint and since it is a real space, we have $\langle T(w), v \rangle = \langle w, T(v) \rangle = \langle T(v), w \rangle$. Substituting this into (1), we obtain $\langle T(v), w \rangle = 0$ for any $v, w \in V$. By (i), $T = 0$.

For our example, consider the linear operator T on $\mathbf{R}^2$ defined by $T(x, y) = (y, -x)$. Then $\langle T(u), u \rangle = 0$ for every $u \in V$, but $T \neq 0$.

ORTHOGONAL AND UNITARY OPERATORS AND MATRICES

13.23. Prove Theorem 13.9: The following conditions on an operator U are equivalent: (i) $U^* = U^{-1}$; (ii) $\langle U(v), U(w) \rangle = \langle v, w \rangle$, for every $v, w \in V$; (iii) $\|U(v)\| = \|v\|$, for every $v \in V$.

Suppose (i) holds. Then, for every $v, w \in V$,

$$\langle U(v),\, U(w) \rangle = \langle v,\, U^*U(w) \rangle = \langle v,\, I(w) \rangle = \langle v, w \rangle$$

Thus (i) implies (ii). Now if (ii) holds, then

$$\|U(v)\| = \sqrt{\langle U(v),\, U(v) \rangle} = \sqrt{\langle v, v \rangle} = \|v\|$$

Hence (ii) implies (iii). It remains to show that (iii) implies (i).

Suppose (iii) holds. Then for every $v \in V$,

$$\langle U^*U(v),\, v \rangle = \langle U(v),\, U(v) \rangle = \langle v, v \rangle = \langle I(v),\, v \rangle$$

Hence $\langle (U^*U - I)(v), v \rangle = 0$ for every $v \in V$. But $U^*U - I$ is self-adjoint (Prove!); then by Problem 13.22 we have $U^*U - I = 0$ and so $U^*U = I$. Thus $U^* = U^{-1}$ as claimed.

13.24. Let U be a unitary (orthogonal) operator on V, and let W be a subspace invariant under U. Show that $W^\perp$ is also invariant under U.

Since U is nonsingular, $U(W) = W$; that is, for any $w \in W$ there exists $w' \in W$ such that $U(w') = w$. Now let $v \in W^\perp$. Then for any $w \in W$,

$$\langle U(v),\, w \rangle = \langle U(v),\, U(w') \rangle = \langle v, w' \rangle = 0$$

Thus $U(v)$ belongs to $W^\perp$. Therefore $W^\perp$ is invariant under U.

13.25. Let A be a matrix with rows R_i and columns C_i. Show that: (i) the ij-entry of AA^* is $\langle R_i, R_j \rangle$; (ii) the ij-entry of A^*A is $\langle C_j, C_i \rangle$.

If $A = (a_{ij})$, then $A^* = (b_{ij})$ where $b_{ij} = \overline{a_{ji}}$. Thus $AA^* = (c_{ij})$ where

$$c_{ij} = \sum_{k=1}^{n} a_{ik} b_{kj} = \sum_{k=1}^{n} a_{ik}\overline{a_{jk}} = a_{i1}\overline{a_{j1}} + a_{i2}\overline{a_{j2}} + \cdots + a_{in}\overline{a_{jn}}$$
$$= \overline{\langle (a_{i1}, \ldots, a_{in}),\, (a_{j1}, \ldots, a_{jn}) \rangle} = \langle R_i, R_j \rangle$$

as required. Also, $A^*A = (d_{ij})$ where

$$d_{ij} = \sum_{k=1}^{n} b_{ik} a_{kj} = \sum_{k=1}^{n} a_{kj}\overline{a_{ki}} = a_{1j}\overline{a_{1i}} + a_{2j}\overline{a_{2i}} + \cdots + a_{nj}\overline{a_{ni}}$$
$$= \langle (a_{1j}, \ldots, a_{nj}),\, (a_{1i}, \ldots, a_{ni}) \rangle = \langle C_j, C_i \rangle$$

13.26. Prove Theorem 13.11:   The following conditions for a matrix A are equivalent:
(i) A is unitary (orthogonal). (ii) The rows of A form an orthonormal set. (iii) The columns of A form an orthonormal set.

Let R_i and C_i denote the rows and columns of A, respectively. By the preceding problem, $AA^* = (c_{ij})$ where $c_{ij} = \langle R_i, R_j \rangle$. Thus $AA^* = I$ if and only if $\langle R_i, R_j \rangle = \delta_{ij}$. That is, (i) is equivalent to (ii).

Also, by the preceding problem, $A^*A = (d_{ij})$ where $d_{ij} = \langle C_j, C_i \rangle$. Thus $A^*A = I$ if and only if $\langle C_j, C_i \rangle = \delta_{ij}$. That is, (i) is equivalent to (iii).

Remark: Since (ii) and (iii) are equivalent, A is unitary (orthogonal) if and only if the transpose of A is unitary (orthogonal).

13.27. Find an orthogonal matrix A whose first row is $u_1 = (1/3, 2/3, 2/3)$.

First find a nonzero vector $w_2 = (x, y, z)$ which is orthogonal to u_1, i.e. for which

$$0 = \langle u_1, w_2 \rangle = x/3 + 2y/3 + 2z/3 = 0 \quad \text{or} \quad x + 2y + 2z = 0$$

One such solution is $w_2 = (0, 1, -1)$. Normalize w_2 to obtain the second row of A, i.e. $u_2 = (0, 1/\sqrt{2}, -1/\sqrt{2})$.

Next find a nonzero vector $w_3 = (x, y, z)$ which is orthogonal to both u_1 and u_2, i.e. for which

$$0 = \langle u_1, w_3 \rangle = x/3 + 2y/3 + 2z/3 = 0 \quad \text{or} \quad x + 2y + 2z = 0$$
$$0 = \langle u_2, w_3 \rangle = \qquad\quad y/\sqrt{2} - z/\sqrt{2} = 0 \quad \text{or} \qquad\quad y - z = 0$$

Set $z = -1$ and find the solution $w_3 = (4, -1, -1)$. Normalize w_3 and obtain the third row of A, i.e. $u_3 = (4/\sqrt{18}, -1/\sqrt{18}, -1/\sqrt{18})$.   Thus

$$A = \begin{pmatrix} 1/3 & 2/3 & 2/3 \\ 0 & 1/\sqrt{2} & -1/\sqrt{2} \\ 4/3\sqrt{2} & -1/3\sqrt{2} & -1/3\sqrt{2} \end{pmatrix}$$

We emphasize that the above matrix A is not unique.

13.28. Prove Theorem 13.12:   Let $\{e_1, \ldots, e_n\}$ be an orthonormal basis of an inner product space V.   Then the transition matrix from $\{e_i\}$ into another orthonormal basis is unitary (orthogonal).   Conversely, if $P = (a_{ij})$ is a unitary (orthogonal) matrix, then the following is an orthonormal basis:

$$\{e_i' = a_{1i}e_1 + a_{2i}e_2 + \cdots + a_{ni}e_n : i = 1, \ldots, n\}$$

Suppose $\{f_i\}$ is another orthonormal basis and suppose

$$f_i = b_{i1}e_1 + b_{i2}e_2 + \cdots + b_{in}e_n, \quad i = 1, \ldots, n \tag{1}$$

By Problem 13.15 and since $\{f_i\}$ is orthonormal,

$$\delta_{ij} = \langle f_i, f_j \rangle = b_{i1}\overline{b_{j1}} + b_{i2}\overline{b_{j2}} + \cdots + b_{in}\overline{b_{jn}} \tag{2}$$

Let $B = (b_{ij})$ be the matrix of coefficients in (1). (Then B^t is the transition matrix from $\{e_i\}$ to $\{f_i\}$.) By Problem 13.25, $BB^* = (c_{ij})$ where $c_{ij} = b_{i1}\overline{b_{j1}} + b_{i2}\overline{b_{j2}} + \cdots + b_{in}\overline{b_{jn}}$. By (2), $c_{ij} = \delta_{ij}$ and therefore $BB^* = I$. Accordingly B, and hence B^t, are unitary.

It remains to prove that $\{e_i'\}$ is orthonormal. By Problem 13.15,

$$\langle e_i', e_j' \rangle = a_{1i}\overline{a_{1j}} + a_{2i}\overline{a_{2j}} + \cdots + a_{ni}\overline{a_{nj}} = \langle C_i, C_j \rangle$$

where C_i denotes the ith column of the unitary (orthogonal) matrix $P = (a_{ij})$. By Theorem 13.11, the columns of P are orthonormal; hence $\langle e_i', e_j' \rangle = \langle C_i, C_j \rangle = \delta_{ij}$. Thus $\{e_i'\}$ is an orthonormal basis.

13.29. Suppose A is orthogonal.   Show that $\det(A) = 1$ or -1.

Since A is orthogonal, $AA^t = I$. Using $|A| = |A^t|$,

$$1 = |I| = |AA^t| = |A||A^t| = |A|^2$$

Therefore $|A| = 1$ or -1.

13.30. Show that every 2 by 2 orthogonal matrix A for which $\det(A) = 1$ is of the form $\begin{pmatrix} \cos\theta & -\sin\theta \\ \sin\theta & \cos\theta \end{pmatrix}$ for some real number θ.

Suppose $A = \begin{pmatrix} a & b \\ c & d \end{pmatrix}$. Since A is orthogonal, its rows form an orthonormal set; hence

$$a^2 + b^2 = 1, \quad c^2 + d^2 = 1, \quad ac + bd = 0, \quad ad - bc = 1$$

The last equation follows from $\det(A) = 1$. We consider separately the cases $a = 0$ and $a \neq 0$.

If $a = 0$, the first equation gives $b^2 = 1$ and therefore $b = \pm 1$. Then the fourth equation gives $c = -b = \mp 1$, and the second equation yields $1 + d^2 = 1$ or $d = 0$. Thus

$$A = \begin{pmatrix} 0 & 1 \\ -1 & 0 \end{pmatrix} \quad \text{or} \quad \begin{pmatrix} 0 & -1 \\ 1 & 0 \end{pmatrix}$$

The first alternative has the required form with $\theta = -\pi/2$, and the second alternative has the required form with $\theta = \pi/2$.

If $a \neq 0$, the third equation can be solved to give $c = -bd/a$. Substituting this into the second equation,

$$b^2 d^2 / a^2 + d^2 = 1 \quad \text{or} \quad b^2 d^2 + a^2 d^2 = a^2 \quad \text{or} \quad (b^2 + a^2) d^2 = a^2 \quad \text{or} \quad a^2 = d^2$$

and therefore $a = d$ or $a = -d$. If $a = -d$, then the third equation yields $c = b$ and so the fourth equation gives $-a^2 - c^2 = 1$ which is impossible. Thus $a = d$. But then the third equation gives $b = -c$ and so

$$A = \begin{pmatrix} a & -c \\ c & a \end{pmatrix}$$

Since $a^2 + c^2 = 1$, there is a real number θ such that $a = \cos\theta$, $c = \sin\theta$ and hence A has the required form in this case also.

SYMMETRIC OPERATORS AND CANONICAL FORMS IN EUCLIDEAN SPACES

13.31. Let T be a symmetric operator. Show that: (i) the characteristic polynomial $\Delta(t)$ of T is a product of linear polynomials (over $\mathbf{R}$); (ii) T has a nonzero eigenvector; (iii) eigenvectors of T belonging to distinct eigenvalues are orthogonal.

(i)   Let A be a matrix representing T relative to an orthonormal basis of V; then $A = A^t$. Let $\Delta(t)$ be the characteristic polynomial of A. Viewing A as a complex self-adjoint operator, A has only real eigenvalues by Theorem 13.8. Thus

$$\Delta(t) = (t - \lambda_1)(t - \lambda_2) \cdots (t - \lambda_n)$$

where the λ_i are all real. In other words, $\Delta(t)$ is a product of linear polynomials over $\mathbf{R}$.

(ii)   By (i), T has at least one (real) eigenvalue. Hence T has a nonzero eigenvector.

(iii)   Suppose $T(v) = \lambda v$ and $T(w) = \mu w$ where $\lambda \neq \mu$. We show that $\lambda\langle v, w\rangle = \mu\langle v, w\rangle$:

$$\lambda\langle v, w\rangle = \langle \lambda v, w\rangle = \langle T(v), w\rangle = \langle v, T(w)\rangle = \langle v, \mu w\rangle = \mu\langle v, w\rangle$$

But $\lambda \neq \mu$; hence $\langle v, w\rangle = 0$ as claimed.

13.32. Prove Theorem 13.14:   Let T be a symmetric operator on a real inner product space V. Then there exists an orthonormal basis of V consisting of eigenvectors of T; that is, T can be represented by a diagonal matrix relative to an orthonormal basis.

The proof is by induction on the dimension of V. If $\dim V = 1$, the theorem trivially holds. Now suppose $\dim V = n > 1$. By the preceding problem, there exists a nonzero eigenvector v_1 of T. Let W be the space spanned by v_1, and let u_1 be a unit vector in W, e.g. let $u_1 = v_1/\|v_1\|$.

Since v_1 is an eigenvector of T, the subspace W of V is invariant under T. By Problem 13.21, $W^\perp$ is invariant under $T^* = T$. Thus the restriction $\hat{T}$ of T to $W^\perp$ is a symmetric operator. By Theorem 13.2, $V = W \oplus W^\perp$. Hence $\dim W^\perp = n - 1$ since $\dim W = 1$. By induction, there exists an orthonormal basis $\{u_2, \ldots, u_n\}$ of $W^\perp$ consisting of eigenvectors of $\hat{T}$ and hence of T. But $\langle u_1, u_i \rangle = 0$ for $i = 2, \ldots, n$ because $u_i \in W^\perp$. Accordingly $\{u_1, u_2, \ldots, u_n\}$ is an orthonormal set and consists of eigenvectors of T. Thus the theorem is proved.

13.33. Let $A = \begin{pmatrix} 1 & 2 \\ 2 & 1 \end{pmatrix}$. Find a (real) orthogonal matrix P for which $P^t A P$ is diagonal.

The characteristic polynomial $\Delta(t)$ of A is

$$\Delta(t) = |tI - A| = \begin{vmatrix} t-1 & -2 \\ -2 & t-1 \end{vmatrix} = t^2 - 2t - 3 = (t-3)(t+1)$$

and thus the eigenvalues of A are 3 and -1. Substitute $t = 3$ into the matrix $tI - A$ to obtain the corresponding homogeneous system of linear equations

$$2x - 2y = 0, \qquad -2x + 2y = 0$$

A nonzero solution is $v_1 = (1, 1)$. Normalize v_1 to find the unit solution $u_1 = (1/\sqrt{2}, 1/\sqrt{2})$.

Next substitute $t = -1$ into the matrix $tI - A$ to obtain the corresponding homogeneous system of linear equations

$$-2x - 2y = 0, \qquad -2x - 2y = 0$$

A nonzero solution is $v_2 = (1, -1)$. Normalize v_2 to find the unit solution $u_2 = (1/\sqrt{2}, -1/\sqrt{2})$.

Finally let P be the matrix whose columns are u_1 and u_2 respectively; then

$$P = \begin{pmatrix} 1/\sqrt{2} & 1/\sqrt{2} \\ 1/\sqrt{2} & -1/\sqrt{2} \end{pmatrix} \quad \text{and} \quad P^t A P = \begin{pmatrix} 3 & 0 \\ 0 & -1 \end{pmatrix}$$

As expected, the diagonal entries of $P^t A P$ are the eigenvalues of A.

13.34. Let $A = \begin{pmatrix} 2 & 1 & 1 \\ 1 & 2 & 1 \\ 1 & 1 & 2 \end{pmatrix}$. Find a (real) orthogonal matrix P for which $P^t A P$ is diagonal.

First find the characteristic polynomial $\Delta(t)$ of A:

$$\Delta(t) = |tI - A| = \begin{vmatrix} t-2 & -1 & -1 \\ -1 & t-2 & -1 \\ -1 & -1 & t-2 \end{vmatrix} = (t-1)^2(t-4)$$

Thus the eigenvalues of A are 1 (with multiplicity two) and 4 (with multiplicity one). Substitute $t = 1$ into the matrix $tI - A$ to obtain the corresponding homogeneous system

$$-x - y - z = 0, \qquad -x - y - z = 0, \qquad -x - y - z = 0$$

That is, $x + y + z = 0$. The system has two independent solutions. One such solution is $v_1 = (1, -1, 0)$. We seek a second solution $v_2 = (a, b, c)$ which is also orthogonal to v_1; that is, such that

$$a + b + c = 0 \quad \text{and also} \quad a - b = 0$$

For example, $v_2 = (1, 1, -2)$. Next we normalize v_1 and v_2 to obtain the unit orthogonal solutions

$$u_1 = (1/\sqrt{2}, -1/\sqrt{2}, 0), \qquad u_2 = (1/\sqrt{6}, 1/\sqrt{6}, -2/\sqrt{6})$$

Now substitute $t = 4$ into the matrix $tI - A$ to find the corresponding homogeneous system

$$2x - y - z = 0, \qquad -x + 2y - z = 0, \qquad -x - y + 2z = 0$$

Find a nonzero solution such as $v_3 = (1, 1, 1)$, and normalize v_3 to obtain the unit solution $u_3 = (1/\sqrt{3}, 1/\sqrt{3}, 1/\sqrt{3})$. Finally, if P is the matrix whose columns are the u_i respectively,

$$P = \begin{pmatrix} 1/\sqrt{2} & 1/\sqrt{6} & 1/\sqrt{3} \\ -1/\sqrt{2} & 1/\sqrt{6} & 1/\sqrt{3} \\ 0 & -2/\sqrt{6} & 1/\sqrt{3} \end{pmatrix} \quad \text{and} \quad P^tAP = \begin{pmatrix} 1 & 0 & 0 \\ 0 & 1 & 0 \\ 0 & 0 & 4 \end{pmatrix}$$

13.35. Find an orthogonal change of coordinates which diagonalizes the real quadratic form $q(x,y) = 2x^2 + 2xy + 2y^2$.

First find the symmetric matrix A representing q and then its characteristic polynomial $\Delta(t)$:

$$A = \begin{pmatrix} 2 & 1 \\ 1 & 2 \end{pmatrix} \quad \text{and} \quad \Delta(t) = |tI - A| = \begin{vmatrix} t-2 & -1 \\ -1 & t-2 \end{vmatrix} = (t-1)(t-3)$$

The eigenvalues of A are 1 and 3; hence the diagonal form of q is

$$q(x', y') = x'^2 + 3y'^2$$

We find the corresponding transformation of coordinates by obtaining a corresponding orthonormal set of eigenvectors of A.

Set $t = 1$ into the matrix $tI - A$ to obtain the corresponding homogeneous system

$$-x - y = 0, \quad -x - y = 0$$

A nonzero solution is $v_1 = (1, -1)$. Now set $t = 3$ into the matrix $tI - A$ to find the corresponding homogeneous system

$$x - y = 0, \quad -x + y = 0$$

A nonzero solution is $v_2 = (1, 1)$. As expected by Problem 13.31, v_1 and v_2 are orthogonal. Normalize v_1 and v_2 to obtain the orthonormal basis

$$\{u_1 = (1/\sqrt{2}, -1/\sqrt{2}), \ u_2 = (1/\sqrt{2}, 1/\sqrt{2})\}$$

The transition matrix P and the required transformation of coordinates follow:

$$P = \begin{pmatrix} 1/\sqrt{2} & 1/\sqrt{2} \\ -1/\sqrt{2} & 1/\sqrt{2} \end{pmatrix} \quad \text{and} \quad \begin{pmatrix} x \\ y \end{pmatrix} = P\begin{pmatrix} x' \\ y' \end{pmatrix} \quad \text{or} \quad \begin{aligned} x &= (x' + y')/\sqrt{2} \\ y &= (-x' + y')/\sqrt{2} \end{aligned}$$

Note that the columns of P are u_1 and u_2. We can also express x' and y' in terms of x and y by using $P^{-1} = P^t$; that is,

$$x' = (x - y)/\sqrt{2}, \quad y' = (x + y)/\sqrt{2}$$

13.36. Prove Theorem 13.15: Let T be an orthogonal operator on a real inner product space V. Then there is an orthonormal basis with respect to which T has the following form:

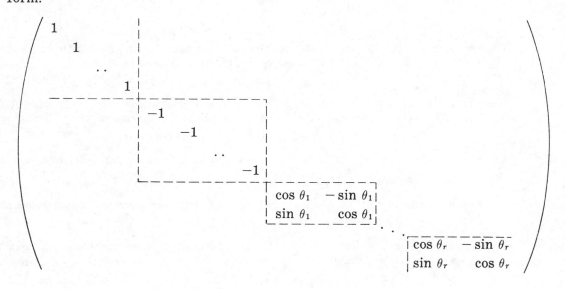

Let $S = T + T^{-1} = T + T^*$. Then $S^* = (T + T^*)^* = T^* + T = S$. Thus S is a symmetric operator on V. By Theorem 13.14, there exists an orthonormal basis of V consisting of eigenvectors of S. If $\lambda_1, \ldots, \lambda_m$ denote the distinct eigenvalues of S, then V can be decomposed into the direct sum $V = V_1 \oplus V_2 \oplus \cdots \oplus V_m$ where the V_i consists of the eigenvectors of S belonging to λ_i. We claim that each V_i is invariant under T. For suppose $v \in V_i$; then $S(v) = \lambda_i v$ and

$$S(T(v)) = (T + T^{-1})T(v) = T(T + T^{-1})(v) = TS(v) = T(\lambda_i v) = \lambda_i T(v)$$

That is, $T(v) \in V_i$. Hence V_i is invariant under T. Since the V_i are orthogonal to each other, we can restrict our investigation to the way that T acts on each individual V_i.

On a given V_i, $(T + T^{-1})v = S(v) = \lambda_i v$. Multiplying by T,

$$(T^2 - \lambda_i T + I)(v) = 0$$

We consider the cases $\lambda_i = \pm 2$ and $\lambda_i \neq \pm 2$ separately. If $\lambda_i = \pm 2$, then $(T \pm I)^2(v) = 0$ which leads to $(T \pm I)(v) = 0$ or $T(v) = \pm v$. Thus T restricted to this V_i is either I or $-I$.

If $\lambda_i \neq \pm 2$, then T has no eigenvectors in V_i since by Theorem 13.8 the only eigenvalues of T are 1 or -1. Accordingly, for $v \neq 0$ the vectors v and $T(v)$ are linearly independent. Let W be the subspace spanned by v and $T(v)$. Then W is invariant under T, since

$$T(T(v)) = T^2(v) = \lambda_i T(v) - v$$

By Theorem 13.2, $V_i = W \oplus W^\perp$. Furthermore, by Problem 13.24 $W^\perp$ is also invariant under T. Thus we can decompose V_i into the direct sum of two dimensional subspaces W_j where the W_j are orthogonal to each other and each W_j is invariant under T. Thus we can now restrict our investigation to the way T acts on each individual W_j.

Since $T^2 - \lambda_i T + I = 0$, the characteristic polynomial $\Delta(t)$ of T acting on W_j is $\Delta(t) = t^2 - \lambda_i t + 1$. Thus the determinant of T is 1, the constant term in $\Delta(t)$. By Problem 13.30, the matrix A representing T acting on W_j relative to any orthonormal basis of W_j must be of the form

$$\begin{pmatrix} \cos\theta & -\sin\theta \\ \sin\theta & \cos\theta \end{pmatrix}$$

The union of the basis of the W_j gives an orthonormal basis of V_i, and the union of the basis of the V_i gives an orthonormal basis of V in which the matrix representing T is of the desired form.

NORMAL OPERATORS AND CANONICAL FORMS IN UNITARY SPACES

13.37. Determine which matrix is normal: (i) $A = \begin{pmatrix} 1 & i \\ 0 & 1 \end{pmatrix}$, (ii) $B = \begin{pmatrix} 1 & i \\ 1 & 2+i \end{pmatrix}$.

(i) $\quad AA^* = \begin{pmatrix} 1 & i \\ 0 & 1 \end{pmatrix}\begin{pmatrix} 1 & 0 \\ -i & 1 \end{pmatrix} = \begin{pmatrix} 2 & i \\ -i & 1 \end{pmatrix} \qquad A^*A = \begin{pmatrix} 1 & 0 \\ -i & 1 \end{pmatrix}\begin{pmatrix} 1 & i \\ 0 & 1 \end{pmatrix} = \begin{pmatrix} 1 & i \\ -i & 2 \end{pmatrix}$

Since $AA^* \neq A^*A$, the matrix A is not normal.

(ii) $\quad BB^* = \begin{pmatrix} 1 & i \\ 1 & 2+i \end{pmatrix}\begin{pmatrix} 1 & 1 \\ -i & 2-i \end{pmatrix} = \begin{pmatrix} 2 & 2+2i \\ 2-2i & 6 \end{pmatrix}$

$\quad B^*B = \begin{pmatrix} 1 & 1 \\ -i & 2-i \end{pmatrix}\begin{pmatrix} 1 & i \\ 1 & 2+i \end{pmatrix} = \begin{pmatrix} 2 & 2+2i \\ 2-2i & 6 \end{pmatrix}$

Since $BB^* = B^*B$, the matrix B is normal.

13.38. Let T be a normal operator. Prove:

(i) $T(v) = 0$ if and only if $T^*(v) = 0$.

(ii) $T - \lambda I$ is normal.

(iii) If $T(v) = \lambda v$, then $T^*(v) = \bar{\lambda} v$; hence any eigenvector of T is also an eigenvector of T^*.

(iv) If $T(v) = \lambda_1 v$ and $T(w) = \lambda_2 w$ where $\lambda_1 \neq \lambda_2$, then $\langle v, w \rangle = 0$; that is, eigenvectors of T belonging to distinct eigenvalues are orthonormal.

(i)   We show that $\langle T(v), T(v) \rangle = \langle T^*(v), T^*(v) \rangle$:

$$\langle T(v), T(v) \rangle = \langle v, T^*T(v) \rangle = \langle v, TT^*(v) \rangle = \langle T^*(v), T^*(v) \rangle$$

Hence by $[I_3]$, $T(v) = 0$ if and only if $T^*(v) = 0$.

(ii)   We show that $T - \lambda I$ commutes with its adjoint:

$$
\begin{aligned}
(T - \lambda I)(T - \lambda I)^* &= (T - \lambda I)(T^* - \bar{\lambda}I) = TT^* - \lambda T^* - \bar{\lambda}T + \lambda\bar{\lambda}I \\
&= T^*T - \bar{\lambda}T - \lambda T^* + \bar{\lambda}\lambda I = (T^* - \bar{\lambda}I)(T - \lambda I) \\
&= (T - \lambda I)^*(T - \lambda I)
\end{aligned}
$$

Thus $T - \lambda I$ is normal.

(iii) If $T(v) = \lambda v$, then $(T - \lambda I)\langle v \rangle = 0$. Now $T - \lambda I$ is normal by (ii); therefore, by (i), $(T - \lambda I)^*(v) = 0$. That is, $(T^* - \lambda I)(v) = 0$; hence $T^*(v) = \bar{\lambda}v$.

(iv)   We show that $\lambda_1 \langle v, w \rangle = \lambda_2 \langle v, w \rangle$:

$$\lambda_1 \langle v, w \rangle = \langle \lambda_1 v, w \rangle = \langle T(v), w \rangle = \langle v, T^*(w) \rangle = \langle v, \bar{\lambda}_2 w \rangle = \lambda_2 \langle v, w \rangle$$

But $\lambda_1 \neq \lambda_2$; hence $\langle v, w \rangle = 0$.

13.39. Prove Theorem 13.16:   Let T be a normal operator on a complex finite dimensional inner product space V.   Then there exists an orthonormal basis of V consisting of eigenvectors of T; that is, T can be represented by a diagonal matrix relative to an orthonormal basis.

The proof is by induction on the dimension of V. If $\dim V = 1$, then the theorem trivially holds. Now suppose $\dim V = n > 1$. Since V is a complex vector space, T has at least one eigenvalue and hence a nonzero eigenvector v. Let W be the subspace of V spanned by v and let u_1 be a unit vector in W.

Since v is an eigenvector of T, the subspace W is invariant under T. However, v is also an eigenvector of T^* by the preceding problem; hence W is also invariant under T^*. By Problem 13.21, $W^\perp$ is invariant under $T^{**} = T$. The remainder of the proof is identical with the latter part of the proof of Theorem 13.14 (Problem 13.32).

13.40. Prove Theorem 13.17:   Let T be an arbitrary operator on a complex finite dimensional inner product space V.   Then T can be represented by a triangular matrix relative to an orthonormal basis $\{u_1, u_2, \ldots, u_n\}$; that is, for $i = 1, \ldots, n$,

$$T(u_i) = a_{i1}u_1 + a_{i2}u_2 + \cdots + a_{ii}u_i$$

The proof is by induction on the dimension of V. If $\dim V = 1$, then the theorem trivially holds. Now suppose $\dim V = n > 1$. Since V is a complex vector space, T has at least one eigenvalue and hence at least one nonzero eigenvector v. Let W be the subspace of V spanned by v and let u_1 be a unit vector in W. Then u_1 is an eigenvector of T and, say, $T(u_1) = a_{11}u_1$.

By Theorem 13.2, $V = W \oplus W^\perp$. Let E denote the orthogonal projection of V into $W^\perp$. Clearly $W^\perp$ is invariant under the operator ET. By induction, there exists an orthonormal basis $\{u_2, \ldots, u_n\}$ of $W^\perp$ such that, for $i = 2, \ldots, n$,

$$ET(u_i) = a_{i2}u_2 + a_{i3}u_3 + \cdots + a_{ii}u_i$$

(Note that $\{u_1, u_2, \ldots, u_n\}$ is an orthonormal basis of V.) But E is the orthogonal projection of V onto $W^\perp$; hence we must have

$$T(u_i) = a_{i1}u_1 + a_{i2}u_2 + \cdots + a_{ii}u_i$$

for $i = 2, \ldots, n$. This with $T(u_1) = a_{11}u_1$ gives us the desired result.

MISCELLANEOUS PROBLEMS

13.41. Prove Theorem 13.13A: The following conditions on an operator P are equivalent:

    (i) $P = T^2$ for some self-adjoint operator T.

    (ii) $P = S^*S$ for some operator S.

    (iii) P is self-adjoint and $\langle P(u), u \rangle \geqq 0$ for every $u \in V$.

       Suppose (i) holds, that is, $P = T^2$ where $T = T^*$. Then $P = TT = T^*T$ and so (i) implies (ii). Now suppose (ii) holds. Then $P^* = (S^*S)^* = S^*S^{**} = S^*S = P$ and so P is self-adjoint. Furthermore,

$$\langle P(u), u \rangle \; = \; \langle S^*S(u), u \rangle \; = \; \langle S(u), S(u) \rangle \; \geqq \; 0$$

Thus (ii) implies (iii), and so it remains to prove that (iii) implies (i).

       Now suppose (iii) holds. Since P is self-adjoint, there exists an orthonormal basis $\{u_1, \ldots, u_n\}$ of V consisting of eigenvectors of P; say, $P(u_i) = \lambda_i u_i$. By Theorem 13.8, the λ_i are real. Using (iii), we show that the λ_i are nonnegative.   We have, for each i,

$$0 \; \leqq \; \langle P(u_i), u_i \rangle \; = \; \langle \lambda_i u_i, u_i \rangle \; = \; \lambda_i \langle u_i, u_i \rangle$$

Thus $\langle u_i, u_i \rangle \geqq 0$ forces $\lambda_i \geqq 0$, as claimed. Accordingly, $\sqrt{\lambda_i}$ is a real number. Let T be the linear operator defined by

$$T(u_i) \; = \; \sqrt{\lambda_i}\, u_i, \quad \text{for } i = 1, \ldots, n$$

Since T is represented by a real diagonal matrix relative to the orthonormal basis $\{u_i\}$, T is self-adjoint. Moreover, for each i,

$$T^2(u_i) \; = \; T(\sqrt{\lambda_i}\, u_i) \; = \; \sqrt{\lambda_i}\, T(u_i) \; = \; \sqrt{\lambda_i}\,\sqrt{\lambda_i}\, u_i \; = \; \lambda_i u_i \; = \; P(u_i)$$

Since T^2 and P agree on a basis of V, $P = T^2$. Thus the theorem is proved.

       Remark: The above operator T is the unique positive operator such that $P = T^2$ (Problem 13.93); it is called the *positive square root* of P.

13.42. Show that any operator T is the sum of a self-adjoint operator and skew-adjoint operator.

       Set $S = \tfrac{1}{2}(T + T^*)$ and $U = \tfrac{1}{2}(T - T^*)$. Then $T = S + U$ where

$$S^* \; = \; (\tfrac{1}{2}(T + T^*))^* \; = \; \tfrac{1}{2}(T^* + T^{**}) \; = \; \tfrac{1}{2}(T^* + T) \; = \; S$$

and
$$U^* \; = \; (\tfrac{1}{2}(T - T^*))^* \; = \; \tfrac{1}{2}(T^* - T) \; = \; -\tfrac{1}{2}(T - T^*) \; = \; -U$$

i.e. S is self-adjoint and U is skew adjoint.

13.43. Prove: Let T be an arbitrary linear operator on a finite dimensional inner product space V. Then T is a product of a unitary (orthogonal) operator U and a unique positive operator P, that is, $T = UP$.   Furthermore, if T is invertible, then U is also uniquely determined.

       By Theorem 13.13, T^*T is a positive operator and hence there exists a (unique) positive operator P such that $P^2 = T^*T$ (Problem 13.93). Observe that

$$\|P(v)\|^2 \; = \; \langle P(v), P(v) \rangle \; = \; \langle P^2(v), v \rangle \; = \; \langle T^*T(v), v \rangle \; = \; \langle T(v), T(v) \rangle \; = \; \|T(v)\|^2 \tag{1}$$

We now consider separately the cases when T is invertible and non-invertible.

       If T is invertible, then we set $\hat{U} = PT^{-1}$. We show that $\hat{U}$ is unitary:

$$\hat{U}^* \; = \; (PT^{-1})^* \; = \; T^{-1*}P^* \; = \; (T^*)^{-1}P \quad \text{and} \quad \hat{U}^*\hat{U} \; = \; (T^*)^{-1}PPT^{-1} \; = \; (T^*)^{-1}T^*TT^{-1} \; = \; I$$

Thus $\hat{U}$ is unitary. We next set $U = \hat{U}^{-1}$. Then U is also unitary and $T = UP$ as required.

       To prove uniqueness, we assume $T = U_0 P_0$ where U_0 is unitary and P_0 is positive. Then

$$T^*T \; = \; P_0^* U_0^* U_0 P_0 \; = \; P_0 I P_0 \; = \; P_0^2$$

But the positive square root of T^*T is unique (Problem 13.93); hence $P_0 = P$. (Note that the invertibility of T is not used to prove the uniqueness of P.) Now if T is invertible, then P is also by (1). Multiplying $U_0 P = UP$ on the right by P^{-1} yields $U_0 = U$. Thus U is also unique when T is invertible.

Now suppose T is not invertible. Let W be the image of P, i.e. $W = \operatorname{Im} P$. We define $U_1 : W \to V$ by
$$U_1(w) = T(v) \quad \text{where} \quad P(v) = w \tag{2}$$

We must show that U_1 is well defined, that is, that $P(v) = P(v')$ implies $T(v) = T(v')$. This follows from the fact that $P(v - v') = 0$ is equivalent to $\|P(v - v')\| = 0$ which forces $\|T(v - v')\| = 0$ by (1). Thus U_1 is well defined. We next define $U_2 : W \to V$. Note by (1) that P and T have the same kernels. Hence the images of P and T have the same dimension, i.e. $\dim (\operatorname{Im} P) = \dim W = \dim (\operatorname{Im} T)$. Consequently, $W^\perp$ and $(\operatorname{Im} T)^\perp$ also have the same dimension. We let U_2 be any isomorphism between $W^\perp$ and $(\operatorname{Im} T)^\perp$.

We next set $U = U_1 \oplus U_2$. (Here U is defined as follows: if $v \in V$ and $v = w + w'$ where $w \in W$, $w' \in W^\perp$, then $U(v) = U_1(w) + U_2(w')$.) Now U is linear (Problem 13.121) and, if $v \in V$ and $P(v) = w$, then by (2)
$$T(v) = U_1(w) = U(w) = UP(v)$$
Thus $T = UP$ as required.

It remains to show that U is unitary. Now every vector $x \in V$ can be written in the form $x = P(v) + w'$ where $w' \in W^\perp$. Then $U(x) = UP(v) + U_2(w') = T(v) + U_2(w')$ where $\langle T(v), U_2(w') \rangle = 0$ by definition of U_2. Also, $\langle T(v), T(v) \rangle = \langle P(v), P(v) \rangle$ by (1). Thus
$$\begin{aligned} \langle U(x), U(x) \rangle &= \langle T(v) + U_2(w'), T(v) + U_2(w') \rangle \\ &= \langle T(v), T(v) \rangle + \langle U_2(w'), U_2(w') \rangle \\ &= \langle P(v), P(v) \rangle + \langle w', w' \rangle = \langle P(v) + w', P(v) + w' \rangle \\ &= \langle x, x \rangle \end{aligned}$$

(We also used the fact that $\langle P(v), w' \rangle = 0$.) Thus U is unitary and the theorem is proved.

13.44. Let $(a_1, a_2, \dots)$ and $(b_1, b_2, \dots)$ be any pair of points in l_2-space of Example 13.5. Show that the sum $\sum\limits_{i=1}^\infty a_i b_i = a_1 b_1 + a_2 b_2 + \cdots$ converges absolutely.

By Problem 1.16 (Cauchy-Schwarz inequality),
$$|a_1 b_1| + \cdots + |a_n b_n| \le \sqrt{\sum_{i=1}^n a_i^2} \sqrt{\sum_{i=1}^n b_i^2} \le \sqrt{\sum_{i=1}^\infty a_i^2} \sqrt{\sum_{i=1}^\infty b_i^2}$$

which holds for every n. Thus the (monotonic) sequence of sums $S_n = |a_1 b_1| + \cdots + |a_n b_n|$ is bounded, and therefore converges. Hence the infinite sum converges absolutely.

13.45. Let V be the vector space of polynomials over $\mathbf{R}$ with inner product defined by $\langle f, g \rangle = \int_0^1 f(t) g(t) \, dt$. Give an example of a linear functional ϕ on V for which Theorem 13.5 does not hold, i.e. there does not exist a polynomial $h(t)$ for which $\phi(f) = \langle f, h \rangle$ for every $f \in V$.

Let $\phi : V \to \mathbf{R}$ be defined by $\phi(f) = f(0)$, that is, ϕ evaluates $f(t)$ at 0 and hence maps $f(t)$ into its constant term. Suppose a polynomial $h(t)$ exists for which
$$\phi(f) = f(0) = \int_0^1 f(t) h(t) \, dt \tag{1}$$

for every polynomial $f(t)$. Observe that ϕ maps the polynomial $tf(t)$ into 0; hence by (1),
$$\int_0^1 tf(t) h(t) \, dt = 0 \tag{2}$$

for every polynomial $f(t)$. In particular, (2) must hold for $f(t) = th(t)$, that is,
$$\int_0^1 t^2 h^2(t) \, dt = 0$$

This integral forces $h(t)$ to be the zero polynomial; hence $\phi(f) = \langle f, h \rangle = \langle f, 0 \rangle = 0$ for every polynomial $f(t)$. This contradicts the fact that ϕ is not the zero functional; hence the polynomial $h(t)$ does not exist.

Supplementary Problems

INNER PRODUCTS

13.46. Verify that
$$\langle a_1u_1 + a_2u_2,\ b_1v_1 + b_2v_2\rangle = a_1\bar{b}_1\langle u_1, v_1\rangle + a_1\bar{b}_2\langle u_1, v_2\rangle + a_2\bar{b}_1\langle u_2, v_1\rangle + a_2\bar{b}_2\langle u_2, v_2\rangle$$

More generally, prove that
$$\left\langle \sum_{i=1}^{m} a_iu_i,\ \sum_{j=1}^{n} b_jv_j \right\rangle = \sum_{i,j} a_i\bar{b}_j\langle u_i, v_j\rangle$$

13.47. Let $u = (x_1, x_2)$ and $v = (y_1, y_2)$ belong to $\mathbf{R}^2$.

(i)   Verify that the following is an inner product on $\mathbf{R}^2$:
$$f(u, v) = x_1y_1 - 2x_1y_2 - 2x_2y_1 + 5x_2y_2$$

(ii) For what values of k is the following an inner product on $\mathbf{R}^2$?
$$f(u, v) = x_1y_1 - 3x_1y_2 - 3x_2y_1 + kx_2y_2$$

(iii) For what values of $a, b, c, d \in \mathbf{R}$ is the following an inner product on $\mathbf{R}^2$?
$$f(u, v) = ax_1y_1 + bx_1y_2 + cx_2y_1 + dx_2y_2$$

13.48. Find the norm of $v = (1, 2) \in \mathbf{R}^2$ with respect to (i) the usual inner product, (ii) the inner product in Problem 13.47(i).

13.49. Let $u = (z_1, z_2)$ and $v = (w_1, w_2)$ belong to $\mathbf{C}^2$.

(i)   Verify that the following is an inner product on $\mathbf{C}^2$:
$$f(u, v) = z_1\bar{w}_1 + (1+i)z_1\bar{w}_2 + (1-i)z_2\bar{w}_1 + 3z_2\bar{w}_2$$

(ii) For what values of $a, b, c, d \in \mathbf{C}$ is the following an inner product on $\mathbf{C}^2$?
$$f(u, v) = az_1\bar{w}_1 + bz_1\bar{w}_2 + cz_2\bar{w}_1 + dz_2\bar{w}_2$$

13.50. Find the norm of $v = (1 - 2i, 2 + 3i) \in \mathbf{C}^2$ with respect to (i) the usual inner product, (ii) the inner product in Problem 13.49(i).

13.51. Show that the distance function $d(u, v) = ||v - u||$, where $u, v \in V$, satisfies the following axiom of a metric space:

[D_1] $d(u, v) \geqq 0$; and $d(u, v) = 0$ if and only if $u = v$.

[D_2] $d(u, v) = d(v, u)$.

[D_3] $d(u, v) \leqq d(u, w) + d(w, v)$.

13.52. Verify the Parallelogram Law: $||u + v|| + ||u - v|| = 2||u|| + 2||v||$.

13.53. Verify the following *polar forms* for $\langle u, v\rangle$:

(i) $\langle u, v\rangle = \frac{1}{4}||u + v||^2 - \frac{1}{4}||u - v||^2$ (real case);

(ii) $\langle u, v\rangle = \frac{1}{4}||u + v||^2 - \frac{1}{4}||u - v||^2 + \frac{i}{4}||u + iv||^2 - \frac{i}{4}||u - iv||^2$ (complex case).

13.54. Let V be the vector space of $m \times n$ matrices over $\mathbf{R}$. Show that $\langle A, B\rangle = \text{tr}(B^tA)$ defines an inner product in V.

13.55. Let V be the vector space of polynomials over $\mathbf{R}$. Show that $\langle f, g\rangle = \int_0^1 f(t)\,g(t)\,dt$ defines an inner product in V.

13.56. Find the norm of each of the following vectors:

(i) $u = (\frac{1}{2}, -\frac{1}{4}, \frac{1}{3}, \frac{1}{6}) \in \mathbf{R}^4$,

(ii) $v = (1 - 2i, 3 + i, 2 - 5i) \in \mathbf{C}^3$,

(iii) $f(t) = t^2 - 2t + 3$ in the space of Problem 13.55,

(iv) $A = \begin{pmatrix} 1 & 2 \\ 3 & -4 \end{pmatrix}$ in the space of Problem 13.54.

13.57. Show that: (i) the sum of two inner products is an inner product; (ii) a positive multiple of an inner product is an inner product.

13.58. Let $a, b, c \in \mathbf{R}$ be such that $at^2 + bt + c \geq 0$ for every $t \in \mathbf{R}$. Show that $b^2 - 4ac \leq 0$. Use this result to prove the Cauchy-Schwarz inequality for real inner product spaces by expanding $||tu + v||^2 \geq 0$.

13.59. Suppose $|\langle u, v \rangle| = ||u|| \, ||v||$. (That is, the Cauchy-Schwarz inequality reduces to an equality.) Show that u and v are linearly independent.

13.60. Find the cosine of the angle θ between u and v if:
(i) $u = (1, -3, 2)$, $v = (2, 1, 5)$ in $\mathbf{R}^3$;
(ii) $u = 2t - 1$, $v = t^2$ in the space of Problem 13.55;
(iii) $u = \begin{pmatrix} 2 & 1 \\ 3 & -1 \end{pmatrix}$, $v = \begin{pmatrix} 0 & -1 \\ 2 & 3 \end{pmatrix}$ in the space of Problem 13.54.

ORTHOGONALITY

13.61. Find a basis of the subspace W of $\mathbf{R}^4$ orthogonal to $u_1 = (1, -2, 3, 4)$ and $u_2 = (3, -5, 7, 8)$.

13.62. Find an orthonormal basis for the subspace W of $\mathbf{C}^3$ spanned by $u_1 = (1, i, 1)$ and $u_2 = (1 + i, 0, 2)$.

13.63. Let V be the vector space of polynomials over $\mathbf{R}$ of degree ≤ 2 with inner product $\langle f, g \rangle = \int_0^1 f(t) \, g(t) \, dt$.
(i)   Find a basis of the subspace W orthogonal to $h(t) = 2t + 1$.
(ii) Apply the Gram-Schmidt orthogonalization process to the basis $\{1, t, t^2\}$ to obtain an orthonormal basis $\{u_1(t), u_2(t), u_3(t)\}$ of V.

13.64. Let V be the vector space of 2×2 matrices over $\mathbf{R}$ with inner product defined by $\langle A, B \rangle = \mathrm{tr}(B^t A)$.
(i)   Show that the following is an orthonormal basis of V:
$$\left\{ \begin{pmatrix} 1 & 0 \\ 0 & 0 \end{pmatrix}, \begin{pmatrix} 0 & 1 \\ 0 & 0 \end{pmatrix}, \begin{pmatrix} 0 & 0 \\ 1 & 0 \end{pmatrix}, \begin{pmatrix} 0 & 0 \\ 0 & 1 \end{pmatrix} \right\}$$
(ii) Find a basis for the orthogonal complement of (a) the diagonal matrices, (b) the symmetric matrices.

13.65. Let W be a subset (not necessarily subspace) of V. Prove: (i) $W^\perp = L(W)$; (ii) if V has finite dimension, then $W^{\perp\perp} = L(W)$. (Here $L(W)$ is the space spanned by W.)

13.66. Let W be the subspace spanned by a nonzero vector w in V, and let E be the orthogonal projection of V onto W. Prove $E(v) = \dfrac{\langle v, w \rangle}{||w||^2} w$. We call $E(v)$ the *projection of v along w*.

13.67. Find the projection of v along w if:
(i) $v = (1, -1, 2)$, $w = (0, 1, 1)$ in $\mathbf{R}^3$;
(ii) $v = (1 - i, 2 + 3i)$, $w = (2 - i, 3)$ in $\mathbf{C}^2$;
(iii) $v = 2t - 1$, $w = t^2$ in the space of Problem 13.55;
(iv) $v = \begin{pmatrix} 1 & 2 \\ 1 & -3 \end{pmatrix}$, $w = \begin{pmatrix} 0 & -1 \\ 1 & 2 \end{pmatrix}$ in the space of Problem 13.54.

13.68. Suppose $\{u_1, \ldots, u_r\}$ is a basis of a subspace W of V where $\dim V = n$. Let $\{v_1, \ldots, v_{n-r}\}$ be an independent set of $n - r$ vectors such that $\langle u_i, v_j \rangle = 0$ for each i and each j. Show that $\{v_1, \ldots, v_{n-r}\}$ is a basis of the orthogonal complement $W^\perp$.

13.69. Suppose $\{u_1, \ldots, u_r\}$ is an orthonormal basis for a subspace W of V. Let $E : V \to V$ be the linear mapping defined by
$$E(v) \;=\; \langle v, u_1 \rangle u_1 + \langle v, u_2 \rangle u_2 + \cdots + \langle v, u_r \rangle u_r$$
Show that E is the orthogonal projection of V onto W.

13.70. Let $\{u_1, \ldots, u_r\}$ be an orthonormal subset of V. Show that, for any $v \in V$, $\sum_{i=1}^{r} |\langle v, u_i \rangle|^2 \le ||v||^2$. (This is known as Bessel's inequality.)

13.71. Let V be a real inner product space. Show that:
(i) $||u|| = ||v||$ if and only if $\langle u + v, u - v \rangle = 0$;
(ii) $||u + v||^2 = ||u||^2 + ||v||^2$ if and only if $\langle u, v \rangle = 0$.
Show by counterexamples that the above statements are not true for, say, $\mathbf{C}^2$.

13.72. Let U and W be subspaces of a finite dimensional inner product space V. Show that: (i) $(U + W)^{\perp} = U^{\perp} \cap W^{\perp}$; (ii) $(U \cap W)^{\perp} = U^{\perp} + W^{\perp}$.

ADJOINT OPERATOR

13.73. Let $T : \mathbf{R}^3 \to \mathbf{R}^3$ be defined by $T(x, y, z) = (x + 2y, 3x - 4z, y)$. Find $T^*(x, y, z)$.

13.74. Let $T : \mathbf{C}^3 \to \mathbf{C}^3$ be defined by
$$T(x, y, z) \;=\; (ix + (2 + 3i)y, \; 3x + (3 - i)z, \; (2 - 5i)y + iz)$$
Find $T^*(x, y, z)$.

13.75. For each of the following linear functions ϕ on V find a vector $u \in V$ such that $\phi(v) = \langle v, u \rangle$ for every $v \in V$:
(i) $\phi : \mathbf{R}^3 \to \mathbf{R}$ defined by $\phi(x, y, z) = x + 2y - 3z$.
(ii) $\phi : \mathbf{C}^3 \to \mathbf{C}$ defined by $\phi(x, y, z) = ix + (2 + 3i)y + (1 - 2i)z$.
(iii) $\phi : V \to \mathbf{R}$ defined by $\phi(f) = f(1)$ where V is the vector space of Problem 13.63.

13.76. Suppose V has finite dimension. Prove that the image of T^* is the orthogonal complement of the kernel of T, i.e. $\operatorname{Im} T^* = (\operatorname{Ker} T)^{\perp}$. Hence $\operatorname{rank}(T) = \operatorname{rank}(T^*)$.

13.77. Show that $T^*T = 0$ implies $T = 0$.

13.78. Let V be the vector space of polynomials over $\mathbf{R}$ with inner product defined by $\langle f, g \rangle = \displaystyle\int_0^1 f(t)\, g(t)\, dt$.
Let D be the derivative operator on V, i.e. $D(f) = df/dt$. Show that there is no operator D^* on V such that $\langle D(f), g \rangle = \langle f, D^*(g) \rangle$ for every $f, g \in V$. That is, D has no adjoint.

UNITARY AND ORTHOGONAL OPERATORS AND MATRICES

13.79. Find an orthogonal matrix whose first row is: (i) $(1/\sqrt{5}, 2/\sqrt{5})$; (ii) a multiple of $(1, 1, 1)$.

13.80. Find a symmetric orthogonal matrix whose first row is $(1/3, 2/3, 2/3)$. (Compare with Problem 13.27.)

13.81. Find a unitary matrix whose first row is: (i) a multiple of $(1, 1 - i)$; (ii) $(\frac{1}{2}, \frac{1}{2}i, \frac{1}{2} - \frac{1}{2}i)$.

13.82. Prove: The product and inverses of orthogonal matrices are orthogonal. (Thus the orthogonal matrices form a group under multiplication called the *orthogonal group*.)

13.83. Prove: The product and inverses of unitary matrices are unitary. (Thus the unitary matrices form a group under multiplication called the *unitary group*.)

13.84. Show that if an orthogonal (unitary) matrix is triangular, then it is diagonal.

13.85. Recall that the complex matrices A and B are unitarily equivalent if there exists a unitary matrix P such that $B = P^*AP$. Show that this relation is an equivalence relation.

13.86. Recall that the real matrices A and B are orthogonally equivalent if there exists an orthogonal matrix P such that $B = P^tAP$. Show that this relation is an equivalence relation.

13.87. Let W be a subspace of V. For any $v \in V$ let $v = w + w'$ where $w \in W$, $w' \in W^\perp$. (Such a sum is unique because $V = W \oplus W^\perp$.) Let $T : V \to V$ be defined by $T(v) = w - w'$. Show that T is a self-adjoint unitary operator on V.

13.88. Let V be an inner product space, and suppose $U : V \to V$ (not necessarily linear) is surjective (onto) and preserves inner products, i.e. $\langle U(v), U(w) \rangle = \langle u, w \rangle$ for every $v, w \in V$. Prove that U is linear and hence unitary.

POSITIVE AND POSITIVE DEFINITE OPERATORS

13.89. Show that the sum of two positive (positive definite) operators is positive (positive definite).

13.90. Let T be a linear operator on V and let $f : V \times V \to K$ be defined by $f(u, v) = \langle T(u), v \rangle$. Show that f is itself an inner product on V if and only if T is positive definite.

13.91. Suppose E is an orthogonal projection onto some subspace W of V. Prove that $kI + E$ is positive (positive definite) if $k \geqq 0$ $(k > 0)$.

13.92. Prove Theorem 13.13B, page 288, on positive definite operators. (The corresponding Theorem 13.13A for positive operators is proved in Problem 13.41.)

13.93. Consider the operator T defined by $T(u_i) = \sqrt{\lambda_i}\, u_i$, $i = 1, \ldots, n$, in the proof of Theorem 13.13A (Problem 13.41). Show that T is positive and that it is the only positive operator for which $T^2 = P$.

13.94. Suppose P is both positive and unitary. Prove that $P = I$.

13.95. An $n \times n$ (real or complex) matrix $A = (a_{ij})$ is said to be *positive* if A viewed as a linear operator on K^n is positive. (An analogous definition defines a positive definite matrix.) Prove A is positive (positive definite) if and only if $a_{ij} = \overline{a_{ji}}$ and

$$\sum_{i,j=1}^{n} a_{ij} x_i \overline{x}_j \geqq 0 \qquad (> 0)$$

for every $(x_1, \ldots, x_n)$ in K^n.

13.96. Determine which of the following matrices are positive (positive definite):

$$\begin{pmatrix} 1 & 1 \\ 1 & 1 \end{pmatrix} \qquad \begin{pmatrix} 0 & i \\ -i & 0 \end{pmatrix} \qquad \begin{pmatrix} 0 & 1 \\ -1 & 0 \end{pmatrix} \qquad \begin{pmatrix} 1 & 1 \\ 0 & 1 \end{pmatrix} \qquad \begin{pmatrix} 2 & 1 \\ 1 & 2 \end{pmatrix} \qquad \begin{pmatrix} 1 & 2 \\ 2 & 1 \end{pmatrix}$$

$$\text{(i)} \qquad\qquad \text{(ii)} \qquad\qquad \text{(iii)} \qquad\qquad \text{(iv)} \qquad\qquad \text{(v)} \qquad\qquad \text{(vi)}$$

13.97. Prove that a 2×2 complex matrix $A = \begin{pmatrix} a & b \\ c & d \end{pmatrix}$ is positive if and only if (i) $A = A^*$, and (ii) a, d and $ad - bc$ are nonnegative real numbers.

13.98. Prove that a diagonal matrix A is positive (positive definite) if and only if every diagonal entry is a nonnegative (positive) real number.

SELF-ADJOINT AND SYMMETRIC OPERATORS

13.99. For any operator T, show that $T + T^*$ is self-adjoint and $T - T^*$ is skew-adjoint.

13.100. Suppose T is self-adjoint. Show that $T^2(v) = 0$ implies $T(v) = 0$. Use this to prove that $T^n(v) = 0$ also implies $T(v) = 0$ for $n > 0$.

13.101. Let V be a complex inner product space. Suppose $\langle T(v), v \rangle$ is real for every $v \in V$. Show that T is self-adjoint.

13.102. Suppose S and T are self-adjoint. Show that ST is self-adjoint if and only if S and T commute, i.e. $ST = TS$.

13.103. For each of the following symmetric matrices A, find an orthogonal matrix P for which $P^t A P$ is diagonal:
  (i) $A = \begin{pmatrix} 1 & 2 \\ 2 & -2 \end{pmatrix}$, (ii) $A = \begin{pmatrix} 5 & 4 \\ 4 & -1 \end{pmatrix}$, (iii) $A = \begin{pmatrix} 7 & 3 \\ 3 & -1 \end{pmatrix}$

13.104. Find an orthogonal transformation of coordinates which diagonalizes each quadratic form:
  (i) $q(x, y) = 2x^2 - 6xy + 10y^2$, (ii) $q(x, y) = x^2 + 8xy - 5y^2$

13.105. Find an orthogonal transformation of coordinates which diagonalizes the quadratic form $q(x, y, z) = 2xy + 2xz + 2yz$.

NORMAL OPERATORS AND MATRICES

13.106. Verify that $A = \begin{pmatrix} 2 & i \\ i & 2 \end{pmatrix}$ is normal. Find a unitary matrix P such that P^*AP is diagonal, and find P^*AP.

13.107. Show that a triangular matrix is normal if and only if it is diagonal.

13.108. Prove that if T is normal on V, then $||T(v)|| = ||T^*(v)||$ for every $v \in V$. Prove that the converse holds in complex inner product spaces.

13.109. Show that self-adjoint, skew-adjoint and unitary (orthogonal) operators are normal.

13.110. Suppose T is normal. Prove that:
  (i) T is self-adjoint if and only if its eigenvalues are real.
  (ii) T is unitary if and only if its eigenvalues have absolute value 1.
  (iii) T is positive if and only if its eigenvalues are nonnegative real numbers.

13.111. Show that if T is normal, then T and T^* have the same kernel and the same image.

13.112. Suppose S and T are normal and commute. Show that $S + T$ and ST are also normal.

13.113. Suppose T is normal and commutes with S. Show that T also commutes with S^*.

13.114. Prove: Let S and T be normal operators on a complex finite dimensional vector space V. Then there exists an orthonormal basis of V consisting of eigenvectors of both S and T. (That is, S and T can be simultaneously diagonalized.)

ISOMORPHISM PROBLEMS

13.115. Let $\{e_1, \ldots, e_n\}$ be an orthonormal basis of an inner product space V over K. Show that the map $v \mapsto [v]_e$ is an (inner product space) isomorphism between V and K^n. (Here $[v]_e$ denotes the coordinate vector of v in the basis $\{e_i\}$.)

13.116. Show that inner product spaces V and W over K are isomorphic if and only if V and W have the same dimension.

13.117. Suppose $\{e_1, \ldots, e_n\}$ and $\{e_1', \ldots, e_n'\}$ are orthonormal bases of V and W respectively. Let $T: V \to W$ be the linear map defined by $T(e_i) = e_i'$, for each i. Show that T is an isomorphism.

13.118. Let V be an inner product space. Recall (page 283) that each $u \in V$ determines a linear functional $\hat{u}$ in the dual space V^* by the definition $\hat{u}(v) = \langle v, u \rangle$ for every $v \in V$. Show that the map $u \mapsto \hat{u}$ is linear and nonsingular, and hence an isomorphism from V onto V^*.

13.119. Consider the inner product space V of Problem 13.54. Show that V is isomorphic to $\mathbf{R}^{mn}$ under the mapping

$$A = \begin{pmatrix} a_{11} & a_{12} & \dots & a_{1n} \\ a_{21} & a_{22} & \dots & a_{2n} \\ \multicolumn{4}{c}{\dotfill} \\ a_{m1} & a_{m2} & \dots & a_{mn} \end{pmatrix} \mapsto (R_1, R_2, \dots, R_m)$$

where $R_i = (a_{i1}, a_{i2}, \dots, a_{in})$, the ith row of A.

MISCELLANEOUS PROBLEMS

13.120. Show that there exists an orthonormal basis $\{u_1, \dots, u_n\}$ of V consisting of eigenvectors of T if and only if there exist orthogonal projections $E_1, \dots, E_r$ and scalars $\lambda_1, \dots, \lambda_r$ such that: (i) $T = \lambda_1 E_1 + \cdots + \lambda_r E_r$; (ii) $E_1 + \cdots + E_r = I$; (iii) $E_i E_j = 0$ for $i \neq j$.

13.121. Suppose $V = U \oplus W$ and suppose $T_1 : U \to V$ and $T_2 : W \to V$ are linear. Show that $T = T_1 \oplus T_2$ is also linear. (Here T is defined as follows: if $v \in V$ and $v = u + w$ where $u \in U$, $w \in W$, then $T(v) = T_1(u) + T_2(w)$.)

13.122. Suppose U is an orthogonal operator on $\mathbf{R}^3$ with positive determinant. Show that U is either a rotation or a reflection through a plane.

Answers to Supplementary Problems

13.47. (ii) $k > 9$;   (iii) $a > 0$, $d > 0$, $ad - bc > 0$

13.48. (i) $\sqrt{5}$,   (ii) $\sqrt{13}$

13.50. (i) $3\sqrt{2}$,   (ii) $5\sqrt{2}$

13.56. (i) $\|u\| = \sqrt{65}/12$,   (ii) $\|v\| = 2\sqrt{11}$,   (iii) $\|f(t)\| = \sqrt{83/15}$,   (iv) $\|A\| = \sqrt{30}$

13.60. (i) $\cos\theta = 9/\sqrt{420}$,   (ii) $\cos\theta = \sqrt{15}/6$,   (iii) $\cos\theta = 2/\sqrt{210}$

13.61. $\{v_1 = (1, 2, 1, 0),\ v_2 = (4, 4, 0, 1)\}$

13.62. $\{v_1 = (1, i, 1)/\sqrt{3},\ v_2 = (2i, 1 - 3i, 3 - i)/\sqrt{24}\}$

13.63. (i) $\{f_1(t) = 7t^2 - 5t,\ f_2(t) = 12t^2 - 5\}$
  (ii) $\{u_1(t) = 1,\ u_2(t) = (2t - 1)/\sqrt{3},\ u_3(t) = (6t^2 - 6t + 1)/\sqrt{5}\}$

13.64. (ii)   (a) $\left\{ \begin{pmatrix} 0 & 1 \\ 0 & 0 \end{pmatrix}, \begin{pmatrix} 0 & 0 \\ 1 & 0 \end{pmatrix} \right\}$,   (b) $\left\{ \begin{pmatrix} 0 & -1 \\ 1 & 0 \end{pmatrix} \right\}$

13.67. (i) $(0, 1/\sqrt{2}, 1/\sqrt{2})$,   (ii) $(26 + 7i, 27 + 24i)/\sqrt{14}$,   (iii) $\sqrt{5}\, t^2/6$,   (iv) $\begin{pmatrix} 0 & 7/\sqrt{6} \\ -7/\sqrt{6} & -14/\sqrt{6} \end{pmatrix}$

13.73. $T^*(x, y, z) = (x + 3y, 2x + z, -4y)$

13.74. $T^*(x, y, z) = (-ix + 3y, (2 - 3i)x + (2 + 5i)z, (3 + i)y - iz)$

13.75. Let $u = \overline{\phi(e_1)}e_1 + \cdots + \overline{\phi(e_n)}e_n$ where $\{e_i\}$ is an orthonormal basis.

(i) $u = (1, 2, -3)$,   (ii) $u = (-i, 2 - 3i, 1 + 2i)$,   (iii) $u = (18t^2 - 8t + 13)/15$

13.79. (i) $\begin{pmatrix} 1/\sqrt{5} & 2/\sqrt{5} \\ 2/\sqrt{5} & -1/\sqrt{5} \end{pmatrix}$,   (ii) $\begin{pmatrix} 1/\sqrt{3} & 1/\sqrt{3} & 1/\sqrt{3} \\ 0 & 1/\sqrt{2} & -1/\sqrt{2} \\ 2/\sqrt{6} & -1/\sqrt{6} & -1/\sqrt{6} \end{pmatrix}$

13.80. $\begin{pmatrix} 1/3 & 2/3 & 2/3 \\ 2/3 & -2/3 & 1/3 \\ 2/3 & 1/3 & -2/3 \end{pmatrix}$

13.81. (i) $\begin{pmatrix} 1/\sqrt{3} & (1 - i)/\sqrt{3} \\ (1 + i)/\sqrt{3} & -1/\sqrt{3} \end{pmatrix}$,   (ii) $\begin{pmatrix} \frac{1}{2} & \frac{1}{2}i & \frac{1}{2} - \frac{1}{2}i \\ i/\sqrt{2} & -1/\sqrt{2} & 0 \\ \frac{1}{2} & -\frac{1}{2}i & -\frac{1}{2} + \frac{1}{2}i \end{pmatrix}$

13.96. Only (i) and (v) are positive. Moreover, (v) is positive definite.

13.103. (i) $P = \begin{pmatrix} 2/\sqrt{5} & -1/\sqrt{5} \\ -1/\sqrt{5} & 2/\sqrt{5} \end{pmatrix}$,   (ii) $P = \begin{pmatrix} 2/\sqrt{5} & -1/\sqrt{5} \\ -1/\sqrt{5} & 2/\sqrt{5} \end{pmatrix}$,   (iii) $P = \begin{pmatrix} 3/\sqrt{10} & -1/\sqrt{10} \\ -1/\sqrt{10} & 3/\sqrt{10} \end{pmatrix}$

13.104. (i) $x = (3x' - y')/\sqrt{10}$, $y = (x' + 3y')/\sqrt{10}$,   (ii) $x = (2x' - y')/\sqrt{5}$, $y = (x' + 2y')/\sqrt{5}$

13.105. $x = x'/\sqrt{3} + y'/\sqrt{2} + z'/\sqrt{6}$, $y = x'/\sqrt{3} - y'/\sqrt{2} + z'/\sqrt{6}$, $z = x'/\sqrt{3} - 2z'/\sqrt{6}$

13.106. $P = \begin{pmatrix} 1/\sqrt{2} & -1/\sqrt{2} \\ 1/\sqrt{2} & 1/\sqrt{2} \end{pmatrix}$, $P^*AP = \begin{pmatrix} 2 + i & 0 \\ 0 & 2 - i \end{pmatrix}$

Appendix A

Sets and Relations

SETS, ELEMENTS

Any well defined list or collection of objects is called a *set*; the objects comprising the set are called its *elements* or *members*. We write

$$p \in A \quad \text{if } p \text{ is an element in the set } A$$

If every element of A also belongs to a set B, i.e. if $x \in A$ implies $x \in B$, then A is called a *subset* of B or is said to be *contained* in B; this is denoted by

$$A \subset B \quad \text{or} \quad B \supset A$$

Two sets are *equal* if they both contain the same elements; that is,

$$A = B \quad \text{if and only if} \quad A \subset B \text{ and } B \subset A$$

The negations of $p \in A$, $A \subset B$ and $A = B$ are written $p \notin A$, $A \not\subset B$ and $A \neq B$ respectively.

We specify a particular set by either listing its elements or by stating properties which characterize the elements in the set. For example,

$$A = \{1, 3, 5, 7, 9\}$$

means A is the set consisting of the numbers 1, 3, 5, 7 and 9; and

$$B = \{x : x \text{ is a prime number, } x < 15\}$$

means that B is the set of prime numbers less than 15. We also use special symbols to denote sets which occur very often in the text. Unless otherwise specified:

$\mathbf{N}$ = the set of positive integers: $1, 2, 3, \ldots$;

$\mathbf{Z}$ = the set of integers: $\ldots, -2, -1, 0, 1, 2, \ldots$;

$\mathbf{Q}$ = the set of rational numbers;

$\mathbf{R}$ = the set of real numbers;

$\mathbf{C}$ = the set of complex numbers.

We also use $\emptyset$ to denote the *empty* or *null* set, i.e. the set which contains no elements; this set is assumed to be a subset of every other set.

Frequently the members of a set are sets themselves. For example, each line in a set of lines is a set of points. To help clarify these situations, we use the words *class*, *collection* and *family* synonymously with set. The words *subclass*, *subcollection* and *subfamily* have meanings analogous to subset.

Example A.1: The sets A and B above can also be written as

$$A = \{x \in \mathbf{N} : x \text{ is odd, } x < 10\} \quad \text{and} \quad B = \{2, 3, 5, 7, 11, 13\}$$

Observe that $9 \in A$ but $9 \notin B$, and $11 \in B$ but $11 \notin A$; whereas $3 \in A$ and $3 \in B$, and $6 \notin A$ and $6 \notin B$.

Example A.2: The sets of numbers are related as follows: $\mathbf{N} \subset \mathbf{Z} \subset \mathbf{Q} \subset \mathbf{R} \subset \mathbf{C}$.

Example A.3: Let $C = \{x : x^2 = 4, x \text{ is odd}\}$. Then $C = \emptyset$, that is, C is the empty set.

Example A.4: The members of the class $\{\{2, 3\}, \{2\}, \{5, 6\}\}$ are the sets $\{2, 3\}$, $\{2\}$ and $\{5, 6\}$.

The following theorem applies.

Theorem A.1:   Let A, B and C be any sets.   Then: (i) $A \subset A$; (ii) if $A \subset B$ and $B \subset A$, then $A = B$; and (iii) if $A \subset B$ and $B \subset C$, then $A \subset C$.

We emphasize that $A \subset B$ does not exclude the possibility that $A = B$.   However, if $A \subset B$ but $A \neq B$, then we say that A is a *proper subset* of B.   (Some authors use the symbol $\subseteq$ for a subset and the symbol $\subset$ only for a proper subset.)

When we speak of an *indexed set* $\{a_i : i \in I\}$, or simply $\{a_i\}$, we mean that there is a mapping ϕ from the set I to a set A and that the image $\phi(i)$ of $i \in I$ is denoted a_i.   The set I is called the *indexing set* and the elements a_i (the range of ϕ) are said to be indexed by I. A set $\{a_1, a_2, \dots\}$ indexed by the positive integers $\mathbf{N}$ is called a *sequence*.   An indexed class of sets $\{A_i : i \in I\}$, or simply $\{A_i\}$, has an analogous meaning except that now the map ϕ assigns to each $i \in I$ a set A_i rather than an element a_i.

SET OPERATIONS

Let A and B be arbitrary sets.   The *union* of A and B, written $A \cup B$, is the set of elements belonging to A or to B; and the *intersection* of A and B, written $A \cap B$, is the set of elements belonging to both A and B:

$$A \cup B = \{x : x \in A \text{ or } x \in B\} \quad \text{and} \quad A \cap B = \{x : x \in A \text{ and } x \in B\}$$

If $A \cap B = \emptyset$, that is, if A and B do not have any elements in common, then A and B are said to be *disjoint*.

We assume that all our sets are subsets of a fixed *universal set* (denoted here by U). Then the *complement* of A, written A^c, is the set of elements which do not belong to A:

$$A^c = \{x \in U : x \notin A\}$$

Example A.5:   The following diagrams, called Venn diagrams, illustrate the above set operations. Here sets are represented by simple plane areas and U, the universal set, by the area in the entire rectangle.

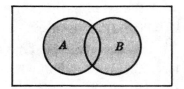

$A \cup B$ is shaded

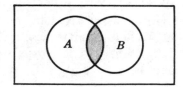

$A \cap B$ is shaded

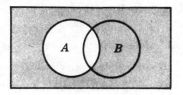

A^c is shaded

Sets under the above operations satisfy various laws or identities which are listed in the table below. In fact, we state

Theorem A.2: Sets satisfy the laws in Table 1.

LAWS OF THE ALGEBRA OF SETS	
Idempotent Laws	
1a. $A \cup A = A$	1b. $A \cap A = A$
Associative Laws	
2a. $(A \cup B) \cup C = A \cup (B \cup C)$	2b. $(A \cap B) \cap C = A \cap (B \cap C)$
Commutative Laws	
3a. $A \cup B = B \cup A$	3b. $A \cap B = B \cap A$
Distributive Laws	
4a. $A \cup (B \cap C) = (A \cup B) \cap (A \cup C)$	4b. $A \cap (B \cup C) = (A \cap B) \cup (A \cap C)$
Identity Laws	
5a. $A \cup \emptyset = A$	5b. $A \cap U = A$
6a. $A \cup U = U$	6b. $A \cap \emptyset = \emptyset$
Complement Laws	
7a. $A \cup A^c = U$	7b. $A \cap A^c = \emptyset$
8a. $(A^c)^c = A$	8b. $U^c = \emptyset, \ \emptyset^c = U$
De Morgan's Laws	
9a. $(A \cup B)^c = A^c \cap B^c$	9b. $(A \cap B)^c = A^c \cup B^c$

Table 1

Remark: Each of the above laws follows from an analogous logical law. For example,

$$A \cap B = \{x : x \in A \text{ and } x \in B\} = \{x : x \in B \text{ and } x \in A\} = B \cap A$$

(Here we use the fact that the composite statement "p and q", written $p \wedge q$, is logically equivalent to the composite statement "q and p", i.e. $q \wedge p$.)

The relationship between set inclusion and the above set operations follows.

Theorem A.3: Each of the following conditions is equivalent to $A \subset B$:

$$\text{(i)} \ \ A \cap B = A \qquad \text{(iii)} \ \ B^c \subset A^c \qquad \qquad \text{(v)} \ \ B \cup A^c = U$$

$$\text{(ii)} \ \ A \cup B = B \qquad \text{(iv)} \ \ A \cap B^c = \emptyset$$

We generalize the above set operations as follows. Let $\{A_i : i \in I\}$ be any family of sets. Then the *union* of the A_i, written $\cup_{i \in I} A_i$ (or simply $\cup_i A_i$), is the set of elements each belonging to at least one of the A_i; and the *intersection* of the A_i, written $\cap_{i \in I} A_i$ or simply $\cap_i A_i$, is the set of elements each belonging to every A_i.

PRODUCT SETS

Let A and B be two sets. The *product set* of A and B, denoted by $A \times B$, consists of all ordered pairs (a, b) where $a \in A$ and $b \in B$:

$$A \times B = \{(a, b) : a \in A, \ b \in B\}$$

The product of a set with itself, say $A \times A$, is denoted by A^2.

Example A.6:   The reader is familiar with the cartesian plane $\mathbf{R}^2 = \mathbf{R} \times \mathbf{R}$ as shown below.   Here each point P represents an ordered pair (a, b) of real numbers, and vice versa.

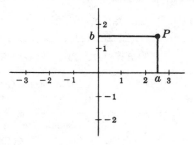

Example A.7:   Let $A = \{1, 2, 3\}$ and $B = \{a, b\}$.   Then
$$A \times B \ = \ \{(1, a), (1, b), (2, a), (2, b), (3, a), (3, b)\}$$

Remark: The ordered pair (a, b) is defined rigorously by $(a, b) \equiv \{\{a\}, \{a, b\}\}$.   From this definition, the "order" property may be proven; that is, $(a, b) = (c, d)$ if and only if $a = c$ and $b = d$.

The concept of product set is extended to any finite number of sets in a natural way. The *product set* of the sets $A_1, \ldots, A_m$, written $A_1 \times A_2 \times \cdots \times A_m$, is the set consisting of all m-tuples $(a_1, a_2, \ldots, a_m)$ where $a_i \in A_i$ for each i.

RELATIONS

A *binary relation* or simply *relation* R from a set A to a set B assigns to each ordered pair $(a, b) \in A \times B$ exactly one of the following statements:

> (i) "a is related to b", written $a R b$,

> (ii) "a is not related to b", written $a \not\!R b$.

A relation from a set A to the same set A is called a *relation in A*.

Example A.8:   Set inclusion is a relation in any class of sets. For, given any pair of sets A and B, either $A \subset B$ or $A \not\subset B$.

Observe that any relation R from A to B uniquely defines a subset $\hat{R}$ of $A \times B$ as follows:
$$\hat{R} \ = \ \{(a, b) : a R b\}$$

Conversely, any subset $\hat{R}$ of $A \times B$ defines a relation from A to B as follows:
$$a R b \ \text{ if and only if } \ (a, b) \in \hat{R}$$

In view of the above correspondence between relations from A to B and subsets of $A \times B$, we redefine a relation as follows:

Definition: A relation R from A to B is a subset of $A \times B$.

EQUIVALENCE RELATIONS

A relation in a set A is called an *equivalence relation* if it satisfies the following axioms:

$[E_1]$ Every $a \in A$ is related to itself.

$[E_2]$ If a is related to b, then b is related to a.

$[E_3]$ If a is related to b and b is related to c, then a is related to c.

In general, a relation is said to be *reflexive* if it satisfies $[E_1]$, *symmetric* if it satisfies $[E_2]$, and *transitive* if it satisfies $[E_3]$.   In other words, a relation is an equivalence relation if it is reflexive, symmetric and transitive.

Example A.9:   Consider the relation $\subset$ of set inclusion. By Theorem A.1, $A \subset A$ for every set A; and if $A \subset B$ and $B \subset C$, then $A \subset C$. That is, $\subset$ is both reflexive and transitive. On the other hand, $\subset$ is not symmetric, since $A \subset B$ and $A \neq B$ implies $B \not\subset A$.

Example A.10: In Euclidean geometry, similarity of triangles is an equivalence relation. For if α, β and γ are any triangles, then: (i) α is similar to itself; (ii) if α is similar to β, then β is similar to α; and (iii) if α is similar to β and β is similar to γ, then α is similar to γ.

If R is an equivalence relation in A, then the *equivalence class* of any element $a \in A$, denoted by $[a]$, is the set of elements to which a is related:

$$[a] \;=\; \{x : a \, R \, x\}$$

The collection of equivalence classes, denoted by A/R, is called the *quotient* of A by R:

$$A/R \;=\; \{[a] : a \in A\}$$

The fundamental property of equivalence relations follows:

Theorem A.4: Let R be an equivalence relation in A. Then the quotient set A/R is a *partition* of A, i.e. each $a \in A$ belongs to a member of A/R, and the members of A/R are pairwise disjoint.

Example A.11: Let R_5 be the relation in $\mathbf{Z}$, the set of integers defined by

$$x \equiv y \quad (\bmod\ 5)$$

which reads "x is congruent to y modulo 5" and which means "$x - y$ is divisible by 5". Then R_5 is an equivalence relation in $\mathbf{Z}$. There are exactly five distinct equivalence classes in $\mathbf{Z}/R_5$:

$$A_0 \;=\; \{\ldots, -10, -5, 0, 5, 10\}$$
$$A_1 \;=\; \{\ldots, -9, -4, 1, 6, 11\}$$
$$A_2 \;=\; \{\ldots, -8, -3, 2, 7, 12\}$$
$$A_3 \;=\; \{\ldots, -7, -2, 3, 8, 13\}$$
$$A_4 \;=\; \{\ldots, -6, -1, 4, 9, 14\}$$

Now each integer x is uniquely expressible in the form $x = 5q + r$ where $0 \leqq r < 5$; observe that $x \in E_r$ where r is the remainder. Note that the equivalence classes are pairwise disjoint and that $\mathbf{Z} = A_0 \cup A_1 \cup A_2 \cup A_3 \cup A_4$.

Appendix B

Algebraic Structures

INTRODUCTION

We define here algebraic structures which occur in almost all branches of mathematics. In particular we will define a *field* which appears in the definition of a vector space. We begin with the definition of a *group*, which is a relatively simple algebraic structure with only one operation and is used as a building block for many other algebraic systems.

GROUPS

Let G be a nonempty set with a binary operation, i.e. to each pair of elements $a, b \in G$ there is assigned an element $ab \in G$. Then G is called a *group* if the following axioms hold:

[G_1] For any $a, b, c \in G$, we have $(ab)c = a(bc)$ (the *associative law*).

[G_2] There exists an element $e \in G$, called the *identity* element, such that $ae = ea = a$ for every $a \in G$.

[G_3] For each $a \in G$ there exists an element $a^{-1} \in G$, called the *inverse* of a, such that $aa^{-1} = a^{-1}a = e$.

A group G is said to be *abelian* (or: *commutative*) if the *commutative law* holds, i.e. if $ab = ba$ for every $a, b \in G$.

When the binary operation is denoted by juxtaposition as above, the group G is said to be written *multiplicatively*. Sometimes, when G is abelian, the binary operation is denoted by $+$ and G is said to be written *additively*. In such case the identity element is denoted by 0 and is called the *zero* element; and the inverse is denoted by $-a$ and is called the *negative* of a.

If A and B are subsets of a group G then we write

$$AB = \{ab : a \in A,\ b \in B\}, \quad \text{or} \quad A + B = \{a + b : a \in A,\ b \in B\}$$

We also write a for $\{a\}$.

A subset H of a group G is called a *subgroup* of G if H itself forms a group under the operation of G. If H is a subgroup of G and $a \in G$, then the set Ha is called a *right coset* of H and the set aH is called a *left coset* of H.

Definition: A subgroup H of G is called a *normal* subgroup if $a^{-1}Ha \subset H$ for every $a \in G$. Equivalently, H is normal if $aH = Ha$ for every $a \in G$, i.e. if the right and left cosets of H coincide.

Note that every subgroup of an abelian group is normal.

Theorem B.1: Let H be a normal subgroup of G. Then the cosets of H in G form a group under coset multiplication. This group is called the *quotient group* and is denoted by G/H.

Example B.1: The set **Z** of integers forms an abelian group under addition. (We remark that the even integers form a subgroup of **Z** but the odd integers do not.) Let H denote the set of multiples of 5, i.e. $H = \{\ldots, -10, -5, 0, 5, 10, \ldots\}$. Then H is a subgroup (necessarily normal) of **Z**. The cosets of H in **Z** follow:

$$\overline{0} = 0 + H = H = \{\ldots, -10, -5, 0, 5, 10, \ldots\}$$
$$\overline{1} = 1 + H = \{\ldots, -9, -4, 1, 6, 11, \ldots\}$$
$$\overline{2} = 2 + H = \{\ldots, -8, -3, 2, 7, 12, \ldots\}$$
$$\overline{3} = 3 + H = \{\ldots, -7, -2, 3, 8, 13, \ldots\}$$
$$\overline{4} = 4 + H = \{\ldots, -6, -1, 4, 9, 14, \ldots\}$$

For any other integer $n \in \mathbf{Z}$, $\bar{n} = n + H$ coincides with one of the above cosets. Thus by the above theorem, $\mathbf{Z}/H = \{\overline{0}, \overline{1}, \overline{2}, \overline{3}, \overline{4}\}$ forms a group under coset addition; its addition table follows:

+	$\overline{0}$	$\overline{1}$	$\overline{2}$	$\overline{3}$	$\overline{4}$
$\overline{0}$	$\overline{0}$	$\overline{1}$	$\overline{2}$	$\overline{3}$	$\overline{4}$
$\overline{1}$	$\overline{1}$	$\overline{2}$	$\overline{3}$	$\overline{4}$	$\overline{0}$
$\overline{2}$	$\overline{2}$	$\overline{3}$	$\overline{4}$	$\overline{0}$	$\overline{1}$
$\overline{3}$	$\overline{3}$	$\overline{4}$	$\overline{0}$	$\overline{1}$	$\overline{2}$
$\overline{4}$	$\overline{4}$	$\overline{0}$	$\overline{1}$	$\overline{2}$	$\overline{3}$

This quotient group $\mathbf{Z}/H$ is referred to as the integers modulo 5 and is frequently denoted by $\mathbf{Z}_5$. Analogously, for any positive integer n, there exists the quotient group $\mathbf{Z}_n$ called the integers modulo n.

Example B.2: The permutations of n symbols (see page 171) form a group under composition of mappings; it is called the *symmetric group* of degree n and is denoted by S_n. We investigate S_3 here; its elements are

$$\epsilon = \begin{pmatrix} 1 & 2 & 3 \\ 1 & 2 & 3 \end{pmatrix} \qquad \sigma_2 = \begin{pmatrix} 1 & 2 & 3 \\ 3 & 2 & 1 \end{pmatrix} \qquad \phi_1 = \begin{pmatrix} 1 & 2 & 3 \\ 2 & 3 & 1 \end{pmatrix}$$

$$\sigma_1 = \begin{pmatrix} 1 & 2 & 3 \\ 1 & 3 & 2 \end{pmatrix} \qquad \sigma_3 = \begin{pmatrix} 1 & 2 & 3 \\ 2 & 1 & 3 \end{pmatrix} \qquad \phi_2 = \begin{pmatrix} 1 & 2 & 3 \\ 3 & 1 & 2 \end{pmatrix}$$

Here $\begin{pmatrix} 1 & 2 & 3 \\ i & j & k \end{pmatrix}$ is the permutation which maps $1 \mapsto i$, $2 \mapsto j$, $3 \mapsto k$. The multiplication table of S_3 is

	ϵ	σ_1	σ_2	σ_3	ϕ_1	ϕ_2
ϵ	ϵ	σ_1	σ_2	σ_3	ϕ_1	ϕ_2
σ_1	σ_1	ϵ	ϕ_1	ϕ_2	σ_2	σ_3
σ_2	σ_2	ϕ_2	ϵ	ϕ_1	σ_3	σ_1
σ_3	σ_3	ϕ_1	ϕ_2	ϵ	σ_1	σ_2
ϕ_1	ϕ_1	σ_3	σ_1	σ_2	ϕ_2	ϵ
ϕ_2	ϕ_2	σ_2	σ_3	σ_1	ϵ	ϕ_1

(The element in the ath row and bth column is ab.) The set $H = \{\epsilon, \sigma_1\}$ is a subgroup of S_3; its right and left cosets are

Right Cosets	Left Cosets
$H = \{\epsilon, \sigma_1\}$	$H = \{\epsilon, \sigma_1\}$
$H\phi_1 = \{\phi_1, \sigma_2\}$	$\phi_1 H = \{\phi_1, \sigma_3\}$
$H\phi_2 = \{\phi_2, \sigma_3\}$	$\phi_2 H = \{\phi_2, \sigma_2\}$

Observe that the right cosets and the left cosets are distinct; hence H is not a normal subgroup of S_3.

A mapping f from a group G into a group G' is called a *homomorphism* if $f(ab) = f(a)f(b)$ for every $a, b \in G$. (If f is also bijective, i.e. one-to-one and onto, then f is called an *isomorphism* and G and G' are said to be *isomorphic*.) If $f: G \to G'$ is a homomorphism, then the *kernel* of f is the set of elements of G which map into the identity element $e' \in G'$:

$$\text{kernel of } f = \{a \in G: f(a) = e'\}$$

(As usual, $f(G)$ is called the *image* of the mapping $f: G \to G'$.) The following theorem applies.

Theorem B.2: Let $f: G \to G'$ be a homomorphism with kernel K. Then K is a normal subgroup of G, and the quotient group G/K is isomorphic to the image of f.

Example B.3: Let G be the group of real numbers under addition, and let G' be the group of positive real numbers under multiplication. The mapping $f : G \to G'$ defined by $f(a) = 2^a$ is a homomorphism because

$$f(a+b) \;=\; 2^{a+b} \;=\; 2^a 2^b \;=\; f(a)\,f(b)$$

In particular, f is bijective; hence G and G' are isomorphic.

Example B.4: Let G be the group of nonzero complex numbers under multiplication, and let G' be the group of nonzero real numbers under multiplication. The mapping $f : G \to G'$ defined by $f(z) = |z|$ is a homomorphism because

$$f(z_1 z_2) \;=\; |z_1 z_2| \;=\; |z_1|\,|z_2| \;=\; f(z_1)\,f(z_2)$$

The kernel K of f consists of those complex numbers z on the unit circle, i.e. for which $|z| = 1$. Thus G/K is isomorphic to the image of f, i.e. to the group of positive real numbers under multiplication.

RINGS, INTEGRAL DOMAINS AND FIELDS

Let R be a nonempty set with two binary operations, an operation of addition (denoted by $+$) and an operation of multiplication (denoted by juxtaposition). Then R is called a *ring* if the following axioms are satisfied:

[R_1] For any $a, b, c \in R$, we have $(a+b)+c = a+(b+c)$.

[R_2] There exists an element $0 \in R$, called the *zero* element, such that $a+0 = 0+a = a$ for every $a \in R$.

[R_3] For each $a \in R$ there exists an element $-a \in R$, called the *negative* of a, such that $a+(-a) = (-a)+a = 0$.

[R_4] For any $a, b \in R$, we have $a+b = b+a$.

[R_5] For any $a, b, c \in R$, we have $(ab)c = a(bc)$.

[R_6] For any $a, b, c \in R$, we have:

    (i) $a(b+c) = ab+ac$, and (ii) $(b+c)a = ba+ca$.

Observe that the axioms [R_1] through [R_4] may be summarized by saying that R is an abelian group under addition.

Subtraction is defined in R by $a - b \equiv a + (-b)$.

It can be shown (see Problem B.25) that $a \cdot 0 = 0 \cdot a = 0$ for every $a \in R$.

R is called a *commutative ring* if $ab = ba$ for every $a, b \in R$. We also say that R is a *ring with a unit element* if there exists a nonzero element $1 \in R$ such that $a \cdot 1 = 1 \cdot a = a$ for every $a \in R$.

A nonempty subset S of R is called a *subring* of R if S itself forms a ring under the operations of R. We note that S is a subring of R if and only if $a, b \in S$ implies $a - b \in S$ and $ab \in S$.

A nonempty subset I of R is called a *left ideal* in R if: (i) $a - b \in I$ whenever $a, b \in I$, and (ii) $ra \in I$ whenever $r \in R$, $a \in I$. Note that a left ideal I in R is also a subring of R. Similarly we can define a *right ideal* and a *two-sided ideal*. Clearly all ideals in commutative rings are two-sided. The term ideal shall mean two-sided ideal unless otherwise specified.

Theorem B.3: Let I be a (two-sided) ideal in a ring R. Then the cosets $\{a + I : a \in R\}$ form a ring under coset addition and coset multiplication. This ring is denoted by R/I and is called the *quotient ring*.

Now let R be a commutative ring with a unit element. For any $a \in R$, the set $(a) = \{ra : r \in R\}$ is an ideal; it is called the *principal ideal* generated by a. If every ideal in R is a principal ideal, then R is called a *principal ideal ring*.

Definition: A commutative ring R with a unit element is called an *integral domain* if R has no *zero divisors*, i.e. if $ab = 0$ implies $a = 0$ or $b = 0$.

Definition: A commutative ring R with a unit element is called a *field* if every nonzero $a \in R$ has a *multiplicative inverse*, i.e. there exists an element $a^{-1} \in R$ such that $aa^{-1} = a^{-1}a = 1$.

A field is necessarily an integral domain; for if $ab = 0$ and $a \neq 0$, then

$$b = 1 \cdot b = a^{-1}ab = a^{-1} \cdot 0 = 0$$

We remark that a field may also be viewed as a commutative ring in which the nonzero elements form a group under multiplication.

Example B.5: The set $\mathbf{Z}$ of integers with the usual operations of addition and multiplication is the classical example of an integral domain with a unit element. Every ideal I in $\mathbf{Z}$ is a principal ideal, i.e. $I = (n)$ for some integer n. The quotient ring $\mathbf{Z}_n = \mathbf{Z}/(n)$ is called the *ring of integers modulo n*. If n is prime, then $\mathbf{Z}_n$ is a field. On the other hand, if n is not prime then $\mathbf{Z}_n$ has zero divisors. For example, in the ring $\mathbf{Z}_6$, $\bar{2}\,\bar{3} = \bar{0}$ and $\bar{2} \neq \bar{0}$ and $\bar{3} \neq \bar{0}$.

Example B.6: The rational numbers $\mathbf{Q}$ and the real numbers $\mathbf{R}$ each form a field with respect to the usual operations of addition and multiplication.

Example B.7: Let $\mathbf{C}$ denote the set of ordered pairs of real numbers with addition and multiplication defined by

$$(a, b) + (c, d) = (a + c, b + d)$$
$$(a, b) \cdot (c, d) = (ac - bd, ad + bc)$$

Then $\mathbf{C}$ satisfies all the required properties of a field. In fact, $\mathbf{C}$ is just the field of complex numbers (see page 4).

Example B.8: The set M of all 2 by 2 matrices with real entries forms a noncommutative ring with zero divisors under the operations of matrix addition and matrix multiplication.

Example B.9: Let R be any ring. Then the set $R[x]$ of all polynomials over R forms a ring with respect to the usual operations of addition and multiplication of polynomials. Moreover, if R is an integral domain then $R[x]$ is also an integral domain.

Now let D be an integral domain. We say that b *divides* a in D if $a = bc$ for some $c \in D$. An element $u \in D$ is called a *unit* if u divides 1, i.e. if u has a multiplicative inverse. An element $b \in D$ is called an *associate* of $a \in D$ if $b = ua$ for some unit $u \in D$. A nonunit $p \in D$ is said to be *irreducible* if $p = ab$ implies a or b is a unit.

An integral domain D is called a *unique factorization domain* if every nonunit $a \in D$ can be written uniquely (up to associates and order) as a product of irreducible elements.

Example B.10: The ring $\mathbf{Z}$ of integers is the classical example of a unique factorization domain. The units of $\mathbf{Z}$ are 1 and -1. The only associates of $n \in \mathbf{Z}$ are n and $-n$. The irreducible elements of $\mathbf{Z}$ are the prime numbers.

Example B.11: The set $D = \{a + b\sqrt{13} : a, b \text{ integers}\}$ is an integral domain. The units of D are ± 1, $18 \pm 5\sqrt{13}$ and $-18 \pm 5\sqrt{13}$. The elements 2, $3 - \sqrt{13}$ and $-3 - \sqrt{13}$ are irreducible in D. Observe that $4 = 2 \cdot 2 = (3 - \sqrt{13})(-3 - \sqrt{13})$. Thus D is not a unique factorization domain. (See Problem B.40.)

MODULES

Let M be a nonempty set and let R be a ring with a unit element. Then M is said to be a (left) *R-module* if M is an additive abelian group and there exists a mapping $R \times M \to M$ which satisfies the following axioms:

$[M_1]$ $r(m_1 + m_2) \;=\; rm_1 + rm_2$

$[M_2]$ $(r+s)m \;=\; rm + sm$

$[M_3]$ $(rs)m \;=\; r(sm)$

$[M_4]$ $1 \cdot m \;=\; m$

for any $r, s \in R$ and any $m_i \in M$.

We emphasize that an R-module is a generalization of a vector space where we allow the scalars to come from a ring rather than a field.

Example B.12: Let G be any additive abelian group. We make G into a module over the ring $\mathbf{Z}$ of integers by defining

$$\overbrace{ng \;=\; g + g + \cdots + g,}^{n \text{ times}} \quad 0g = 0, \quad (-n)g = -ng$$

where n is any positive integer.

Example B.13: Let R be a ring and let I be an ideal in R. Then I may be viewed as a module over R.

Example B.14: Let V be a vector space over a field K and let $T : V \to V$ be a linear mapping. We make V into a module over the ring $K[x]$ of polynomials over K by defining $f(x)v = f(T)\,(v)$. The reader should check that a scalar multiplication has been defined.

Let M be a module over R. An additive subgroup N of M is called a *submodule* of M if $u \in N$ and $k \in R$ imply $ku \in N$. (Note that N is then a module over R.)

Let M and M' be R-modules. A mapping $T : M \to M'$ is called a *homomorphism* (or *R-homomorphism* or *R-linear*) if

$$\text{(i) } T(u+v) \;=\; T(u) + T(v) \quad \text{and} \quad \text{(ii) } T(ku) \;=\; kT(u)$$

for every $u, v \in M$ and every $k \in R$.

Problems

GROUPS

B.1. Determine whether each of the following systems forms a group G:

(i) G = set of integers, operation subtraction;

(ii) $G = \{1, -1\}$, operation multiplication;

(iii) G = set of nonzero rational numbers, operation division;

(iv) G = set of nonsingular $n \times n$ matrices, operation matrix multiplication;

(v) $G = \{a + bi : a, b \in \mathbf{Z}\}$, operation addition.

B.2. Show that in a group G:

(i)   the identity element of G is unique;

(ii) each $a \in G$ has a unique inverse $a^{-1} \in G$;

(iii) $(a^{-1})^{-1} = a$, and $(ab)^{-1} = b^{-1}a^{-1}$;

(iv) $ab = ac$ implies $b = c$, and $ba = ca$ implies $b = c$.

B.3. In a group G, the powers of $a \in G$ are defined by

$$a^0 = e, \;\; a^n = aa^{n-1}, \;\; a^{-n} = (a^n)^{-1}, \quad \text{where } n \in \mathbf{N}$$

Show that the following formulae hold for any integers $r, s, t \in \mathbf{Z}$: (i) $a^r a^s = a^{r+s}$, (ii) $(a^r)^s = a^{rs}$, (iii) $(a^{r+s})^t = a^{rt+st}$.

B.4. Show that if G is an abelian group, then $(ab)^n = a^n b^n$ for any $a, b \in G$ and any integer $n \in \mathbf{Z}$.

B.5. Suppose G is a group such that $(ab)^2 = a^2 b^2$ for every $a, b \in G$. Show that G is abelian.

B.6. Suppose H is a subset of a group G. Show that H is a subgroup of G if and only if (i) H is non-empty, and (ii) $a, b \in H$ implies $ab^{-1} \in H$.

B.7. Prove that the intersection of any number of subgroups of G is also a subgroup of G.

B.8. Show that the set of all powers of $a \in G$ is a subgroup of G; it is called the *cyclic group* generated by a.

B.9. A group G is said to be *cyclic* if G is generated by some $a \in G$, i.e. $G = \{a^n : n \in \mathbf{Z}\}$. Show that every subgroup of a cyclic group is cyclic.

B.10. Suppose G is a cyclic subgroup. Show that G is isomorphic to the set $\mathbf{Z}$ of integers under addition or to the set $\mathbf{Z}_n$ (of the integers modulo n) under addition.

B.11. Let H be a subgroup of G. Show that the right (left) cosets of H partition G into mutually disjoint subsets.

B.12. The *order* of a group G, denoted by $|G|$, is the number of elements of G. Prove **Lagrange's theorem:** If H is a subgroup of a finite group G, then $|H|$ divides $|G|$.

B.13. Suppose $|G| = p$ where p is prime. Show that G is cyclic.

B.14. Suppose H and N are subgroups of G with N normal. Show that (i) HN is a subgroup of G and (ii) $H \cap N$ is a normal subgroup of G.

B.15. Let H be a subgroup of G with only two right (left) cosets. Show that H is a normal subgroup of G.

B.16. Prove Theorem B.1: Let H be a normal subgroup of G. Then the cosets of H in G form a group G/H under coset multiplication.

B.17. Suppose G is an abelian group. Show that any factor group G/H is also abelian.

B.18. Let $f : G \to G'$ be a group homomorphism. Show that:
(i) $f(e) = e'$ where e and e' are the identity elements of G and G' respectively;
(ii) $f(a^{-1}) = f(a)^{-1}$ for any $a \in G$.

B.19. Prove Theorem B.2: Let $f : G \to G'$ be a group homomorphism with kernel K. Then K is a normal subgroup of G, and the quotient group G/K is isomorphic to the image of f.

B.20. Let G be the multiplicative group of complex numbers z such that $|z| = 1$, and let $\mathbf{R}$ be the additive group of real numbers. Prove that G is isomorphic to $\mathbf{R}/\mathbf{Z}$.

B.21. For a fixed $g \in G$, let $\hat{g} : G \to G$ be defined by $\hat{g}(a) = g^{-1}ag$. Show that G is an isomorphism of G onto G.

B.22. Let G be the multiplicative group of $n \times n$ nonsingular matrices over $\mathbf{R}$. Show that the mapping $A \mapsto |A|$ is a homomorphism of G into the multiplicative group of nonzero real numbers.

B.23. Let G be an abelian group. For a fixed $n \in \mathbf{Z}$, show that the map $a \mapsto a^n$ is a homomorphism of G into G.

B.24. Suppose H and N are subgroups of G with N normal. Prove that $H \cap N$ is normal in H and $H/(H \cap N)$ is isomorphic to HN/N.

RINGS

B.25. Show that in a ring R:
(i) $a \cdot 0 = 0 \cdot a = 0$, (ii) $a(-b) = (-a)b = -ab$, (iii) $(-a)(-b) = ab$.

B.26. Show that in a ring R with a unit element: (i) $(-1)a = -a$, (ii) $(-1)(-1) = 1$.

B.27. Suppose $a^2 = a$ for every $a \in R$. Prove that R is a commutative ring. (Such a ring is called a *Boolean ring*.)

B.28. Let R be a ring with a unit element. We make R into another ring $\widehat{R}$ by defining $a \oplus b = a + b + 1$ and $a \cdot b = ab + a + b$. (i) Verify that $\widehat{R}$ is a ring. (ii) Determine the 0-element and 1-element of $\widehat{R}$.

B.29. Let G be any (additive) abelian group. Define a multiplication in G by $a \cdot b = 0$. Show that this makes G into a ring.

B.30. Prove Theorem B.3: Let I be a (two-sided) ideal in a ring R. Then the cosets $\{a + I : a \in R\}$ form a ring under coset addition and coset multiplication.

B.31. Let I_1 and I_2 be ideals in R. Prove that $I_1 + I_2$ and $I_1 \cap I_2$ are also ideals in R.

B.32. Let R and R' be rings. A mapping $f : R \to R'$ is called a *homomorphism* (or: *ring homomorphism*) if

$$\text{(i)} \quad f(a + b) = f(a) + f(b) \quad \text{and} \quad \text{(ii)} \quad f(ab) = f(a) f(b),$$

for every $a, b \in R$. Prove that if $f : R \to R'$ is a homomorphism, then the set $K = \{r \in R : f(r) = 0\}$ is an ideal in R. (The set K is called the *kernel* of f.)

INTEGRAL DOMAINS AND FIELDS

B.33. Prove that in an integral domain D, if $ab = ac$, $a \neq 0$, then $b = c$.

B.34. Prove that $F = \{a + b\sqrt{2} : a, b \text{ rational}\}$ is a field.

B.35. Prove that $D = \{a + b\sqrt{2} : a, b \text{ integers}\}$ is an integral domain but not a field.

B.36. Prove that a finite integral domain D is a field.

B.37. Show that the only ideals in a field K are $\{0\}$ and K.

B.38. A complex number $a + bi$ where a, b are integers is called a *Gaussian integer*. Show that the set G of Gaussian integers is an integral domain. Also show that the units in G are ± 1 and $\pm i$.

B.39. Let D be an integral domain and let I be an ideal in D. Prove that the factor ring D/I is an integral domain if and only if I is a prime ideal. (An ideal I is *prime* if $ab \in I$ implies $a \in I$ or $b \in I$.)

B.40. Consider the integral domain $D = \{a + b\sqrt{13} : a, b \text{ integers}\}$ (see **Example B.11**). If $\alpha = a + b\sqrt{13}$, we define $N(\alpha) = a^2 - 13b^2$. Prove: (i) $N(\alpha\beta) = N(\alpha)N(\beta)$; (ii) α is a unit if and only if $N(\alpha) = \pm 1$; (iii) the units of D are ± 1, $18 \pm 5\sqrt{13}$ and $-18 \pm 5\sqrt{13}$; (iv) the numbers $2, 3 - \sqrt{13}$ and $-3 - \sqrt{13}$ are irreducible.

MODULES

B.41. Let M be an R-module and let A and B be submodules of M. Show that $A + B$ and $A \cap B$ are also submodules of M.

B.42. Let M be an R-module with submodule N. Show that the cosets $\{u + N : u \in M\}$ form an R-module under coset addition and scalar multiplication defined by $r(u + N) = ru + N$. (This module is denoted by M/N and is called the *quotient module*.)

B.43. Let M and M' be R-modules and let $f : M \to M'$ be an R-homomorphism. Show that the set $K = \{u \in M : f(u) = 0\}$ is a submodule of f. (The set K is called the *kernel* of f.)

B.44. Let M be an R-module and let $E(M)$ denote the set of all R-homomorphisms of M into itself. Define the appropriate operations of addition and multiplication in $E(M)$ so that $E(M)$ becomes a ring.

Appendix C

Polynomials over a Field

INTRODUCTION

We will investigate polynomials over a field K and show that they have many properties which are analogous to properties of the integers. These results play an important role in obtaining canonical forms for a linear operator T on a vector space V over K.

RING OF POLYNOMIALS

Let K be a field. Formally, a polynomial f over K is an infinite sequence of elements from K in which all except a finite number of them are 0:

$$f = (\ldots, 0, a_n, \ldots, a_1, a_0)$$

(We write the sequence so that it extends to the left instead of to the right.) The entry a_k is called the kth coefficient of f. If n is the largest integer for which $a_n \neq 0$, then we say that the *degree* of f is n, written

$$\deg f = n$$

We also call a_n the *leading coefficient* of f, and if $a_n = 1$ we call f a *monic polynomial*. On the other hand, if every coefficient of f is 0 then f is called the *zero polynomial*, written $f = 0$. The degree of the zero polynomial is not defined.

Now if g is another polynomial over K, say

$$g = (\ldots, 0, b_m, \ldots, b_1, b_0)$$

then the *sum* $f + g$ is the polynomial obtained by adding corresponding coefficients. That is, if $m \leqq n$ then

$$f + g = (\ldots, 0, a_n, \ldots, a_m + b_m, \ldots, a_1 + b_1, a_0 + b_0)$$

Furthermore, the *product* fg is the polynomial

$$fg = (\ldots, 0, a_n b_m, \ldots, a_1 b_0 + a_0 b_1, a_0 b_0)$$

that is, the kth coefficient c_k of fg is

$$c_k = \sum_{i=0}^{k} a_i b_{k-i} = a_0 b_k + a_1 b_{k-1} + \cdots + a_k b_0$$

The following theorem applies.

Theorem C.1: The set P of polynomials over a field K under the above operations of addition and multiplication forms a commutative ring with a unit element and with no zero divisors, i.e. an integral domain. If f and g are nonzero polynomials in P, then $\deg(fg) = (\deg f)(\deg g)$.

NOTATION

We identify the scalar $a_0 \in K$ with the polynomial

$$a_0 = (\ldots, 0, a_0)$$

We also choose a symbol, say t, to denote the polynomial

$$t = (\ldots, 0, 1, 0)$$

We call the symbol t an *indeterminant*. Multiplying t with itself, we obtain

$$t^2 = (\ldots, 0, 1, 0, 0), \quad t^3 = (\ldots, 0, 1, 0, 0, 0), \quad \ldots$$

Thus the above polynomial f can be written uniquely in the usual form

$$f = a_n t^n + \cdots + a_1 t + a_0$$

When the symbol t is selected as the indeterminant, the ring of polynomials over K is denoted by

$$K[t]$$

and a polynomial f is frequently denoted by $f(t)$.

We also view the field K as a subset of $K[t]$ under the above identification. This is possible since the operations of addition and multiplication of elements of K are preserved under this identification:

$$(\ldots, 0, a_0) + (\ldots, 0, b_0) = (\ldots, 0, a_0 + b_0)$$

$$(\ldots, 0, a_0) \cdot (\ldots, 0, b_0) = (\ldots, 0, a_0 b_0)$$

We remark that the nonzero elements of K are the units of the ring $K[t]$.

We also remark that every nonzero polynomial is an associate of a unique monic polynomial. Hence if d and d' are monic polynomials for which d divides d' and d' divides d, then $d = d'$. (A polynomial g *divides* a polynomial f if there is a polynomial h such that $f = hg$.)

DIVISIBILITY

The following theorem formalizes the process known as "long division".

Theorem C.2 (Division Algorithm):   Let f and g be polynomials over a field K with $g \neq 0$. Then there exist polynomials q and r such that

$$f = qg + r$$

where either $r = 0$ or $\deg r < \deg g$.

Proof: If $f = 0$ or if $\deg f < \deg g$, then we have the required representation

$$f = 0g + f$$

Now suppose $\deg f \geqq \deg g$, say

$$f = a_n t^n + \cdots + a_1 t + a_0 \quad \text{and} \quad g = b_m t^m + \cdots + b_1 t + b_0$$

where $a_n, b_m \neq 0$ and $n \geqq m$. We form the polynomial

$$f_1 = f - \frac{a_n}{b_m} t^{n-m} g \tag{1}$$

Then $\deg f_1 < \deg f$. By induction, there exist polynomials q_1 and r such that

$$f_1 = q_1 g + r$$

where either $r = 0$ or $\deg r < \deg g$. Substituting this into (1) and solving for f,

$$f = \left(q_1 + \frac{a_n}{b_m} t^{n-m} \right) g + r$$

which is the desired representation.

Theorem C.3: The ring $K[t]$ of polynomials over a field K is a principal ideal ring. If I is an ideal in $K[t]$, then there exists a unique monic polynomial d which generates I, that is, such that d divides every polynomial $f \in I$.

Proof. Let d be a polynomial of lowest degree in I. Since we can multiply d by a non-zero scalar and still remain in I, we can assume without loss in generality that d is a monic polynomial. Now suppose $f \in I$. By Theorem C.2 there exist polynomials q and r such that

$$f = qd + r \quad \text{where either } r = 0 \text{ or } \deg r < \deg d$$

Now $f, d \in I$ implies $qd \in I$ and hence $r = f - qd \in I$. But d is a polynomial of lowest degree in I. Accordingly, $r = 0$ and $f = qd$, that is, d divides f. It remains to show that d is unique. If d' is another monic polynomial which generates I, then d divides d' and d' divides d. This implies that $d = d'$, because d and d' are monic. Thus the theorem is proved.

Theorem C.4: Let f and g be nonzero polynomials in $K[t]$. Then there exists a unique monic polynomial d such that: (i) d divides f and g; and (ii) if d' divides f and g, then d' divides d.

Definition: The above polynomial d is called the *greatest common divisor* of f and g. If $d = 1$, then f and g are said to be *relatively prime*.

Proof of Theorem C.4. The set $I = \{mf + ng : m, n \in K[t]\}$ is an ideal. Let d be the monic polynomial which generates I. Note $f, g \in I$; hence d divides f and g. Now suppose d' divides f and g. Let J be the ideal generated by d'. Then $f, g \in J$ and hence $I \subset J$. Accordingly, $d \in J$ and so d' divides d as claimed. It remains to show that d is unique. If d_1 is another (monic) greatest common divisor of f and g, then d divides d_1 and d_1 divides d. This implies that $d = d_1$ because d and d_1 are monic. Thus the theorem is proved.

Corollary C.5: Let d be the greatest common divisor of the polynomials f and g. Then there exist polynomials m and n such that $d = mf + ng$. In particular, if f and g are relatively prime then there exist polynomials m and n such that $mf + ng = 1$.

The corollary follows directly from the fact that d generates the ideal

$$I = \{mf + ng : m, n \in K[t]\}$$

FACTORIZATION

A polynomial $p \in K[t]$ of positive degree is said to be irreducible if $p = fg$ implies f or g is a scalar.

Lemma C.6: Suppose $p \in K[t]$ is irreducible. If p divides the product fg of polynomials $f, g \in K[t]$, then p divides f or p divides g. More generally, if p divides the product of n polynomials $f_1 f_2 \ldots f_n$, then p divides one of them.

Proof. Suppose p divides fg but not f. Since p is irreducible, the polynomials f and p must then be relatively prime. Thus there exist polynomials $m, n \in K[t]$ such that $mf + np = 1$. Multiplying this equation by g, we obtain $mfg + npg = g$. But p divides fg and so mfg, and p divides npg; hence p divides the sum $g = mfg + npg$.

Now suppose p divides $f_1 f_2 \ldots f_n$. If p divides f_1, then we are through. If not, then by the above result p divides the product $f_2 \ldots f_n$. By induction on n, p divides one of the polynomials $f_2, \ldots, f_n$. Thus the lemma is proved.

Theorem C.7 (Unique Factorization Theorem): Let f be a nonzero polynomial in $K[t]$. Then f can be written uniquely (except for order) as a product

$$f = k p_1 p_2 \ldots p_n$$

where $k \in K$ and the p_i are monic irreducible polynomials in $K[t]$.

Proof: We prove the existence of such a product first. If f is irreducible or if $f \in K$, then such a product clearly exists. On the other hand, suppose $f = gh$ where f and g are nonscalars. Then g and h have degrees less than that of f. By induction, we can assume

$$g = k_1 g_1 g_2 \ldots g_r \quad \text{and} \quad h = k_2 h_1 h_2 \ldots h_s$$

where $k_1, k_2 \in K$ and the g_i and h_j are monic irreducible polynomials. Accordingly,

$$f = (k_1 k_2) g_1 g_2 \ldots g_r h_1 h_2 \ldots h_s$$

is our desired representation.

We next prove uniqueness (except for order) of such a product for f. Suppose

$$f = k p_1 p_2 \ldots p_n = k' q_1 q_2 \ldots q_m$$

where $k, k' \in K$ and the $p_1, \ldots, p_n, q_1, \ldots, q_m$ are monic irreducible polynomials. Now p_1 divides $k' q_1 \ldots q_m$. Since p_1 is irreducible it must divide one of the q_i by the above lemma. Say p_1 divides q_1. Since p_1 and q_1 are both irreducible and monic, $p_1 = q_1$. Accordingly,

$$k p_2 \ldots p_n = k' q_2 \ldots q_m$$

By induction, we have that $n = m$ and $p_2 = q_2, \ldots, p_n = q_m$ for some rearrangement of the q_i. We also have that $k = k'$. Thus the theorem is proved.

If the field K is the complex field **C**, then we have the following result which is known as the fundamental theorem of algebra; its proof lies beyond the scope of this text.

Theorem C.8 (Fundamental Theorem of Algebra): Let $f(t)$ be a nonzero polynomial over the complex field **C**. Then $f(t)$ can be written uniquely (except for order) as a product

$$f(t) = k(t - r_1)(t - r_2) \cdots (t - r_n)$$

where $k, r_i \in \mathbf{C}$, i.e. as a product of linear polynomials.

In the case of the real field **R** we have the following result.

Theorem C.9: Let $f(t)$ be a nonzero polynomial over the real field **R**. Then $f(t)$ can be written uniquely (except for order) as a product

$$f(t) = k p_1(t) \, p_2(t) \cdots p_m(t)$$

where $k \in \mathbf{R}$ and the $p_i(t)$ are monic irreducible polynomials of degree one or two.

INDEX

Abelian group, 320
Absolute value, 4
Addition,
  in $\mathbf{R}^n$, 2
  of linear mappings, 128
  of matrices, 36
Adjoint,
  classical, 176
  operator, 284
Algebra,
  isomorphism, 169
  of linear operators, 129
  of square matrices, 43
Algebraic multiplicity, 203
Alternating,
  bilinear forms, 262
  multilinear forms, 178, 277
Angle between vectors, 282
Annihilator, 227, 251
Anti-symmetric
  bilinear form, 263
  operator, 285
Augmented matrix, 40

Basis, 88
  change of, 153
Bessel's inequality, 309
Bijective mapping, 123
Bilinear form, 261, 277
Binary relation, 318
Block matrix, 45
Bounded function, 65

$\mathbf{C}$, 4
$\mathbf{C}^n$, 5
Cayley-Hamilton theorem, 201, 211
Canonical forms in
  Euclidean spaces, 288
  unitary spaces, 290
  vector spaces, 222
Cauchy-Schwarz inequality, 4, 10, 281
Cells, 45
Change of basis, 153
Characteristic,
  equation, 200
  matrix, 200
  polynomial, 200, 203, 210
  value, 198
  vector, 198
Classical adjoint, 176
Co-domain, 121
Coefficient matrix, 40
Cofactor, 174

Column,
  of a matrix, 35
  rank, 90
  space, 67
  vector, 36
Companion matrix, 228
Complex numbers, 4
Components, 2
Composition of mappings, 121
Congruent matrices, 262
Conjugate complex number, 4
Consistent linear equations, 31
Convex, 260
Coordinate, 2
  vector, 92
Coset, 229
Cramer's rule, 177
Cyclic group, 325
Cyclic subspaces, 227

Decomposition,
  direct sum, 224
  primary, 225
Degenerate bilinear form, 262
Dependent vectors, 86
Determinant, 171
Determinantal rank, 195
Diagonal
  matrix, 43
  of a matrix, 43
Diagonalization,
  Euclidean spaces, 288
  unitary spaces, 290
  vector spaces, 155, 199
Dimension, 88
Direct sum, 69, 82, 224
Disjoint, 316
Distance, 3, 280
Distinguished elements, 41
Division algorithm, 328
Domain,
  integral, 322
  of a mapping, 121
Dot product,
  in $\mathbf{C}^n$, 6
  in $\mathbf{R}^n$, 3
Dual
  basis, 250
  space, 249

Echelon form,
  linear equations, 21
  matrices, 41

Echelon matrix, 41
Eigenspace, 198, 205
Eigenvalue, 198
Eigenvector, 198
Element, 315
Elementary,
  column operation, 61
  divisors, 229
  matrix, 56
  row operation, 41
Elimination, 20
Empty set, 315
Equality
  of matrices, 36
  of vectors, 2
Equations (see Linear equations)
Equivalence relation, 318
Equivalent matrices, 61
Euclidean space, 3, 279
Even
  function, 83
  permutation, 171
External direct sum, 82

Field, 323
Free variable, 21
Function, 121
Functional, 249

Gaussian integers, 326
Generate, 66
Geometric multiplicity, 203
Gram-Schmidt orthogonalization, 283
Greatest common divisor, 329
Group, 320

Hermitian,
  form, 266
  matrix, 266
Hilbert space, 280
Hom (V, U), 128
Homogeneous linear equations, 19
Homomorphism, 123
Hyperplane, 14

Ideal, 322
Identity,
  element, 320
  mapping, 123
  matrix, 43
  permutation, 172
Image, 121, 125
Inclusion mapping, 146
Independent
  subspaces, 244
  vectors, 86
Index
  of nilpotency, 225
  set, 316
Injective mapping, 123
Inner product, 279
Inner product space, 279
Integers modulo n, 323

Integral domain, 322
Intersection of sets, 316
Invariant subspace, 223
Inverse,
  mapping, 123
  matrix, 44, 176
Invertible,
  linear operator, 130
  matrix, 44
Irreducible, 323, 329
Isomorphism of
  algebras, 169
  groups, 321
  inner product spaces, 286, 311
  vector spaces, 93, 124

Jordan canonical form, 226

Kernel, 123, 321, 326

l_2-space, 280
Line segment, 14, 260
Linear combination
  of equations, 30
  of vectors, 66
Linear dependence, 86
  in $\mathbf{R}^n$, 28
Linear equations, 18, 127, 176, 251, 282
Linear functional, 249
Linear independence, 86
  in $\mathbf{R}^n$, 28
Linear mapping, 123
  matrix of, 150
  rank of, 126
Linear operators, 129
Linear span, 66

Mapping, 121
  linear, 123
Matrices, 35
  addition, 36
  augmented, 40
  block, 45
  change of basis, 153
  coefficient, 40
  column, 35
  congruent, 262
  determinant, 171
  diagonal, 43
  echelon, 41
  equivalent, 61
  Hermitian, 266
  identity, 43
  multiplication, 39
  normal, 290
  rank, 90
  row, 35
  row canonical form, 42, 68
  row equivalent, 41
  row space, 60
  scalar, 43
  scalar multiplication, 36
  similar, 155
  size, 35

Matrices (cont.)
  square, 43
  symmetric, 65, 288
  transition, 153
  transpose, 39
  triangular, 43
  zero, 37
Matrix representation,
  bilinear forms, 262
  linear mappings, 150
Maximal independent set, 89
Minimal polynomial, 202, 212
Minkowski's inequality, 10
Minor, 174
Module, 323
Monic polynomial, 201
Multilinear, 178, 277
Multiplication of matrices, 37, 39

N (positive integers), 315
n-space, 2
n-tuple, 2
Nilpotent, 225
Nonnegative semi-definite, 265
Nonsingular,
  linear mapping, 127
  matrix, 130
Norm, 279
  in $\mathbf{R}^n$, 4
Normal operator, 286, 290, 303
Normal subgroup, 320
Normalized vector, 280
Null set, 315
Nullity, 126

Odd,
  function, 73
  permutation, 171
One-to-one mappings, 123
Onto mappings, 123
Operations with linear mappings, 128
Operators (*see* Linear operators)
Ordered pair, 318
Orthogonal
  complement, 281
  matrix, 287
  operator, 286
  vectors, 3, 280
Orthogonally equivalent, 288
Orthonormal, 282

Parallelogram law, 307
Parity, 171
Partition, 319
Permutations, 171
Polar form, 264, 307
Polynomials, 327
Positive
  matrix, 310
  operator, 288
Positive definite,
  bilinear form, 265
  matrix, 272, 310
  operator, 288

Primary decomposition theorem, 225
Prime ideal, 326
Principal ideal, 322
Principal minor, 219
Product set, 317
Projection operator, 243, 308
  orthogonal, 281
Proper
  subset, 316
  value, 198
  vector, 198

Q (rational numbers), 315
Quadratic form, 264
Quotient,
  group, 320
  module, 326
  ring, 322
  set, 319
  space, 229

R (real field), 315
$\mathbf{R}^n$, 2
Rank,
  bilinear form, 262
  linear mapping, 126
  matrix, 90, 195
Rational canonical form, 228
Relation, 318
Relatively prime, 329
Ring, 322
Row,
  canonical form, 42
  equivalent matrices, 41
  of a matrix, 35
  operations, 41
  rank, 90
  reduced echelon form, 41
  reduction, 42
  vector, 36

Scalar, 2, 63
  mapping, 219
  matrix, 43
Scalar multiplication, 69
  of linear mappings, 128
  of matrices, 36
Second dual space, 251
Self-adjoint operator, 285
Set, 315
Sgn, 171
Sign of a permutation, 171
Signature, 265, 266
Similar matrices, 155
Singular mappings, 127
Size of a matrix, 35
Skew-adjoint operator, 285
Skew-symmetric bilinear form, 263
Solution,
  of linear equations, 18, 23
  space, 65
Span, 66
Spectral theorem, 291
Square matrices, 43

Subgroup, 320
Subring, 322
Subset, 315
Subspace (of a vector space), 65
  sum of, 68
Surjective mapping, 123
Sylvester's theorem, 265
Symmetric,
  bilinear form, 263
  matrix, 65
  operator, 285, 288, 300
System of linear equations, 19

Trace, 155
Transition matrix, 153
Transpose,
  of a linear mapping, 252
  of a matrix, 39
Transposition, 172
Triangle inequality, 293
Triangular,
  form, 222
  matrix, 43
Trivial solution, 19

Union of sets, 316

Unique factorization, 323
Unit vector, 280
Unitarily equivalent, 288
Unitary,
  matrix, 287
  operator, 286
  space, 279
Universal set, 316
Upper triangular matrix, 43
Usual basis, 88, 89

Vector, 63
  in $\mathbf{C}^n$, 5
  in $\mathbf{R}^n$, 2
Vector space, 63
Venn diagram, 316

$\mathbf{Z}$ (integers), 315
$\mathbf{Z}_n$ (ring of integers modulo n), 323
Zero,
  mapping, 124
  matrix, 37
  of a polynomial, 44
  solution, 19
  vector, 3, 63